THE UNIVERSITY OF CHICAGO

THE
TESTAMENT OF SOLOMON

EDITED FROM MANUSCRIPTS
AT MOUNT ATHOS, BOLOGNA,
HOLKHAM HALL, JERUSALEM,
LONDON, MILAN, PARIS AND
VIENNA

WITH INTRODUCTION

A DISSERTATION
SUBMITTED TO THE FACULTY
OF THE
GRADUATE DIVINITY SCHOOL
IN CANDIDACY FOR THE DEGREE OF
DOCTOR OF PHILOSOPHY
(DEPARTMENT OF NEW TESTAMENT AND EARLY CHRISTIAN LITERATURE)

BY

CHESTER CHARLTON McCOWN

TO H. D. M.

WHOSE CONTINUED ASSISTANCE AND ENCOURAGEMENT

HAVE MADE THIS WORK POSSIBLE

Preface.

A new text of the *Testament of Solomon* has long been needed. Of the published texts, Fleck's was a careless and inaccurate transcription of a single manuscript, while Istrin's, which was indispensable for understanding the history of the work, is buried in Russian. Of unpublished manuscripts several were found which take us much nearer the original than did any of those already printed. Conybeare's investigation, while resulting in an excellent discussion and translation, labored under the disadvantage of depending upon Fleck, and, because of lack of fuller materials, could not avoid erroneous conclusions. In consequence of the paucity of materials there was a great variety of opinion as to the origin, character, and value of the document.

This edition cannot aspire to present all the materials nor to answer all the questions involved. It is hoped, however, that no accessible manuscripts have been missed, and that the materials available have been set forth in such a manner as to put scholars in possession of all data necessary for accurate conclusions.

When the task was begun, the intention was to edit the text of Fleck's manuscript with introduction, commentary, and translation; but as the number of manuscripts discovered increased, the commentary and translation were abandoned, since it was plain that the volume would be swollen beyond due proportions. The Introduction has in size far exceeded the writer's expectation and desire, and constitutes in part a commentary.

The work here published has been under way for many years. Forced by ill health to leave the mission work in India to which he had intended to give his life, the writer determined to devote himself to New Testament study, to which he had been especially attracted during his theological course under the instruction of Professor D. A. Hayes of Garrett Biblical Institute. Directed by the *Expository Times* he went to Heidelberg to work under Professor Adolf Deissmann. The latter with his characteristic great-heartedness received the unknown student, and after a few months suggested the *Testament* as a subject worthy of investigation. Professor Albrecht Dieterich also promised to take an interest in the work. Upon Professor Deissmann's removal to Berlin and the untimely and lamented death of Professor Dieterich the writer decided to go to Berlin. There, beside further guidance from the former and the inspiration of the lectures of Professors Norden and von Wilamowitz-Moellendorff, he had the highly prized advantage of suggestions from Professor Hermann Diels, who read as much of the manuscript as was then written.

As it became necessary to return to America, the further prosecution of the task was interrupted except for occasional intervals during vacations until the writer had the good fortune to remove to Chicago where, in time snatched from pedagogical duties, the work was continued and practically completed under the supervision of Professor E. J. Goodspeed. The manuscript has since been read by Professors E. D. Burton and H. Windisch. Dr. Montague Rhodes James went through it very carefully and made numerous suggestions which have been gladly used. At an early stage of the work encouragement and direction were thankfully received from the late Dr. Eberhard Nestle, from Professors von Dobschütz and E. Kurz, and especially from Dr. James. These obligations are acknowledged, but not so fully as they are felt, in the footnotes and bibliography.

In 1920—21 the writer was Thayer Fellow of the American School of Oriental Research in Jerusalem. The manuscript was put into the hands of the publisher as he was on his way to Palestine. In browsing among the manuscripts of the Great Greek Monastery in Jerusalem he had the good fortune to discover two manuscripts, one of the *Testament*, one of the legend of

Solomon's dealings with the demons. Although the printing of the *Testament* has been delayed for various reasons, it was not possible to incorporate the results of the study of these manuscripts in the text. A collation of one, called MS N, and a copy of the other, called MS E, have been printed in the Appendix (see pp. 112—128 and 102*—120*) and a list of emendations suggested by MS N will be found on p. 121*f.

On the way to Palestine the writer passed through Milan and took occasion to visit its famous library and inspect the manuscript, Ambrosianus No. 1030, in which fragments of the *Testament* are found, described below, pp. 20f. Nothing new was discovered. The fragments seem to have been cut of some manuscript, perhaps for the sake of, what was on the *recto*, which, in the case of Uᴘ, contains rules for gematric prognostication. This fragment ends with the word $\dot{\eta}\mu\acute{\epsilon}\varrho\alpha\nu$, p. 7*, l. 15. It follows the W text.

For the patience and wisdom of the editor of the series, Professor Windisch, in dealing with many perplexing problems that have arisen and for the skill and carefulness of the publisher in overcoming the technical difficulties of a complicated critical apparatus the writer cannot express too high appreciation.

The task was practically completed at the beginning of the war. The course of events which has prevented publication until now has given further time for revision of the manuscript and, it is hoped, thus contributed to more careful conclusions.

The work is given to the public with the hope that it may assist others, as it has the writer, to a better understanding of the devious ways of the ancient book maker and copyist and a better insight into the working of the popular mind in antiquity, and so advance the study of the *genus humanum*.

Berkeley, California Dec. 24., 1921.

Chester Charlton McCown.

Contents.

Seite

INTRODUCTION.

I. General character and contents . . . . . . 1—9
1. General character 1. 2. The popular faith 1. 3. Contribution to history of Christianity 2. 4. Contribution to Jewish history 3. 5. The motifs of the work 3—5. 6. Contents of MSS 6—9.

II. Description of the manuscripts. . . . . . . 10—28
1. MS D 10. 2. MS H 11. 3. MS I 12. 4. MS L 13ff. 5. MS P 15ff. 6. MS Q 18. 7. MS S 18. 8. MS T 18ff. 9. MS U 20f. 10. MS V 21—25. 11. MS W 25ff. 12. Athos MS 27. 13. Other MSS 28f.

III. Modern editions, translations, and treatises . . 28—30
1. Fabricius 28. 2. Fleck 28. 3. Bornemann 28f. 4. Fürst 28f. 5. Migne 29. 6. Conybeare 29. 7. Notices in periodicals 29. 8. Istrin 29. 9. Kurz 29. 10. Harnack and Kohler 29f. 11. Salzberger 30. 12. Ginzberg 30.

IV. The textual history of the *Testament* . . . . 30—38
1. The manuscript families 30f. 2. Relationships and relative dates of the recensions 32—34. 3. Evolution of the *Testament* 35f. 4. Textual value of the manuscripts and their use in reconstructing the text 36ff.

V. Language and style . . . . 38—43
1. MS D 38f. 2. Rec. C 39f. 3. Rec. B 40. 4. Rec. A and the original *Testament* 40. 5. Letter of Adarkes to Solomon 40f. 6. Is the *Testament* a translation? 42f. 7. Tentative conclusion 43.

VI. The chief ideas of the *Testament* . . . . . . 43—51
1. Demonology 43—46. 2. Astrology 46. 3. Angelology 46f. 4. Magic and medicine 47f. 5. Solomon 48f. 6. Apocalyptic element 49f. 7. Jesus Christ 50f.

VII. Sources and relationships of the subject matter 51—90
1. Syncretism 51f. 2. The universal human element 52. 3. Assyrian and Babylonian influences 52ff. 4. Iranian influence 54ff. 5. Egyptian elements 55—59. 6. Jewish elements and relationships 59—66. 7. Hellenistic elements and relationships 66ff. 8. Christian elements and relationships 68—78. 9. Arabic folklore 78—82. 10. Unique mater in Rec. A 82. 11. Unique mater in Rec. B 82f. 12. Unique matter in Rec. C 83ff. 13. Unique matter in MS D 85f. 14. Solomon's seal 86f. 15. Summary and conclusions 87ff.

Contents.

		Seite
VIII.	The Testament in literature and history . . .	90—104

    1. Solomonic books of healing and magic among the Jews 90—94. 2. Solomonic books among the Arabs 94. 3. Among Christians 94—104.

IX. The date of the Testament and its recensions . 105—108

    1. Previous opinions as to date 105 f. 2. Conclusions 106 f. 3. Date of the original Jewish ground work 108. 4. Date of the recensions 108.

X. Authorship and provenience . . . . 108—111

    1. Authorship: Opinions 108 f. 2. Autorship: Conclusions 109. 3. Provenience 109 f. 4. Provenience of the recensions 111.

Appendix . . . . 112—126

    A. Manuscript N with a list of variant readings pp. 112—123. B. Manuscript E pp. 123—126.

BIBLIOGRAPHY . . . . 127—136
    I. Editions and reprints 127
    II. Translations 127
    III. Treatises and discussions 128
    IV. General bibliography with abbreviations . . . 128—136

    1. Dictionaries, encyclopedias, and periodicals 128 ff. 2. Modern authors 130—136.

TEXTS WITH CRITICAL APPARATUS . . . . 1*—122*
    Sigla et Compendia 3*
    Original Text of Testament 5*
    Text of Recension C 76*
    Text of Manuscript D Περὶ τοῦ Σολομῶντος . . 88*
    Conspectus Titulorum . . . . : . . 98*
    Sigilla Anuli Salomonis 100*
    Text of Manuscript E Διήγησις περὶ τοῦ Σολομῶντος 102*
    Emendationes in Textum 121*
    Corrigenda 122*

INDEXES . . . . 123*—166*
    I. Grammar and syntax 123*
    II. Angelology, Astrology, Demonology, Magic . . 130*
    III. Greek words 134*
    IV. Modern Greek words 161*
    V. Subjects and Persons 161*
    VI. Quotations from Ancient Authors 165*

THE TESTAMENT OF SOLOMON.

INTRODUCTION.

I. GENERAL CHARACTER AND CONTENTS.

1. The *Testament of Solomon* is a combination of folktales and a magician's *vade-mecum*. In its interpretations of Scripture and its legends of biblical personages it reminds one of the Haggadah. In its stories of demons and their activities it is similar to the *Arabian Nights*. Its magical formulae and recipes relate it to the execration tablets, the amulets, and the magical papyri of antiquity, and to the medical recipe books of the Middle Ages. The same combination of naïve popular science and laboriously learned philosophy runs indirectly into the Faust literature, and directly into the *Clavicula Salomonis*, the "Key of All Mysteries"[1]. It is a product of those three pseudo-sciences which have brought more disappointed hopes and abject terrors to mankind than any others: astrology, demonology, and magic.

2. It is as a leaf from the common man's thinking that the *Testament* has its chief value. Its superstitious puerilities arouse intense interest, when one thinks of them as recording the hopes and fears of the vast majority of mankind. The "Meditations" of Marcus Aurelius and the "Confessions" of St. Augustine open the door to the innermost thoughts of two great personalities who have done much to mould the life of their own and all succeeding generations. Books like the *Testament* help one to understand the psychological reactions of the great shadowy

---

[1] Cf. *infra*, p. 14 and n. 1.

army of men who followed these leaders afar off. They explain why the philosophical emperor, who had learned "not to give credit to what was said by miracle-workers and jugglers about incantations and the driving away of demons and such things"[1], should have allowed two lions to be cast into the Danube with elaborate ceremonies and costly sacrifices, in the vain hope of winning success for the Roman arms, and should have consulted the Chaldeans to cure Faustina's infatuation for a gladiator[2]. In spite of their absurdities demonology and magic had a tremendous hold upon the great body of mankind. The *Testament* is doubly welcome, since unfortunately we have too few first hand sources in this field[3].

3. The document also makes a contribution to a most important chapter in the early history of Christianity, coming as it probably does from the fourth century, or earlier, and embodying much older materials. One of the prominent motifs in the work is the conception of Christ as conqueror of demons. The Christian compiler combines a simple, unhesitating faith in the efficacy of the pagan formulae he cites with an inconsistent trust in the superior power of *Christus invictus*. Dion Cassius ascribes the famous thunder storm that miraculously refreshed the Roman legions and discomfited their enemies during the Marcomannic war to the magic arts of an Egyptian sorcerer[4]. The Christians claimed the marvel came in answer to the prayers of the 'Thundering Legion', and made the incident a powerful argument for the new faith[5]. Our author, combining the two contradictory points of view, stands as a representative of the great majority of the Christians of his time, to whom their faith

---

[1] *Meditations* I 6.
[2] Dill, *Roman Society from Nero to Marcus Aurelius*. London: Macmillan, 1905, pp. 446—450; Lucian, *Alexander* 48.
[3] The *Test* in some measure fills the gap in our knowledge of ancient superstitions left by the missing books of Hippolytus' *Refutatio* (II and III).
[4] *Hist.* LXXI 8.
[5] Eusebius (*HE* v 5) quotes as his authority Claudius Apollinaris, who addressed an apology to Marcus Aurelius. Tertullian makes the same apologetic use of the story. Cf. the account of Dion with that of Xifilinus in *Dio Cassius Cocceianus* ed. Bossewain, III 259 f.

was but another superstition superimposed upon the old. It was impossible all at once to replace the old sensuous paganism with a spiritual and ethical monotheism. During the long struggle Christianity was fearfully debased and weakened. How much of the old was carried over into the new religion the *Testament of Solomon* helps one partly to realize.

4. Another important service the *Testament* renders in that it represents, so far as it is Jewish, "pre-Talmudic demonology"[1], and one might add, Palestinian demonology. It is, to be sure, much more than a Christian revision of a Jewish work. A profusion of both Christian and pagan ideas and materials are to be found in it, and until these are indicated, the document must be used with caution[2]. However, when once these elements are eliminated, as they can be with some certainty, the *Test* comes to be of real assistance in reconstructing the thought world of the Palestinian Jew in the first century of our era, and it is, therefore, important not only for the student of church history, but for the New Testament and the Jewish scholar.

5. A complete table of contents is given at the end of this section. The aim of the present paragraph is to call attention to the main ideas that enter into the construction of the work. In the two chief recensions the story in brief is as follows: In response to his prayers Solomon receives his famous magic ring, in order that he may protect a favorite workman on the Temple, who is being tormented by a demon. By means of the ring the King calls the demon before him, learns the powers and activities of all the demons, the formula, or angelic name, which frustrates each, and in addition many secrets of nature and of the future. The demons are used to perform various tasks in connection with the building of the temple. The story ends with an account of Solomon's fall because of his love for a Shunamite girl, and of the consequent loss of his power over the demons. This simple framework, without plot or progress of thought, allows the introduction of a bizarre medley of stories

---

[1] Dr. Kohler, art. "Demonology" in *JE* IV 518 a.
[2] V. *infra* III 12, a criticism of Ginzberg's use of the *Test*.

about demons. The writer's chief interest is medico-magical. He writes to make known to the world what the diseases and ills are which demons bring to mankind, and how their malevolent designs are to be frustrated. His angelology is only a foil to his demonology, for God's messengers come to earth solely for the purpose of counteracting demonic agency. The *motif* of temple building, which introduces the story, is well maintained throughout, entering into almost every section. Yet, while ostensibly primary, it is really subordinate; it is part of the background against which the author can display his demonological knowledge. Another *motif* is the wisdom and glory of Solomon. This also is kept continually in mind throughout the entire narrative. In one brief section the demons are for the moment entirely forgotten, while the magnificence of Solomon's buildings, the wealth of his treasury, and the homage rendered him by other nations are described. Though the "Queen of the South" is introduced as a sorceress (γόης), it is without a trace of the Jinn of the Bilkis legend. However, Solomon's power is due to his ring, his wisdom and magnificence to what the demons have taught him and done for him, and thus the whole is brought within the writer's circle of ideas. Another very natural interest betrays itself. No doubt many an inquiring mind had asked how the magicians came to know the secret names and incantations by which the demons could be laid. In a well known Egyptian legend, Isis, the divine sorceress, wishes to learn the secret, allpowerful name of Re. She causes him to be bitten by a serpent, and he must reveal the name before she can cure him[1]. The question which inspired the Egyptian story is more satisfactorily answered by the *Testament*. Solomon's magic ring forces the revelations, and the wise king before his death writes all this hidden lore in a "Testament", which is handed down to future generations, that they may be able to escape the wiles of their demonic tormentors. It is in this connection that the

---

[1] Erman, *Handbook of the Egyptian Religion*, p. 154 ff. Unfortunately the name is not pronounced aloud, and the reader never learns it.

motivation for the story of Solomon's fall is not unskillfully supplied. According to one manuscript[1], a demon foretells the sad end of the King's glory, and, when the prophecy is fulfilled, the chastened monarch, satisfied of the truth of all that the demons have told him, writes it down. Thus, with all its variety of contents, the work is a real unity, owing to the writer's preponderating interest in magic and demonology[2].

6. The following inventory of the contents of the recensions of the *Testament* is intended to show in the most concise manner what the various forms of the work contain. By comparison of the numbers in this list with those of the "Comparative Table" opposite it will be plain at once what part of the total material each manuscript contains. References to chapter and section or to pages of the Greek text will, it is hoped, render the rapid survey of the latter easier.

The "Comparative Table" is intended to show the material contained in each manuscript, and thus to illustrate the relations of the manuscripts one to another. The divisions of the manuscripts into families, or recensions, here adopted is supported by other considerations, as will appear later. Yet the proof offered by this table is so simple and decisive that further evidence is hardly necessary.

In the table the figures at the left refer to the sectional numbers in the conspectus of contents on the opposite page. The letters, a, b, and c, used in the columns pretaining to the manuscripts, stand for Recensions A, B, and C, and indicate that the recension contains the material of the section in question. Where one of the letters: d, h, i, l, p, etc., appears, it indicates that in that section the manuscript shows material peculiar to it. The cipher: o indicates that the section is wanting through the carelessness of the scribe or accident to the manuscript, not by intentional omission on the part of the editor of the recension.

---

[1] P, XV 14 f., the only complete MS. But see MS N in appendix.

[2] Schürer, *GJV* III 419, is hardly right in calling the *Test* "Unterhaltungsliteratur".

6 Contents of the Recensions.

a) Prefatory matter (not originally part of *Test*)

1. Title
2. Doxology
3. David's sin with Bathsheba, D I 1—3 [1]
4. Failure of God's attempt to stop David, D I 4—6
5. Nathan's reproof of David, D I 7—11
6. Solomon's birth, reign, power, and wisdom, D I 12 f.
7. Solomon's prayer; command to build Temple, UVW [2], Prol. 1—5
8. Building of Temple, D II 1; cf. *Test* I 1

b) Testament proper, matter common to majority of MSS

9. The favorite slave, or chief architect, I 1; D II 2
10. His affliction by a vampire, I 2 [3]; D II 2
11. Solomon's prayer about the matter, I 3; D II 3
12. Solomon examines the slave, I 3 f.; D II 3 f.
13. Solomon's supplication for him, I 5; D II 5
14. The answer, a magic ring, I 6 f.; D II 6 f.
15. The inscription on the ring (not original) [4]
16. Solomon gives the ring to the slave, I 8 f.; D II 8 f.
17. The capture of the demon, Ornias, I 10—14; D II 10—13.
18. Solomon examines Ornias, II 1—9, D III 1—4
19. Ornias fetches Beelzebul, who is examined, III 1—7 [5]
20. Onoskelis summoned and examined, IV 1—12
21. Asmodaeus summoned and examined, V 1—5
22. Asmodaeus further examined, V 6—13 [6]
23. Beelzebul re-examined, VI 1—11 [7]
24. Lix Tetrax, VII 1—8 [8]
25. The seven sister vices, VIII 1—12
26. Phonos, IX 1—7 [9]

c) Testament proper continued in Recensions A and B

27. Punishment of Phonos, IX 8
28. Kyon, or Rhabdos, and the green stone, X 1—11
29. Leontophoron, XI 1—7

---

[1] For compendia employed to indicate MSS see below, II.

[2] U contains only a few lines in § 4 and again in Nos. 52 and 53.

[3] About the middle of I 2 HI and PQ unite.

[4] The inscription on the ring in HI and T is found also in an amulet in V (V^r) not connected with the *Test*.   [5] Q resumes in section 40 below.

Comparative Table.

No.	D.	Rec. A. H.	Rec. A. I.	Rec. A. L.	Rec. B. P.	Rec. B. Q.	Rec. C. S.	Rec. C. T.	Rec. C. U.	Rec. C. V.	Rec. C. W.	Migne col.	Text p.
					a) Prefatory matter (not originally part of *Test*)								
1.	d	h	i	o	b	b			c		c	1316 A	98* f.
2.		a	a		a	a						1316 A	5*, 99*
3.	d												88*
4.	d												88*
5.	d												89*
6.	d												89*
7.								c	c	c			78* f.
8.	d	a	a	l	b	b			c		c	1316 A	90*
					b) Testament proper, matter common to majority of MSS								
9.	d	a	a	l					c		c		5* f., 90*
10.	d	a	a	l	b	b			c		c	1316 A	6* f., 201
11.	d								c		c		8* f., 90*
12.	d	a	a	l	a	a			c		c	1316 B	8* f., 90*
13.	d	a	a	a	a	a			a		a	1317 A	9* f., 90*
14.	d	a	a	l	b	b			c		c	1317 B	10*, 90*
15.		a	a	l	b	b	c	a	c		c	1317 B	100* f.
16.	d	a	a	l	a	a			a		a	1317 B	11*, 90*
17.	d	a	a	l	a	a			a		a	1317 C	11* ff., 90* f.
18.	d	a	a	a	a	a			a		a	1317 D	13*, 91*
19.		a	a	a	a	o			a		a	1320 B	16*
20.		a	a	a	a	o			a		a	1320 D	18*
21.		a	a	a	a	o			a		a	1321 C	21*
22.		a	a	a	a	o			o		o	1321 D	22*
23.		a	o	a	ap	o			o		o	1324 C	25*
24.		a	o	a	a	o	c		ca		ca	1325 C	28*
25.		a	o	a	a	o			a		a	1328 B	31*
26.		a	o	a	ap	o			a		a	1329 B	35*
					c) Testament proper continued in Recensions A and B								
27.		a	o	a	a	o						1329 B	37*
28.		a	o	a	a	o						1332 A	37*
29.		a	o	a	a	o						1332 C	39*

6 In V 12 f. L has a different text. Sections 22 and 23 are wanting in VW, probably because of parablepsia. In V 8 MS I ends.

7 In VI 3—9 P has its peculiar text.

8 In VII 6 S has only a few lines of a magic formula in the form in which it appears in Rec. C.

9 In IX 7 P has a considerable interpolation.

30. Koryphe drakonton, XII 1—6
31. Obyzuth, XIII 1—7
32. Pterodrakon, XIV 1—8 [1]
33. Enepsigos and the origin of the *Test*, XV 1—15
34. Kynopegos, XVI 1—7
35. The cave spirit, XVII 1—5
36. The thirty-six *decani*, or clements, XVIII 1—41 [2]
37. Treatment of *decani*, XVIII 42 (of all demons, XVIII 42—44, D III 5—9.
38. Solomon's power and glory, XIX 1f. [3]
39. Saba, Queen of the South, XIX 3
40. Quarrelsome father and son; Ornias' prophecy, XX 1—21 [4], D IV 1—18
41. The "Queen of the South" in the Temple, XXI 1—4, D VI 1—8
42. Ephippas, pest and wind demon of Arabia, XXII 1—20, D VI 9—11
43. Ephippas and the corner-stone, XXIII 1—4, D VI 9—11
44. Ephippas, Abezethibu, and the air-pillar, XXIV 1—5, D VI 12—14
45. Abezethibu examined, XXV 1—9 [5]
46. Solomon's fall through the Shunamite, XXVI 1—7 [5]
47. The writing of the *Test*, XXVI 8 (H XXVI 8f.) [5]
48. Closing doxology, H XXVI 10 [5]

d) Close of MS D

49. Solomon and the demon prince, Samael, VII 1—6
50. The glory and wisdom of Solomon, VIII 1—7

e) New material in Recension C

51. The request and promise of Phonos, IX 8
52. Magical recipe, IX 9—10 [6]
53. List of demons and their signs, X 1—53 [6]
54. Onoskelu summoned and examined (second account) XI 1—6 [7]
55. The request and promise of Onoskelu, XI 7—9 [7]
56. Solomon's conversation with Paltiel Tzamal, XII 1—6 [7]
57. Paltiel Tzamal secures a "new testament," XIII 1—12
58. The preservation of the "great mystery," i. e., Rec. C, XIII 13f.
59. Solomon's conclusion and signature, XIII 15
60. Subscription of copyist of MS V (partly cryptographic)

---

[1] MSS HL omit XIV 3—XVI 1.
[2] In XVIII 4 P has an unique text. L breaks off at the end of XVIII 28.
[3] In XIX P has numerous additions.
[4] MS Q reappears in XX 10. P often has a longer text than H.
[5] In many sections H presents a highly abbreviated text, in XXVI 8—10 an inflated one. The B text is here probably better.

Comparative Table.

No.	D.	Rec. A. H.	I.	L.	Rec. B. P.	Q.	Rec. C. S. T. U. V. W.	Migne col.	Text p.
30.		a	o	a	a	o		1333 A	41*
31.		a	o	a	a	o		1333 C	43*
32.		o	o	o	a	o		1336 C	45*
33.		o	o	o	a	o		1337 A	46*
34.		a	o	a	a	o		1340 A	48*
35.		a	o	a	a	o		1340 D	49*
36.		a	o	a	a	o		1341 A	51*, 91*
37.	d	a	o	o	p	o		1348 A	59*
38.		a	o	o	p	o		1348 A	59*
39.		a	o	o	p	o		1348 B	60*
40.	d	a	o	o	a	a		1348 C	60*, 92*
41.	d	a	o	o	p	b		1348 D	64*, 94*
42.	d	a	o	o	a	a		1352 A	65*, 95*
43.	d	a	o	o	a	a		1353 D	69*, 95*
44.	d	a	o	o	a	a		1356 A	70*, 95*
45.		a	o	o	a	a		1356 B	71*
46.		a	o	o	b	b		1357 A	73*
47.		h	o	o	b	b		1357 B	74*
48.		h	o	o					75*

d) Close of MS D

| 49. | d | | | | | | | | 96* |
| 50. | d | | | | | | | | 96* |

e) New material of Recension C

51.							c c c c		77*
52.							c c c c		77*
53.							c c c c		78*
54.							c o c c		83*
55.							c o c c		84*
56.							t o c c		84*
57.							c c		85*
58.							c c		87*
59.							c c		87*
60.							v		99*

---

6 Sections 52 and 53 are found in the *Clavicula Salomonis* in the same codex as L and T⁰, Harl. 5596, here called Tᵈ. MS U ends with X 11.

7 Sections 54—56 are found as an unrelated fragment in Harl. 5596, in this case called T⁰.

II. DESCRIPTION OF THE MANUSCRIPTS.

The manuscripts are here described in the briefest manner that seemed consistent with the desire to put the reader in possession of the main facts necessary to estimate their relative importance and their relationships. They are taken up in the order in which they appear in the foregoing table, that is, following the alphabetical order of the letters which have been chosen to symbolize them, which is also the order of priority in the development of the *Test*.

1. D Dionysius monastery, Mt. Athos, No. 132, ff. 367ʳ—374ᵛ, XVI cent.; entitled περὶ τοῦ Σολομῶντος; published by Istrin, cf. Edition No. 4; collated by photograph [1], from which the title is missing; pages of *Test* deleted by transverse lines [2].

Istrin gives no description of the manuscript. The photograph shows it to have been carefully and correctly written and well preserved; it seems to be in small format. The hand is heavy, round, and beautifully clear, with the customary ligatures and abbreviations. Orthography and punctuation (comma, question mark, and period) are exceptionally good. The iota subscript is lacking. The $β$ is often written like an v. In one instance an omitted word was added at the bottom of the page; in another the order of two clauses was reversed by putting the letter $β$ before the first, $α$ before the second [3]. Otherwise there are no important corrections or erasures. A later hand has added marginal notes giving some of the subjects mentioned in the text. The title given by Istrin appears to have been written above the ornamental head-piece, and only the lower part of the letter $π$ appears in the photograph. The Solomonic writing, which fills eight leaves, was wrongly bound. The leaves are in the order 367—371, 374, 373, 372. The page on which

---

[1] Secured during the summer of 1914 through Dr. Heinrich Jantsch, Leipzig-Marienbrunn, by whose permission it is used.

[2] It does not appear to be noticed by Lambros in his *Catalogue*.

[3] κέκτημε occurs for κέκτημαι, I 10; σιτεία for σιτία II 2, 4; φησί is always written with the grave accent.

the next selection begins appears to be 375. The writing covers only about two-thirds of f. 374ᵛ, something having been erased from the remainder of the page. F. 366ᵛ contains the conclusion of a religious or ecclesiastical writing which I do not recognize¹. On f. 375ʳ begins a selection described in another hand as εἰς τοὺς αἱρετικοὺς, λόγ(οι) λδ΄, φύλλα ε΄².

2. H Private library of the Earl of Leicester, Holkham Hall, Norfolk, England, No. 99, described in the catalogue as "Opuscula theologica varia, on paper, Quarto XV and XVI cent." The *Test* is of the XV cent.; cm. 16×21.5; 35 ff., unnumbered; f. 1 recto and f. 35 verso blank, making 68 pages; entitled διήγησις περὶ τῆς διαθήκης σολομῶντος, etc.; well preserved, unpublished³. The writing is large, round, and clear; γ and ν, ε and σ may easily be confused. Ligatures and abbreviations are frequent; iotacism often appears; the iota subscript is rare. The punctuation, which is intelligently used, consists mainly of the period, placed sometimes higher, sometimes lower. Corrections and erasures are rare. It is the only manuscript which boasts rubrics placed before the chief divisions of the story. The title and the

---

1 The page begins, χαίρουσα παραστῆς, τὰς ἀϊδίους | ἐκείνους (in -ας corr.) καὶ θείας ἐλλάμψεις πλου|σίως ἀεὶ δεχομένη ..., and ends, οὐ δὴ | καὶ ἡμεῖς μετρίως μὲν ἐνταῦθα, πλου|σίως δὲ ἐκεῖ ταῖς σαῖς ὁσίαις εὐχαῖς ἐπι| τύχοιμεν· χάριτι τοῦ Κ(υρίο)υ καὶ Θ(εο)ῦ καὶ σ(ωτῆ)ρ(ο)ς ἡμῶν Ἰ(ησο)ῦ· χ(ριστο)ῦ· ᾧ|πρέπει πᾶσα δόξα|τιμή, etc.

2 It is called Ἔκθεσις κατ᾽ ἐπιτομὴν τοῦ τῶν ἰακωβϊτῶν δόγματος· καὶ τῶν ἄλλων ὧν ποιοῦσι παρὰ τὴν|ἐκκλησιαστικὴν καὶ ὀρθόδοξον πίστιν τε καὶ παράδοσιν· συγγραφεῖσα παρὰ δημητρίου μητροπο|λίτου κυζύκου· ἐκ προτροπῆ(ς)) τοῦ φιλοχρίστου | κωνσταντίνου τοῦ πορφυρογεννήτου υἱοῦ λέον|τος τοῦ σοφοῦ· ἐν ᾖ καὶ περὶ τῶν χατζιτζαρίων: — | Inc.: Ἐπειδή σου τὴν ὑπερφυῆ καὶ τῷ ὄντι βασιλικωτάτην φύσιν ἐξαίρετόν τί χρῆμα Θ(εὸ)ς τῷ κόσμῳ ἐδωρήσατο...: the page ends with καὶ πρὸς τὸν τῶν ἰακωβιτῶν διανέστησεν ἔλεγχον ὡς ἂν μὴ|καὶ οὗτοι διεστραμμένα καὶ βλάσφημα δόγματα.

3 Professor Deissmann very kindly made inquiries concerning the *Test* while lecturing in Cambridge in 1907. Dr. M. R. James informed him of the Holkham Hall MS, and later was so kind as to send me a copy of the first nineteen pages. In January, 1908, I went to Holkham and, through the generosity of the owner and the goodness of the librarian, Alexander I. Napier, Esq., was allowed to collate the MS in the library of the Hall. It is published by permission of the owner.

initial letters of the lesser sections are also in red. In XXII 10, 11 ς for σ has been mistaken for ι.

Aside from the *Test* the contents of the codex are theological and ecclesiastical. There is nothing to indicate its provenience except a tract copied in the same hand as the *Test* and called in the catalogue "Johannes Canabutii magistri ad principem Aeni et Samothraciae"[1]. This seems to point to Greece.

3. I Bibliothèque Nationale, Paris, Supplément grec, No. 500, XVI cent., paper, cm. 16×22; ff. 78—82; entitled σολομῶντος, etc., with διαθήκη τοῦ added in a careless hand in the upper margin of the page; well preserved; published by Istrin, cf. Edition No. 4.

The writing is fine, slender, and somewhat crowded; ligatures are extremely frequent and intricate, abbreviations and compendia numerous. Iotacism is comparatively rare; Attic orthography appears occasionally; e. g., φρίττω (II 1); the iota subscript is wanting; the punctuation (comma and period), the division of words, and the use of breathings and accents correct. Corrections and erasures are very rare. Although a broad margin has been left, marginal variants and glosses are wanting. The title with a conventional ornamental head-piece above it, the magical inscription of the ring, and occasional initial letters of sections are rubricated.

The codex contains a miscellaneous collection of classical, philosophical, ethical, theological, and biblical writings, including Ecclesiastes and Canticles, some of them unfinished. The *Test* follows the two Solomonic works just mentioned. Unfortunately, as with some of the other works, the copyist soon became weary of the stories of the many demons and broke off in the middle of a sentence and a column, when he had written about one sixth of the *Test*.

The well known Greek scholar, Minoïdes Minas, whose name appears on one of the fly leaves at the back, owned the codex; and through his heirs it came into the Bibliothèque Nationale in

---

[1] Johannes Canabutzes was a Graeco-Italian from Chios, first half of the fifteenth century, Krumbacher, *BLg*.

1864. Minas had been under commission from the French government to seek manuscripts in European Turkey, Asia Minor, and especially at Mt. Athos. Where he acquired this one is unknown. Doubtless it was somewhere in the Levant[1].

4. L Harleian MSS, British Museum, No. 5596; 58 ff., paper. cm. 23×34, XV cent., described in the printed catalogue as "Geomantica, exorcismi, divinationes et huius modi," with the addition in the written "Class-catalogue" of the words "quaedam Salomonis;" well preserved, unpublished. Four fragments are used as follows: 1) ff. 8^r—18^r, the title, originally missing, supplied by a later hand in Latin: "Quomodo Solomon aedificaturus templum cum spiritibus colloquitus fuit, et multa edoctus," 2) f. 7^r—7^v, 3) f. 33^r, and 4) ff. 39^v—41^r. (On the last three fragments, which are designated by T, see below.)

The writing is low, broad, round, and heavy; it is somewhat run together, yet it is regular, very clear, and not without beauty. Abbreviations and ligatures are frequent, compendia less so. Iotacism is not frequent. The iota subscript does not appear. The comma (rather infrequent), the period, and, at the end of the more important sections, a triple period make up the punctuation. Erasures, corrections, and Greek glosses are wanting. A later hand has added in Latin, besides the title, occasional marginal notices and translations, and has marked by a cross and circle those peculiar directions for the use of the *Test* as a magical remedy for disease which render this MS unique. The MS also has the distinction of being the only one written in columns, two to the page. They are seven to eight centimeters wide, and contain twenty lines. In fragment 1) no colors are used except on the seal of Solomon. It is painted

---

[1] In a personal letter, dated April 10, 1908, M. Omont very kindly gave me information regarding the three MSS of the *Test* found in the Bib. Nat. Regarding this one he says: "Suppl. gr. 500. Provient de Minoïde Mynas, no. 35 d'une list de ses manuscrits, mais sans qu'on puisse autrement préciser l'origine orientale du volume." My wife copied the MS in Paris in 1907. I compared the copy with the original then and again in Heidelberg, where it was sent through the customary diplomatic channels to the University library for my use.

with silver over red, as are the titles of the sections in the *Clavicula* (see below), and the numbers as well as the article (ὁ) before each name in the list of fifty-one demons (Fragment 4). The rather coarse, yellow paper of the codex is beginning to decay. At one spot in the lower half of the inner column many of the leaves have rubbed until a few letters have disappeared.

Harleian MS 5596 is entirely filled with magical, astrological, and demonological matter, evidently written by a mediaeval magician for practical use in his profession. The largest part (ff. 18—44^r) is taken up by the Greek form of the *Clavicula Salomonis*[1]. In it Fragments 3) and 4), which appear respectively in Recensions A and C in other MSS of the *Test*, are found. The first seven leaves of the codex contain various brief magical, geomantical, and astrological excerpts and observations, ending with Fragment 2), which is the second form of the Onoskelis story, found in Recension C of the *Test*. Two other of these excerpts bring this MS into relation with MS V, which contains a copy of Recension C; viz., ἕτερα τοῦ Πυθαγόρου ἡλιάδι (sic)[2], f. 5^v, col. 2, and a "Pythagorean table," πλινθῆς (sic) α[3], f. 6^v, col. 2, both also found in MS V. I have discovered only one other MS in which the *Clavicula* and the *Test* appear together, and that is MS W, in which there are three very badly written pages of the former and a complete copy

---

[1] This well known magico-astrological work, though mediaeval in its present form, is based on older materials. The Harleian MS contains the longest Greek copy I have seen. The ὑγρομαντεία in Munich MS. 70, ff. 240—253 (cf. *CCAG* VII 3, 3, f. 240), is well written, but shorter. *Paris. graec.* 2419 (= MS W) has, as remarked above, only a fragment, and that miserably written. It is to this last that Reitzenstein refers in *Poim.* 187, n. 1. Other Greek MSS, known to me only through catalogues, are Turin C VII 15, f. 75^v (*CCAG* IV 16), called ἑρμανεία; Mt. Athos, Dionysios monastery, (Lambros, *Cat* I 400) No. 3816.4 (282), f. 28^v—37^r, entitled τὸ κληδὴν τῆς πάσης τέχνης τῆς ὑγρομαντείας, ... συντεθὲν παρὰ τοῦ Σολομῶντος, κ. τ. λ. Latin, French, Italian, and English MSS of the *Clavicula* are numerous. Cf. the translation from Latin into English by S. L. M. Mathers, *Clavicula Salomonis*, London, 1889. Seligsohn in *JE*, art. "Solomon, Apocryphal Works" (XI 447), accepts a Hebrew original. He knows no Greek form.

[2] MS V, f. 274 (cf. *CCAG* IV 41, Bon. Univ. 3632).

[3] MS V, f. 274^v, closing the ἐπιστολὴ Πυθαγόρου.

of Recension C of the latter. Fragment 1), or L, contains about two-thirds of the *Test*, ending in the middle of a column. While on a brief visit to England in January and February, 1908, I undertook to go through all the Greek MSS of magical contents in the British Museum, as well as all the Solomonic literature in Latin, French, and English. In the course of the search I came across the Onoskelu story, then the longer fragment of the *Test* (L), and later the other pieces in the *Clavicula*. Unfortunately I have been able to get no light on the provenience of the codex. But it certainly has Italian relationships, since the "Pythagorean" letter and table are found in several other Italian MSS [1] besides V, and S of Vienna which is closely related to V [2].

5. P Bibliothèque Nationale, Anciens fonds grecs, No. 38 (Colbert 4895); XVI cent., paper, cm. 15.5×20.5; 24 ff. in three quaternions; well preserved; entitled διαθήκη σολομῶντος, etc.; published by Fleck, reprinted in part by Fürst, and entire by Migne; cf. Editions Nos. 1, 2, and 3.

The manuscript has been carefully and intelligently written. The handwriting is somewhat unskilful and angular in appearance, but easily readable. The letters are ligatured as ordinarily in the sixteenth century, but compendia and abbreviations are rare, even such words as θεός and Ἱεροσόλυμα being often written out in full. Iotacism is very rare. The iota subscript, the accents, and the breathings are almost always correctly given. Unfortunately the punctuation, consisting of the comma, and the period at various heights, is most profusely employed and, as Fürst says, "verstößt gegen jede auf bestimmte Grundsätze basierte Abzeichnung der Satzteile" [3].

Not only has the manuscript been carefully written, but part of it has also been through the hands of a corrector. A large number of letters which seemed uncertain to the co-

---

[1] Cf. *CCAG* IV (codd. Ital.) 15 (Taurin. 5, f. 39ᵛ), 31 (Mutin. 11, f. 77), 53 (Neapol. 19, f. 44), 75 (Florent. = Laurent. 29, f. 38); also Milan (Ambros.) 1030, f. 247. [2] Cf. *CCAG* VI 33. [3] *Orient* V, col. 596 note.

pyist were marked with three dots, in other instances he left part of a line vacant for the insertion of the proper words. Two such cases occur on the first page, where blacker ink, smaller and more crowded letters, and more numerous abbreviations show that the words were put in later [1]. In one case the corrector hit upon the right text; in the other he missed. On f. 2[12] a similar blank was left, but the corrector was too uncertain to put his conjecture in the text; it remains on the margin. Unfortunately he failed to go carefully through the entire manuscript, and not all of the uncertain places received his attention. Occasional corrections were made in the course of the writing[3]. Initial letters of sections are enlarged, and in two or three instances the closing lines of paragraphs have been left partly blank. No attempt has been made to rubricate or decorate the manuscript. It contains only the *Test*.

As to the provenience of the codex little can be made out. It belonged to the library of M. le President de Mesmes according to the catalogue printed by Montfaucon in 1739[4]. Henri de Mesmes died in 1596, his son, Jean-Jaques, who inherited his manuscripts, in 1642. In 1679 Colbert bought about 215 manuscripts from the Duchesse de Vivonne, great-granddaughter of the former[5], among them the *Test*, as the list shows[6]. The manuscripts of Colbert came into the *Bibliothèque du Roi* in 1732[7]. In the catalogue of the *Bibliothèque Royale* (later *Nationale*) of 1740[8] it is mentioned as "No. 38 olim Colbert." Back of the library of de Mesmes it cannot be traced. Above the beginning of the text on the first page is written "Codex Colb. 4895 Regius 2913 3", preceded by a short word ending in many flourishes. Of this, to me illegible, part of the superscription

---

[1] In I C. 3, 4.
[2] In C. I 9. Similar blanks are left in II 3, XXVI 3, 4. Marginal notes are found in IV 5, V 19, VII 3, VIII 7, 9, 10, IX 6, XIII 2, 3, XVIII 27, 37, XIX 1, XX 1.
[3] Cf. XVIII 33, XXVI 2. The only serious omission due to carelessness is in XXI 3 f.   [4] *Bib. bib. mss.*, II, p. 1327.
[5] Cf. Delisle, *Cab. des. msc.*, I, pp. 469, 471, and Omont, *Inv.* IV, pp. XXI, XXX.   [6] It is *msc. lat.* 9364 f. 11 in the *Bib. Nat.*   [7] Delisle, *op. cit.* p. 439.
[8] *Cat. codd. mss. bib. reg.*, voll. 1—4, Paris, 1739—1744.

M. Omont says: "'Cent': ce numero est une code d'inventaire des manuscrits de la duchesse de Vivonne; il provient très vraisemblablement des de Mesmes"[1]. This manuscript has been occasionally noticed by scholars. Du Cange used it in his *Glossarium* published in 1688[2], referring to "Salomonis Testamentum ex Codd. Reg. 1843[3] et Colbert," and adding "vide notas nostras as Zonarae Annal. p. 83"[4]. In these *Notae*, published in 1687, he gives the title almost as in P with the remark, "legimus apographum ex Bibliotheca Thuanea." Either this is a slip of the memory, or else the "apographum" was merely a copy of the title. The library of Jaques August de Thou (died 1617) was sold in 1680, most of the ancient manuscripts being acquired by Colbert. But none of the printed catalogues of the library of de Thou show any copy of the *Test*[5].

Other references to the *Testament* are secondary and rest upon Du Cange[6] or Gaulmin, until finally Fleck came across the manuscript and published it in 1837. His edition[7] has been the basis of all subsequent labors upon this piece of Solomonic literature, until the publication of Istrin[8].

---

1 In the personal letter above referred to, p. 13, u. 1.
2 *Gloss. ad script. med. et infin. graec.* (Paris, 1688), II, col. 32, in "Index Auctor. Graec. ined." 3 Now *Par. gr.* 2419, see below MS W.
4 *Zonarae Annalia* ed. Du Cangius, Parisiis 1686—7, 2 vols.
5 Cf. Delisle, Cab. des msc., I, p. 471; Omont, *Inv.* IV, p. XXX; *Biographie Universelle* (Paris 1826), XLV, p. 505 and n. 17; *Nouvelle Biographie Universelle* (Paris 1866), XLV, p. 229; Maichell, *Intro. ad hist. lit. de praecip. bibl. Paris.*, p. 60. Concerning this M. Omont, in the letter already mentioned, says: "Bien que le ms. 38, comme vous le verrez provienne de De Mesmes et non de De Thou, je crois cependant que c'est lui auquel Du Cange fait allusion à la p. 9 des notes du t. II de Zonaras. En tous cas, il n'y avait pas de ms. du Testament de Salomon dans le Catalogue imprimé au XVIIe siècle de la Bibliothèque de De Thou."
6 So the references by Hemsterhuis in *Thomas Magister* (Lugd. Bat. 1757), p. 636, and *Etymolog. Mag.* (ed. Gaisford, Oxford 1848), p. 142, 7, depend upon the *Glossarium*. Fabricius reprinted the title from *Zonaras*. On a slip pasted on the inside of the cover of the codex one reads: "Testamentum Salomonis, Fictitium, non semel laudatum a Gauminio in Notas ad Psellum de operat. Daemonum. 4895.'" This is a mistake. On Gaulmin's quotations see below on the use of MS W. 7 Edition No. 1; cf. *infra Intro* III 1.
8 Edition No. 4; cf. *infra Intro* III 4.
UNT. 9: McCown.

6. Q Andreas Convent, Mt. Athos, No. 73, ff. 11—15: XV cent.; published by Istrin, cf. Edition No. 4[1].

Although Istrin has given no description of the manuscript or critical apparatus, it is evident from the number of omitted letters which he has supplied in brackets, as well as from the frequent longer lacunae that it was carelessly copied from a defective exemplar.

The manuscript contains only about one third of P; viz., the first ninety and the last two hundred thirty-seven lines, cc. III 1—XX 9 being omitted. The omission occurs near the bottom of f. 12^r, many pages, evidently, having dropped out of its exemplar.

7. S Vienna, codex philos. graec. 108; paper, cm. 19×25; XVI cent.; well preserved; the greater part unpublished. Contains two unpublished fragments: 1) copies of the twelve seals said in MSS VW to have been found on the ring of Solomon, f. 361^v; 2) one of the recipes found in the same recension (VII 7), f. 167^v [2].

The codex contains much astrological matter, and many Solomonic amulets and selections. It has a large number of amulets like those in MS V, and long selections of magical content written in the peculiar cryptography to be found in that manuscript. They must, therefore, be of related origin, S having been copied from V or its exemplar. I have not learned anything concerning its provenience.

8. T British Museum, Harleian MS No. 5596; cf. supra, No. 4.

This manuscript has already been fully described. A different letter, T, is used to designate the three fragments which are

---

[1] I attempted to secure a photograph of this manuscript, as of MS D, but none was sent. No reason was given for the failure.

[2] Cf. CCAG VI (Codd. Vindobon.), p. 1. Some of the Solomonic matter is edited in the catalog. The names of the *decani* from ff. 357 ff. (p. 73 ff.), bear practically no resemblance to those in the *Test* XVIII, yet the materials are ultimately related; cf. *infra* p. 56. I studied the codex in Berlin, where it was very kindly sent to the imperial library for my use.

not incorporated in the incomplete copy of the *Test* found in this manuscript, and which belong to different recensions.

T⁰ (or simple T) designates a fragment containing the variant story of Onoskelis (Rec. C, XI), and part of Solomon's conversation with Paltiel Tzamal (Rec. C, XII 1—4, and 6 — in part —). It begins without title in the middle of col. 1 on f. 7ʳ, being separated from a magic formula which precedes it by a slight space, and ends in the middle of col. 2 on the *verso* of the same leaf. The remainder of the column is blank. The *Test* begins at the top of the next column, f. 8ʳ¹.

Tʳ designates a fragment from the *Clavicula* containing a representation of a seal and inscription which, according to MSS HI, was that on Solomon's ring. The seal, an elongated six-sided figure containing ten circles and various magical characters with the word σαβαωθ, takes up the greater part of the first column on the page (f. 33ʳ), and following it are given certain instructions and the inscription (cf. infra p. 2/3.), which runs over into the second column, under the rubric περὶ τοῦ δακτυλιδίου. The *Test* in this manuscript (L), contains a somewhat different but closely related version of the inscription on the seal.

Tᵈ designates a section in the *Clavicula* which contains the list of fifty (or fifty-one) demons which makes up a considerable portion of the unique matter in Rec. C. It runs from f. 39ᵛ¹ (bottom) to f. 41ᵛ¹ (top), and bears the rubric, ἕτερα πράξης (sic) τῆς αὐτῆς. The previous section has for its rubric, ἕτερα πράξης τοῦ καθρέπτου (modern Greek, *mirror*). It is an exorcism of a certain female demon and her people (ἡ κυρὰ βασίλισσα ἡ συμπίλια ὁμοῦ με τοῦ λαοῦ της . . . ἐσύ καὶ οἱ ἄρχοντές σου) in order that they may perform certain services for the magician, particularly that they may answer truthfully any questions he may ask. It is written in very late Greek with an Italian flavor, much more modern than the already late Greek of the list of fifty demons. Tᵈ is followed by a list of the demons and angels that rule each hour of the day, and another of the ruling planets and the work proper to each hour of the day. Both of these subjects had already been covered more briefly in an earlier part of the *Clavicula*; that is, the writer is

2*

here adding to the *Clavicula* matter of various kinds that belongs to the same sort of magic, but was not found in his copy. The last two sections he probably found in another recension of the *Clavicula*, for they appear without great difference of text in the Munich codex[1]. The origin of the list of fifty demons will be discussed later[2]. The text of T^d covers about one fifth of Rec. C.

9. U Ambrosian library, Milan, No. 1030 (H 2 inf.); paper, cm. 16×22.6; ff. 1—378; XVI cent.; two fragments: 1) f. 233^v, (= U^d), 2) f. 252^v (= U^p).

As this manuscript is known to me only through the catalogue[3] and a photograph of the page on which Fragment 1) is found, a full description of it is impossible. As to the handwriting of the page photographed, however, and general contents, it closely resembles manuscripts V and W, discussions of which follow. It has two pages from the *Clavicula*[4], here called ὑγρομαντεία as in Munich MS No. 70, the "Pythagorean" letter[5] and table found in Harl. MS No. 5596 and Bologna University MS 3632, and some astrological matter found in the Bologna manuscript[6].

The manuscript contains several unfinished fragments, some of them, like those from the *Test*, "transversis lineis deleta." I should judge that the scribe filled up odds and ends of time and space by copying little sections from other manuscripts. Thus he started in on the list of demons, and when he had reached the bottom of the page stopped. He probably had W or its exemplar before him, for he usually follows the W text.

U^d designates a fragment which, like T^d, contains the list of demons given in Rec. C. In this case, however, it is a mere fugitive fragment, with no relation to what precedes or follows, except as it is all of astrological character, and it does not com-

---

[1] Cod. 70, ff. 243^r—246^r; ff. 240^r—243^r. [2] Cf. infra VII 12.
[3] *CCGBA*, II 1096. The photograph was obtained through Dr. H. Jantsch, as was that of MS D; cf. *supra*, p. 10, n. 1. [4] Cf. *supra*, p. 14, n. 1.
[5] Cf. *supra*, pp. 14, ns. 2—3. Here it reads, πυθαγόρου ἡλιοδώρῳ χαίρειν· πολλὰ παθὼν, κτλ.
[6] περὶ τῶν ζ΄ βατανῶν (sic), f. 250; περὶ βοτανῶν ιβ΄ ζωδίων καὶ τῶν ζ΄ πλανητῶν, f. 246^r.

plete the list, ending with § 11. It bears the title, Δαίμων σφραγισάμενος ὑπὸ σαλυμῶνος τάδε εἶπε. Δαιμονίων δυνάμεις καὶ ὀνόματα.

Up I have chosen to designate a little fragment which begins very abruptly in the middle of a sentence in § 5 of the "Prologue" to Recension C, with the words, πρὸς αὐτόν· σολομὼν, σολομὼν, κύριος ὁ θεός σου ἐρεῖ. The catalogue does not quote farther, nor give the *explicit*.

10. V Bologna, Library of the University, MS No. 3632; 475 ff., paper, cm. 21.9×29.6; XV cent.; written by a physician, John of Aro (or the son of Aro, or Aron); *Test*, entitled Διαθήκη τοῦ σοφωτάτου σολομῶντος, κτλ., ff. 436ᵛ—441ᵛ; dated (f. 441ᵛ) December 14, 1440[1]. Unpublished[2].

The codex is poorly preserved. The leather of the halfleather binding is torn away, and the book is almost in pieces. The rough, gray paper is becoming discolored, yet the writing is distinct. One would not form a high estimate of the education of Dr. John from his handwriting, for it is loose, careless, and irregular, and his lines run up hill. His spelling is equally unsatisfactory. No distinction is made between, ει, η, ι, οι, and υ; between α and ε; or between ο and ω. Often β and υ, occasionally α and ει[3] are interchanged. The accents are usually placed on the right syllable, but no attention is paid to the distinction between acute, grave, and circumflex, the last appearing even on ε. The breathings also are interchanged. The iota subscript is wanting. The punctuation, consisting of comma and period, is in general not bad, but not entirely consistent. Abbreviations, ligatures, and compendia are extremely frequent. Well known words or forms are abbreviated by leaving off the last few

---

1 Cf. *CCAG* IV (codd. Ital. praeter Flor. etc.) 46. Olivieri, "Indice", 452.

2 Through the customary diplomatic channels the officials of the University Library at Heidelberg very kindly secured the loan of this MS for a period of three months from February to May, 1908, and later the extension of the time for three months more, transferring it also to Berlin, where I had gone for the summer semester. This gave opportunity for a careful study of the whole codex.

3 Probably because the ligature for ει closely resembles a common form of α.

letters. The title, the subscription, and the initial letters of the chief sections are rubricated. Corrections, erasures, and marginal notes are wanting. The contents of the codex are instructive both as to the medical practice and the religious beliefs of the Middle Ages, for they include all sorts of pseudo-scientific biological information, pages of medico-magical formulae, partly in cryptography [1], and long astrological treatises. The codex is rendered unique by its cryptography and by the large number of illustrations, poorly drawn and highly colored, including drawings of animals and plants, and magical and astrological figures.

The *Test* stands in gathering μ of the codex, being preceded by 1) λαβύρινθος τοῦ σοφοῦ σολομῶντος, f. $435^{r\,2}$, and 2) περὶ βοτανῶν τῶν ιβ´ ζωδίων ἑρμοῦ τοῦ τρισμεγίστου καὶ περὶ βοτανῶν τῶν ζ´ πλανήτων, f. $435^{v\,3}$. Following the *Test* comes ὀνειρόκριτος ὁ σηρημ [4] καὶ ἕτερος ὀνειρόκριτος καὶ πάλιν ἕτερος κατ᾽ ἀλφάβητον. After the letter π of this third ὀνειρόκριτος the codex ends (f. 475). Two further writings mentioned in the πίναξ (f. 16ᵛ) are wanting; 1) εὐχὴ τοῦ ἁγίου κυπριάνου καὶ ἑτέρου (sic) τοῦ ἁγίου γριγορίου, and 2) καὶ ἕτερες τέχναις τοῦ σολομῶντος [5]. None of these items were originally in the πίναξ, but the writings themselves are in the same hand as the greater part of the book. They evidently were not a part of the original plan of the copyist. The codex contains also the "Pythagorean" matter found in Harl. 5596 [6], but in this case the copyist saved himself trouble by pasting in six leaves, the first five of which, containing the "Pythagorean" letter, were written in another hand, Dr. John continuing on the sixth. The titles of the

---

1 Cf. *infra*, p. 23 and n. 1.
2 Cf. Berthelot, *Col. alch.* I 156 f., Texte grec I XX 39 f. (from MS 299, St. Mark's, Venice, f. 102ᵛ, XIV or XV cent.); I have found it also in Munich MS 395 (Hardt, IV 228), and Brit. Mus. Add. MS 34060, f. 162ᵛ. The Bologna MS lacks the text which in three different forms accompanies the *Labyrinth* in the above three MSS.
3 Cf. *CCAG* IV 134, VI 83, VII 29; Fr. Boll in *N JBB kl Alt* XXI (1908), 110 n. 2; see below p. 26 on MS W.
4 See below on MS W, p. 26, n. 2.   5 Was this the *Clavicula*?
6 Cf. *supra*, p. 14 and ns. 2—3 and p. 20 and n. 5.

writings which were pasted in are an original part of the πίναξ, and therefore, probably of the plan. From the similarity of subject matter it is plain, I think, that T, U, and V are very closely related.

The *Test* covers the lower two thirds of f. 436ᵛ, on which it begins. After fifteen lines at the top of the succeeding page, all the remainder is occupied by the twelve seals which were engraved on Solomon's ring, with an additional circle in which the description of the seals given in the text is repeated [1]. The next six pages are written solid, the writing space averaging cm. 17.5×25. On f. 441ᵛ the first eleven centimeters of the writing space are occupied by a circular figure intended to represent a magic writing of Solomon which is mentioned in the text (Rec. C XIII 14), and bearing the superscription, αὖτ(η) ἡ βούλ(α) ἣν ἐφόρεσ(ε) σωλομὸν ἐπάνο τη σκευει αυτου. Beside it stands another, empty circle. There follow the concluding five lines of the *Test*, and then the subscription, consisting of seven lines, the first five of which are in the cryptographic character peculiar to this MS and Vienna 108.

The subscription, reduced to ordinary characters, is given in the Text, p. 212. Lines five and six read, ἐγράφη παρ' ἐμοῦ Ἰω⟨αννου⟩ ἰατροῦ τοῦ αρο ἐν ἔτει ͵ϛϡμθ' (ἰνδικτιόνος) δ' ἐν μηνὶ Δεκε⟨μ⟩βρίῳ ιδ'. The name, Ἰωάννου is abbreviated to Ἰω, the remainder of the line up to and including αρο being in cryptographic characters. On f. 362ʳ the name is given again in cryptographic characters, this time spelled out in full, as follows: ιοάνου ιατρου του αρον. On f. 327ʳ it is found again thus: ιοανου του αρό του ιατρου. There can be no doubt as to the reading of the characters, since by a combination of two lists of words and their equivalents in different parts of the codex a key is formed to the cryptography [2]. *Aro* I take as a place name, but am unable to locate it.

As to date there is no difficulty, since that part of the subscription exhibits only the common abbreviations. The world

---

[1] Called Vˢ in the apparatus crit., cf. p. 214.
[2] The writer has in preparation an article on this cryptography.

year 6949 corresponds to 1440—1. The indiction, four, fits that year according to the table given by Gardthausen. The date is, therefore, December 14, 1440. On f. 269ᵛ (bottom) one reads the date ͵ϚϠλθ´, and on f. 327ʳ after the name, ͵Ϛϡνβ´; that is, 6939, or 1430—1, and 6952, or 1443—4. Although the meaning of the accompanying notice is not clear to me, I take it for an astronomical remark[1]. That on f. 327ʳ has the appearance of having been added to the page at the lower margin after the original writing had been completed. As we have already seen, the codex falls into two parts, the second beginning with gathering μ, f. 435, and there is no reason why the first part may not have been written last, yet I incline to think the date was added after the writing.

There are several other writings in the codex which in the πίναξ are called πρᾶξις Σολομῶντος, all of them having to do with magic. The references to Solomon, however, were added after the first writing of the index, and it would seem that after writing the latter part of the codex, the scribe came to the conclusion that Solomon was the great source of all magical science and proceeded to give him due credit. The *Test* may well have been the cause of this opinion.

Most of the writings marked πρᾶξις Σολομῶντος have no relation to the ancient king, except that they are magical. However, on ff. 360—361 is a considerable collection of amulets, two of which bear his name. In the one it is simply a part of the incantation[2]. The other, a circle four centimeters in dia-

---

[1] The three notices read, after correction as to orthography, as follows: 1) f. 327ʳ: μνήσθητι, κύριε, τὴν ψυχὴν τοῦ δούλου σου Ἰωάνου τοῦ Ἀρδ τοῦ ἰατροῦ + (ἔτει) ͵Ϛϡνβ´ (εἰσὶν) ὦ ⚹ ἧς τ(ους) ·) (· (l. ὁ χρόνος εἰς τοὺς ἰχθύας); at lower margin in faded ink: ξβ´ ͵ϚϠξε´. 2) f. 62ʳ: Ἰωάνου ἰατροῦ τοῦ Ἀρόν· ἡ μὲν ἡ χεῖρ ἡ γράψασα σέπεται τάφῳ, τὸ δὲ γραφὲν εἰς τοὺς αἰῶνας μένει. + εβρετε βρεμα εκ θεου ελενι (l. εὕρεται βλέμμα ἐκ θεοῦ ἐλεεινοῦ?) + Γαληνοῦ. 3) f. 269ᵛ (not in cryptography): ἔτει ͵ϚϠλθ´ κύκλ(ου) κγ´ (σελήνης) (ἡμέρα?) δ´ θεμελ(ίῳ) ξ´ (ἰνδικτιῶν)ος θ´. Cf. Gardthausen, *Gr. Pal.* II 495.

[2] The same amulet is found in S (= Vind. phil. gr. 108), f. 361ʳ, on the page preceding the copies of the twelve seals of Solomon (cf. supra p. 15). The amulet consists of a circle decorated within and without with magic signs and containing the following: ιωηλ βοηθει (within a triangle). ιδου σολομ(ον) υιος

meter, bears the title, τοῦ σολομῶντος μεγ(άλου), and it contains within it the inscription which, according to H and I, belongs on Solomon's magic seal, and which is given in the *Clavicula* in Harl. 5596 (= T ʳ), and in a slightly different form in the *Test* in that manuscript (L). The Bologna version has been designated as Vʳ¹.

As to the provenience of the codex I have been able to learn nothing more than has been already intimated. The cryptography of the manuscript is sufficiently like the stenography of Cod. Vat. Graec. 1809 to make one think of the monastery of Grottaferrata² as some way the source of Dr. John's knowledge of stenography. Yet the inference that he was connected with the monastery would be extremely uncertain. He may have gotten the stenography indirectly or even have developed it independently upon the basis of more ancient systems. That the manuscript is Italian in origin there can be no doubt.

11. W Bibliothèque Nationale, Paris, Anc. fonds grecs, No. 2419, XV cent. paper, cm. 27×37, 342 ff., written by George Mediatēs. *Test* entitled διαθήκη τοῦ σοφωτάτου σολομῶντος, κτλ., ff. 266ᵛ—270ᵛ. Well preserved. Unpublished³.

The codex resembles very closely the foregoing. The writing is somewhat more regular and less hasty in most of the codex. Iotacisms are almost as numerous; doubled letters are almost always written singly, even where they belong to different words. As to all other points W is just a trifle better than V. W omits occasional phrases that are found in V, sometimes apparently through carelessness, sometimes because they were unintelligible.

As to contents again there is great similarity, but in W the

δα(βι)δ δρακοντος γλοσ(σ)α εχων βασιλεος εγγκεφαλον. Beneath is written the following prescription for the use of the amulet: αυτ⟨η⟩ η βουλα γρα⟨ψε⟩ ομοιων κροκον και κηναβαρι και μαγνητη και βαστα ενθα εισι χριματα (και εσι ακηνητος add. Bol; more correct spelling adopted where MSS differed).

1 Cf. Text p. 100*. 2 See M. Gitlbauer, *Überreste*, 1 Fasc. p. 3.

3 On this MS cf. Omont, *Inv*, II 256f. I copied the *Test* in Paris in May and June, 1907.

alchemistic and astronomical interests outweigh the biological and the magico-medical. Berthelot says of it, "Ce manuscrit in-folio ... est des plus précieux pour l'histoire de l'Astronomie, de l'Astrologie, de l'Alchimie, et de la Magie au moyen âge; c'est une réunion indigeste de documents de dates diverses et parfois fort anciens, depuis l'Almageste de Ptolémée et les auteurs arabes jusqu'aux écrivains de la fin du moyen âge"[1]. The codex contains three pages from the *Clavicula*, and some "Hermetic" and "Pythagorean" writings. The fact which connects it most clearly and indubitably with Bologna 3632 is that the *Test* is immediately preceded by the Hermetic work on the planets and the twelve signs of the zodiac, and followed, though not immediately, by two of the "dream books" which also appear in the Italian manuscript[2]. The very position of the beginning of the *Test* on the page is the same in the two manuscripts. As in V, so in W, the *Test* begins about one third down the page, and at the bottom of the next page are found the large seals that in this recension belong on Solomon's ring. Either the one was copied from the other, or both followed very closely the same exemplar. The decision of this question can best be left to a later section (III 4) where the text will be discussed.

As to the provenience of the codex, M. Omont has given me the following information[3]: "Grec 2419: Provient du cardinal Nicolas Ridolfi († 1550), puis du maréchal Pierre Strozzi († 1558) et de Catherine de Medicis, après la mort de laquelle (1589), il resta sous scellés jusqu'à son entrée dans la bibliothèque du Roi en 1599. Au fol. 340ᵛᵒ, le bibliothécaire de Ridolfi, Matthieu Devaris, a écrit cette note sur l'origine du ms.: αὕτη ἡ μεγάλη βίβλος, ἣν ἐκόμισέ τις Ἕλλην ἐν Βαλνεαρίᾳ διατρίβοντι τῷ δεσπότῃ, περιέχει ἀστρονομικά τινα καὶ ἰατρικὰ καὶ ἄλλα διάφορα. Nᵒ 35. [Deleted by a transverse line.] Nᵒ 44 vigesim. quart. (Ce sont deux numéros successifs de la bibliothèque du Cardinal Ridolfi; s. e. *capsae*. τῷ δεσπότῃ désigne ici le maitre de De-

---

[1] *Col. alch.* I, Intro., I, 205; MS described, pp. 205—211.
[2] Cf. *supra*, p. 22. The titles of the "dream books" as given by Omont (*loc. cit.*) are *Oneirocrites Syrim* and *Manuelis Palaeologi oneirocrites*.
[3] In the letter already referred to above, p. 13, n. 1, p. 17, n. 1.

varis, le cardinal Nicolas Ridolfi.)" W, then, like V, came from Italy. The name of the writer was George Mediates (or, Meidiates), as appears from a subscription found on f. 288. From a *Paschalion* on f. 275 running from 1462 to 1492 the conclusion is drawn that the codex was written about 1462. The codex has been frequently used by scholars. Gaulmin in all probability took from its the excerpts he quoted in his notes on Psellus *de oper. daem*[1]. From it Du Cange prepared a very considerable list of chemical and astrological abbreviations and tachygraphic signs[2]. In more recent times Berthelot has taken from it some important chapters in his *Collection des Anciens Alchimistes Grecs*, while Reitzenstein refers to it several times in his *Poimandres*. Aside from Gaulmin I know of no publication which refers to the *Test*.

12. Βιβλιοθήκη μόνης Κουτλουμουσίου, Χαρτ. 16. XVI (Φ. 431), ... 4. διαθῆκαι Σολομῶντος. Ἅπαντα ἐν τῇ καθωμιλημένῃ.

This reference is taken from Lambros' Catalogue of the MSS on Mt. Athos, No. 3221, p. 287. I attempted to secure a photograph, but was unsuccessful, and know only this reference to the manuscript.

13. While studying in Berlin, Paris, London, Heidelberg, Munich, and smaller places on the Continent, I made search for other manuscripts and for. translations of the *Test*, but without success. None of the catalogues which I was able to consult gave indications of its presence in any form. Through the kindness of Dr. A. F. R. Petsch, then professor in Heidelberg, and later in the University of Liverpool, inquiries were mady by friends of his in the libraries at St. Petersburg and Moscow, but without success. Dr. F. C. Conybeare was so kind as to search in the Vatican Library. Though he was under the impression that a Latin manuscript was in existence[3], he was

---

1 See above, p. 17, ns. 6, 7.
2 *Gloss.*, "Notarum characteres, Notae aliae," coll. 19—22, in vol. II.
3 At Florence; see the *Guardian*, Mar. 29, 1899, p. 442. Dr. Conybeare

unable to verify that supposition or to find any other manuscripts. No doubt such exist and will be found, but no others are available at present [1].

III. MODERN EDITIONS, TRANSLATIONS, AND TREATISES.

1. Fabricius [2] deserves mention before all others, because he first attempted a systematic collection of materials bearing on the *Test*. As already indicated [3], he gathered his excerpts from Gaulmin and Du Cange, whose quotations he prints in full with some attempt at emendation.

2. Fleck rather inaccurately copied the *editio princeps* [4] from MS P, mistaking many letters, and so causing himself and those who have had to depend upon his edition much difficulty. He evidently was not familiar with sixteenth century ligatures. While it has not seemed necessary to note his misreadings in the critical apparatus of the present edition, some of the more important have been included as samples of his errors [5].

3. Apparently the first scholar to concern himself with the text which Fleck had printed was Bornemann. In 1843 and in 1846 he published conjectural emendations of the text, showing no little ingenuity, and in some obvious cases finding the original, though missing it in every real difficulty, as is usual with such conjectures. In 1844 he published a complete translation in German [6], marked by the same learning and good sense shown in his "Conjectanea".

4. Fürst [7] was the next to deal with the *Test*, printing the Greek text after Fleck, with a German translation, also in 1844.

---

was so kind also as to send me a reference to Chachanov's *History of Georgian Literature* (I 170 ff.), where mention is made of Georgian manuscripts of the *Test*. Unfortunately the work was to be found neither in Berlin, London, nor Chicago, and I have not seen the pages in question.

1 The index to Omont, *Inv* refers to Anc. fonds grecs 2511 as having a copy of the *Test*, but it is merely a copy of Prov. XXV 1—XXIX 29. Two Jerusalem MSS discovered later are discussed in the appendix.

2 Cf. Bibliogr. III 1. 3 Supra p. 17, n. 6, p. 27, ns. 1, 2; Bibliogr. IV.
4 Cf. Bibliogr. I 1. 5 Cf. c. I 2, II 6, IV 4. 6 Cf. Bibliogr. III 1 and II 1.
7 Cf. Bibliogr. I 2 and II 2.

The work, however, was not completed. Little attention was given to emending the text, but no small learning was expended on its proper translation and interpretation, though, rather strangely, the title is rendered "Bund", not "Testament", or "Vermächtniss."

5. In Migne's *Patrologia Graeca*[1] a reprint of the text from Fleck with a Latin translation was appended to Psellus, because of the fact that Gaulmin had quoted the *Test* in his *Notae* to Psellus' *de oper. daem.* The reprint shows the usual additional typographical errors, but in a few cases Fleck's more obvious mistakes were corrected. The article in Migne's *Dictionaire des Apocryphs* (Bibliogr. III 3) adds nothing new.

6. Chronologically next in order is Dr. F. C. Conybeare's translation with introduction in the old *Jewish Quarterly Review*[2], which is marked by the famous rationalist's usual careful scholarship and independence of judgment. He did all one could do with Fleck's edition. However, I am inclined to differ from him on questions of date and origin.

7. As a result of the publication of Conybeare's translation there appeared two brief articles in the *Manchester Guardian*[3], one by Dr. Montague Rhodes James, and the other by Dr. Conybeare, and a brief review in the *Theologische Literaturzeitung* by Schürer[4], who differed with Conybeare as to the Jewish origin of the *Test*.

8. In the same year that Dr. Conybeare's translation appeared, the Russian scholar, Istrin, presented the text of the fragmentary manuscripts which I have called I and Q, and of the interesting story called MS D[5]. His introduction indicates the true relationship, as I believe, between D and the *Test*.

9. A brief notice of Istrin's publication and a review by Dr. E. Kurz appeared in the *Byzantinische Zeitschrift*[6].

10. Harnack has a brief notice in his *Altchristliche Literatur*[7], and Schürer a considerable one in his *Geschichte des jüdischen Volkes*, which includes a valuable collection of materials[8]. To

---

1 Cf. Bibliogr. I 3. 2 *Ibid.* II 4 and III 4. 3 *Ibid.* III 5 and 6.
4 *Ibid.* III 7. 5 *Ibid.* I 4 and III 8. 6 *Ibid.* III 9 and 10.
7 Vol. I 858. 8 *GJV* III 419f., *HJP* II III 154f.

Dr. Kohler's article in the *Jewish Encyclopedia* [1] I owe the interesting suggestion that the *Test* represents pre-Talmudic demonology. Other encyclopedia articles make no special contribution [2].

11. In Salzberger's dissertation on the *Salomosage* much space is dedicated to the *Test* [3]. He accepts Conybeare's conclusions as to authorship and date, and accordingly takes the *Test* as representative of early Jewish-Christian demonology and folklore, making no attempt to distinguish Hellenistic elements. He has evidently used Conybeare's translation without reference to the Greek text [4].

12. Ginzberg's *Legends of the Jews* [5] contains a section devoted to the *Test*. It is a paraphrase and epitome rather than a translation, but follows the text of Fleck rather closely. One error is sufficiently serious to deserve mention: the aerial column of c. XXIV is confused with the cornerstone of c. XXIII. As unfortunately the notes and references, which, according to the preface [6], were to have appeared in the last volume, are lacking, there is nothing to indicate the source from which the story was taken. As a piece of entertaining writing the work may have a place, but it is a hindrance rather than a help to the study of ancient Jewish thinking because of its uncritical confusion of older and later materials. Ginzberg was not justified in using the *Test* without first sifting out the considerable non-Jewish elements more carefully than he does.

IV. THE TEXTUAL HISTORY OF THE *TESTAMENT*.

1. The manuscript families. — On the textual evidence alone, without reference to wider considerations of language and subject matter, which will be taken up later, the various

---

[1] IV 518, art. „Demonology". [2] Cf. Bibliogr. III 3 and 12.
[3] Bibliogr. III 13.
[4] This appears from his citing only Conybeare (p. 9, n. 9) and from his use of *"Flasche"* for ἀσκός (p. 97), following Conybeare's "flask" in secs. 119—123, though the latter once has "leather flask" (119).
[5] Bibliogr. II 5. [6] Vol. I XV.

MSS divide themselves into four clearly marked classes or recensions[1].

a) MS D differs from the rest in that it is not a "Testament." Of magico-medical formulae there are none. It is simply a biography of Solomon in which the demonological interest outweighs all others, quite closely resembling in many features the *Arabian Nights*. It clearly belongs to the "literature of entertainment," where Schürer wished to class the whole *Test*[2].

b) MSS H, I, and L (Rec. A) stand very close together, H and I agreeing in a beginning which is entirely different from that in the other MSS, H and L (after I drops out) in the long omission, cc. XIV 3—XVI 1. L might deserve to be put by itself as a separate recension, for it has at a late period undergone a special revision. A magician has endeavored to make the work more useful for members of his profession by introducing directions for the use of the more important magical formulae in the cure of some disease, probably demon possession. He has also made some further changes in the opening sections. However, all these alterations, marked by modern Greek forms[3], are so easily detached from the remainder and affect it so little that there is no need to separate it from H and I as a textual witness.

c) MSS P and Q (Rec. B), again, clearly stand together almost from beginning to end. The title and the opening sentences are good illustrations of their close similarity throughout. This recension, in P at least, is marked by two explanations of the writing of the *Test*[4], by a shorter beginning and ending, and by more extended accounts of many of the demons[5].

d) MSS V and W with the fragments S, T, and U group

---

1 The variety of recensions is not at all remarkable in popular literature such as this; cf. the remarks of Krumbacher, "Studien zur Legende des heil. Theodosius," in *Sitzungsber. d. bay. Akad. d. Wiss., philos., philol. u. hist. Cl.*, 1892, Heft II, p. 225.

2 Since this is not a *Test*, I have not called it a recension, but refer to it as MS D. See above, p. 5, n. 2.   3 Such as ἤτον ἕνας, I 1.

4 See XV 14 and XXVI 8; no great weight can be attached to this, since c. XV is wanting in HILQ by accident or scribal error.

5 See cc. XIX, XX, and XXVI.

themselves as an entirely different recension (C), which has undergone a thorough revision. The *Prologue*, as I have called it, in order to bring the chapter and verse divisions into line with the other recensions, and the altered title, but especially the entirely different ending from IX 8 on are sufficient evidence. This recension is more interested in demonology as a means for revealing nature's treasures and mysteries than in its medical aspect as emphasized in the original *Test*. It is marked by scribal omissions [1].

2. The relationships and relative dates of the recensions. —
a) MS D represents the story which formed the basis of the *Test*. The recensions have just been considered in what the writer regards as their chronological order. It is inconceivable that any one should take the *Test* as found in Recs. A, B, or C, and, by eliminating all the magico-medical element and the "testament" motif, reduce it to the simple tale of Solomon's birth and greatness, his temple building and dealing with demons, which appears in MS D. On the other hand, the very close resemblances between MS D and Recs. A and B as to general outline and even as to text in places, e. g., in the story of the old man and his son, c. XXI, proves the closest possible relationship, and, therefore, the dependence of the *Test* upon the story as found in MS D.

Yet D in its present form cannot have been the basis of the *Test*. It occasionally shows a fuller, secondary text, e. g., in the threat of the old man to cease working if Solomon did not condemn his son (D IV 2). Especially is this true of D VII. The question of c. VII 1, ἔστι καὶ ἕτερον δαιμόνιον; and its answer, εἰσὶ μὲν πολλά, ὦ βασιλεῦ, after the statements of c. III 4—8 that all the demons had been brought in and set to work in the temple are manifestly a later addition. There is no reason why c. VII should not have been put into the *Test* if it had lain before its writer. It is evident, then, that MS D represents a revision of the work that formed the original of the *Test*.

---

[1] See cc. I 4, 11, 14; V, VI, etc. The language of C is more consistently late than in any of the other recensions; see below, V 2.

The question as to whether cc. I, II, and VIII were part of this original is harder to answer. The editor of the *Test* could not well include cc. I and II in a "testament," which must have been written in the first person to have entirely consistent. The abrupt beginning of Rec. B is probably due to truncating the original story in order to eliminate these elements, which do not fit the new plan. C. VIII could easily have been put into the first person and left in the *Test*. Yet it seems entirely possible that it was in the original and was omitted by the editor of the *Test* merely because it did not interest him, or perhaps because it did not suit the pathos of the fall. It is not inconsistent with the remainder of D, but rather comes as a fitting conclusion to a narrative of which the account of the sin of David and the birth of Solomon was the beginning[1]. I am inclined, therefore, to regard D I—VI, VIII as the original basis for the *Test;* with certain changes which we cannot follow and the addition of c. VII, D received its present form. The making of the *Test* was a much more complicated process.

b) Recensions A and B are both revisions of the original *Test*. The question of priority in this case is much more difficult. It is plain that A is secondary at its beginning, because it is much fuller than B (c. I 1 f.). Again at its conclusion, A, here represented by H only, is much fuller, and probably represents an expansion (C. XXVI 8—10). In the main, however, A has the shorter text in so many places where B presents fuller information regarding the demons[2], that one cannot but conclude that Rec. A has the claim to priority in most cases, and is nearest the original *Test*[3].

c) Recension C is a revision of Recension B. The nature of the material in the added chapters of C, as well as the fact that in the fragments, especially in T, much of it occurs in, or in

---

[1] The transposition of sentences in c. VIII does not affect these conclusions, as it may have occured in the exemplar from which MS D was copied, or in the copying of D without touching the original. But see MS E in appendix.

[2] Cf., for example, VI 4 f., XVI 4 f., XVIII 42, XX 6, etc.-

[3] Rec. A presents omissions due to careless copying or a defective exemplar; e. g., XIV 3—XVI 1.

connection with, the *Clavicula*, which is a mediaeval product, establishes the character of this recension as secondary and late. The interesting account in C XIII of the origin of a καινὴ διαϑήκη which is to be given to the world as a deception and a snare, while the true, original *Testament* is to be preserved in one copy only until "the expected parousia of God," when it is again to be spread abroad, is plainly intended to establish faith in this recension as the real original article over against Rec. B, which it was to supplant. The numerous agreements of B and C prove that the latter was based upon the type of text found in the former[1], yet in some cases C has a more primitive text than the present MS representatives of B (MSS PQ) offer.

d) Illustration will serve to make the relationships of the recensions clearer. A good example is to be found in c. III 7. Here Rec. A (HIL) gives a text which is entirely fitting and intelligible: ἀπῄτουν δὲ τοῦτον ἀδιαλείπτως ἐγγυϑέν μοι προ-⟨σ⟩εδρεύειν. This became nonsense by misreading into ἁπάντων δὲ τούτων οὐ διαλιπο⟨, as V shows (W omits this much). P, wishing to leave nothing unintelligible, altered to ἅπαντες δὲ οἱ δαίμονες ἔγγισϑέν μου προεδρεύουσι, which in itself is good, but does not fit the context which follows in § 8. Another example of B's improvement upon a text which seemed unintelligible is found in II 8, where both V and W, as W in the previous case, omitted the difficult words. In c. XVIII 42 the editor of B expands a short section which in A merely closes the account of the thirty-six *decani* into an entirely new narrative of Solomon's treatment of demons in general. On the other hand, in the latter part of the *Test*, where H alone represents Rec. A, there are a number of sections in which the text of H is so brief as to be almost unintelligible, and, as it seems to me, shows evidence of hasty abbreviation[2]. In these sections I have given B the preference, as also in the conclusion (c. XXVI 7—8), where H has an expanded text.

---

[1] Examples may be found on almost any page; cf. c. VII. This account of the writing of a "New Testament" may be compared with IV Ezra XIV 26, 42, 45 f.

[2] Cf. XXII 3, 11, XXIV and XXV *passim*.

3. The evolution of the Testament: summary of conclusions. — A number of stories about Solomon in which demons played a large part were gathered into a tale, *d*, a revision of which lies before us in MS D[1]. Some one who was interested in the magical cure of diseases then conceived the idea of the *Test*, and decapitated the story of *d*, leaving it to begin abruptly as in Rec. B with the tale of a demon who plagued the King's favorite workman during the temple building. The editor added a more fitting conclusion in the story of Solomon's fall as found in Rec. B. The original *Test*, then, consisted of the beginning and ending as in Rec. B (MSS PQ), but with the body of the work mainly as in Rec. A (MSS HIL)[2]. The present beginning of Rec. A resulted from an attempt to remove the abruptness of the first sentence, being constructed by piecing together from later sections items regarding the favorite workman. This redacteur also thought himself able to construct a conclusion with greater parenetic value. Rec. B is another independent working over of the original *Test*, with certain interesting additions. Whereas redacteur A was mainly concerned with making the story read better, redacteur B was in possession of fuller knowledge regarding many of the demons mentioned, and accordingly added to or replaced several sections[3]. Finally a student of demonological literature with a theological and scientific bent discovered some fragments which he thought Solomonic and which appeared to him to have greater value than a good part of the *Test*. So taking Rec. B he constructed another *Test*, putting in a preface, or prologue, containing certain prayers of Solomon, removing the abruptness of the beginning much as redacteur A did, and replacing the latter two-thirds of the *Test* by his new material. In the story of Onoskelu (Rec. C XI) he

---

[1] Istrin in his introduction to the MSS which he edited came to the same conclusions regarding the relation of MS D to the *Test* as those expressed above, and I am in part indebted to him for this theory, and especially for the discovery of MS D.

[2] The text printed at the top of the page in this edition is an attempt to reconstruct this original *Test*.

[3] These are printed in brackets thus: ⌈ ⌉, or placed in the critical apparatus at the bottom of the page.

presents a variant form of a tale which he allows to remain in the earlier, unaltered part under the name of Onoskelis (c. IV)[1]. He seeks to give authority to his version by representing that it was feared and secretly preserved at the request of a great demon, Paltiel Tzamal, who wished to prevent the publication of its great mysteries, and that the well known, current form of the *Test* had been specially written for Hezekiah, thus utilizing an early tradition[2]. MS L represents an interesting step in another direction, the attempt to make the work of greater practical value as a physician's *vade mecum*, or book of prescriptions. Its reading with the proper rites would cure the possessed[3].

4. The textual value of the MSS and their use in reconstructing the text. — Although MS D represents the original story from which the *Test* was evolved, it possesses no primary textual value, since it is not the *Test*, and, though its contents are similar, its text is rarely that of the *Test*. The attempt here is to reconstruct the original *Test* out of which Recs. A and B have grown. MS D is printed separately at the end of the volume.

Our MSS of Rec. C come from a class of men of rather low mentality and poor Greek education. The numerous omissions are textually of little moment, because the redacteur was interested in different matters from the originator of the *Test*, and the scribes were careless. Since, as we have already shown above (IV 2 c, d), C is derived from B, their agreement can have little weight *per se* against acceptable readings found in A alone. Where, however, Recs. A and C agree, they represent the original text. Without C it would have been much more difficult to show that B was secondary. While neither V nor W could have been copied the one from the other[4], they may have come from the same exemplar. Where it was unintelligible or corrupt,

---

[1] In the critical apparatus to c. IV readings from c. XI of C have been distinguished by adding a superior letter o to the letters T, V, and W.

[2] Rec. C XIII; cf. Josephus, *Hypomnesticon* c. 74, Suidas, s. v. Ἐζεκίας; see below VIII 3c (3). [3] Cf. II 5, 6; IV 12; V 8, 9, 12f.

[4] I can find no words in W omitted by V which the scribe of W might not have added by guess, while the reverse (words in V omitted by W) often

V sometimes reproduces conscientiously where W omits or emends, for W had the more intelligent copyist. Accordingly V has been given the greater weight except where mistakes appear to have arisen from carelessness or misunderstanding.

Rec. B represents a learned, and in MS P a very careful, revision [1]. Occasionally P alone preserves the true text owing to the greater intelligence with which it has been handled. Yet it must be used with great caution, since both redacteur B and scribe P have taken great liberties with the text in making additions, alterations, and omissions. Q shows more errors than P, but fewer intentional changes.

The MSS of Rec. A have been rather mechanically copied. In some instances the scribes have not taken the liberty to drop or emend what they could not understand, but have reproduced it letter for letter [2]. There are omissions due to carelessness, one so long as probably to have been caused by a missed or missing leaf in the exemplar. In general H appears to have suffered least from intentional revision, but to have been in less skilful hands than I [3]. Both were conscientiously copied by scribes who knew little of magic. Therefore the better instructed L occasionally presents a preferable reading, although he was somewhat careless and illiterate and his practical directions often vitiate his text. In c. I I have followed MS I, since it alone preserves the first person, which the original *Test* ought to have shown throughout [4], and also since it appears to me, following

---

occurs, where other MSS make it possible to determine the true text; e. g., IV 5 (φύσεως), II 9, IV 12. W omits by homoeoteleuton, IV 12, of intention, II 9, VIII 9, where the passage seemed unintelligible. Therefore V could not have copied from W. But I do not believe W could have made out the true text from V's unwarranted expansion in II 6 (φοβούμενος ... προσψαῦσαι), nor is he likely to have omitted the right words in IX 9.

1 In one case at least P omits a difficult passage where H and L are unintelligible; viz., V 7; it omits difficult lines in V 4, cf. VW; it makes a glaring omission by homoeoteleuton in XXI 3f., and a minor one in IX 6.

2 Cf. II 2, 3 (HIL), 6 (H), V 6 (HL), XVIII 4 (HL).

3 Cf. XXII 7 and XXIV 3—5 (H); XIV 3—XVI 1 (HL). In V 4, 5, IX 6 H appears to have read '/. (= ἐστίν) as ϳ (= δέ).

4 L maintains the third person for Solomon consistently, I the first; the others vary, but in general begin with the third and change to the first.

a suggestion of Dr. Goodspeed, that H exhibits an attempt to make clearer the somewhat unusual language of I regarding the favorite slave. Here, however, as in the concluding sections, Rec. A shows signs of undue expansion, and in constructing the text of the *Test*, which always appears at the top of the page, I have followed Rec. B. Again, in certain sections toward the end, I have thought that Rec. A gave evidence of abridgment, and in these places, especially since the carelessly written H is here the only MS of Rec. A, I have given Rec. B the preference[1]. In general, then, unless weighty reasons appeared to the contrary, H has been made the basis of this edition. The rule adopted has been, 'When in doubt, follow H.'

In concluding this section it should be noted that we cannot claim to have the original *Test* in our reconstructed text. Such an admission would be called for on a priori grounds alone. But we have evidence on the subject, for, in the quotation from the *Test* which occurs in the *Dialogue of Timothy and Aquila*[2], the Jew insists that Solomon οὐκ ἔσφαξεν ἀλλὰ ἔθλασεν, while in the *Test* as we now have it, although the Shunamite says σφάξαι (MS H) or σύντριψον (MSS PQ)[3], Solomon merely says ἔθυσα (MS H) or ὅπερ καὶ ἐτέλεσα[4]. If we could find the original MS, many such differences would appear, but not enough to vitiate our general conclusions regarding the work[5].

V. LANGUAGE AND STYLE.

This section will be made quite brief, as the grammatical index will supplement it by presenting the evidence for the positions taken.

1. MS D. — As to language and style there are decided

---

1 Cf. *supra*, IV 2 b, d. MS N has valuable readings. See appendix.
2 *Anec. Oxon.* Class. Ser. VIII 70, c. XIII 6; cf. *infra*, VIII 3 d) (2) (e).
3 C. XXVI 4.   4 C. XXVI 5.
5 In general the effort has been made to print the text as the author may be supposed to have written it, following the ordinary practice of the early Christian centuries as to spelling and grammar. As to ν moveable the classical rule has been followed for the sake of simplicity.

differences between the recensions. In this regard, as well as from the diplomatic standpoint, MS D is far superior to the rest. An educated Greek has edited and written it. The outstanding inaccuracy in his grammar is the use of the nominative absolute, or rather *nominativus pendens*, not a serious blunder[1], which occurs a few times. Once ἅμα is used with τό and the infinitive[2]. Otherwise tenses and cases are on the whole corretly used. The optative, subjunctive, imperative in both second and third person, and a future participle of purpose are found. Late forms and usages are rare. For the dative πρός with the accusative is frequent. In IV 9 οὐκέτι ἴδῃς is a (Homeric and) late usage, subjunctive for future, which has contributed to such a future as εἰσενέγκομεν in VI 2[3]. βούλεσαι replaces βούλει in IV 11[4].

As to style, the constant use of the historical present and the occasional omission of λέγει or φησί after the name of the speaker in dialogue lends vivacity, while the conversations are short and to the point. The writer has a fairly large vocabulary, including a considerable number of particles. There is a heaping up of epithets and synonymous words when opportunity offers[5]. Specially noteworthy is the constant use of the circumstantial participle in various relations. The author is fond of dropping in a verb to separate the article and attributives from their noun[6]. The use of βασιλεία = "Majesty," and κράτος = "Excellency" in direct address is Byzantine.

2. Rec. C. — This, the latest recension, is at the antipodes from MS D. How far its present condition is due to scribal carelessness and ignorance we cannot say, but probably they are partly accountable for its very poor Greek. Errors, such as the accusative for the dative, and late forms, such as -αν as ending of the accusative singular in the third declension with an analogous nominative, e. g., σφραγῖδα, abound, and there are several Latinisms. The first sentence is an unattachable genitive absolute. The editor was fond of compound tenses. As to style[7]

---

1 Cf. Moulton, *Proleg.* 69. 2 C. III 5. 3 Cf. Dieterich, *Unters.* 243 ff.
4 *Ibid.* 249. 5 C. I 2, 13; IV 6, 7, 9, 18.
6 C. IV 2, VI 14, VII 2, 4, 5. 7 See Prologue 1, 2; c. XIII 4, 12.

the additions show somewhat ambitious attempts at fine writing, e. g., in the prayers of the Prologue and in the closing chapter. The same trick appears as in D, of dropping the verb in between attributives and their nouns.

3. Rec. B. — Rec. B is more correct as to grammar and simpler as to style than Rec. C. Between A and B there is little difference, but in its additions B, especially MS P, shows a tendency to more "correct" usage, but also to compound words, and in one instance it has a decided Latinism, πρωτομαΐστωρ [1].

4. Rec. A and the original *Testament*. — The editorial additions to Rec. A have some glaring errors, particularly in MS L, but, if we may judge from this recension, the *Test* was originally a very simple piece of writing in fairly correct Koinē Greek. It paid no attention to refinements of rhetoric or lexicography, but told its story in a straightforward, paratactic style, such as one might expect from a man of small education and mental ability in recounting an interesting series of stories. On the whole the grammar is that of the New Testament, with developments along the lines taken by the Koinē such as would seem to point to a period subsequent to the New Testament. The disappearance of the optative, the aorist subjunctive for the future, the increase in the use of prepositions and compound words, and the numerous locutions which are characterized by the Atticists as vulgar constitute the evidence on this point. Real Semitisms do not appear in the *Test*. That the καὶ ἐγένετο construction may be called such I cannot believe [2]. Another so-called Semitism, the demonstrative repeating the relative, occurs, but it is a mere blunder due to an attempt to repair a garbled passage [3].

5. Letter of Adarkes to Solomon. — The letter of the Arabian King in c. XXII contains two peculiarities, the absence of the name of the sender from the introductory formula and in MS D the use of direct address, βασιλεῦ Σολομῶν, χαίροις. Unfortunately the two treatises which have appeared on the

---

[1] C. I 2.   [2] Contrast Conybeare, *JQR* XI 6, and Moulton, *Proleg.* 16f.
[3] C. I 9, Rec. C; cf. Moulton, *op. cit.* 94f.

subject of Greek letter formulae[1] do not carry the subject far enough into the Byzantine period to aid us here, and the extant letters have too often been handed down without the introductory formula[2].

So far as the evidence goes, the use of variations of the customary formula, ὁ δεῖνα τῷ δεῖνι χαίρειν, does not mark any particular era. The use of χαίροις with the vocative seems a sign either of servility or of poor breeding, for three of the instances known to me from the papyri are from people of little culture, while the ancients particularly reprobated the use of the first person and direct address[3]. Perhaps the editor of D thought such familiarity entirely legitimate between kings, or wished to represent the Arabian king as inferior to Solomon[4].

To account for the absence of the senders's name three theories are possible: either βασιλεὺς Ἀράβων Ἀδάρκης has fallen out by haplography, or the MS D form was original and the present text of A and B is a correction to the third person, or the writer has used the form which was customary in copies of letters[5]. Other evidence for the secondary character of the present text of D seems too strong to allow the second alternative. For the first speaks the fact that the MSS differ decidedly as to the lines immediately preceding the letter. More decisive, however, seems the consideration that such a writer could hardly be expected to be precise as to letter formulae, particularly as the identity of the sender is plainly indicated in the text.

Unfortunately in any case we reach the negative conclusion that the peculiarities of the letter formulae give no aid in determining the date of the recensions.

---

1 Gerhard and Ziemann, see Bibliography IV *infra*.
2 See Hercher and Migne, *PG*.
3 Apollonius Dyscolus, *de const.* II 9, III 14, ed. Bekker, 112, l. 27—113, l. 10, 232, ll. 18 ff.; Scholiast to Dionysius Thrax, 550, ll. 14—23, ed. Hilgard. Ziemann found six examples of χαίροις to which add *Ox P* 112 (I 177, III/IV cent.) and the optative εἴης, Migne, *PG* 161, cols. 688, 692, 697; and nine examples of χαῖρε to which add *Ox P* 1156 (VIII 258, III cent.); *op. cit.*, 295.
4 Ziemann, *op. cit.*, 296 f., suggests also the possibility of Latin influence.
5 Cf. Ziemann, *op. cit.*, 285 f.; petitions and memorials give no precedent for such a form, cf. *ibid.*, 259—266.

6. Is the *Testament* a translation? — Dr. M. Gaster argues that the *Test* is translated from Hebrew[1]. Such a view is naturally suggested by the large number of Hebrew names of angels and demons, to say nothing of the fact that Solomon, the great Jewish wise man, is the hero of the story. Dr. Gaster finds evidence of translation in the expression τῷ ἀγγέλῳ τοῦ θεοῦ τῷ. καλουμένῳ Ἀφαρώφ, ὃ ἑρμηνεύεται Ῥαφαήλ, ... καταργοῦμαι[2]. He believes that we have here a misunderstanding of the word *Shem-ha-meforash, perush* having been taken to mean "interpretation." Aside from the precariousness of argument from a single case such as this, the decisive fact is that this expression is an editorial addition found only in MS P. HL present a shorter and simpler text, ὑπὸ τοῦ ἀγγέλου Ῥαφαήλ (καταργοῦμαι). There is no reason why HL should have omitted the phrases of P if they had stood in the original *Test*, for they are perfectly intelligible, with only an element of mystery in the word Ἀφαρώφ such as this sort of literature loves. The editor of Rec. B contributed this out of his fund of magical knowledge[3].

As it seems to me, the strongest evidence for translation from a Semitic original is to be found in Rec. A in the list of *decani*, the thirty-six στοιχεῖα, where all from the twentieth on call themselves ῥύξ (H, XVIII 24—40), or ῥίξ (L, XVIII 24—28). This word surely is a transliteration of רוּחַ. But even such a transliteration does not prove that the whole *Test* was originally written in Hebrew or Aramaic. This particular section, which is plainly of Egyptian origin, has been partially revised by a Jew before it was taken over into the *Test*[4].

Another possible piece of evidence is to be found in the clause ἀπόγονος δέ εἰμι ἀρχαγγέλου τῆς δυνάμεως τοῦ Θεοῦ[5]. Ouriel is not the "power of God," as in Recs. B and C, but the "light of God." It might be thought that originally גַבְרִיאֵל stood in the text and was translated by some one who failed to recognize it as a proper noun. The copyists, feeling the need of some name, have made various "corrections." Such a supposi-

---

1 "The Sword of Moses," *JAS* 1896 p. 155, 170.   2 C. XIII 6.
3 Cf. *infra* VII 11.   4 Cf. *infra* VII 5.   5 C. II 4.

tion would be entirely probable if the language of the *Test* elsewhere gave evidence of translation. It is more likely the passage was written by one who knew no Hebrew.

7. Tentative conclusion. — It seems much more natural to explain all apparent indications of Semitic origin as due to the fact that the writer of the *Test* has used materials already translated from languages unfamiliar to him. Did the heathen compiler of the great Paris magic papyrus translate the biblical material he used? Did the writers of the Synoptic Gospels translate their sources from Aramaic? No one so alleges. Our tentative conclusion, then, at this stage of the investigation, must be that the native language of the writer of the *Test* was Greek. So far a study of the language of the work has taken us. For a more precise answer as to its origin we must analyze its chief ideas and their sources.

VI. THE CHIEF IDEAS OF THE *TESTAMENT*.

The *Test* is a collection of astrological, demonological, and magical lore, brought together without any attempt at consistency. The writer attempts no science or philosophy of demonology; indeed he is a compiler rather than an author.

1. Demonology[1]. No general statement is made as to the origin of demons, and the data given in particular cases disagree. Some are fallen angels[2], others are the offspring of angels and the daughters of men[3]. One is the spirit of a murdered giant, one is perhaps born of a *bath qol*[4]. They dwell in deserts, tombs, precipices, caves, chasms, and at cross roads[5].

As to their nature certain intimations are given. Most of them are embodied spirits. Of one this is distinctly stated[6], while a number are minutely described, generally as griffins combined of animals and birds, or of animals and man. One is a wind merely, but when put into a sack he acts like a man[7]. They can, within limits, assume different forms[8]. They are an-

---

1 Cf. Index II.   2 C. VI 2.   3 C. V 3.
4 C. XVII 1, IV 8.   5 C. IV 5; VIII 4.   6 C. IV 4.
7 Cc. XXII, XXIII.   8 C. IV 4; II 3.

thropomorphically conceived. Onoskelis quails before a threatened beating[1], Asmodaeus is bound and beaten[2], Kunopegos almost faints from thirst[3], Akephalos Daemon sees through his breasts and is blinded when the seal is pressed upon him[4]. Some are female, and the writer probably thought it possible for both males and females to have offspring[5]. They have all the physical as well as psychical passions of mankind.

Though they thus resemble human beings so closely, they have a certain likeness also to the angels. They escape many of the physical limitations of men, in that they may assume various forms and are supernaturally crafty and powerful. They know the future, and several of them tell Solomon of coming events. How this is possible is explained by Ornias, who relates that the demons fly up to the gates of heaven and overhear the decisions announced to the great concourse of angels there; then, coming down, they make use of their knowledge to injure mankind. However, this foreknowledge is gained at great risk, for, having no place to light at the gate of heaven, they become weary and fall, and these falling demons are what men call shooting stars[6].

No systematized demonic hierarchy is known. Beelzebul, as chief of the whole tribe of demons[7], is summoned to assist Solomon in dealing with them. He has a vicegerent, named Abezethibou, like himself a fallen angel, who is the great spirit of rebellion against God and the good. Beelzebul apparently now rules upon earth and Abezethibou in Tartarus, though the latter is "nourished in the Red Sea," where he was confined on the overthrow of Pharaoh and his host[8]. He is haled before Solomon by Ephippas, not by Beelzebul, and may, therefore, be thought of as independent of the latter[9]. Beelzebul is plainly

---

1 C. IV 11.   2 C. V 6.   3 C. XVI 5.   4 C. IX 3.
5 C. V 4; Rec. B certainly so thought; cf. VI 6; XXII 20.
6 C. XX 14—17.
7 Cc. III, VI. Βεελζεβούλ, the form occurring in the majority of NT MSS and adopted by Tischendorf, Nestle, and von Soden, is the form of Recs. BC. H has Βεελζεβουήλ, said by Legge to be the Coptic form (*PSBA* XXIII 248).   8 Cc. VI 3; XXV.   9 Cc. VI 5, 6; XXIII 2; XXIV 1.

identified with the ἄρχων τῶν δαιμονίων of the Gospels¹, for he trembles before "Emmanuel of the Hellenists"². But he is not "Lucifer, star of the morning"³; his star is Ἑσπερία⁴. Except in C. III, where he is first summoned, and in C. VI, where he is examined, Beelzebul is a figurehead. Only Kunopegos, a sort of Poseidon, mentions the fact that he, with all the demons, is subject to Beelzebul's direction, and at intervals comes to land to consult him; it was on one of these trips that Beelzebul arrested him and brought him before Solomon⁵.

Many interesting demonic figures appear, such as Ornias, Asmodaeus, Lix Tetrax, Pterodrakon, the dog Rhabdos, the three headed dragon called κορυφὴ δρακόντων, Leontophoron the demon of Gadara, three liliths, or Empusas, called Onoskelis, Enepsigos, and Obyzuth, seven stars that are κοσμοκράτορες τοῦ σκότους, and other thirty-six with the same high sounding title who are the *decani*. Limitation of space forbids their further discussion here. They cause all kinds of diseases and bodily defects, from seasickness to epilepsy, being particularly dangerous to women in childbirth and to infants. They destroy fields, flocks, houses, ships, and human lives, and will finally bring the end of the world⁶. The thirty-six *decani* are entirely of this sort⁷. Demons are sources also of moral evil, inspiring heresies, idolatry, lust, theft, envy, hatred, murder, war, and kinred evils. The seven spirits who call themselves κοσμοκράτορες are of this kind⁸. So far as the writer of the *Test* has thought the matter out, evil does not reside in the flesh, nor in matter, nor can it be ascribed to God; sins are the result of demonic incitement. How or when the angels came to sin we are not told. In any case there is no real dualism in the *Test*. Though Beelzebul rules "the spiritual hosts of wickedness," they and he are completely subject to God and to the divinely ordained means for their subjugation. Mention is made of demons in Tartarus, but no punishment for them seems to be known ex-

---

1 Cf. Mk III 22; = Mt XII 24; = Lk XI 16.   2 C. VI 8.
3 Is XIV 12 AV; ἑωσφόρος ὁ πρωΐ ἀνατέλλων LXX.
4 C. VI 7.   5 C. XVI 3, 5.   6 Only in P VI 4, ἀπολῶ τὸν κόσμον.
7 C. XVIII.   8 C. VIII.

cept that which Solomon and the magic revealed in the *Test* can inflict.

2. Astrology. — A large proportion of the demons in the *Test* have some definite astrological relationship. Demons and men are said to reside in a star[1], or a sign of the zodiac[2], or a phase of the moon[3], and mortals seem to be particularly liable to injury from demons who are συναστροί with them, that is belong to the same star[4]. The author seems to think of the influence of the stars as wholly baleful. Asmodaeus says, "through the stars I ⌈scatter⌉ madness after women"[5], and that suggests the prevailing notion. There is, I believe, no reference to prediction by means of astrology.

One chapter (XVIII), a list of the thirty-six *decani*, is a piece of astrological material taken over bodily. In this case each δεκανός is thought of as a demon causing certain diseases, which are recorded, and the means for counteracting them are detailed. Here the astrological entity does not *belong* to the demon, or the demon to it, but *is* the demon. On the other hand one may doubt whether the stars are thought of as living beings, for in XX 17 it is said, "the stars are founded in the firmament" so that they cannot fall. It would seem that astrological influences are operative, not of themselves, but through the demons that "dwell" in each star or sign. In other words, the astral deities of paganism have become demons[6]. It is interesting to note also that the pillar of cloud of the ancient Israelites is transferred to the heavens, for, as Dr. James has pointed out[7], the pillar suspended in air[8] is the Milky Way.

3. Angelology[9]. — The angelology of. the *Test* is entirely undeveloped. Aside from Michael and Raphael no angels appear as actual actors. Numerous angel names, including many that are familiar and many not elsewhere discovered, are scattered

---

1 Cc. V 4, VI 7, VII 6, *et passim*. κεῖμαι and ὁδεύω are the verbs used. ἄστρον seems to mean any astrological entity. An astrological papyrus fragment at Munich has points of affinity with the *Test*, see *Archiv f. Pap.-Forschung* I (1900—1) 492 ff.   2 C. II 2.   3 C. IV 9.   4 C. IV 6.   5 C. V 8.

6 Cf. the attempt to combine the polytheistic and polydaemonistic viewpoints in VII 6.   7 Cf. Bibliogr. III 5.   8 C. XXIV 5.   9 See Index II.

through the book, but they are charms rather than designations of real beings. They are given solely for their apotropaic value. Considering the fact, however, that the two great archangels do actually appear, it is likely that the author believed in the actual existence of great numbers of angels, just as he did of demons, and thought that each appeared, when his name was called, to subdue the demon subject to him[1]. Aside from the use of the word ἀρχάγγελος there is no allusion to an angelic hierarchy.

4. Magic and Medicine. — The prime interest of the writer of the *Test* was medical. For him demons were what bacilli are to the modern physician, and his magical recipes and angel names are his pharmacopoeia. The one case where he embarks upon a piece of magical mysticism only serves to emphasize this fact. For when, at Solomon's request that he speak περὶ τῶν ἐπουρανίων, Beelzebul tells him the recipe whereby he may see the heavenly dragons circling 'round and hauling the chariot of the sun[2], he is at once rebuked and silenced. Evidently this was forbidden magic, although it might well be true. There is likewise a story of obtaining wealth through a demon[3], but such suggestions bear fruit only for the beautifying of the temple[4]. Such use of demons is evidently dangerous.

As in his demonology, so also in his magic the author combined various and inconsistent views. He has full confidence in the power of the magic name, which, in most cases, is an angel name. To subjugate Onoskelis Solomon "spoke the name of the Holy One of Israel"[5]. Men are led astray, says Asmodaeus, "because they do not know the names of the angels which are ordained over us"[6]. In the original *Test* Ephesia grammata are infrequent, except in the list of the thrity-six *decani*[7]. Here there appear some well known angel names, a few that are possibly real names, but not a few ὀνόματα ἄσημα in the best manner of the magic papyri and "Gnostic" amulets. Since these *voces mysticae* are less numerous in the former part of the

---

[1] As Raphael does, II 7 f. Cf. *Test Dan* VI 1.   [2] C. VI 10f.
[3] C. IV 7.   [4] C. X 5—9.   [5] C. IV 12.   [6] C. V 5; cf. XXVI 8 H.
[7] C. XVIII, esp. secs. 15f., 21, 29, 32; cf. also VII 6, likewise a piece of unregenerate Hellenistic magic.

section, it would appear that a Jewish editor had undertaken the task of removing the heathen elements, but had become weary before he was done.

Likewise there appear the well-known apotropaic materials, such as iron, lead, wood from a wrecked ship, spittle, certain organs of animals, and kinds of plants[1], and the common magical devices, such as the use of the cause to cure the ill, i. e., the name of the demon to drive the demon away or a fishbone to cure a person who has swallowed one[2], the drinking of potions or sprinkling them about, and the writing of amulets or hanging them in the house[3]. Surely these methods of aversion are fundamentally inconsistent with monotheism and with the view that the angels are appointed to frustrate the demons. The ring of Solomon differs only in that it was probably thought to contain the ineffable name[4].

5. Solomon. — Few figures have bulked larger in the folklore of Jews, Mohammedans, and Christians than Solomon. In the *Test* he is already the wise man and magician *par excellence*, the favorite of God, endowed by him with divine σοφία, which includes insight into the crafty wiles of his demonic captives. He uses the demons for one purpose only, to assist in building and beautifying the great Temple at Jerusalem, this labor being the usual form of punishment adopted for them. Solomon's glory, the visit and gifts of the Queen of Sheba, and the gifts of other kings are described in some detail; but all this is only temporary, for the wise king, deceived by Eros, held by the bonds of Artemis as the demons prophesied[5], is eventually led

---

[1] See II 6, V 12, IV 8, XVIII 28, VII 3, V 9f., 13, VI 10, XVIII 20, 33. I am much in doubt whether the means used by Raphael in II 8 to subdue Ornias is the application of parts of the κήτη θαλάσσης (as with Asmodaeus of the fish), or the casting of the μοῖρα (in astrological fashion?), or both as in the restored text. I do not find μοῖραν ῥίπτειν in Vettius Valens as an astrological phrase, but Dr. Conybeare so understands it (*JQR* XI 18 and n. 2).

[2] C. XVIII 35.   [3] Cf. c. XVIII.

[4] Cf. *infra* VII 14. Cf. Charles' interesting view that the sealing of the 144,000 in Rev VII 4—8 was to secure them against demonic attack (*Studies in the Apocalypse*, 1913, pp. 118—32).

[5] C. VIII 9, 11. That Solomon was not regarded as a model of perfection is indicated by the statement that the murder of his brothers was caused by Ἀπάτη.

by the Shunamite to sacrifice locusts to the gods of the Jebusites, and thus loses all his power. How soon he dies is not indicated, but at his death, convinced by the fulfilment of their prophecies that all the demons had said was true, he writes the *Test* and leaves it to the Children of Israel.

The chief part of Solomon's magical equipment is his ring, which is given to him by Michael at God's command in answer to the king's prayer[1]. Either in his own hand, or that of his best beloved servant, or even the demon Ornias it at once subdues every demon. The editors have removed the original statement as to the inscription, if there was one[2]. What became of the ring after Solomon's fall is not stated.

Several features of the Solomonic legend receive their first known literary expression in the *Test*. To quote Salzberger, „Immerhin wird es hier zum ersten Male ausgesprochen, daß Sal. Geister beim Tempelbau verwendet habe und daß er, durch die Liebe zu einer Jebusiterin in heidnischen Kult verstrickt, der Macht über die Geister verlustig gegangen und ihnen zum Gespött geworden sei. Zu beachten ist auch, daß die „Königin des Südens" bereits als eine Zauberin (γόης) auftritt"[3].

6. Apocalyptic element. — The apocalyptic element in the *Test* is very slight[4]. Certain prophecies by the demons and their speedy and exact fulfilment are related in order to prove the trustworthiness of the demons' revelations in general, and, in particular, of their statements regarding their own activities and the means for their frustration[5]. In some cases these prophecies extend far beyond Solomon's time, particularly in certain references to Christ as one who will subdue individual demons[6]. The only section which may be called measurably apocalyptic

---

1 C. I 5—7.   2 Cf. *infra* VII 14.   3 *Salomosage* 11.

4 Dr. James, *TS* II 29 *The Testament of Abraham*, says, "The names 'Testament' and 'Apocalypse' are convertible terms. In the case of the Apocalypses of Adam, Moses, and Isaiah we have positive evidence of this fact, and it is known that most, if not all, extant 'Testaments' have a large Apocalyptic element. The Testaments of Job and Solomon come nearest to transgressing this rule, but even they do not actually transgress it."

5 Cc. V 5; VI 3, 5; VIII 11; XII 4.   6 Cc. XI 6; XII 3.

in tone¹ is found in that part of the *Test* which is preserved only in MS P, and, therefore, while there is no doubt that the original *Test* had a prophecy in this place, it seems very likely that it resembled the one in V 5, and contained at least no such detailed reference to Christ as is now there found².

Did the writer of the *Test*, then, know nothing of the apocalyptic hopes of Judaism and Christianity? At best these hopes had little meaning for him. He makes no reference to that element in Apocalyptic for which we would most naturally look, the expectation of the final overthrow and eternal binding of Beelzebul and his hosts³. Aside from a single mention of the συντέλεια⁴, the writer has his eyes on his muckrake and sees no happier future for the world than in the continued use of his wretched recipes.

7. Jesus Christ. — One of the outstanding inconsistencies of the *Test* is its introduction of Christ as the "angel" who subdues certain demons. Whether these passages are Christian interpolations in a Jewish document will be discussed later⁵. We are now concerned with the religious standpoint of the writer who gave the *Test* its present form⁶.

It is probable that VI 8 contains a reference to Christ. Certainly Rec B so understood it, and the phrase παρὰ δὲ Ἕλλησιν Ἐμμανουήλ is natural from the pen of a Christian who was without knowledge of Hebrew, but familiar with the use of the term Immanuel in Christian circles, as in XI 6. Yet the text is so corrupt and the MSS agree so little that the meaning cannot be certainly made out. The garbled allusion to the "place of a skull" and "the wood" in XII 3 is so unintelligible as to afford no light on the author's views, but is plainly of Christian origin.

Unmistakable is the reference in c. XI to the incident of the Gadarene demoniac who had a legion of devils. But what is the meaning of ἐν τρισὶ χαρακτῆρσι κατάγεται περιηχούμενος,

---

1 C. XV 8—12.   2 Cf. *infra* VII 11.
3 Jub X 8; I En X 6, 12; XIV 5; XVI 6; Mt XXV 41.   4 C. XXV 8.
5 Cf. *infra* VII 11.
6 With this discussion cf. Conybeare in *JQR* XI 5—12.

in section 6? P probably understood it to refer to χμδ' (= 644), the numerical value of Ἐμμανουήλ, already introduced in VI 8 and XI 6[1]. Can the three characters mean the trinity? In XVII 4 is mentioned ὁ μέλλων κατελθεῖν σωτήρ. Οὗ τὸ στοιχεῖον ἐν τῷ μετώπῳ may be a reminiscence of Apoc XXII 4, καὶ τὸ ὄνομα αὐτοῦ ἐπὶ τῶν μετώπων αὐτῶν. The sign is the cross, as the next line shows, not a number as Conybeare concluded from P's frequent introduction of χμδ'[2]. Another distinctively Christian passage is much milder in the A form than in Rec B, which, as Conybeare points out, is distinctively patripassian in character[3]. Rec A mentions the virgin birth, an adoration by angels, and the crucifixion. The allusions to the permanent immaculacy of the Virgin and to the victory of Christ over Satan in the Temptation in XV 10f. cannot be used to define the position of the originator of the Test[4].

Dr. Conybeare's characterization of the Christianity of the Test as "equivocal" is far more true of the original than it was of Rec B, which he had before him[5]. The nature of the writer's faith can be better understood after an investigation of the sources and relationships of his subject matter, to which we now turn.

VII. THE SOURCES AND RELATIONSHIPS OF THE SUBJECT MATTER.

1. Syncretism of the *Testament*. — To set forth what the present writer has collected for the purpose of interpreting the *Test* and determining its sources and relationships would require a large volume. Yet what has been gathered has only touched the fringe of that great body of material bearing on magic, demonology, astrology, and kindred superstitions which has recently appeared, much of it since this work was first under-

---

1 So Conybeare understood, *op. cit.* 28, n. 6.
2 *Op. cit.* 34, § 71. Diog. Laert. 6. 102 uses στοιχεῖον for "sign" of the zodiac. 3 C. XXII 20; Conybeare *op. cit.* 11.
4 Cf. *supra* sec. 6, *infra* VII 11.   5 *JQR* XI 11.

taken¹. The purpose is to introduce here only what is absolutely germain to the subject of the section. One point is clear beyond cavil: Like other magic the *Test* is thoroughly eclectic. It borrows and combines elements, often contradictory, from all the nations that contributed to the civilization about the eastern Mediterranean, without any apparent consciousness of their sources. The whole course of the succeeding discussion will offer illustrations of this patent fact.

2. The universal human element. — In one direction caution is necessary, perhaps especially in the realm of comparative magical and mythological study. Similarities are not always an evidence of borrowing. Take an example from the story of Lix Tetrax. As the demon in the form of a sand storm whirl-wind approaches Solomon, he lays it by spitting on the ground². In a modern Bengali charm for a whirl-wind exactly the same means is used to stay the demon³. Did the *Test* borrow from India or the Bengali from the *Test*? Manifestly neither. Spitting is almost universally apotropaic⁴. And what is more natural than that spittle should magically lay a dust storm. So in many instances from widely separated localities the human mind under similar circumstances has reached similar conclusions. With this caution in mind we can proceed to notice the instances of real borrowing.

3. Assyrian and Babylonian influence. — The great civilization on the Euphrates deeply affected Hellenistic, Jewish, and Christian demonological and magical beliefs. Babylonia is one of the few countries in which theology and demonology, religion and "her bastard daughter, magic," seem from the first to have gone hand in hand⁵. There are no indications that the official cultus ever regarded magic as alien. Rather, the exorcism of

---

1 See, for example, *ERE*, arts. "Ancestor Worship," "Baalzebub," "Birth", "Charms and Amulets," "Cross," "Demons and Spirits," "Disease and Medicine," "Divination," "Evil Eye," "Keres," and the literature there referred to.

2 C. VII 3.

3 In a little collection of charms sent the author by former pupils, Babu Probodh Chandra Mallik and Babu Shusil Chandra Karuli. One must spit on his own breast, however.   4 Cf. Conybeare, *op. cit.* 23, n. 3.

5 Farnell, *Greece and Babylonia*, 300 f.

countless demons seems to have been one of the regular duties of the priesthood, and, to judge from the relative proportion of magical texts among those that have been preserved, one of the most important duties[1]. Nowhere do we find a ranker growth of demonological beliefs than in Babylonia. Every possible ill or accident that could happen, "a toothache, a headache, a broken bone, a raging fever, an outburst of anger, of jealousy, of incomprehensible disease"[2], all were ascribed to demonic agency, and were to be averted or cured by means of incantations.

This is precisely the atmosphere of the *Test*. But it is also that of Hellenistic superstition[3], and such a general similarity of tone proves no direct relationship between the *Test* and the Euphrates valley. Can we find more definite evidence of dependence?

A peculiar resemblance appears between one class of Babylonian demons and a figure in the *Test*: the *ašakku marsu* and Ephippas, the wind demon of Arabia. Since the similarity is somewhat vague, I call attention to it with some hesitation. Ephippas is an early morning blast of wind that kills man and beast[4], or, according to MS D, "uproots houses and trees and hills, and destroys men"[5]. The *ašakku marsu* is „der Dämon der auszehrenden Krankheit" according to Jastrow[6], but Sayce[7] and Thompson[8] render the word "fever." The following from Thompson's translation of the *Ašakku* series shows interesting similarities with Ephippas' activities:

---

1 Zimmern, *Bab. Hymnen*, 13; cf. Jastrow, *Rel. Bab. Ass.*, 253—93, Germ., I 273—392, Rogers, *Rel. Bab. Ass.* 144—159; Weber, *Dämonenbeschwörungen*. The chief part of the hymns that have been preserved consists of incantations.

2 Rogers, *op. cit.* 145.   3 Cf. *infra* VII 7.

4 C. XXII 2 f.   5 MS D VI 1.

6 *Rel. Bab. Ass.* I 348 ff.; he is uncertain as to what disease is meant.

7 *Hibbert Lect.* 1887, 477; Sayce translates thus: "The plague-demon burns up the land like fire. The plague-demon like the fever (*ašakku*) attacks a man. The plague-demon in the desert like a cloud of dust makes his way. The plague-demon like a foe takes captive a man. The plague-demon like a flame consumes a man. The plague-demon, though he hath neither hands nor feet (cf. Ephippas), ever goes round and round. The plague-demon like destruction cuts down the sick man."

8 *Devils and Evil Spirits* II 31. Cf. Rogers, *Rel. Bab. Ass.* 147.

.... the evil Fiend,
The roaming windblast . . . . . ¹
The evil Spirit which in the street creates a storm wind . . . ²
The evil Fever hath come like a deluge, and
Girt with dread brilliance it filleth the broad earth,
Enveloped in terror it casteth fear abroad;
It roameth through the street, it is let loose in the road . . . ³
An evil ghost(?) hath assailed the land,
And perturbed the people of the land above and below:
A pestilence, a plague that giveth the land no rest,
Hath cast desolation upon it.
The great Demon, Spirit, and Fiend, which roameth the broad places for men,
The angry, quaking storm [which if one] seeth
He turneth not nor looketh back again . . . . . ⁴
Fever (ašakku) hath blown upon a man as the wind-blast⁵.

That this is the closest parallel between the *Test* and Assyro-Babylonian demonology is significant. Granting that Babylonian, or, at least, Semitic superstition may have contributed to the figure of Ephippas, we still can assert only that the *Test* rests ultimately upon that great mass of Sumerian-Semitic beliefs of which we have the earliest and fullest illustrations from the Babylonian tablets, but not that it has borrowed directly⁶.

4. Iranian influence. — To Mazdaism is to be ascribed the questionable honor, not of introducing demonology and angelology into Judaism⁷, but of decidedly directing its development⁸. The *Test* has not been so deeply affected as has the New Testament Apocalypse, for example, in its war between Michael and the Dragon⁹, nor even as Paul¹⁰; for there is no dualism in our text. Its writer knows Beelzebul only as "ruler of the

---

1 *Op. cit.* 5.   2 *Ibid.* 9.   3 *Ibid.* 11.   4 *Ibid.* 13.

5 *Ibid.* 31. It is, perhaps, worthy of note that Ephippas is caught in an ἀσκός, a sack. However silly it may seem, is it not possible that a popular etymology connected *ašakku* and ἀσκός?

6 The lilith, who appears in three forms (cf. *supra* p. 45), is an international figure, and, therefore, no evidence of Babylonian influence.

7 So Perles, *Bousset's Rel. des Judentums*, p. 36.

8 Moulton, *Early Zoroastrianism* 304 ff., 325 ff., *HDB* IV 991 f.; Mills, *Zarathuštra* 436; Bousset, *Rel. des Jud.* 387; Clemen, *Prim. Christ.* 111 ff. = *Religionsgesch. Erkl.* 85 ff., where earlier literature is cited. See particularly Grünbaum, "Beiträge" in *ZDMG* XXXI, 256; Dibelius, *Geisterwelt*, 183 ff., 190 ff.

9 Cf. Moulton, *HDB* IV 992.   10 ὁ θεὸς τοῦ αἰῶνος τούτου, 2 Co IV, 4.

demons"[1]. He has no doubt that God can empower Solomon or any one who knows the angelic names to frustrate and bind any and all demons. The archangels, though their names appear, never are grouped together as seven, and the one group of seven demons has no Parsi coloring[2]. Yet one cannot read the Persian sacred writings without being struck by the *Test*[3]. And, furthermore, the *Test* has adopted one Mazdian demon, Aēšma daēva, or Asmodaeus[4], very much in his Magian character. Plainly the demon of the *Test* is the same as that of Tobit[5], but the writer did not have Tobit before him or he would not have used the heart and gall, instead of the heart and liver, of the fish as his φάρμακα. His additional details, such as the name of the fish, γλάνος, show that, while he may have had the story of Tobit in his mind, he was drawing upon the developing Jewish folklore which had its fount in the original source and eventuated in the Talmudic Asmodaeus[6].

In another direction we naturally look for Persian influence to manifest itself, namely on the Solomonic legend. The Mohammedans identified Solomon with Yima, the Jamshīd of Firdausi, because he had taken over so many traits of the Persian hero,

---

1 C. II 9.   2 C. VIII; cf. *infra* VII 6, p. 60.

3 See the *Vendīdād*, the "anti-demoniac law," (Moulton, *Early Rel. Poetry of Persia*, 12), esp. the incantations of Fargards XIX and XX, and the account in XXII of Angra Mainyu's creation of 99, 999 diseases (*SBE* IV 203—235), and Darmesteter's discussion, *ibid.* LXXXV—XCV.

4 Moulton, *Early Rel. Poetry of Persia* 68 f., accepts the derivation from Aēšma Daēva, as does Stave, *JE* I 220 f., and Marshall, *HDB* I 172. Ginzberg, *JE* II 219, though admitting the identity, denies the derivation; cf. Clemen, *Prim. Christ.* 112, n. 7 = *Rel.-Gesch. Erkl.* 86, n. 7. Moulton's theory that Tobit is a Magian legend revamped by a Jew in its present form (*Early Zoroast.* 246—253) is accepted by Simpson, Charles' *Apoc. and Pseudep. of the OT* I 185 f. On the influence of the Aḥikar cycle see J. Rendell Harris, "The Double Text of Tobit," *AJT* III (1899) 541—554, and Clemen, *loc. cit.,* who quotes Fries, *ZNTW* 1905 168, which I have not at hand.

5 *Test* V; Tob III 8, 17; V 7 f.; VI 13—17; VIII 2 f.

6 A. is more plainly the "wrath demon" in the *Test* than in Tob. There is no reference to Egypt in the *Test*, cf. Tob VIII 3. Is the uncertain phrase πλήρης ὁδοὺς πικρίας (*Test* V 13) an attempt to render the "wounding spear" of Aēšma (*Yt* I 32)? ¹Cf. *SBE* IV p. LXVII, *JE* II 217 f.

particularly his renown as a builder[1]. The Talmudic story of Solomon combines elements from the legends of Takhma Urupa, who made Ahriman his horse until his wife betrayed him[2], of Yima, the prosperous king and great builder, who, like Takhma Urupa, "ruled over the Daēvas and men, the Yātus and Pairikas," but sinned and fell before the usurping Azhi Dahāka[3], and of Thraētaona, the first healer, the inventor of magic, the fiend-smiter[4]. In the *Test*, however, we catch the story midway in its development. There has arisen, as yet, no demonic being to depose the king, and the *Test* lacks, therefore, the most characteristic detail which the Talmud borrowed from Persia[5].

The evidence, then, justifies the conclusion that Persian influences are at work upon the folklore from which the *Test* drew its inspiration, and have affected our text in part directly, in part through Tobit and, no doubt, other Apocrypha. Yet the *Test* cannot come from circles where, as in Babylon, for example, Magian influence was dominant.

5. Egyptian elements. — Egypt is pre-eminently the land of magic, but not of demonology[6]. Her "Book of the Dead" almost from its inception had the purpose of magically insuring the happiness of the dead in the hereafter; and the ancient inhabitants of the Nile valley were so much concerned with the future life that their magical texts gave little attention to avert-

---

1 Salzberger, *Salomosage* 5; *SBE* IV 18, n. 3.
2 *Yt* XIX 29 (*SBE* XXIII 292 f.; cf. *ibid.* 252, n. 1).
3 *Yt* XIX 31—38 (*ibid.* 293—295, 297, and n. 5).   4 *Vend.* XX (*SBE* IV 219).
5 The legends of the *Shāhnāmeh* (cf. Atkinson, 5—34, the only version of Firdausi available to me) with the allusions in the *Dādīstān-ī-Dīnīk* (XXXIX 16f., *SBE* XVIII 127f.), *Bundahish* XXIII : (*SBE* V 87), and elsewhere throw much light on the references in the earlier literature, but they have probably been influenced in their turn by the developed Jewish and Musulman tales; cf. Darmesteter, *Le Zend Avesta* II 624, cited by Moulton, *Early Zoroast.* 150. *Bundahish* XXXIV 4f. (*SBE* V 149f.) is particularly interesting because it brings Dahāk into connection with Scorpio, much as the *Test* connects certain demons and zodiacal signs. Cf. a closer parallel to Solomon and Asmodaeus in King Mukunda and the hunchback in the *Pañchatantra* (Benfey II 124—127; cf. I 129f.).
6 Cf. *ERE* IV 584—590, 749—753 (Foucart), III 430—433 (Naville); Wiedemann, *Mag. und Zaub.*; Breasted, *RTAE* 281 f., 296, *et pas.*, Erman, *Äg. Rel.*, c. VI, 148—164.

ing ill from the living. Yet enough has been preserved to show that the fear of evil spirits, especially the ghosts of the dead, was abroad here as in Babylonia and Persia, even thought the official texts reflect but little of it. Egyptian demonology is so lacking in definite color and in general so much like that of Babylonia and Greece that one can hardly hope to show from this side any distinctive Egyptian traits in the *Test*. In the times when the *Test* was written it was of the variegated mixture that we call Hellenistic [1].

When we turn to astrology, however, the case is different, for one of the longest sections in the *Test*, that having to do with the thirty-six *decani* [2], is distinctly Egyptian. It has been generally accepted since Letronne that astrology is not, as the ancients supposed, of Egyptian origin, but rather that Babylonia was its native land [3]. As Boll, however, has shown [4], having been adopted by the Egyptian priesthood and actively practised by them, it came to be so thoroughly at home and so mixed with Egyptian elements as to be really native, "in ihrer *Eigenart* autochthon, wenn auch in allem rein ägyptischen Inhalt von sehr spätem Ursprung" [5]. Particularly is this true of the *decani*. They were originally, not Babylonian [6], but Egyptian divisions of the equator [7], which were given an astrological significance. "Nur diese (the Egyptian astrology) hat die 36 Dekane personifiziert: alle andere Dekandarstellungen in Indien oder bei den Arabern gehen darauf in letzter Linie zurück," says Boll [8]. This sentence is especially noteworthy for our purpose, for the *Test* has fully personified the *decani*.

Various lists of *decani* have come down to us [9]. With

---

1 Erman, *op. cit.* 227 ff.   2 C. XVIII.
3 M. Letronne, *Sur l'Origine du Zodiaque Grec*, Paris 1849, esp. p. 2. Cf. Riess, in *Pauly-Wissowa* II 1808, art. "Astrologie"; Cumont, *Or. Rel.* 133 f., 163; *Astrol.* 74 ff.   4 *Sphaera* 372 f.   5 *Ibid.* 373.
6 Bouché-Leclerq, *Astrol. Gr.* 215—240.
7 Boll, *op. cit.* 316, 336, n. 2.   8 *Ibid.* 216 f.
9 See the comparative table in Bouché-Leclerq, *op. cit.* 232 f., and that in Budge, *Gods of the Egyptians* II 304—308; also articles by G. Daressy, *Annales du Service des Ant. de l'Égypt*, I 79—90, III 175, 236—9, X 21 ff., 180 ff.; by Ahmed bey Kamal, *ibid.* IX 192.

these the names in the *Test* do not at all agree, but seem rather for the most part to be Hebrew, or, perhaps, mock Hebrew[1]. Yet the *Test's* account of the activities of these siderial spirits is not original invention, for, at the beginning, the two chief lists, one given by Pitra from a Moscow and a Vienna MS[2], and one given by Kroll from another Vienna MS[3], agree with the *Test* in certain essential particulars. The names in Vind. 108 and its fellow, Par. 2419, do not correspond with any other list, just as those of the *Test* do not. The peculiarity of the names in the last, therefore, need not trouble us. That the activities ascribed to the several decans should not agree in all the lists is not strange, in view of the confusion in the Egyptian lists[4]. While there is much closer resemblance between Pitra's and Kroll's documents than between either of them and the *Test*, still they differ in many important particulars. They all agree on the fundamental proposition, which Celsus described as an Egyptian belief, that the decans rule diseases, each of a certain part of the body[5]. In the case of the first decan all three agree that it is the head, although the *Test* adds κροταφούς, which M-V puts under the second. Vind. 108 has πάθη ὀφθαλμῶν under the second decan, while the *Test* has it unter the third. Under the third both M-V and Vind. 108 have among other things toothache. All three agree that the fourth decan rules diseases of the throat. From this point on there are still fewer similarities between the three accounts, yet these we have indi-

---

1 The allusion of Origen, *contra Cels.* VI 30, to οἱ ἑπτὰ ἄρχοντες δαίμονες is not applicable to the *decani*. There is, to be sure, an Antiochus excerpt which mentions the ζ' δεκανῶν σχῆμα (Boll, *Sphaera* 57), but this either means the Pleiades, or, as seems to me more probable, it is a mistake for the seven planets (cf. *ibid.* 280), which are sometimes connected with the thirty-six *decani* (*ibid.* 302). See Bouché-Leclerq, *Astrol. Gr.* 224—230.

2 *Analecta* V, 2, 285, from Mosquensis 415 and Vindobon. Medic. 23, ol. 50, referred to as M-V.

3 *CCAG* VI 73—78, from Vind. Graec. 108 (= MS S, cf. *supra* II 7, p. 18) with the seals for each decan; there is also given a parallel list of names from Par. 2419 (= MS W, cf. *supra* II 11, p. 26).

4 Cf. Bouché-Leclerq, *op. cit.* 230, n. 3.

5 *Contra Cels.* VIII 58. Cf. Bouché-Leclercq, *loc. cit.*, quotation from Firmicus, and ch. XV, "La Médicine Astrol.," pp. 517—542.

cated are more than fortuitous. They evidently rest upon a common tradition. But M-V has for the first few names the Hellenistic transliteration of the old Egyptian names[1], and therefore serves to connect this common tradition with Egypt.

We are safe, then, in concluding that this chapter of the *Test* comes from Egyptian sources, presenting probably a Jewish revision of a list of *decani*. The editor has made it more nearly monotheistic than the other accounts mentioned above, in regarding the decans as demons who cause disease, rather than deities who "rule" ($\kappa v \varrho \iota \varepsilon \acute{v} \varepsilon \iota$) or cure ($\iota \tilde{a} \tau a \iota$) the parts affected. Yet he has failed to purge out all the heathen elements, such as the amulets and *voces mysticae*[2]. Other evidence of Egyptian influence I am unable to find.

6. Jewish elements and relationships. — a) That Judaism is one main source of the *Test* is apparent on every page. The background, the plot, and the principal characters are Jewish. Solomon, wise man, builder, and glorious king, the Queen of Sheba, and the Shunamite girl[3] are all familiar Old Testament figures, though sometimes presented here in strange connections. In pre-Christian times Solomon was already on the way to become a magician, both in the canonical books and in the Apocrypha[4]. Josephus shows this conception of the king gradually developing, his exorcisms and the remedial or magical plants he had recommended being already in practical use by Jewish magicians[5]. His ring, his power over demons, and his use of them on the Temple become commonplaces of Jewish legendary lore. His glory and his fall are put in telling contrast by the editors of the Old Testament as they are by the *Test*.

b) The angelology and demonology of the *Test* are practically those of the Apocrypha and Pseudepigrapha. Our text contains the view, based upon Gen VI 1—4 and found in Ethiopic Enoch VI—VII, XV—XVI and Jubilees VII 21 ff., X 5, that the angels who fell and their offspring became

---

[1] Bouché-Leclercq, *Astrol. gr.* 232 f., Budge, *Gods* II 304—308, beginning with No. 27, p. 307.   [2] Cf. *supra* VI 4.
[3] Cant VI 12, VII 1.   [4] See fuller discussion below, VIII 1 a), b).
[5] *Ant* VIII 25; quoted below VIII 1 d).

demons[1]; but much of it seems rather to follow the belief found in the Similitudes (I En XXXVII—L XXI; cf. Charles, *Enoch* p. 107) that demons have existed since the creation. The Pseudo-Philonic Jewish work *de antiquitatibus biblicis*, dating from the latter part of the first century A. D., in its *citharismus regis Dauid contra daemonium Saulis*, unites this view with another found in the *Test* as to the origin of certain demons. According to a badly tangled passage Onoskelis is born of an echo. In the *Citharismus* David addresses the demon thus:

> Et factum est tunc nomen in compaginatione extensionis quod appellatum est superius caelum . . . (There follows a reference to the creation of the earth but not of animals and man.) Et post haec facta est tribus spirituum vestrorum. Et nunc molesta esse noli, tanquam secunda creatura; si quominus, memorare Tartari in quo ambulas. Aut non audire . . . . Aut immemores quoniam de resultatione in chaomate nata est vestra creatura.

Less apposite is a parallel Dr. James notes from Dieterich, *Abraxas*, p. 17, γελάσαντος δὲ τοῦ θεοῦ ἐγεννήθησαν θεοὶ ἑπτά[2].

In spite of great differences in detail the general manner in which each demon's work is described in I En LXIX 1—12[3] may well have contributed to the demon portraits in the *Test.* The section on the seven κοσμοκράτορες (c. VII) is based upon exactly the same conceptions of evil and of demons as the list of seven vices in Test. Reuben III 3—6; yet the lists do not agree except that the third in each has to do with μάχη, apparently a mere coincidence. Jub X 7—9, which tells how God commanded the angels to imprison nine tenths of the evil spirits in "the place of condemnation", and left one tenth free under

---

1 See above VI 1. Cf. Grünbaum, "Beiträge," *ZDMG* XXXI 225.

2 Dr. James printed the *Citharismus* with three other Pseudo-Philonic fragments in *TS* II 3, *Apocrypha Anecdota*, Cambridge, 1893, without being aware of their origin. Dr. L. Cohn called attention to the source in *JQR* X (1898) 277—332 in an article entitled "An Apocryphal Work Ascribed to Philo of Alexandria." The text I have quoted Dr. James communicated in a letter of July 8, 1916, after making a further collation of MSS. James and Cohn agree as to the date. See below VIII 1 c) for the concluding sentence of the so-called song.

3 From the "Apocalypse of Noah." One might think the *Test* depended particularly upon this work, were it not that the rest of the sections Charles ascribes to it (*Enoch*, pp. 24 f.) do not at all agree with the *Test*, e. g. as to sorcery and witchcraft, I En VIII, IX.

command of Mastema, explains the statement of Beelzebul in *Test* VI 3 that his second in command rules his race in Tartarus. Not only its demonology in general but certain particular figures of our text are well known in Jewish mind. Tobit has made Asmodaeus at home in the Jewish folklore. The lilith also came to belong to Judaism as it did to other nations.

Judaism, however, gave more attention to angels than to demons. While here the *Test* differs in emphasis, the view point is the same. Among the Jews as in our text exorcism was one of the chief means of healing, so much so that in antiquity the Jew became almost as famous for magical arts as the Chaldean. "The Graeco-Roman world regarded the Jews as a race of magicians"[1]. Angel names, of which so many occur in the Pseudepigrapha, were often used in incantations. The Jews were fully persuaded of the power of the "name"[2], and they also thought of the angels as specially commissioned to protect the righteous from the machinations of demons.

There are thus many similarities between the *Test* and Jewish folklore and superstition of the beginning of the Christian era. But that our document is dependent in a literary way upon the Apocrypha or Pseudepigrapha does not at all appear. I have discovered but two quotations from Jewish literature, one the passage touching the corner stone[3], the other the phrase τὴν τῶν σῶν θρόνων πάρεδρον σοφίαν[4], taken from the Wisdom of Solomon, and a possible allusion to the same book[5]. In the passages describing Solomon's glory and the Temple, where one would expect quotation, there is only a free development of the biblical accounts[6]. One might mention elements of Jewish thinking which are absent from the *Test*, such as the coming of the Messiah to destroy all the demons[7]. We must, then,

---

[1] Ludwig Blau, *JE* VIII 255 f., art. "Magic." He says, *ibid.* 255, "The frequency of allusions to it in the Bible indicates that the practice of magic was common throughout ancient Israel." Cf. his *Altjüd. Zauberwesen*, one of the classics on the subject, also Bousset, *Rel. Jud.* 391 and Schürer *GJV* III 408 f.
[2] Heitmüller, *Im Namen Jesu* 176—80.
[3] C. XXIII 4; Ps CXVIII 22; Mt XXI 42 and parallels, I Pt II 6.
[4] C. III 5; Sap IX 4.   [5] C. V 3; Sap VII 1.
[6] C. XIX, XXI.   [7] Cf. I En LXIX 27.

conclude that, while the writer of our document operated with much the same beliefs as the Apocryphal and Pseudepigraphic writers, he is not in a literary way dependent upon any Jewish literature. On the other hand so many traits connect him with the rabbinical writings that we must suppose him to live during or after the first century of the Christian era.

c) Turning to the Talmud we find parallels to many of our stories[1]. The account of Benaiah's capture of Asmodaeus by the use of a magic ring and chain, a bundle of wool, and a skin of wine[2] reminds one of the slave's capture of Ornias (I 10—14) and again of Ephippas (XXII 9—16), for the ring is used in both cases. It is pressed upon Ornias and seals Ephippas in his sack, while in the rabbinic legend Benaiah cries to Asmodaeus, "The name of the Lord is upon thee." Ephippas is caught in the sack instead of by drinking wine from it. Asmodaeus shows a knowledge of the future and laughs at men's foolish plans, just as Ornias does[3]. The idea that the demons know the future is found elsewhere in the Talmud. In *Hagiga* 16a the collocation of ideas is much the same as in the *Test.* "The rabbans taught: The demons possess six characteristics, three like the ministering angels, and three like the sons of men. Three like the ministering angels: they have wings like the ministering angels and they fly from one end of the world to the other like the ministering angels and they know what is determined for the future (מה שעתיד להיות) like the ministering angels. They know! Do you come to that opinion? Rather they hear it from behind the curtain like the ministering angels. Three like the sons of men: they eat and drink like the sons of men, they propagate themselves like the sons of men, and they die like the sons of men"[4]. The *Aboth* of R. Nathan

---

1 Ginzberg, *Legends* IV 165—9.

2 *Gittin* 68a; Ginzberg, *loc. cit.*; *JE* XI 443 f.

3 C. XX 6—18; cf. a story of the angel of death related by Brecher, *Transcendentale, Magie und magische Heilarten im Talmud*, Wien 1850, p. 58 f., from Suca 53a.

4 Goldschmidt III 2 839, Streane, 92; cf. *Test* XX 16 for "hearing behind the curtain."

adds: "Many say: They change their appearance according to every form as they wish, and they see and are not seen"[1]. This passage is instructive in that it describes the demonology of the *Test* and reduces it to a system which apparently our writer was not able to construct.

d) While, however, there are many resemblances between Jewish angelology, demonology, magic, and mythology and the *Test*, it must not forthwith be taken as proved that it is a Jewish work. It certainly was not a product of rabbinic Judaism such as is seen in the Babylonian Talmud, and later Jewish speculation. Samael appears only in MS D, the angel of death, Malak ha-Moweth, of the Zohar and Qelippoth not at all[2]. Asmodaeus is an entirely different character, his place being taken by Ornias and the New Testament Beelzebul[3].

The mists of Jewish tradition come to surround Solomon with a halo which only begins to appear in the *Test*[4]. Among the many later traits not found in our document, one which might easily have been used is the statement in Targum Sheni Esther that "Solomon ruled over the wild beasts, over the birds of heaven, and over the creeping beasts of the earth, as well as over the devils, the spirits of the night; and he understood the language of all these according as it is written, 'and he talked with the trees,'" instead of 'of the trees,' I Kg IV 33[5].

One of the most decisive illustrations of the difference between the *Test* and later Judaism is the account of the fall of Solomon. The subject was one which the Jewish theologians in the early Christian centuries discussed with some heat[6]. The *Test* in its attitude stands midway between the Tannaim and the Amoraim, in that, while Solomon falls, it is under the pressure of a passion which seems not to be regarded as ille-

---

[1] A. Wünsch, "Die Zahlensprüche in Talmud u. Midrasch", *ZDMG* LXVI 416 f.; *Aboth di R. Nathan* 37 3. [2] Cf. Meyer, *Qabbalah* 430 f., 432—7.
[3] See Grünbaum's characterization of the Talmudic Asmodaeus in *ZDMG* XXXI 216, following *Git* 68 a, b, and *Pes* 110 a.
[4] Cf. Eisenmenger, *Entd. Jud.* I 441; Faerber, *K. Sal.*; Salzberger, *Salomosage*; *JE* XI 438 ff., 448.
[5] Salzberger, *op. cit.* 93 f, from f. 440, ed. David p. 8.
[6] Faerber, *K. Sal.* 4—19, Salzberger, *Salomosage* 12 f.

gitimate, and his worship of idols was not conscious and brazen, but consisted merely in crushing certain locusts before idols, for he "did not consider the blood of the locusts"[1]. This charitable estimate quite befits a writer who wished his work accepted as a valuable medical treatise from Solomon's own hand. That in the *Test* Asmodaeus has nothing to do with the king's fall at once differentiates the work from the Talmud and proves that it had no close connection with those popular cycles of Solomonic myth from which the rabbis probably drew their stories. Moreover, in the *Test* there is, on the one hand, no hint that the king lost his throne along with his power over the demons; and, on the other, no restoration of his power, while the ring, which is the chief means by which he gains his power over the demons, is not indispensible, as it is in the Talmudic legends[2]. The connection of a Shunamite girl with Solomon's fall is unique. It must have been suggested by the name in Cant VI 12; VII 1, and it would seem to hint at an interpretation of Canticles otherwise unknown to me[3], and entirely

---

[1] C. XXVI 5. The *Test* takes the attitude of the Half-Tannaites; Faerber, *op. cit.* 8f.

[2] See *Gittin* 68a, b. Salzberger, *op. cit.* 115 is hardly justified in making the *Test* present a later development of the ring legend than the Talmud, if that is what he means. Josephus (*Ant* VIII 2 5) presupposes a ring of Solomon. The often published passage from the great Paris magical papyrus (Suppl. grec. 574) is no doubt borrowed from Jewish, not Christian magicians. Dieterich believes the section cannot be earlier than the time of Eupolemus, and probably comes from the Essenes (*Abraxas* 142ff., *Leid. pap.* 780ff.). In any case this papyrus, written in the III or IV cent. A. D., but embodying much older material, stands beside Josephus as a witness to the prominence of Solomon and his ring in magic during the earliest centuries of the Christian era. No satisfactory explanation of the clause ὁρκίζω σε κατὰ τῆς σφραγῖδος ἧς ἔθετο Σολομὼν ἐπὶ τὴν γλῶσσαν τοῦ Ἱερημίου καὶ ἐλάλησεν (11. 3039f.) has been advanced. Professor Deissman (*Licht* 187, n. 15, *LAE* 257, n. 10) thinks it may allude to some legend connected with LXX Jer I 6—10. Is it not more likely that the name Jeremiah is a mistake for some demon or dragon name that has been misread? In one of the phylacteria of the Bologna MS which contains the *Test* is the line ἰδοὺ Σ. υἱὸς Δαβὶδ δράκοντος γλῶσσαν ἔχων βασιλέως ἐγκέφαλιν (cf. *supra* II, p. 24, n. 2). One can go no farther than to suggest the possibility of a connection. I can discover no Essenic material in the *Test*, unless indefinite prescriptions of "cleanness" can be supposed to be such (VI 10, XIII 2).

[3] See my article in *Jl. Palest. Or. Soc.*, I 116—121.

contradictory to that which became customary in Jewish and Christian circles.

A comparison of the *Test*, then, with Jewish thought in the same field confirms the statement which Dr. Kohler makes, that our document is pre-Talmudic[1]. It is, moreover, closer to the Palestinian than to the Babylonian Talmud[2]. If Loewe is right in his contention that it was Galilean, not Judean, rabbis who believed in demonology and magic[3], we have just the line of tradition we should expect in a Christian work, which would be connected with Palestine rather than Babylon, and with Galilee rather than Judea.

e) One offshoot of Jewish magic remains to be considered. Perhaps the most interesting and valuable of recent publications in this field is Montgomery's *Aramaic Incantation Texts from Nippur*, inscriptions from a series of magic bowls in rabbinic Aramaic, Syriac, and Mandaic, intended to protect the houses and families of the clients, and dating from the sixth century A. D. Some are distinctly heathen, all are decidedly eclectic, mingling Babylonian, Jewish, and Hellenistic elements, but the majority show Jewish influence and were prepared for Jews. Strangely enough, in view of the place of origin, Persian demonology has left no trace, but "Egypto-Hellenistic magic is one of the prime sources of our texts"[4]. How is the *Test* related to this remarkable series of incantations?

In many respects the similarity is great. We find the same kind of angel names ending in -el[5], the same trust in their efficacy[6], and the same conception of demons as the causes of ills and diseases of all sorts. The sealing of demons is mentioned in most of the texts[7], and Solomon's seal is referred to in some[8]. In a related text Grünbaum found the phrase "jinn of Solomon"[9].

---

1 Cf. *supra* I 4.

2 Grünbaum (*ZDMG* XXXI 215) and Perles (*Bousset's Rel. d. Jud.* 35 f.) call attention to the difference. The *Test* comes nearer to the soberer views of the former, as is natural in a Christian work, which would not show direct Babylonian influence. 3 *ERE* IV 612f. 4 *Op. cit.* 115, cf. 116.

5 *Ibid.* 96 ff.; see review by the writer, *AJT* XIX (1915) 292 ff.

6 *Ibid.* 56 ff., 111. 7 Cf. *ibid.* 127, 133, 165, 191, 231 f.

8 *Ibid.* 170, 173, 232, 248. 9 *Ibid.* 80, גינא דשלמוה.

On the other hand there are decided differences. The magician is not concerned with individual demons or angels. Personal names of demons are few; rather they are addressed as classes, "Demons and Devils and Satans and Liliths"[1], while the angels, even more than in the *Test*, come to be mere charms, not personalities. The black art is personified, and "the Curse and the Vow, and Arts and Practices" are adjured[2]. Certain familiar names appear which the *Test* lacks; for example, Metatron[3], Abraxas[4], and Hermes[5]. Rather more of plainly Hellenistic magic enters into the Aramaic texts; for example, Zeus and Okeanos[6]. Heathen deities appear more distinctly: Sames, Sin, Bel, and Nirig[7]. The charms are much more elaborate than any in the *Test*.

From this hasty comparison it is evident that Montgomery's texts and ours belong to the same world, that of syncretistic Hellenism, but not to the same part of that world, nor to the same era. The *Test* comes from an earlier, or at least a less highly developed stage in the history of magic, and, strange as it may appear, shows really less of Hellenistic influence on its magic, if not on its demonology, than do the Semitic texts.

7. Hellenistic elements and relationships. — No one familiar with the magic papyri can fail to identify the *Test* as a Hellenistic work. Upon the basis of primitive Greek and Roman animism the popular mind had constructed by the time of the early Empire a magic that borrowed from all the races, Babylonian, Persian, Indian, Jewish, and Egyptian, that had contributed to its civilization, and yet was thoroughly naturalized[8]. It is in this world that the *Test* belongs.

---

1 *Ibid.* 225; cf. 68. Such summaries are frequent and long, cf. pp. 188f., 218. The magician wishes to include all possible evil spirits.

2 *Ibid.* 237, *et passim.*   3 *Ibid.* 207, cf. 98, 113.

4 *Ibid.* 148, 196, 232, cf. 57.   5 *Ibid.* 147, 196, 207, cf. 123, 113.

6 *Ibid.* 197, cf. 113.   7 *Ibid.* 238, in a heathen charm, cf. 70f.

8 Cf. art. "Demons and Evil Spirits (Greek)" in *ERE* IV 590—4 by A. C. Pearson and art. "Dämonen u. Dämonische" in *Realenc.* IV 408—19 by J. Weiss, with bibliographies.

Onoskelis is no doubt, the well known Greek female demon, although the manner of her birth can be paralleled from both Greek and Jewish sources[1]. Enepsigos is probably Hekate[2]. One demon I have identified with Lix Tetrax, two of the original *Ephesia grammata*, in part because, while the name is corrupted, it is in the *Test* connected with a wind as it is in a Cretan tablet of the fourth century B. C.[3]. In any case the section is Hellenistic, as the charm βουλταλά· θαλάλ· μελχάλ· shows; the demon also cures fever, a heathen, not a Jewish or Christian idea. Kynopegos may be identified with Poseidon[4]. Akephalos Daemon appears in the magic papyri[5]. The idea of demons as the cause of disease was familiar to the Greek mind, for the Κῆρες were the ancient Greek form of microbe[6]. The similarity of views on this subject among men widely separated in time and place is illustrated by the fact that Plato, Apuleius, and the Talmud all agree in regarding demons as partly human, partly supernatural in their nature[7].

The magic of the *Test* is not outwardly so different from that of the magic papyri, and the writer was familiar with the praxis of the latter, as VI 10 and XVIII show. But ὀνόματα ἄσημα rarely appear, and when they do they are an evidence that the section in which they occur has come from Hellenism; nor do the incantations and amulets have the elaborateness that characterizes them in the papyri. The angel, a messenger of God, is the agent of healing and protection. No black magic, nor *defixiones* appear. The *Test*, then, differs from the magic papyri chiefly in that it is the work of a Christian using heathen

---

[1] C. IV. Cf. Roscher, *Lexicon*, s. v. Ὀνόσκελις; J. Harrison, *Proleg.* 202f.; Gruppe, *Gr. Myth.* 1306 and n. 17, 769; Lucian *ver. hist.* II 46; *supra* VI 1, VII 6 b.   [2] She is a moon goddess, called μυριώνυμος, and has three forms.

[3] Ziebarth in *NGG* 1899, 131, Wünsch, *Rh. Mus.* LV (1900) 73ff. The writer is preparing an article in defense of this identification.   [4] C. XVI.

[5] Lond. P 46 145ff., *Gr. Pap. Br. Mus.* I 69f.; Deissmann, *Licht* 194, *LAE* 139. Of course the headless ghost is an international figure (cf. Washington Irving's *Legend of Sleepy Hollow*), but allusions to fire and lightning in both accounts make the identification certain.

[6] Harrison, *Proleg.* 163ff., Bouché-Leclerq, *Astrol. Gr.* 24 n. 1.

[7] *Sympos.* 202e; Apuleius *de Socr.* XIII. Cf. *supra* VII 6.

materials rather than that of a heathen working on Jewish or Christian matter.

The passages in the papyri which mention Solomon merely show that his fame as a magician was spreading beyond the limits of Judaism and Christianity [1]. One is inclined to think that some legend of Solomon's dealing with demons is back of the line that speaks of Solomon's laying his seal on the tongue of Jeremiah [2].

8. Christian elements and relationships.

a) Relation to the New Testament. — The thought of our text regarding Christ has already been sufficiently discussed [3]. As to demonology the New Testament is not sufficiently detailed to permit a comparison of individual figures except in the case of Beelzebul, who is a purely New Testament character, so far as our knowledge goes, and who has been fully adopted into our text [4]. In general it is quite evident that Paul and the writers of the Synoptic Gospels believed in demonic activities such as are described in the *Test* [5]. They differ in the essential point that Christ's is the only name to use in exorcism, and, according to Luke, it could safely be invoked only by real Christians [6]; all magic books were to be burned [7].

New Testament language has been adopted by our writer in the phrases $\sigma\tau o\iota\chi\epsilon\tilde{\iota}\alpha\ \varkappa o\sigma\mu o\varkappa\rho\acute{\alpha}\tau o\rho\epsilon\varsigma\ \tau o\tilde{\upsilon}\ \sigma\varkappa\acute{o}\tau o\upsilon\varsigma$, applied to the seven spirits of evil [8], or $\sigma\tau o\iota\chi\epsilon\tilde{\iota}\alpha\ o\acute{\iota}\ \varkappa o\sigma\mu o\varkappa\rho\acute{\alpha}\tau o\rho\epsilon\varsigma\ \tau o\tilde{\upsilon}\ \sigma\varkappa\acute{o}\tau o\upsilon\varsigma\ (\tau o\tilde{\upsilon}\ \alpha\grave{\iota}\tilde{\omega}\nu o\varsigma)\ \tau o\acute{\upsilon}\tau o\upsilon$ applied to the thirty-six *decani* [9], and $\dot{\alpha}\rho\chi\alpha\grave{\iota}\ \varkappa\alpha\grave{\iota}\ \dot{\epsilon}\xi o\upsilon\sigma\acute{\iota}\alpha\iota\ \varkappa\alpha\grave{\iota}\ \delta\upsilon\nu\acute{\alpha}\mu\epsilon\iota\varsigma$ as designations of angelic beings [10]. Dr. Conybeare has collected and discussed a considerable number of words and phrases common to our text and

---

[1] Par MP 850, 853, 3040.
[2] Cf. Deissmann, *opp. citt.* 184, 252, Dieterich, *Abraxas* 139; cf. *supra* p. 64, n. 2. [3] Cf. *supra* V 7. [4] Cf. *supra* VI 1 and p. 44, n. 7.
[5] Dibelius, *Geisterwelt*, 37—114.
[6] Mk IX 38ff.; Lk IX 49f.; Ac XIX 13—17.
[7] Ac XIX 19. [8] C. VIII 2.
[9] C. XVIII 2, combining Gal IV 3, 9; Col II 8, 20 with Eph VI 12. MS P omits $\tau o\tilde{\upsilon}\ \alpha\grave{\iota}\tilde{\omega}\nu o\varsigma$ as do the best witnesses in Eph VI 12.
[10] C. XX 15, Eph. I 21; Col I 16; II 15 and I Pt III 22 are combined; but MS P, putting $\varkappa o\sigma\mu o\varkappa\rho\acute{\alpha}\tau o\rho\epsilon\varsigma$ for $\delta\upsilon\nu\acute{\alpha}\mu\epsilon\iota\varsigma$ has the order of Eph VI 12.

the New Testament[1]. He comes to the conclusion, with which we must on the whole agree, that the similarity of phrase is due to common environment. "Paul merely glances at a system of belief which the *Testament* sets before us in lengthy detail"[2]. But the environment of our writer includes the New Testament. Not as if he had first hand acquaintance with it. That is excluded by those passages which deal with its incidents or ideas. When he describes the "Gadarene" demon, Leontophoron, he refers only to the outstanding features of the story which any one would remember who had heard it read or told[3]. Likewise in mentioning Jesus he alludes only to characteristic features of Christian doctrine which would impress themselves on a hearer who was δεισιδαιμονέστερος. The story of the rejected cornerstone, combining as it does Ps CXVIII 22 and Is XXVIII 16 after the manner of I Pt II 6f.[4], but referring them to an actual stone, reads like anti-Christian polemic from the Jewish side. Certainly our writer was not familiar with the Christian application of these verses, if he was a Christian.

After weighing the evidence one is driven to the conclusion that the author of the *Test* had the same relation to the New Testament that we have found him sustaining to the Old Testament and the apocryphal literature. All this constitutes part of the background of his thinking, and he had a superficial knowledge of it derived from hearing it read in the Sabbath worship, or mentioned in sermons and discussions; an occasional phrase or quotation sticks in his mind, or he may borrow from other better instructed magicians; but he is not working with copies of any of this literature before him. He composes freely without literary trammels. It is auricular knowledge with an absence of literary dependence rather than a very early date which makes the *Test* at once like and unlike the New Testament[5].

---

1 *JQR* XI 5 f.   2 *Ibid*. 6.   3 C. IX; cf. *supra* VI 7, p. 50.
4 C. XXII 7 f., XXIII 2—4. Cf. Mt XXI 42 and parallels; see above VII 6, p. 61 f., also IX 2 and n. 16, p. 102.
5 Cf. Conybeare, *JQR* XI 10; "The allusion [to the miracle of Gadara] is not of such a kind as to involve our Gospel text in its present form, but rather reflects the oral tradition which went before it."

b) Relation to the early Church. — To what class of Christians would such a work as the *Test* appeal? One would expect to find much Gnostic material in such a work, especially in view of the fact that so many so-called "Gnostic amulets" have been preserved, many of them coupling the name of Solomon with Abraxas and similar words of power[1]. In fact, Dr. Conybeare concludes, "It is probable.... that the *Testament* was the favourite book of the Ophiani, or of some analogous sect which combined a belief in Emmanuel with a mass of pre-existent Jewish superstitions"[2]. With this we cannot agree.

The passage on which Dr. Conybeare seems to base this judgment appears to me directly to contradict it. The seven ruling demons, faith in whom Origen ascribed to the Ophiani[3], are, to be sure, just the sort of beings in which the author of the *Test* believes. But these seven, which with the "mother" play so important a part in Gnosticism[4], are certainly the seven planets. In the *Test* the only group of seven which appears is to be identified with the Pleiades[5]; they have none of the characteristics of the Gnostic seven[6], nor is there any "mother" mentioned with them. Sophia is personified in Proverbs and Wisdom as in the *Test* long before her appropriation by Gnosticism.

The prohibition of the invocation of angels' names "um irgend eine Sache" in the *Second Book of Jeū*[7] is a direct attack upon such practices as the *Test* sought to further. A similar condemnation of heathen magic and astrology appears in *Pistis Sophia*[8],

---

1 In the British Museum is a bronze nail with the inscription, ABARAXAS. ASTRAEL IAO SABAO (drawing of a serpent) SOLOMONO; cf. H. B. Walters, *Cat. of the Bronzes in the Br. Mus., Greek, Roman, and Etruscan*, p. 370, No. 3194. Henzen, *Bull. d. Inst. di Corr. Arch.* 1849 p. 11 cites from a magic nail the inscription, AO SABAO SOLOMONO. Wessely, *Eph. Gram.* 22, 202, cites ιαο σολομων σαβαο from Montfaucon *Tab.* 164. 2 *Op. cit.* 14.

3 *Contra Cels.* VI 30, Conybeare, *JQR* XI 13.

4 Cf. Bousset, *Hauptprobl.* c. I, pp. 9—58.

5 So Bousset, *op. cit.* 21 n. 2, decides; as does also Conybeare himself, *op. cit.* 24 n. 2, though suggesting the planets as an alternative.

6 Cf. Bousset, *op. cit.* 27.   7 Schmidt, *K-Gn. Schriften*, 305, 30f.

8 *Ibid.* pp. 15—18, 167.

but, as Dieterich pointed out, the Gnostic insisted he had the key to the true science[1], and it was this that gave Gnostic amulets such tremendous vogue. Now one of the striking facts about the original *Test* is that, outside the chapter on the thirty-six decani (XVIII), which, as we have seen, is of Egyptian origin[2], it contains practically none of the names which are commonly found on Gnostic amulets, or are regarded as characteristic of Gnosticism; such names as Abraxas and Ialdaboth. The distinctly Gnostic elements belong to sections which have been assigned on other grounds to the later recensions[3].

The one piece of cosmic mysticism occurring in the *Test*, the directions for seeing "the heavenly dragons dragging the chariot of the sun"[4], presents a contrast to *Pistis Sophia* c. 136, which describes the sun as a great dragon with his tail in his mouth[5]. The words and phrases in the list of the *decani*[6] which have a Gnostic sound may be in part really of Gnostic origin; for example, ἰαέ· ἰεώ· υἱοὶ Σαβαώθ[7], κάλλιόν ἐστι Σολομῶν ἕνδεκα πατέρων[8], Ἰοῦδα ζιζαβοῦ[9]. Some, perhaps all, are borrowed by Gnosticism and the *Test* from the same sources, Judaism, heathenism, and Christianity[10]. None of the characteristic features of the Gnostic systems, such as dualism, emanations, syzygies, and mystic names being found in the *Test*, and there being so few allusions of any kind to Gnostic language, the conclusion must be that our text has not come under Gnostic influence.

One story in the *Test* brings it into touch with Ethiopia. From Ethiopia comes a story of Solomon's fall which closely parallels that in the *Test*. In the Talmud it is Asmodaeus who temporarily deposes the King by seizing his ring. In this Ethiopian legend Pharaoh's daughter seduces him. She urges him to worship her idols; he refuses. She entices him until finally he promises on oath that he will do whatever she wishes. Then

---

1 *Abraxas*, 151 f. and n. 2.   2 Cf. *supra* VII 5.
3 Cf. *infra* VII 11 and 12.   4 C. VI 19.
5 Schmidt, *K-Gn. Schriften* 233 18 f.   6 C. XVIII.
7 *Ibid.* § 16.   8 *Ibid.* § 18, P only.   9 *Ibid.* § 21.
10 E. g., Σαβαώθ, Ἀδωναΐ; cf. § 17.

she ties a thread across the middle of the door of the temple of her gods (that is, across the door half way up), brings three locusts, sets them in the temple of her gods, and says to him, "Come to me stooping so as not to break the woolen thread, kill these locusts before me, and twist their necks." When he complies, she says to him, "From now on I will do thy will, since thou hast made offering to my gods and hast prayed to them." The writer, moved by the same apologetic tendency as in the *Test*, explains that he acted thus on account of his oath in order that he might not perjure himself, although he knew that it was a sin to enter the idol temple[1].

The parallels between this legend and that in the *Test* are too striking to be overlooked. Furthermore, Ethiopic magic and demonology as a whole are much like those of the *Test*. "Very great importance is attached in (Ethiopic) magic spells to the knowledge of names and the power resident in them; and in this potent element of the magician's art Jewish, Christian, and pagan ideas curiously meet.... In Abyssinia, Biblical sacred names, together with a large number of fanciful appellations much resembling those in the Jewish Kabbala, were magically pronounced for the purpose of warding off the power of demons and all kinds of diseases"[2]. The use of slips of paper as amulets to be tied to the person or wall[3], the prominence of Michael, the use of angelic names against demons and diseases[4], the lilith-like Werzelya[5], and the power of Solomon over demons almost make the impression that it is the *Test* which Margoliouth is describing[6]. Remembering also the similarity of the *Test* and Ethiopic Enoch one might be led to the conclusion that the

---

[1] Prof. Dr. Carl Bezold, *Kebra Nagast, Die Herrlichkeit der Könige, nach den HSS. in Berlin, London, Oxford, and Paris*, c. 64, in *Abh. der philos-philol. Klasse der königl. bayer. Ak. d. Wiss.* 23. Bd., 1 Abt., München 1905, 60f. Salzberger, *Salomosage* 96, says the same story is found in Kisā'ī; cf. *infra* § 9, p. 80.

[2] G. Margoliouth, "The Use of Charms and Amulets in Ethiopia," *ExT* XXI 9 (June 1910) 403. [3] *Ibid.* 404. Cf. *Test* XVIII 22—42. [4] *Loc. cit.*

[5] Montgomery (*AITN* 261 f.) gives several parallels to the story of Christ's meeting with a lilith. In Canaan *Aberglaube* 27 f. the story in told of Solomon.

[6] *Op. cit.* 405.

Test must have come from the land from which the Ethiopic church received its legends, that is, from Egypt.

Lest one should infer too much, it is to be noted that legends similar to those in our text are to be found in other parts of the Christian world. Dr. Conybeare has discovered a parallel to the story of the corner stone which human agency could not lift[1] in life of St. Nino, the mother of the Georgian church[2]. In the Georgian life of the saint and the Armenian history of the Georgians is a story of a cedar column, the seventh and last necessary to the erection of the first church in the newly converted kingdom, which the king and all his people were unable to move, but which, in the early morning, after the defeat of the hosts of evil by St. Nino's prayers, is moved by invisible hands to the base prepared for it[3]. In Rufinus' *Ecclesiastical History* the same story is told of the "Iberians" and their king, but the miracle is heightened by leaving the pillar suspended above its base[4]. One might think of a combination of the stories of the corner stone and the aerial column in this last legend, but the connection is very tenuous.

Dr. James writes to me: "I would add two more references to your bit of *testimonia*. In the Syriac *Obsequies of the Virgin*, Wright, *Contributions to the Apocryphal Literature of the NT*, 1865, p. 42, is the story of the old man and his son [*Test* XX] — the end of it only, and in different guise, but unmistakably the same tale. It is from a fifth century MS (see p. 12). Also in a tract called *Inventiones Nominum* which I printed in *Journal of Theological Studies*, 1903, p. 224, § 27, is, 'Tres sunt Orniae.... Tercius est Ornias princeps demoniorum.' In one MS this is emended to 'Ornias princeps Lacedaemoniorum' in allusion to I Macc. XII 7; but I feel sure it *is* an emendation. It is interesting to find an allusion in Latin."

Returning from these excursions to outlying fields of Christian thought and life we find every reason for believing

---

1 *Test* XXII 7, XXIII.　2 *Guardian*, Mar. 29, 1899, 442.
3 *Stud. Bibl.* V (1908) 38—41, and 83f., edited by Miss Wardrop and Dr. Conybeare. The accounts are full of wild stories of demons and exorcisms.
4 *Ibid.* 60, *Eccl. hist.* I x; Migne, *PL* XXI 482.

that the *Test* belongs in the ordinary current of Christian faith and practice. From Paul on down the church fathers believed in the real existence and the dangerous powers of demons[1]. "Aus dem tiefsten Gefühl heraus, von der Hilflosigkeit und niedergedrückten Stimmung, wie dieser Glaube sie erzeugt hatte, eine Rettung gefunden zu haben, schreibt ein Christ des II. Jahrh. (Clemens Alex., Theodoti Exc. 71, 72) die Worte: 'Verschieden-artig sind die Gestirne und ihre Kräfte, heilsame, schädliche, rechte, linke.... Von diesem Widerstreit und Kampf der Kräfte rettet uns der Herr und gibt uns Frieden vor dem Kampfe der Kräfte und der Engel, den die einen für, die anderen wider uns führen'"[2]. Origen also seems to believe fully in the "powerful names" known by "the Egyptians, or by the Magi among the Persians, or by the Indian philosophers called Brahmans," as he does in the power of the name of God and of Jesus and of angel names[3]. That Christians practise sorcery or exorcism by demonic names he indignantly denies; it is the name of Jesus which drives out demons. Jesus has freed the Christian from all superstitious fears[4].

If such was the case with the leaders in the Christian church, how can we expect that the rank and file of their followers should fully grasp and consistently apply the one great idea in which Christian magic differed from heathen, that Christ's was the sole name of power to use for all purposes of healing and protection? The newly converted idolater cannot at once rise to the full heights of Christian spirituality[5]. The ancient church replaced the heathen deities with the crucifix

---

[1] Cf. von Dobschütz, *ERE* III 413—30, art. "Charms and Amulets (Christian)," very strangely H. L. Pass, *ibid.* IV 578—83, art. "Demons and Evil Spirits (Christian)" treats only of angels, but see now VIII 277f., art. "Magic." See also Heitmüller, *Im Namen Jesu*, 291—5. [2] Wendland, *Kultur* 81.
[3] *Contra Cels.* I 24f. cf. V 45. οὕτως οὐ τὰ σημαινόμενα κατὰ τῶν πραγμάτων ἀλλ' αἱ τῶν φωνῶν ποιότητες καὶ ἰδιότητες ἔχουσί τι δυνατὸν ἐν αὐταῖς πρὸς τάδε τινὰ ἢ τάδε. I 25 20, *KV Com.* II 76. [4] *Ibid.* VIII 57f.
[5] Experience as a missionary in India has vividly impressed upon the writer's mind the difficulties which converts to Christianity have in acquiring its point of view. But modern western Christianity is not without illustrations of the same problem.

and the images of the saints and madonna, and the old abradacadabra with angel names[1]. At a very early time on Christian amulets the Lord's Prayer, verses from the Psalms, and other familiar passages replaced the heathen myths and incantations[2]. Similarly the writer of the *Test* is making a brave, though but partially successful, attempt to put Christian (i. e., Jewish and Christian) ideas in the place of heathen. This whole movement is most illuminatingly set forth in an excerpt quoted by F. C. Burkitt from the Syriac homily *De magis, incantoribus, et divinis*, in which "the writer complains that his fellow-Christians, even the clergy, resorted to Magicians *and Jews*. He says (col. 395): 'Instead of the blessings of the Saints, lo, they carry about the incantations of the magicians, and instead of the holy cross, lo, they carry the books of devils.... One carries it on his head, and another round his neck, and a child, who knows nothing at all, carries about devils' names and comes (to church)..... Polluted and abominable priests take refuge in the names of demons...'"[3] Magic grew in power in the church, especially from the fourth century on, and was officially recognized in the sixth and seventh[4]. Our text is a document of this progressive paganizing of official Christianity rather than the product of some obscure heretical sect.

c) Relation to mediaeval Christianity. — That the *Test* belongs to orthodox Christianity is further demonstrated when one turns to study the preservation of the ideas for which it stands in the European world. Illustrations are too numerous to present in detail. The Queen of Sheba will serve as one. Kraus has collected many references of Byzantine writers to the fabled queen, which show that in using her the *Test* was following, or inaugurating, Christian tradition[5].

---

1 Cf. Heitmüller, *Im Namen Jesu*, 252f.
2 Cf. Deissmann, *Licht*, 24, 167, 297, *LAE* 39, 232, 415ff.
3 In *PSBA* XXIII (1901) 77f. The homily is "ascribed in MSS to S. Ephraim and edited as his by Lamy (vol. II, col. 393—426), but ... in my opinion is more likely to be the work of Isaac of Antioch (*circ.* 450 A. D.)"
4 Cf. von Dobschütz, *ERE* III 414.
5 "Die Königin von Saba in den byz. Chroniken," *BZ* XI (1902) 120ff.; cf. Nestle, *BZ* XIII (1904) 492f.

As to Solomon there was in the beginning some difference of opinion among Christian writers. Early anti-Jewish polemics, like the *Dialogue of Timothy and Aquila*, for example [1], find Solomon used to offset the claims of Jesus. Not only did their Jewish opponents apply many a Messianic passage to the wise son of David, but they made the claim that he had anticipated and excelled Jesus in his power over demons, thus undermining the Christian argument that Jesus was the Messiah because he had broken the power of Satan, and weakening the Christian appeal to a world that was languishing under the oppressive fear of demonic activities. To offset this Jewish claim these Christian writers bitterly attacked the memory of the wise king, maintaining that his was only a temporary victory over the demons, who overcame him at the end of his life. Leontius of Constantinople argues at some length that Christ's greatness is manifest in his power over demons while he was here on earth. In the midst of his description of the cure of the Gadarene demoniac he abruptly turns the request of the "Legion" to enter the swine to account in this fashion: Τίνι εἶπεν ὁ λεγεὼν τῶν δαιμόνων· Εἰ ἐκβάλῃς ἡμᾶς, ἐπίστρεψον ἡμῖν εἰς τὴν ἀγέλην τῶν χοίρων εἰσελθεῖν; Σολομῶντι, τῷ τὰ Ἰεροσόλυμα κτίσαντι, ἢ τῷ Δεσπότῃ Χριστῷ, τῷ τὰ σύμπαντα ἐν τῇ χειρὶ βαστάζοντι; Ἀλλ' ἐροῦσιν εὐθέως οἱ φιλοδαίμονες Ἰουδαῖοι· Τί οὖν; ὁ Σολομῶν οὐκ ἐδεσπότευσε τῶν δαιμόνων; οὐχὶ πάντας ὑφ' ἓν ὡς ἕνα συνέκλεισεν; οὐχὶ μέχρι τῆς σήμερον τοῦτον δεδοίκασιν; Ἀλλ' ὦ Ἰουδαῖοι μαγγανοδαίμονες, μάτην ταῦτα προβάλλεσθε· μόνος γὰρ ὁ Δεσπότης Χριστὸς κραταιῶς τὸν ἰσχυρὸν ἔδησε, καὶ τὰ σκεύη αὐτοῦ διήρπασε. Σολομῶν γάρ, οὐ μόνον οὐκ ἐδέσποσε τῶν δαιμόνων βασιλικῶς, ἀλλὰ καὶ ὑπ' αὐτῶν ἐδεσποτεύθη πρὸς τὰ τέλη καταφθαρείς. ἀγαπήσας γὰρ τὸν τῆς πολυγαμίας ἔρωτα, τῇ τοῦ διαβόλου μαστροπότητι δελεασθείς, ... ἐρρύπωσε τὸν τῆς θεογνωσίας θάλαμον. . . . . Πῶς οὖν δαιμόνων δεσπότης, ὁ τῶν δαιμόνων δοῦλος;[2]

---

[1] Cf. *infra* p. 103 f.
[2] From the homily *In mediam Pentecostem*, Migne, *PG* 86, col. 1980; According to Loofs, *Das Leben usw. des Leont. v. Byz.*, summarized by Krumbacher, *BLg* p. 54 f., this Leontius was a Constantinopolitan presbyter who lived

Similarly in the *Disputatio* of Pseudo-Gregentius, in reply to the claim of Herban the Jew that Solomon had ruled all the demons the archbishop replies: Σολομῶν ἐταπείνωσε δαίμονας; οὐκ οἶδας τί διαγορεύεις. πρὸς καιρὸν μὲν ἠσφαλίσατο τούτους ἐν τοῖς ἀγγείοις καὶ σφραγίσας κατέχωσεν. ἀλλά γε τὸ τηνικαῦτά μοι σκόπει, ὅτι νητῶς καταπολεμηθεὶς ὑπ' αὐτῶν τῶν δαιμόνων καὶ ἡττηθεὶς περὶ σωτηρίαν αὐτοῦ ἐκινδύνευσεν, ὡς ἡ γραφὴ μαρτυρεῖ[1].

The original *Test* shows no suspicion of a conflict of claims between Solomon and Christ, but in c. XV 10—12 Rec. B (MS P) attempts to combine the Jewish and Christian viewpoints. As to the glorious king's sad end, these early fathers think of him as falling a prey to the demons through the seduction of women, or vice versa. But the majority of Christian writers, like Josephus[2], ascribe his fall into idolatry to his love for women without the interposition of demonic agency[3]. The *Test* in one place takes the former view[4], but in the closing chapter apparently the latter. Here again our text shows its early date.

The conception of Solomon as a great magician who was powerful over demons and disease is witnessed to by scores of amulets and incantations, and especially by such books as the *Clavicula*[5]. Many of the demons of the *Test* lived on. Asmo-

---

about 485—542. Cf. Gelzer, *Leont. v. Byz.*, etc., and *Hist. Ztschr.* LXI (1899) 1—32, Fabricius, *Bib. Graec.* VIII 319 ff.

1 Migne, *PG* 86, col. 644 A. Gregentius was bishop of the Homerite church in Taphar in southern Arabia in the early part of the sixth cent. The *Disputatio* is not authentic, but may contain historical materials. Cf. Smith and Wace, *DCB*, Krumbacher, *BLg* 59, Bardenhewer, *Patrol.* 477. The mention of ἀγγεῖα makes connection between the Arabic type of tradition and the *Test*; cf. XV 9, XVIII 43, XXV 7, where the word is found only in MS P, and XVI 7, where Recs. A and B both should probably have it, though A reads φυλακήν.

2 *Ant* VIII 7 5; cf. 1 Kg XI 43.

3 Georgius Syncellus, P 181, V 145, B 341; Georgius Hamart., *Chron.* II 43 (Migne *PG* 110, 252—64); Glycas, *Ann.*, Migne *PG* 158 353 f.; Joseph. *Hypomn.* 74, (Migne *PG* 106 89 D). 4 C. VIII 8, 10.

5 Solomonic amulets can be found in many museums as well as in a large number of mediaeval MSS. They occur in Syriac, Arabic, and Hebrew, and in Latin, Greek, and modern European languages; e. g., Sachau, *Verz. Syr. HSS. Berlin* I 367, No. 10n, f. 54b: Sol. on horseback attacking Asmodaeus;

daeus goes through many transformations[1]. Obyzut appears in the Abyzu of Pradel's *Griechische und süditalienische Gebete*, while Ornias appears in the same documents[2]. Gaulmin and Migne were right in bringing the *Test* and Psellus together. The great Byzantine's περὶ ἐνεργείας δαιμόνων διάλογος is but the effort of a master mind to systematizise the ideas which the *Test* merely registers. Withal, this whole complex of Byzantine demonology and magic makes the impression of being a more highly developed form of the conceptions with which our text is operating. The roots of the tree run back to the Sumerians, the Babylonians, the Iranians, and the Pelasgians, the *Test* stands for the blossom, Psellus gives us the ripened fruit dissected and analyzed.

9. **Relation to Arabian folklore.** — Arabic literature, since it is especially rich in demon lore and Solomonic myth, invites particular comparison with the *Test*. In general Arabian beliefs and practices in the field of demonology and magic are not essentially different from those of our text except in one feature which Islam inherited from heathenism, the idea of the Jinn,

---

Schwab, *Dict.* 421, "ΣΦΡΑΓΙΣ ΘΕΟΥ; sur une hématite figurant un Salomon à cheval, perçant de sa lance un ennemi terrassé, avec la legende ΣΟΛΩΜΩΝ, au Cabinet des Medailles et Antiques de la Bibliothèque Nat. II 3039". The late Prof. Nestle wrote me of a Sol. on horseback as an amulet against *malocchio*, published by Bienkowski in *Eranos Vindobonensis*, 1893, 288. Amulets in MSS are well illustrated by those in *cod. Bonon. univ.* 3632, cf. *supra* p. 24. Cf. Heim "Incantamenta magica," in *Jbb. für class. Philol. Sup.* XIX (1893) pp. 463 —576, Nos. 56 = 169, 61, 62, 236, 237, and Sorlin Dorigny, "Sal. als Reiter," in *Rev. des Études Grecs* IV (1891) 217—296. The pilgrim of Bordeaux in the IV cent. was shown the "crypta ubi S. daemones torquebat," Schürer *GJV* III 418, from Tobler, *Palaest. descript.* (1869) 3, Pal. Pil. Text Soc., *Bordeaux Pilg.* 20. Dr. Conybeare drew my attention to Gannurini's ed. of St. Silvia's *Perigrinatio* (IV cent.), according to which the ring was kept in the Church of St. James (p. 96 and 95 n. 2). The tradition was that Vespasian took it to Rome, whence Constantine returned it (*ibid.* 96 n. 3), cf. Petri diaconi *liber de locis sanctis, ibid.* 117; see Pal. Pil. Text Soc., *The Pilgrimage of S. Silvia to the Holy Places*, 64 and 125.

1 As Markolf, Morolf, Kitovras, Saturn; cf. Fr. Vogt, *Die deutschen Dichtungen von Sal. u. Markolf*, I; J. M. Kemble, *The Anglo-Saxon Dialogue of Sol. and Saturn.*

2 Cf. Index I, s. v. "Dämonen," and Reitzenstein, *Poim.* 297 ff.

which are often kindly and beneficent creatures[1]. In our writer's mind there is properly no place for any good among demons, although he is once or twice betrayed by his pagan materials into referring to their healing powers. The wild exuberance of Arab fancy as we see it in the *Thousand and One Nights* is another mark of differentiation.

The Quran and even more the *Arabian Nights* have made all the world familiar with Solomon's authority over the Jinn and with the latter's terrible forms and powers. In the Quran are allusions to the fallen angels, Hārūt and Mārūt[2], and to the devils who were subject to Solomon, some as builders, and others bound in fetters[3]. In the *Nights* we find full accounts of how Solomon placed rebellious Jinn in bottles, or in cucurbites of copper, poured lead over them, and sealed them with his ring[4], with tales of their later escape from these prisons[5].

According to the Quran the Jinn are not allowed to listen at the gates of heaven, but God has placed the stars there as weapons for the angels to throw at them if they make the attempt. In the *Nights* the Jinniyah Maymunah "made for the firmament, thinking to listen by stealth to the converse of the angels," and when she ascended "skywards till she drew near the heaven of the world, the lowest of the heavens," she found an Ifrit there before her[6]. In another story "Allah suffered his angelic host to shoot down the Ifrit with a shooting star[7].

---

[1] Cf. Wellhausen's account of primitive Arabic beliefs, *Reste* 148—67, and Canaan, *Aberglaube* 6—27, for modern demonology; also *Encycl. of Islam*, I 1045 f., art. "Djinn," by D. B. Macdonald.

[2] Sura II 97 ff., *SBE* VI (Quran I) 14; Sale *ad loc.* quotes the legend substantially as told in Midrash Yalkut c. 44, see St. Clair-Tisdall and Muir, *Sources of Islam*, 30 f., and Weil, *Bibl. Leg.* 208 ff. Zohra resembles Shunamite in her activities.

[3] Sura XXXVIII 35 ff., *SBE* IX (II) 179, cf. Sale, *ad loc.*; XXVII 7, *SBE* IX (II) 101. [4] Lane-Poole III 110 f., Burton VI 84, Nights 566 f.

[5] Burton VI 85. The most famous is that of the "Fisherman and the Jinn," Burton I 38; cf. MacDonald's transcription from Galland's MS in *Or. Stud. Th. Nöldeke gewidmet*, also separately published. [6] Burton III 223 f.

[7] Burton, I 224, Night 22; cf. Quran, Sura XXXVII 6—9, *SBE* IX (II) 168; III 31, *ibid.* VI (I) 50 and n. 2; LXVII 5, *ibid.* IX (II) 293; LXXII 8 f., *ibid.* 305; Burton VI 100, Night 571, VIII 293, Night 870.

The likeness and unlikeness of the conceptions in the *Test* are apparent.

Salzberger's dissertation on the *Salomosage*, although it does not reach the fall of the king, presents a rich collection of legends, particularly with regard to his relations to the demons. He gathers them under four rubrics, the punishment of the demons, their appearance before Solomon, the description of certain individuals, especially Saḫr, and Solomon's ring[1]. Two descriptions of the appearance of the devils as they are marshalled before the king are given from three Berlin MSS of Kisa'i. The portrayal of demonic forms as given "nach dem korrecteren und vollständigeren Text der dritten Berliner Handschrift des Kisa'i"[2] would seem most strikingly like that in the *Test*, were it not that the other two MSS give in a longer and shorter form descriptions which are still more similar[3]. Solomon inquires from the demons, just as in the *Test*, what their activities are, and, having learned, chains them so they may injure mankind no more. The ring, as in the *Test*, is brought down from heaven, and by its aid Solomon becomes master of the demons.

Yet, with all these close resemblances, there are also great differences between the *Test* and the Arabic legends. All the Jewish stories of Solomon's glory and wisdom, his wonderful ring, the building of the Temple by the aid of the demons, and his dealings with the queen of Sheba have grown marvellously under the fructifying fancy of the Arabs. Beside the marvels of the Quran and its commentaries, and especially the *Arabian Nights* the *Test* is dull and tame[4]. Most of the features in which we found Jewish legend to have evolved beyond the *Test* are to be found in still more highly developed form among the Arabs; for example, Solomon's power over the animals is greatly extended[5];

---

1 (1) *op. cit.* 98f., 113ff.; (2) 99—112; (3) 112—115; (4) 115—29.

2 *Ibid.* 99, Mg. 40, f. 72b.

3 *Ibid.* 105ff.; Pm. 627, f. 160a f. gives the longer form, which most resembles the *Test*; Spr. 86, f. 226aff. the shorter.

4 Cf., for example, Lane-Poole, III 51f., 110f., 239, 317, 329, 454.

5 In the Quran he knows the language of the birds; Sura XXVII 16, *SBE* IX (II) 100.

Saḫr is the Talmudic Asmodaeus, but worse; Iblis, the devil, whose refusal to worship Adam leads to his fall[1], is not, like Beelzebul in the *Test*, subject to Solomon, but carries a step farther that independence and insolence which Asmodaeus shows in the Jewish legends; the king's fall has quite a different aspect in the Quran[2].

The ring also, as Salzberger shows, develops a new character in Arabic legend different from that which it has in the *Test*, evolving along the lines suggested by the Talmudic story of Asmodaeus' theft of it[3]. Kisa'i is the first to describe it fully[4] It is so glorious that no one can look at it without repeating the Moslem creed, and has four considerable legends engraved upon it[5]. It is either brought by Gabriel, or of itself comes from the throne of God and appears upon Solomon's hand.

Solomon's fall according to Kisa'i was due to conscious or unconscious idolworship, which, if I understand Salzberger, was connected with the sacrifice of locusts[6]. This tradition, then, connects the *Test* on the one hand with Ethiopia, and on the other with Arabia. Since Ethiopia was closely connected with Arabia in Christian history, we have probably to think of a Palestinian Jewish tradition which never found its way to Babylon, nor, so far as I know, into official Palestinian Jewish literature, but passed by way of the Jewish colonies in southern Arabia into Ethiopian and Mohammedan legend, and directly from Palestinan Judaism into our Christian work, for we cannot suppose that the *Test* arose in Arabia. This being so, one of the links that would connect our text with Egypt is broken.

These examples are sufficient to illustrate both the likeness and the unlikeness of the *Test* to Arabic literature. They show how Arabic legend, where it resembles our work, has developed its

---

1 Sura II 33 f.; VII 19 ff.; XV 30 ff.; XVII 63 f.; XVIII 47 ff.; XXXVIII 75 ff., *ibid.* VI (I) 5, 138 f., 246 f., IX (II) 8, 20, 181.
2 Sura XXXVIII 33 f., *ibid.* IX (II) 178 and n. 2.
3 *Salomosage* 115—9.   4 *Ibid.*, from Mq. 40 f. 70b—72b.
5 In the *Nights* an oath by the names on Solomon's ring is peculiarly powerful, Burton III 224 f., Night 177; cf. VII 317 n.
6 *Op. cit.* 96; refers to Pm. 627, f. 151b—155a.

ideas farther and in a different manner, and how in many particulars it rests upon the sort of Jewish tradition seen in the Talmud.

10. Unique matter in Recension A. — Having studied the material relationships of the *Test* as a whole we now undertake the same task for the individual recensions. As Rec. A is nearest the original, it has little matter that calls for comment. Its expansions are of a purely narrative sort[1]. MS L alone has undergone a considerable revision by a mediaeval magician, who added nothing new, but merely mutilated the document. The single addition of importance in this recension is the inscription on the ring[2].

11. Unique matter in Recension B. — The peculiarities of Rec. B, and particularly of MS P, the only complete MS of this recension, consist in the main of unimportant interpolations and alterations. There are, however, a few additions of moment. These may be classed under four heads: (1) those which show familiarity with demonological tradition; e. g., the reference to the ghosts of the giants[3], to the female demon Obyzuth as πνεῦμα μυριώνυμον καὶ πολύμορφον[4], and to Enepsigos, another female demon, as μυριώνυμος[5], the allusion to a cycle of legend regarding Ἐλβουρίων and οἱ ἑπτὰ δαίμονες[6], the added charms in XVIII 23, 27 f., further information regarding Abezethibu[7]; (2) those which are Gnostic in character; e. g., the allusions to the eleven fathers and the eleventh aeon[8]; (3) those which have a cabalistic tendency; e. g., the introduction of Apharoph for Raphael, of χμδ´ for Emmanuel, and of χμ´ for Raphael[9], and

---

1 Cf. c. I 1 f. and XXVI 8—10. 2 Cf. infra VII 14. 3 C. XVII 1.
4 C. XIII 3; cf. Ἑκάτη μυριώνυμε Par MP 2745, Orph. Hymn. *passim*, Ἐκ. πολυώνυμε Par MP 2815; her many names are given in *cod. Par.* 2316, f. 432, cf. Reitzenstein, *Poim.* 299 (one is Ἀβιζά), Pradel, *Gr. Geb.* 23 (275) (Ἀβυζοῦ), Montgomery, *AJTN* 260 (No. 42), 262, Gaster in *Folklore* XI 133, Avezuha; πολυώνυμε is frequent. For πολύμορφος cf. Par MP 2726, 2799, of Hekate and Selene; *cod. Par.* 2316 f. 318ᵛ (Reitzenstein, *Poim.* 297) Στραγγαλιὰ πολύμορφε. 5 C. XV 2. 6 C. IX 7.
7 C. XXV 1—5, possibly omitted by accident from Rec. A. See also additions in VI 4. 8 C. XVIII 18, 31.
9 C. XIII 6, XV 11. See other additions in XVIII 3, 23, XXII 8, XXIII 4.

(4) those which show familiarity with Christianity. Additions are found in every section that refers to Christ; viz., VI 8, XI, XII 3, XVII 4, and XXII 20. The additions in the first three passages are not important. The remaining two, however, seem to be due to an attempt to make the Christianity of the *Test* less "equivocal," since in XVII 4 the "becoming man" of the Savior is mentioned, and in XXII 20 the one to be born of a virgin and crucified is called ὁ μονάρχης θεός. These additions lead to the belief that in XV 10 f., where Rec. A is wanting by accident, the positive Christian ideas advanced, viz., that it is the son of God who is to be stretched on the tree, that his mother is never to know man, and that he is especially fit to receive dominion over all the demons because he overcame the devil (διάβολος rarely occurs in the *Test*) are probably the work of the B redacteur. This conclusion is supported by the fact that the *Test* elsewhere makes no attempt at systematic thought or generalization. At any rate we cannot definitely claim these ideas for the original writer, and must conclude that B is not only much better instructed in the faith, but also later.

12. Unique matter in Recension C. — Rec. C deserves a special investigation of much greater proportions than can be given here, in order to determine its sources and relationships. As we have already seen, its language is late, and the codices in which it is found as well as its unique material relate it to the *Clavicula*[1].

Many problems I must leave to others. Why is Beelzebul called Eltzianphiel[2]? What is the meaning of Onoskelu's birth ἀπὸ φωνῆς βηρσαβεὲ ἱππικῆς χρηματικῆς[3]? Whence comes the idea of the bird that flies over God's head? One of the most interesting and baffling sections is that which we have called the "Prologue". In spite of defective grammar the editor has

---

1 Cf. *supra* II 4, IV 2 c.   2 Rec. C XI 1; cf. Τζιανφιέλ, X 1.

3 *Ibid.* XI 6. Dr. James writes, "I am clear that χρηματικῆς has something to do with χρεμετίζειν, *neighing of horse*, and I compare Jer. V 8, ἵπποι θηλυμανεῖς ἐγενήθησαν, ἕκαστος ἐπὶ γυναῖκα τοῦ πλησίον ἐχρεμέτιζον. When David sinned with Bathsheba, βηρσαβεέ, he was a ἵππος θηλυμανής. See *Test* V 8, θηλυμανεία.

been able to select from some source certain high sounding prayers, which; I think, have no parallels in the LXX, the New Testament, or the early fathers. Possibly he borrowed from some, to him well known, liturgy.

The magical cup and table in c. XI 7 ff. are related to the "marvelous cup of crystal middlemost of which was the figure of a lion faced by a kneeling man grasping a bow with arrow drawn to the very head, together with the food-tray of Sulayman, the son of David" in the story of "Sinbad the Seaman and Sinbad the Landsman" from the *Arabian Nights*[1]. The added magical formulae connect this recension more closely than the others to the magical literature of the Middle Ages on the one hand, and to the magical papyri on the othero The word Agla (XIII 6), which by *notarikon* stands for "thou art mighty forever, O Lord," indicates dependence upon Jewish cabalism, and probably a relatively late date, for the word is not in the magic papyri, so far as I can discover, but is a favorite in the Middle Ages[2].

The magical recipe of c. IX 9f. and the list of fifty demons in c. X have many marks which show that they are later than the original *Test* and have arisen in a different circle. The list is not concerned solely or primarily with the cure of diseases; it relates the powers, some good, some evil, of each demon, and implies that these powers are under the control of him who knows the demon's seal. Furthermore, each demon rules a certain number of inferiors. These ideas are to be found, on the one hand, in Gnosticism, which details the number of spirits ruled by each $ἄρχων$[3], and, on the other, in mediaeval

---

[1] Seventh Voyage in the Calcutta edition, Burton VI 80.

[2] The word is an acrostic from the first four words of the second blessing of the Shemoneh 'Esreh: אתה גבור לעלם אדני. Since this liturgy and also the practice of *notarikon* are early, one can argue as to date only on general probabilities; cf. *JE* I 235, IX 270—82; Schwab, *Dict.* s. v. אגלא. It occurs often in Horst, *Zauberbib.*, I 127, II 90, 103, 121, 123 ff., etc.; in Mather's *Key*, p. 7; in Harl. MS 5596 (cf. *supra* II 4) f. 30a¹ in an incantation to secure treasure: $ὁρκίζω ὑμᾶς, δαίμονες, εἰς τὰ ὀνόματα τοῦ θεοῦ τὸ τετραγράμματον ὅπερ ἐστὶν ἀγλα· ἀγλαατά· ἀγλαΐ· ἀγλαώρ$; also f. 30b², 32b²; often in Latin *Clavicula*. [3] Cf. p. 85, n. 2.

magic[1]. The resemblance between c. X and the language of *Pistis Sophia* regarding the five ἄρχοντες and the ψῆφοι and σφραγῖδες of the thirteenth αἰών[2], and the various χαρακτῆρες, σφραγῖδες, and lists of names in chapters 5—40 and 45—52 in the *First Book of Jeu*[3] is most striking. Furthermore, there are close resemblances between the magical figures of the Coptic papyri, the *Clavicula*, both Latin and Greek, and the unique sections of this recension.

We cannot attempt to trace the connecting links between these widely separated branches of magic, which, no doubt, go back to a common source in Hellenistic syncretism. The facts presented are an interesting illustration of the wide wanderings of superstitions, and the tenacity with which they maintain their forms in their migrations.

13. Unique matter in MS D. — On internal grounds and by comparison with Recs. A and B we have decided that MS D c. I—VI and VIII present in general the form of the original story of Solomon out of which the *Test* was developed[4]. From what sources did this legend come? As it now stands, it is quite plainly a Christian redaction of Jewish *midrashim* regarding Solomon, Palestinian, perhaps Galilean, in origin, rather than Babylonian[5]. That the legend of c. I is ultimately Jewish is suggested by Nathan's stopping to bury a dead countryman, a trait borrowed from Magianism[6]. Traces of later influences are to be found in c. VII[7]. The story of Solomon's flying through the air appears in Jewish mythology, where he is said to have ridden on an eagle[8], but in Mohammedan legend, according to the Quran on a wind[9], and in the

---

1 Cf. Trinity Col. (Cambridge) MS 1404 in French; Harl. (Br. Mus.) 6483, which contains "all the names, orders, and offices of all the spirits Sol. ever conversed with" (f. 1). 2 Cc. 138 ff., Schmidt, *K-Gn. Schr.* 235 ff.
3 *Ibid.* 260—97, 308—29. 4 Cf. *supra* IV 2. 5 Cf. *supra* VII 6 d), p. 64 f.
6 Cf. Tob I 19, II 3 ff. Dr. James points out to me that the story is found in Ps.-Epiphanius, *Vitae Prophetarum*, see ed. Schermann (Teubner 1907), pp. 4, 54, 89, Migne, *PG* 43, col. 425, and thinks this is its probable source. For D it would then be indirectly Jewish, I suppose. Calish, *JE* IX 176, says the rabbis are practically silent as to Nathan. 7 Cf. *supra* IV 2.
8 Grünbaum, *ZDMG* XXXI 23.
9 Suras XXXI 81, XXXIV 11, XXXVII 35, *SBE* IX (II) 52, 151, 179.

Arabian Nights on a magic carpet[1]. If the story originally referred to Asmodaeus' usurpation of the throne, then we have also Jewish sources. This chapter, then, would seem to be an addition from a Jewish-Mohammedan type of tradition. All the remainder of this version we have already traced to Jewish sources [2].

From considerations of textual and literary criticism we concluded that D in its present form was late, but that its archetype (*d*) was the starting point for the *Test*[3]. From its language and style we concluded that it was Byzantine[4]. Our conclusions based upon a study of its subject matter accord with this and take us one step further: an originally Jewish document or cycle of legends has been thoroughly worked over by an educated Christian in early Byzantine times. Since there are no Christian elements in those parts of *d* which were taken over into the *Test*, and the quality of the Christianity in Rec. A is much poorer than in D, it is natural to conclude that *d* had nothing Christian in it when it was transformed into the *Test*.

14. Solomon's seal. — The origin of the seals supposedly engraved on the ring of Solomon is of subordinate importance, since they are in any case secondary additions in our MSS. The simplest form is that found in Rec. B, which attempts no reproduction, but merely says the inscription was a pentagram. Since this is the western type of the tradition, it cannot have been original[5].

Rec. A presents an interesting formula consisting for the most part of unintelligible words and containing those combinations of vowels so common in Hellenistic magic. MS L alone reproduces the seal with the legend in the form of a circle, the formula appearing around the circumference, while the interior contains magic signs. In the manuscript in which L is found, Harl. 5596, the *Clavicula* contains a seal of different shape on

---

1 Burton III 267. 2 *Supra* VII 6. 3 *Supra* IV 1, 2, 3. 4 *Supra* V 1.
5 Cf. *JE* XI 438 ff., 448, Grünbaum, *Neue Beiträge z. sem. Sagenkunde* 251. The text of the inscriptions as given in our MSS will be found below, p. 100 f. Canaan, *Aberglaube*, p. 112 f., *et passim*, gives the seal of Solomon as usually the sixpointed star among modern Arabs, but also the five.

which the same legend was to be written. In Bologna University MS No. 3632 (V of the *Test*) there is found among many such "pentacles" a circle inscribed τοῦ σολομῶντος μεγάλου, within which is written the same legend. No doubt the editor of Rec. A got his seal from some such collection. The wording of the inscription would seem to link it to the older amulets and magic papyri, but in any case it is younger than the *Test*, which shows little trace of such influence.

In Rec. C twelve large seals are found, the first a rectangle with various transverse lines and magic sings, the remaining eleven round and also containing various mystical symbols. In the fifth and the ninth are figures that look like the signs for Virgo and Scorpio, in the seventh for Aquarius, in the eighth for Pisces; the third, fourth, and fifth contain among others modifications of the Christian monogram ☧. The fact that these same seals are found in a Vienna MS which does not contain the *Test* is, I think, indicative of their origin. We must conclude that the original *Test* contained no description or reproduction of the seal.

15. Summary and conclusions. — If our previous conclusions are correct, the original Jewish stem of the present *Test* consisted of the narrative parts of chapters I, II, XX, XXII, XXIII, and XXIV, i. e., of those parts which are common to the *Test* and MS D. Upon this parent stem have been grafted (1) certain sections which describe the demons more fully, (2) two brief references to the work as a *Test*, which give it the name (XV 13 f., XXVI 8), other considerable sections containing demonic prophecies whose later fulfilment is represented as constituting the basis for Solomon's faith in their testimony, and which, therefore, are intended to validate the work to the public (XII 4, XV 12 ff., XX 21)[1], and (4) additions made merely for the story's sake or intended to link the parts of the story together (VI 3, 5 f., XIX, XXI, XXII 7 f., 17).

In this division of the *Introduction* we have given attention mainly to the origin of the first of these four classes of additions,

---

[1] Note also the late (P) addition XV 8—11.

which includes the demonological, astrological, and magical elements in the work[1], additions marked by the questions τίς εἶ σύ; τίς καλεῖσαι; ποίῳ ζῳδίῳ κεῖσαι; ποίῳ ἀγγέλῳ καταργεῖσαι; It is for the sake of answering these questions that the *Test* was written. As we have seen, the material for the answers has been drawn through Judaism from Babylonia in Ephippas (XXII) and possibly in the lilith-like Obyzuth (XIII) and from Persia in Asmodaeus (V); from Hellenistic Egypt come the decani although the section has been much altered by Jewish or Christian revisers (XVIII); from Hellenistic Greek mythology come Onoskelis (IV), Lix Tetrax (VII), Akephalos Daemon (IX), Enepsigos (= Hekate, XV), Kunopegos (= Poseidon, XVI), and possibly the dog, Rhabdos (X, = ? Cerberus) and Pterodrakon (XIV = ? Typhon)[2], from Hellenistic mysticism the recipe for a cosmic revelation (VI 10f.); from (perhaps Galilean) Jewish sources come the seven κοσμοκράτορες[3], the giant, Machthon[4], the demon of the Red Sea, Abezethibou (XXV), and probably the Shunamite (XXVI); from Christian, or Jewish-Christian sources in part, come Beelzebul (III, VI 1—9), Leontophoron, the demon of Gadara (XI), and perhaps the demon of epilepsy called κορυφὴ δρακόντων, beside the charms which include some allusion to Christ (XV 10f., XVII 4).

What sort of a man could have held such inconsistent and ill-digested views drawn from all these diverse sources. He cannot have been a heathen for he knows Judaism and Christianty, the Old Testament and the New too well. He cannot have been a Jew because of the Christian elements. Dr. Conybeare suggests that we have here as in the *Testaments of the Twelve Patriarchs*, "a Christian recension of a Jewish book"[5]. Although I cannot agree with Schürer that there are no Jewish passages in the book[6], Dr. Conybeare's hypothesis does not seem to

---

[1] MS D shows that some of this was in the original story, *d*.

[2] Azazel, the serpent tempter of Eve, has human hands and feet in the *Apoc. of Abraham* XXIII, Bonwetsch p. 33; cf. Hughes, *Ethics Jew. Apoc.*, 211.

[3] C. VIII; it has some Hellenistic and Christian additions.

[4] Is he a Titan rather than one of the Nephilim?

[5] *JQR* XI 13 f.   [6] *Th. Litztg.* 1899 110.

meet the facts in the case. There is too much Christian material in the *Test*. Particularly is it to be noted that, in both places where the word *testament* occurs (XV 14, XXVI 8), it is closely connected with passages which are Christian in tone; c. XV 10f. in the form in which we have it is the most characteristically Christian section in the entire work; c. XXVI 8 in Rec. B, which we believe to represent the original here, is less markedly so than is MS H with its reference to the "Jews," and yet we have discovered that the whole of the last chapter is based on a legend which otherwise comes to us from a Christian source. Moreover, the demonology of the work, which so much resembles that of the New Testament and the pseudepigrapha which were accepted in the Christian church, and the language with its resemblances to that of the New Testament even in passages where there is no quotation or direct allusion point to a Christian origin. The absence too of smaller inconsistencies from the narrative, especially of Rec. A, the impossibility of finding the joints in the mending, point to unity of authorship for the *Test* as such. We conclude, then, that while the original story *d* was probably Jewish, the demonological document which first called itself a *Testament*, best represented in Rec. A, was a Christian work.

The man who composed our *Test* bears no distinctive marks of any heterodox circle, yet he was no thorough-going Christian. He was above all a magician, and it is as such that he collected this bizarre potpourri of fragments from almost every nation that had contributed to Mediterranean civilization. He must have been a Greek Christian, familiar, perhaps from childhood, with the language of the Septuagint and New Testament, familiar also with many legends of Jewish origin, but entirely familiar too with the demonology and magic of the heathen world, to which he belonged almost as truly as he did to Christianity. For him Christ is not yet master of the whole world; nevertheless, Christ's is a name to conjure with, and, when he is at a loss for a powerful angel name, the new savior comes into the exorcism. He is a half-hearted Christian in a world where Christianity is not yet the conquering religion. This is the more evident when one compares Recs. B and C, which introduce elements which reveal the period when Christianity had conquered, and was absorbing its former foes and their superstitions.

VIII. THE TESTAMENT IN LITERATURE AND HISTORY.

1. Solomonic books of healing and magic among the Jews. —
a) The literary starting point for all the later legends regarding Solomon's wisdom is to be found in III Reg III. Here, as Benzinger points out, it is the judicial wisdom of the ruler that is in the writer's mind[1]. In c. V 9—14, on the other hand, it is "religiöse Lebensweisheit"[2]. Furthermore, Benzinger believes that in comparing Solomon's wisdom with that of the children of the East and the wisdom of the Egyptians the writer intended to imply that Solomon knew magic and astrology, for these ancients were famous for such knowledge, as the records of the Exodus, for example, testify. How far back may we place this earliest reference to Solomon's magical knowledge? The verses in question can hardly belong to the earlier sources of the Books of Kings as Kautzsch seems to imply[3], but rather to the final redaction of the book[4]. The least that one can say is that it must date before the Septuagint translation. More than two centuries, therefore, before Christ, in the leading circles of Palestinian Judaism, Solomon is already a magician. The interpolator of the passage may not have thought of him as the author of magical books, but surely many readers would understand from the allusion to the wisdom of the ancients and Egypt that ᾠδαί meant, not psalms, but *carmina*, incantations, and that the discourses ὑπὲρ τῶν ξύλων must include their medical, or what amounted to the same thing, their magical uses[5].

---

[1] *Könige*, p. 23f., on I Kg V 9—14.
[2] I Kg V 9—14 (Heb), IV 29—34 (Eng).
[3] According to markings adopted in *Heil. Schr. des AT*.
[4] So Benzinger, *loc. cit.* Stade and Schwally in Haupt's polychrome Hebrew Bible color it as a "non-Deuteronomic addition of unknown origin." Cf. Steuernagel, *Einl. AT* 356, and *ZATW* 1910 70, whose suggestions require a very late date.
[5] Cf. Salzberger, *Salomosage*, 5 ff., for an analysis of the biblical passage.

b) The next reference to Solomon's magical powers, in Wisdom VII 17—22, makes no allusion to writings; indeed the context does not call for it. But it does plainly involve the ascription to the supposed writer of knowledge of astrology, of the nature of beasts and spirits, as well as of men, of the ἐνέργεια στοιχείων, the διαφοραὶ φυτῶν, and the δυνάμεις ῥιζῶν, of "all things that are either secret or manifest"[1]. The Wisdom of Solomon, then, is a witness to the acceptance of the legend of Solomon's astrological, demonological, and magical accomplishments in Alexandrian Judaism in the first century B. C., and, let it be noted, by a thoroughly educated and highly cultured Jew of the Dispersion.

c) A still further allusion to Solomon's authority over demons is found in Pseudo-Philo, *de antiquitatibus biblicis*, in *Citharismus regis Dauid contra daemonium Saulis*, which we have already quoted. The lines which concern us here should run, according to Dr. James, as follows: Arguet autem te metra nova unde natus sum de quo nascetur post tempus de lateribus meis qui vos domabit. Dr. James says, "In this last sentence it seems at first sight as though we had a prophecy of Messiah, and a possible Christian touch. But a little consideration will show, I think, that the 'vanquisher of demons' who is to spring from David is not Messiah, but Solomon the king of Genies, the wizard whose spells produced such marked effects in the time of Josephus, the hero, too, of the *Testament of Solomon*, where he figures almost solely as the restrainer and chastiser of mischievous spirits"[2].

d) The next mention of Solomon's power as a magician is the decisive one, without which one might doubt the interpretations adopted above. There can be no doubt as to Josephus' meaning on the whole when he relates the following: ⟨44⟩ συνετάξατο δὲ καὶ βιβλία [περὶ] ᾠδῶν καὶ μελῶν πέντε πρὸς τοῖς χιλίοις, καὶ παραβολῶν καὶ εἰκόνων βίβλους τρισχιλίας· καθ'

---

[1] Following the translations by Siegfried in Kautzsch, *APAT* I 490, and Holmes in Charles, *APOT* I 546.
[2] *TS* II 3 (1893) *Apoc. Anec.* 183 ff.; cf. *supra* VII 6 b), and p. 60 n. 2.

ἕκαστον γὰρ εἶδος δένδρου παραβολὴν εἶπεν, ἀφ' ὑσσώπου ἕως κέδρου. τὸν αὐτὸν δὲ τρόπον καὶ περὶ κτηνῶν καὶ τῶν τ' ἐπιγείων ἁπάντων ζῴων καὶ τῶν νηκτῶν καὶ τῶν ἀερίων· οὐδεμίαν γὰρ τούτων φύσιν ἠγνόησεν οὐδὲ παρῆλθεν ἀνεξέταστον, ἀλλ' ἐν πάσαις ἐφιλοσόφησε καὶ τὴν ἐπιστήμην τῶν ἐν αὐταῖς ἰδιωμάτων ἄκραν ἐπεδείξατο. ⟨45⟩ παρέσχε δ' αὐτῷ μαθεῖν ὁ θεὸς καὶ τὴν κατὰ τῶν δαιμόνων τέχνην εἰς ὠφέλειαν καὶ θεραπείαν τοῖς ἀνθρώποις. ἐπῳδάς τε συνταξάμενος αἷς παρηγορεῖται τὰ νοσήματα, τρόπους ἐξορκώσεων κατέλιπεν, οἷς ἐνδούμενα τὰ δαιμόνια ὡς μηκέτ' ἐπανελθεῖν ἐκδιώκουσι. ⟨46⟩ καὶ αὕτη μέχρι νῦν παρ' ἡμῖν ἡ θεραπεία πλεῖστον ἰσχύει· ἱστόρησα γάρ τινα Ἐλεάζαρον τῶν ὁμοφύλων, Οὐεσπασιανοῦ παρόντος καὶ τῶν υἱῶν αὐτοῦ καὶ χιλιάρχων καὶ ἄλλου στρατιωτικοῦ πλήθους, τοὺς ὑπὸ τῶν δαιμονίων λαμβανομένους ἀπολύοντα τούτων. ὁ δὲ τῆς θεραπείας τρόπος τοιοῦτος ἦν. ⟨47⟩ προσφέρων ταῖς ῥισὶ τοῦ δαιμονιζομένου τὸν δακτύλιον, ἔχοντα ὑπὸ τῇ σφραγῖδι ῥίζαν ἐξ ὧν ὑπέδειξε Σολομών, ἔπειτ' ἐξεῖλκεν ὀσφρομένῳ διὰ τῶν μυκτήρων τὸ δαιμόνιον, καὶ πέσοντος εὐθὺς τἀνθρώπου μηκέτ' εἰς αὐτὸν ἐπανήξειν ὥρκου, Σολομῶνός τε μεμνημένος καὶ τὰς ἐπῳδάς, ἃς συνέθηκεν ἐκεῖνος, ἐπιλέγων . . . . ⟨49⟩ γινομένου δὲ τούτου σαφὴς ἡ Σολομῶνος καθίστατο σύνεσις καὶ σοφία . . .[1]

We have quoted the passage at length, because we believe that, having it before the eye and remembering the previous Jewish allusions to Solomonic incantations, one cannot but accept Albrecht Dieterich's conclusion that Josephus means to imply that books were in circulation under Solomon's name which gave the magical, or medicinal, virtues of plants after the plan of the works later written by Pamphilus and called εἰκόνες κατὰ στοιχεῖον[2]. And surely the ἐπῳδαί had long ago been written down.

e) The Mishna says that Hezekiah hid the "book of recipes"[3],

---

[1] Ant VIII 44—49 (Naber) = VIII 2 5.
[2] Abraxas 142 f., Leid. Pap. 780 ff.
[3] In the Gemara, Berakoth 10a (Goldziher I 35), Pesachim 56a (ibid. II 520): רפואה. גנז ספר רפואות means Heilung, in the plural Arzeneien, Heilmittel, Levy-Fleischer, s. v.; cf. Jer XXX 13. See also A. Wünsch, ZDMG LXVI (1912) 414.

which, according to Maimonides and Rashi meant a book which Solomon had written; Maimonides holding that it was a book of magic[1], Rashi that the evil consisted in its leading men not to pray to God for their healing[2]. Otherwise rabbinic literature does not refer to such Solomonic works; evidently this sort of tradition was avoided in official Judaism.

f) After Talmudic times I know of no reference to such books until we reach the Jews of the Middle Ages. In fact Moses takes the place of Solomon in Jewish literature and becomes the representative wise man, as Solomon does for the Christians[3]. Steinschneider gives citations from writers of the twelfth and following centuries who look upon Solomon as the source of all wisdom, including medicine, magic, and astrology[4]. In particular, Sheintob ben Isaac of Tortosa (1260) in his paraphrase of Zahravi's *Tasrif*, called ספר השמות (XI cent.)[5], gives "eine Schilderung der Weisheit Salomo's (namentlich in der Naturkunde), unter dessen Namen in Zahrawi ein Verband (רטיה) erwähnt werde, der auf weißer Marmortafel an der Wand seines Palastes eingegraben war, wie verschiedene Rezepte (נוסחאות ופוקחות), die von den Späteren (האחרונים) erläutert worden; Scheintob hat 'hier in Marseille' den Christen mehr davon erläutert, als er in Zahrawi fand"[6]. We have here possible the contract with the demons[7], and certainly the magical recipes said to have been written on the temple gates[8]. Steinschneider

---

1 Surenhusius, *Mishna* II 149, *de Paschati* IV 9. Maimonides says: "Haec Mishna est ex Tosaphta, quam exponam propter utilitatem illius; ספר רפואות *liber medicinae*, erat liber qui tractabat de medicis quibus se sanare non permittebat Lex, uti sunt ejusmodi res quae proponebantur per figuras; erant enim Astrologiae periti nonnulli quorum dicto homines faciebant suo tempore imagines ac figuras quasdam, qui aliquibus damnum (sic) vel utilitatem adferebant; haec autem figura in lingua Graeca vocabatur $\tau \acute{\varepsilon} \lambda \varepsilon \sigma \mu \alpha$ . . . . . Prolixius esse volui in hisce, eo quod mibi exposuerant, quod Shelomo composuisset librum medicinae.
2 Grünbaum, *ZDMG* XXXI 200.
3 Kohler in *JE* IV 518; cf. Gaster, *Sword of Moses*.
4 *Hebr. Übers.* 936, ns. 225 and 226; 849 f.
5 *Ibid.* 740 ff. Zahravi is called Açararius, Azaravi, etc.
6 *Ibid.* 743. Is Scheintob borrowing from the Christian tradition, or vice versa? See below VIII 3 b) (2).
7 Cf. *infra* VIII 3 d) 2) (d).   8 Cf. *infra* VIII 3 c) 2).

is only partly right in trying to relieve his compatriots of the responsibility for the ascription of such works to Solomon¹. The Christians, however, developed the tradition far more than did the Jews from whom they received it.

2. Solomonic books among the Arabs. — A single reference in the Quran and the comments thereon show that among the Jews of Mohammed's time magical books of Solomon were known. Sura II 95 ff. reads: "And when there came unto them a prophet from God confirming that *scripture* which was with them, some of those to whom the scriptures were given cast the book of God behind their backs as if they knew it not: and they follow *the device* which the devils devised against the kingdom of Solomon; and Solomon was not an unbeliever, but the devils believed not, they taught men sorcery." The context supports Sale's interpretation drawn from Yahya and Jallalo'ddin, that this device against the kingdom of Solomon consisted in the devils' attempt to blacken the character of Solomon by writing books of sorcery, hiding them under his throne, and after his death pretending he had had in them the recipes by which he obtained his power².

3. Among Christians. —

a) The power of Salomonic exorcisms. — One line of Christian tradition goes back to Josephus and follows him more or less closely, recounting merely the power of the exorcisms he had composed. Origen, who writes "a Salomone scriptis adjurationibus solent daemones adjurari. Sed ipsi qui utuntur adjurationibus illis, aliquoties nec idoneis constitutis libris utuntur: quibusdam autem et de Hebraeo acceptis adjurant daemonia," may be merely paraphrasing Josephus, or he may have had personal knowledge of Solomonic works³. The first I have discovered to quote Josephus expressly is Georgius Monachus

---

1 *Op. cit.* 936. An interesting reference to Jewish magic, Burton, *Nights* II 234.

2 Cf. Sale *ad loc.* Palmer's note, *SBE* VI (Qu II) 14, does not so well explain the passage, which is concerned solely with books.

3 *In Mattheum comm. ser.* (tract. 33) 110, Migne *PG* 13, 1757, in discussion of Mt XXVI 63.

Medical wisdom from Solomon. 95

(c. 850)[1], who is followed by Cedrenus (c. 1100)[2], Zonaras (c. 1150)[3], and Glycas (after 1150)[4].

b) Solomon the ultimate source of medical wisdom. — Other Christian writers start from the Old Testament notices of Solomon's wisdom, developing the tradition in various directions. In the first place, according to Theodoret (386/393—458), he was wiser than the most famous wise men to whom the Hellenistic world looked back. In his *Quaestiones in III Reg.*, Qu. X he asks, Πῶς νοητέον τὸ "Ἐπλήθυνεν (cod. α, ἐπληθύνθη) ἡ σοφία Σολομῶντος ὑπὲρ τὴν φρόνησιν πάντων τῶν υἱῶν ἀρχαίων, καὶ ὑπὲρ πάντας φρονίμους Αἰγύπτου;" He answers, Ἐκ παραλλήλου δεῖξαι αὐτοῦ τὴν σοφίαν ὁ ἱστοριογράφος ἠθέλησεν. Τούτου χάριν καὶ τῶν πάλαι γεγενημένων σοφῶν ἀορίστως ἐμνήσθη .... Τούτους, φησίν, ἅπαντας ὁ Σολομῶν ἀπέκρυψεν, ἅτε δὴ θεόθεν τῆς σοφίας τὸ δῶρον δεξάμενος[5]. Procopius of Gaza, without acknowledging his debt, quotes Theodoret almost word for word[6]. Georgius Monachus[7] and after him Georgius Cedrenus[8] give a slightly different version of Theodoret, adding also a part of Theodoret's *Quaest.* XVIII.

In the second place Theodoret represents the wise king as the source from which the ancients derived their knowledge of medicine. He asks, Πῶς νοητέον τὸ "Ἐλάλησε περὶ τῶν ξύλων....", and answers, Καὶ τὰς φύσεις, καὶ τὰς δυνάμεις, καὶ τῶν βοτανῶν, καὶ τῶν δένδρων, καὶ μέντοι καὶ τῶν ἀλόγων ζῴων πεφυσιολογηκέναι αὐτὸν εἴρηκεν· ἐντεῦθεν οἶμαι καὶ τὰς ἰατρικὰς βίβλους συγγεγραφότας ἐρανίσασθαι πάμπολλα..... καὶ τοῦδε τοῦ ζῴου τόδε τὸ μόριον τίνος πάθους ἀλεξιφάρμακον· οἷον ἡ τῆς ὑαίνης χολή, ἢ τὸ λεόντειον στέαρ, ἢ τὸ ταύ-

---

[1] Or Hamartolos; *Chron.* II 42 4, Migne *PG* 110 249 C; cf. Krumbacher, *BLg* 352—8.
[2] Migne, *PG* 121 156 Bf. and 196 CD; cf. Krumbacher, *BLg* 368 f., Gelzer, *Sext. Jul. Afr* II 1 357—84.
[3] *Ann.* II 8, Migne, *PG* 134 168 B, cf. Roger Bacon, *Opera inedita*, ed. Brewer London 1859, vol. I, App. p. 526.
[4] Migne *PG* 158 349 C; cf. Krumbacher, *BLg* 380—5.
[5] Migne, *PG* 80 676 AB.
[6] *Com. ad III Reg.* II 45, Migne, *PG* 87 : 1 1152.
[7] *Chron.* II 42 1 f., Migne, *PG* 110 249 A.   [8] Migne, *PG* 121 197 Df.

ρειον αίμα, ή τῶν ἐχνιδῶν αἱ σάρκες. Περὶ τούτων γὰρ οἱ σοφοὶ τῶν ἰατρῶν συγγεγράφασιν, ἐκ τῶν Σολομῶντι συγγεγραμμένων εἰληφότες τῶν πρώτων τὰς ἀφορμάς¹. Procopius of Gaza quotes Theodoret as far as πάμπολλα². Anastasius Sinaites repeats both question and answer almost word for word³. So far as I have discovered, no others use the first part of the reply ending with πάμπολλα, but Georgius Monachus, Cedrenus, and Glycas weave into their account of Hezekiah's suppression of Solomon's books the sentence, ἀφ' ὧν οἱ τῶν Ἑλλήνων ἰατροσοφισταὶ σφετερισάμενοι καὶ τὰς ἀφορμὰς εἰληφότες τὰς οἰκείας συνεστήσαντο τέχνας, or its equivalent⁴.

c) Hezekiah's suppression of Solomon's books.

1) Origin of the legend. — The question naturally arose as to what had become of all the proverbs, odes, and scientific writings of Solomon. So far as the sources show, this question was first raised and answered by Hippolytus in his commentary on Canticles, portions of which are preserved in Armenian, Syriac, Slavic[5], and Georgian[6]. The last mentioned version contains a discussion, the essence of which has been handed down also in a quotation or summary found in the *Quaestiones* of Anastasius Sinaites.

In *Quaest.* XLI Anastasius collects several ancient references to Solomon's books and wisdom. Beginning with an unacknowledged quotation from Theodoret[7], he reproduces Sap VII 16—21 and III Reg IV 26—29, and then adds the following:

---

1 *In III Reg. Quaest.* XVIII, Migne, *PG* 80 681 AB. Does Jerome have this tradition in mind? Cf. *Quaest. Hebr. in libr. III Reg.* (Migne, *PL* 23 1365 C): Disputavit enim de naturis lignorum, jumentorum, reptilium, et piscium, de vi videlicet et naturis illorum....

2 *Com. ad III Reg* IV 33; Migne, *PG* 87:1 1153.

3 *Quaest.* XLI; cf. *infra* p. 97 n, 1. It is the first part of the ἀπόκρισις and immediately follows a quotation from Θεοδωρήτου ἐπισκόπου Κύρου, which stands at the end of *Quaest.* 40.

4 *Chron.* II 42 4 (Migne *PG* 110, 249 B) for G. Monachus; Migne, *PG* 121 200 B, 224 C for Cedrenus; Glycas (*ibid.* 158 348 D) has, τὰς τοῦ Σ. βίβλους, ἀφ' ὧν καὶ οἱ τῶν ἰατρῶν παῖδες ἀφορμὰς ἔλαβον.

5 Bonwetsch, *KVCom* I 343—74.

6 Bonwetsch, *Hippolyts Kom. z. Hohelied* in *TU* NF VIII (23) H. 2, 22 f.

7 Cf. *supra* n. 3.

Ἱππολύτου ἐκ τοῦ εἰς τὸ ᾆσμα ᾀσμάτων. Καὶ ποῦ πᾶσα ἡ πλουσία αὕτη γνῶσις; ποῦ δὲ τὰ μυστήρια ταῦτα; καὶ ποῦ αἱ βίβλοι; ἀναφέρονται γὰρ μόναι αἱ παροιμίαι καὶ ἡ σοφία καὶ ὁ ἐκκλησιαστὴς καὶ τὸ ᾆσμα τῶν ᾀσμάτων. τί οὖν; ψεύδεται ἡ γραφή; μὴ γένοιτο. ἀλλὰ πολλὴ μέν τις ὕλη γεγένηται τῶν γραμμάτων, ὡς δηλοῖ τὸ λέγειν ᾆσμα ᾀσμάτων· σημαίνει γὰρ ὅτι ὅσα περιεῖχον αἱ πεντακισχίλιαι ᾠδαὶ ἐν τῷ ἑνὶ διηγήσατο. ἐν δὲ ταῖς ἡμέραις Ἐζεκίου τὰ μὲν τῶν βιβλίων ἐξελέγησαν, τὰ δὲ καὶ περιώφθησαν ....[1] Perhaps Jerome has this in mind when he says, Aiunt Hebraei cum inter cetera scripta Salomonis quae antiquata sunt, nec in memoria duraverunt, et hic liber [Eccl.] obliterandus videretur... ex hoc uno capitulo [XII] meruisse auctoritatem [2].

That general encyclopedia, the *Hypomnesticon*, written by the otherwise unknown Josephus Christianus, mentions πεντακισχιλίας παροιμίας written by Solomon among the books referred to in the Scriptures but not now found [3]. Michael Glycas gives a badly garbled account of it all, making Hezekiah's revision fall after the Exile and Ezra's labors, and naming ὁ σοφώτατος Ψέλλος as his authority, evidently by mistake [4].

2) The writings on the temple gate. — In view of Hezekiah's iconoclastic zeal as to the brazen serpent, it was inevitable that some one should suggest that he had also suppressed the magical writings of Solomon. Two Christian writers present an independent tradition, somewhat like that of Sheintob already mentioned [5]. Georgius Syncellus (c. 800) in his ἐκλογὴ χρονο-

---

[1] *KVCom* I 343; Migne, *PG* 89 589; cf. *supra* p. 96 n. 6. Anastasius' floruit is placed by Krumbacher (*BLg* 64 ff.) between 640 and 700. The *Quaestiones* in their present form are not original, but that does not affect our material, for it is all quoted.   [2] *Com. in Eccl* XII 13 f.

[3] Cap. 120, *PG* 106 124 A. The date of the *Hypomnesticon* is still unsettled. Schürer, *GJV* III 420, refers to Gutschmidt, *Kleine Schriften* V 618, who places it in the tenth century, and the "more accurate researches". of Diekamp, *Hippolytus von Theben* (1898) 145—151, who decides for 800 at the latest, possibly a much earlier date. To the writer it appears that aside from certain evident interpolations it may belong to the fifth century.

[4] *PG* 158 349 A; cf. 122, 537, 540 for Psellus' opinion.

[5] Cf. *supra* p. 93. The story in Ez VIII 7—11 does not appear to have played any part in these speculations.

γραφίας, when speaking of Solomon's reign, merely describes most concisely his wisdom and fall; when he comes to Hezekiah, after expanding IV Reg XVIII 4, he adds, Ἐζεκίας μὲν οὖν ὁ βασιλεὺς Ἰούδα μετὰ τὸ κατασκάψαι τὰ εἰδωλεῖα καὶ τὰ ἄλση ἐκκόψαι καὶ τὸν χαλκοῦν ὄφιν ἐξαλεῖψαι τοὺς εὑρισκομένους εἰδωλολατροῦντας ἐξ Ἰουδαίων ἐθανάτου. τοσοῦτον γὰρ τῇ εἰδωλολατρείᾳ συνείχοντο ὥστε τῶν θυρωμάτων ὄπισθεν ζωγραφεῖν τὰ βδελύγματα τῶν ἐθνῶν καὶ προσκυνεῖν αὐτοῖς, καὶ ἵνα παρ' Ἐζεκίου ψηλαφᾶν πεμπομένων κρύβοιντο ἀνοιγομένων τῶν θυρῶν. ἦν δὲ καὶ Σολομῶντος γραφή τις ἐγκεκολαμμένη τῇ πύλῃ τοῦ ναοῦ παντὸς νοσήματος ἄκος περιέχουσα, ᾗ προσέχων ὁ λαὸς καὶ τὰς θεραπείας νομιζόμενος ἔχειν κατεφρόνει τοῦ θεοῦ· διὸ καὶ ταύτην Ἐζεκίας ἐξεκόλαψεν ἵνα πάσχοντες τῷ θεῷ προσέχωσιν[1]. Suidas abbreviates the account and puts βίβλος ἰαμάτων for γραφή[2].

3) Solomon's magical books suppressed.' — Turning to Anastasius Sinaites again we make the interesting discovery that he ascribes the account of the reforming activity of Hezekiah to Eusebius. The final section in *Quaest.* XII runs as follows: Εὐσεβίου Παμφίλου ἐκ τῆς ἀρχαιολογικῆς ἱστορίας. Τὰς δὲ βίβλους τοῦ Σολομῶντος, τὰς περὶ τῶν παραβολῶν καὶ ᾠδῶν, ἐν αἷς περὶ φυτῶν καὶ παντοίων ζώων φυσιολογήσας, χερσαίων, πετεινῶν τε καὶ νηττῶν, καὶ ἰαμάτων πάθους παντός, γραφείσας αὐτῷ, ἀφανεῖς ἐποίησεν Ἐζεκίας, διὰ τὸ τὰς θεραπείας τῶν νοσημάτων ἔνθεν κομίζεσθαι τὸν λαόν, καὶ περιορᾶν αἰτεῖν, καὶ παρορᾶν ἐντεῦθεν παρὰ θεῷ τὰς ἰάσεις[3].

The *Hypomnesticon* of Josephus, which in chapter 120, as we have seen, tells of Hezekiah's revision of Solomon's proverbs, says in c. 74, εἰσὶ δὲ καὶ ἕτεροι πλεῖστοι λόγοι, οὓς ἀπέκρυψεν ὁ εὐσεβὴς βασιλεὺς Ἐζεκίας, οὐδὲν ὄφελος ἐπὶ πολλοῖς εὑρίσκεσθαι λόγοις[4].

The account given by Georgius Monachus of Solomon's wisdom combines part of the Eusebian quotation with express

---

1 B 376f., P 200, V 160. See Gelzer, *Sext. Jul. Afr.* II 176—249, Krumbacher, *BLg* 339 ff.   2 *Lex.* s. v. Ἐζεκίας.   3 *PG* 89 592 Df.; cf. *supra* p. 96 f.
4 *PG* 106 89 C. C. 74, which is in a part of the work that recounts the deeds of Old Testament characters, is itself a record of the reign of Solomon.

indication of its origin, with extracts from Theodoret and Flavius Josephus, as we have seen[1]. Georgius Cedrenus practically repeats Monachus, but with the addition of a clause βιβλίον Σολομῶντος ἰαματήριον παντὸς πάθους ἐγκεκολαμμένον, apparently borrowed from Syncellus or Suidas; he mentions no authority[2]. Glycas presents on the whole an independent account of Solomon's wisdom and literary activities, but like Anastasius, he appeals to the authority of Eusebius; he says, τὰς τοῦ Σολομῶντος βίβλους, ἀφ' ὧν καὶ οἱ τῶν ἰατρῶν παῖδες τὰς ἀφορμὰς ἔλαβον.... παρὰ δὲ Ἐζεκίου κεκαῦσθαί φησιν ὁ πολυμαθὴς καὶ πολυΐστωρ Εὐσέβιος[3].

Is this appeal to the authority of Eusebius deceptive? We may not be sure of the date of the *Quaestiones* of Anastasius in their present form, but, whoever the writer of *Quaest.* XII is, he quotes accurately from Theodoret, and from a lost work of Hippolytus. Is not the presumption in favor of accepting his testimony regarding Eusebius, and supposing that he is quoting from some lost work of the great historian[4]? That Eusebius should make such a statement cannot seem at all strange in view of the reference by Origen to "a Salomone scriptis adjurantionibus"[5]

4) One further reference to the tradition that Hezekiah took summary measures with Solomon's medico-magical writings is of particular interest to us, since it is found in Rec. C of the *Test* (c. XIII 1—12) and, indeed, forms its *raison d'être*. If this

---

[1] I discover no marks to indicate its date; the quotation above is more closely related to Glycas than Georgius Monachus, yet the similarity may be due merely to likeness of literary method.

1 *Chron.* II 42 4), *PG* 110 249 B, sec 273 B; cf. *supra* p. 96.

2 *PG* 121 200 B, 224 C. Both Monachus and Cedrenus mention the suppression of the books in their accounts of Solomon and again under Hezekiah.

3 *PG* 158 348 Df.

4 Although no "archaeological history" by Eusebius is known to historians of Christian literature, Bonwetsch, in his chapter on "Die vornicänische Litt. in altslav. HSS." in Harnack, *Altchr. Lit.* I 900, mentions a Russian MS in the Synodal library at Moscow (cod. 339 [1001] 4^0 s; 17, f. 310) which has "Eusebeios(?) Pamphilos, aus der Archaeologie(?)," and strangely enough it begins, "Das Buch aber des Salomo, welches von den Sprichwörtern handelt." It at least has some mention of Solomon.   5 See above, VIII 3 a), p. 94.

legend was already found in Eusebius, as it was in the Mishna, there were plenty of channels through which redacteur C might have obtained it. Yet the mention of „burning" and "hiding" (c. XIII 4, 8 f.) suggests that Rec. C comes from the time of Cedrenus and Glycas, for the earlier writers do not use the word καταχαύειν.

d) Solomonic books of incantations in the Middle Ages. —
1) Solomonic books of magic and astrology found in mediaeval manuscripts. — In spite of these records of the sad fate of Solomon's medico-magical literary efforts, such books continued to flourish. The long lists given by M. Seligsohn in his article, "Solomon-Apocryphal Works", in the *Jewish Encyclopedia* is by no means exhaustive. Indeed Solomon's reputation became such that any thing connected with magic or astrology or science might be ascribed to him[1]. The most popular of the works which are consistently handed down under his name is the *Clavicula*, or Ύγρομαντεία, as some of the Greek copies have it. The two are not exactly the same, but along with the *Sepher Raziel*[2], the *Semiphoras*[3], and others of the sort, are of a well marked type. They consist mainly of prayers and incantations intended to accomplish various purposes, usually by commanding demonic aid. The prayers are usually interlarded with barbaric names, and there are many pentacles, or magical drawings, each of which gives power over the demon to which it belongs, or serves as an amulet for some specific purpose. Lists of the angels and demons who rule the days and hours are given.

None of these works is like the *Test*. It is much older in language than any of the Greek works of this sort, and differs from them all as to purpose; for, aside from Rec. C, which has

---

[1] See above II 4, 8, 10, 11, pp. 13 and p. n. 1. 18 f., 21 ff, 25 ff. Professor von Dobschütz in a personal note first called my attention to the fact that in the Ambrosiana the *Physiologus* of Aristotle is ascribed to Solomon; *Cat. Codd, Gr. Bibl. Ambr.* I 104, cod. 89, 183. In Lambros, *Cat. of the MSS on Mt. Athos* are illustrations of this, see Pinax A; s. v. Σολομωνική. On the *Clavicula* cf. Reitzenstein, *Poim.* 186 f., and Steinschneider, *Heb. Üb.* 938.

[2] See Steinschneider, *op. cit.* 937.   [3] Scheibel, *Das Kloster* III, 289 ff.

drawn upon them in part, the *Test* is interested in the demons primarily as the causes of disease. The writer wishes to disclose their nature, relationships, and activities for the same reason that a doctor studies diseases, that he may counteract them. These other books are technical works for the professional astrologer and magician, not concerned with the cure of diseases, in fact rarely showing any medical interest, but anxious rather to show how the demons may be used to gain wealth, power, and happiness. The list of fifty demons in Rec. C (c. X) is characteristic of this type of literature. With it compare the list of thirty-six *decani* in Recs. A and B (XVIII) to gain a sharp definition of the contrast. When, therefore, the Christian writers refer to a Solomonic "book of healing" they are not thinking of the *Clavicula*, nor of any of the similar works. The *Test* is the one Solomonic work which fits the term. Having thus cleared the way, we are ready to consider the evidence that goes to show that such a book was actually in use during the Middle Ages.

2) Literary references to contemporaneous Solomonic medical works.

(a) The citations above which mention medico-magical books of Solomon might be supposed not to imply first hand knowledge of any such works. There are others, however, which show that they were well known. Following the brief quotation given above[1] the *Hypomnesticon* continues, τοὺς δὲ δαιμόνων ἐκφευκτικούς, καὶ παθῶν ἰατρικούς, καὶ κλεπτῶν φωρατικοὺς [λόγους] οἱ τῶν Ἰουδαίων ἀγύρται παρ' ἑαυτοῖς φυλάσσουσιν ἐπιμελέστατα, τῶν πιστῶν τῆς ἁγίας ἐκκλησίας τούτοις οὐ κεχρεμένων διὰ τὸ τῇ Χριστοῦ πίστει καθοσιοῦν ἑαυτοὺς δεδιδάχθαι. The man who wrote this is not depending upon what he has read, but describes what he knows of personal observation. There is no reason why such a sentence could not have been written in the fifth century.

(b) The next allusion is equally direct and unambiguous. Nicetas Acominatus, or Choniates, who was a high official at

---

[1] See above VIII 3 c) 3), p. 98.

the Byzantine court about 1200 and wrote his *History* from personal recollections[1], knew an interpreter and sycophant at the court, Aaron by name, who was also a magician. He relates of him, ἑάλω δὲ καὶ βίβλον Σολομώντειον ἀνελίττων ἥτις ἀναπτυσσομένη τε καὶ διερχομένη κατὰ λεγεῶνας συλλέγει καὶ παρίστησι τὰ δαιμόνια συχνάκις ἀναπυνθανόμενα, ἐφ' ὅτῳ προσκέκληνται· καὶ τὸ ἐπιταττόμενον ἐπισπεύδοντα περατοῦν, καὶ προθύμως δρῶντο τὸ κελευόμενον[2]. This describes accurately parts of the Ὑγρομαντεία and the Latin *Clavicula*, as well as the new material in Rec. C. The list of fifty demons (c. X) is intended to accomplish just the end of calling in certain demons and the hosts they command, while Paltiel Tzamal uses almost the language of Nicetas in describing the obedience Solomon may expect[3]. It is no doubt a book of this sort, not the *Test*, which Aaron used, for no mention is made of healing.

(c) Michael Glycas, in the passage already referred to[4], has a description of Solomon's magical books which we have reserved for separate discussion, because in it he takes a path of his own. His statement is as follows: ἐφυσιολόγησε δὲ Σολομῶν καὶ περὶ λίθων .... ἀλλὰ καὶ περὶ δαιμόνων ἐτέθη βιβλίον αὐτοῦ, ὅπως τε κατάγονται, καὶ ἐν οἵοις εἴδεσι φαίνονται, φύσεις δὲ τούτων καὶ ἰδιότητας ἔγραψε, πῶς τε δεσμοῦνται καὶ πῶς ἐμφιλοχωροῦντες ἀπολύονται. ὅθεν ἔργα τούτοις ἀχθοφόρα ἐπέταττεν, ὑλοτομεῖν τε, ὡς λόγος, ἠνάγκαζε, καὶ κατωμαδὸν τὰ ἄχθη φέρειν παρεβιάζετο, ᾠδηκότα τε σπλάγχνα ἢ ἐπῳδαῖς ἢ βοτάναις περιτιθεὶς ἐθεράπευσεν. ἀλλ' ὁ γε θεῖος Ἐζεκίας θεῷ ἑαυτὸν ἀνατιθεὶς καὶ πάντα τῆς ἐκεῖθεν προνοίας ἐξαρτήσας τῶν ὑπὲρ φύσιν τῷ Σολομῶντι φιλοσοφηθέντων ὠλιγώρησεν. This βιβλίον περὶ δαιμόνων is the *Test* in everything but name. The latter is throughout concerned with bringing down demons; their forms, natures, and peculiarities are most carefully described. One of the chief purposes of the work is to tell how they are discovered in their lurking places and bound or destroyed. A special feature is the labor to which each demon is con-

---

[1] Krumbacher, *BLg* 281—6. [2] Migne, *PG* 139 489 A (= P 95).
[3] Rec. C XII 4 f. [4] Cf. *supra* p. 95 and p. 96 n. 4; Migne, *PG* 158 349 B.

The title Testament. 103

demned, one of the most striking instances being that of Leontophoron, who is sentenced to the task of cutting wood for the Temple[1]. Cures by the means Glycas mentions are to be found[2]. One cannot avoid the conclusion that it is the *Test* which is here described, either from Glycas' own knowledge, or after some popular account[3]. That he does not name the title need not trouble us[4].

(d) The next allusion is dubious. In the *Decretum Gelasianum* mention is made of a *Salomonis interdictio*, or as the later texts have it *contradictio*[5]. In the *Decretum* in the next line as a separate item and in the *Collectio Herovalliana* in the same and the following lines mention is made of *phylacteria*, which contain the names, not of angels, but of demons. In pseudo-Isidor, *de Muneris*, a line intervenes between the *contradictio* and *phylacteria*. Probably, therefore, the two are distinct works, and the second is no doubt the *Clavicula*, which is characterized by seals and amulets. We must at least postulate the possibility that the *interdictio* is the *Test*, since in this sort of literature there is a tendency to assimilate titles[6]. It is entirely possible, however, that the *Test* never became sufficiently known in the West to call for a pronouncement against it.

(e) The most important notice we have reserved to the last. In the *Dialogue of Timothy and Aquila* the Christian says, Γνῶθι δὲ Ἰουδαῖε, ὅτι [Σολομῶν] προσεκύνησεν, καὶ ἀκρίδα ἔσφαξεν τοῖς γλυπτοῖς. The Jew replies, οὐκ ἔσφαξεν ἀλλὰ ἔθλασεν ἐν τῇ χειρὶ ἀκουσίως. ταῦτα δὲ οὐ περιέχει ἡ βίβλος τῶν βασιλέων, ἀλλ' ἐν τῇ διαθήκῃ αὐτοῦ γέγραπται. The Christian accepts the correction: ἐν τούτῳ γὰρ ἔστην πιστοποιῶν, ὅτι οὐκ ἐν χειρὶ ἱστοριογράφου ἐφανερώθη τοῦτο, ἀλλ' ἐκ τοῦ

---
1 C. XI 7.   2 C. XVIII 29, 15, etc.

3 Glycas names Psellus as authority for the "contemning" of the books of Solomon; probably he means Eusebius, cf. *supra* p. 97 and n. 4. In this account Glycas is true to the character Krumbacher (*BLg* 380—5) gives him as being a popular, rather than a learned, writer.   4 See below (e).

5 Cf. E. von Dobschütz, "Das Decretum Gel. etc.." TU (1912) 13, ll. 332—5, 84, ll. 112 f., 74, ll. 242—5; cf. p. 319.

6 See James in *TS* II 2 p. 9 on the convertibility of the titles "testament" and "apocalypse."

στόματος αὐτοῦ τοῦ σολομῶντος ἐγνώθη τοῦτο[1]. This allusion is of value, not only for the sake of the help is gives us in dating the *Test*, as we shall see in the next section of our discussion, but also because the title appears here[2], and from the reference to the locusts we can be sure beyond a doubt that it is our *Test* to which reference is made; we also see that the *Test* was held in high honor in Christian circles.

(f) Summary: the Christian use of the *Testament*. — One might expect to find more allusions to the *Test* in early Christian literature and more evidence of its use. But it was one of those books which circulated among the people without attracting literary attention. Moreover, it represents a passing, though very important, phase of theological development. As the world became more and more Christianized, it could not but prove unsatisfactory to Christian thinking, even in the revised form of Rec. B, and it had no vital attraction which could overcome the fatal weakness of its inconsistent combination of paganism and Christianity. The allusions to it in *Timothy and Aquila*, in the *Hypomnesticon*, and in Glycas are all we could rightly expect in view of its character[3].

---

[1] F. C. Conybeare, *Anecdota Oxon*. Classical ser. VIII 70.

[2] In connection with the title διαθήκη it should be noted that magical literature is perfectly familiar with a *covenant* which S. made with the demons; cf. Schlumberger in *Rev. des Ét. Gr*. V (1892) 87 διαθήκην ἣν ἔθεντο [δαίμονες] ἐπὶ μεγάλου Σολομῶνος καὶ Μιχαήλου τοῦ ἀρχαγγέλου, the same is quoted by Wessely, *Wiener Studien* VIII (1886) 179; see *Atti e Memorie della RR. Deputazioni di Storia per le provincie dell' Emilia*, N. S., vol. V, Part I, Modena 1880, p. 177, Pellichioni, "Un filaterio esorcistico"; it was copied by Amati from a gold plate in a dealers shop, and is now lost. Vasiljev, *Anecdota*, 332, has a reference to their oath. Bezold, *ZA* XX 3—4 (Aug. 1907) pp. 405 f., gives "Eine arab. Zauberformel gegen Epilepsie," from the margin of ff. 24b—27a of cod. (113) Sachau 199 (Königl. Bibl. Berlin) which mentions the contract between Solomon and the devils. Strangely Fürst translated the title *Bund Salomos*; cf. *supra* p. 28f.

[3] One gathers a wrong impression from Dr. Conybeare's note (*JQR* XI 32, n. 6 to § 65) to c. XV 8—11: "This prophecy roughly corresponds to the one which Lactantius, *Instit. Div*., lib. iv. c. 18, quotes from an apocryphal *Book of Solomon*." Even more misleading is another statement (*ibid*. 11): "The apocryphal Book of Solomon, used by Lactantius in his *Institutions*, was so far Christian as to speak both of the birth from a virgin of Emmanuel and of the crucifixion." But the passage he evidently refers to (c. 18 32f., Vienna *Corpus* XIX 359f.) is

IX. THE DATE OF THE *TESTAMENT* AND ITS RECENSIONS.

1. Previous opinions as to date. — Having studied our document on the linguistic and material sides and investigated its sources and relationships, we are prepared to attempt to date it. It will be an advantage first to summarize previous opinion on this point.

a) Fleck regarded the *Test* as a Byzantine work belonging to the Middle Ages, but advanced no arguments to substantiate his conclusion [1]. Likewise Istrin, who discovered MS D and recognized it as the basis of the *Test*, regarded the latter as belonging to the Middle Ages (c. 1200), though containing pre-Christian elements [2].

b) Bornemann concluded that it belonged to the early fourth century, since its demonology resembled that of Lactantius in his *Institutions* [3]. Toy accepts this verdict without investigation [4]. Harnack merely refers to the *Test* in this fashion: "Verschiedene 'Testamente', so das des Salomo, deren Alter nicht zu bestimmen ist, und die vielleicht gar nicht in die ersten Jahrh. gehören" [5]. Schürer makes no attempt to fix the date, but thinks the passage from Leontius is especially to be considered in this connection [6].

c) After careful investigation Dr. Conybeare concludes, "It is impossible to say when and where the Christian elements present in the *Testament* were worked into it, but the stress

---

only a loose epitome of III Reg IX 6—9a, with the addition of the phrase "et persecuti sunt regem suum dilectissimum et cruciauerunt illum in humilitate magna" (*ibid.* p. 360, II. 32 ff.). It may well come from some Christian apocryphon (as Roensch supposed) which summarized O. T. history, or even from a *Book of Solomon*, but it can hardly have any connection with the *Test*. *In humilitate magna* does not necessarily imply the virgin birth, while *in ultionem sanctae crucis* (*ibid.* p. 359, l. 10) presents an anti-Semitism to which our document has no parallel.

1 "Est hoc monumentum *Byzantinum* .... Per mediam vero, quae dicitur, aetatem hic liber late sparsus in mythologiae Salomoneae fonte est habitus." Quoted from Fleck's preface in Migne, *PG* 122, 1315.
2 *Gr. Spiski Zab. Sol.*, 18 f.
3 In introduction to his translation, cf. Bibliography II 1.
4 *JE* XI 448 f., art. "Sol., Testament of." He evidently knows nothing of Conybeare's work on the *Test*. 5 *Gesch. altchr. Litt.* I 858.
6 *GJV* III 419; cf. *supra* VII 8c), p. 76.

laid on the name Emmanuel and on its numerical value, on the writing of the name on the forehead, the use of the word ταννσθείς, the patripassian conceptions, all have a very archaic air, and seem to belong to about 100 A. D." "In its original [Jewish] form" it may be "the very collection of incantations which, according to Josephus, was composed and bequeathed by Solomon"[1]. Kohler accepts Conybeare's results and, as we have already seen, regards our document as representing pre-Talmudic demonology[2]. Salzberger adopts the views of Kohler and Conybeare[3].

2. Conclusions. — Which of these dates can we adopt? Unfortunately there are in the work no historical allusions which can aid us. Yet one piece of external evidence immediately proves the late date adopted by Fleck and Istrin untenable, I mean, of course, the mention of the *Test* in the *Dialogue of Timothy and Aquila*[4]. Conybeare's manuscript of the *Dialogue* belongs to the twelfth century, and he says of the work, "The title affixed to TA describes the debate as having taken place in the days of Archbishop Cyril, and to this date belong the allusions to the Trinity in foll. 75 v⁰, 101 v⁰, 103 r⁰. But this title really no more than marks the time at which the work assumed its present form." The materials are in part much older[5]. Since, however, we have no way of proving that the allusion to the *Test* belongs to the older stratum, our *terminus ad quem* must be set about the time of Cyril (died 444), that is at 400.

As to the *terminus a quo* we must conclude that it is 100 A. D., at which date Dr. Conybeare would place the *Test*, regarding the Jewish original as still earlier. But what Conybeare regards as the "Jewish original" was a book of incantations, while we have found the original to be only a story containing no exorcisms, as MS D shows, and the *Test* as such to have been a Christian work[6]. The book which Eleazar in Josephus' story

---

1 *JQR* XI 12.   2 *JE* IV 578, art. "Demonology."   3 *Salomosage* 10.
4 Cf. *supra* VIII 3 d) 2) (e), p. 103.
5 *Op. cit.* XI, XXXIV; cf. also LVI n. 2.
6 Cf. *supra* VII 15, p. 87 ff., VII 13, p. 85, IV 2, p. 32.

used may be represented by the *Hygromanteia*, or *Clavicula*; it cannot have been the *Test*, for a Jew would not have used such a Christian work, nor is it likely to have been written so early.

Can we now date our document more precisely within the limits 100—400 A. D.? We are left to depend upon general considerations of language and subject matter. In view of the lateness of our manuscripts we cannot be absolutely sure of the linguistic evidence, but, as we have seen, it seems to point to a time when the Koinê was in full sway, after the New Testament was written [1], which merely confirms the general conclusion we have already reached.

As to the type of thought and the materials entering into the work, we come to conclusions differing from Conybeare's. The items upon which he most relies are found to belong to a secondary recension. The relation to the New Testament we have explained, by supposing the *Test* to depend, not upon pre-Gospel Synoptic tradition, but upon imperfect, perhaps auricular, knowledge of the written Gospels [2]. The allusion to the corner stone [3], which might seem to imply a date before the idea of Christ as the corner-stone became common Christian property, proves nothing, for in the fourth and the sixth century we have the applicaton of the same Old Testament passages to an actual corner stone [4]. Rec. B belongs to the time when Christianity was conuqering the world, but the original *Test* to the age of Alexander Severus and his *lararium* with Apollonius, Christ, Abraham, and Orpheus on an equal footing [5]. As Conybeare well shows, its demonology is much like that which Celsus and Origen described [6]. As it appears to the writer, without attempting to be too precise, the conditions of language and

---

1 Cf. *supra* V 4, p. 40.
2 See quotations above, IX 1 c), p. 106 n. 1, and VII 11, p. 82 f., 8 a), p. 68.
3 C. XXII 7 f., XXIII 2—4, cf. *supra* VII 8 a), p. 68.
4 Nestle, *ExT* XIV (1903) 528, "The Stone which the Builders Rejected," quoting the Pilgrim of Bordeaux and Antonius of Piacenza from "Itinera Hierosolymitana," ed P. Geyer, in vol. XXXVIII of the *Vienna Corpus*, pp. 23, 173.
5 Cf. *supra* VII 15, p. 87. 6 *JQR* XI 7 ff., 12 ff.

and subject matter are best met by supposing the *Test* to have been written early in the third century.

3. Date of the original Jewish ground work. — Josephus shows that ideas of Solomon's character and his dealings with demons such as are found in *d* (the prototype of MS D and the *Test*) were common among the Jews already in the first century A. D., although they do not appear in the Talmud until the third century[1]. Therefore *d* may be as early as the first century of the Christian era. At present our data allow no more precise date.

4. Date of the Recensions. — Rec. A, which differs but little from the original, probably underwent trifling changes with every transcription. The concluding sections (XXVI 8—10) belong to Byzantine times. For MS L the same man was probably editor and copyist, in mediaeval times. Rec. B may well belong to the fourth or fifth century, when Christianity was conscious of her conquest of the world, and her theology was being carefully formulated. Rec. C, although probably containing very old material, presents also much that smacks of the Middle Ages, and is apparently not much older than the manuscripts that preserve it[2]. It may well belong to the twelfth or thirteenth century.

X. AUTHORSHIP AND PROVENIENCE.

1. Authorship: Opinions. — As to the kind of individual who wrote the *Test* there are at least four possibilities: he may have been either a Jew or a Christian; if a Jew, either Aramaic or Greek speaking; if a Christian, either Jewish or Greek in origin. Gaster believes that originally the *Test* was written in Aramaic[3]. Harnack[4], Conybeare, and Kohler[5] think it to be

---

[1] Salzberger, *Salomosage* 92 f.
[2] Cf. *supra* VII 12, p. 83 and VIII 3 c) 4), p. 99.
[3] *JAS* 1896 p. 155, 170.
[4] *Gesch. altchr. Lit.* I 858; it is included under "die von den Christen angeeignete und z. Th. bearbeitete jüdische Litteratur."
[5] See IX 1 b), c) p. 105 and ns. 1 f., p. 106.

a Christian revision of a Jewish work. Toy concludes, "the author of the *Testament* is a Greek speaking Jewish Christian"[1]. Schürer held it to be the work of a Christian with "no Jewish places" in it[2].

2. Authorship: Conclusions. — We have found Gaster's assumption of an Aramaic original untenable[3]. Our new materials render the opinion that the *Test* was originally Jewish likewise impossible. Only the ground work, *d*, which was not a "testament", and certain of the materials were Jewish[4]. Was the author, then, a Christian of Jewish or Gentile origin? A final answer can hardly be given. On the one hand, the abundance of Jewish material and the Jewish trust in angel names, on the other the plainly Christian and heathen elements worked into the warp and woof of the document point in opposite directions. However, if the date for which we have just argued is correct, there is no reason why a Greek Christian should not have written the whole work, for he would be heir of both Jewish and Gentile materials and much more likely than a Jewish Christian to combine them in his faith[5]. In the third century also Christian Jews would be few. The probabilities, therefore, are in favor of Greek Christian authorship.

3. Provenience. — So far as I am aware, no one has attempted to decide from what part of the ancient world the *Test* came — perhaps wisely, for no certain conclusion can be reached. Three regions suggest themselves: Palestine, Egypt, and the province of Asia. Much is in favor of the first, particularly if one think of Galilee, where Judaism and Hellenism were in the closest contact, and where Christianity took its rise and won its first conquests[6]. Again, as we have seen, some of the materials come from Egypt, and some appear in Ethiopia, which was Christianized from

---

1 *JE* XI 449. 2 *Th. Litztg.* XXIV (1898) 4, col. 110.
3 See above V 6f., p. 42f. 4 See above IX 2 and n. 6, p. 106.
5 See Deissmann's argument regarding the archangel inscription at Miletus, *Licht* 333f., *LAE* 453ff.
6 See above VII 6e), p. 65f.

Egypt[1], while the only early literary allusion to the work by name is Egyptian[2]. One would think that the sand storm demon, Lix Tetrax, had originated in a land like Palestine or Egypt, where such storms were familiar phenomena[3]. Yet from Ac XIX 19 we see that "Asia" was probably as much a center of magic as Agypt, and if its climate had permitted, we should no doubt have an abundance of magical papyri from that region also.

Against Palestine is the fact that its popular Christianity was no doubt Aramaic rather than Greek speaking, while the *Test*, which is not the work of a leader in the church but of some uninstructed individual, is nevertheless thoroughly Greek in its language and much of its material. Against Egypt the strongest argument is the absence of Gnostic influence and of specific resemblances to the magic papyri. Against Ephesus or some part of "Asia" no decisive objections appear[4]. In its favor are the only two geographical terms in the document, Lydia and Olympus[5]. The very fact that the sand storm receives as its name two of the *Ephesia grammata* points — very weakly, to be sure — in the same direction. Like Egypt, Asia was a meeting place for all the currents of ancient thought.

We are dealing only with probabilities; in a work that borrows so impartially from all lands, no marks are decisive. As it seems to the writer, the probabilities are to be ranged in ascending order, Galilee, Egypt, Asia. Farther one cannot go until more light is thrown upon the whole subject of demonology, magic, and astrology, as well as on Christian origins.

---

1 Harnack, *Mission and Expansion* II 179, but see above VII 8b), p. 68f., VII 9, p. 70.

2 *Dial. of Tim. and Aquila*, see above VIII 3d) 2) (e), p. 103f. and IX 2, p. 106. 3 C. VII.

4 Perhaps because Asian magic material is scant. Gnosticism was there, but less vigorous. The Milesian inscription offers a point of contact.

5 That is, outside Palestine; c. VIII 4; Olympus might point to Greece, but other reason sare lacking. Where is the "great mountain"? Is it Hermon? Cf. I En VI 4, Montgomery, *AITN* 126.

4. Provenience of the recensions. — As to the place of origin of Recs. A and B I see no possibility of arriving at a conclusion, unless Rec. B may be thought of as western on account of its western form of Solomon's seal, the pentegram [1]. The manuscripts of Rec. C are so thoroughly Italian that one is tempted to suppose the recension originated in Greek-speaking southern Italy. MS D is, as we have seen, Byzantine in origin [2], but whether from Asia Minor or Europe one cannot say.

---

1 See above VII 14, p. 86.   2 See above V 1, p. 38f.

APPENDIX.

A. Manuskript N with a list of variant readings.

N. Library of the Greek Patriarchate, Jerusalem, Sancti Saba, No. 422; XV or XVI cent., paper, cm. 11×15; beginning and end of codex lacking; as recently numbered, ff. 49^r—93^v. Catalogue, vol. B, p. 541 [1]:

This manuscript I discovered while spending the winter of 1920—21 in Jerusalem as fellow of the American School of Oriental Research. I had called for the codex to examine the imperfect copy of the *Narratio Iosephi* with which it begins, but in leaving it through came suddenly upon the familiar matter of the *Test*. As the first page of the latter is wanting, the title did not get into the catalogue. Indeed the codex is so abominably written that a number of its selections are not mentioned.

As now bound sheets α—ε contain the *Narratio Iosephi*, beginning with c. I 4 [2]. Then begins a new subject and a new numbering, in a smaller but similar hand. Of this sheet α and two leaves of β remain. With sheet γ the second page of the *Test* begins and it ends on f. 5^v of sheet η. F. 88 I found folded into the latter part of the codex. The missing first page evidently was the last of sheet β and in rebinding was lost.

The learned author of the catalogue remarks that the copy of the *Narratio Iosephi* is λίαν ἀνορθόγραφον. It is even more

---

[1] Ἱεροσολυμιτικὴ βιβλιοθήκη, ἤτοι κατάλογος τῶν ἐν ταῖς βιβλιοθήκαις τοῦ ἁγιοτάτου ἀποστολικοῦ θρόνου τῶν Ἱεροσολύμων ... κωδίκων ... ὑπὸ Α. Παπαδοπούλου Κεραμέως. 4 vols. Petrograd 1899.

[2] Tischendorf, *Evangelia apocrypha*. ed. alt. Leipzig, 1876, p. 461.

true of the *Test*. The copyist either understood Greek very imperfectly, or, what is more likely, had before him a manuscript which he read with the greatest difficulty, but which he tried to copy accurately. The result is a manuscript which often makes no sense at all. Not only are there occasional mistakes of haplography and dittography and constant iotacism, but cases and endings are constantly confused, words are wrongly combined and divided, and all rules of accentuation are repeatedly broken. Worst of all, $ν$ is added to almost any word ending in a vowel and even introduced within words.

Nevertheless, since we already have excellent manuscripts of the *Test*, this one proves to have considerable value, for, aside from the missing first page, it contains a complete text of Rec. B. It adds another witness to the long section cc. XIV 3—XVI 1, which is wanting in all manuscripts but P. It has the longer form of P in cc. IX 7, XI 6, XIII 3, 6, XVI 4f., XVII 1, 4, XVIII 4, 18, 23, 27f., 31, 42f., XX 4, 6, 8 (in part), 13, 15, XXII 3, 8, 11, 20, XXIII 4 (in part), XXIV 3ff., and XXV. N follows P in every one of the four instances where it introduces a numerical equivalent for a sacred name (VI 8, XI 6, XIII 6, XV 11), and in all the passages where P improves the theology of the *Test*, especially XIII 3, XVII 4, and XXII 20. This is sufficient to prove that it belongs to the B recension.

However, in a considerable number of instances N does not support P. In a very few cases N follows Q against P, e. g. XX 13. In a number of places it supports C against B, e. g. V 4f. In VII 5 it follows C in a few words which P omits. It often confirms the text of A, e. g. II 3, III 5, XXII 11, 12, but especially in c. XVIII, where it repeats the peculiar word $ῥίξ$, or $ῥύξ$, though often corrupting it. In VI 4—9, where P makes numerous additions for the purpose of reconstructing the theology and perfecting the demonology of the section, N follows the A recension in the main. It is certainly much nearer the original than P, but in some expressions, such as $πευτηκή$, $οὑ̃$ $καὶ\ ψῆφος\ \overline{χμδ}$ and $τὶς\ τῶν\ καλῶς\ ζώντων$, it prepares the way for P. In II 8, also, it seems a step nearer the original than P and in passages like II 1 and 3 ($καὶ\ λεβόμενος$) it suggests the error which led to diverse corruptions in the different recensions.

The most important contribution made by the manuscript to the text of the *Test* is in the concluding sections. Here H seems so prolix that I had lost faith in it and chosen the B text as nearer the original. Manuscript N, however, coincides with H in part and thus shows that P and Q represent an unduly abbreviated text. In this and a few other instances, where the textual evidence was evenly balanced, N has served as additional weight to tip the scales in favor of a reading I had put into the margin or has suggested a new reading. These emendations will be found on page 121*.

Manuscript N makes certain additions of its own, e. g. in XVIII 16, 22, and XXVI 5. None of them are such as to indicate additional knowledge in matters demonological or magical. The only one of any considerable size or interest is in c. XVIII, where each of the thirty-six decani is equated with ten days of a Coptic month[1]. The copyists have not understood the intention of the interpolator and have confused and corrupted his statements, but it is quite easy to reconstruct the entire scheme. This matter adds another connection between the *Test* and Egypt, but since there is not the slightest trace of it in any of the other manuscripts, it is quite impossible to suppose that the original *Test* contained it. It rather shows what we might have expected had the *Test* come from Egypt.

The chief textual fruits of the discovery of manuscript N, then, are the list of emendations already mentioned and the confirmation of the strange word ῥύξ in c. XVIII. But the greatest value of the manuscript lies in its corroboration of the general scheme of recensions and manuscript relationships already adopted. The fact that it fits in so well goes far to support the confidence that any subsequent discoveries will not invalidate the conclusions reached in the *Introduction*.

The list of variant readings appended will illustrate the character of the manuscript and give the basis for the emenda-

---

[1] See *Intro*, above pp. 57 ff.

Lectiones variae ex MS N.

tions suggested. Variations merely of spelling, order, and stereotyped phrases, such as καὶ εἶπον, have been passed by. Only where they confirmed some disputed reading or were different enough to be of value in determining manuscript relationships have they been noted. Otherwise it would have been necessary to print the entire manuscript. Even the orthography has been corrected when it was too misleading. Except where some other manuscript is specifically indicated, N has been collated with P.

Lectiones variae ex MS N (= Sancti Saba 422)
cum Rec. B comparatae.

Incipit MS N (f. 49^r) c. I 5, p. 10*, l. 1 τῆς ψυχῆς (+ αὐτοῦ) ἐξομολογούμενος νυκτὸς κ. ἡμέρας cum rec. B   2 μοι B, om. N   3 ἐξουσιάσει N | § 6. ἐγένετο — N   4 με — N | προσέρχεστε καθ' ἑκάστην ἡμέραν καὶ ἐδόθη   5 χάρις B, — N   § 7. 7 Σολ. βασιλεὺς υἱοῦ | 8: ἦν 9 τά τε ... αρσ. κ. οἰκοδ. τὸν ναὸν τοῦ κυρίου ἐν τῇ σφραγίδι ταύτῃ (om. glos. de anuli signo) § 8. p. 11*, l. 1 γενομ. πάλιν ἐδοξ. ll. 2—5 ἐκάλεσεν τὸ παιδάριον ὁ σολ. κ. ἔδωκεν αὐτὸν τὸν δακτυλίδιον καὶ φήσας αὐτὸν ἐὰν ἡμέραν ἐπιστῇ τὸ ... δακ. (f. 49^v) ὃ ἔλαβον παρὰ κυρίου κ. Μιχαὴλ τοῦ ἀρχ. καὶ λαμβάννοι τὸ πεδάριον τὸ δακ. κ. φάσας τὸ χαλεπὸν δαιμόνιον ῥήψας τὸ δακ. ἐποὶ τοῦ στῆθος αὐτοῦ τοῦ δαιμονίου λέγων δεῦρο   6 παραγενοῦ | καὶ μηδὲν διαλογιζόμενος τὸ μέλλο σοι φράσε   § 10. p. 12*, 1 φλέγον § 11. l. 3 τὰ ῥηθέντα | βασ. Σολ.   4 ἐπὶ τοῦ στήθους τ. δαίμονος   5 καὶ ... Σολ. — N | § 12. καὶ εἶπεν ὁ δ. τὸ πεδάριον   6 πεποίηκας   7 s. καὶ δώσω (f. 50^r) σοι τὸ ἀργ. ... γῆς καὶ μὴ ἀπ. με cum A   § 13. l. 10 ἰσδραήλ (sic passim) | μὴ σου ἀνάξομεν | σε ἀγάγω   § 14. l. 12 χαίρον κ. ἀγαλόμενος κ. εἶπε τῷ βασιλεῖ· βασ. Σολ   p. 13*, l. 1 ἡμῖν δέσποτα | πρὸς τ. θυρῶν. τ. βασ. σου δεόμενος κ. κραυγάζων   3 μὴ αὐτὸν ἀπαγάγης με π. σολομόν C. II. ἀκ. ταῦτα ὁ βασ. Σολ.   6 αὐτοῦ κ. ἐξῆλθεν εἰς τὰ πρ. τῆς βασιλείας αὐτοῦ κ. εἶδον   8 καλ. — N | § 2. κ. εἶπεν αὐτὸν ὁ βασ. σολ. (f. 50^v) | εἰς ποῖον ζώδιον οἰκεῖσαι; κ. εἶπεν   p. 14*, l. 1 δι' ἐπιθυμιῶν τῶν γυναίων ἐπὶ γῆν παρθένον τὸν ζώδιον κεκληκότας   3 § 3. εἰς — N | μεταβαλλόμενος, ποτὲ μὲν ὅς ἄνθρωπος ἔχων ἐπιθυμίαν ἐνὶ πέδον θηλυκὸν εὔχοσμον ἁπτόμενος· ἀλγῶσιν πάνυ   5 πάλιν — N   6 ποτέ ... (cum HI) ἐνφαίνομαι ὑπὸ πάντων τῶν σι δαιμονίων καὶ λεβόμενος (l. κελευόμενος) § 4. l. 7 τῆς ... ἀρχαγγ.: μιχαήλ. κ. εἶπεν ὁ βασιλεὺς σολομόν· ὑπὸ ποίου ἀγγέλου καταργεῖσαι; ὑπὸ οὐρειήλ ἀρχαγγέλου τῆς δυνάμεως τοῦ θεοῦ § 5. p. 15*, l. 1 τῆς f. 51^1 3 γιαλόν | § 6. τὸ σήνδιριν προσφαῦσαι καὶ ἐφήμισε μιν   5 ἐάσομεν· ἀναφέρο καγώ σοι   § 7. l. 6 ηὐξάμην ... μοι: ἐπαρεκάλεσε τ. ἀρχ. Οὐ. τοῦ ἐλθ.   § 8. l. 8 κῆτος ἐκ. τ. θαλ. etc. c. B p. 16*, l. 2 κακείνῃ οὕτος etc. cum textu, μεγ. κ. θρασύ   3 κόψαι | τελεῖν § 9. l. 4 κύριον τ. θ. ... γῆς σαβαώθ   5 παρεῖναι τ. Ὀ. σὺν τῇ μοίρᾳ 7 ὧδε — N | πάντων τῶν

8*

C. III. βελζεβούλ constanter scr. N | Βεελ. τὸν ἄρχοντα τῶν δαιμονίων 11 σύ μοι φῇς p. 17*, § 4. l. 1 ὡς etc. c. textu, μεγάλως 3 πρὸς σολομῶντα | § 5. ὁ δὲ εἶδεν ὁ βασ. σολ. 4 τ. θεὸν c. textu 5 θεός: + τοῦ ... γῆς c. L | Σολ., f. 52ʳ | τὸν σὸν θρόνον 6 εἰς ἐμὲ — N 9 § 7. ἀπήγουν ... φάντ.: ἅπαντα ἐγὼ ποιῶ ἀδιαλ. καὶ ἐμφανιζόμενος ἕκαστος τὴν ἐργασίαν αὐτοῦ
C. IV. l. 4 εἴη ἔστι ἐν ἐμῖν θηλείαι 5 εἶναι, ὦ δεσπότης, ἐβουλ. 6 ἐδειξέ μοι: ἐν τάχει ἤνεγκε ἐνμπροστεν μοῦ | καὶ ἔχουσα περκαλὴν 7 δέμας: δεπειε | εὐχρόστου 8 § 3. αὐτῆς ,.. αὐτῇ: αὐτοῖ ἔφη (bis) ἐγὼ σολ. § 4. 9 ἠνοσκαιλεῖ | σεσομεπεποιημένον p. 19*, § 5. l. 2 εἰς ἔγγονος σκολεικοιάζο αὐτ. 3 μοι ἔστιν | φράγγες § 6. l. 4 με εἶναι (— νομιζ.) 5 μελαχρ. | μου 6 λαθρέως κ. φανερά 7 βλάπτοι 7s. κακουργοῖ 9 πορίζουσι p. 20*, § 8. l. 1 αὐτὸν (f. 53ʳ) ποθ. γεννᾶται. ὁ δὲ 2 φωνῆς ἀκερέου τ. κ. σῆχον ἀν(θρώπ)ον μολήβου 3 § 9. δὲ ἐγὼ πρὸς αὐτήν· ποῖον ἄστρον 4 πανσέληνον ἄστρον 5 πλέον διωδευδν. καὶ εἶπον ἐγὼ σολ. πρὸς αὐτήν· ποῖος ἄγγελος καταργεῖ σε. κ. εἶπε· ἐσὺ βασιλεύς 6 § 11. εἰς φλέβην 7 στρατ. φωνήσας πρὸς αὐτὴν ξίφει κροῦσαι. ὁ δὲ εἶπεν· λέγω σοι, βασ., ὑπὸ § 12. l. 9 τὸ ὄνομα ἁγίου ἰωήλ 10 διὸ c. A | αὐτὴν — N | εἰς ... καν. om. c. W
C. V. p. 21*, l. 4 δαίμονα ... πονηρὸν — N § 2. 6 ἀπειλ. βλ. βλέψας πρός με κ. ἔφη· τίς ἦν καὶ αὐτῶν 7 § 3. οὗτος τετ. οὗτος (f. 53ᵛ) ἀποκρίθη 9 ὁ υἱὸς ἧς ἄν., ἐγὼ 11 γηγενήν | § 4. καὶ νῦν τό p. 22*, l. 1 φωλεύη ἐν τῷ οὐρανὸν c. C 1s. διὰ τὸν δρακόντων παίδας 3 καὶ ὁ τοῦ θεοῦ πατρὸς ὁ θρόνος ἐστὶν καὶ τὸ ἀξ. μέχρι τὴν σήμερον ἐν τῷ ουρ. 5 § 5. ἐρωτᾶν, κ. σοῦ γὰρ τὸ β. διαρ. ἐν κ. etc. c. textu 6 προσχωρήσει καὶ 7 βασ. ἡμ. ἔχεις cum C | ἔχομεν τινα θροπότιταν etc. c. A § 6. l. 11 δεσ. αὐτ. (f. 54ʳ) καὶ ἐκελ. αὐτὸν ἐκῄζεσται κ. ἀπολογεῖσθαι τίς καλ. κ. ἐκῃζεσται τί ἐστιν § 7. p. 23*, l. 1 καλ. παρὰ βροτοῖς· εἰ δὲ μὴ παρὰ κακούργων ἀν(θρώ)πων etc. c. textu § 8. l. 4 διὰ τῶν ἐπὶ πλεῖστον ἄστρων καὶ τριγαμίας κ. ὡς ἑπτὰ καὶ ἐφον. κ. δαμάζω § 9. N c. P sed scr. ποῖον ἄγγελον, om. τοῦ θρόνου 11. 9—10 ἐπὶ .. καπν.: 3 λέγεται γλαναίος ὁ ἐπὶ μερικῶν ἀνθράκων (f. 54ᵛ) καπν. ἢ κάλαμος στύρακος ὑποκαιόντων ἀσμόδιον § 10. p. 24*, l. 1 (fin.) ὃς στὸ ὄνομα κεκλ. κλάνος 2 ποτ. τῇ(ς) συρίας εὑρ. διότι κἀκεῖνα τὰ μέρη ἐξήλωσα πάντοτε κατοικὴν καὶ ἐν π(ᾶν) τῷ κόσμῳ πλὴν οὐκ ἤμην, κύριέ μου § 11. l. 6 δεσμεύσαντος 7 ἀληθὴς ἐστιν | ἀξιῶ δέ σε: ἕνα δὲ ἀεὶ | μή με κατ. bis § 12. l. 9 σίδηρον φορέσας ἀλλὰ ... ποιήσας (f. 55ʳ) 10 ἀνατρ. τ. ποσίν σου εἰς ὑπουργίαν τοῦ ναοῦ τῆς οἰκοδομῆς 11 ὑδρίας δέκα δοθῆναι αὐτόν p. 25*, l. 1 αὐτὸν 2 s. τὸ δαιμόνιον ἀσμόδιος § 13. l. 4 σοφίαν ταύτην τ. δουλ. σου | χολὴν καὶ καλάμμα στύρακος λύων ὑποκαίων 6 ἡ φωνὴ ὀδῦς πικρίας
C. VI. l. 9 προσκ. τῆς ἐνδοξότερον καὶ ἐπηρώτησα αὐτ. λέγων· ὁ δὲ βελζεβουὴλ 10 ἄρχης 11 μόνομαν ὑπολελειφθέν 12 οὐράνιος — N 8 § 3. καὶ μετ᾽ ἐμὲ δεύτερος λέγε θὰν ἤγουν δεύτερος θεός 4 καρτῶ τὰ ἐν ταρτάρῳ δεσμὰ cum A p. 26*, l. 2 ἐλ. καὶ εἰς θρίαμος | §§ 4—9. N cum A | § 4 τί ἐστιν ἡ πραξίς σου 4 τοὺς δαίμονας | ἀνθρώπων 5 εἰς ἐπιθυμίας ἐγύρω | ἐν πολ. ἐγύρας 6 ἀποστέλω | ἐπάγω — N § 5. l. 7 s. ὃν ... γένο⟨ς⟩ σου τὸν ... τρεφόμενος c. L 8 ἐγὼ αὐτὸν οὐκ

ενεγγον προς (— σε) c. L 9 έφήπας κακεινος δέσμω δὲ θεὶς αὐτὸς ἀπὸ τὸν βυθὸν τῆς θαλάσσης § 6. l. 10 ἐκεινος ὁ υἱός σου 11 τῆς θαλ. τῆς ἐρ. 12 οὐ γὰρ p. 27*, l. 1, § 7. ἡ δὲ εἶπον αὐτόν· σὺ δὲ ποῖον ἄστρον οἰκεισαι 2 ἑσπέρειον § 8. l. 3 φράσον | ποιῶν ἀγγέλων | τοῦ ἁγίου τιμίου ὀνόματος τοῦ παντ. θ. καλούμενον παρὰ ἀνθρώποις ἐβραιστὶ πεντηκῆ οὔ καὶ ψῆφος χμδ. ἔστιν δὲ νόητον ἑλληνιστὶ ἐμ., τὸν δεδοκόταρομέον. ἐὰν δὲ μή τις τῶν καλῶν ζωόντων ὁρκίσει τὸν ἐλεθεῖ τὸ μέγα ὄνομαν τοῦ θεοῦ τῆς δυν. (f. 56ᵛ) § 9. l. 9 ἐν ... αὐτὸν — N | ἠλάλαξαν φωνὴν πάντες οἱ δαιμ. διὰ τ. βασ. αὐτῶν c. B‛ § 10. l. 11 αὐτὸν ἐπηρώτησα | βούλει ἀφ. λαβεῖν 12 τὴν c. A | ἔφη ... βασ. 13 θαλασσίους p. 28*, l. 2 οἰκ. ἐρ. etc. N c. P 3 ἡμέρας | τοὺς (1°)

C. VII. 1. 8 πρὸ ... μου: πρός με 13 ἐπὶ πολλῆς ἀναστάντα με πτῆσε p. 29*, l. 2 αὖβρα ἐκείνη § 4. 5 κάγὼ f. 57ᵛ § 5. l. 9 στρόφους ... ἀγροὺς: στρωφώνο κ. πῦρ αὐτὸν εἰποῆ στῆον κ. ἐν πυρὶ ἀγρ. 10 οἴκους ἐνμπυρίζω καὶ κατάγω 11 ὑποδύων ἡμέρας (— εἰς ... καὶ) § 6. p. 30*, l. 1 ποῖον ἄστρον οἰκεῖσαι 2 τοῦ ἐν τοῦ νότου εὐ⟨ρι⟩σκόμενος 4 εἴδοντα πολλοὶ τῶν ἀνθρ. ἔχοντο εἰς τὸ μητρητέον 5 βούλ· τἆλλα· θαλλάλ· μέλχαλ § 7. l. 8 ἡμιτριταῖος παύεται 9 καταργ. 10 ζαζαηλ P. 31*. c. VIII. l. 4 τὸ δόντα μοι τοιαύτην ἐξ. 6 ἦλθον πρός με | συνπλεκόμενα, ἔμορφα τὸ εἴδει § 2. l. 8 ἐθαυ(- μασα in fine pag.) f. 58ᵛ εἰ δὲ ὁμοθυμαδὸν εἶπον μιᾷ φωνὴν ἔφησαν 9 τὰ λγ στοιχεῖα οἱ κοσμοκράτορες τοὺς σκότους | § 3. καὶ εἰσὶν οἱ πρῶτοι | ἐγώ εἰμι ὁ vel ἡ statim om. N p. 32*, l. 1 κλοθὸν ἢ ἔστι μαχία | τετάρτη λεγομένη 2 ἡ δύναμις 4 § 4. θεὰ 6 § 5. αὐτὸν 7 ἀρξ. ἀπὸ τῆς πρώτης 3 πλέκω (bis) λέγω αὐτὰ ὧδε κακεῖς ἐρέσεις ἐρεθίζω 9 ἀγγ. τὸν κατ. με λαμεχελαλ 10 ἐρήσις ῥῆδον 11 τοῦ τόπου — N p. 33*, l. 1 βαρηχηαήλ § 7. l. 2 καὶ πάντα π. μαχ.: μάχην ἐστὶν τὸ ὄνομά μου | εὐσχ. περιεξ.: εὐχή μόνος ἠσχῆσε κ. περησχοιθέναι ποιῶ § 8. l. 5 μερίζω· χωρίζω (— ἀπομερ.) 8 βαλθησύχ | ordinem sectionum habet N ut A p. 34*, l. 3 ρηδῆλ | § 10. δύναμις καλοῦμαι· τυρ. ἀνιστῶ 5 καθὲ παρέχων 7 ὅτε ἐκελεύστων ἀρτ. δεσμῆς ἢ δὲ ἀκ. μελλήσει] 8 ὡς φιλ. — N | ἐμοὶ δὲ καται ἀντῆς ἐποιθειμοίαν τῆ⟨ς⟩ σοφίας 10 ἴχνος αὐτῆς 11 ἐπειδὴ σύντομαι ἐκελ.΄ 12 κ. ἔτ. ... πεντ : ἐπεὶ διακοσίας πηχῶν πεντ. τὸ μῆκος p. 35*, l. 1 ἔφησα ... καὶ δεινῶς γογγήσε τὰ κελεστέντα αὐτ. κατ.

C. IX. l. 3 N post θεὸν (mss. CP) add. τοῦ οὐρανοῦ καὶ τῆς γῆς | ἔτ. δαίμον 4 ἀν. μὲν: ὡς ἔχων § 2. l. 5 ἰδὸν αὐτὸν εἶπον c. W | λέγει ͵.. καλ.: τί λέγεις 6 καλοῦμαι — N | ἐμαυτὸν 7 ποιήσασθαι: περιποιῆσαι 8 ποιῆσαι: τὴν αὐτὴν ἔχω | οἷαν ὡς: ἔνηαν § 3. l. 11 ἐγόγγυζεν | *οἴμοι: ἡμῖν p. 36*, l. 2, § 5. ἡδονὴν: ἀδόδειν | ἤκουσε θέλω δὲ 3 ἢ μὴ φωνὴ ἡμῖν 4 βοβοὶ 5 γιν. δ. ἡμ. 7 § 6. ἀωρίαις | πλεῖον πορεύομαι καὶ τὸ 12 ἐκποιῶν p. 37*, l. 1, § 7. N cum P; ... οὐδὲ γὰρ οὔπω, .. ἐπευχόντων αὐτὸν ... ἐλθὼν εἶπον τὸν ἴδιον ὄνομαν ... § 8. l. 2 μεχρίου πάλιν ἀνάξω πρός με

C. X. l. 4 ἦλθε πρός με κύων. τὸ σχ. μεγ. 7 §. 2. γενόμενος | ἀθέσματα 9 ἀθέσματα 10 κατασχῶν p. 38*, l. 3, § 3. τοὺς φρενεῖν ἀνθρώπους τοὺς τῶν ἐμῶν 8 § 5. τὸν λίθον πρ. μεταλευόμενον 12 § 6· ὃς δ' ἂν ἐπιστρέψῃς καὶ δείξῃ σου 13 τὸ δακτυλίδιον 14 ἄγαγέ μοι ὧδε

τὸν δαίμοναν | § 7. καὶ ἔδειξεν αὐτὸν ὁ δαίμων τὸν (bis) πρ. λ. 16 ἤνεγκεν § 8. ll. 17 ss. cum. P: τὰ δύο... (— ὁμοίως)... τηρεῖται... λαμπάδας πυρὸς... παραπέμποι... τεχν. p. 39*, l. 9, § 9. ᾖρον | πετάλου 4 ἀναφωρέσιν · | ἦν δὲ ὁ λιθ. ἐκεῖνος ὥσπερ κερασίου τοῦ θυσιαστηρίου ὁμοιούμενον § 11 l. 9 καταργεῖσαι | βάρη ἐὼν
C. XI. l. 11 πρός με λέοντος etc. cum P 12 πν. εἰμὶ πν(εύμα)τι μηδ. § 2. l. 13 ἐγὼ δὲ ἐν πᾶσι p. 40*, l. 1 κατάκειμε | ἐφόρμομεν 3 § 3. ἐκβάλω 4 δεικτηκὸν (f. 63ᵛ) δέ εἰμι | ὑπ' ἐμὲ λεγεῶν 6 § 4. τί σου ἡ ἐργασία καὶ τί τὸ ὄνομά σου | λεοντόφρον 7 § 5. πῶς οὖν καταργεῖς 8 ἔχεις 11 § 6. εἰς τὸ μέγαν ὄν. τ. θ. σαβαώθ 12 καταργῇ μὲν τὰ τῆς δυνάμεώς σου 11 ἔχων πολλὰ παθῶν p. 41*, l. 2 κατὰ τοῦ — N 3 κακαταργοῦσα § 7. l. 5 αὐτὸν δὲ τὸν λεοντόφρονα 6 εἰς ἀπόκαψιν
C. XII. l. 8 ἦλθε πρός με δρακόντων τρικέφ. φοβεροχθρῶς § 2. l. 10 τρικέφαλον καὶ τρίβολον 11 νήπια | ἐπιδένω καὶ κουφένω κ. πάλιν ἐν τῇ τρ. μου κεφ, ὑπόδυνα κ. τύπτω 13 τὸ εἰκ. — N | κ. τρίζ. — N p. 42*, l. 2, § 3. σιωμένης | ἡ προωριστον § 4. l. 7 ἀνάγω | ἔσω — N Ἀραβίας: + ὅστις καὶ ἀσκὸν ἐκεῖσε καὶ καταβληθεὶς κοσμηστὴ ἀπὸ τῆς Ἀρ. 12 § 6. τί ἐστιν τὸ ὄνομά σου 13 πληθουρ. | ναὸν, εἶχεν γὰρ χ. α.
C. XIII. p. 43*, l. 1 καὶ πρὸς τῷ κυρίῳ τῷ θεῷ ἰσδραὴλ ἐκελ. | ἦλθε πρός με 2 καὶ αὐτὸν λυσίτριχον § 2. l. 4 ἡ δὲ... σύ — N 5 μαθεῖν... ὄντα: καὶ ἔφη· ἄκουσον τὰ κατ' ἐμέ 6 ταμή σου 7 προσκαθείσας 8 μαθεὶς § 3 l. 9 κ. ἐλέγξαι αὐτ. P: — N 10 τίς εἶ σύ: λέγε μοι παρὰ τοῖς ἀν(θρώπ)οις πῶς καλεῖσαι | ὀβηζθγελαουθ. 11 καθεύδομαι | κόσμον: + ἐπὶ ταῖς νύκταις 12 ἀποστοχαζόμενος p. 44*, l. 1 λίαν ἀναχώρισας | κ. νῦν με εἶναι: μὲν εἰμίν | δεκτηκὰ μέρη | οὐκ ἐποίησας — N § 4. l. 4 στόματα χαλινοδεσμία § 6. l. 8 ποῖον ἄγγελον 9 (— ὑπὸ) τὸν ἄγγελον τ. θ. τὸν καλούμενον βαραφάν,... ὁ κ. νῦν καταργούμενος εἰς τ. ἅπαν χ. ἐὰν... καὶ ἐπιγινώσκει γ. ἐπιγράψει τότε etc. § 7. l. 12 ἔμπροσθεν — N p. 45*, l. 1 βλέπουσιν καὶ 2 δύναμιν καὶ (f. 67ʳ) κρατέωσιν τὴν δεδομένην μοι παρὰ
C. XIV 3, l. 11 πολλαῖς — N 12 ἐμόρφοις | τοῦ ξείλου (f. 67ᵛ) τούτου 13 § 4. ἀπέρμε 14 ἐβάσταζεν ἡ ἐφόρησα] 15 ἔρος 16 τὴν γυναῖκαν ἐκείνην p. 46*, l. 1, § 5. θέλεισον | μονον — N .2 καταροσόμενα 4 συγγενέσθαι § 6. l. 7 ἅπερ: ἅπτην 10 ποῖον ἄγγελον καταργείη σε 12 βαζαζόθ
C. XV 3, l. 15 ἦλθε πρός με γύνη § 2. l. 19 ἐνείψυχος § 3. l. 21 μεταβ. καὶ γίνομαι ὡς 22 καὶ γίνομαι — N § 4. l. 24 εἰς τὴν σελ. § 5. l. 26 ἕτερον δὲ παλ. παρ' αὐτὸν κατάγομεν κ. φαιν. p. 47*, l. 5, § 7. αὐτὴν ἀλείσεσιν τρεῖς κ. καταδεσμεύσας μὲ τὴν ἄλλησον καὶ σφραγισάμενος τῇ σφραγίδην § 8. l. 9 συνλευσθ.: σκελευθήσεται § 9. l. 13 κατακλεῖς § 10. l. 16 πολλοῖς καιροῖς 17 ὅμοιος ὡς ἐν σειεῖ ὑμῆ ὁ πάντα ἡμᾶς κατ. § 13. l. 25 ἀποασεβῶν p. 48*, l. 3, § 15. παραδωθῆναι
C. XVI. l. 5 καὶ... δαιμ. — N 8 ἀποδεχ. χρυσίον κ. ἀργύριον. ἐτοιοῦτον εἰμὶ | τὰ ἀλόμενα τ. ὕδατος 10 § 2. εἰς κῦμα μέγαν 14 οὕτως... σωματ.: οὐ γὰρ εἰμὶ ἐπιθυμῶ σώματος § 3. l. 16 ἄρχων τῶν δαιμόνων ζεῖ καὶ βασιλεύει εἰς 18 σκέψιν (f. 71ʳ) τινὰ ζῆν p. 49*, l. 1, § 4. δόξαν καὶ — N 4 ὄνομα ἀλ. νατῆα· ἀποστ. δὲ 10 § 6. Ἰαμέθ: μηάσθαι

Lectiones variae ex MS N. 119

C. XVII. 1. 15 ἦλθε ὀμβρός μου 16 χεροσπάθην χαλκὴν p. 50*, l. 1 ὁ
2 πνεῦμα γίγαντος 3 τῶν ὀνομάτων γιγ. § 3, 1. 9 κατατρώγει § 4.
12 f. ὁ μελ. σωτὴρ καλεῖσθαι παρ' ἀν(θρώπ)οις 14 ἐπιστρέψῃ ἡττήσει
16 § 5, ἀπέκλεισα
C. XVIII, 1. 1f. ἦλθον ὀμπρός μου λ̄ζ πνεύματα 4 θεριοπρ.. σφηγγόσωμα, πυροειδῆ, τυποσώματα, βοωπρόσωπα, ὀθεοπρόσωπα, πτηνοπρόσωπα
§ 2. 1. 7 τοῦ κοσμοκράτορος | τοῦ αἰώνος § 3. l. 8 ἀλλ' οὐδὲ κατακλ.
ἡμῖν p. 52*, l. 1f. pro ἐγὼ... Ῥύαξ praebet Ν φαρμουθίου καλοῦμαι. ad
marg. adscr. ἀπὸ κρίου πρώτο⟨υ ἕως⟩ δεκά⟨του⟩ 3 κροτ. οκηλέβω | ἐγκλ.
'Ρ.: ἐγῶ κλήροσι ἄκας § 6. 1. 4 φαρμουθῆ κριοῦ. ὁ δευτ. ἔφη· β̄ ᾱ (1. ἀπὸ)
ῑ ᾱ ε̄ ὡς κ̄· ἐγὼ δευτ. καλ. βαρ. 6 ἐγκλ. Βαρ. — Ν 7 § 7. φαρμουθῆ
κριοῦ γ̄ ἀπὸ κ̄ ἕως λ̄. ὁ τρίτος | ἀρατοήλ 8 καὶ σφόδρα βλάπτω | ἀρατοσαήλ 10 § 8. πάχο ταύρον ἀπὸ πρώτου ἕως δεκάτου | ῥοπεῖ | λῆμα
κ. συνοχᾶς κ. συνδονᾶς ἐκπέμπων 12 § 9. πάχο ταυρίου β̄ ἕως κ̄ 13 κηριξουδάλ | καὶ σφηνόσια (f. 74ʳ) κορῶ ἐπιτελῶ | ἐὰν... ἀναχωρῶ — Ν
p. 53, l. 2, § 10. πάχο ταύρου γ̄· ἕως κ̄ | σφοδραήλ | παρίσθμια P, παρθεμνια 3 ὄπισθ. P, πιστότερον | βαηλ 4 σφοδραήλ | § 11. παύνι
διδίμου ᾱ· ἕως (κ̄ eras.) ᾱ 5 σφαδορ 6 ἐπιπήξω 7 σφαδορ | § 12. παύνι
διδίμου ἕως κ̄ 9 βελζεβουλ

§ 13. l. 10 παύνι διδίμου γ̄ ἕως η'· κ̄ ἕως λ̄ | ουρταήλ 11 ἰὰθ
σαβάθ | κουρταήλ 12 § 14. ἐπιφημή (f. 74ᵛ) καρκίνου β̄ | μεταθι
14 § 15. ἐποιφημη καρκίνου ἀπὸ β̄ ἕως ῑᾱ καὶ η'· κ̄· | ἐντέκατος | κανικοταιήλ 16 κ. τ. τ. ὀν. (P) — Ν p. 54*, l. 2 πλύνας δάφνας 3 § 16.
ἐπηφημὶ καρκίνου γ̄· ἀπὸ κ̄ ἕως τὸν λ̄ 4 σαφθορωθαήλ | ἐκβάλω 6 ἰαέ
... Σαβ. — Ν, v. infra | ἃς φορέεσι ἐπὶ τ. τρ. ἢ κ. τὰς πρὸ τ. οὓς εἴθη | post
ἀναχωρῶ add. τὴν μέθην διαλύω. μεσόρηον λέοντος ᾱ ἀπὸ πρώτου ἕως δέκα.
ἄκουσον, βασιλεῦ σο⟨λο⟩μόν, τὰ ὀνόματα ὅπου θέλη φορέεσι ὁποῖός ἐστιν·
τῶν ἀγγέλων τὰ ὀνόματα· ἰαεῶ· ἰελεῶ· ἰωελέτ· σαβαῶν ἠθὼθ βαέ (om. Ν
supra l. 6)

8 § 17. βωθο(πο eras.) θήλ 9 ἀθοναήθ...βωθωθήλ | § 18. μεσορείου
λέοντος β̄· ἀπὸ ᾱ ἕως η'· κ̄ 10 Δερ. καλ. — Ν 11 ἐπάγω: ἐκπιῶν, ὄνομα
δέ μοι ροκλίδ 12 ὅτι κολεῖ καλλιῶ ἐστὶν 13 § 19. μεσόριον λέοντος γ̄ ἀπὸ
εἰκουστοῦ λ̄ 14 κωμετήλ p. 55*, l. 1 κουμεταήλ | § 20. θὼθ πάρθη
ἀπὸ ᾱ ἕως δεκάτου 3 πυρετ(ῆς) ἐνάτης 4 ἐπιέχριε τὸν τράχηλον κ.
λέγων τὴν σπονδὴν ταύτην 5 ἀναχώρει ἀπὸ τοῦ πλάσματος (f. 76ʳ) τοῦ
θεοῦ τοῦ ὑψίστου τὸν θρόνον ἀναχωρεῖ ἀπὸ... θεοῦ

7 § 21. θὼθ πάρθη β̄ ἀπὸ ῑᾱ ἕως κ̄ | ἐροπαήλ 8 σπασμοὺς 9 ὅπου
δ' ἂν εὕρω 10 εἰς τοῦ οὓς τοῦ σπάχωντος εἰς τὸ δεξιὸν ἐκ τρίτου τ. ὀν.
ταῦτα· ἰουδαρζῆ· βαβωυννηδονηδέ 11 § 22. ὁ ὄγδη κ. δεκ. παρθένου γ̄ ἀπὸ
εἰκοστὸν πρῶτον ἕως λ̄ ὄγδο καὶ 12 βολδομιχ p. 56*, l. 2 τούτου P:
+ ὁρκίζω σε βολομόχ κανς (l. κατὰ τῆς) δυναστείας αὐτῶν ἀναχώρισον ἀπὸ
τοῦ οἴκου τούτου | § 23. ζηγὸς ᾱ ἀπὸ ᾱ ἕως ῑ 3 ἐγώ, κ(ύρι)ε σολομῶν,
καλ. ροὺξ μαδέρον | χαρτ. ἀβηβηλίου σφηνειραφαήλ· ἀναχωρίν με δούρον
4 § 24. φανὸφ ζηγὸς β̄ ἀπὸ ῑᾱ (l. οἱ?) κ̄ᾱ ἕως λ̄ 5 κήρηξ νουθάθ 6 φο-

νουβωήλ 7 (f. 77ʳ) § 25. φαωφῆ ζηγὸς β̄ ἀπὸ η κ̄ᾱ ἕως λ̄ 8 γράψει
... ῥορίξ, δ. οὐσ(ουσ)λάθ(?) κ. περιάψη
10 § 26. om. N 12 § 27. ἀθοὺρ σκορπήος β̄ ἀπὸ ῑᾱ ἕως η κ̄ ο η·
κ̄· γ̄· ἐγώ, κήριξ σολομόν, καὶ. ἐφθάδα p. 57*, l. 1 ἐ⟨ν⟩λάμνο κασσιτηρήω
| ἐφθαδὰ | τ. ἰοχ. — N 2 § 28. ἀθοὺρ σκορπίο νγ̄ ἀπὸ η κ̄ᾱ ἕως λ̄ ὁ η
κ̄δ̄ ἔφη· ἐγώ, κήριξ σολ., ἀκτόμεν καλ. 4 ὕλο | ἀρν. μαρμαρώθ, ἀκτόμε
διωξ. 5 § 29. χοίαν τοξότης ᾱ ἕως ῑ | ἐγώ, κήριξ σολ., καλ. ἀνατρέθ
7 ἀρ. χαρ. ἀποδιώξων ἀνατρέθ | § 30. χοιακον τοξότου β̄ ἀπὸ η κ̄η̄ ἕως
λ̄, ὁ η κ̄ς̄ καὶ ἕτερα δέκατος· ἐγώ, κήριξ σολ., καλ. ἐνόθ. 9 ἀλλαζολ...
ἐνοῦθ καὶ γράψει χαρτ. 10 § 31. χήακα τοξώτης γ̄ ἀπὸ κ̄β̄. λ̄· οη κ̄ζ̄
ἔφη· ἐγώ κήριξ σολ, ὤφθη καλ. 11 ὑπατικοὺς | αἱμ.: ἐνμωρραγκὰς φιλῶ
12 ἑῶν P (1°): ἑώλ, (2°): ἑῶ | ἀξηωφήθ | δὸς πίει τοῦ πάσχοντος
14 § 32. τίβη ἐγοκέρου κέρατον· οη κ̄η̄ ἔφη· ἐγώ, κήριξ σολ., ἅρπας καλ.
15 γράψει εἰς φύλλον δαφνις κόκο φνῆ δίσμος (+ μῶς eras) καὶ 16 § 33.
τοβηέθ κέρατος β̄ γ̄ ἀπὸ ῑβ̄ εἰκοστὸς οη κ̄θ̄ ἔφη· ἐγώ, κήριξ σολ.. καλ. (nomen om.) p. 58*, l. 1 σε κανοστίρ 2 μαρμαρώθ | § 34. πο β̄ (l. τοβ)
ἐγόκαιρος τω γ̄ ἀπὸ εἰκοστοῦ πρώτου ἕως λ̄. ὁ λ̄ ἔφη· ἐγώ, κήριξ σολ., καλ.
ἠφησικεράθ 3 ποιῶ τοῖς ἀνθρώποις 5 βοηθεῖτε, φεύγω καὶ ἀναχωρῶ
καὶ ἀναπληρῶν ἡμερῶν ἑπτά | § 35. μεσει δρηχόου ᾱ ἀπὸ ᾱ ἕως ξ̄, ὁ λ̄ᾱ
ἔφη· ἐγώ, κήριξ σολ., καλ. ἀλλεβωρίθ 7 νυκτὸς φαγήσας καὶ ὀστέον ἀπὸ
8 § 36. μεσει· χηρῆ δρηχώου β̄ ἀπὸ ᾱ ἕως λ̄, ὁ λ̄β̄ ἔφη· ἐγώ, κήριξ σολ., καλ.
ἰχθήος 10 § 37. μεση δρηχώου β̄ γ̄ ἀπὸ κ̄ᾱ ἕως λ̄, ὁ τριασκοστὸς τρίτος ἔφη·
ἐγώ, κήριξ σολ, καλ. ἀγωχώνηον 11 σπαργάνοις κατὰ φάραγγι 12 κούργος· οὔργος· ῥογος· ὀος ὅς
14 § 38. φαμενόθ ἰχθήος ἀπὸ ᾱ ἕως ῑ, ὁ τριακ. τεταρ. ἔφη· ἐγώ, κήριξ
σολ., καλ. ῥης (nomen om.) 15 α ἢ β 16 § 39. φαμενὸθ ἰχθήος β̄ ἀπὸ ῑᾱ
ἕως κ̄, ὁ τρ. πέπτος ἔφη· ἐγώ (bis), κήρης σολ., καλ. ῥὶξ φηνόθ 18 § 40.
φαμενόθ ἰχθήος γ̄ ἀπὸ κ̄ᾱ· λ̄· ὁ τρ. ἐκ. ἔφη· ἐγώ· κήριξ σολ, καλ. βιανακήθ
p. 59*, l. 2 ἐπήφθονον 3 μηλτον· ἀρθουνα· ἐνᾱθ 6 ὑδροφονεῖν | § 42.
N cum P, atque § 43, sed post κατέκλεισα add. ἄλλους δὲ εἰς ἀγγεῖα ἀπέκλεισα, et in § 44 ὑελῶν pro φιάλῳ, et τόπους εἴτήμασα ... κλιθεῖναι

C. XIX. N cum P. § 1. σολ. ὁ βασ. | παντὸς ἀνθρώπου τοῦ ὑπὸ
— ὅλον § 2. πᾶς τῶν βασιλέων τ. γ. πάσης | θεωρεῖν | δοθ. ἡμῖν
ἐπροσφέρασι δῶρα, χρυσ. κ. ἀργ. πολύ | κ. πολ κ. διαφ. ἐκόμιζον προσφορὰς
εἰς τὸν ναὸν κυρίου τοῦ θεοῦ χαλκ. τε καὶ | ξύλα σεπτὰ προσφέρομεν εἰς
p. 60*, § 3. ἐν οἷς — N | σάβα ἡ βασ. | ἐδόξαζον τὸν θεὸν

C. XX. 1. 7 γέρας μου | λέγε ... ἔφη: ὁ γέρων λέγων § 2. 1 6 προσωπ ... μοι: πρός σε εἶμι ἐκοδήσον με § 3. l. 12 ἐλθόντος ἐπηρώτησα
τὸν νέον· ἀληθῶς οὕτως ἔχει § 4. l. 13 om. πατέρα 14 om. ἐπιπεπλησμένος et π(ατέ)ρα ... βασιλεῦς 15 ἀθέσμιτα p. 61*, l. 1, §. 5. οὖν
| ἀκ. τοῦ νέου 3 ἀλλ' εἶπεν· οὐχὶ ἀλλὰ θανατωθήτω

§ 6. πρεσβύτην | τ. δαίμονα ἐλθεῖν καὶ ἀνήγειλέν μοι καὶ λέγοντά
μοι οὕτως· ἐγω δὲ σολ. (+ ἀκούσας ταῦτα eras) ἐθυμ. λίαν διὰ | εἰπέ μοι,

Lectiones variae ex MS N. 121

ὦ κατάρατε § 7. 1 9 ἔτι τρεῖς | τελευτήσει 10 ἀνελεῖ | § 8. ταῦτα οὕτως ἔχει. (f. 72ʳ) ὁ δὲ ἔφη· ἀληθῶς ταῦτα § 9. l. 12 ἐλθ. τ. γηρ (μεταστῆναι eras.) εἰς τὸ μέσον μετὰ καὶ τοῦ 13 φιλίαν τρ. ἅμα καὶ εἰς τὸν τροφὴν αὐτ. παρασχόμε § 10. l. 14 τὸν νέον τ. υἱόν σου καὶ ἐπιμελοῦμαι αὐτοῦ 15 οἱ δὲ προσκυν. p. 62*, l. 5, § 12. ὠπτάμεθα | ἀπὸ τ. θ. 6 § 13. εἰς τὸ ὀν. τ. τεθ. (c. Q) ὥστε φαίνεσθαι | ἐπὶ τοῖς ἀν(θρώπ)οις (— φύσεως) § 14. l. 9 ἐν 10 ἐν μέσῳ | μιγενητο § 15. cum P | ὡς ἄτον μὴ | — ἀτονοῦμεν § 16. p. 63*, l. 2 δοκοῦσιν οἱ ἄνθρωποι καὶ θεορούντες ἡμᾶς ὅτι ἄστερες ἐπίπτουσιν 3 § 17. οὐ οὕτως δὲ 4 ἀλλὰ ἐκπίπτομεν ἐπὶ (ex ἀπό corr.) τὴν γῆν διὰ 5 πολλῇ 6 πόλεις: πολλοὺς § 19. l. 11 οὐκ... πενθοῦντα: ἔμελλον ἐπεροτᾶν αὐτὸν καὶ ἐλθὸν πρός με ὁ ἄν(θρωπ)ος κατὰ πένθος καὶ μελλανόμενος τὸ πρόσωπον καὶ πλήτον ἐαυτοῦ τὸ σόμα § 20. l. 14 παρακαθέζομαι | ἡμέραι § 21. l. 16 Ἰσραήλ

C. XXI. l. 1 δοξάζουσα καὶ αὐτὴ τὸν 2 ἣν εἰκοδόμουν τετελειομένον | ἔδωκε σίκλον χρυσίου κ. ἀργ. κ. χαλκοῦ ἐκλεκτοῦ μυρ. 3 § 2. εἶδε | τὰς ἀναφόρας 5 λίθους τοὺς τιμίους ὥσπερ λυχνοὺς ἀστραπτ. 6 λυχνικοῦ λίθου 7 § 3. κριθειδανόμενο 8 λησειδώτου | πλόκην περιπλεμένην 9 στάδιον δεκάξι ταύρους 10 § 4. N cum C 12 καὶ... γῆς P: — N

C. XXII. p. 65*, l. 1 ἀπεστ. δὲ μὲ ὁ βασ. ἀράβων ὀνόματι ἀρδάκης | ἡ δὲ... οὕτως — N 2 βασιλεῦ σολομῶν τοῦ ἰῆλ, ἰδοὺ ἤκουσ. πάντα περὶ σου καὶ παν. τὰ πέρατα, etc. cum Q § 4. l. 14 εἰρηνεύσεις πᾶσαν ἀραβίαν | ταύτην τὴν δικαιοσ. p. 66*, l. 1 § 5. ὑποτεταγμένοι ὑπαρχίαν ἀπολέσις 2 καὶ πᾶσα ἡ γῆ μου — N
4 § 6. ἀκούσας καὶ ἀναγνοὺς 5 πτύξας αὐτὴν 6 § 7. καὶ ... συνεπλ. — N 7 ἀκρογων. μέγας ἐκλεκτὸς (— κείμενος) | ὅντινα βάλομεν εἰς § 8. l. 10 οἱ συνπουργῶν τὸν λίθον ἐπὶ τὸ αὐτὸν ὅτε ἀνάγη τὸν λίθον ἐπὶ τὸ αὐτῶ καὶ λιθῆναι αὐτὸν ἐπὶ τὸ πτερυγ. 12 τ. θεματ. αὐτῷ — N | ἐκεῖνος πάνυ — N | § 9. μνησθείς: γνοὺς N 13 ἀρδάκου 14 τὴν μετά σε 15 § 10. ἐπὶ τοῦ 16 πνέει — N § 11. p. 67*, l. 3 κ. σφραγ. τ. δακτ. cum H | ἐπίσαξω και. τὴν καμ. κ. θέσε τ. ἀσκὸν ἐπὶ τὴν καμ. κομίσεις ἐνθ. | τάξεται | θησαυροὺς μὴ ἀπο ἀλύσεις
§ 12. l. 5 Τότε: τοῦτον N | τὰ τελεσμένα | καὶ ... ἀσκὸν — N 7 ἥκιστ. καὶ ἅρα δυνατόν τ. πν. τ πον. συλ. | § 13. καὶ ὄρθρου mecum 8 ἐνωπ.... πνοῆς καθὺς τ. ἀσκὸν ... ἐπεθ. τὸ στόμα τοῦ ἀσκοῦ τῶ δακτυλίδιον 10 τοῦ δακτ. ... στόμα P: — N 11 § 14. σταθεὶς εὐθέως p. 68*, l. 1 § 15. κ. οὕτως ἐπέμενεν ὁ 2 πλέον ἐν τ. χώρᾳ ἐκ. 3 § 16 ἐπέσαξεν τὴν καμ. ὁ παῖς κ. ἐπέθηκεν τ. ἀσκ. ἐπὶ τ. καμ. 5 καὶ εὐφ. ἐδόξαζον

§ 17. l. 9 με § 18 1 13 πεφυσημένος § 19. l. 15 εἰμι ὁ λεγ. ἐφήπτας p. 69*, l. 1, § 20. ναί, κήρι σολομῶν βασιλεῖ, ἔφιπτ. | σταυρωθ. (f. 88ʳ) ἐπὶ ξύλον, ὁ καὶ προσκυνήσαντες ἄγγελον ἀρχάγγελον

C. XXIII. εἶπον ἐγὼ σολομῶν βασ. πρὸς αὐτόν 5 μεφέρειν | ἔπητα ἄλλα § 2. 1. 10 στήσεις | βούλει: + κήρη βασ. σολ. 11 § 3. ἵνα ἀναγάγει σε κ. φυσηθεὶς ὁ ἀσκ. ἐν τοῦτο κ. ὑποδέδοκεν τὸν λίθον p. 70*, l. 1 ἔθετο ἐπάνω εἰς τὰς γονίας τοῦ ναοῦ § 4. l. 3 ἡ ῥέθεισα | κ. τὰ λοῖπα: τοῦτον οὐκ ἔστιν ἄλλον ἀλλήνα τοῦ θεοῦ τὸ θέλημαν κατισχύσαι etc. cum P

C. XXIV, § 4. p. 71*, l. 2 *ὁ κίονας ὑπερμεγέθη σπόδρα διὰ τὸν ἀέρα* 4 *βαστάζοντα* — N

C. XXV. *βασιλεὺς σολ.* (f. 89ᵛ) | *τὸν ἕτερον δαίμοναν τὸν ἂν ἐλθὼν* 8 *καὶ σὺ τίς εἶ κ. τί σου* § 2. 10 *ἀβεζεβιθοῦ* | *καὶ ἤμουν πότε μὲν καθεζόμενος* 12 § 3. *πνεῦμα περοτὸν ἐπιβ.* 13 ss. *ἐγώ . . . καρδίαν*: *ἐγώ εἶμι ὁ σκληρύνας τὴν καρδίαν φαραῶν καὶ τῶν θεραπόντων αὐτοῦ κατὰ τὸν μονισὴν τὸν ἰσραηλίτον.* § 4. *ἐγὼ ἐκεῖνος ὃ ἐπικ. . . . οἱ μαχόμενοι* (f. 90ʳ) *τῷ βασιλεῖ ἐγύπτου* p. 72*, § 6. 1 4, *ἐποίησα καταδιῶξαι ὀπίσω τὸν υἱὸν ἰσραὴλ καὶ ἐγένετο ἐν τῷ ἐγγύζειν αὐτοὺς ἐν τῇ ἐρυθρᾷ θαλ. διέρηξεν ὁ θεὸς τὴν θάλασσαν καὶ διεπέρασεν τοὺς υἱοὺς ἰ*(*σρα*)*ὴλ* 6 *τότε . . . ἐκεῖ*: *παρημῶν* 7—10 § 7. *καὶ διεγένετο καὶ ἐκάλυψεν καὶ ἔμειναν* 11—14 § 8. *ἀλλὰ παραμέναι αὐτοὺς βαστάζον τὸν κίονα ἤγουν τὸν στεῖλον ὃν ἐκ τῆς ἐρυθρᾶς θαλάσσης ἐκόμισαν καὶ ὤμοσαν. . . . ὁ θεὸς τοῦ ἰηλ ὃς παρεδ. ἡμᾶς ἀποχειρό σου οὐ . . . τοῦτον ἐπὶ τῆς γῆς . . .* § 9. . . . *τὸν* (f. 91ʳ) *θεὸν τοῦ οὐνοῦ καὶ τῆς γῆς καὶ . . . κυρίου μετὰ πάσην εὐπρεπίαν καὶ ἐμνήστ*(*ην*) *ἐν . . .*

C. XXVI. 1 1, p. 73* *τῆς βασιλείας μου ἐ γυνέκες καὶ ἄλλες πολλὲς μοι γυνέκες οὐκ* 2 *πορεύθει* 3 *ἐκεῖ*: *ἐκ τὸ βασίλειον αὐτοῦ* 4 *ἐβουλ. δοξάσε αὐτ. πρὸς* § 2. 1. 5 *μοι* | *σομανήτην* 6 *μολόχου* 7 *ἀγαπᾷς* 8 *τὸν μέγαν θεὸν* (f. 91ᵛ) *τὸν καλούμενον ῥ. κ. μ. ἐὰν ἀγαπᾷς τὴν παρθένον τίς δὲ ἔστιν ἡ ὑποθ. τοῦτο με ἀνάγγασε προσκυνεῖσε καὶ ποιῆσαι;* § 4. *. . . ὁμοιωθῇς τοῖς ἔθ*[*ν*]*εσιν τῶν . . . ἡμ. ἐμὴ πυθ. οὐδαμῶς θύσω θεοὺς ἀλλ. καὶ παρεβίασε* hoc a loco cum H

N cum H comp. 12 Σολ.: + *τοῦ βασιλέως ἰηλ ἀνάγκασε αὐτὸν προσκυνῆσαι τοῖς θεοῖς ἡμῶν καὶ ἐὰν μὴ βουληθῇ ἐπακοῦσαί σου* 12 *αὐτῷ* in *αὐτῶν* corr. N 13 *ὁμ. τοῖς θεοῖς ἡμῶν καὶ τῷ* | *καὶ αὐτὰς σφάξαι ὑπὸ τὰς χεῖρας σου καὶ λέγον ἐν ὀνόματί σου ραφᾶ κ. μολόχ* p. 74*. pro sec. 5 praebet ms. N textum hunc: *ἐγὼ παρενόχλουν τοῖς ⟨ἰ⟩εβουσαίοις διὰ τὸ ἀγ τ. παρθένον ταύτην τὴν ὠραίαν εἰς ὑπερβολὴν καὶ καλὴν τὴν ὄψιν σφόδρα καὶ εἶναι αἶνις*(?) *ἀγαθὴν ἐνόπιόν μου. καὶ εἶπεν πρός με· ἀθέσμιτός μου ἐστίν, βασιλεῦ, καὶ κοιμηθῆναι μετὰ μοῦ ἔθνη ἀλλοτριῶ· ἀλλὰ προσκύνησον τοῖς θεοῖς τοῦ πατρός μου καὶ ἰδοὺ καὶ ἐγὼ δούλ*⟨*η*⟩ *ἐνώπιόν σου. Ἐν δὲ τὸ πιστεῖναι μὴ ἐπεκαθῆσαν μὴ δι' ὕλης τῆς νυκτὸς λέγων· πῶς λαλεῖς ἀγαπᾷν με καὶ οὐκ ἀκούεις τῆς φωνῆς τῆς δούλ*⟨*ης*⟩ *σου. Εἰ γοῦν βούλῃ προσκυνῆσαι τοῖς θεοῖς τοῦ πατρός μου, μὴ ἔστω σοι σχολιὸν τοῦτον· λάβε δὲ ἐν τῇ χειρί σου ἀκρίδες ε̄ καὶ ἄρρας σφάξον ὅπως* (f. 92ᵛ) *λήψεις με εἰς γυναῖκαν· καὶ ἔσομαι ἐγὼ καὶ ὁ λαός μου μετὰ σοῦ. ἐγὼ δὲ ὁ τάλας ὡς διτελος* (sic) *καὶ οὐδὲν ὅρμησα τῆς ἀκρίδος τὸ αἷμα καὶ σφάξας εἰς τὰς χεῖρας μου ἐν ὀνόματι μολόχ καὶ ραφᾶ εἰπὼν καὶ ἔλαβα τὴν γυναῖκαν καὶ ἦγον αὐτὴν εἰς τὸν οἶκον τ. βασ. μου*

p. 74*. § 6. N cum P. *ἐξ οὗ . . . Μολοχ*: *καὶ ἐν τῷ εἶναι με ἐν αὐτῇ ἠνέγγασεν ἡ γυνὴ ἐκείνη οἰκοδομῆσαι ναοὺς τοῖς βαὰλ καὶ ἥρα ἐγὼ τὸν ραφᾶν κ. τὸν μολόχ*

§ 7. N cum H. *πάνη* — N | *αὐτήν·* + *καὶ ἀπέστη τὸ πνεῦμα ἀπ' αὐτοῦ διὰ τὸ πορευθῆναι με ὀπίσο τῆς ἀθεμίας μου* | *καὶ ἐσκοτίσθη τὸ* πν. μου καὶ ἐσκορπίσθην τὸ σπέρμα μου κ. ἐδοθ. τῷ δούλῳ μου Ἱεροβάμ δέκα σκῆπτρα. τὰ δὲ δύο σκῆπτρα ἀπομείναντες πρός με διὰ δᾶδ τὸ πν̄α (l. τὸν πρ̄α) μου· διὰ τοῦτο ἐλέησεν ὁ θεὸς καὶ τὰ δύο σκῆπτρα ἴασε τὸ πεδίον μου τούτων σινηκαν παριθέντα (sic) μοι ὑπὸ τῶν δαιμ. καὶ ἐμνήσθην ὅτι ὅσα εἶπον ἀληθῶς εἶπον· ἔφησα γάρ μοι περὶ τούτων· ὑπό τ. χείρας μου δισάτει τελευτῆσαι καὶ ἐκλείπη ἐκ προσώπου τοῦ (ἡλίου) §§ 8 et 9. N cum H. τοῖς ἴηλ καὶ ἀφῆκαν αὐτὴν εἰς μνημ. ὅτι προ τελ. μου μακαριούσε με ὥστε οὖν φυλαχθῆναι τὴν διαθήκην μου πρὸς ἡμᾶς (p. 75*) μυστ. μεγ. (f. 93ᵛ) κατὰ παντὸς ἀκαθάρτου πν̄ς ὥστε γινώσκειν ὑμᾶς | ἰσραὴλ ἱποτάξε ἐπ᾿ ἐμὲ πάντα τὰ δαιμ. ὥστε εἶναι σφραγίδα | ταῦτα οὖν ... δακτ. τοῦ θεοῦ (§ 9) — N | προσετέθει πρὸς τοὺς πρ̄ας | ἐν ἰλη̄μ — N | οὐ ὑπὸ θρόνου ad finem om. N, sed add. ᾧ πρέπει τιμὴ καὶ προσκύνησις εἰς τοὺς αἰῶνας τῶν αἰώνων· ἀμήν

B. Manuscript E.

A Narrative Concerning Solomon the Prophet.

E. Library of the Greek Patriarchate, Jerusalem, Sancti Saba, No. 290; XVIII cent., paper, cm. 17×21,7; 204 ff.; unpublished. Catalogue, vol. B, p. 415.

The first one hundred thirty-eight leaves of the manuscript were written by Gerasimos, a monk from Chios in 1719 at the μόνη τοῦ ἁγίου ἐνδόξου προφήτου Ἡλίου τοῦ Θεσβίτου (f. 48ʳ and 139ᵛ), probably, therefore, at Mar Elias near Jerusalem. The "Narrative Concerning Solomon", however, is in a section of the book which was written by other, and it would appear to me somewhat older hands, although nearly every work in this latter part of the codex is strongly marked by modern Greek forms.

The "narrative", found on ff. 177ᵛ—191ʳ, is in a clear strong hand, comparatively easy to read. It is not free from errors, but is immeasurably superior to MS N, to those of Rec. C, or even to L. It is unique in that it is not merely marked by occasional late Greek forms, as are several of the others, but is entirely written in Modern Greek of a style much more colloquial than modern newspaper Greek. Aside from its relation to the *Test*, it has some value as a sample of colloquial Greek of the XVII or XVIII century.

Its nearest relative is MS D. In other words it is not a "testament" at all, but a story. Certain sections read like a paraphrase of MS D into Modern Greek. Indeed, it occasionally uses the very phrases of D, for example in D c. IV 6—9, 13f., 16¹. Moreover it follows the outline of MS D, beginning with the story of David's sin, and then recounting the beginning of the building of the Temple, the favorite slave's difficulty, the capture of Ornias, the sending of Ornias and the slave to capture the demons, and their work upon the temple². All of D cc. IV—VII 3 is repeated in E, often almost word for word³. From this point on, however, E parts company with all the other accounts. It tells how Samael was examined and replies and is set to work in exactly the manner of the *Test*⁴. Then it goes on to narrate how, after the Temple was finished, Solomon shut all the demons up in vessels, how the Temple was dedicated, how later the Chaldeans came and released the demons, and how later still Jesus came and by the cross overcame them all, adding that this was the symbol engraved on Solomon's ring and that anyone who properly uses this sacred symbol may escape all their attacks⁵.

The differences between E and D go still farther than this conclusion. The resemblance between the introductory sections telling of Solomon's parentage is after all superficial. The account of the devil's frustration of Nathan's attempt to forestall David's sin (D c. I 4—6) is entirely lacking in E and the account of Nathan's parable and David's repentance is quite different⁶. When (D c. III 4) Ornias and the slave are sent to bring in the other demons, they bring Beelzebul, who is examined as in the *Test*. Here MS E uses material from the accounts of both Beelzebul and Asmodaeus, in something like this order, *Test* cc. III 6, IV 1—3a, V 8f. VI 4, 7f., 9 (part). Then it resumes the matter and order of D (c. III 8)⁷.

There are fewer resemblances in language between E and the *Test* than between D and E, and yet in the account of Beelzebul the same words are often used and the likenesses are such

---

1 E, c. V 3—6, 8ff.   2 E, c. I—IV 1, 12.   3 E, c. V—IX 4.
4 E, c. IX 7—10.   5 E, cc. X—XII.   6 E, c. I 6—9.
7 C. IV 11 ff.

as very strongly to suggest some kind of literary dependence. This is particularly true if one omits the account of Onoskelis and Asmodaeus from the *Test*, an account which breaks into the very middle of the examination of Beelzebul (cc. III 7—VI 1a). On other grounds also this appears like an interpolation, for only in these chapters does Beelzebul figure prominently.

Just how it comes about that some traits which plainly belong to Asmodaeus are ascribed to Beelzebul it is difficult to explain. That Raphael and the gall of a fish called $\gamma\lambda\iota\alpha\nu\acute{o}\varsigma$ belong to Asmodaeus cannot be disputed[1]. It is plain also that the writer of E is combining two accounts from the fact that in two separate places he introduces the means by which the demon is to be laid[2]. He must have known two descriptions of the chief demon and he preferred the name Beelzebul because of its use in the Gospels. MS E is more definitely Christian than any other of these documents.

We have in our manuscripts a "synoptic problem" rendered even more complicated by the discovery of E. The resemblances in phrasing and in order are too close to permit of an oral theory, but on the other hand, the differences are such as to preclude the conclusion that the *Test* was derived directly from either D or E or either of them from the other. Rather we must go back to an original "narrative", *d* which included a brief account of Solomon's parentage, the building of the Temple, the capture of Ornias, the use of demons in the building, the incident of the father and son, the gifts from foreign monarchs, the letter of the Arabian king, the capture of Ephippas, and the placing of the cornerstone and the aerial column. This *d* possibly had also some reference to Samael, for he appears in both E and D. Both the introductory account of Solomon's birth and the concluding reference to Samael where developed differently in the two editions.

E steps in to make the connection between *d* and the *Test*. In c. XVII is a nameless demon whose "work" is exactly that of Samael in E and who is frustrated in the same way, by the

---

[1] E, c. IV 7.   [2] E, c. IV 7 and 9.

sign of the cross[1]. The demon is, moreover, "shut up ... like the other demons" (XVII 5), an idea especially prominent in E[2]. As the *Test*, which was *ex hypothese* written by Solomon, could not tell of the future escape of the demons from their vessels, the writer had a demon foretell it and the power of the coming Son of the Virgin to overcome them again (XV 8—12), all of which is given in much fuller detail in E. The relations may be explained by supposing E to be based upon *e*, a manuscript derived from *d* and forming the original also from which the *Test* was developed. E, of course, represents a considerable expansion of *e*. A great deal of liberty must be allowed to editors and copyists in such literature as this. This will explain changes and omissions of all kinds. The use of various sources is also to be expected. In one passage E mentions Jeremiah, Baruch, and Abimelek, and evidently depends on the *Paralipomena of Jeremiah*[3].

In the transcripton of E which follows[4] I have tried to be as faithful to the manuscript as possible, only correcting obvious errors and not trying even to introduce consistency.

---

[1] E, c. IX 8f. [2] E, c. X 2. [3] E, c. XI 1f. [4] See pp. 102*—120*.

BIBLIOGRAPHY.

I. Editions and reprints.

1. Fleck, Dr. F. F„ Wissenschaftliche Reise durch das südliche Deutschland, Italien, Sicilien und Frankreich, II 3, Anecdota maximam partem sacra. Leipz. 1837, pp. 113—40. (= Fl) MS P only
2. Fürst, J., Der Orient, 5. Jahrgang, 1844, 7. Jahrgang, 1846, Literaturblatt, Sp. 593, 663, 714, 741. Incomplete. (= Fü) Reprint of Fleck
3. Migne, Abbé J. P., Patrologia graeca, vol. 122, Paris 1864, coll. 1315—58. Reprint of Fleck. (= Mg)
4. Istrin, V. M., Griečeski spiski zabesania Solomona (Greek Manuscripts of the Testament of Solomon) Odessa 1898, 50 pp.[1] Printed also in the Yearbook of the historical-philosophical Society at the Imperial Newrussian University (at Odessa) VII, Byzantine Division IV (Odessa 1899), pp. 49—98. (Russian) Contains MSS D, I, and Q. (= Is)

II. Translations.

1. Bornemann, Dr. Friedrich August, Zeitschrift für die historische Theologie herausg. von Dr. C. F. Illgen, vol. XIV, Leipzig 1844, part 3, pp. 9—56. German. (= Bn)
2. Fürst, J., Der Orient 1844, 1846. Cf. *supra*, Edition 2. German. Incomplete. (= Fütr)
3. Migne, Abbé J. P., Patrologia graeca, vol. 122; cf. *supra*, Edition 3. Latin. (= Mgtr)
4. Conybeare, F. C. "The Testament of Solomon", Jewish Quarterly Review XI (No. 41), London October 1898, pp. 15—45. English. (= Crtr)
5. Ginzberg, Louis, The Legends of the Jews, translated from the German manuscript by Henrietta Szold, 4 vols. Philadelphia 1913, vol. IV Bible Times and Characters from Joshua to Esther, pp. 150ff.

---

1) This was very kindly sent to me by the author, whose address I owed to Prof. E. Kurz.

III. Treatises and discussions.

1. Fabricius, Johannes Albert, Codex pseudepigraphicus veteris testamenti, Hamburg 1713, I 1036 ff.
2. Bornemann, Dr. Friedrich August, "Conjectanea in Salomonis Testamentum", in Biblische Studien von Geistlichen des Königreichs Sachsen herausg. von Dr. Kauffer, 2. Jahrgang, Dresden u. Leipzig 1843, pp. 43—60, 4. Jahrgang, 1846, pp. 28—69. (= Bncn)
3. Migne, Abbé, Dictionaire des Apocryphes, vol. II (= Enc. theol., vol. XLI), Paris 1853, pp. 839 ff.
4. Conybeare, F. C., Introduction to translation 4, above II 4
5. James, M. R., in the Guardian, vol. 54, pt. I, No. 2780, London March 15, 1899, p. 367
6. Conybeare, F. C., ibid., March 29, 1899, p. 442
7. Schürer, E., Theol. Literaturzeitung, 1899, 110, review of Conybeare's translation and the introduction thereto
8. Istrin, V. M., introduction to text, above Bibliography I 4
9. Krumbacher, K., Byz. Ztschr. VII (1900), p. 634
10. Kurz, E., ibid. X, p. 238
11. Schürer, E., Geschichte des jüdischen Volkes, 4. Aufl., Leipzig 1909 III 419 ff. (= JGV) = The History of the Jewish People in the Time of Jesus Christ, New York 1891, II 1. c. 153 ff. (= HJP)
12. Toy, C. H., Jewish Encyclopedia, New York 1907, XI 448, art. "Solomon, Testament of"
13. Kohler, K., Jewish Encyclopedia: IV 518, in art. "Demonology"
14. Salzberger, Georg, Die Salomosage in der semitischen Literatur: ein Beitrag zur vergleichenden Sagenkunde. I. Teil: Salomo bis zur Höhe seines Ruhmes, Diss. Heidelberg, Berlin 1907, pp. 9—12, 94—97, 99

IV. General Bibliography (including Abbreviations).

These lists include not only works referred to, but also a few others to which the writer has been especially indebted.

1. Dictionaries, encyclopedias, periodicals, and collections.

AJT = American Journal of Theology, Chicago 1897 ff.
Anecdota Oxoniensia, Classical Series, Part VIII, Oxford 1898: F. C. Conybeare, The Dialogues of Athanasius and Zacchaeus and of Timothy and Aquila
Archiv für Papyrusforschung, ed. by Ulrich Wilcken, Leipzig 1900 ff.
B = Corpus Scriptorum Historiae Byzantinae, editio emendatior et copiosior consilio B. G. Niebuhrii instituta, auctoritate Academiae Litterarum Regiae Borussicae continuata, Bonnae 1828—1878
Biographie universelle, Paris 1826
BZ = Byzantinische Zeitschrift, hersg. von Karl Krumbacher, Leipzig 1892 ff.

Bibliography. 129

CCAG = Catalogus codicum astrologorum graecorum, 7 vols., Bruxelles 1896 —1908

CCGBA = Catalogus codicum graecorum bibliothecae Ambrosianae digesserunt Aemidius Martini et Dominicus Bassi, Mediolan. 1906

Catalogus codicum mss. bibliothecae regiae, 4 vols., Paris 1739—44

Encyclopaedia of Islam, a dictionary of the geography, the ethnography and biography of the Muhammadan peoples, ed. by M. Th. Houtsma, T. W. Arnold, R. Basset and R. Hartmann, vol. I A—D, Leyden-London 1913

ERE = Encyclopedia of Religion and Ethics, ed. by James Hastings, Edinburgh 1908, 8 vols. up to 1916

ExT = The Expository Times, ed. by James Hastings, Edinburgh 1889 ff.

Folklore, a quarterly Review of myth, tradition, institution and custom, London 1890 ff.

Griechische Urkunden aus dem Berliner Museum, hersg. von Wilcken, Krebs und Viereck, Berlin 1892 ff.

HDB = Dictionary of the Bible, ed. by James Hastings, 5 vols., Edinburgh 1898—1904

Jahrbücher für klassische Philologie, ed. by Alfred Fleckeisen, 43 vols., Leipzig 1855—97

JAS = Journal of the Royal Asiatic Society, London 1834 ff.

JE = The Jewish Encyclopedia, ed. Isidore Singer, 12 vols., New York 1907—

JQR = Jewish Quarterly Review, First Series, ed. by L. Abrahams and C. J. Montefiore, 50 vols., London 1888—1908

KVCom = Die griechischen christlichen Schriftsteller der ersten drei Jahrhunderte hersg. v. der Kirchenväter-Commission der königl. Preußischen Ak. der Wissenschaften, Leipzig 1897 ff.

Migne, J. P., *PG* = Patrologiae cursus completus, Series Graeca, Paris 1857—65

Migne, J. P., *PL* = Patrologiae cursus completus, Series Latina, Paris 1844—90

NGG = Nachrichten der königl. Gesellschaft der Wissenschaften zu Göttingen, Berlin 1860 ff.

N Jbb kl Alt = Neue Jahrbücher für das klassische Altertum, Leipzig 1898 ff.

Nouvelle Biographie universelle, Paris 1866

Der Orient, ed. by J. Fürst 1840 ff.

Orientalische Studien Th. Nöldeke gewidmet, ed. Carl Bezold, Gießen 1906

P = Corpus byzantinae historiae, ed. Labbaeus, 43 parts, Paris 1648—1711, 1819

Palestine Pilgrims' Text Society, vol. I, Itinerary from Bordeaux to Jerusalem, Bordeaux Pilgrim, trans. by A. Stewart, London 1896

Palestine Pilgrims' Text Society, vol. I, The Pilgrimage of S. Silvia of Aquitania to the Holy Places, tr. by John H. Bernard, London 1896

Pauly-Wissowa = Paulys Realencyclopädie der class. Altertumswissenschaft, hersg. von G. Wissowa, Stuttgart 1894 ff.

PSBA = Proceedings of the Society of Biblical Archaeology, London 1879 ff.

Realenc. = Herzog-Hauck, Realencyclopädie für protestantische Theologie u. Kirche, 24 vols., Leipzig 1896—1913

Religionsgeschichtliche Versuche u. Vorarbeiten, hersg. v. A. Dieterich u. R. Wünsch, Gießen 1903 ff.

UNT. 9: McCown.   9

Revue des études grecs, Paris 1888 ff.
Rh Mus = Rheinisches Museum, Leipzig 1833 ff.
SBE = Sacred Books of the East, ed. by F. Max Müller, 50 vols. 1879—1894
Sophocles, E. A., A Greek dictionary of the Roman and Byzantine periods[3], Boston 1888
Studia Biblica et Ecclesiastica, Essays chiefly in biblical and patristic criticism by members of the University of Oxford, Oxford 1885 ff.
Studi Italiani di filolog. classica, Firenze-Roma 1893 ff.
TL = Theologische Literaturzeitung, Leipzig 1876 ff.
Thuanus, Catalog. bibliothecae Thuanae a Petro et Jac. Puteanis etc., Paris 1679
TS = Texts and Studies, ed. by J. Armitage Robinson, Cambridge 1893 ff.
TU = Texte u. Untersuchungen, ed. by Adolf Harnack, Leipzig 1883 ff.
V = Bibliotheca Veterum Patrum Antiquorumque Scriptorum Eccl. ed. A. Gallandius, 14 vols. and app., Venice 1765– 81, 2 ed. 1788
Vienna Corpus = Corpus scriptorum ecclesiasticorum Latinorum, Vindobon. 1866 ff.
ZA = Zeitschrift für Assyriologie, ed. by Carl Bezold, Straßburg 1886 ff.
ZATW = Zeitschrift für die alttestamentliche Wissenschaft, ed. by D. Bernhard Stade, Gießen 1881 ff.
ZDMG = Zeitschrift der deutschen morgenländischen Gesellschaft, Leipzig 1847 ff
ZNTW = Zeitschrift für die neutestamentliche Wissenschaft, ed. by E. Preuschen Gießen 1900 ff.

2. Modern Authors.

Atkinson, James, see Sháh Námeh
Bardenhewer, Otto, Patrologie[3], Freiburg im Breisgau 1910
Benfey, Theodor, Pañtschatantra: fünf Bücher indischer Fabeln, etc., 1859
Benzinger, I., Die Bücher der Könige, Kurzer Handcommentar zum Alten Test. hersg. v. D. Karl Marti, IX Freiburg i. B. 1899
Berthelot, M., and Ruelle, C. E., Collection des anciens alchimistes grecs 2 vols., Paris 1887—88
Blaß, Fr., Grammatik des nt. Griechisch[2], Göttingen 1902, the same, 3 ed.
Blaß, Fr., Hermeneutik u. Kritik, Paläographie, Buchwesen u. Handschriftenkunde, in einleitenden u. Hilfsdisziplinen, vol. I of Müller's Handbuch de kl. Altertumswissenschaft
Blau, Ludwig, Das altjüdische Zauberwesen (Jahresbericht der Landes-Rabbiner schule in Budapest, 1897—98). Budapest 1898
Boll, Franz, Sphaera: neue griechische Texte u. Untersuchungen zur Geschicht der Sternbilder, Leipzig 1903
Bonwetsch, G. Nathanael, Die Apocalypse Abrahams, Das Testament der vierzi(Märtyrer, Leipzig 1897, in Studien zur Geschichte der Theol. u. der Kirche hersg. von N. Bonwetsch u. R. Seeberg
Bonwetsch, G. Nathanael, Hippolytus, *KVCom I*, Leipzig 1897
Bonwetsch, G. Nathanael, Hippolyts Kom. z. Hohelied auf Grund von N. Marr Ausgabe des grusinischen Textes = *TU* XXIII (NF VIII) 2
Bouché-Leclerq, A., L'Astrologie grecque, Paris 1899

Bousset, Wilhelm, Hauptprobleme der Gnosis, Göttingen 1907
Bousset, Wilhelm, Die Religion des Judentums im neutestamentlichen Zeitalter[2], Berlin 1906
Breasted, James Henry, *RTAE* = Development of Religion and Thought in Ancient Egypt, Morse Lectures, New York 1912
Budge, E. A. Wallis, The Gods of the Egyptians: or Studies in Egyptian mythology, 2 vols., Chicago 1904
Burton, Richard F., A Plain and Literal Translation of the Arabian Nights' Entertainment, now entitled The book of the Thousand Nights and a Night, with introduction, explanatory notes on the manners and customs of Moslem men and a terminal essay upon the history of the Nights. Printed by the Burton Club for private subscribers only, Bagdad ed. limited to one thousand numbered sets of which this is number 410, [1885—87]
Canaan, T., Dr. med., Aberglaube u. Volksmedicin im Lande der Bibel, Hamburg, 1914, in Abh. des Hamb. Kolonialinstituts, Bd. XX, Reihe B. Völkerkunde, Kulturgesch. u. Sprachen, Band 12
Chachanov, A. S., Očerki po Istorii Gruzinskoĭ Slovesnosti, Mosco 1895
Charles, R. H., The Book of Enoch, transl. from Professor Dillmann's Ethiopic Text, etc., Oxford 1893
Charles R. H., *APOT* = The Apocrypha and Pseudepigrapha of the Old Testament, etc. 2 vols., Oxford 1913
Clemen, Carl, Religionsgeschichtliche Erklärung des Neuen Testaments: die Abhängigkeit des ältesten Christentums von nichtjüdischen Religionen u. philosophischen Systemen, Gießen 1909 = Primitive Christianity and its Non-Jewish Sources, transl. by Robert G. Nisbet, Edinburgh 1912
Conway, Moncure Daniel, Solomon and Solomonic Literature, London-Chicago 1899
Conybeare, Frederic C., cf. Dial. Tim. and Aquila, in Anecdota Oxon.
Conybeare, Frederic C., "The Testament of Solomon", JQR XI (1898) 1—45
Cumont, Frank, The Oriental Religions in Roman Paganism, Chicago 1911
Cumont, Frank, Astrology and Religion among the Greeks and Romans, New York and London 1912
Deißmann, Adolf, Bible Studies, Edinburgh 1901
Deißmann, Adolf, *Licht* vom Osten, Tübingen 1908 = *LAE* = Light from the Ancient East, New York and London 1910
Delisle, Leop., Le cabinet des msc. de la bibliothèque imperiale, Paris 1868
Dibelius, Martin, Die Geisterwelt im Glauben des Paulus, Göttingen 1909
Dieterich, Albrecht, Abraxas: Studien zur Religionsgeschichte des spätern Altertums, Leipzig 1891
Dieterich, Albrecht, *Leid Pap* = Papyrus Magica Musei Lugdunensis Batavi quam C. Leemans edidit, etc., in Fleckeisen's Jahrbücher, Suppl. XVI, Leipzig 1887, pp. 747—829
Dieterich, Karl, *Unters* = Untersuchungen zur Geschichte der griechischen Sprache von der hellenistischen Zeit bis zum 10. Jahrh. n. Chr., Byzantinisches Archiv als Ergänzung der Byzantinischen Zeitschrift, Heft 1, Leipzig 1898

Du Cange, Carolo du Fresne, Glossarium ad scriptores mediae et infimae Graecitatis, etc., Lugduni 1688; effigies recens, Vratislaviae 1891, 2 vols. in one

Eisenmenger, Entdecktes Judentum, 2 vols., Königsberg 1711

Erman, Adolf, Die ägyptische Religion, Handbücher der königl. Museen zu Berlin, Berlin 1905 = A Handbook of Egyptian Religion, London 1907

Fabricius, Ioh. Alb., Bibliotheca Graeca, etc., 12 vols., Hamburg 1790—1809

Fabricius, Ioh. Alb., Codex pseudepigraphicus vet. test. (Bibl. III 1)

Faerber, R., König Salomo in der Tradition: ein hist.-krit. Beitrag zur Geschichte der Haggada, der Tanaiten u. Amoräer, Teil I. Diss. Straßburg, Vienna 1902

Farnell, Lewis Richard, Greece and Babylonia, a comparative sketch of Mesopotamian, Anatolian, and Hellenic religions, Edinburgh 1911

Gannurini, lob. F., S. Hilarii tractatus de mysteriis et hymni et S. Silviae Aquitanae perigrinatio ad loca sancta, Petri diaconi liber de locis sanctis, Romae 1887

Gardthausen, Viktor Emil, Griechische Palaeographie[2], 2 vols., Leipzig 1911—13

Gaster, M., Sword of Moses, London 1896; printed separately and in Journal of the Royal Asiatic Society, January, 1896, pp. 144—198, April, pp. I—XXXV

Gelzer, Heinrich, Sextus Julius Africanus u. die byzantinische Chronographie, Leipzig 1880—85

Gerhard, G. A., Untersuchungen zur Gesch. des griechischen Briefes, I. Heft, Die Anfangsformel, Inaugural-Diss. Heidelberg, Tübingen 1903, also in Philologus LXIV (NF XV) 1905

Ginzberg, Louis, Legends of the Jews, trans. from the German manuscript by Henrietta Szold, 4 vols., Philadelphia 1909—13

Gitlbauer, M., Studien zur griechischen Tachygraphie, Berlin 1903

Giltbauer, M., Die Überreste griechischer Tachygraphie in Codex Vat. Graec. 1809, in Denkschr. der kaiserl. Ak. der Wissenschaften, Philos.-hist. Cl., 1 Fasc. vol. XXVIII Vienna 1878, 2. Abt. 1—110, Plates I—XIV, 2 Fasc. Vienna 1884, 2. Abt. 1—48, Plates I—XXVIII. Also published separately

Goldschmidt, Lazarus, B Tal. — Der babylonische Talmud, etc., (Heb & German) Berlin 1897

Grünbaum, Max, Beiträge zur semitischen Sagenkunde, in ZDMG XXXI

Grünbaum, Max, Neue Beiträge zur semitischen Sagenkunde, Leiden 1893

Gruppe, Otto Friedrich, Griechische Mythologie u. Religionsgeschichte, München 1906, in Müller's Handbuch der kl. Altertumswissenschaft V 2

Gutschmid, Hermann Alfred, Freiherr von, Kleine Schriften hersg. v. Franz Rühl, 5 vols., Leipzig 1889—1894

Hardt, J., Catalogus codicum mss. biblioth. regiae Bavariae, 5 vols., Monac. 1806—12

Harnack, Adolf, Geschichte der Altchristlichen Litteratur bis Eusebius, 2 vols., Leipzig 1893

Harnack, Adolf, The Mission and Expansion of Christianity in the First Three Centuries[2], 2 vols., New York 1908

Harrison, Jane Ellen, Prolegomena to the Study of Greek Religion[2], Cambridge 1908

Heitmüller, Wilhelm, Im Namen Jesu, eine sprach- u. religionsgeschichtliche Untersuchung zum Neuen Testament, speziell zur altchristlichen Taufe, Göttingen 1903
Hemsterhuis, Thomas Magister, Ludg. Bat. 1757
Hercher, Rudolf, Epistolographi Graeci, Paris 1873
Horst, G. C., Zauberbibliothek, 6 vols., Mainz 1821—26
Hughes, H. Maldewyn, Ethics of Jewish Apocryphal Literature, London n. d.
James, Montague Rhodes, The Testament of Abraham, *TS* II 2
James, Montague Rhodes, Apocrypha Anecdota, *TS* II 3
Jannaris, A. N., Historical Greek Grammar, etc., London 1897
Jastrow, M., Jr., Die Religion Babyloniens u. Assyriens, 2 vols. in 3, Gießen 1905, 1912; sometimes referred to as German edition of The Religion of Babylonia and Assyria, Boston 1898
Kautzsch, E., Die Heilige Schrift des Alten Testaments, 2 vols., Tübingen 1909—10
Kautzsch, E., *APAT* = Die Apocryphen u. Pseudepigraphen des Alten Testaments, 2 vols., Tübingen 1900
Kemble, J. M., The Anglo-Saxon Dialogue of Salomon and Saturn, London 1848
Kenyon, F. G., *GrPBMus* = Greek Papyri in the British Museum, 5 vols., London 1893—1917
King, Charles William, The Gnostics and their Remains, Ancient and Mediaeval, London 1864
Krumbacher, Karl, *BLg* = Geschichte der Byzantinischen Literatur, von Justinian bis zum Ende des oströmischen Reiches ², München 1897, in Müller's Handbuch der kl. Altertumswissenschaft IX, 1
Krumbacher, Karl, Studien zur Legende des heil. Theodosius, in Sitzungsber. d. bay. Akad. d. Wiss., Philos., philol. u. hist. Cl., 1892, Heft 2, p. 225 ff.
Lambros, Spyr. C., Catalogue of the Greek Manuscripts on Mount Athos, 2 vols., Cambridge 1895, 1900
Lane-Poole, The Thousand and One Nights .... transl. by Edward William Lane, ed. by Stanley Lane-Poole, 1859
Letronne, M., Sur l'origine du zodiaque grec, etc., Paris 1840
Levy-Fleischer, Levy, Jacob, and Fleischer, Heinrich Leberecht, Neuhebräisches u. Chaldäisches Wörterbuch über d. Talmudim u. Midraschim, Leipzig 1876 —89
Maichell, D., Introductio ad hist. liter. de praecip. bibliothecis Parisiensibus, 2 vols., Cantab. 1721
Mathers, S. L. M., The Key of Solomon the King, trans. and ed., London 1889
Meyer, Isaak, Qabbalah: The philosophic writings of Solomon ben Yehuda ibn Gebirol, etc., Philadelphia 1888
Mills, Lawrence H., Zaraθustra, Philo, the Achaemenids and Israel, Chicago 1906
Montfaucon, Bernard de, Bibliotheca bibliothecarum mss. nov., 2 vols., Paris 1739
Montgomery, James A., *AITN* = Aramaic Incantation Texts from Nippur, University of Pennsylvania, The Museum, Publications of the Babylonian Section III, Philadelphia 1913

Moulton, James Hope, Early Religious Poetry of Persia, Cambridge 1911
Moulton, James Hope, Early Zoroastrianism, Hibbert Lectures 1912, London 1913
Moulton, James Hope, *Proleg.* = A Grammar of New Testament Greek, Vol. I Prolegomena, Edinburgh 1906
Naber, Samuel Adrian, Flavii Iosephi opera omnia post Im. Bekkerum recogn., 6 vols., Leipzig 1888—1896
Olivieri, "Indice dei codici greci delle bibliotheche Universitaria e Communale di Bologna", in Studi Ital. di filol. class. III 1895
Omont, Henri, Inventaire sommaire des msc. grecs de la bibliothèque nationale, 4 vols., Paris 1886—98
Perles, Felix, Bousset's Religion des Judentums im nt. Zeitalter kritisch untersucht, Berlin 1903
Pitra, Johannes Baptista Cardinalis, Analecta sacra et classica spicilegio solesmensi, 5 vols., Parisiis 1876—82
Pradel, Fritz, Griechische u. süditalienische Gebete, Beschwörungen u. Rezepte des Mittelalters, in "Rel.-gesch. Versuche u. Vorarbeiten" III 1907, 253—403, also separately paged
Reitzenstein, R., Poimandres, Studien zur griechisch-ägyptischen u. frühchristlichen Literatur, Leipzig 1904
Rogers, Robert William, The Religion of Babylonia and Assyria: especially in its relation to Israel, New York-Cincinnati 1908
Roscher, W. H., *Lexicon* = Ausführliches Lexikon der griech. u. röm. Mythologie, 3 vols. in 6, Leipzig 1884—1900
Sachau, Karl Eduard, Verzeichnis der syr. Handschriften der königl. Bibliothek zu Berlin, Berlin 1899
St. Claire-Tisdall, W., Sources of Islam, A Persian treatise, translated and abridged by Sir William Muir, Edinburgh 1901
Sale, George, The Koran, commonly called the Alkoran of Mohammed, translated into English from the original Arabic, with explanatory notes taken from the most approved commentators, to which is prefixed a preliminary discourse, London n. d.
Salzberger, Georg, Die Salomosage in der semitischen Literatur: Ein Beitrag zur vergleichenden Sagenkunde, I. Teil: Salomo bis zur Höhe seines Ruhmes, Diss. Heidelberg, Berlin 1907
Sayce, A. H., Hibbert Lectures 1887, Lectures on the Origin and growth of Religion as illustrated by the religion of the ancient Babylonians[4], London 1897
Scheibel, J., Das Kloster, etc., 12 vols., Stuttgart 1845—49
Schlumberger, G., Sillographie de l'empire byzantine, Paris 1884
Schmidt, Carl, Gnostische Schriften in koptischer Sprache aus dem codex Brucianus hersg., etc., in *TU* VIII. (1892) Heft 1/2
Schmidt, Carl, Koptisch-Gnostische Schriften, I. Band, *KVCom* XIII, Leipzig 1905
Schürer, Emil, *GJV* = Geschichte des jüdischen Volkes im Zeitalter Jesu Christi, 3 vols., Leipzig 1901—11 = *HJP* = A history of the Jewish People in the Time of Jesus Christ, 2nd and rev. ed., 5 vols., New York 1891

Schwab, Moyse, *Voc. Ang.* = Vocabulaire de l'angélologie d'après les mss. hebreux de la Bib. Nat., extrait des mémoires présentés par divers savants à l'Académie des insciptions et belles-lettres, 1ère Série, tome X, 2e partie, Paris 1897

Smith, William and Wace, Henry, *DCB* = Dictionary of Christian Biography, Literature, Sects and Doctrines, etc., 4 vols., Boston 1887—1897

Stade, Bernhard and Schwally, Friedrich, The book of Kings: critical ed. of the Hebrew text printed in colors, etc., Leipzig 1904, in "The sacred books of the Old Testament", ed. by Paul Haupt, Part 9

Steinschneider, Moritz, Die hebräischen Übersetzungen des Mittelalters u. die Juden als Dolmetscher, Berlin 1893

Steuernagel, Carl, Lehrbuch der Einleitung in das Alte Testament, etc., Tübingen 1912

Streane, A. W., חגיגה, a Translation of the treatise Chagigah from the Babylonian Talmud, Cambridge 1891

Surenhusius, G., Mishna: sive totius Hebraeorum juris, ritum, etc., 6 vols. in 3, Amstel. 1698—1703

Tamborñino, Julius, De antiquorum daemonismo, in "Relig.-gesch. Versuche u. Vorarb." 1908—09, Heft 3

Thompson, R. Campbell, The Devils and Evil Spirits of Babylonia, etc., 2 vols., London 1903—04 (Luzac's "Semitic Text and Translation Series" XIV and XV)

Thompson, R. Campbell, Semitic Magic: its origins and development, London 1908

Thumb, A., Die griechische Sprache im Zeitalter des Hellenismus, Straßburg 1901

Thumb, A., Handbuch der neugr. Volkssprache 2, Straßburg 1910

Vasiljev, Alex., Anecdota Graeco-Byzantina, ed. by S. A. Sokolovsky, 1893

Vogt, Fr., Die deutschen Dichtungen von Salomon u. Markolf, Halle 1880

Walters, H. B., Catalogue of the Bronzes in the British Museum, London 1899

Wardrop, Margery, "Life of St. Nino", in Studia Biblica V 1908

Weber, Otto, Dämonenbeschwörungen bei den Babyloniern u. Assyrern, in "Der Alte Orient", VII 4, Leipzig 1906

Weil, G., The Bible, the Koran, and the Talmud; or Biblical Legends of the Mussulmans, compiled from Arabic sources, and compared with Jewish traditions, transl. from the German, London 1846

Wellhausen, J., Reste arabischen Heidentums gesammelt u. erläutert 2, Berlin 1897

Wendland, Paul, Die Hellenistisch-römische Kultur in ihrer Beziehung zu Judentum u. Christentum, Tübingen 1907, in Handbuch zum Neuen Testament I 2

Wessely, Carl, Ephesia grammata, Jahresber. des Franz-Joseph-Gymnasiums in Wien 1886

Wessely, Carl, Griechische Zauberpapyri von Paris u. London, in Denkschriften der kaiserl. Ak. der Wissenschaften, philos.-hist. Classe, vol. XXXVI Part 2, Wien, 1888, pp. 27—208

Wessely, Carl, Neue griechische Zauberpapyri, in Denkschriften der kaiserl. Ak. d. Wiss., philos.-hist. Cl., vol. XLII, Part II, Wien 1894

Wiedemann, K. Alfred, Magie u. Zauberei im alten Ägypten, in "Der alte Orient" VI 4, Leipzig 1905

Wünsch, R., Antike Fluchtafeln, in Lietzmann's "Kleine Texte für theologische Vorlesungen u. Übungen", 20, Bonn 1907

Wünsch, R., Sethianische Verfluchungstafeln aus Rom, Leipzig 1898

Ziemann, F., De epistularum graecarum formulis sollemnibus (Diss. phil. Halenses XVIII), 1911

Zimmern, Heinrich, Babylonische Hymnen u. Gebete in Auswahl, in "Der alte Orient" VII 3, Leipzig 1905

ΔΙΑΘΗΚΗ ΣΟΛΟΜΩΝΤΟΣ

TEXTS

WITH

CRITICAL APPARATUS

Sigla et compendia in apparatu critico et in textu adhibita

Uncis rotundis ( ) circumduxi vocabula vel litteras, quae in codice compendio scripta sunt, velut ($ἡμέρα$) = $δ$.

Uncis rotundis ( ) in apparatu critico circumdedi numeros sectionum interpretationis a Conybeare scriptae.

Uncis fractis 〈 〉 circumdedi ea quae in codice perierunt vel a scriptore omissa sunt.

Uncum fractum < post vocabulum posui cuius terminatio a scribente omissa est.

His signis ⌜ ⌝ inclusi lectiones in suspicionem vocatas, ubicumque errorem primarium vel interpolationem praesuppono.

Asteriscu * in textu apparatuque insignivi manuscriptorum editionumque initium et paginarum numeros.

+ vel add. = addit, addunt
— vel om. = omittit, omittunt
cf. = confere(ndum)
cod(d). = codex, codices
conj. = conjicit, -unt (quidam scriptores recentiores)
cor(r). = corrigit, -unt
ego = proponit editor
exp. = explicit, -unt
f., ff. = folium, folia
inc. = incipit, -iunt
ins. = insere, -it

i. q. = idem quod
l. = lege(ndum) vel linea
leg. = legit, -unt
MS (ms.) = codex manuscriptus
MSS (mss.) = codices manuscripti
n. = nota
pr. = praemittit, -unt
rec. = recensio
s., ss. = sequens, sequentes
tr. = transpone(ndum), -it, -unt
v. = vide(ntur)

A = Rec. A, i. q., MSS H1L
B = Rec. B, i. q., MSS PQ(N)
C = Rec. C, i. q., MSS STUVW
C⁰ = narratio altera de Onoskelu ex rec. C
D = Dionysii monasterii (Athos) cod. 132, cf. supra p. 10
E = Monasterii Sancti Saba (Hierosol.) cod. 290, cf. App. infra p. 125
H = Holkham Hall, cod. 99, cf. p. 11

I = Bib. Nat., Suppl. grec cod. 500, cf. supra p. 12
L = Harl. cod. 5596, cf. supra p. 13
N = Monasterii Sancti Saba (Hierosol.) cod. 422, cf. App. infra p. 112
P = Bib. Nat., Anc. fonds grec, cod. 38, cf. supra p. 15
Q = Andreae monasterii cod. 73, cf. supra p. 18
S = Vind. Phil.-graec. cod. 108, cf. p. 18

T = Harl. cod. 5596 fragmenta, cf. p. 18
U = Bib. Ambros. cod. 1030, cf. p. 20
V = Bib. Bonon. Acad. cod. 3632, cf. p. 21
W = Bib. Nat., Anc. fonds grec, cod. 2419, cf. p. 25
c = corrector

d = de li daemonis, C^d, cf. supra p. 19
o = narratio alt. de Onoskelu, C^o, cf. p. 19
r = phylacterium, H^r, L^r, C^r, cf. pp. 19, 25, et n. 1
s = descriptio altera de XII signis, cf. p. 23 et n. 1

Bn = Bornemann, versio, cf. Bibliographiam
Bncn = Bornemann, "Conjectanea"
Cr = Conybeare
Fl = Fleck

Fü = Fürst
Is = Istrin
Mg = Migne
tr = versio, velut Mgtr = versio in Migne, *Patrologia graeca*, vol. 122

ΔΙΑΘΗΚΗ ΣΟΛΟΜΩΝΤΟΣ

HIPQ Εὐλογητὸς εἶ, κύριε ὁ θεός, ὁ δοὺς τῷ Σολομῶντι τὴν ἐξουσίαν ταύτην· σοὶ δόξα καὶ κράτος εἰς τοὺς αἰῶνας· ἀμήν.

PQ I. Καὶ ἰδοὺ οἰκοδομουμένου τοῦ ναοῦ πόλεως Ἱερουσαλὴμ

5 HI I. Καὶ ἰδοὺ ἀνοικοδομουμένης τῆς Ἱερουσαλὴμ καὶ ἐργαζομένων τῶν τεχνιτῶν, ἓν παιδίον ἔχων προθυμίαν μεγίστην ἐπὶ τὴν τοῦ ναοῦ οἰκοδομήν, ὃς ἐποίει τοὺς τεχνίτας προθυμοτέρους πρὸς ἐρ-

L I. Βουλόμενος ὁ Σολομῶν υἱὸς Δαυεὶδ ἀνακτίσαι καὶ οἰκοδομῆσαι τὴν Σιών, κελεύσας κατὰ τόπον καὶ κατὰ χώραν τοῦ συναχ-
10 θῆναι τεχνίτας ἄνδρας τοῦ ἐργάζεσθαι εἰς τὸν ναὸν τοῦ θεοῦ, μέσον δὲ τῶν τεχνιτῶν ἦτον ἕνας νέος πολλὰ ἄξιος καὶ πολλὴν προθυμίαν ἔχων κατὰ τῆς οἰκοδομῆς τοῦ θείου ναοῦ· διὸ καὶ ἀπὸ τοῦ βασιλέως

VW I. Ἐργαζομένων δὲ τῶν τεχνιτῶν εἰς τὴν τοῦ ναοῦ οἰκοδομὴν ἦν τις ἐκεῖσε παῖς νέος ἄλκιμος σφόδρα καὶ ἀρχιτεχνίτης, ὃν
15 ἠγάπα ὁ βασιλεὺς πάνυ διὰ τὸ εἶναι αὐτὸν φρένιμον καὶ ἐπιεικῆ.

Titulum primarium eruere non possum: v. conspectum titulorum codd. mss. infra, pp. 98* s. Benedictionem vel doxologiam scr. mss. HIPQ; app. crit. v. infra, p. 99*.
Parallela ad c. I cf. infra in ms. D II 1—18.

MSS PQ = Rec. B: c. 1, l. 4 inc. ms. P in f. 1ʳ; Fl p. 113, Mg col. 1316; ms. Q in f. 11ʳ; Is p. 29. (2) ⟨Κ⟩αὶ Is (Q) | οἰκονομουμένου P | Ἱεροσολύμων P, Ἱεροσολὴμ Q

MSS HI = Rec. A: c. I, l. 5 inc. ms. H in f. 1ʳ, ms. I in f. 78ʳ 6 ἦν γὰρ παιδίον ἓν ἔχων H | ἔχον Is (p. 29 n. 1) | ἐπὶ τὴν οἰκ. τ. ναοῦ H | 7 ὃς ... ἐργασίαν I, καὶ ἦν διάγων ὥστε ποιοῦν τ. τεχ. πρὸς τὴν ἐργ. προθύμως H

MS L: c. I, l. 8 inc. ms. L in f. 8ʳ col. 1

MSS VW = Rec. C: c. 1, l. 13 inc. hae lineae ms. V in f. 436ᵛ, ms. W in f. 266ᵛ fin. initium mss. VW v. infra, Rec. C, p. 76* 14 ἦν δέ τις V
15 ἀγαπᾶ V | ἐπιεική V, ἐπιοικὴν W

6* τὸ παιδίον καὶ Ὀρνίας I, 1—2

PQ καὶ ἐργαζομένων τῶν τεχνιτῶν ἐν αὐτῷ, 2. ἤρχετο ὁ Ὀρνίας τὸ δαιμονικὸν κατὰ ἡλίου δυσμὰς καὶ * ἐλάμβανε τὸ ἥμισυ τοῦ μισθοῦ

HI γασίαν, καὶ οἱ ἀκούοντες ἔχαιρον πάντες ἐπὶ τῇ τοῦ παιδὸς προθυμίᾳ. ἦν δὲ ἀγαπώμενος ἄγαν παρ' ἐμοῦ Σολομῶντος, καὶ
5 ἐλάμβανε παρὰ πάντας τοὺς τεχνίτας διπλοῦν τὸν μισθὸν καὶ τὰ σιτίδια διπλᾶ. καὶ ἐπέμενον χαίρων καὶ εὐφραινόμενος ἐγὼ Σολομῶν καὶ εὐλογῶν τὸν θεὸν ἐπὶ τῇ τοῦ ναοῦ οἰκοδομῇ.
2. Φθονήσαντος δὲ τοῦ δαίμονος ἐπὶ τὴν τοῦ παιδὸς προθυμίαν, ἤρχετο καθ' ἑκάστην ἡμέραν ὁ δαίμων καὶ * ἐλάμβανε
10 τὸ ἥμισυ κτλ.

L πολλὰ ἦν ἀγαπώμενος, καὶ τὰ σιτία καὶ τὸν μισθὸν διπλοῦν ἐλάμβανεν ὑπὲρ πάντας τοὺς τεχνίτας· καὶ ἔχαιρεν ὁ βασιλεὺς ἐπὶ τὴν τοῦ παιδὸς προθυμίαν.
2. Φθονηθεὶς δὲ ὁ νεώτερος ὑπὸ τοῦ δαίμονος, ἤρχετο ἀόρατος
15 VW ἔπεμπε δὲ αὐτὸν ἀπὸ τῆς τραπέζης αὐτοῦ βρώματα καθ' ἑκάστην ὁ * βασιλεὺς καί ἐν τῷ δείπνῳ ἀπεδίδου αὐτὸν τὸν μισθὸν ἐπὶ τὸ διπλάσιον.
2. Τοῦτο δὲ τὸ παιδάριον περὶ ἡλίου δυσμὰς ἐπιέζετο ὑπὸ χαλεποῦ δαίμονος Ὀρνίου λεγομένου. ἐλάμβανε δὲ τὸ τοιοῦτον δαιμόνιον

MSS PQ = Rec. B. 1 τεχνιτῶν ἐν αὐτῷ Q: τεχν., ἐν αὐτοῦς P, τεχ. ἐν αὐτοῖς Fl, τεχ., ἐν αὐτοῖς BnMgtr | § 2. ἤρχετο ego: ἔρχεται (Fl) in ἤρχεται cor. P^c, ⟨ἔ⟩ρχετο Is(Q)   2 δαιμονικὸν B: in δαιμόνιον corr. P^cFl | δυσμᾶς Q, pr. τὰς P, δεσμὰς (δυσμάς) Fl
*MSS HIPQ = Recc. AB. 2 τ. μισθοῦ — A

MSS HI = Rec. A. 3 οἱ ... προθυμίᾳ I: τοὺς ἀκούοντας ὥστε χαίρειν πάντας ἐπὶ τὴν τ. π. προθυμίαν H   4 δὲ καὶ I | ἠγαπιμένος H | ἄγαν I: λίαν H | παρ' ἐμοῦ I: ὑπὸ τοῦ H   5 διπλὸν I   6 σιτίδια conj. Diels: σιτείδια I, σιτήδια Is, στατίδια H | ἐπέμενον ego: ἐπέμενεν H, ἤμουν I | καὶ ... Σολ. — H   7 τὴν τ. ν. οἰκοδομήν H
§ 2. 8 ἐπὶ — H   9 ἡμέραν ὁ δαιμ. — H | * cf. textum rec. B, l. 2
10 post ἥμισυ textus recensionis A cum rec. B includitur

MS L. 11 πολλὰ ἦν ego: πολλὴν ms.   12 ἔχαιρον ms.

MSS VW = Rec. C. 15. 16 αὐτὸν mss.: l. αὐτῷ   16 * W f. 267^r
§ 2. 19 δαίμονος: δαιμονίου V | Ὀρν. λεγ.: ὀνόματι Ὀρνίου V

HIPQ ⌈τοῦ πρωτομαΐστορος παιδαρίου ὄντος⌉ καὶ τὰ ἥμισυ σιτία. *
καὶ ἐθήλαζε τὸν ἀντίχειρον τῆς δεξιᾶς αὐτοῦ χειρὸς * ἐφ' ἑκάστην ἡμέραν. καὶ ἐλεπτύνετο τὸ παιδίον ὅπερ ἦν ἀγαπώμενον
ὑπ' ἐμοῦ σφόδρα.

5 L καὶ ἐλάμβανε τὸ ἥμισυ τῶν μισθῶν τοῦ παιδὸς ὅτι ἄρα ἐπεδίδοντο αὐτῷ καθ' ἑκάστην ἑσπέραν. μετὰ τὸ ἀποδιδόναι καὶ
ἀφεθῆναι τοῦ ἔργου ἤρχετον τὸ πονηρὸν πνεῦμα καὶ [ἠλάλαζε·
εἶτα λέγει ὁ ἀναγινώσκων ἐκ τρίτου μεγαλόφωνος ἐπάνου τοῦ *
ὀχλουμένου· εἶτα] ἐλάμβανε τὸν τοῦ παιδὸς δεξιᾶς χειρὸς δάκτυ-
10 λον καὶ ἐβύζανεν αὐτόν. *

VW τὸ ἥμισυ μέρος τοῦ μισθοῦ αὐτοῦ ὃν ἐλάμβανε παρὰ τοῦ
βασιλέως καθεμίαν ἡμέραν. καὶ οὐ μόνον τοῦτο ἐποίει ἀλλ' ἔτεμε
καὶ τὸν δάκτυλον τῆς δεξιᾶς αὐτοῦ χειρὸς καὶ ἐξεθήλαζε τὸν
ἀντίχειρον τοσοῦτον ὥστε τὸ παιδάριον ἀσθενεῖν καθ' ἑκάστην
15 ἡμέραν καὶ λεπτύνεσθαι.

MSS HIPQ = Recc. AB. 1 τοῦ ... ὄντος: om. A, l. fortasse ἑνὸς τῶν
παιδαρίων μου, cf. D II 2 | πρωτομαϊστόρον Q | παιδαρίον ὄντος Q, conj.
Bn: παιδαρίου, οὕτως P | κ. τὰ ἥμ. σιτ. B: τῶν σιτείων αὐτοῦ I. τοῦ σιτείου
αὐτοῦ H | * H f. 1ᵛ   2 τ. ἀντίχειρα ... χειρὸς ἐθήλαζεν B | ἐθήλαζεν
ἐν I per geminationem | * I f. 78ᵛ | ἐφ' HQ: ἀφ' P | ἐφ' ἑκάστην ἡμέραν H: — I, ἐφ' ἑκάστης ἡμέρας PQ   3 παιδιον A: παιδάριον B | ὅπερ
... αὐτῷ (§ 3, p. 8*, l. 2): — Q   4 ὑπ' (ὑπὲρ H) ἐμοῦ σφόδρα A: παρὰ τοῦ
βασιλέως πάνυ P

MS L. 5 τὸ μισθίον ms. | ὅτι ego: εἴτι ms, l. forte ἅτινα | ἐπιδίδον
τὸ ms.   6 ἑκάστῃ ἑσπέρα ms.   8 * f. 8ʳ²   10 ἐβύζανεν: in marg. lat. scr.
man. rec. sugebat | * a sect. 3 ms. L cum rec. A (mss. HI) includitur, cf.
p. 8*, l. 1

MSS VW = Rec. C.   11 ὅν: ὅ mss.   12 καθεμίαν ego: καθὴν vel
καθεμ- mss. l. fortasse καθ' ἑκάστην   13 καὶ (1°) — V | δάκτυλον ... τοσοῦτον: δεξιὸν δακτ. ἤγουν τὸν ἀντίχειραν, καὶ ἐξεθηλ. W | καὶ (2°) — V
14 ἀσθενεῖ V | καὶ ante καθ' ponit V

HILPQ 3. Ἐγὼ δὲ Σολομῶν ἐν μιᾷ τῶν ἡμερῶν ἀνακρίνας τὸ παιδάριον εἶπον αὐτῷ· »οὐχὶ ὑπὲρ πάντας τοὺς τεχνίτας τοὺς ἐργαζομένους ἐν τῷ ναῷ τοῦ θεοῦ σὲ ἠγάπησα καὶ ἐπεδίδουν σοι ἐν διπλῷ τὸν μισθὸν

5 VW 3. Καὶ δὴ ἐν μιᾷ τῶν ἡμερῶν ὁ βασιλεὺς Σολομῶν ⟨ἰδὼν⟩ καὶ ⟨ἐκπετάσας⟩ τὰς χεῖρας εἰς τὸν οὐρανὸν εἶπεν· »θεὲ θεῶν καὶ μόνε βασιλεῦ βασιλέων, ἀποκάλυψόν μοι τὴν τοῦ παιδὸς πᾶσαν βάσανον διὰ τὸ ὄνομά σου τὸ φοβερὸν καὶ πανάγιον.« ἦλθε δὲ φωνὴ λέγουσα· »πρόσειπε εἰς τὸ δεξιὸν οὖς τοῦ παιδὸς
10 τάδε· »δαφνών· μαγατά· παλιπούλ·« ἔγγραφον δὲ ποίησον ἐν ἀγεννήτῳ χάρτῃ ταῦτα· *** καὶ παραδοὺς πυρὶ ὑποκάπνισον αὐτῷ, ἔχων δὲ καὶ βοτάνην τὴν λεγομένην κισσὸν καὶ λίθον ἰασαφήτην ἐν τῇ χειρί σου· καὶ ἐν πέμπτῃ ὥρᾳ τῆς νυκτὸς ἐρώτησον τὸν παῖδαν, καὶ ἀναγγελεῖ σοι ἅπαντα.« ταῦτα ἀκούσας
15 Σολομῶν καὶ ποιήσας ἀπαραλλάκτως ἠρώτησε τὸν παῖδαν. *

MSS HILPQ = Recc. AB. § 3. (3) 1 ὁ δὲ βασιλεὺς σολομῶν LP | ἐν: καλέσας P | ἐν ... ἡμερῶν: ὁρῶν τὸν νεότερον ὃν ἠγάπα ὁ βασιλεὺς σφόδρα ἐν ἀθυμίᾳ κατέσχον σκυθρωπάζων καὶ τῇ ὄψει παρελαγμένος ἐκάλεσεν αὐτὸν L | ἀνακρίνας ... αὐτῷ A: τὸν παῖδα ἐπηρώτησεν αὐτὸν λέγων P, καὶ ἀνακριν. οὕτως εἰπών· τί ὅτι σὺ λυπούμενον βλέπω σε L   2 ὑπερ A: παρὰ B   3 τ. ἐργαζ. ... θεοῦ — L | ἐργαζ. ... ναῷ in spatio puro a prim. man. relicto adscr. P^c 4 ἀγαπῶ B, ποθῶ L | καὶ διπλὰ τὰ μισθία καὶ τὰ σιτία ἐπιδίδωσι L | κ. ἐπεδίδου(⟨ν⟩ James) σὺ (l. σοι) H, κ. δίδωμί σοι I, διδούς σοι P (-σοι) Q | ἐν διπλῷ IB: διπλοῦν H | τοὺς μισθοὺς B

MSS VW = Rec. C. § 3. 6 ἰδών, ἐκπετάσας supplevit James   7 βασιλεὺς τῶν βασ., ἀποκαλ. με πᾶσαν βασ. τὴν τ. παιδ. V   9 καὶ ταῦτα εἰπὼν ἦλθε φωνὴ κτλ. W | παιδός: παιδάριον V   10 ἔγραφον W | * V f. 437^r 11 χάρτην mss. | *** omitto sigilla magica mihi insensibilia   12 κισσὸν ego: κύσαν mss.   13 ἰασαμφήτην V, l. ἰάσπιδα? | ἐν πέμπτῃ ... νυκτὸς W: τῆς νυκτὸς ὥρα ē V   14 ἀνάγκελή V, ἀνηγγέλη W   15 * a sect. 4 mss. VW (rec. C) cum recc. AB includuntur

3—5 Σολομών καὶ τὸ παιδίον 9*

ιὶ τὰ σιτία· καὶ πῶς ἐφ᾽ ἑκάστην * ἡμέραν λεπτύνῃ;« 4. τὸ δὲ
αιδίον εἶπεν· »δέομαί σου, βασιλεῦ, ἄκουσόν μου τὰ συμβάντα
ιι. μετὰ τὸ ἀπολυθῆναι ἡμᾶς ἐκ τοῦ ἔργου τοῦ ναοῦ τοῦ θεοῦ
ιτὰ ἡλίου δυσμὰς ἐν τῷ ἀναπαύεσθαί * με, ἔρχεται πονηρὸν
ιιμόνιον * καὶ ἀφαιρεῖ ἀπ᾽ ἐμοῦ τὸ ἥμισυ τοῦ μισθοῦ μου
ιὶ τὸ ἥμισυ τῶν σιτίων μου, καὶ λαμβάνει μου τὴν δεξιὰν χεῖρα καὶ
ηλάζει μου τὸν ἀντίχειρον. καὶ ἰδοὺ * θλιβομένης μου τῆς
υχῆς τὸ σῶμά μου λεπτύνεται καθ᾽ ἑκάστην ἡμέραν.
5. Καὶ ταῦτα ἀκούσας ἐγὼ ὁ βασιλεὺς Σολομῶν εἰσῆλθον εἰς

MSS HILPQ = Recc. AB. 1 σιτία IB: συτίδια H, + διπλάσιον B | κ.
ὅς: σὺ δὲ L, καὶ — P | ἐφ᾽ ἑκάστης ἡμέρας (τε P) καὶ ὥρας B | * Mg
|17 | λεπτύνῃ P: λεπτύνης A (-εις) Q
MSS HILPQVW = Recc. ABC. § 4. (4) l. 1 τὸ δὲ (καὶ τὸ I) παιδίον
l: τὸ δὲ παιδάριον B, ὁ δὲ νεότερος L, ὁ δὲ W, ἡ δὲ V   2 εἶπεν HIVW ·
ιη πρὸς τὸν βασιλέα B, ὑπολαβὼν τῷ βασιλεῖ λέγει L, pr. ἡσυχῇ καὶ πραεία
ῇ φωνῇ C | δέομαι... μοι: ἄκουσον, ὦ θεῖε βασιλεῦ C | βασιλεῦ: — L.
·. δέσποτα HI | μου A: — PC, δὴ Q | τὰ συμβάντα μοι A: τὰ συμβ. τῷ
ῥ.παιδαρίῳ Q, pr. καὶ ἐρῶσί (l. σοι) πάντα I, + καὶ ἐρῶσιν πάντα H, + ὁ
νόμενος καὶ στιγνάζοντα L, + rubricam ἀπόκρισις τοῦ παιδὸς πρὸς σολο-
ῶντα περὶ τοῦ δαίμονος τοῦ ὀρνίαν H | post τὰ συμβ. in spatio puro mi-
ιre a man. prim. relicto (om. μοι) adscr. καὶ ὅσα ἔχει τὸ παιδάριον P^c   3 μετὰ
ιν ἀπόλυσιν ἡμῶν HI | ἡμᾶς: + πάντας B | ἐκ: ἀπὸ B, — C | τῆς
ιγασίας H | τὸν τοῦ ναοῦ ἔργον (— τοῦ θεοῦ) L | τοῦ θεοῦ τῶν ναῶν V
ιῦ (3°) — W   4 καὶ μετὰ HI | δυσμὰς Q | ἐν: μετὰ H, — V | ἐν
. με: καὶ ὀψίας γενομένης L | ἀναπανθῆναι HI | * H f. 2^r | μοι P |
ἔρχεται V | πον. δαιμ. LC: πον. (-ῶν H) πνεῦμα H1, ἕν τῶν πονηρῶν
ιμονίων (-όνων Q) B   5 * P f. 1^V | καὶ ἀφαιρ.... ἀντίχειρον (l. 7):
ιὶ τὰ ἥμισυ τῶν μισθόν μου λαμβάνων· καὶ μετὰ ταῦτα θυλάζοντά μοι (in
arg. lat. scr. man. rec. θηλάζοντα, sugendum) τὸν δάκτυλον τῆς δεξιᾶς χειρὸς
υς πρωί L | ἀφαίρεται HI, διαφερητε (l. διαφαιρεῖται) V | ἀπ᾽ ἐμοῦ — C
καὶ (1°)... μου: καὶ τὰ ἥμισυ σιτία B | καὶ (2°)... χεῖρα: εἶτα λαμβ.
ιὶ τ. δεξ. μου χεῖρα B, — C | κ. θηλαζ.: θηλαζ. δὲ (— V) καὶ C   7 τὸν
ντίχειρά μου B, τὸν τῆς δεξιᾶς μου χειρὸς (+ τὸν V) ἀντίχειραν C | καὶ
ού: ἐκ δὲ τοῦ φοβοῦ L | * L f. 8^v1 | θλιβ.... ψυχῆς LC: θλιβ. τ. ψυχ.
ου HI, θλιβομένη μου ἡ ψυχή B, + οὕτως W, + καὶ οὗτος V, + οὕτω B
ου — LC   8 λεπτ.: — H, λεπτύνεσθαι C | καθ᾽: ἐφ᾽ I | ἡμέραν: + ὡς
ιᾶς, δέσποτα, καὶ οὐκ ἔχω που δρᾶσαι καὶ ἀποστὰν (sic) ἀπ᾽ ἐμοῦ τὸ πο-
ιρὸν καὶ κάκιστον δαιμόνιον, τοιούτως (ω supra o scr. prim. man.) πάσχον-
ος) L
§ 5. (5) l. 9 Καὶ — LC | ἐγὼ — L | ὁ β. Σολ. IL: Σολ. ὁ βασ. H,
βασ. — BC | εἰσῆλθα Q, εἰσῆλθε L, ἦλθον HI | ἐν τῷ ναῷ C | εἰς
.. αὐτῷ (p. 10, l. 2); ἐκ τὸν ναὸν τοῦ θεοῦ εἰς τὸν οἶκον αὐτοῦ· ἐν λύπῃ
ολλ(ῇ) καὶ ἐξ ὕλης τῆς ψυχῆς ἐξομολογούμενος καὶ προσευχόμενος L

τὸν ναὸν τοῦ θεοῦ καὶ ἐδεήθην ἐξ ὅλης μου τῆς ψυχῆς ἐξομολογούμενος αὐτῷ νύκτα καὶ ἡμέραν ὅπως παραδοθῇ ὁ δαίμων εἰς τὰς χεῖράς μου καὶ ἐξουσιάσω αὐτόν. 6. καὶ ἐγένετο ἐν τῷ προσεύχεσθαί με πρὸς τὸν θεὸν τοῦ οὐρανοῦ καὶ τῆς γῆς ἐδόθη
5 μοι * παρὰ κυρίου Σαβαὼθ διὰ Μιχαὴλ τοῦ ἀρχαγγέλου δακτυλίδιον ἔχον σφραγῖδα γλυφῆς λίθου τιμίου· 7. καὶ εἶπέ μοι·
»λάβε, Σολομῶν υἱὸς Δαυείδ, δῶρον ὃ ἀπέστειλέ σοι κύριος ὁ θεὸς ὁ ὕψιστος Σαβαώθ, καὶ συγκλείσεις πάντα τὰ δαιμόνια τά τε θηλυκὰ καὶ ἀρσενικὰ καὶ * δι᾿ αὐτῶν οἰκοδομήσεις
10 τὴν Ἰερουσαλὴμ ἐν τῷ τὴν σφραγῖδα ταύτην σε φέρειν τοῦ θεοῦ.«

MSS HILPQVW = Recc. ABC. 1 καὶ — V | ἐδεόμην C | μου — A | τῆς — IW | ἐξομολ. αὐτῷ (τὸν θεὸν H, — L) W: τῶ θεῶ καὶ ἐξομολογούμην αὐτῷ C, — B   2 νύκταν κ. ἡμερ. HL, νύκτα κ. ἡμέρα I, νυκτὸς κ. ἡμέρας B, νυκτὸς κ. ἡμέρος V, compendiis scr. W | ὅπως: πῶς Q | παραδώσει κύριος ὁ θεὸς τὸ δαιμόνιον εἰς κτλ. L | παραδοθῇ: παραδοθεῖν H, + μοι B, + με V   3 τὰς — P | μου: αὐτοῦ L, — Q | ἐξουσιάζω Q, ἐπεξουσιάσει L | § 6. καὶ: κ om. W in literis rubricandis | ἐγένετο: ἐν τὸ γένετο H   4 με: om. sed προσεύχεσθαί scr. I, μοι P, αὐτὸν L, + καθ᾿ ἑκάστην ἡμέραν καὶ νύκταν C | πρὸς τὸν θεὸν HI: τὸν κύριον L, τῶ θεῶ C, — B | τοῦ ... γῆς ILC: — B, κ. τ. γῆς — H, + μετὰ συντετριμμένης καρδίας ἐξ ὅλης τῆς ψυχῆς αὐτοῦ L   5 μοι: αὐτῶ L | * I f. 79ʳ | παρὰ κυρ. Σαβ.: — L, + χάρις B | διὰ ... Ἰερουσαλὴμ (l. 9 f): σφραγῆς· ὑπὸ μιχαὴλ τοῦ ἀρχαγγέλου· λέγων· ποίει οὕτως σολομῶν καὶ δῶς αὐτῶ τὸ δακτυλίδιον· τιμιώτερον εἰσὶν λίθου τιμίου L, add. L glossam de anuli signo, v. infra, p. 100* et fig. p. 101* | ἀρχαγγ. αὐτοῦ P | δακτύλιον C   6 ἔχον IQBn: ἔχων HPW, ἔχω V | σφραγῖδας W, compendio scr. forte idem V | γλυφῆς: κολαπτὴν I | λίθου τιμίου: λίθιδος τιμὴν C, pr. ἐκ B, add. glossam de anuli signo Hl, v. infra, p. 100* | § 7. μοι: μου P, με Q   7 Σολ.: + βασιλεῦ P, βασιλεὺς Q | υἱὲ VW | δῶρον — HI | δ HIP: ὃν Q, ὕπερ C | ἀποστέλλει I, ἀπέστιλάν σι V | ὁ θεὸς HB: — IC | κυρ. Σαβ. ὑψ. Ἰσραὴλ C   8 ὁ ὑψ. — Q | καὶ συγκλ.: ἵνα συγκλείσις C | πάντας τοὺς δαίμονας Q | δαιμ. τῆς γῆς P 9 τά τε ... ἀρσεν. (ἀσερν. Η) HI: τὰ ἀρσηνηκὰ κ. θυλικὰ V, — W, ἄρσενα κ. θήλεα B   9 καὶ δεῖ μετ᾿ αὐτῶν ἀνοικοδομῆσαι P | Q f. 11ᵛ | δι᾿: μετ᾿ Q | ἀνοικοδομήσεις QV   10 τὴν Ἰερουσ.: ναὸν κυρίου τοῦ θεοῦ σου, add. glossam de anuli signo C, v. infra, p. 101* | ἐν . . θεοῦ ego: τὴν σφραγῖδα ταύτην σε φέριν τοῦ θεοῦ I, φέρειν σε τ. σφρ. ταυτ. τ. θ. (add. glossam de anuli signo, v. infra, p. 100*) B, τῇ σφραγίδῃ ταύτη ᾗ ἔδωκέ σοι ὁ θεός H, ἐν δὲ τὸ τὴν σφρ. ταυτ. φορεῖν cum sequentibus conjuncta C, λαβὼν ὁ σολομῶν τὴν σφρ. cum sequentibus conjuncta L

8. Καὶ περιχαρὴς γενόμενος ὕμνουν καὶ ἐδόξαζον τὸν θεὸν τοῦ οὐρανοῦ καὶ τῆς γῆς· καὶ τῇ ἐπαύριον ἐκέλευσα ἐλθεῖν πρός με τὸ παιδίον καὶ ἀπέδωκα αὐτῷ τὴν σφραγῖδα, 9. καὶ εἶπον αὐτῷ· ›ἐν ᾗ ἂν ὥρᾳ ἐπιστῇ σοι τὸ δαιμόνιον ῥῖψον τὸ δακτυλίδιον τοῦτο εἰς τὸ στῆθος τοῦ δαίμονος λέγων αὐτῷ· ›δεῦρο καλεῖ σε * ὁ Σολομῶν,‹ καὶ δρομαίως παραγίνου πρός με μηδὲν λογισάμενος ὧν μέλλει σοι φοβῆσαι.‹ 10. Καὶ ἰδοὺ κατὰ τὴν εἰθισμένην ὥραν ἦλθεν ὁ Ὀρνίας τὸ

MSS HILPQVW = Recc. ABC. § 8. (6) l. 1 Καὶ — LV | περιχ.... ἐπαυρ.: εὐχαριστήσας κύριον τὸν θεὸν τ. οὐρ. εἴτις (l. ὅστις) εἰσακούει τὴν δέησιν καὶ προσευχὴν τῶν προσευχομένων καὶ τὸ ζητούμενον, οὐκ ἔστιν ὡς (ἔστην ἕως) L | γενομ.: + ἐγὼ σολομῶν B, + (ὁ βασιλεὺς H) ἐπὶ τοῦτο (τοῦτον H) πάλιν HI | κ. ἐδοξ. — HI | τὸν — P | τοῦ θεοῦ V 2 τοῦ ... γῆς — HI | παύριον W | ἐκελ. ἐλθ. (ἐωσθὴν H, 1. ἐπελθεῖν?) ... παιδ. (l. 3) HI: ἐκελ. τὸν παῖδαν (τὸ παιδάριον V̇) V̈W, ἐκάλεσα τὸ παῖδα (νεὸν L) BL 3 καὶ — L | ἀπέδωτο L, ἐπέδωκα P | αὐτῷ: — L, αὐτὸν W | τὴν σφραγῖδα A: τὸ δακτυλίδιον B, τὸ δακτύλιον (-ίῳ V) VW, + ταύτην I, + τοῦ θεοῦ L | § 9. κ. εἶπον αὐτῷ IPW (αὐτὸν) H (εἶπεν) L: — Q, κ. φήσας αὐτῷ V, + λάβε τοῦτο καὶ B 4 ἐν ... δαίμονος (l. 5): πορεύου ἐπὶ τὸ ἔργων σου· μετὰ δὲ ἀφεθῆναι τοῦ ἔργου καὶ ἑσπέρα⟨ν⟩ ἤδη γενέσθαι καὶ ἐλθόν⟨τος⟩ τοῦ πονηροῦ πνεύματος ὅπως ποιῆσαι τὸ πρότερον· ῥῆψε τὸ δακτυλίδιον ἐπάνω τούτου L | ἐν ἴα ὥρ < V | ὥραν H | ἐπιστῇ σοι: ἐπιστήσει H, ἐπεστή σοι I, ἔλθῃ πρός σε B, σοι — C | ῥιψ... δαιμ. H (ῥ. τουτ. τ. δακτ... δαιμονίου) Q; (εἰς τὸ in mg. sin.) στηθ. τ. δαιμονίου ῥ. τουτ. τ. δακτ. P, ῥ. αὐτῷ ἐπὶ τ. στ. τ. δαιμ. (+ τὸ δακτ. V) δ καὶ ἔλαβον τοῦτο παρὰ θεοῦ Σαβαὼθ C, ῥ. τ. δακτ. τουτ. δ ἔλαβον παρὰ κυρίου σαβαὼθ· καὶ ῥίψον αὐτὸ εἰς τ. στηθ. τ. δαίμονος I 5 λέγων αὐτῷ HC: καὶ εἰπὲ αὐτῷ IB, εἶτα εἰπέ L, + ἐπ' ὀνόματι (-τος Q) τοῦ θεοῦ B 6 * P f. 2ʳ | ὁ: — C, + βασιλεὺς B | Σολ.: + ἐν ὀνόματι κυρίου τοῦ θεοῦ παντοκράτορος (— καὶ ... φοβῆσαι) L | δρομαῖος P, δρομαίος I | παραγένου V, ἔρχου B | δραμὼν παραγ. πρός με δρομαίως ἐπειπὼν καὶ ταῦτα πρὸς τὸν δαίμοναν φαθαλά· πιστηφούμ (πιστιρούμ V)· ἀλακαρτανάκ· C | μηδὲν ... φοβ (l. 7) (pr. καὶ) C: μὴ διαλογιζόμενος ἃ μέλλει σοι λέγειν I, καὶ μὴ ἀμελήσεις εἰς ἅπερ (t. 3ʳ) μέλλει σοι λέγειν H, μηδὲν δειλιάσας (δειλιάζων Q) ἢ (μὴ δὲ P) φοβηθεὶς (-ῆς P) ἐν ᾧ μέλλεις ἀκούειν παρὰ (ὑπὸ P) τοῦ δαίμονος. (7) καὶ λαβὼν τὸ παιδάριον τὸ δακτυλίδιον ἀπῆλθεν B

§ 10. l. 8 Pro § 10 habet L hoc: λαβὼν δὲ ὁ νεανίας τὸ δακτυλίδιον πορευθῆς ἐπὶ τοῦ θείου ἔργου· ἐργαζόμενος εἶτα ἑσπέρα γενέσθαι· καὶ ἐκ τοῦ ἔργου σχολάσαντες· ἦλθον πάντες οἱ τεχνῆτ(αι)· ἐπὶ τὰς κατοικείας αὐτῶν· ἦλθε δὲ καὶ ὁ νέος ἐπὶ τὴν κατοικείαν αὐτοῦ, καὶ ἐλθὼν ὁ πονηρότ(ατος) δαίμων καθὼς τὸ σύνηθες, τούτου | εἰθισμ. Kurz: ἤθισμ. BC Is, ὁρισμ. HI | εἰσῆλθεν VW

χαλεπὸν δαιμόνιον ὡς πῦρ φλεγόμενον ὥστε λαβεῖν κατὰ τὸ ούνηθες τὸν μισθὸν τοῦ παιδαρίου. 11. τὸ δὲ παιδάριον κατὰ τὸ ῥηθὲν αὐτῷ παρὰ τοῦ Σολομῶντος ἔρριψε τὸ δακτυλίδιον ἐπὶ τὸ στῆθος τοῦ δαίμονος λέγων αὐτῷ· »δεῦρο καλεῖ σε ὁ Σολομῶν,« καὶ ἀπῄει δρομαίως πρὸς τὸν Σολομῶντα. 12. ὁ δὲ δαίμων ἐκραύγασε λέγων τῷ παιδαρίῳ· »τί τοῦτο ἐποίησας; λάβε τὸ δακτυλίδιον καὶ ἐπίδος αὐτὸ πρὸς Σολομῶντα, κἀγώ σοι δώσω τὸ ἀργύριον καί τὸ χρυσίον πάσης τῆς γῆς· μόνον μή με ἀπαγάγῃς πρὸς Σολομῶντα.« 13. καὶ εἶπεν αὐτῷ τὸ παιδάριον· »ζῇ κύριος ὁ θεὸς τοῦ Ἰσραήλ, οὐ μή σε ἀνέξομαι ἐὰν μὴ ἀπαγάγω σε πρὸς Σολομῶντα.« 14. * καὶ ἦλθε τὸ παιδάριον καὶ εἶπε τῷ Σολομῶντι· »βασιλεῦ Σολομῶν, ἤγαγόν σοι τὸν

MSS HILPQVW = Recc. ABC.   1 φλέγων HI | ὥστε ... Σολ. (l. 7) — Q | ὅπως τε λάβῃ P | κατὰ τ. συνηθ.: — P, post παιδάριον ponit C 2 § 11. τὸ ... δαίμονος: ἐν τῷ ἅμα ῥήψας τὴν σφραγῖδα αὐτοῦ ἄνω τούτου L | κατὰ ... Σολ.: — C, cf. not. ad l. 5   3 τὸ ῥηθὲν: τὸ ῥηθέντ < H, τὸ ῥηθέντι I, τῷ ῥηφθέντι Is, τὸ προσταχθὲν P | αὐτῷ: αὐτοῦ H, — P | Σολ. H: βασιλέως Σ. I, βασιλέως P | τὸ δακτ.: τὴν σφραγίδαν C   4 ἐπὶ: παρὰ H | δαιμονίου P | λεγ. αὐτ. I: καὶ λεγ. αὐτὸ H, εἶτα λέγ < L, καὶ εἶπεν PVW | ὁ: — C, + βασιλεὺς P   5 Σολ.: + ἐν τῷ ὀνόματι κυρίου τοῦ θεοῦ παντοκράτορος L, + ἐπεῖπεν δὲ καὶ τὰ ῥηθέντα ὀνόματα C | καὶ ... Σολομῶντα: — LC | ἀπῄει Kurz: ἀπόιει HI, ἀπίει Is, ἀπῆγε P, ἀπήγαγε Bucn | τὸν — I | Σολ. HI: βασιλέα P | § 12. Pro § 12 habet L hoc: ἀκούσας (f. 9ʳ¹) ταῦτα ὁ δαίμων βρυχιζόμενος λέγ(ει:) τίς ἐστὶν οὗτος ὁ σολομῶν   6 ἐκραύγασε IP: ἐκραύγαξεν H, ἀνέκραξεν C | λεγ. τ. παιδ. I: λέγων· παιδάριον PVW, τ. παιδ. — H | ἐποίησας: + πρός με P   7 δακτύλιον W | κ. ἐπιδ. αὐτὸ (αὐτὸν H) HI: — BC | πρὸς Σολ.: IVW: πρ. τὸν Σ. H, ἀπ' ἐμοῦ P | κἀγώ σοι δώσω H1: κἀγὼ ἀποδώσω P, ἐγώ σοι δώσω Q, καὶ δώσω σοι C   8 τὸ ἀργ. κ. — B | πάσης — B | μόνον: ἐὰν W, + λάβε τοῦτο ἀπ' ἐμοῦ καὶ B | μὴ: μοι H   9 ἀγάγῃς VW | ἀπάγῃς με B | Σολομῶνα P | § 13. (8) Pro § 13 habet L hoc: καὶ ὁ νεανίας· ἔλθε καὶ εἶδε | καὶ ... παιδ. HI (— αὐτῷ) V; τὸ δὲ παιδ. λέγει (εἶπε W) πρὸς τὸν δαίμονα BW   10 τοῦ: — HW, μου V | Ἰσρ. — H | σε: — W, σου Q | ἐὰν ... Σολ.: ἀλλὰ δεῦρο ἐλθέ P, ἀλλὰ δεῦρο ἀκολουθῇ μοι Q   11 σε ἀγάγω C | § 14. Pro § 14 habet L: ὁ δὲ ἀκόλουθος γενόμενος ὁ δαίμων ἦλθε ἐπὶ τὴν βασιλικὴν οἰκίαν | * H f. 3ᵛ | hic scr. H rubricam hanc: ἔλευσις τοῦ χαλεποῦ δαίμον⟨ος⟩ ὀρνίαν πρὸς σολομῶν⟨τα⟩ | ἦλθε: ἐλθὼν (ἐλθὸν P) δρομαίως B   12 καὶ εἶπε HIC: χαίρων (χαῖρον P) πρὸς τὸν βασιλέα λέγων (λέγον P) B, pr. πρὸς τὸν Σολομῶντα χαῖρον (-ων W) βαστῶν (καὶ βαστάζων W) τὸν δαίμοναν C | τῷ Σολομῶντι H: τῷ βασιλεῖ I, — BC | βασ. Σολ. IC: — HB | σοι HI: — BC

δαίμονα καθώς ενετείλω μοι, και ιδού στήκει προ των πυλών έξω δεδεμένος και κράζων μεγάλη τη φωνή διδόναι μοι το αργύριον και το χρυσίον πάσης της γης του μή με απαγαγείν αυτόν προς σέ.«

5 II. Και ταύτα ακούσας εγώ Σολομών αναστάς από του θρόνου μου είδον τον δαίμονα φρίσσοντα και τρέμοντα και είπον αυτώ· »τίς εί σύ, ⌐και τίς ή κλήσίς σου;⌐« ο δαίμων είπεν· »Ορνίας καλούμαι.« 2. και είπον αυτώ· * »λέγε μοι εν ποίω ζωδίω κείσαι.« και αποκριθείς ο δαίμων λέγει· »Υδροχόω· * και τους εν

MSS HILPQVW = Recc. ABC. 1 καθ' ένετ.: βασιλεύ, ως εκέλευσας Β | μή (l. μοι) ένετ. V | μοι: + δέσποτα BC | στηκ. HI: στήκεται Β, ηστίκη V. ηστήκει W | προ IB: προς Η, παρά C | τ. πυλ. I: τον πυλώνα Η, των θυρών (+ της αυλής Β) της βασιλείας σου BC 2 έξω HI: — BC | δεδεμ. κ. κραζ. I (— και) Η: δεόμενον κραυγάζει VW, κράζων κ. δεόμενος Ρ, κραυγάζων κ. δεόμενος Q | φώνην μεγάλην Η | διδούς Ρ | μοι IQ: εμοί Ρ, με C, — Η | το άργ. . . . χρυσ. HB: τ. χρ. κ. τ. άργ. IW, το χρ. κ. πάντας τους θησαυρούς V 3 πάσης HIW: — BV | του . . . σε — VW | του IB: και Η | με — Β | απαγ. με I | αγαγείν Ρ

C. II. parallela v. infra in MS D III 1—10. (9) l. 5 Και ταύτα . . . τρέμοντα: ιδών δε ο σολομών την τοιούτην εκπετάσας τας χείρας αυτού εις τον ουρανόν· ευχαριστήσας κύριον τον θεόν ουρανού και γης ποιητήν τον τα πάντα κτήσαντα· και δύναται ότι ποιήματα και κτήματα αυτού εισίν τα πάντα L | Και ΗΒ: — IC | άκ. ταυτ. — Β | εγώ HI: — BC | Σολ. HIB: — C, pr. ο Η | αναστ. HI: ανέστη Β, ανέστην C | από: ειπό V, επί W 6 μου: αυτού Β, + και εξήλθεν έξω εις τα πρόθυρα της αυλής των βασιλείων αυτού και Ρ, + και εξήλθεν (έξω . . . καλούμαι, l. 8, omissis) Q, + και εξήλθον εις τα πρόθυρα τα βασιλικά και C | είδον: εθεώρει Ρ | φρίττοντα I, φρίττων Η | τρέμων. Η | * P f. 2^v | και (2°): είτα L | είπον HIW: λέγει LPV 7 αυτώ IP: αυτόν HC, — L | τίς εί σύ AP: — C, + και πόθεν εί L | κ. τίς . . . σου A: — P, τίς καλεί W (-ής) V | ο δαιμ. είπεν: ο δε έφη PC | εγώ Ορν. P 8 καλ. PC: καλούμεν L, — HI | § 2. (10) κ. είπον αυτ. ego: κ. είπ < αυτώ ο βασιλεύς V, κ. είπον W, είπον ούν αυτώ I, εγώ δε αυτόν λέγων Η, είπε δε ο σολομών L, ο δε (και ο Ρ) σολ. λέγει Β | * Mg 1320 | μοι: + ουν VW, + ώ δαίμων Β | εν C: — AB | ποίω ζωδ. κεισ. P: ποίων ζωδίων κεισ. Q, πριν εξωδιώκω (εξαδιώκω Η, εξεδιώκω L) σε A, + λέγε μοι πού αγωνίζεσε L 9 και . . . λέγει: κ. απεκρίθη το δαιμόνιον και είπεν C, λέγει δε L, ο δε είπεν Β | λέγει Η: — I: | Υδροχόω κ. τους: — LVW per homoeoarcton | ιδρωοχρώς, ιδροχόω (p. 14, l. 1) Η, ιδρονχρώς, υδροχρώο (p. 14, l. 1) I, υδρωχρώο L, compendio scr. W | * I f. 80^r | των κεμιμένων Q, εν Υδροχόω — PQ

Ὑδροχόῳ κειμένους δι' ἐπιθυμίαν τῶν γυναίων ἐπὶ τὴν Παρθένον ζῴδιον κεκληκότας ἀποπνίγω. 3. εἰμὶ δὲ καὶ ὑπνοτικόν, εἰς τρεῖς μορφὰς μεταβαλλόμενος, ποτὲ * μὲν ὡς ἄνθρωπος ἔχων ἐπιθυμίαν εἴδους παιδίων θηλυκῶν ἀνήβων, καὶ ἁπτομένου μου 5 ἀλγῶσι πάνυ. ποτὲ δὲ ὑπόπτερος γίνομαι ἐπὶ τοὺς οὐρανίους τόπους. ποτὲ δὲ ὄψιν λέοντος ἐμφαίνω. 4. ἀπόγονος δέ εἰμι * ἀρχαγγέλλου τῆς δυνάμεως τοῦ θεοῦ, καταργοῦμαι δὲ ὑπὸ Οὐριὴλ τοῦ ἀρχαγγέλου.« 5. ὅτε δὲ ἤκουσα ἐγὼ Σολομῶν τὸ ὄνομα τοῦ ἀρχαγγέλου ηὐξάμην καὶ ἐδόξασα τὸν θεὸν τοῦ οὐρανοῦ καὶ τῆς

MSS HILPQVW = Recc. ABC. 1 κειμένους HP: κειμένος I, κείμαι C, καιομένους conj. Cr | δι'... κεκληκ. ego (τῶν γονέων monuit Diels, γυναικῶν vel γυναίων »certe recte« James): δι' ἐπιθ. τῶν γονέων ἐπί τι (τὴν W) παρθένῳ ζωδίῳ (ζώδιον W) καικληκότα C, δι' ἐπιθυμιῶν τὸν λόγον (-ων H) ἐπὶ τὴν παρθένον (-ων H) τὸ (τὴν L, ὅτι H) ἐξόδιον (ἐξωδίων H) κεκληκότος (κεκληκῶ L) A, δι' ἐπιθυμιῶν γυναίων (γυναικῶν Q) ἐπὶ τὴν παρθένων (spatium purum minus reliquit P) τῷ ζῳδίῳ κέκληται B, τῷ ζῳδ. κεκλ. pro glossa marg. habet Cr 2 ἀποπν. BW: εἰπεπνήγο V, ἐπάγω A, pr. τούτους B | § 3. εἰμί..., ὑπνοτ.: — A | εἰμί: εἰ μὴ PQVFl | ὑπνωτικὸν P, ὑπνοτικῶν Q, ὑπνοτικός monuit Diels, forte recte 3 εἰς B: — C, καὶ εἰς τοῦτο A | μεταβαλ. A: μεταβάλλομαι B, μεταλαμβανόμενος C | ποτὲ μὲν: ὁπότ'αν B | * H f. 4ʳ | ὡς: ὅς V, οἱ B | ἄνθρωποι B | ἔχων (+ τὴν W) ... ἀνηβ. C: ἔχων ἔτι (ἔτει H, ἐπὶ L) εἰμὶ (ἡμεῖν H, — L) ἕνι τα δον (μετὰ δῶν L) θυλικὸν (-ῶν L) εὔοσμον (εἶμι L) A, ἔρχωνται εἰς ἐπιθυμίας (-ίαν Q) γυναικῶν ἐγὼ μεταμορφοῦμαι εἰς (ὡς Q) θῆλυ εὔκοσμον B 4 καὶ — C | ἁπτ. μου B: ἀπὸ ὄμουν V, ἀπὸ ὦμον W, δι' αὐτῶν H, δι' αὐτόν l. fortasse ἀπ' ἐμοῦ, vel ἀπ' ὤμων, vel ἀπομνώμενοι 5 ἀλγ. πάνυ HIV: ἀλγῶ σοι π. W, οἱ ἄνθρωποι καθ' ὕπνον ἐμπαίζω αὐτοῖς (αὐτούς Q) B | πάνυ — L | δὲ: — Q, + πάλιν B | ὑποπτ.: γνιότερον C | γένομαι HIQ | ἐπὶ: ὑπὸ B, πρὸς W | ἐπὶ ... τοπ.: καὶ τ. ἐπουρανίους ἐπὶ εἰσέρχομαι τοπ. L 6 τοπ.: κόλπους W | ποτὲ (δὲ — H) ... ἐμφ. HI: πότε δὲ καὶ ὡς λέων (λέοντας Q) B, πότε μὲν ὄψει (καὶ πότε ὄψιν W) λέοντος ἐπιφέρομαι C, add. glossam marginaliam in textum insertam: ὑπὸ πάντων (+ δὲ L) τῶν δαιμονίων (δαιμόνων H) λαβόμενος A, quam in καὶ (— Q) κελεύομαι ὑπὸ πάντων τῶν δαιμόνων corrigere voluit B | § 4. ἀπογ. ... θεοῦ H (— ἀρχαγγ.) I: — C | δὲ — P | * L f. 9ˣ² 7 ἀρχ.... θεοῦ: — L, pr. τοῦ Q, ἀρχ. Οὐριὴλ etc. P | καταργ... ἀρχαγγ. I (— δὲ) H: — P | δὲ — Q | Οὐριὴλ τ. ἀρχ. ego: Μιχ. τ. ἀρχ. A, + τῆς δυνάμεως τοῦ θεοῦ (supra omissa) L, τ. ἀρχ. Οὐριὴλ τ. δυν. τ. θεοῦ Q, τ. δυν. τ. θεοῦ οὐρουὴλ τοῦ (bis V) ἀρχαγγέλου C 8 § 5. (11) ὅτε (ὅταν I) ... Σολ.: HI: ἐγὼ (+ δὲ P) Σ. ἀκούσας B, ἐγὼ δὲ ἀκούσας ὁ Σ. C, πότε οὖν Σ. L | τὸ ὀν. τ. ἀρχ. IBC: — HL, + μιχαὴλ I 9 ηὐξαμ. A; εὐξάμενος BC | καὶ — LB | ἐδοξ. HIB: δοξάσας C. — L | τ. θεὸν: pr. κύριον Q, + καὶ κύριον P | τὸν ... γῆς: τὸ ὄνομα τοῦ κυρίου C, τὸν θεὸν τὸν δόντα μοι τὴν χάριν ταύτην· καὶ εἶδα πνεύματα ἀσώματα· εἰς σχῆμα μεταβαλλόμενα σεσωματωμένα L

γῆς, καὶ σφραγίσας αὐτὸν ἔταξα εἰς τὴν ἐργασίαν τῆς λιθοτομίας, τοῦ τέμνειν λίθους τοῦ ναοῦ ἀρθέντας διὰ θαλάσσης Ἀραβίας τοὺς κειμένους παρὰ αἰγιαλόν. 6. φοβουμένου δὲ αὐτοῦ τοῦ σιδήρου προσψαῦσαι ἔφη μοι· »δέομαί σου, βασιλεῦ Σολομῶν, * ἐασόν με ἐν ἀνέσει εἶναι, κἀγώ σοι ἀναγαγῶ πάντας τοὺς δαίμονας.« 7. μὴ θέλοντος δὲ αὐτοῦ ὑποταγῆναί μοι, ηὐξάμην τὸν ἀρχάγγελον Οὐριὴλ ἐλθεῖν μοι εἰς βοήθειαν· καὶ εὐθέως * εἶδον τὸν ἀρχάγγελον Οὐριὴλ ἐκ τοῦ οὐρανοῦ κατερχόμενον πρός με. 8. καὶ ἐκέλευσε ἀνελθεῖν ἐκ τῆς θαλάσσης κήτη καὶ ἐξήρανεν

MSS HILPQVW = Recc. ABC. 1 σφραγίσαν H | αὐτὸν: + μετὰ δακτυλιδίου εἶτα λαμβάνει ὁ ἀναγινώσκων μεθετέρων λίθων βαρυτάτων· καὶ ἐπιθένεν ἐπάνω τοῦ ὀχλουμένου ἕως βοῆσαι· ὅταν βοήσει ὁ ὀχλούμενος· ὑπόταξον τὸ πνεῦμα τὸ ἀκάθαρτον τοῦ ἐξελθεῖν· καὶ εἶπεν αὐτῷ ἔξελθε ἀπὸ ὀνόματι τοῦ ἐπουρανίου βασιλέως θεοῦ ἡμῶν· καὶ τῆς σφραγίδος τῆς δωθήσης τῷ βασιλεῖ σολομῶν⟨τι⟩· καὶ σφραγίσας αὐτὸν L | ἔταξα: + αὐτὸν C | τὴν — LC | τῆς — L | λιθοτόμου C 2 τοῦ τεμν. ... ναοῦ — L | τέμνειν HIP: τεμεῖν W, τέμνει V, κόπτειν Q | τοὺς λιθ. P | τ. ναοῦ: ἐν τῷ ναῷ B, — C | ἀρθεντ. HI (-τος) L: ἀχθέντας B, τοὺς συναχθέντας VW | διὰ: ὑπὸ L | Ἀραβ. BC: ἀρράβω L, ἀνάγων H, ἀναλαβὼν I 3 τοὺς... αἰγιαλ.: — C | ἀγιαλλόν Q | § 6. φοβ. δὲ αὐτ. H(L): φοβούμενος δὲ αὐτὸς W (αὐτοὺς) I (— αὐτὸς) P, ἐφοβεῖτο οὖν Q | φοβουμ. ... προσψαυσ.: φοβούμενος δὲ αὐτὸ⟨ς⟩ τὴν ἀπόφασιν τοῦ βασιλέως περὴ τὸν λήθ⟨ων⟩ ἦνα μὴ πρὸς ψαύσι τὸ σύδίρον φοβούμενος V, φοβουμένους δὲ αὐτοῦ· λάβε ὁ ἀναγινώσκον σίδηρον (in marg. lat. signum O+ scr. man. rec.) ἄλυσσον ἐπίθες ἐπὶ τοῦ ὀχλουμένου τῷ τραχείλω καὶ δῆσον σφόδρα ἕως οὐ βοήσει· φοβουμένου δὲ αὐτοῦ etc. L | τοῦ σιδήρου A: τὸ σιδήρω W, τὸν σίδηρον B 4 προσψαῦσαι LQW: οὐ προσάψωμαι I, οὐ προσψαύσω μεν H, post προς spatio puro VI litt. relicto ad marg. sin. man. prim. scr. πάντ < ἢ πρὸς ταῦτα P, quod Fl τραυτὸν εἰπὸς ταῦτα legit | ἔφη μοι L (μιν) H: καὶ λέγει μοι P, λέγει Q, ἔφη ὁ δαίμων W, ὁ δέμων ἔφη V, ἔφη δὲ ὁ ὀρνίας I | σου: σοι W | * L f. 9^VI. 5 με: μοι W, — L | ἐν ἀνεσ. IL: ἔναν ἔσοι H, ἄνετον BC | εἶναι: ἦν αα H, + μοι L, + με B | ἀναγαγῶ IP: ἀνανάγω in ἀνάγω corr. H, ἀγαγῶ C, ἄγω L, εὐαγγέλω Q | πάντα τὰ δαιμόνια BC 6 § 7. μὴ ... μοι: καὶ μὴ θέλοντα (-τες W) ὑποταγῆναι cum δαιμόνια conjuncta C ·| θέλων A | αὐτοῦ: αὐτοὺς HL, αὐτὸς I | ὑποταγόν μοι L | ηὐξαμ. ... βοηθ.: ηὐξαμ.: pr. ἐγὼ δὲ C, εὐξάμενος B, εἰξαμ- V | ηὐξαμ. ... βοηθ.: ηὐξάμην τὸν θεὸν καὶ κατελθὼν τὸν ἀρχάγγελον οὐρουέλ ὑποταγήν μοι· εἰς βοήθειαν L | τὸ ἀρχάγγελον V, τοῦ ἀρχαγγέλου B 7 οὐρουηλ IW | ἐλθεῖν·: pr. τοῦ C, συνελθεῖν B | μοι HLQ: με P, — IC | * P f. 3^r 8 τ. ἀρχ. Οὐρ.: αὐτὸν C | οὐρουὴλ IC, οὐρουὲλ L | τῶν οὐρανῶν B | ἐρχόμενον | πρός με — L 9 § 8. (12) ἐκελ. LB: ἐκέλευσα C, ἐκάλεσεν HI, + ὁ ἄγγελος B | ἀνελθ. (καὶ ἦλθον L) ... κήτη A: κήτη (κῆτον W) θαλλάσσης ἐλθεῖν ἐκ τῆς ἀβύσσου BC | καὶ ... μερίδα A: — BC | ἐξήρεν H

αὐτῶν τὴν μερίδα ⌈καὶ ἔρριψεν αὐτοῦ τὴν μοῖραν⌉ ἐπὶ τῆς γῆς, κἀκείνως καὶ οὕτως ὑπέταξε τὸν δαίμονα τὸν Ὀρνίαν τὸν μέγαν, τοῦ κόπτειν λίθους καὶ συντελεῖν εἰς τὴν οἰκοδομὴν τοῦ ναοῦ ὃν ᾠκοδόμουν ἐγὼ Σολομῶν. 9. καὶ πάλιν ἐδόξασα τὸν θεὸν 5 τοῦ οὐρανοῦ καὶ τῆς γῆς καὶ ἐκέλευσα περιέναι τὸν Ὀρνίαν εἰς τὴν μοῖραν αὐτοῦ καὶ ἔδωκα αὐτῷ τὴν σφραγῖδα λέγων· »ἄπελθε καὶ ἄγαγέ μοι ὧδε τὸν ἄρχοντα τῶν δαιμονίων.«

III. Ὁ δὲ Ὀρνίας λαβὼν τὸ δακτυλίδιον ἀπῆλθε πρὸς τὸν Βεελ*ζεβοὺλ καί ἔφη αὐτῷ· »δεῦρο καλεῖ σε ὁ Σολομῶν.« 2. ὁ 10 δὲ Βεελζεβοὺλ λέγει αὐτῷ· »λέγε μοι, * τίς ἐστιν οὗτος ὁ Σολομῶν ὃν σὺ λέγεις;« 3. ὁ δὲ Ὀρνίας ἔρριψε τὸ δακτυλίδιον εἰς τὸ στῆθος τοῦ Βεελζεβοὺλ λέγων· »καλεῖ σε Σολομῶν ὁ βασι-

---

MSS HILPQVW = Recc. ABC. 1 αὐτὸν L | μερίδαν H, μεριπα L | καὶ ... μοῖραν B: — A | ἔρριψεν αὐτὸν C | τὴν μοῖραν ... συντελεῖν (l. 3) — C   2 κἀκείνως κ. οὕτως ego: κακείνως κ. οὗτος H, κἀκεῖνος κ. οὗτος L. καὶ οὕτως L, καὶ Q, κἀκείνη et postea spatium purum VII litt. habet P, »καὶ οὕτως« scheint Glossen« Diels | ὑπέταξε: ὑπέταξα I, ἐκέλευσεν Q, + τὸ δαιμόνιον τὸ μέγα καὶ ἐκέλευσεν P | τ. Ὀρ. τ. μεγ. HL: tr. I, τὸν μέγαν καὶ θρασὺν (θρασὺ Q) τ. Ὀρν. B   3 τοῦ — L | τοὺς λίθους P | καὶ ... Σολ.: πρὸς τὸν ναόν B | συντελῶν L | εἰς LV   4 ὃν A: ἦν C | Σολ.: pr. βασιλεύ(ς) H, βασιλεύς V | § 9. καὶ πάλιν ... γῆς — C | πάλιν: οὕτως ἐγὼ Σολ. B | ἐδόξασαν L   5 τῆς — Q | γῆς: + ποιήτην B | ἐκέλευσα ... δαιμονίων (l. 7): ἐκέλευσα τὸν ὀρνίαν συνπαρήνε μοι τὸν ἄρχονταν τῶν δαιμονίων καὶ δέδοκα αὐτὸν, τὴν σφραγίδαν W | ἐκέλευσεν P | περιέναι (περιεῖναι L) ... τὴν (— L) μοιρ. αὐτ. (αὐτὸν I, αὐτῶν H) A: τὸν Ὀ. παρῆναι μη σὺν τῖ μύρα αὐτοῦ V, ἐλθεῖν τὸν Ὀ. σὺν τῇ μοίρᾳ αὐτοῦ B   6 ἔδοκεν H, δέδωκα CL | αὐτῷ: αὐτὸν C, αὐτοῦ LB | τὸ σφραγίδιον B | λέγων: φήσαν αὐτόν V, καὶ εἶπον I   7 καὶ — L | ἀναγαγέ I | ὧδε: ὢ I | τ δαιμ.: pr. πάντων I, + πάντων P, λαβεῖν ἀπὸ τῆς βασιλείας μου Q

C. III. MSS HILPVW = Recc. ABC. (13) c. III—XX 9 Ὁ δὲ ... γενέσθαι om. Q   8 δακτύλιον C   9 constanter scr. βελζεβουήλ H, βεελζεβουέλ L | βεζεελθεουλ in βεελζεβουλ corr. V | * H f. 5^r | Βεελζ.: + τὸι ἔχοντα τὴν βασιλείαν ἐπὶ τῶν δαιμόνων P, ὃς ἦν ἔξαρχος τῶν δαιμονίων C add. insuper ἔχων τὸ τὸ βασιλεῖ ἂν τω V | καὶ — P | ἔφη αὐτῷ IPC λέγει HL, + αὐτὸν H, + ὁ (— V) ὀρνίας C | ὁ (1°) HI: — LPC § 2. 10 λέγει αὐτῷ (— αὐτ. H) A: ἀκούσας ἔφη αὐτῷ P, ἀκούσας εἶπεν (| λέγε IPC: εἰπέ H, ἀνήγγελέ L | * L f. 9^{v2} | τίς: τί H, pr. τί ἐστὶν L οὗτος AP: αὐτὸς C | ὃν: ὢν I | σὺ: + μοι C   11 λέγεις: φῆς μοι P § 3. τὸ δακτύλιον V, τῶ δακτυλίω W | εἰς AP: ἐπὶ C   12 τω σθῆθος V τὸ στήθει W | βελζεβοὺλ W, βελζεβουήλ V | λέγων: λέγει αὐτόν H + αὐτῶ I | λέγων ... βασιλ. — L | δεῦρο καλεῖ HI | καλεῖς (— σε) | Σολ. ὁ βασ. PV (pr. ὁ) I: βασ. σολ. H (pr. ὁ) W

III, 4—7   ἔλευσις τοῦ Βεελζεβούλ   17*

λεύς.« 4. * καὶ ἀνέκραξεν ὁ Βεελζεβοὺλ ὡς ἀπὸ πυρὸς φλογὸς καιομένης μεγάλης καὶ ἀναστὰς ἠκολούθησεν αὐτῷ μετὰ βίας καὶ ἦλθε πρός με. 5. καὶ ὡς εἶδον ἐγὼ τὸν ἄρχοντα τῶν δαιμονίων ἐρχόμενον, ἐδόξασα τὸν θεὸν καὶ εἶπον· * »εὐλογητὸς εἶ, κύριε ὁ θεὸς ὁ παντοκράτωρ ὁ δοὺς τῷ παιδί σου Σολομῶντι τὴν τῶν σῶν θρόνων πάρεδρον σοφίαν καὶ ὑποτάξας εἰς ἐμὲ πᾶσαν τὴν τῶν δαιμόνων δύναμιν.« 6. καὶ ἐπηρώτησα αὐτὸν καὶ * εἶπον· »λέγε μοι, τίς εἶ σύ;« ὁ δαίμων * ἔφη: »ἐγώ εἰμι Βεελζεβοὺλ τῶν δαιμονίων ὁ ἔξαρχος.« 7. ἀπῄτουν δὲ τοῦτον ἀδιαλείπτως ἐγγύθεν μοι προσεδρεύειν καὶ ἐμφανίζειν μοι τὴν κατὰ τῶν δαιμόνων φαντασίαν. αὐτὸς δέ μοι ἐπηγγείλατο πάντα

MSS HILPVW = Recc. ABC. 1 § 4. * V f. 438ʳ | κ. ἀνεκ. HI: εἶτα κράξας L, ἀνεκ. δὲ PC | ὁ Βεελζ.: τὸ δαιμόνιον φωνὴν μεγάλην L, + φωνῇ μεγάλῃ P | ὡς ... μεγαλ. L (— μεγαλ.) H: καὶ ἔρριψε φλόγα πυρὸς καιομένην μεγάλην P, λέγων ταῦτα· ὡς ἀπὸ πυρὸς φλογὸς καιομένης μοι μεγάλης C, ὡς ἀπὸ φλογὸς καιόμενος I, add. rubricam: ἡ ἔλευσις βελζεβουὴλ πρὸς σολομῶντα H   2 ἠκολ. αὐτῷ I (αὐτὸν) H: ἠκολούθ < αὐτῶ L, ἠκολούθει τῷ δρνία PC | μετὰ βίας — P   3 καὶ ... με — C | καὶ — L | ἦλθε IP: ἀπῆλθεν HL | με I: τὸν σολομῶντα HL, σολομῶνα P | § 5. (14) κ. ὡς εἶδον H (— ὡς) I: ὡς δὲ εἶδον P, καὶ (+ ὡς V) ἰδὼν δὲ C, ἰδὼν δὲ L | ἐγὼ HIC: — P, ὁ σολ. L, + σολ. HI   4 ἔρχομ.: — P, + πρός με HI, + τὸν βεελζεβοὺλ C, + καὶ I | ἐδόξασε L | κύριον τ. θεὸν τοῦ οὐρανοῦ καὶ γῆς ποιητὴν P | εἶπεν L | * P f. 3ᵛ   5 εἶ, κύριε: κύριος IL | θεός: + τοῦ οὐρανοῦ καὶ τῆς γῆς L | δοὺς ... σοφ. καὶ — I | σου — C   6 τῶν σ. θρόνων HW: τὸν σὸν θρόνον L, τὸ σὸν θρον- V, τῶν σοφῶν P   7 πᾶσαν — H | τ. δαιμ. A: τοῦ διαβόλου PC | τ. δυν. τ. διαβ. P | § 6. (15) κ. ἐπηρωτ. HI (ex -ωτητα corr.) Pᵒ: ἐπηρωτ. δὲ C, κ. ἐπηρώτησεν H | * I f. 81¹ | αὐτῶν H, αὐτὴν V   8 κ. εἶπον PC (— καὶ) H: — I, λέγων L | * W f. 268ʳ | λέγε μοι — L | μοι — P | τίς εἶ σύ: τίς εἰσὶν L | σύ — PW | ὁ δαίμων: καὶ H | * H f. 5ᵛ | ἔφη· »ἐγὼ: λέγει· ἐγὼ I, λέγω H   9 Βεελζ.: pr. ὁ IL, + ὁ PV | δαιμ.: δαιμόνων HI, + πάντων W | ὁ — LPW | ἔξαργος: ἄρχων V, ἀρχή W | § 7. ἀπητ. ... προσεδ. ego: ἀπητ. ... ἀδιαλυπτ. (-λήπτως Is, -λειπτως Kurz) ἔγγυθέν μοι προεδρεύειν I, ἀπήτην ... ἀδιαλήπτως ἔγκυθέν μοι προεδρεύειν H, ἀπήτουν δὲ οὗτον ἀδιαλήπτως προεδρεύειν ἐγγιθέν μοι L, ἀπάντ(ων) δὲ τούτ(ων) οὐ διαλιπο < ἐγκηθέν μοι προσεδρέβειν V, (ἀπητ. ... ἀδιαλ. — W) ἐνγγικστά μου προσεβρεύειν (β forte in δ corr.) W, ἅπαντες δὲ οἱ δαίμονες ἐγγιστέν μου προεδρεύουσι P   10 ἐμφανίζει LW, ἐφανίζει V, ἐμφανίζω P | μοι — IP | τ. κατὰ (μετὰ L) τ. δαιμ. φαντ. A: ἑκάστου δαίμονος τ. φαντ. P, ἑνὸς ἑκάστου δαίμονος φαντασίας C   11 αὐτ. ... ἐπηγγ. (ἐπειγγειλε L) ... πνευμ. AP: ἐπηγγ. μοι δὲ αὐτ. παντ. τ. δαιμόνια C

C. III, 5. Sap. IX 4
UNT. 9: McCown.   2 *

τὰ ἀκάθαρτα πνεύματα ἀγαγεῖν πρός με δέσμια. καὶ ἐγὼ πάλιν ἐδόξασα * τὸν θεὸν τοῦ οὐρανοῦ καὶ τῆς γῆς εὐχαριστῶν αὐτῷ πάντοτε. IV. Ἐπυθόμην δὲ τοῦ δαίμονος εἰ ἔστι δαιμόνων θήλεια. 5 τοῦ δὲ φήσαντος εἶναι ἐβουλόμην εἰδέναι. 2. καὶ ἀπελθὼν ὁ Βεελζεβοὺλ ἔδειξέ μοι τὴν Ὀνοσκελίδα μορφὴν ἔχουσαν περικαλλῆ, ⌜καὶ δέμας γυναικὸς εὐχρώτου, κνήμας δὲ ἡμιόνου.⌝ 3. ἐλθούσης δὲ αὐτῆς πρός με εἶπον * αὐτῇ· »λέγε μοι σὺ τίς εἶ.« 4. ἡ δὲ ἔφη· »ἐγὼ Ὀνοσκελὶς καλοῦμαι, πνεῦμα σεσωματοποιημένον * 10 φωλεῦον ἐπὶ τῆς γῆς· ἐν σπηλαίοις μὲν ἔχω τὴν κατοίκησιν,

MSS HILPVW = Recc. ABC. 1 ἀγαγῶν L | πρός με: μιαι W | δεσμ. ἀγ. με V | δεσμ. LPV: δίσμοια H (δέσμια conj. James), δεδεμένα l, — W | ἐγὼ PC: — A 2 * L f. 10ʳ¹ | τοῦ... γῆς: τὸν παντοκράτορα σαβαώθ L | εὐχ. αὐτ. παντ. H (παντα <) V: καὶ εὐχαριστῶ αὐτ. παντ. P, — ILW C. IV. MSS HILPVWTºVºWºGlm = Recc. ABCCº; cf. infra Rec. C XI 1—6, supra *Intro.*, IV 1d), 2c), pp. 31—33. l. 4 (16) Ἐπυθ. δὲ: pr. εἶτα L, + ἐγὼ C | δὲ — P | τοῦ δαιμ.: pr. παρὰ P, pr. καὶ ἠρώτησα τὸν δαίμονα βεελζεβοὺλ I | δαιμ. — H | ἐπυθ. δὲ τ. δαιμ.: ἐρωτηθεὶς δὲ ὁ βεελζεβοὺλ (ἐπερώτησα δὲ ἐγὼ τὸν β. Wº) ὃς ἐντζανφιὲλ (ἐλτζιανφηὲλ Vº) καλεῖται παρ' ἐμοῦ (ὃς... ἐμοῦ: ὁ καὶ τζιανφιὲλ Tº) Cº | εἰ εἰσιν Vº | εἰ — Tº | δαιμ. θηλ. ego: δαιμ. θυλια ἔγγιος I, θύλιαν H, θήλεα ἔγγιος ἡμῆν L, ἐν αὐτοῖς θήλειαι P, καὶ θήλεια (θήλεα Tº) δαιμόνια Cº (— καὶ) CGlm 5 τοῦ: τούτου LTº | δὲ: + μοι PCW° | ἐβουλόμην: pr. καγὼ W, κἀγὼ εἶπον· ἤθελον P | εἰδέναι AP: ἰδεῖν CCºGlm | § 2. ὁ — PV | ὁ Βεελζ. AC: ὁ τοιοῦτος Wº, ὅτι οὗτος Vº, ὅτι οὕτως Tº, — Glm, + ταχὺ P 6 ἔδειξ. μοι A: ἤνεγκέ μοι Tº, ἤνεγκε πρός με P, ἤνεγκε ἔμπροσθέν μου CVºWºGlm | Ὀνοσκ. AP: ὀνοσκελοῦν WCºGlm (-λοῖ V), + καλουμένην TºWº (-ενη) Vº | ἔχουσα HLTºVVº | περικαλλῆ Kurz: περικαλῆ HIPIs, -αλήν WWºGlm (sic), περιπερκαλή L 7 καὶ ... ἡμιον. — A, add. rubric. ἔλευσις τῆς ὀνοσκελίδας πρὸς σολομῶντα H | δέμας ego: δέμαν V, δέρμα W James, δεσμὰ P, σῶμαν Cº | κνημ. δὲ ἠιον. Wº (μιώνου) W (ἡμιῶν) VVº: μνήμιος δὲ ἡμίονος Tº, καὶ κερατίζουσα τὴν κεφαλὴν P | κνήμην Glm | § 3. (17) Glm deest 8 δὲ — Tº | πρός με IL (μεν) H: καὶ ἰδὸν W, — PVCº | εἶπον AW: ἔφην PCº, ἔφι V | * Mg 1321 | αὐτὴν LWCº | λέγε μοι: λέγων VºWº | σὺ — P | τίς εἶ σύ H | § 4. ἡ δὲ ἔφη: ἐκείνη εἶπεν L 9 ἔφη: pr. μοι PC, + μοι VºWº, ἔφην W | ἐγὼ: ἐ I, ἐγὼ Is. | Ὀνοσκ. P: ὀνοσκελῆς Vº, -λ(ῆς) V, ὀνοσκελίδα A, ὀνοσκελοῖ TºWWº | σεσωματων. Wº, σεσωματοπηεμμένα Vº, σεσωματωπεποιημένον P, σεσωματωμένον πεποιημένον HL, σεσωματωμένον ITº, πεποιημένον W (-μένω) V, σεβωματω(?) πεποι .Fl | * H f. 6ʳ 10 φωλεῦον P: φολεύων HWº, φολεύω LCTºVº, φολέον I, + δὲ TºVº | ἐν σπηλαίοις ἐπὶ τῆς γῆς L | ἐν ... κατοικ. I (ἔχον) H: σπήλαιον οἰκῶ (οἶκον V) (ἐν σπηλαίοις Tº) ἔνθα χρυσίον κεῖται CCº, σπήλαιον μοι χρύσιον ἔνθα κεῖμαι P | μὲν — L ἔχω δὲ πολυποίκιλον τρόπον. 5. ποτὲ μὲν ἄνθρωπον * πνίγω, ποτὲ δὲ ἀπὸ τῆς φύσεως σκολιάζω αὐτούς. * τὰ δὲ πλεῖστά ἐστί μοι οἰκητήρια κρημνοὶ σπήλαια φάραγγες. 6. πολλάκις δὲ καὶ συγγίνομαι τοῖς ἀνθρώποις ὡς γυναῖκα εἶναί με νομίζοντες, πρὸ πάντων δὲ τοῖς μελιχρόοις ὅτι οὗτοι συναστροί μού εἰσιν, καὶ γὰρ * τὸ ἄστρον μου οὗτοι λάθρα ** καὶ φανερῶς προσκυνοῦσι καὶ οὐκ οἴδασιν ὅτι ἑαυτοὺς βλάπτουσι καὶ πλεῖόν με κακοῦργον εἶναι ἐρεθίζουσιν· 7. θέλουσι γὰρ διὰ τῆς μνήμης χρυσίον πορίζειν. ἐγὼ δὲ παρέχω ὀλίγον τοῖς καλῶς με προσκυνοῦσιν.«

MSS HILPVWT°V°W° = Recc. ABCC°. 1 ἔχω: ἔχων H | πολυπ. τροπ, APC°: καὶ πολυποίκιλα τρόπαια (forte ex τρόπα corr.) C | § 5. μὲν HIPT°: δὲ LCV°W° | ἀνθρώπους PCC° | δι' ἀγχόνης πνίγω ἀνθρώπους C | * P f. 4ʳ | πνίγω: + δι' ἀγχόνης P, + ὡς δι' ἀγχόνης V°W° 2 αὐτοὺς ὑπὸ T° | τῆς — H | φύσεως: — W, + εἰς ἀγκώνας P, ἐπὶ ἐγκών(ων) CT°, (-όνων) W°, ἐπὶ ἐγκώνω V° | σκολιάζω LT°: σκελιάζω HIIs, σκωλιάζω V°, σκολιάζων V, σχολιάζων WW°, σκωλήκια (ad marg.), φωλεύω (in textu P) | αὐτοὺς — P | * T° f. 7ʳ² | τὰ δὲ HP: — ICC°, τοὺς δὲ L | πλειστ... οἰκητ.: πλ. ἴσταμαι οἰκητήριον H, πλείστους ἔτεσιν οἰκητήρια L, πλεῖστα μοι οἰκητήρια εἰσι P (— εἰσι) T°, πλεῖστα δέ ἐστίν μοι οἰκητήρια κεκρυμμένα VW. πλεῖστα μοι δὲ ἔσται οἰκητήρια W°, πλ. ἔσται (in ἔστη corr.?) μὴ οἰκητήρια V°, πολλάκις δὲ οἰκῶ I   3 κρημν. σπηλ. φαραγγ. P: κρύμνοις σπήλαιον φάραγγες H, ἔχω κρημνοὺς καὶ σπηλαίοις φαραγγες L, ἐν κρυμνοῖς ἐν σπηλαίοις ἐν φαράγγοις I, σπήλαια καὶ κρήμνους καὶ φάραγχαι C, — C° 4 § 6. καὶ — HL | γύνη P | εἶναί με νομ. (l. νομίζουσι?) H: νομ. με εἶναι I, ἦμαι νομ. L, με εἶναι CC°, δοκοῦσα εἶναι P   5 πρὸ παντ. ILPC: πρὸς πάντα H, πρὸ (πρὸς T°W°) δὲ τῶν ἄλλων C° | τοῖς μελιχ. P: τοὺς μελιχρόους CV°W°, τοὺς μελαχρόους HT°, τοὺς μελανοχρόους L (ex μελαχρ. corr.) I, τοὺς μελαντοχρόους (in textu, μελιχρόους ad marg.) Is | ὅτι — L | ὅτι οὗτοι HI: οὗτοι γὰρ PCC°, + καὶ CW°, + μου καὶ V° | συναστ. μού εἰσιν ILT°W°: εἰσιν συν. μου H | μου: μοι P, — CV°   6 καὶ ... ἀστρ.: κ. τὸ ἄστρο T° | γὰρ — L | * I f. 81ᵛ | προσκ. λαθ. κ. ἐναργέως (φανερός V) CW° | λαθ. προσκ. οὗτοι T° | ** L f. 10ʳ² | φανερᾶ HL   7 καὶ οὐκ ... προσκυν. (l. 9f): — C° | οὐκ οἰδ. ὅτι — I | ὅτι — L | ἑαυτῶς C, αὐτοὺς P | βλαπτ. AP: ἀπατῶνται C | καὶ πλεῖον ... προσκυν. (l. 9s.): — I | πλεῖον... ἐρεθ.: πλ. ... ῥεθίζουσιν H, πλείων μεν κακούργος εἶναι ρεθίζουσιν L, πλεῖον με κακουργεῖν ἐρεθίζουσι P, πλημελῶς κακούργους ἐρεθίζουσα C   8 § 7. θελ. PV: θέλουσα W, θέλοντες HL | γὰρ — L | διὰ ... χρυσίον: αὐτοὺς μνήμην τοῦ χρυσίου L   9 ποριζ. HLP: πορίζεσθαι C | ἐγὼ ... προσκ. HP: ἐγὼ γὰρ παρέχων ὀλ. τοῖς καλεῖς· μὲν προσκ. L, τούς τε παρέχειν ὀλίγοις, τοῖς καὶ καλουμένοις, προσκ. W, τῆς τε δὲ παρέχιν ὀλήγης τῆς κεκαλουμένης προσκυνούσῃ V

περὶ τῆς Ὀνοσκελίδος

8. Επηρώτησα δὲ αὐτὴν πόθεν γεννᾶται. ἡ δὲ εἶπεν· »ἀπὸ φωνῆς ἀκαίρου τῆς καλουμένης ἤχου οὐρανοῦ ⌈μολύβδου φωνὴν ἀφέντος⌉ ἐν ὕλῃ ἐγεννήθην.« 9. εἶπον δὲ αὐτῇ· »ἐν ποίῳ ἄστρῳ διέρχῃ;« ἡ δὲ εἶπεν· »ἐν πανσελήνῳ, διότι καὶ ἐν σελήνῃ τὸ πλείονα ὁδεύω.« 10. ἐγὼ δὲ εἶπον· »ποῖος ἄγγελός ἐστιν ὁ καταργῶν σε;« ἡ δὲ ἔφη· »ὁ καὶ ἐν σοί, βασιλεῦ.« 11. κἀγὼ εἰς χλεύην αὐτὰ λογισάμενος ἐκέλευσα στρατιώτην κροῦσαι αὐτήν. ἡ δὲ ἀνακράξασα εἶπεν· ⌈»λέγω σοι, βασιλεῦ, ἐγώ, ὑπὸ τῆς δεδομένης σοι σοφίας τοῦ θεοῦ.« 12. καὶ εἶπον τὸ ὄνομα τοῦ Ἁγίου Ἰσραὴλ καὶ⌉ ἐκέλευσα αὐτὴν νήθειν τὴν κάνναβιν * εἰς τὰ

MSS HILPVWT°V°W° = Recc. ABCC°. § 8. (18) 1 ἐπερώτων L | δὲ — H | αὐτήν: αὐτοὺς C, + ἐγώ (κἀγὼ P) Σολομῶν PCC° | γεννᾶται A: γεννάσε T°, γεναστ < V°, γενάσται V, γενᾶσθαι WW°, γεννᾷσα (σα transversa linea del.) P | εἶπεν AT°: μοι ἔφη P (ἔφησε) C, ἔφη μοι V°, ἔφη W° 2 ἀκαίρου ... οὐραν.: ἀκαιρ. τ. καλ. ἐγχοανῆς C, ἀκροατῆς καλουμένης (-μενον L) ἤχον οὐ(ρα)νοῦ A, ἀκαίρου τοῦ καλουμένου ἤχου ἀν(θρώπ)ου P, βηρσαβεδὶ (βειρσαβεέ V°, βηρωβεέ T°) ἱππικῆς (+ καὶ V°W°) χρηματικῆς C°, explicit narratio parallela codd. mss. T°V°W° | μολύβδου: μολύγδον H, βολβίτου conj. Cr, μολίβδους Bncn | φωνῆς HL | ἀφέντος P: ἀφέντες C, ἀφιέντες A 3 ἐν ὕλῃ: ἐκήνῃ V, ἐκεῖνοι W | § 9 (19) εἶπον HI: ἔφησα C, ἔφη LP | δὲ: δ' ἐγὼ P, + ἐγὼ C | αὐτὴν W, αὐτῶ L | ἐν — PC | ἐν π. ἀστρ.: ἐκ τῶν ἄστρων L 4 δὲ: + μοι P | ἐν (1°): — PC | πανσελ. ILP: πάντι σελήνῳ H, π(ανσέλην)ος C, + ἄστρῳ P | διὸ I | διότι ... σελήνη — C per homoeoteleuton | ἐν σελήνῃ I: ἐν σελήνῳ HL, ἡ σελήνη P 5 πλείω I | ὁδεύω W: ὁδέβω V, ὁδεύων H, ὁδεύει P, ποιῶ καὶ ὁδεύω L | § 10. ἐγὼ δὲ — W | εἶπον HIW: λέγω PL, + δὲ W, + αὐτὴν LW, + πρὸς αὐτὴν P | ἔφη δὲ ἐγὼ αὐτὴν V | καὶ ποῖος ἐστὶν ὁ ἄγγελος ὁ P | ποῖος: pr. καὶ L | ἐστιν: δ' ἐς H, — C | ὁ — H | καταργῶ V 6 ἡ δὲ HIPW: ὁ δὲ L, καὶ V | ἔφη HLV: εἶπε PW, λέγει I, + μοι P | ὁ καὶ ... κἀγὼ — L | ὁ — H | καὶ — PC | βασιλ. W: βασιλεὺς V, βασιλεύσῃ I, βασιλεύειν H, βασιλεύων P § 11. 7 χλεύην ILPW: χλέβην H, χλέβη V | αὐτὰ IL: αὐτῶν H, — PC | στρατιώτας C 8 λέγω: ἐγὼ P | βασιλεὺς V, βασιλεὺς σολομῶν L | ἐγώ I: κἀγὼ HL, — PC | ὑπὸ: ἀπὸ C | ὑπὸ τῆς: ἀπάτης L 9 σοι: ἧς V, — L | τοῦ: ἐκ C | § 12. κ. εἶπον ego: κ. ὑπὸ P, εἶπον HIC, ἦ L, ὑπὸ (in textu, εἶπον ad marg.) Is | τὸ ὄνομα — P 10 ἁγίου Ἰ(σρα)ὴλ A: ἀγγέλου Ἰωὴλ PC, ἁγίου Ἰωὴλ Is | (20) καὶ C: ἐγὼ δὲ P, διὸ A | ἐκέλευσα: ἐκάλεσα C | νήθειν: νήθη V, + κλώθειν W, ἠδυνήθειν H | τὴν κάνναβιν Bncn: τ. κάναβιν LP, τ. κανάβην IW, τ(ὴν) κανάβη V, ἐν τῇ κανάβῃ H | * L f. 10ᵛⁱ | εἰς ... κάνναβιν (p. 21, l. 3): εἶτα λαβὼν σχοινίον δήσας τοῦ ὀχλουμένου ἀσφαλῶς L, — W | τὰ σχοινία HV: τασχινί(αν) I, τὰς σχοινίας Is, τὰς σχοίνους P

σχοινία τοῦ ἔργου τοῦ ναοῦ τοῦ θεοῦ. καὶ οὕτως σφραγισθὲν καὶ δεθὲν κατηργήθη ὥστε ἱστάναι νύκτα καὶ ἡμέραν νήθειν τὴν κάνναβιν. V. Καὶ ἐκέλευσα * ἀχθῆναί μοι ἕτερον δαίμονα· καὶ ἤγαγέ μοι Ἀσμοδαῖον τὸν πονηρὰν δαίμονα δεδεμένον. 2. καὶ ἐπηρώτησα αὐτόν· »σὺ τίς εἶ;« ὁ δὲ ἀπειλητικὸν βλέμμα ῥίψας λέγει· »σὺ δὲ τίς εἶ;« 3. καὶ εἶπον αὐτῷ· »οὕτως τετιμωρημένος ἀποκρίνῃ;« ὁ δὲ τῷ αὐτῷ βλέμματι προσχὼν εἶπέ μοι· »πῶς ἔχω σοι ἀποκριθῆναι; σὺ μὲν υἱὸς ἀνθρώπου εἶ, κἀγὼ ἀγγέλου, καὶ διὰ θυγατρὸς ἀνθρώπου ἐγεννήθην, * ὥστε οὐδὲν ὑπερήφανον ῥῆμα οὐρανίου γένους πρὸς γηγενῆ. 4. τὸ ἄστρον μοι·

MSS HILPVW = Recc. ABC. 1 τ. ἐργ. τ. ν.: ἐν τῷ ἔργῳ τοῦ κτίσματος P | τοῦ ναοῦ τοῦ θεοῦ τὸ ἔργων V | οὕτως P ls: οὗτος HI | σφραγ. H: σφραγιστ(εν) V, σφραγίσας IP   2 καὶ δεθὲν ego: κ. δοθὲν V, κ. διωθὲν H, κ. δήσας αὐτὴν P, — I | κατηργ. HIV: ἑκατηργ. P, + τὸ δαιμόνιον V | ἱστάνε V, ἵστασθαι in ἱστάναι corr. P | νύκτα κ. ἡμ. ν. τ. κανάβειν IV, νυκτὸς κ. ἡμέρας ν. τ. καναβ. P, νήθυν τ. κανάβειν ἡμέραν κ. νύκταν H 3 κάνναβιν FlMg
C. V. MSS HILPVW = Recc. ABC. 4 (21) Καὶ (1°): τότε L | * H f. 7ʳ, P f. 4ᵛ | ἐτ. δαιμ. HW: pr. καὶ W, ἐτ. δαιμόνιον PVls, ἕτερα δαιμόνια IL, add. rubric. ἔλευσις ἀσμοδίου πρὸς σολομῶν(τα) H | κ. ἡγ. μοι — L | ἤγαγε ... δεδεμ. HI (— ἡγ. μοι) L: εὐθέως μοι προῆλθεν ὁ δαίμων ἀσμόδιος (ex -αιος corr.) δεδεμένος P, ἔστιν ἐνταῦθα C   5 § 2. ἐπηρώτων C 6 δὲ — H | ἀπειλ. βλ. ῥιψ. ego: ἀπολυτικὸν βλέμα ῥίψας H (ῥιψ.: προεπιστρέψας πρός με) L, ἀπηλικὸν ὄμ(μ)α ῥίψας C, βλοσυρὸν βλέμα βλέψας IBls (βλέμμα Kurz), μετὰ θυμοῦ καὶ ὀργῆς ἐμβλέψας με P   7 λέγει HI: ἔφη PC, — L | σὺ ... αὐτῷ — A | δὲ — C | § 3. αὐτὸν C | οὕτως PW: οὗτος V, καὶ οὕτος A | τετιμ. P: τετιμωρημένα C, τετηρημένος IL (-ωμενος) H   8 ἀποκρ. APV: ἀπεκρίθην W, + μοι P, + λέγ < L | δὲ + πάλιν H | τῷ ... προσχ.: τῶ αὐτῶ βλέμματι προσχ. I, τὸ αὐτὸ βλέματι H, τὸ (— V) αὐτοῦ βλέμματι προσχῶν W (πρόσσχήν) V, μετ᾽ ὀργῆς P | εἶπε HI: ἔφη C, λέγει P | μοι — C | πῶς: pr. ἀλλὰ PC   9 ἔχω — P | ἀποκριθῶ P | μὲν: γὰρ P, + γὰρ C | ἀνθρ. υἱὸς P | εἶ — LC | κἀγὼ A: ἐγὼ δὲ PC | ἀγγέλου G: ἀγγέλου σπορᾶ P, ἄγγελός εἰμι (ἤμην H) A 10 καὶ IL: — HP | καὶ ... γηγενῆ (I. 11) — C | θυγ. ἀνθρ. IP; θυγατέρων ἀνθρώπων HL | ἐγενν. LP: ἐγεννήθης I (pr. σὺ) H | * I f. 82ᵛ | ὥστε ILP: ὅτε H | οὐδὲν — L   11 γηγενῆ L: γηγενήν I, γαγενάν l. ls errore, γηγενουν vel -ους H, γηγενεῖς P (in textu) ls | § 4. τὸ: pr. διὸ καὶ P, pr. νὺν δὲ C

C. V 3: Sap. VII 1. Gen. VI 1—4

ἐν οὐρανῷ φωλεύει καὶ οἱ ἄνθρωποί με καλοῦσιν ἅμαξαν, οἱ δὲ τὸν δρακοντόποδα· διὰ τοῦτο καὶ μικρότερα ἄστρα συμπάρεισι τῷ ἐμῷ ἄστρῳ, καὶ γὰρ τοῦ πατρός μου τὸ ἀξίωμα καὶ ὁ θρόνος μέχρι σήμερον ἐν τῷ οὐρανῷ ἐστιν. 5. πολλὰ δὲ μή με 5 ἐρώτα, Σολομῶν, καὶ * γὰρ τὸ βασίλειόν σου διαρραγήσεται ἐν καιρῷ καὶ αὕτη σου ἡ δόξα προσκαιρός ἐστι καὶ ὀλίγον * χρόνον βασανίσαι ἡμᾶς ἔχεις, καὶ πάλιν νομὴν ἔχωμεν * ἐπ᾽ ἀνθρωπότητα ὥστε σέβεσθαι ἡμᾶς ὡς θεούς, μὴ γινωσκόντων τῶν ἀνθρώπων τὰ ὀνόματα τῶν καθ᾽ ἡμῶν τεταγμένων ἀγγέλλων.«
10 6. Ἐγὼ δὲ Σολομῶν ἀκούσας ταῦτα ἐπιμελέστερον αὐτὸν δεσμεύσας ἐκέλευσα ῥαβδίζεσθαι καὶ ἀπολογηθῆναι τίς καλεῖται καὶ τίς ἡ ἐργασία αὐτοῦ. 7. ὁ δαίμων εἶπεν· »ἐγὼ Ἀσμοδαῖος

MSS HILPVW = Recc. ABC. 1 φωλεύει IPC: φολεύειν Η, πολιτεύει L, φωτεύει FIIs | φολεύη ἐν τῷ οὐ(ρα)νῷ C | καὶ HIV: δ W, + αὐτὸ P | οἱ ἄνδρες καὶ πᾶς ἄν(θρωπ)ος με L | οἱ (1°) — P | με Α: — PW, εἰμι(ε) V | καλοῦσιν: λέγουσιν Ρ | ἅμαξα V | τὸν — IW 2 δρακοντ. ΗΙC: δρακοντόπαιδα LP | διὰ ... ἄστρῳ: πλησιάζομαι σὺν τῷ ἄστρῳ αὐτοῦ P | συμπάρεισι IL: συμπάρην H, παρίστανται C 3 τ. ἐ. ἀστ. C: τὸ ἐμὸν ἄστρον Α | καὶ γὰρ ... ἐστιν: — Ρ, καὶ ὁ τοῦ πατρὸς θρόνος ἐστὶν τὸ ἀξίωμα ἐν οὐρανῷ C | γὰρ IL: — H | μου HL: — I | θρόνον H, + μου L 4 μέχρι: + τῇ H | μεχ. σημ. — I | τῷ — I | ἐστιν᾽: δὲ H | § 5. πολ. δὲ: καὶ πολ. Ρ | μή με I: μὴ μεμε L, μοι μὴ Ρ, μοι Η, μὴ C 5 ἐρώτα PC: ἐπερώτας (-ωτὰς L) A | Σολ. Α: — PC | κ. γὰρ Α: ὅτι καὶ Ρ | * H f. 7ᵛ | γὰρ — C | σου τ. βασ. PC | διαρ. ἐν καιρ. ILC: ἐν καιρ. διαραγ. Η, πρὸς χρόνους μικροὺς διαρήγνυται (διαρρ. Pᶜ) P 6 αὕτη ... δόξα ILC: ἡ δόξα σου αὕτη Η | προσκ. ἐστιν ἡ δόξα σου P | προσκ. ἐστι: πρὸς καιρὸν εἰσὶν L, προσκ. δὲ Η, ἀποχωρίσει C | ὀλ. χρ. ὀλίγα P | * L f. 10ᵛ² 7 βασ. ἡμ. ἔχεις C: ἡμ. τυραννήσεις P, βασ. με ἔχεις Α | νομὰν V | ἔχωμεν HL: ἔχομεν (post ἀνθρωπ.) I, ἕξομεν P, εὕρομεν V, εὕρωμεν W | " V f. 438ᵛ | ἐπ᾽ Α: εἰς Ρ, πρὸς C, + τὴν PC 8 θεοὺς: + ὄντας PV, ὄντες W | γινώσκοντα Η, -οντες W, -οντος V | τῶν: τὸν Η, — L 9 τὰ — L | καθ᾽ ἡμῶν HIV: καθεμένων L, μεθ᾽ ἡμῶν W, καθ᾽ ἡμᾶς Ρ § 6. MSS HILP = Recc. AB. (22) c. V, 6—VI, 10 ἐγὼ δὲ ... τοῦ ἡλίου om. C (= VW) per homoeoarcton 10 ταῦτα ἀκ. Ρ | αὐτ. δεσμ. HL: αὐτ. ἐδέσμευσα καὶ I, δεσμ. αὐτ. Ρ, + καὶ πάλιν περίσφι(γ)ξον αὐτοῦ τοῦ ὀχλουμένου τὰς χεῖρας· καὶ ἐξόρκισον αὐτοῦ τοῦ ἐξελθεῖν· καὶ τύψας τῇ κεφαλῇ τοῦ ὀχλουμένου μετὰ καλάμου· καὶ μετὰ ἀρτίκου λέγει ἔξελθε πονηρὸν δαιμόνιον ἐπ᾽ ὀνόματι τοῦ κ(υρίο)υ· καὶ τοῦ παιδὸς σολομῶντος· καὶ L 11 ῥαβδ.: αὐτὸν ῥανδιζ. Η, αὐτὸν ὀργίζεσθαι L, μαστίζεσθαι βουνεύροις Ρ | ἀπολογεῖσθαι P | τίς: πῶς I | καλεῖ σε (1. καλεῖσαι) Η 12 αὐτοῦ — H § 7. ὁ δὲ ἔφη μοι Ρ

C. V 7: cf. Tob. III 8; VI 14 f.

V, 7—10 ἀπόκρισις τοῦ Ἀσμοδαίου 23*

καλοῦμαι ⌈περικλυτός· οἰδαίνομαι⌉ κακουργίαν ἀνθρώπων ἐν ὅλῳ τῷ κόσμῳ. νεονύμφων ἐπίβουλός εἰμι· παρθένων κάλλος ἀφανίζω καὶ καρδίας ἀλλοιῶ.« 8. ἔφην δὲ αὐτῷ· *»μόνη αὕτη σου ἡ ἐργασία;« * ὁ δὲ πάλιν λέγει· »διὰ τῶν ἄστρων ⌈στρώνω
5 θηλυμανίας καὶ ἔπειτα εἰς τρικυμίας⌉ καὶ ἕως ἑπτὰ ἐφόνευσα.« * 9. καὶ οὕτως ὥρκισα αὐτὸν τὸ ὄνομα κυρίου Σαβαώθ· »φοβήθητι, Ἀσμοδαῖε, τὸν θεὸν καὶ εἰπέ μοι ἐν ποίῳ ἀγγέλῳ καταργῆσαι.« ὁ δαίμων λέγει· »Ῥαφαὴλ ὁ παρεστὼς ἐνώπιον τοῦ θεοῦ· διώκει δέ με καὶ ἧπαρ μετὰ χολῆς ἰχθύος ἐπὶ κροκίνων
10 ἀνθράκων καπνιζόμενον.« 10. ἐπηρώτησα πάλιν αὐτὸν λέγων· »μὴ κρύψῃς ἀπ᾽ ἐμοῦ ῥῆμα, ὅτι ἐγώ εἰμι Σολομῶν υἱὸς Δαυείδ,

MSS HILP = Recc. AB. 1 καλοῦ I | περικλυτός ego: περίκρυτος I, περύκρυτος H, περικρίτην L, παρὰ βροτοῖς P, 1. forte περίκριτός (i. q. περὶ et κριτός), excellentissimus? | οἴδαιν... κόσμῳ: — P | οἰδαίνομαι ego: εἰ δαί νε μαι H, εἰδένεμαι καὶ L ἠδύνομαι I | κακουργίας I | ἐν .. κόσμῳ ante περικλυτός ponit I 2 νεονυμφ... παρθ.: καὶ ἡ ἐργασία μου ἐστὶ τὸ τοὺς νεονύμφους ἐπιβουλεύειν μὴ συμμιγῆναι, καὶ παντελῶς ἀποχωρίζω διὰ πολλῶν (f. 5ʳ) συμφορῶν, καὶ γυναικῶν παρθ. P | ἐπίβολος I | παρθ.: παρνα, θ supra π et ο supra α (2°) scr. H | κάλλος P: κάλος HI, καλῶς L | καὶ — I | 3 § 8. (23) ἔφη H | δὲ: δ᾽ ἐγὼ P | ἔφην δὲ αὐτῷ: καὶ πάλιν εἴπον L | * hic explicit pagina non omnino scripta cod. ms. I
MSS HLP = Recc. AB. 3 καὶ μόνη L μόνων H | αὕτη .. ἐργ.: σου ἡ ἐργ. ἔστιν αὕτη P 4 L f. 11ʳ¹ | πάλιν — P | λέγει P: λέγων H, ἔφη L, + μοι P | διὰ τῶν ... ἐφόνευσα: περιφέρω ἀνθρώπους εἰς λύσσαν (Mg 1324) καὶ εἰς ὄρεξιν, ἔχον(τες) τὰς γυναίκας αὐτῶν πάλιν εἰς ἑτέρας ἑτέρων ἀπέρχεσθαι ἐν νυκτὶ καὶ ἡμέρᾳ, ὥστε καὶ τὴν ἁμαρτίαν ἐπιτελεῖν καὶ εἰς φόνους ἐμπλακήσεσθαι P | στρώνω ego: ἴστρον L, — H, cf. Dieterich, Unters. p. 220, 230 f., 1. fortasse οἰστρῶ? 5 θυλιμανίας L, — H 6 H f. 8ʳ | § 9. (24) καὶ ... αὐτὸν: ὥρκισα δὲ αὐτῷ P | τῷ ὀνόματι L | φοβηθ.: λέγων pr. P, add. L 7 τ. θεὸν ἀσμοδαῖε P | ἐν — P | ἐκ ποίου ἀγγέλου L | καταργῇ σύ P 8 ὁ δαιμ. λεγ.: ὁ δὲ ἔφη P | λέγων H | διὰ ῥαφαὴλ τοῦ ἀρχαγγέλου τοῦ παρεστῶτος ἐνώπιον τοῦ θρόνου τοῦ θεοῦ P | παρεστικὸς L 9 με δὲ H | καὶ — P | ἰχθύος ἧπαρ καὶ χολὴ P | ἧπαρ — L | (με)τὰ χολῆς L: σὺν χολὴν H | ἐπὶ κορκίνων ἀνθρ. καπν. H, καπνιζόμενος ἐπὶ κορκίνου ἀνθρ. L, ἐπὶ μυρικίνῳ ἄνθρακι ἐπικαπνιζόμενα P, + καὶ λαβὼν καὶ λαβὼν (sic) ὁ ἀναγινώσκων τὴν ἁγίαν διαθήκην ταύτην· ἰχθύος χολὴν καπνίσας (III litt. perierunt, fortasse ὑπὸ vel τὸν) ὀχλούμενον λέγ(ων)· διώκει σε ῥαφαὴλ ὁ παρεστικὸς ἐνώπιον τοῦ θεοῦ· λέγ(ε) τοῦτο τρεῖς καὶ ἄρξου L
10 § 10. ἐπερώτων δὲ αὐτὸν L | πάλιν ἐγὼ P | λέγων H: λέγω L, — P 11 ὅτι ... Δαυείδ: ὅτι ἐγὼ ἔλαβα ἐξεσίαν τοῦ χειρῶσαι πάντας τοὺς δαίμονας L, + βασιλέως Ἰ(σρα)ὴλ P

C. V 9: cf. Tob. VI 17 f.; VIII 2 f.

καὶ εἰπέ μοι τὸ ὄνομα τοῦ ἰχθύος οὗ σὺ σέβῃ.« ὁ δὲ λέγει· »τὸ ὄνομα κέκληται γλάνις·· ἐν τοῖς ποταμοῖς τῶν Ἀσσυρίων εὑρίσκεται· μόνος γὰρ ἐκεῖ γεννᾶται, ὅτι κἀγὼ ἐν τοῖς μέρεσιν ἐκείνοις εὑρίσκομαι.« 11. καὶ λέγω αὐτῷ· »οὐδὲν ἕτερον παρά σου, 5 Ἀσμοδαῖε;« καὶ εἰπέ μοι· »ἐπίσταται ἡ δύναμις τοῦ θεοῦ τοῦ διὰ τῆς αὐτοῦ σφραγῖδος δεσμεύσαντός με ἀλύτοις δεσμοῖς ὅτι ἅπερ σοι εἶπον ἀληθῆ εἰσιν. ἀξιῶ δέ σε, βασιλεῦ Σολομῶν, μή με κατακρίνῃς εἰς ὕδωρ.« 12. ἐγὼ δὲ μειδιάσας εἶπον· »ζῇ κύριος ὁ θεὸς τῶν πατέρων μου * σίδηρα ἔχεις φορέσαι καὶ πηλὸν ποιή-
10 σεις εἰς ὅλην τὴν σκευὴν τοῦ ναοῦ ἀνατρίβων τὴν χορηγίαν τῆς κώμης.« καὶ ἐκέλευσα γενέσθαι ὑδρίας δέκα καὶ περιχώννυσθαι αὐτόν.

MSS HLP = Recc. AB. 1 οὖ σὺ σέβῃ: οὗ οὐ σεύει H, οὗ σέβης L, ᾦ σὺ σέβῃ | ὁ δὲ λέγει H; ὁ δὲ ἔφη P, — L | τ. ὀν. κεκλ. γλάνις: τὸ ὀν. καίκτητε γλάνος H, ὀνόματι γλάνος P, λέγεται ὁ ἰχθὺς· γλαῦκος L 2 γλάνις vel γλανίς conj. Bncn | εὑρισκ. ἐν τ. ποτ. ἀσσυρίας P | τοῖς — H | τῶν — H |
* L f. 11¹² 3 μόνος .. γενν. H: μόνοις ἐν τοῖς ὕδασι ἐκείνοις γενᾶται L, — P | ὅτι κἀγὼ H: ὅτι ἐγὼ L, διότι καὶ P | ἐν τ. μερ. ἐκ.: ἐν ταῖς μέρεσιν ἐκείναις H, ἐν ἐκείναις ταῖς ἡμέραις L, εἰς ἐκεῖνα τὰ μέρη P 4 εὑρισκ. HL: καταπεριπολεύω P | § 11. (25) κ. λέγω αὐτῷ (αὐτὸ) H: ἐγὼ δὲ λέγω πρὸς αὐτὸν P, ὁ δὲ σολομῶν L | ἕτερον HP: ἑτέρῳ L, ἑταῖρον vel ἔτυμον conj. Bncn | σου HL: σοι P 5 Ἀσμοδ. HLBncn: ἀσμοδίῳ P | κ. εἶπε HL: ὁ δὲ ἔφη P | μοι — L | ἐπίσταμαι L, ἐπίστασαι H | τοῦ διὰ ... δεσμ. H: διὰ τ. σφρ. αὐτοῦ δεσμ. L, τοῦ διὰ τῆς ἐκείνου σφρ. δεσμεύσας P, ἡ διὰ ... δεσμεύσασα Crtr 6 με — H | * H f. 8ᵛ 7 σοι P James: σὺ HL | εἴπω H | εἶπον σοι P | εἰσιν P: εἶναι HL | ἀξιῶ δέ σε H: ἀξιῶ σε δὲ L, δέομαί σου P | σολ. βασ. L 8 § 12. μειδιάσας HP: θαυμάσας L ζῇ ... φορέσαι: κύριος ὁ θεὸς τῶν πατ. μου ποίησον σίδηρον ὥσπερ μανιάκην καὶ βαλὼν τοῦ ὀχλουμένου εἰς τὸν τράχηλον αὐτοῦ καὶ ἀναγινώσκων τὴν ἄνων (l. ἄνω) ταύτην διαθήκην· εἶτα λέγει ὁ ἀναγινώσκων· ὅτι σίδηρα ἔχεις φορέσε (l. -σαι) L 9 * P f. 5ᵛ | ἔχεις φορ. H: φορέσω σε P | καὶ: pr. ἀλλὰ P | supra τὸν πηλὸν adscr. ποιήσεις 10 εἰς: ἐφ' H | κατασκευὴν P | ἀνατρίβουν L | τ. χορ. τ. κωμ. H: τ. χορ. τοῦ ναοῦ L, τοῖς ποσί σου P, l. fortasse τ. χορ. ταῖς κόμαις? 11 κ. ἐκελ.: ἐκελ. δὲ L | γενέσθαι H: ἀχθῆναι L, δοθῆναι αὐτῷ P | δέκα ὑδρ. φέρειν ὕδωρ P | καὶ ... αὐτόν — P | περιχωναισθαι H | αὐτόν: + καὶ λαβὼν ὁ ἀναγινώσκων ἐκ τῶν τεσσάρων γονιῶν τοῦ ναοῦ· τοῦ δεσποτικοῦ χωριγην (f. 11ᵛ¹) ἐκ τῆς ἐπικειμένης ὕλης καὶ τύχους (l. τείχους) καὶ τρίψας αὐτὸν καὶ ποιήσας ψηλόν· εἶτα λαβὼν ὑδρίας δέκα γεμᾶται ἐπὶ τὴν χορηγίαν καὶ σταλάξας ἀπὸ ἑκάστης ὑδρίας καὶ πηλὸν χρίσας ἐπὶ τὸ μέτοπον τοῦ ὀχλουμένου καὶ τὸν πόγωνα καὶ τῶν δύο ὀτίων· εἶτα ἀπογυμνώσας τὸν ὀχλούμενον καὶ ἀνατρίψας αὐτοῦ ὅλον τῶ σώμα μετὰ τῆς χωριγίας ἀπὸ τοῦ ἀμφαλοῦ καὶ ἄνω εἶτα ὁ ἀναγινώσκων· πάλιν τὴν ἄνω ταύτην διαθήκην L.

καὶ δεινῶς στενάξας ὁ δαίμων τὰ κελευσθέντα αὐτὸν κατειργάζετο. τοῦτο δὲ ἐποίησε διότι καὶ τὸ προγνωστικὸν εἶχεν ὁ Ἀσμοδαῖος. 13. καὶ ἐδόξασα τὸν θεὸν ἐγὼ Σολομῶν τὸν δόντα ͅοι τὴν ἐξουσίαν ταύτην· τὸ δὲ ἧπαρ τοῦ ἰχθύος καὶ τὴν χολὴν ͅετὰ κλάσματος ⌐στύρακος λευκοῦ ὑπέκαιον τὸν Ἀσμοδαῖον¬ διὰ ͅὸ εἶναι αὐτὸν δυνατόν, καὶ κατηργεῖτο αὐτοῦ ἡ φωνὴ ⌐καὶ τλήρης ὁδοὺς πικρίας.¬

VI. Καὶ ἐκέλευσα πάλιν παραστῆναι ἔμπροσθέν μου τὸν Βεελζεβοὺλ καὶ προσκαθίσας ἔδοξέ μοι ἐπερωτῆσαι αὐτόν· »διὰ ͅί σὺ μόνος ἄρχων τῶν δαιμόνων;« 2. ὁ δὲ λέγει μοι· »διὰ ͅὸ μόνον με ὑπολειφθῆναι τῶν οὐρανίων ἀγγέλων. ἐγὼ γὰρ ἤμην ἐν πρώτοις οὐράνιος ἄγγελος ὁ προσαγορευόμενος Βεελζεδούλ. 3. καὶ μετ᾽ ἐμοῦ δεύτερος ⌐ἄθεος ὃν ἐπέταμε¬ ὁ θεός, καὶ ͅῦν κατακλεισθεὶς ὧδε ⌐κρατεῖ τὸ¬ ἐν Ταρτάρῳ τῷ δεσμῷ ἐμοῦ

MSS HLP = Recc. AB. 1 δεινῶς: πικρῶς Η | αὐτὸν L: μοι P, — Η | ͅατειργ. LP: κατηρτίζετο Η 2 δὲ — L | ἐποίησε HLBn: ἐποίησα P | ͅιότι: ὅτι L | καὶ — Η | τὸ προγν. εἶχεν Η: προγινώσκων· εἶχεν L, τὰ ͅέλλοντα ᾔδει προγνωστικὸς ὤν, τὸ χαλεπὸν δαιμόνιον P | ὁ — Η 8 § 13. ͅαὶ — L | ἐγὼ σολ. ἐδοξ. τ. θ. τοῦ οὐρανοῦ κ. τῆς γῆς Η | ὁ σολ. L : ἐξουσ. ταυτ. HL: σοφίαν τοῦ δούλου αὐτοῦ P. + ἵνα ὑπογνῶσι ἡμῖν οἱ ͅαίμονες L | χόλην αὐτοῦ P 5 μετὰ ... ὑπέκαιον: μ. κλασ. σωρακλώλου vel στυρακ-) εἶπεν καὶ Η, μ. κλάστομα· συρωκλωκοῦ καὶ εἶπον L, μ. καλα-ͅίου στύρακος λύων ὑπέκαιον P | λευκοῦ ego: l. forte λωτοῦ | τῷ ἀσμο-ͅῳ Η 6 καὶ P: — HL | κατηργείτω P, κατήργηται Η, κατήργειτον L ἡ ... πικρίας (— καὶ) Η: ἡ φ. κ. πλήροις ὁδοῦ πικ. L, ἡ φόρην ὃς πι-ͅία P, ἡ ἀφορητος πικρία P^c (ad marg.)
C. VI. MSS HLP = Recc. AB. (26) 8 παραστῆσαι Η | ἔμπρ. μου: μοι μπρ. P 9 Βεελζ.: + τὸν ἄρχοντα τῶν δαιμονίων P | προσκ. ... αὐτόν HL: ἐπικαθήσας ἐπὶ βήματος ἐνδοξοτέρου ἔφην αὐτῷ P, + καὶ εἶπον αὐ-ὸν Η 10 ἄρχων: ἄρχης Η | § 2. λέγει HL: ἔφη P 11 τὸ: τὸν L | πελήφθην Η, ὑπέληφθα L | ἀγγελ.: + τῶν κατελθόντων P 12 ἤμην P: ͅὶν Η, εἰμὶ L | ἐν πρωτ.: ἐν πρότης HL, ἐν τῷ πρώτῳ οὐρανῷ P | οὐ-ͅάνιος Η: οὐρανοῦ L, πρῶτος P | ἄγγελος HP: μὴ L

§ 3. MS P textum alium praebet hunc: καὶ νῦν κρατῶ πάντων τῶν ἐν ᾧ ταρτάρῳ δεσμῶν (δεσμένων Fl, δεδεμένων Mg). ἔχω δὲ καὶ γόνον καὶ ερπιπολεύει ἐν τῇ ἐρυθρᾷ θαλάσσῃ, καὶ ὡς ἴδιον τινὰ καιρὸν ἐπανέρχεται ρός με ὑποτασσόμενος, καὶ τὰ ἑαυτοῦ ἔργα πρός με ἀνακαλύπτει, καὶ στη-ͅζω αὐτὸν ἐγώ.
MSS HL = Rec. A. l. 13, § 3. ἄθεος ὃν ἐπέταμε ego: ἀθάε ἐπὶ τομὴν Η, θαὲ, ἐπὶ τὸ μὴν L | ὁ — L 14 κατὰ κλειθεῖς L | κρατεῖ τὸ ego: ͅρατεῖτε Η, κρατῶ τε L; l. forte κρατῶ τό? | ἐν τῷ ταρτάρῳ δεσμῷ L

γένος· καὶ τρέφεται ἐν τῇ Ἐρυθρᾷ θαλάσσῃ· ὃς ἐν καιρῷ ἰδίῳ ἐλεύσεται εἰς θρίαμβον.« 4. καὶ εἶπον αὐτῷ· »τίνες εἰσὶν αἱ πράξεις σου;« καὶ εἶπέ μοι· »κἀγὼ καθαιρῶ διὰ τυράννων καὶ τὰ δαιμόνια ποιῶ παρὰ ἀνθρώποις σέβεσθαι καὶ τοὺς ἁγίους καὶ
5 τοὺς ἐκλεκτοὺς ἱερεῖς εἰς ἐπιθυμίαν ἐγείρω. ** καὶ φθόνους ἐν πόλεσι καὶ φόνους ἀποτελῶ καὶ πολέμους ἐπάγω.« 5. καὶ εἶπα αὐτῷ· »προσένεγκέ μοι τὸν ἐν τῇ Ἐρυθρᾷ θαλάσσῃ ὃν εἶπας τρεφόμενον.« ὁ δὲ λέγει· »οὐκ ἀνενέγκω πρός σε οὐδένα. ἐλεύσεται δέ τις ὀνόματι Ἐφιππᾶς ὃς ἐκεῖνον δεσμεύσει καὶ ἀναγάγει
10 ἐκ τοῦ βυθοῦ.« 6. καὶ εἶπον αὐτῷ· »λέγε μοι πῶς ἐκεῖνός ἐστιν ἐν τῷ βυθῷ τῆς Ἐρυθρᾶς θαλάσσης καὶ τί τὸ ὄνομα αὐτοῦ.« ὁ δὲ ἔφη· »μή με ἐρωτᾷς· οὐ δύνασαι παρ' ἐμοῦ μαθεῖν, αὐτὸς γὰρ ἐλεύσεται πρός σε διὰ τὸ καὶ ἐμὲ πρός σε εἶναι«.

MSS HL = Rec. A. 1 γένους L | Ἐρυθ. — H | ὃς: ὡς HL

§ 4. MS P. (27) ἐγὼ σολομῶν ἔφην πρὸς αὐτὸν λέγων· βεελζεβούλ, τίς (f. 6ʳ) ἐστὶν ἡ πρᾶξις σου; ὁ δὲ λέγει· ἐγὼ βασιλεῖς ἀπολῶ· συμμαχῶ μετὰ ἀλλοφύλων τυράννων· καὶ τοὺς ἐμοὺς δαίμονας ἐπιβάλλω πρὸς τοὺς ἀνθρώπους ἵνα εἰς αὐτοὺς πιστεύωσι καὶ ἀπόλλωνται· καὶ τοὺς ἐκλεκτοὺς δούλους τοῦ θεοῦ, ἢ ἱερεῖς καὶ πίστους ἀνθρώπους εἰς ἐπιθυμίας ἁμαρτιῶν πονηρῶν καὶ αἱρέσεων κακῶν καὶ ἔργων παρανόμων διεγείρω, καὶ ὑπακούουσί μοι, καὶ εἰς ἀπόλειαν φέρω αὐτούς. καὶ φθόνους καὶ φόνους καὶ πολέμους καὶ ἀρρενοβατίας καὶ ἕτερα κακὰ τοῖς ἀνθρώποις ἐνεργῶ, καὶ ἀπολῶ τὸν κόσμον.
§ 5. (28) εἶπον οὖν αὐτῷ· προσάγαγέ μοι τὸν σὸν γόνον ὅνπερ λέγεις ὅτι ἐστὶν ἐν τῇ θαλάσσῃ τῇ ἐρυθρᾷ. ὁ δὲ λέγει· ἐγὼ αὐτὸν οὐ φέρω πρὸς σέ· ἐλεύσεται δὲ πρός με ἕτερος δαίμων ὀνόματι ἐφιππᾶς, (Mg 1325) αὐτὸν δεσμεύσω καὶ αὐτὸς ἐκ τοῦ βυθοῦ ἀναγάγει πρός με. § 6. ἐγὼ δὲ λέγω πρὸς αὐτόν· πῶς ἔστιν ὁ υἱός σου ἐν τῷ βυθῷ τῆς (FlMg, τοῖς MS) θαλάσσης καὶ τί τὸ ὄνομα αὐτοῦ; ὁ δὲ ἔφη· μή με ἐπερωτᾷς, οὐ γὰρ δυνήσῃ παρ' ἐμοὶ μαθεῖν· αὐτὸς γὰρ ἐλεύσεται πρὸς σὲ δι' ἐμοῦ κελεύσματος καὶ εἴποι σοι φανερῶς.

MSS HL = Rec. A. 1. 2, § 4. αὐτῷ: αὐτὸν H   3 καθαιρῷ ego: καθαίρω HL | τύρανον H   4 τὰ δαιμόνιαν H, τοὺς δαίμονας L | σεβ. π. ἀνθρ. L   5 * H f. 9ᵛ | ἐγύρω L, ἔγειρον H | ** L f. 12ʳ¹   6 φόνον ἐν πολ. κ. φθόνους L | ἀποτελῶν κ. πολ. ἐπάγω H, ἀποστελῶ ἐν πολέμοις· ἐπάγω καὶ πόνους καὶ οὐκ ἔστιν τοῖς ἀνθρώποις· οὐδὲν καλὸν οὐ (l. δ) δύναμαι ποιῆσαι αὐτῷ L | § 5. κ. εἶπα αὐτῷ H: ὁ δὲ βασιλεὺς λέγει L   7 τὸν ... τρεφομ.: τὸν ... ὡς εἶπας τρεφομένας H, ὃν εἶπας γένους τὸ ἐν τῇ ἐρ. θαλ. τρεφομένους L   8 οὐκ (ἀνέγκω) ... οὐδ. H: ἐγὼ αὐτῶ οὐκ ἀνενέγκω πρὸς σὲ L   9 Ἐφιππᾶς (cf. P): ἔφιππος H, ἐφηπτας L | ὃς ἐκεῖνον ego: ὡς ἐκεῖνος HL | δεσμ. καὶ H: δεσμεύσας L | ἀνάγει L   10 § 6. αὐτὸν H   11 τῷ ... θαλ. L: τῇ ἐρυθρᾷ θαλάσσῃ H | τί — L   12 παρ' H: περὶ L   13 τὸ ego: τοῦτο HL

7. Είπον δὲ αὐτῷ· »λέγε μοι ἐν ποίῳ ἄστρῳ προσοικεῖσαι.« ὁ δὲ λέγει· »τὸ καλούμενον παρὰ ἀνθρώποις Ἑσπερία.« 8. ἐγὼ δὲ λέγω· »φράσον μοι ὑπὸ ποίου ἀγγέλου καταργεῖσαι.« ὁ δὲ * ἔφη· * »ὑπὸ τοῦ παντοκράτορος θεοῦ· καλεῖται δὲ παρ' Ἑβραίοις Πατικῆ, ὁ ἀφ' ὕψους κατελθών· ἔστι δὲ τῶν Ἑλληνιστῶν Ἐμμανουήλ, οὗ δέδοικα τρέμων. ἐάν τίς με ὀρκίσῃ τὸ Ἐλωΐ, μέγα ὄνομα τῆς δυνάμεως αὐτοῦ, ἀφανὴς γίνομαι.« 9. ἐγὼ δὲ Σολομῶν ἀκούσας ταῦτα ἐκέλευσα αὐτὸν Θηβαῖα μάρμαρα πρίζειν. ἐν δὲ τῷ ἄρξασθαι πρίζειν αὐτὸν ἠλάλαζον ὅλα τὰ δαιμόνια μεγάλῃ τῇ φωνῇ διὰ τὸν βασιλέα Βεελζεβούλ· 10. ἐγὼ δὲ Σολομῶν ἐπηρώτων αὐτὸν λέγων· »εἰ βούλει ἄφεσιν λαβεῖν, διήγησαί μοι περὶ τῶν ἐπουρανίων.« ἔφη δὲ ὁ Βεελζεβούλ· »ἄκουσον, βασιλεῦ· ἐὰν θυμιάσῃς στακτὴν καὶ λίβανον καὶ βολβοὺς θαλάσ-

---

§ 7. sectionem hanc om. ms. P. § 8. (29) MS P: ἐγὼ πρὸς αὐτὸν λέγω· λέγε μοι ὑπὸ ποίου ἀγγέλου καταργῇ σύ. ὁ δὲ ἔφη· ὑπὸ ἁγίου καὶ τιμίου ὀνόματος τοῦ παντοκράτορος θεοῦ, τῷ καλουμένῳ παρ' Ἑβραίοις πευστικῷ, οὗ ἡ ψῆφος χμδ´· παρὰ δὲ Ἕλλησι ἐμμανουήλ: καὶ ἐάν τις τῶν Ῥομαίων ὀρκίσῃ με τὸ μέγα ὄνομα τῆς δυνάμεως ἐλεῆθ ἀφανὴς (f. 6ᵛ) γίνομαι. § 9. (30) ἐγὼ σολομῶν ταῦτα ἀκούσας ἐξεπλάγην καὶ ἐκέλευσα αὐτὸν πρίζειν μάρμαρα θηβαῖα. ἐν δὲ τῷ ἄρξασθαι αὐτὸν πρίζειν τὰ μάρμαρα οἱ ἕτεροι δαίμονες ἀνεκραύγασαν φωνὴν μεγάλην, ἀλαλάζοντες διὰ τὸν βασιλέα αὐτῶν βεελζεβούλ. § 10. textum similiorem habent cod. mss. HLP.

MSS HL = Rec. A. 1 § 7. προσοικεῖσαι L: καλεῖσαι Η 2 ὁ δὲ ... Ἕσπερ. Η: — L | § 8: ἐγὼ ego: ὁ HL 3 φράσον ego: ςφρασον Η, φράσω L | ποίων ἀγγέλων Η | * Η f. 10ʳ 4 * L f. 12ʳ² | τοῦ L: — H | καλεῖται ego: καλοῦμαι HL 5 πατικῇ Η, πατηκεῖ L | ὁ (James, οὐ ms.) ... Ἐμμαν. Η: παρὰ δὲ ἕλληνας ἐμμανουήλ καὶ ἀφ' ὕψους κατελθεῖν L 6 οὐ δέδηκα τρεμ. Η, οὐδὲ διατρέμον L | τίς με: τοῖς μοι Η | τις ὀρκ. με L | τῶ ἐλωιθ Η, ἐν τῶ ἐλωΐ L 7 γένομαι L, ἐγένομαι Η | § 9. Σολ. — L 8 αὐτὸν Η: τοῦτον L | Θηβαῖα Η: βριβάϊα L 9 ἐν ... αὐτὸν (αὐτός) Η: εἶτα ὁ ἀναγινώσκων· ἐγγίσας τοῦ ὀχλουμένου ἐπὶ τοῦ στήθους λέγων ἐκ τρίτου μεγαλοφώνος L | ἠλάλαξαν Η | ὅλα — L 10 φωνῇ· λέγων L

MSS HLP = Recc. AB. 1. 10 §. 10 (31) ἐγὼ δὲ HP: ἀκούσας ταῦτα ὁ L 11 ἐπηρώτησα P | αὐτ. πάλιν λεγ. L | βούλει HL: θέλεις P | ἀφ. λαβ.: ἄφεσιν λαβῶν L, ἀφ. εκροῖν (l. ἔχειν) Η, λαβεῖν ἄνεσιν P | διηγησόν L 12 περὶ P: τὴν Α | ἔφη ... Βεελζ.: ἔφη ὁ βασιλεὺς Η, ἐφοβήθη δὲ ὁ βεελζ. καὶ εἶπεν L, λέγει δὲ βεελζ. P | ἄκουσον, βασ. P: — Η, ἀκ. βασιλεὺς καὶ λαβῶν ὁ ἀναγινώσκων· νάρσιν· καὶ κρόκον· καὶ καπνίσας τὸν (f. 12ᵛ¹) ὀχλούμενον· καὶ λέγει ὁ βεελζεβουὲλ· L 13 βολβ. θαλ.: β. θαλασσίους P. βόλους θαλ.. Α

σης, νάρδον τε καὶ κρόκον, καὶ λύχνους ἄψῃς ἑπτὰ ἐν σεισμῷ, οἰκίαν ἐρείσεις. ἐὰν δὲ * καθαρὸς ὢν ἄψῃς ὄρθρου ἐν ἡλίῳ ἡμέρας, ὄψεις τοὺς δράκοντας τοὺς ἐπουρανίους πῶς εἰλοῦνται καὶ σύρουσι τὰ ἅρμα τοῦ ἡλίου.« 11. ἐγὼ δὲ Σολομῶν ἀκούσας
5 ταῦτα ἐπετίμησα αὐτὸν καὶ εἶπον· »σιώπησαι καὶ πρίζε τὰ μάρμαρα καθὼς προσέταξά σοι.«
VII. Καὶ εὐλογήσας τὸν θεὸν ἐγὼ Σολομῶν ἐκέλευσα παρεῖναί μοι ἕτερον δαίμονα· καὶ ἦλθε πρὸ προσώπου μου. καὶ ἦν τὸ πρόσωπον ἐπιφέρων ἐν τῷ ἀέρι ἄνω ὑψηλὸν καὶ τὸ ὑπόλει-
10 πον τοῦ σώματος εἰλούμενον ὡσεὶ κοχλίας. 2. καὶ ἔρρηξε στρατιώτας οὐκ ὀλίγους καὶ ἤγειρε * καὶ λάβρον κονιορτὸν ἀπὸ τῆς γῆς καὶ ἀνέφερεν ἄνω καὶ πολλὰ ἔρριπτεν ἐπὶ τὸ ἐμὲ θαμβεῖσθαι, καὶ εἶπον· ⌜»τίνα ἔχω ἐρωτῆσαι;« ἕως ἐπὶ πολύ. 3. καὶ ἀναστάν-

MSS HLP = Recc. AB. 1 νάρδιν L | ἀνάψῃς L | ἐν σεισμῷ: — H, ἐν εἱρμῷ conj. dubitanter Cr 2 οἰκ. ἐρεισ. P: οὖν καὶ ἂν ὡρίσῃς H, οὐκείαν ὁρώσεις L | δὲ — L | * H f. 10ᵛ | καθ. ὢν P: καθαρὸν A | ἀνάψῃς L 3 ἡμέρας ego: ἐνημέραν H, ἡμέρᾳ L, ἡμ (compendia mihi inenodabilia), l. fortasse ἡμέρᾳ vel ἡμερῶν P, ἡμμένου (ἡμετέρου, ἡμετέρῳ?) Fl | pro ἐν ἡλ. ἡμ. l. ἐν ὕλῃ ἐνήμενος(?), cf. Test. XII Patr., Levi XVIII 3 | ὄψοι P | τοὺς (1°): τότε P | δράκοντας HP: διακόνους L | οὐρανίους P 4 σύρουσι HP: ἐσυρνουσι L | ἡλίου LP: θεοῦ H, forte recte
MSS HLPVW = Recc. ABC. § 11.(32) 4 ἐγὼ HPC: ὁ L | ἐγὼ ... ἀκουσ. bis scr. V 5 ταῦτα ἀκουσ. P | ταῦτα ... σοι — C | ἐπετίμησεν L, ἐπετίμουν H | κ. εἶπον· »σιωπ. καὶ ego: κ. ἐσιώπα καὶ ἐλάλουν αὐτόν H, σιωπῆσαι καὶ L, κ. εἶπον, σιώπα μοι ἕως τούτου καὶ P 6 καθὼς προσετ. σοι: καλὸς προέταξά σοι· λέγε ὁ σολομῶν L, ὡς προσετ. σοι P, κατὰ τὸ ὁρισθὲν σοι H

C. VII. MSS HLPVW = Recc. ABC. 7 Καὶ: εἶτα L | Καὶ ... θεὸν: bis scr. V, + τοῦ οὐρανοῦ B | ἐγὼ Σολ.: — L, + καὶ H | τότε ἐκέλευσεν L | παρεῖναι: περίνε L 8 ἕτερα δαιμόνια· καὶ ἦλθον ἕτερον δαιμόνιον ἐπὶ προσώπου L | κ. ἦν ... ἐπιφερ. A: ὃς ἦν ἐπιφ. τ. προσ. P, ὅπερ ἦν (— V) ἡμιπρόσωπον C 9 ἐν ... ὑψηλὸν P (— ἄνω) C: ἐν τὸ ἀρενόφει H, τὸ ἄρενω· ὄψιν L | τὸ λοιπὸν σῶμα· L | ὑπόλοιπον P: ὑπόλειπον HC 10 σώματος H: πνεύματος PC | ὡσεὶ κοχ. P: ὡς εἰ κόχλον H, ὡς κοχλύος L, ὡς κοχλίας C | § 2. ἔρρηξε ... ὀλιγ. A: ὀλίγους διέρρηξεν PC 11 κ. ἤγειρε κ. λαβ. κον. ego: κ. εἴγειρεν κ. λαῦρον οὐκ ὀνιορτόν H, κ. ἔγειρεν δὲ καὶ λαύραν καὶ (— V) κον. C, ἤγειρε δὲ καὶ φοβερὸν κον. P | ἀπὸ HC: ἐπὶ LP | πολλὰ A: πάλιν PC 12 ἐν τῷ θαυμάσθαι με L, ἐν τῷ ἐμὲ θαμβηθῆναι C | ἐμὲ: ἡμᾶς P | θαμβῆσαι P 13 καὶ ... ἐρωτῆσαι — C | κ. εἶπον H: κ. εἶπεν P, — L | ἐρωτίσω H | ἕως ... μου ego: καὶ δὴ ὃς ἐπεὶ πολὴ ἀνείσταντά με V, κ. δὴ ὡς ἐπὶ πολὺ ἀναστάντος μοι W, ἐφ' ἐπὶ πολὺ καὶ ἀν. μου H, ἕως ἐπὶ πολλὴ· καὶ ἀν. μου L, ὡς ἐπὶ πολὺ, καὶ ἀναστάντα με [in textu, κ(αὶ) ἀναστὰς ad marg.] P

VII, 3—6 Λὶξ Τέτραξ 29*

τος μου ἔπτυσα χαμαὶ * κατ' ἐκεῖνον τὸν τόπον καὶ ἐσφράγισα τῷ δακτυλιδίῳ τοῦ θεοῦ, καὶ οὕτως ἔστη ἡ αὔρα. τότε ἠρώτησα αὐτὸν λέγων· »σὺ τίς εἶ;« καὶ οὕτως κονιορτὸν τινάξας ἀπεκρίθη μοι· »τί θέλεις, βασιλεῦ Σολομῶν;« 4. ἀπεκρίθην δὲ αὐτῷ· »εἰπέ μοι τί λέγεις κἀγώ σε ἐρωτᾶν θέλω.« οὕτως δὲ εὐχαριστῶ τῷ θεῷ τῷ σοφίσαντί με πρὸς τὰς βουλὰς αὐτῶν ἀποκρίνεσθαι. ἔφη δέ μοι ὁ δαίμων· »ἐγὼ καλοῦμαι Λὶξ Τέτραξ.« 5. εἶπον δὲ αὐτῷ· »τίς ἡ πρᾶξίς σου;« ἔφη δέ· »ἀνθρώπους σκορπίζω καὶ στρόφους ποιῶ καὶ πῦρ ἅπτω καὶ ἀγροὺς ἐμπυρίζω καὶ οἴκους καταργῶ. ἐπὶ πλεῖστον δὲ ἔχω τὴν πρᾶξιν ἐν θέρει. ἐὰν δὲ καιρὸν εὕρω, ὑποδύνω εἰς γωνίας τοίχων νύκτα καὶ ἡμέραν· ἤδη γὰρ γόνος εἰμὶ τοῦ μεγάλου.« 6. εἶπον * δὲ αὐτῷ·

MSS HLPVW = Recc. ABC. 1 § 3. ἔπτυσα C (ad marg.) P: πτύσας A, πτύσαι P (in textu) | * H f. 11ʳ | κατ'... θεοῦ H: καὶ κατ'... τὸ δακτυλίδιον τ. θ. L, κατ' ἐκείνου τοῦ τόπου καὶ ... θεοῦ (in textu) P (— τοῦ θεοῦ) V, χαμαὶ κατ' ἐκείνου τοῦ τ⟨ό⟩π⟨ον⟩ κ(αὶ) ἐ P (ad marg.), καὶ ἐσφρ. τ. δακτ. κατ' ἐκεῖνον τοῦ τόπου W   2 οὕτως PC: οὗτος A | ἔστη C: ἔστην (ex ἔστιν corr.) P, ἐστὶν L, ἔσται H | αὔρα LP: λαύρα C, λαύρα τοῦ δαίμονος σιωπῶν H, + ἐκείνη LC | τότε κἀγὼ H | ἐπηρώτησα C   3 τίς εἶ σύ H | κ. οὕτως L: κ. οὗτος H, κ. τούτῳ (τοῦτο V) πάλιν C, ἄρα (αὔρα conj. Fl) οὕτω πάλιν P | τινάξας AP: τὴν ἄξαν V, ῥίψας W   4 μοι: + ὁ δαίμων καὶ εἶπεν L | τί με.θέλεις ἐπερωτᾶν C | βασ. Σολ.: — L, add. rubric. ἀπόκρησις τοῦ δαίμονος ἠλὶξ πρὸς σολομ⟨ῶν⟩ H | § 4. ἀπεκρίθην ... ἀποκρίνεσθαι — H | ἀπεκριθ. ... οὕτως δὲ: ἐγὼ δὲ εἶπον L | ἀπεκρ. δὲ αὐτ. (— δὲ) P (+ λέγων) V: καὶ εἶπον W   5 τί ἂν λέγῃς C | δὲ: τ(οὺς) C   6 τοῦ θεοῦ W | τὸ σοφήσαντος V, τοῦ φήσαντος W | αὐτῶν P: αὐτοῦ C, ἡμῶν L | ἀποκρίνεσθαι P: ἃς ἀποκρ. μοι L, τοῦ ἀποκριθῆναί μοι C   7 (33) δέ LPC; — H | μοι LP: — HC | ὁ δαιμ. A: τὸ πνεῦμα C, — P | καλοῦμαι AC: εἰμι P | Λὶξ Τέτραξ (nomina duo celeberrimarum literarum Ephesiarum) ego: ἡ λὶξ τέφρας H, εἰς λὲξ· τεφράσθαι (cum sequentibus — ἀνθρώπων — conjunctus) L, θλὶξ τέφρας C, τὸ πνεῦμα τῆς τέφρας (τέφραν falso Fl) PFlMgtrCrtr   8 § 5. εἶπον δε ... ἔφη δὲ — A | εἶπον δὲ αὐτῷ PV: καὶ ἐπηρώτησα αὐτόν W | ἔφη δέ C: ἡ δὲ ἔφη P | ἀν(θρώπ)ων L   9 σκορπίζω C: σκοτίζω AP | καὶ στροφ. ... ἅπτω: — P, + ἀπιστίω (l. ἀπίστως) C | ἀγροὺς: + πυρὶ A   10 καταργῶ PC: κατάγω A | ἐπὶ πλεῖστον P: κατὰ πλίστην H, κατὰ πληθὴν L, τὰ πλεῖοτα C | δὲ PW: — AV | θέρην L   11 ἐὰν AC: ὅταν P | καιρόν: κερῶ V | ὑποδύνω HC: ὑποδύνομαι P, τόπον (f. 13ʳ¹) παιδινὸν L, τοίχων HC: τυχῶν L, τριχῶν P, τειχῶν Fl | νυκτὸς καὶ ἡμέρας PV, ἡμέρας καὶ νυκτὸς W   12 ἤδη ... μεγάλου PC: καὶ γὰρ συγγενῆς εἰμὶ τοῦ (— L) μεγάλου δαίμονος A | § 6. * W f. 268ᵛ | καὶ εἶπον αὐτὸν A | δὲ C: οὖν P | αὐτῶν V

»ἐν ποίῳ ἄστρῳ κεῖσαι;« ὁ δὲ εἶπεν· »εἰς αὐτὸ τὸ ἄκρον τοῦ
κέρατος τῆς σελήνης τὸ ἐν τῷ νότῳ εὑρισκόμενον ἐκεῖ μου τὸ
ἄστρον. διότι τὰ σφάλματα τοῦ ἡμιτριταίου προσετάχθην ἀνι-
μᾶσθαι. διὰ τοῦτο ἰδόντες πολλοὶ τῶν ἀνθρώπων εὔχονται εἰς
5 τὸν ἡμιτριταῖον ἐν τοῖς τρισὶν ὀνόμασι τούτοις· »βουλταλά·
θαλλάλ· μελχάλ·« καὶ ἰῶμαι αὐτούς.« 7. εἶπον δὲ αὐτῷ ἐγὼ
Σολομῶν· »ὅτε οὖν θέλεις κακουργεῖν, ἐν τίνι καταργεῖσαι;«
⌈ὁ δὲ ἔφη· »ἐν τῷ ἀγγέλῳ ᾧ καὶ ὁ ἡμιτριταῖος * παύεται.«
ἐπηρώτησα δὲ αὐτόν· »ἐν ποίῳ ὀνόματι καταργεῖσαι;« ὁ δὲ εἶπεν·
10 »ἐν τῷ ὀνόματι τοῦ ἀρχαγγέλου Ἀζαήλ.⌉« 8. καὶ ἐπεσφράγισα

MSS HLPVW = Recc. ABC. 1 ἐν — P | σὺ κεῖσαι H, συνοικῆσαι L
| εἶπεν LW: ἔφη PV, λέγει H | εἰς... σελ. τὸ scr. posteaque supra εἰς scr.
ἐν et in αὐτῶ τῶ ἄκρω τ. κ. τ. σ. τῶ corr. P^c | αὐτὸ HP: — LC 2 κέρα-
τος τ. σελ. PC: καιράτου τῆς γῆς H, κέρκου τῆς ☾ (= γῆς) L | τὸ... εὑ-
ριχ. ego: τῷ ἐν τ. ν. εὑρισκομένῳ BC, τὸν ἐν τὸ τόπω εὑρισκομένους H, ἐν
τόπω εὑρισκόμενος L | ἐκεῖ μου: ἐκείνου L | μου HC: μοι ἐστὶ P 3 τὰ
σφαλμ. τ. ἡμ. προσετ. P (— τὰ) V: σφαλ. τ. ἡμ. εἰμὶ ἐγὼ καὶ προετάχθεν W,
τὰ ἡμέτερα τριταίει (ἡμέτερα τριταία L) σφαλ. προστάτης (-την H) A |
σφαλμ.: σπάοματα conj. Cr 4 ἰδόντες... ἡμιτριταῖον PC: εἶδον πολλοὺς
τῶν ἐθνῶν ἔχοντα πρός με τριταῖον (-αίων H) A 5 * Mg 1328 | ἐν...
τούτοις P: ἐν τούτοις τῆς τρισὶν H, ἐν τούτοις τρισὶν ὀνόμασιν L, ἐν τοῖς δυ-
σὶν ὀνόμασιν τούτοις ἣ καὶ τρισὶν ἅτινα εἰσὶν ταῦτα W, (— ἅτινα εἰσὶν) V |
βουλ.... μελχάλ P: βουλ· ταλ· θαλάλ· H, βουλ· ταγιθαμαν· μελχαγ· rubric.
scr. W, βουλ· ταγιθαμάν· μελχαγί· V, καὶ κράτει τοὺς δύο δατύλους τοῦ
ὀχλουμένου καὶ εἰπὲ οὕτως εἰς τὸ δεξιὸν ὠτίον ἑπτάκις· βουςταλ. θαλάλ· L
| in cod. ms. Vindobon. phil.-graec. no. 108, f. 167^V (S) scriptum est incanta-
mentum hoc: ὁ μιτριτεος (l. ἡμιτριταῖος) ⟨κατά⟩ργηται ἐν τὸ ὀνόματι ⟨το⟩ῦ
⟨ἀ⟩ρχαγγέλου ἀζαζηηλ· τὸν βουλ· τὸν ταγηθαμαν· τὸν μὲλχαγϊ (literae in
uncis fractis inclusae compendiis cryptographicis scriptae sunt) 6 αὐτούς AP:
τούτους C | § 7. εἶπον APW: ἔφη K | δὲ: οὖν H | αὐτῷ PC: — A
7 Σολ. πρὸς αὐτὸν H | ὅτε HP: ὅταν LC | οὖν — L | θέλεις HP:
θέλει L, ἔλθῃς C | κακουργεῖν... καταργεῖσαι ego: κακουργεῖν, ἐν τίνι
κακουργεῖς PC, καταργῇ πῶς καταργῆσαι ἣ καὶ τοῦ μητριταίου παύεται H,
τίς καταργήσοισε· καὶ τὸν τριταῖον· ἐν ποίω ἀγγέλω καταργῆσαι θέλει με L
8 ὁ δὲ ... καταργεῖσαι (l. 9): — A | δέ μοι P | ᾧ P: ὁ C | ἡμιτριταῖος
W: μιτριτέος V, τριταῖος P | ⊢ P f. 7^V | ἐπαναπαύεται P 9 αὐτόν:
αὐτῶ V, + καὶ εἶπον P | ποίῳ δέ P | καταργ. — P | ὁ δὲ εἶπεν C: καὶ
εἶπεν μοι A, ὁ δὲ ἔφη P 10 ἐν τῷ ὀνομ. C: — P | ἐν τῷ ἀρχαγγέλῳ A
| Ἀζαήλ AP: ἀζαζήλ C, ἀζαζηηλ S (v. supra) | § 8. κ. ἐπεσφραγ.: κ. ἐπισ-
σογραφίσασα H, εἶτα ἐσφράγησα L, κ. ἐσφράγισα C, κ. ἐπεκαλεσάμην τὸν ἀρχάγγελον ἀζαηλ, καὶ ἐπεσφραγ. P

τὸν δαίμονα καὶ ἐκέλευσα αὐτὸν λίθους ἁρπάζειν καὶ εἰς τὰ ὑψηλὰ τοῦ ναοῦ ἀκοντίζειν * τοῖς τεχνίταις· καὶ ἀναγκαζόμενον τὸ δαιμόνιον τὰ προστεταγμένα αὐτῷ ἐποίει.

VIII. Κἀγὼ δὲ πάλιν ἐδόξασα τὸ θεὸν τὸν δόντα μοι τὴν ἐξουσίαν ταύτην καὶ ἐκέλευσα ἄλλον δαίμονα παρεῖναί μοι. * καὶ ἦλθον πνεύματα ἑπτὰ συνδεδεμένα καὶ συμπεπλεγμένα, εὔμορφα τῷ εἴδει καὶ εὔσχημα. 2. ἐγὼ δὲ Σολομῶν ἰδὼν αὐτὰ ἐθαύμασα καὶ ἐπηρώτησα αὐτά· »τίνες ἔστε;« οἱ δὲ εἶπον· »ἡμεῖς ἐσμεν στοιχεῖα κοσμοκράτορες τοῦ σκότους.« 3. καί φησιν ὁ πρῶτος· »ἐγώ εἰμι ἡ Ἀπάτη.« ὁ δεύτερος· »ἐγώ εἰμι ἡ Ἔρις.«

MSS HLPVW = Recc. ABC. 1 τ. δαίμονα C: τὸ δαιμόνων H, αὐτῶ L, τὸν ἄγγελον scr. P, mox ἄγγελον transversa linea deleto δαίμονα scr. prim. man. | ἐκέλ. αὐτὸν: προσέταξε τοῦτο L | λίθους μεγάλους PC | ἁπάζειν H | ἁρπάζειν λίθους καὶ εἰς τὰ ὑψηλὰ μέρη τοῦ τείχους ἀκοντήζει L 2 τ. ναοῦ — C | * L f. 13^{r2} | τ. τεχν. P: τοὺς τεχνίτας AC, + κελεύσας τὸν ὀχλούμενον ἐπιτιθέναι· ἐν τῶ ὄμω αὐτοῦ λίθους μέγας: εἶτα ὁ ἀναγινώσκων ἐπίθες αὐτῶ φέρειν· ἔνδω τοῦ ναοῦ· ἀπ᾽ ἔξωμεν L | ἀναγκαζόμενος ὁ δαίμων A 3 προστεταγ. P: προσταγμένα L, προσταχθέντα C | αὐτῷ HC: — LP | ἐποίει HP: ἐνεργεῖν L. ἐπάγει C

C. VIII. MSS HLPVW = Recc. ABC. (34) 4 κἀγὼ δὲ HP: κἀγὼ σολομῶν L, καὶ ἐγὼ C | πάλιν — L | θεὸν τοῦ οὐρανοῦ H | μοι τὴν — C 5 καὶ ἐκέλευσα ... σκότους (l. 9) textum ex ms. W exscr. Gaulminius (Glm) in notis ad Psellum, de oper. daem., Migne PG 122, 824 D, n. 11 | ἄλλον :.. μοι A: παρεῖναί μοι ἕτερον δαίμονα C (δαιμόνιον) P, add. rubric. περὶ τὸν ἑπτὰ δαιμόνων H 6 * f. 12¹ H | ἑπτὰ πν(εύμ)ατα H | πν. ἐπ. θηλυκὰ P | συνδεδ. LPG: συνδεόμεθα H, + ἀλλήλων L | κ. συμπεπλ. P: κ. ἐμπεριπλεγμ(εν)α H, — LC 7 εὐμ. τ. εἴδει HC: εὐμ. τὸ εἶδος P, ἄμορφα τὰ εἴδη L | κ. εὐσχ. P: κ. ἄσχημα A, — C | § 2. ἐγὼ δὲ HP: κἀγὼ C, κἀγὼ δὲ L | ἰδὼν αὐτά: εἶδον αὐτὰ καὶ H, ἰδόντα τοῦτα L, ἰδὼν ταῦτα C | ἰδὼν — Glm | αὐτὰ — P 8 ἐθαυμ. κ.: — P, ἐθαυμ. τὰς ἐναλλαγὰς αὐτῶν καὶ L | ἐπερώτουν L | αὐτά PC: αὐτὸν H, αὐτοὺς L, pr. καὶ W, — Glm, + λέγω V, + λέγων W | τίνες: τίνος L, pr. ὑμεῖς P, pr. καὶ ὑμεῖς C | οἱ δὲ εἶπον H: καὶ εἶπον μοι L, αἱ δὲ ὁμοθυμαδὸν μιᾷ φωνῇ ἔφησαν P, εἰ δὲ μοθημαδῶν φων(ὴν) ἐφησαν μιᾶ V, οἱ δὲ ὁμοθημαδ(ῶν) ἔφησαν μιὰ φωνὴ καὶ εἶπων W | ἡμεῖς ἐσμεν — L 9 στοιχ. κοσμ. c. σκοτ. H: τὰ λεγόμενα στοιχεῖα οἱ κοσμ. τ. σκοτ. τούτου C, ἐκ τῶν τριάκοττα τριῶν στοιχείων τοῦ κοσμοκράτορος τοῦ σκοτ. P, στοιχία τοῦ κοσμοκράτορος τὸ ὄργανον τοῦ θη (l. θεοῦ?) L, sequitur in textu character magicus luna similis radios habens septem parallelos alio melius depicto in marg. rect. | add. nomina daemonum haec Gaulminius: Ἀπάτη, Ἔρις, Κλώθων, Ζάλη, Πλάνη, Δύναμις 9 § 3. καὶ ... πρωτ. HV: κ. ὁ μὲν πρῶτος ἔφη W, ἔφησε δὲ ἡ πρώτη P | § 3. om. L 10 ὁ δευτ. HC: ἡ δευτέρα P, — H, + εἶπεν C | ἡ Ἔρις PC: ὁ ἀὴρ H

ὁ τρίτος· »ἐγώ εἰμι ἡ Κλωθώ.« ὁ τέταρτος· ἐγώ εἰμι ἡ Ζάλη.«
ὁ πέμπτος· »ἐγώ εἰμι ἡ Πλάνη.« ὁ ἕκτος· »ἐγώ εἰμι ἡ Δύναμις.«
ὁ ἕβδομος· »ἐγώ εἰμι ἡ Κακίστη. 4. καὶ τὰ ἄστρα * ἡμῶν ἐν
οὐρανῷ * φαίνονται μικρὰ καὶ ὡς θεοὶ καλούμεθα· ὁμοῦ ἀλλασ-
5 σόμεθα καὶ ὁμοῦ οἰκοῦμεν ποτὲ μὲν τὴν Λυδίαν, ποτὲ δὲ τὸν
Ὄλυμπον, ποτὲ δὲ τὸ μέγα ὄρος.« 5. ἐπηρώτων δὲ αὐτοὺς ἐγὼ
Σολομῶν, ἀρξάμενος ἀπὸ τοῦ πρώτου· »λέγε μοι τίς σου ἡ ἐργασία.«
καὶ λέγει· »ἐγὼ Ἀπάτη· ἀπάτην πλέκω καὶ κακίστας αἱρέσεις ἐνθυμίζω. ἀλλ᾽ ἔχω τὸν καταργοῦντά με ἄγγελον Λαμεχιήλ.« 6. ὁ
10 δεύτερος λέγει· »ἐγώ εἰμι ἡ Ἔρις· ἐρίζω φέρων ξύλα λίθους ξίφη
τὰ ὅπλα μου τοῦ τόπου. ἀλλ᾽ ἔχω ἄγγελον τὸν καταργοῦντά

MSS HLPVW = Recc. ABC. **1** ὁ τριτ. HC: ἡ τρίτη P, + υπ < (1. εἶ-
πεν) V | ἡ Κλωθώ ego: ὁ κλοθῶ H, κλοθοῦ ὅ ἐστι μάχη P, ὁ κλόθον V,
ὁ κλώθον W | ὁ (τέταρτ)ος HC: ἡ τετάρτη P, + ὑπε V | Ζάλη P: μάχη H,
supra δύναμις primum scriptum et postea deletum scr. ζάλη W, δύναμις V
2 ὁ (πέμπτ)ος HC: ἡ πέμπτη P, + ὑπ(εν) V | ἡ Πλάνη C: ζα· H, ἡ δύνα-
μις P, cf. infra § 9 | ὁ (ἑκτ)ος HC: ἡ ἕκτη P, pr. καὶ V, + εἶπεν C | ἡ
Δύναμις C: ἡ πλάνη HP **3** ὁ (ἑβδομ)ος HC: ἡ ἑβδόμη P, pr. καὶ V, + εἶπεν C
| ἡ Κακίστη P (-ην) H: ὁ κάκιστος πάντων C | § 4. καὶ — C | * V f. 439ʳ |
ἡμῶν εἰσιν C | ἐν τῷ οὐρανῷ C **4** * P f. 8ʳ | φαιν. μικρὰ A: εἴσιν,
ἑπτὰ ἄστρα μικροφανῆ ἐν ὁμονοίᾳ P, ἑπτὰ ἄστρα (— W) μικροφανῆ C |
και .. καλουμ. A: κ. ὡς θεὰς καλ. P, — C | ὁμοῦ PC: — A | ἀλλασσ.:
ἀλασσώμ. W, ἀλασῶμ. V, ἀλλεσώμ. L. ἀλλασσοῦμ. P, — H **5** οἰκούμενα C
| ποτὲ μὲν C: ποτὲ P, παρὰ A | Λυδίαν: λύδαν H, λυδα L | δὲ HC:
— LP | τ. Ὄλυμπ. P: τ. ὄλυνπον H, τὴν ὀλ. C, τοῦ ἔμπον L **6** ποτὲ δὲ
HPC: καὶ ποτὲ L, + καὶ C | τὸ — PV | § 5. (35) ἐπηρώτησα P | ἐπ.
... Σολ.: — C | αὐτοὺς L: αὐτὰς P, αὐτὸν H **7** ἀρξ. ... πρῶτον L: ἀρξ.
ἀπὸ τῆς πρότης H, ἀρξ. δὲ εγω ἀπὸ τοῦ (πρώτ)ον εἶπον W, ἀρξ. δὲ ἐγὼ ἀπὸ
τὸν (πρώτ)ον λεγὸ V, μιᾷ ἑκάστῃ, ἠρξάμην δὲ ἀπὸ πρώτης ἕως τῆς ἑβδό-
μης P | * L f. 13ᵛ¹ | λέγε ... ἐργασ. — P | μοι AV: — W | σου HC:
— L **8** κ. λέγει A: ἡ πρώτη ἔφη P, ὁ (πρώτ)ος λεγ· V, κ. ὁ μὲν ποῶτος
εἶπ(εν) W | Ἀπάτη: pr. ἡ W, + εἰμι P | ἀπάτην ego: ἀπατῶ PC, om. per
haplographiam A | * H f. 12ᵛ | καὶ ... ἐνθυμ. H: αἱρέσεως κακίστις ἐνθυμ. L,
ὧδε (ᾧ in ras.) κἀκεῖ· αἱρέσειις ἐρεθίζω P, πλεκολογῶ (πλοκ- V) τὸ δὲ καὶ
ἐρεθίζω C **9** τὸν ... ἄγγελον LPC: ἀγγ. τὸν κατ. με H | Λαμεχιήλ C:
γλαμεχιὴλ H, χλαμεὴλ L, λαμεχαλαλ P | § 6. (36) ὁ δευτ. λέγει H: καὶ ὁ
δ. ἔφη C, ὁμοίως καὶ ἡ δευτέρα ἔφη P | sectionem om. L **10** εἰμι — W
| εἰμι ἡ Ἔρις PC: ἡμίρρης H | ἐρίζω ... ξίφη C: ἔρις ἐρίδων (ad marg.
καὶ ἔρις τῶν)· φέρω ξύλα λίθους, ξίφει P, ἐρρίδων ξύλα φαίρων· λίθους δὲ
ξίφη H **11** μον PC: — H | τοῦ τόπου HP; τοιαῦτα C | ἀλλ᾽ ἔχω:
ἔχω δὲ H

με Βαρουχιήλ.« 7. ὁμοίως καὶ ὁ τρίτος ἔφη· »ἐγὼ Κλωθώ· κυκλίσκομαι καὶ πάντα ποιῶ μάχεσθαι καὶ μὴ εἰρηνεύειν εὐσχημόνως περιέξουσιν. ⌈καὶ τί πολλὰ λέγω;⌉ ἔχω ἄγγελον τὸν καταργοῦντά με Μαρμαρώθ.« 8. καὶ ὁ τέταρτος ἔφη· »ἐγὼ ποιῶ ἀνθρώπους μὴ σωφρονεῖν· μερίζω· χωρίζω· παρακολουθούσης μοι καὶ τῆς Ἔριδος ἀποχωρίζω ⌈ἀδελφοὺς καὶ ἄλλα πολλὰ ὅμοια τούτοις ποιῶ.⌉ ⌈καὶ τί πολλὰ λέγω;⌉ ἀλλ' ἔχω ἄγγελον τὸν καταργοῦντά με τὸν μέγαν Βαλθιούλ.« 9. ὁ πέμπτος ἔφη· »ἐγὼ Πλάνη εἰμί, βασιλεῦ * Σολομῶν, καὶ σὲ πλανῶ καὶ ἐπλάνησά σε * καὶ ἐποίησα ἀποκτῆναι τοὺς ἀδελφούς. ἐγὼ πλανῶ ὑμᾶς τάφους ἐρευνᾶν

MSS HLPVW = Recc. ABC. 1 Βαρουχιήλ C: βαρουχιαηλ H, βαρουχιαχήλ P | § 7. (37) ὅμ. καὶ HP: — LC | ὁ τριτ. LC: ἡ τρίτη P, ἡ τρίτων H | ἐγώ εἰμι C | Κλωθώ ego; κλοθώ H, κλώθω L, κλωθοῦ (supra ω scr. o) P, ὁ κλώθων W, ὁ κλοθ < V 2 κυκλίσκομαι (i. q. κυκλίζω) LC: καὶ ἀλίσκομαι H, καλοῦμαι P, l. fortasse κικλήσκομαι | καὶ .. μαχεσθ.: ὃ ἐστι μάχη P | πάντα HC: πάντας L | κ. μὴ εἰρην.: — P | εἰρην. C: ἐρην. H, — L | εὐσχημ. περιεξ. ego: εὐσχημ. πέζουσιν H, εὐχη μόνος περιέξουσα L, εὐσχημόνους χύσαι (vel χόσαι) καὶ περισχηθῆναι (supra η - 1° — scr. ε) ποιῶ P, οὐ σχημόνους (falso) περισχεθῆναι ποιῶ Fl, — C 3 κ. τί πολ. λεγ. PC: — A | ἔχω: pr. καὶ A, pr. εἰ μὴ V, pr. ἀλλ' W | τ. κατ. με ἀγγ. L 4 Μαρμαρώθ V: μαρμαροώθ W, μαρμαράθ P, μαρτυρώθ H, μετύρον L | § 8. (38) κ. ὁ τετ. C (— καί) L: ἡ δὲ τετάρτη H, ὁμοίως καὶ τετάρτη P | ἔφη: εἶπεν H | ἐγὼ ἡ ζάλη· C | τοὺς ἀνθρ. P 5 μὴ σωφρ. PC: μισοκακεῖν A | μερίζω A: μετρίζω P, — C | χωρίζω: + ἀπομερίζω P, + ἀποχωρίζω C | παρακολ. μοι PC: παρακολουθοῦσιν H, — L | κ. τ. Ἐρ. — L 6 ἀποχωρ. ... ποιῶ (— ἀποχωρ.) L: ἀποσχίζω (ad marg. χωρί scr. P_c, i. q. ἀποχωρίζω) ἄνδρα ἀπὸ τῆς συγκοίτου αὐτοῦ καὶ τέκνα ἀπὸ γονέων καὶ ἀδελφοὺς ἀπὸ ἀδελφῶν P, ἀποσχίζω ἄνδρας ἀπὸ τοὺς συνγκενοῖς (l. συγγενεῖς, σονγκητ < V, l. συγκοίτ(ους)) αὐτῶν (αὐτοῦ V) καὶ γονεῖς ἀπὸ τέκνων καὶ ἀδελφοὺς ἀπὸ ἀδελφάς C 7 καὶ .. λέγω PC: — A, + κατ' ἐμοῦ P | ἀλλ' HW; καὶ L, — PV | τὸν scr. bis L 8 τ. μέγα HP: τ. μέγα L, — C | Βαλθιούλ P: μαχιθιούμ C, μελχοῖ H, μελχονήλ L | § 9. (39) πεμπτ. LC: ἡ πέμπτη HP, pr. ὁμοίως καὶ P, pr. καὶ C | ἔφη — W | Δύναμις operaque illius (§ 10) pro quinto, at Πλάνη operaque huius pro sexto habet P | Πλάνη PC: πλάνα H, πλάνος L, pr. ἡ W, pr. εἰμι P | εἰμί AV: — PW 9 * P f. 8^V | Σολ.: + εἰμι C | σε: — L, + δὲ P | σὲ ἐπλάνησά scriptis et post σὲ signo omissionis posito super ἐπλάνησά ad marg. sup. δὲ πλανῶ, ὡς καὶ adscr. P^c | πλανῶ AP: πλανήσω C | κ. ἐπλαν. σε — L | κ. ἐπλαν. ... ἀδελφ.: ἐπ' ἐσχάτων τῶν ἡμερῶν τῆς ζωῆς σου C | * H f. 13^1 | ἐποίησά σε L 10 τὸν ἀδελφὸν σου P | ὑμᾶς L: ἡμᾶς HP, πάντας C | τάφους ... εὐσεβείας — A | ταφ. ἐρευν. P: καὶ τοὺς ταφ. ἐρευνῶ (-να V) C
UNT. 9: McCown.

τὰ ἑπτὰ πνεύματα

καὶ διορυκτὰς διδάσκω, καὶ ἀποπλανῶ ψυχὰς ἀπὸ πάσης εὐσεβείας, καὶ ἕτερα πολλὰ φαῦλα * ποιῶ. ἔχω δὲ τὸν καταργοῦντά με ἄγγελον Οὐριήλ.« 10. ὁμοίως δὲ ὁ ἕκτος ἔφη· »ἐγὼ Δύναμις· τυράννους ἀνιστῶ, βασιλεῖς καθαιρῶ, * καὶ πᾶσι τοῖς ὑπεναντίοις 5 παρέχω δύναμιν. ἔχω ἄγγελον τὸν καταργοῦντά με Ἀστεραώθ.« 11. ὁμοίως καὶ ὁ ἕβδομος ἔφη· »ἐγώ εἰμι Κακίστη, καὶ σέ, βασιλεῦ, κακώσω ὅτε κελευθῶ Ἀρτέμιδος δεσμοῖς· ⌈διὰ ταῦτα γάρ σε διαπρᾶξαι ἔχεις τὴν ἐπιθυμίαν ὡς φίλτατος, ἐμοὶ δὲ κατ᾽ ἐμαυτὴν ἐπιθυμίαν τὴν σοφίαν.⌉ ἐὰν γάρ τις σοφός, οὐκ ἐπι10 στρέψει ἴχνος πρὸς μέ.« 12. κἀγὼ δὲ Σολομῶν ἀκούσας ταῦτα ἐσφράγισα αὐτοὺς τῷ δακτυλιδίῳ τοῦ θεοῦ καὶ ἐκέλευσα αὐτοὺς ὀρύσσειν τοὺς θεμελίους τοῦ ναοῦ· * καὶ ἐτάξατο τὸ μὲν μῆκος

MSS HLPVW = Recc. ABC. 1 κ. διορύκτας διδ. P: κ. ριορείκτα διδάσκων V, — W   2 ἔτ. ποιῶ φαυλ. πολ. H | πολλὰ.— L | φαῦλα AP: φαντάσματα C | * Mg 1329 | ποιῶ: ἐν ἐμοὶ P | ἔχω δὲ LPV: ἔχων δὲ H, ἀλλ᾽ ἔχω W | ἀγγ. τ. κατ. με C   3 Οὐριήλ P: οὐρουήλ A, οὐριχά C | § 10. (40) ὁμοίως δὲ HP: καὶ C, — L, + καὶ H | ὁ ἕκτος LC: ἡ ἕκτη HP | de inversione sectionum 9 et 10 in ms. P v. supra | ἐγὼ: + δὲ H,° + δὲν L, + εἰμι P, + ἡ C | Δυν. . . . ἀνιστῶ ego: δύναμαι (— H) τυρ. ἀνιστάναι A, δύναμις· δυνάμαι τυρ. ἀνιστῶ P, δύναμις· ὁμοῦ τυρ. ἀνιστῶ C   4 καθαιρῶ P: καθαιρεῖν L, — HC | * L f. 13ᵛ² | κ. πᾶσι . . . ἀγγ. τὸν — H | πᾶσι LP: — C | τοὺς ὑπεναντίους W   5 παρέχων W | ἔχω δὲ C | τὸν κατ. με ἀγγ. L | καταργοῦντα μαι ὑπὸ ἀγγέλου H | Ἀστεραώθ W(?)P (-αὲθ) V: ἀσταραqαθ(?) P, περαώθ H, περεώθ L   6 § 11. (41) ὁμοι. καὶ HPV: καὶ W, — L | ὁ ἑβδ. LC: ἡ ἑβδόμη P, ζ H | εἰμι LP: ἡ H, + βασιλεὺς L | εἰμι . . . πρός μέ (l. 10): ἡ (καλοῦμαι V) ζάλη· ζαλίζω· σκοτίζω πάντας ἀνθρώπους ἀπὸ τῆς εὐθείας ὁδοῦ, καὶ ἑτέρας (ἔχω καὶ ἑτέρας ἐνεργείας καὶ W) κακουργίας ἔχω οὐκ ὀλίγας. ἔχω δὲ τὸν ἄγγελον τὸν (— W) καταργοῦντά με, μέγαν κανωνήλ (κανγρρυήλ W) C | βασ. H: βασιλεὺς L, αὐτὸν P   7 κακώσω A: κακῶ P | ὅτε . . . δεσμοῖς A: ὅτι κελευστῶ ἀρτέμιδος δεσμούς, ἡ δὲ ἄκρις με λύσει P (cf. XXVI 4ff.) | κελευσῶ conj. F1Cr | διὰ . . . φίλτατος: δι αὐτῆς γάρ σε δεῖ πραξαι τὴν ἐπιθυμίαν P   8 διαπρᾶξαι (aor. inf. act.) ego: διὰ πρᾶξαι H, διὰ πράξας L | ἔχεις L: ἔχων H | ἐμοὶ . . . τῆς σοφίας H, ἐμοὶ . . . ἐπιθυμῶμην τὴν σοφίαν L, ἐμῇ δὲ κατ᾽ ἐμαυτῆς τὴν σοφίαν P   9 σοφὸς τὶς H | ἐπιστρέψῃ P, ἐπιστρέ L   10 ἴχνος αὐτῆς A | § 12. (42) κἀγὼ A: ἐγὼ P | κἀγὼ . . . ταῦτα: καὶ C | ταῦτα A: καὶ θαυμάσας P   11 ἐσφραγ. AP: σφραγίσας C | αὐτοὺς HC: αὐτὰς LP | τῷ: — L, pr. ἐν P | τοῦ θεοῦ A: — PC | καὶ HP: — LC, + ἐπειδὴ σύντομαι ἦσαν P | αὐτοῖς L, αὐτὰς P   12 ὀρύσσειν PW: ὀρύσσαν H, ὀρεισηⱽ, ὀρύην L | τὸ θεμέλιον L, ἐν τοῖς θεμελίοις H | τ. ναοῦ: καὶ δρυσσον W, κ. ὀρείσον V, + τοῦ θεοῦ P | * H f. 13ᵛ | καὶ ἐτ. τ. μὲν μηκ. H (— τὸ) L: τὸ μὲν γὰρ μηκ. C | κ. ἐτ. . . . πεντ.: ἐπεὶ διακ. πεντ. πηχ. ἦν τ. μηκ. P.

πήχεις διακοσίους πεντήκοντα· καὶ πάντα τὰ κελευσθέντα αὐτοῖς κατηργάζοντο. IX. Καὶ πάλιν ᾔτησα περιελθεῖν ἕτερα δαιμόνια, καὶ προσενέχθη μοι δαιμόνιον, ἄνθρωπος μὲν πάντα τὰ μέλη αὐτοῦ, ἀκέφαλος δέ. 2. καὶ εἶπον αὐτῷ· »λέγε μοι σὺ τίς εἶ, καὶ πῶς καλεῖσαι.« ὁ δὲ δαίμων ἔφη· »Φόνος καλοῦμαι· ἐγὼ γὰρ κεφαλὰς κατεσθίω, θέλων * ἐμαυτῷ κεφαλὴν ποιήσασθαι, καὶ οὐ χορτάζομαι· * ἐπιθυμῶ κεφαλὴν ποιῆσαι οἷαν ὡς καὶ σύ, βασιλεῦ.« 3. ταῦτα ἀκούσας ἐγὼ ἐσφράγισα αὐτὸν ἐκτείνας τὴν χεῖρά μου κατὰ τοῦ στήθους αὐτοῦ. καὶ ἀνεπήδησεν ὁ δαίμων καὶ ἔρρηξεν ἑαυτὸν καὶ ἐγόγγυσεν εἰπών· »οἴμοι· ποῦ ἐπέτυχον προδότην Ὀρνίαν; οὐ βλέπω.« 4. κἀγὼ εἶπον αὐτῷ· »καὶ πόθεν βλέπεις;«

MSS HLPVW = Recc. ABC. 1 πήχας διακοσίας πεντ. H, πήξας ὂν L, πηχῶν v̄ C | κ. παντ. ... κατηργ.: ἔφησα δὲ αὐτὰς εὐτόνους εἶναι, καὶ κοίμους γογγύσασαι τελέσαι τὰ κελευσθέντα αὐταῖς κατηργάζοντο P | κελευθέντα A, κελεστέντα V | αὐτοῖς A: αὐτοῦ V, — W   2 κατηργ.: ἐποίουν W C. IX. (43) 3 Κ. πάλιν H: καὶ L, ἐγὼ δὲ σολομῶν δοξάσας τὸν θεὸν (+ πάλιν C) CP, add. super θεὸν prim. man. κ(ύριο)ν P | ᾔτησα ego: αἴτησα L, ᾐτισάμην W, ἐτισαμ· V, ἔταξα H, ἐκέλευσα P | περιελθεῖν H: τοῦ ἐλθεῖν καὶ L, παρεῖναι μοι P, παραστῆναί μοι καὶ C | ἐτ. δαιμ. A: ἕτερον δαιμόνιον P, ἕτερον δαιμον < V, ἕτερος δαίμον W   4 δαιμόνιον P: δαιμόνια L, — HC | μὲν A: ἔχων P, — C | πάντα τὰ H: ὅλα τὰ L, τὰ πάντα PC | αὐτοῦ — P   5 ἀκεφ. δὲ C | § 2. καὶ: κἀγὼ P | εἶπον αὐτῶ H (pr. ἰδὼν) P: ἰδὸν αὐτὸν εἶπον W, ἰδὼν αὐτῶ εἶπα V, λέγει τούτον L | λέγε μοι — L | σὺ — H | κ. πῶς καλ. A: κ. π. καλεῖ C, — P   6 δὲ — H | δαίμων — PC | ἔφη LW: εἶπεν PV, λέγει L, + δαιμόνιον εἰμί PC, add. adhuc εἶπον οὖν αὐτῶ· τίς. ὁ δὲ ἔφη P | Φόνος δὲ C | ἐγὼ καλοῦμαι φθόνος P | γὰρ LP: δὲ H, — C | κεφαλ.: + ἡδέως PC   7 θέλων HP: θέλον L, θέλω C | * L f. 14ʳ¹ | ἐμαυτῶ HP: ἐμαυτοῦ L, ἐμαυτὸν W, ἐμαυτῶν V | ποιήσασθαι HC: ποιησθαι L, περιποιήσασθαι P | χορτάζω P   8 * P f. 9ʳ | ἐπιθυμῶ: pr. ὡς L, + δὲ PC | ποιῆσαι A: περιποιήσασθαι C, τοιαύτην ἔχειν P, + μοι L | οἷαν ὡς: ἰὰν ὡς H, ἵνα ὡς L, οἷαν P, ἤνπερ C | καὶ σύ: καὶ ἐσύ L | βασιλεῦ A: — PC   9 § 3. ταῦτα δὲ H | ἐγὼ σολομῶν PC | ἐσφραγ.: ἐσφάλησα L | τ. χειρ.: τὰς χεῖρας H   10 κατὰ: ἐκ H | καὶ (1°) — H | ἔρρηξεν H: ῥήξας L, διέρηξεν C, ἔρριψεν P   11 ἑαυτὸν P: αὐτὸν vel αὑτὸν HC, αὐτὴν L | ἐγογγ. P: γόγγισαν H, ἐκό[κ]κυσεν αὐτῶ C, — L | εἰπών PC: εἶπον H, εἶπεν L, pr. αὐτῶ C | οἴμοι PL: εἰμί C, ἡμῖν H | ἐπέτυχον πρ. Ὀρν. L: ἐνέτυχον πρ. Ὀρν. H, πάρειμι, ὦ προδότα Ὀρνία PC   12 οὐ — L | § 4. κ. εἶπον αὐτω H: (βλέπω) καγὼ καὶ εἶπον αὐτὸν L, ἔφην δὲ αὐτῶ ἐγὼ σολομῶν P, εἶπον δὲ ἐγὼ σολ. C | καὶ A: λέγε μοι C (+ γὰρ) P | * H f. 14ʳ

ὁ δὲ ἔφη· »διὰ τῶν μαστῶν μου.« * 5. κἀγὼ δὲ Σολομῶν τὴν ἡδονὴν τῆς φωνῆς αὐτοῦ ἀκούσας καὶ θέλων μαθεῖν ἐπηρώτησα αὐτόν· »πόθεν λαλεῖς;« ὁ δὲ ἔφη· »ἡ ἐμὴ φωνὴ πολλῶν ἀνθρώπων φωνὰς ἐκληρονόμησεν· ὅσοι γὰρ ἐν ἀνθρώποις βωβοὶ καλοῦνται, 5 ⌈τούτων ἐγὼ κατέκλεισα τὰς κεφαλάς.⌉ ὅτε παιδία γίνονται δέκα ἡμερῶν, τότε τῆς νυκτὸς κλαίοντος τοῦ παιδίου γίνομαι πνεῦμα καὶ διὰ τῆς φωνῆς ἐπεισέρχομαι. 6. ἐν ἀωρίαις δὲ πλεῖον τὸ συνάντημά μου βλαβερόν ἐστιν. * ἡ δὲ δύναμίς μου ἐν ταῖς χερσί μου τυγχάνει καὶ ὡς ἐπὶ ξύλου λαβὼν ταῖς χερσί μου κε-
10 φαλὰς ἀποτέμνω καὶ προστίθημι ἐμαυτῷ„, καὶ οὕτως ὑπὸ τοῦ πυρὸς τοῦ ὄντος ἐν ἐμοὶ διὰ τοῦ τραχήλου καταδαπανῶ. ἐγὼ εἰμι ὁ πυρῶν τὰ μέλη καὶ τοῖς ποσὶν ἐπιπέμπω καὶ ἕλκη ἐμποιῶ.

MSS HLPVW = Recc. ABC. 1 μαστῶν LC: μασθῶν V, παθῶν P |
* W f. 269ʳ | § 5. κἀγὼ AP: ἐγὼ C | δὲ: οὖν P, γοῦν V | Σολ. — C
2 ἀκούσας ante τὴν ἡδ. ponit C | ἡδονὴν A: ἄνοδον P, ἐδοδὴν (l. ἐδωδὴν?
sic) C, l. fortasse αὐδὴν | αὐτοῦ PC: τούτου L, — H, + ἀκούην V | κ.
θέλων P: καὶ (— V) θέλω C, ἤθελον H, ἤθελα L | μαθεῖν: pr. αὐτὸν H,
εὐδηλότερον P | ἐπηρ. αὐτὸν A: ἐπηρ. (+ δὲ W) αὐτ. λέγων C, — L
3 λαλεῖ L | ὁ δὲ ἔφη H: ἔφη δέ μοι PC, καί λέγει μοι | ἡ ἐμὴ φωνὴ H
(ἐμοί) L: ἐγώ, σολομῶν, ἡμεῖ φωνὴν C, ἐγὼ βασιλεῦ σολομῶν ὅλως φωνὴ
εἰμί P | πολλῶν .. ἐκληρον. H (-ησα) L: ἡ πολλὰς φωνὰς κληρονομήσασα C,
πολλῶν γὰρ ἀνθρώπων φωνὰς κατεκληρονόμησα P   4 ἐν ἀνθρωπ. AC:
ἄν(θρωπ)οι P | καλ. βοβοὶ C, καλ. κωφοὶ P   5 τούτων ... ἡμερῶν C:
— A | τὰς κεφαλὰς κατεκλ. P | γιν. δ. ἡμ. C: γεννῶνται, καὶ ἡμερῶν ὀκτὼ
φθάσωσι P   6 τότε PC: τό(τε?) L, οὗτος H, + ἐγὼ A | τῆς A: — PC |
νυκτὸς post παιδίου ponit P | παιδὸς L | γένομαι A | φωνῆς αὐτοῦ P
7 ὑπεισέρχομαι C | § 6. ἀωρίαις: ἀορίαις H, ὁρίαις P, ad marg. ἐν
ἀωρι < Pᶜ, ἀορία L, ἀορίας C | δὲ: καὶ P | πλεῖον A: πάνυ PC,
= διακονῶ· καὶ P   8 ἐστιν: δὲ H | * L f. 14ʳ² | ἡ δὲ ... τυγχάνει C
(— τυγχ.) A: om. P per homoeoarcton, καί enim scr. in fine lineae (ἐστὶν
καὶ) et rursus in initio lineae alterae (καὶ εὐθέως λαβὼν) | δὲ — L   9 τυγ-
χάνει ... χερσί μου C: om. A per homoeoteleuton | ὡς ... μου C:
εὐθέως λαβὼν ταῖς χερσί μου ὡς ἐπὶ ξίφος P | τὴν κεφαλὴν P   10 προσ-
τίθημι (-ημοι) L: πρὸς τέθημος H, προστιθῶ PC | ἐμαυτῷ PV: ἐμαυ-
τὸν W, ἐν αὐτῷ A | τοῦ — P   11 ὄντος — C | καταδαπανῶ L: δα-
πανῶ L, καταδαπανᾶται PC   12 ὁ πυρ. ... ἐπιπέμπω A: ὁ τὰς πυρώσεις τὰς μεγάλας καὶ (τοὺς V, τὰς W) ἀθεραπεύτους ἐν τ. ποσὶν ἐπιπέμπων
P (ἐπιπέμπω) C | κ. ἕλκη ἐμπ. HP: κ. ἔγκαι ἐπιῶ V, κ. ἕλκη ἐνεμπιῶ
L, — W

X, 7—X, 2   κύων ὀνόματι Ῥάβδος   37*

7. καὶ διὰ τῆς ἐμπύρου ἀστραπῆς καταργοῦμαι.« 8. κἀγὼ ἐκέλευσα αὐτὸν εἶναι μετὰ τοῦ Βεελζεβοὺλ μέχρι καὶ τούτου φίλος παραγένηται.
X. Καὶ ἐκέλευσα παρεῖναί μοι ἕτερον δαιμόνιον. καὶ ἦλθε πρὸ προσώπου μου ἔχων τὸ σχῆμα * ὡς κύων μέγας, καὶ ἐλάλησέ μοι φωνὴν μεγάλην· »χαῖρε, ὦ βασιλεῦ Σολομῶν.« 2. καὶ ἐκπληκτικὸς ἐγενόμην καὶ εἶπον αὐτῷ· »τίς εἶ σύ, κύον;« ὁ δὲ λέγει· »κύων δοκεῖς εἶναί με· πρὸ γὰρ σοῦ, βασιλεῦ, ἤμην ἐγὼ ἄνθρωπος. κατηργασάμην δὲ ἐν τῶ * κόσμῳ ἔργα πολλὰ ἄθεσμα καὶ καθ᾽ ὑπεροχὴν ἴσχυσα καὶ ἄστρα οὐρανῶν κατασχεῖν, καὶ

MSS HL = Rec. A. § 7. cum mss. HL textus legitur   1 ἔμπυρ. H: ἰπείρου L
MS P interpolationem maiorem praebet pro § 7 hanc: κἀγὼ σολομῶν ἀκούσας ταῦτα, εἶπον αὐτῷ· λέγε μοι οὖν πῶς ἐπαφίης τὸ πῦρ, ἀφ᾽ ὧν ἀποπέμπεις ἐξ αὐτῶν. ἔφη δέ μοι τὸ πνεῦμα ἀπὸ τῆς ἀνατολῆς· ὧδε γὰρ οὕτω supra τ scr. π ut in οὕπω corr.) εὑρέθη κἀκεῖνος ἐλβουρίων ὡς ἐπεύχων τὸ πῦρ· καὶ λυχναψί(ας) (-ίαν Fl falso)- αὐτῷ οἱ ἄνθρωποι ἐπιτελοῦσι, κἀκείνου τὸ οὕνομα ἐπικαλοῦνται (* f. 9ᵛ) οἱ ἑπτὰ δαίμονες ἐνώπιόν μου κἀκεῖνος θεραπεύει αὐτούς: εἶπον δὲ αὐτῷ εἰπέ μοι τὸ ὄνομα αἰτοῦ. ὁ δὲ ἔφη οὐ δύναμαι σοι εἰπεῖν· ἐὰν γὰρ εἴπω αὐτοῦ τὸ ὄνομα ἀθεράπευτον ἐμαυτὸν ποιῶ· ἀλλ᾽ ἐκεῖνος ἐλθὼν ἐπὶ αὐτό (α ex τ corr.) τὸ ὄνομα. καὶ ταῦτα ἀκούσας ἐγὼ σολομῶν εἶπον αὐτῶ εἰπέ μοι οὖν ὑπὸ ποίου ἀγγέλου καταργῇ σύ. ἡ δὲ διὰ τῆς ἐμπύρου ἀστραπῆς ἔφη.
MSS VW (Rec. C) textum praebent hunc: κἀγὼ σολομῶν ἀκούσας ταῦτα, εἶπον (εἶπα αὐτῷ V) λέγε μοι, οὖν, ἐν ποίῳ ἀγγέλω (ἐπὶ ποίου ἀγγέλου V) καταργεῖσαι. ὁ δὲ ἔφη· διὰ τοῦ ἐμπύρου ἀγγέλου.
MSS HLP = Recc. AB. 1 § 8. hoc a loco mss. codd. VW (i. q. recensio C) extum diversum habet, cf. infra, pp. 76*—87*. κἀγὼ H: καὶ ἐγώ L, καὶ προσκυνήσας ἐγὼ κυρίῳ τῷ θεῷ τοῦ ἰ(σρα)ὴλ P   2 εἶναι μετὰ τ. Βεελ. H: ἐν τηρήσει εἶναι ὑπὸ τοῦ βεελ. P, διὰ τοῦ βεελζεβουὲλ ἐπιεῖναι L | μέχρι κ. τ. φιλ. A: μέχρις ὅτου ἴαξ P   3 παραγ. P: ἐπιγίνεται L, παραγέγονεν H
C. X. (47) 4 ἐκέλευσα (1. -σε) L | ἕτερα δαιμόνια L   5 μου: — L, + δαίμων L | ἔχων ... μέγας: κύων· τὸ σχῆμα ἔχων (* Mg 1332) μέγα P τὸ — H | σχῆμα: + αὐτοῦ L | μοι — P   6 φωνῇ μεγάλῃ καὶ εἶτεν P | χαίροις L | ὦ L: ὁ H, κύριε P | § 2. κ. ἐκπ. ἐγ. κ.: κ. ἐκπληκτος ἐγ. κ. H, καὶ ἀκούσας ἐγὼ ἐκπληκτικὸς ἐγ. κ. L, ἐκπληκτικὸς δὲ γεγονὼς ἐγὼ σολομῶν P   7 σύ — P | κύων P | ὁ δὲ λέγει H: καὶ εἶπεν μοι L, ὁ δέ μοι ἔφη P   8 κύων .. με H (μοι) L: καὶ κύων σοι δοκῶ εἶναι P | πρὸ LP: πρὸς H | βασιλεὺς A, βασιλεῦ σολομῶν P | ἐγὼ ἀνθρ. ἤμην P 9 κατηργ. ... ἴσχυσα A: κατεργασάμενος ἀθέμιτα ἐν τῷ κόσμῳ πολλὰ καθ᾽ ὑπερβολὴν φιλολογήσας ὑπερίσχυσα P   10 οὐρανῶ L | κατασχῶν A

C. X 2 Rev. XII 4; cf. Dieterich, Abraxas 118ff.

πλείονα κακὰ ἔργα κατασκευάζω. 3. ἐγὼ οὖν βλάπτω ἀνθρώπους τοὺς τῷ ἐμῷ ἄστρῳ παρακολουθοῦντας καὶ εἰς ἐξηχείαν τρέπω, καὶ τὰς * φρένας τῶν ἀνθρώπων διὰ τοῦ λάρυγγος κρατῶ καὶ οὕτως ἀναιρῶ.« 4. καὶ εἶπον αὐτῷ· »τί σου τὸ ὄνομα;« ὁ δὲ ἔφη· »Ῥάβδος.«

5. Κἀγὼ εἶπον αὐτῷ· »τίς σου ἡ ἐργασία καὶ τί μοι δοκεῖς κατορθῶσαι;« ὁ δαίμων ἔφη· »δός μοι ἄνθρωπον σὸν καὶ ἀπαγάγω αὐτὸν ἐν τόπῳ ὄρους καὶ ἐπιδείξω αὐτῷ λίθον πράσινον μετασαλευόμενον ἐν ᾧ * κοσμήσεις τὸν ναὸν τοῦ θεοῦ.« 6. κἀγὼ δὲ ἀκούσας ταῦτα ἐπέταξα ⌜πορευθῆναι⌝ τὸν οἰκέτην μου ἅμα αὐτῷ ἔχοντα τὸ δακτυλίδιον τῆς σφραγῖδος τοῦ θεοῦ * μετ' αὐτοῦ καὶ εἶπον αὐτῷ· »ἄπελθε μετ' αὐτοῦ καὶ οὗ δ' ἂν ἐπιδείξει σοι τὸν λίθον τὸν πράσινον, σφράγισον αὐτὸν τῷ δακτυλιδίῳ κατασκόπευσον τὸν τόπον ἀκριβῶς, καὶ ἄγαγέ μοι ⌜τὸ δακτυλίδιον⌝.« 7. ὁ δὲ ἀπελθὼν ἔδειξεν αὐτῷ τὸν λίθον τὸν πράσινον, καὶ ἐσφράγισεν αὐτὸν τῷ δακτυλιδίῳ τοῦ θεοῦ, καὶ ἤγαγον τὸν λίθον τὸν πράσινον πρός μέ. 8. καὶ ἔκρινα περισφραγίδας τὰ

MSS HLP = Recc. AB. 1 πλείονα θεῶν ἔργα κατασκεύασα P | § 3. οὖν Α: γὰρ P 2 τὸ ἐμὸν ἄστρῳ L | εἰς ἐξηχίαν τρ. LP, ἐξηχίαν πρέπω H 3 τὰς ... ἀνθρ. A: τοὺς φρενητιῶντας ἀνθρώπους P | * H f. 15ʳ 4 οὕτως H: οὗτος H | ἀναιρῶ αὐτὸν H | § 4. (48) κ. εἶπον αὐτ. L: ἔφην δὲ αὐτῷ ἐγὼ σολομῶν P 6 § 5. κἀγὼ: καὶ P | αὐτῷ — P | τίς: καὶ τί P | καὶ — L | μοι (με L) δοκεῖς A: δύνασαι P 7 δαίμων A: δὲ P 8 ὄρους — H | δείξω P | αὐτῷ P: αὐτὸν H, — L 9 * P f. 10ʳ | κοσμεῖ H | ναόν: + κυρίου P | § 6. (49) κἀγὼ P ἐγὼ P 10 δὲ: — H, + σολομῶν P | ἐπέταξα H: ὑποπροεταξα L, ὑπέταξα P | πορευθῆναι P: — A | ἅμα αὐτῷ HP: ἅματο L 11 ἔχοντα P: ἔχοντι H, κραττοῦντα L | τὸ δακτ. A: δακτύλιον P | * L f. 14ᵛ² — μετ' αὐτ. P: μετὰ τούτ(ους) L, — H 12 κ. εἶπον αὐτ. — L | ἀπελ. ... καὶ — L | ἄπελθε H: ἀπέλθατε L | μετ' αὐτοῦ ego: μετ' αὐτῶν H, μετὰ τούτου L | οὗ δ' ἂν ego: οὐδὰν H, ὃ δ' ἂν P, — L | ἐπιδείξει σοι P (σον) H· ἀποδεί ημιν vel ἀποδείκμιν L 13 τὸν (1° et 2°) — L | αὐτὸν HP: τούτου L | τῷ δακτ. Α: μετὰ τοῦ δακτυλιδίου τούτουP 14 τὸν τόπον ... αὐτὸν (l. 16) — H | ἀκριβ. τ. τοπ. P | τὸ δακτ. L: τὸν δαίμονα ἐνθάδε P fortasse recte 15 § 7. ὁ δὲ ἀπ. L: καὶ P | αὐτῶν P: αὐτοῖς L | τὸν πρασ. λιθ. P 16 αὐτὸν P: αὐτῷ L | τ. δάκτυλ. τ. θ. Α: — P | κ. ἤγαγον ... με H (—πρὸς μέ) L: κ. ἤναγκε τὸ δαιμόνιον πρὸς με P 17 § 8. ἔκρινα: + αὐτὸν A, + ἐγὼ σολομῶν P | περισφραγῆσαι L | * H f. 15ᵛ

MS P pro textu τὰ δύο ... τεχνίταις (l. 17 ss.) praebet haec: τοὺς δύο τῇ δεξιᾷ τὸν ἀκέφαλον, ὁμοίως καὶ τὸν κύνα προσδεδέσθαι ἐκεῖνον τὸν μέγαν, καὶ τὸν μὲν κύνα τηρεῖν τὸν διάπυρον πνεῦμα ὡς λαμπάδας νυκτὸς καὶ ἡμέρας διὰ τοῦ λαιμοῦ παραπίπτειν τοῖς ἐργ. τεχνίταις

δύο δαιμόνια τὸν ἀκέφαλον καὶ τὸν κύνα δεθῆναι καὶ τὸν λίθον ἡμέραν καὶ νύκτα ὥσπερ λαμπάδα περιφέρειν τοῖς ἐργαζομένοις τεχνίταις. 9. Καὶ ⌈ἦρα ἐγὼ ἐκ τοῦ μετοικισμοῦ ἐκείνου τοῦ λίθου διακοσίους σίκλους ἐν τοῖς ἀναφορεῦσι⌉ τοῦ θυσιαστηρίου· ἦν δὲ ὁ λίθος ὡσεὶ πράσου τὸ εἶδος ὅμοιος. 10. κἀγὼ δὲ Σολομῶν δοξάσας κύριον τὸν θεὸν καὶ περικλείσας τὸν θησαυρὸν τοῦ λίθου ἐκέλευσα * τοὺς δαίμονας μάρμαρα κόπτειν εἰς τὴν οἰκοδομὴν τοῦ ναοῦ. 11. καὶ ἐπηρώτησα αὐτὸν τὸν κύνα· »διὰ ποίου ἀγγέλου καταργεῖσαι;« ὁ δὲ ἔφη· »διὰ τοῦ μεγάλου Βριαθοῦ.«

XI. Καὶ ἐκέλευσα πάλιν παρελθεῖν ἐμοὶ ἕτερα δαιμόνια· καὶ ἦλθε βρυχώμενος ὡς λέων ὀρθὸς καὶ σταθεὶς ἀπεκρίθη μοι λόγῳ· * »βασιλεῦ Σολομῶν, ἐγὼ καὶ τὸ σχῆμα ἔχω ** τούτου, πνεῦμα δυνάμενον μηδόλως δεθῆναι. 2. ἐγὼ πᾶσι τοῖς ἀνθρώποις τοῖς

MSS HL § 8 l. 1 δύο — H | τὸν κύνα τε καὶ ἀκεφ. L   2 νύκταν κ. ἡμέραν L | ὥσπερ ... τεχνίταις H: κρατοῦντες τὸν λίθον ἵνα τοῖς ἐργ. τεχν. λάμπῃ ὡς λαμπάδα L
MSS HLP = Recc. AB. 3 § 9. ἦρα ... ἀναφορεῦσι cum dubio ego: l. fortasse εἶαρ ἐκ τ. μετ. ἐκ. τ. λιθ. ἔτρεχεν ἐν τοῖς ἀναφεροῦσιν ἐπὶ τοῦ θυσ.? | ἐγὼ σολομῶν P | μετοικ. A: μετάλλου P | τ. λιθ. ἐκ. L   4 διακ. σικλ. P: ἔτρεχον A | ἀναφορ. P: ἀνωφέρεσιν H, ἀναφέρεσιν L | ἦν ... πράσον — P   5 πράσου ego: κερασίου A | ὅμοιος A: ὁμοιούμενον P | § 10. καὶ ἐγὼ H   7 λίθου ἐκείνου P | κελεύσας L | * L f. 15^{r1} | ἐκέλευσα δὲ πάλιν P | εἰς τ. οἰκ. L: ἐν τοῖ οἰκοδομοῖ H, εἰς τὰς οἰκοδομὰς P 8 τ. ναοῦ A: τῶν ἔργων τοῦ θεοῦ P | § 11. καὶ εὐξάμενος τῷ κυρίῳ ἐγὼ σολομῶν ἐπηρ. P | αὐτὸν — P | διὰ π. ἀγγ. καταργ. L: διὰ ποίου ἄγγελον κατ. H, ποίῳ ἀγγέλῳ καταργῇ σὺ P   9 ὁ δὲ ἔφη — H | δὲ: + δαίμων P | διὰ τ. μεγ. Βριαθοῦ (l. Βριαρίου?) H: διὰ τ. μεγ. βριαθαουηλ L, τῷ μεγάλῳ βριεώ P, Βριαρίῳ coniecit Bn
C. XI. (51) 10 καὶ εὐλογήσας κύρι⟨ον⟩ τὸν θεὸν τοῦ οὐρανοῦ καὶ τῆς γῆς ἐκελ. P | πάλιν — P | παρελθεῖν ἐμοὶ ego: παρελθῆναι μοι H, ἀνελθεῖναι μοι L, παρεῖναι μοι P | ἕτερον δαίμονα P   11 βρυχ. ... ὀρθὸς H: δαιμόνιον τὸ σχῆμα αὐτοῦ λέοντος ὀρθοβρυχόμενος L, πρὸ προσώπου μου λέοντος σχῆμα βρυχόμενος P | λόγῳ A: λέγων P   12 * H f. 16^r | Σολ. — P | ἐγὼ ... τούτου H: ἐγὼ δὲ τούτου τοῦ σχήματος (ad marg. sin. Marc. 5. 4 scr. man. rec.) L, τὸ μὲν σχῆμα τοῦτο δ ἔχω P | ** P f. 10^v | πνεῦμα ... δεθῆναι ego: καὶ πνεῦμα δυνάμεως μηδόλως σθῆναι (l. στῆναι?) H, οὐδ' ὅλως δυνάμενος δεθῆναι L, πνεῦμα εἰμὶ μηδόλως δυνάμενον νοηθῆναι P 13 § 2. καὶ λέγει ἐγὼ L | πᾶσιν P, πάσῃ H, πάσης L | τοῖς (1°) H: — PL | τοῖς (2°) ... κατακειμ. H: τ. ἐν νοσήμασι P, κατακ. ἐν νοσήματι L

C. XI 1 Mk. V 4

ἐν νοσήματι κατακειμένοις ἐφορμῶμαι παρεισερχόμενον, καὶ ἀνένδοτον ποιῶ τὸν ἄνθρωπον ὡς μὴ δυνηθῆναι ἰαθῆναι αὐτοῦ τὴν αἰτίαν. 3. ἔχω καὶ ἑτέραν πρᾶξιν· ἐμβάλλω τοὺς δαίμονας τοὺς ὑποτεταγμένους μοι λεγεῶνας, δυτικὸν ⌈γάρ εἰμι τοῖς τόποις,⌉ 5 ὄνομα δὲ πᾶσι δαίμοσι τοῖς ὑπ᾽ ἐμὲ * ὂν λεγεῶνες.« 4. καὶ ἐπηρώτησα αὐτόν· »τί σου τὸ ὄνομα;« ὁ δὲ ἔφη· »Λεοντοφόρον, Ἄραψ τῷ γένει.« 5. καὶ εἶπον αὐτῷ· »πῶς καταργεῖσαι μετὰ τοῦ λεγεῶνός σου, ἢ ποῖον ἄγγελον ἔχεις;« * ὁ δαίμων εἶπεν· »ἐὰν εἴπω σοι τὸ ὄνομα οὐκ ἐμαυτὸν δεσμεύω μόνον ἀλλὰ * καὶ 10 τὸν ὑπ᾽ ἐμὲ λεγεῶνα τῶν δαιμόνων.« 6. ἐγὼ δὲ εἶπον αὐτῷ· »ἐγὼ ὁρκίζω σε τὸ ὄνομα τοῦ μεγάλου θεοῦ τοῦ ὑψίστου· ἐν ποίῳ ὀνόματι καταργεῖσαι μετὰ τοῦ λεγεῶνός σου;« ὁ δαίμων εἶπεν· »ἐν τῷ ὀνόματι τοῦ μετὰ πολλὰ παθεῖν ὑπομείναντος

MSS HLP = Recc. AB. 1 ἐφορμ. P: ἀφορμόμενος L, ἐμορφόμενος H | παρεισερχόμενον P: περιερχόμ(ενο) < H, περιεισερχόμενος L | ἀνενδ. A: ἀνενδότερον P 2 δυνηθῇ H | ἰαθῆναι ego: ἰασθῆναι L, — HP | αὐτ. τ. αἰτίαν A: αὐτῷ τὴν δίαιταν P, + ταύτην L 3 § 3. καὶ: pr. δὲ P | πρᾶξιν A: δόξαν ἐγὼ βασιλεῦ, P | εἰσβάλλω L | ἐμβ. τ. δαιμ.: δαίμονας ἐμβάλλω (ἐκβάλλω Fl)· ἔχω δὲ P 4 δυτικὸν A: δεκτικὸν P | γάρ supplevi:· — AP | εἶμι: add. inter εἶμι et τοῖς signum omissionis at super lineam compendium mihi inodabile, fortasse l. καὶ vel δὲ vel γὰρ P | τ. τοπ. P: τοὺς τόπους A, cf. Cr, p. 28 5 ὄνομα A: ἅμα P | τοῖς πᾶσι P | τοῖς: super lineam adscr. τ(ῶν) P | * L f. 15ˣ² | ὂν λεγεῶνες ego: ὢν λεγεώνας H, λεγεώνων P, οὐ λέγω L | § 4. κ. ἐπηρ. αὐτ. A: + λέγω L, ἐγὼ δὲ σολομὼν ἀκούσας ταῦτα ἐπηρ. αὐτ. P 6 τι .. ὀν. HP: τὸ σὸν ὀν. πῶς καλεῖται L | ἔφη μοι H | Λεοντοφόρον P: λεοντόφρον A, l. fortasse Λεγεωνοφόρον, sed cf. supra § 1 7 Ἄραψ A: ῥὰθ P, ῥαδινός coni. Bn | τῷ γένει P: ᾧ γένη L, τὸ γένος H | § 5. κ. εἶπον A: εἶπον δὲ P | καταργῇ συ P 8 τοῦ A: τῆς P | ἢ HP: καὶ εἰς L | ἔχεις H: — L, τὸν καταργοῦντα σε P | * Mg 1333 | ὁ δ. εἶπεν H: ἔφη δὲ μοι P, — L 9 ἐὰν δὲ L | εἴπω σοι ego: εἴπωσι P, ὅποσοι H, εἴποσοι L | ὄνομά μου A | ἐμαυτῶ L | δεσμεύεις H, forte recte | * H f. 16ᵛ 10 ὑπ᾽ A: ἐπ᾽ P | § 6. ἐγὼ δ. εἶπ. A: ἔφην δὲ P 11 ἐγὼ .. ὀν.: ἐξορκίζω˙ σε κατὰ L | μεγ. .. ὑψίστου H: θεοῦ του (+ compendium = τῶν?) ὤντος τοῦ ὑψίστου L, θεοῦ σαβαὼθ P | ἐν A: τοῦ εἰπεῖν σε P 12 ὄνομα L | καταργῇ συ P | τοῦ λεγ. A: τῆς δυνάμεως P | ὁ δ. εἶπεν A: εἶπε δέ μοι τὸ πνεῦμα P 13 ἐν ... Ἐμμανουὴλ (p. 41ᵛ, l. 1) H: ὁ μεγάλοις (μέγας ἐν Crtr) ἀνθρώποις ἔχων πολλαπαθεῖν ὑπ᾽ ἀνθρώπων οὗ τὸ ὄνομα ψῆφος χμδ, ὃ ἐστιν ἐμμανουὴλ P | ὑπομειν. — L

§ 3. Mk. V 13; Mt. VIII 32; Lk. VIII 31 f.
§ 6. Mk. IV 35—V 20; Mt. VIII 23 - 34; Lk. VIII 22—39.

ὑπὸ τῶν ἀνθρώπων, οὗ τὸ ὄνομα Ἐμμανουήλ, ὃς καὶ νῦν ἐδέρμευσεν ἡμᾶς καὶ ἐλεύσεται κατὰ τοῦ ὕδατος κρημνῷ βασανίσαι ἡμᾶς· ἐν δὲ τρισὶ χαρακτῆρσι κατάγεται περιηχούμενος.« 7. κἀγὼ δὲ κατέκρινα αὐτοῦ τὸν λεγεῶνα φέρειν ἀπὸ τοῦ δρυμοῦ ξύλον, τὸν δὲ Λεοντοφόρον καταπρίζειν αὐτὰ * λεπτὰ τοῖς ὄνυξι καὶ ὑποκάτω τῆς καμίνου τῆς ἀσβέστου ῥίπτειν. XII. Κἀγὼ προσκυνήσας τὸν θεὸν τοῦ Ἰσραὴλ ἐκέλευσα προελθεῖν ἕτερον * δαίμονα. καὶ ἦλθε πρὸ προσώπου μου δράκων τρικέφαλος φοβερόχροος. 2. καὶ ἐπηρώτησα αὐτόν· »σὺ τίς εἶ;« ὁ δὲ ἔφη· »πνεῦμα τρίβολον ἐν τρισὶ κατεργαζόμενον ἐγὼ ἔργοις· ἐν κοιλίαις γυναικῶν τυφλῶ τὰ παιδία καὶ ὦτα ἐπιδινῶ καὶ ποιῶ αὐτὰ βωβὰ καὶ κωφά, καὶ τύπτω τοὺς ἀνθρώπους κατὰ τοῦ σώματος καὶ ποιῶ καταπίπτειν καὶ ἀφρίζειν καὶ τρί-

---

MSS HLP = Recc. AB. 1 οὐ ἐστὶν τὸ ὄν. αὐτοῦ ἐμμαν. L | νῦν — P 2 κ. ἐλευσ. Α: ὃς καὶ τότε ἐλευσόμενος P | κρημ. βασαν. L: κριμμῶ βασ. Η, κρημνοβατίσει (l. -ήσει) P, κρηνοβαπτίσει FI 3 δὲ P: — Α | τοῖς τρισὶ P | καταγ. περιηχ. Η: κατάγουσαι (-ούσαις Cr) περιηχούμενον P, εἰσὶν καταργούμεθα περιηγούμενος L | § 7. κἀγὼ δὲ Η: ἐγὼ δὲ L, κἀγὼ σολομῶν ἀκούσας ταῦτα καὶ δοξάσας τὸν θεὸν P 4 * P f. 11ʳ | αὐτοῦ τ. λεγεῶνα P: αὐτὸν Α | φέρειν .. ξύλον Α: ξυλοφορεῖν ἀπὸ δρυμοῦ P 5 τ. δὲ Λεοντ. ego: τὸν δὲ λεοντόφρον Η (-τόφρων) L, αὐτὸν δὲ τὸν λεοντόμορφον κατέκρινα P | καταπρ. HP: κυπήξει L | αὐτὰ — P | * L f. 15ᵛ¹ | ὄνυξι L: ἄνυξι Η, ὀδοῦσιν P | κ. ὑποκ. Α: εἰς ὑπόκαυσιν P 6 ῥίπτειν Α: εἰς τὸν ναὸν κυρίου τοῦ θεοῦ P
C. XII. (54) 1. 7 κἀγὼ Α: καὶ P | προσκυν. HP: παρεκάλεσα L, + κύριον P | τοῦ — L | καὶ ἐκέλευσα L | προελθ. Η:- παρεῖναι μοι P, ἵνα καὶ ἕτερα δαιμόνια ἐλθεῖν ἐν ἡμῖν L 8 * Η f. 17ʳ | μου — P | δρακ. τρικεφ. P: δράκων τὸ κέφαλος L, δράκον τὸ κέφαλον Η 9 φοβεροχ. LP: — Η | § 2. δὲ: δαίμων L, + μοι P 10 τρίβολον ego: τριόβολον Α, τριβάλαιον εἰμὶ P, τριβολαῖον (τρι et βολαῖος) conj. Bncn | ἐν HP: — L | κατεργ. ἐγὼ ἔργοις: κατεργαζόμενος ἐγὼ ἔργοις Η (— ἔργοις) L: πράξεσι κατεργαζόμενον· ἐγὼ δὲ P 11 ἐν LP: — Η | κοιλίαις Α: κοιλίᾳ P, + τῶν L | τυφλώνω Α | παιδία LP: νήπια Η | ἐπιδένω Α 12 αὐτὰ — P | βωβὰ P: ὁδοδῆ Η (-δεῖ) L, λωβὰ conj. Fü | κωφά: + καὶ ἐμοὶ γ(ὰρ) πάλιν ἐν τῇ τρίτῃ μοι κεφαλῇ ὑπόδυνα P 13 κατὰ: + τὸ εἰκώδες P, ἀκωδὸς in textu, »εἰκώδος — εἰκώδες« ad marg. Fl, conj. ἀκηδές (unbewachten Teilen) Fü, ἄκωλος (limbless part) Cr, l. fortasse τὸν εἰκόνα? | καὶ φρίζει καὶ τρίζει L | κ. τρίζ. — Η

C. XII 2. Mt. XVII 15; Mk. IX 18.

ζειν τοὺς ὀδόντας. 3. ἔχω δὲ τρόπον ἐν ᾧ καταργοῦμαι ὑπὸ τοῦ σημειομένου τόπου ἐγκεφάλου, ἐκεῖ γὰρ προώρισεν ἄγγελος τῆς μεγάλης βουλῆς με παθεῖν, καὶ νῦν φανερῶς ἐπὶ ξύλου οἰκήσει, ἐκεῖνός με καταργήσει ἐν οἷς καὶ ὢν ὑποτέταγμαι. 4. ἐν δὲ τῷ 5 τόπῳ ἐν ᾧ ἤρθη, βασιλεῦ Σολομῶν, στήσει κίονα πορφυροῦν * ἐπὶ τοῦ ἀέρος δῶρα μεμορφούμενον Ἐφιππᾶς ἀπὸ τῆς Ἐρυθρᾶς θαλάσσης ἀγαγὼν ἀπὸ τῆς ἔσω Ἀραβίας. ἐν δὲ τῇ ἀρχῇ τοῦ ναοῦ ὅνπερ ἤρξω κτίζειν, βασιλεῦ Σολομῶν, ἀπόκειται χρυσίον πολύ, ὅπερ ὀρύξας ἆρον.« 5. κἀγὼ Σολομῶν ἀποστεί-
10 λας τὸν παῖδά μου εὗρον καθὼς εἶπέ μοι τὸ δαιμόνιον καὶ σφραγίσας τὸ δακτυλίδιον ᾔνεσα τὸν θεόν. 6. εἶπον οὖν αὐτῷ· »λέγε μοι πῶς καλεῖσαι.« καὶ ὁ δαίμων ἔφη· »κορυφὴ δρακόντων.« καὶ ἐκέλευσα αὐτὸν πλινθουργεῖν εἰς τὸν ναὸν τοῦ θεοῦ.

MSS HLP = Rec. AB. 1 ὀδοντ. LP: ὀδυν. H | § 3. ἐν ᾧ HP: ὡς L | καταργοῦν H | τοῦ ... τόπου L (— τοῦ) H: σημειουμένης τῆς ἱ(ερουσα)λήμ, εἰς τὸν λεγόμενον τόπον P   2 ἐγκεφάλου H: ἐν κεφάλω L, κεφάλαιον P | προόρισεν L, προόρισόν H, προώριστο P | ὁ ἀγγελ. P | ἄγγελον H   3 με παθεῖν — P | φανερὸν L | τ' ἐπὶ P | οἰκήσει: ἥμισι L   4 καταργήσει L: καταργῆσε H, καταργεῖ P | ἐν οἷς καὶ ὢν L: ἐν εἰς ὃν καὶ H, ἐν ᾧ P | ὑποτέταμαι H | § 4. (55) δὲ: ὦ L   5 ἤρθη: καθέζει P | βασ. Σολ.: ὁ βασιλεὺς L | στήσῃ H, στήκει P, στήσης L | κίονα ... μεμορφ.: κίων ἐπὶ τοῦ ἀέρος πορφυροδανόμενος P | πορφυροῦν L: πορφύριον H | * H f. 17ᵛ   6 * L f. 15ᵛ² | μεμορφούμενον ego: μεμορφουμένου L, μαιμορφομένου H | ὁ δαίμων ὁ λεγόμενος ἐφιππᾶς P | ἐφοίποις H, ἔφιππος L   7 ἀγαγὼ L, ἀναγὼν H, ἀναγαγὼν P | Ἀραβίας: + ὅστις καὶ εἰς ἀσκὸν κατακλεισθείς, κομισθήσεται ἔμπροσθέν σου P | δὲ — A   8 ὅνπερ P: οὐ περ L, περ H | ἀπόκειται ... Σολ. — L | * P f. 11ᵛ | χρυσίον .. ὅπερ P: χρόνον πολὴν ὅνπερ H   9 ἆρον P: φαίρον H § 5. κἀγὼ δὲ H | ἀποστείλας ... δαιμ. καὶ — H   10 τὸ παιδίον L | καὶ εὗρεν L | εἶπε P: ἤρηκε L | τὸ δαιμ. P: ὁ δαίμων L | τὸ δακτ. A: τῷ (forte ex τὸ corr.) δακτυλιδίῳ P   11 ᾔνεσα P: καὶ ἔνεσα H, καὶ ὕμνησα L § 6. (56) εἶπον .. αὐτ: P: δὲ (vel κὲ, l. καὶ) εἶπον αὐτ. H, ἔπειτα δὲ εἶπον πρὸς τὸν δαίμον⟨α⟩ L   12 λέγε .. καλ: H: τί σὺ λέγεις P, σὺ τίς εἶ L | κ. ὁ δ. ἔφη L (— καὶ) P: ὁ δὲ ἔφη H | κορ. δρακ. P (κορυφὴν) H: κορυφὴν δράκοντος L, + εἰμι P   13 πλινθ. (ex πλιθ. corr.) P: λεπτουργεῖν H, λεπτουργεῖν L | εἰς A: ἐν P   14 τ. θεοῦ A: εἶχεν χεῖρας ἀν(θρώπ)ων P

---

§ 3. Mk. XV 22; Mt. XXVII 33; Lk. XXIII 33

XIII. Καὶ ἐκέλευσα παρεῖναί μοι ἕτερον δαίμονα. καὶ ἦλθε πρὸ προσώπου μου γύνη μὲν τὸ εἶδος, ⌜τὴν δὲ μορφὴν κατέχουσα ἅμα τοῖς μέλεσιν αὐτῆς λυσίτριχος⌝ ταῖς θριξίν. 2. καὶ εἶπον πρὸς αὐτήν· »σὺ τίς εἶ;« ἡ δὲ ἔφη· »καὶ τίς σύ, ἢ τίνα χρείαν ἔχεις μαθεῖν τὰ κατ᾿ ἐμοῦ πράγματα ποῖά εἰσιν ὄντα; * ἀλλ᾿ εἰ θέλεις μαθεῖν, πορεύθητι ἐν τοῖς ταμείδις τοῖς βασιλικοῖς καὶ· νιψάμενος τὰς χεῖράς σου πάλιν καθέσθητι ἐπὶ τοῦ θρόνου σου καὶ ἐρώτησαί με, καὶ τότε μαθεῖς, βασιλεῦ, τίς εἰμι ἐγώ.« 3. καὶ τοῦτο ποιήσας ἐγὼ Σολομῶν καὶ καθίσας ἐπὶ τοῦ θρόνου μου ἠρώτησα αὐτὴν καὶ εἶπον· »τίς εἶ σύ;« ἡ δὲ ἔφη· * »Ὀβυζούθ, ἥτις ἐν νυκτὶ οὐ καθεύδω, ἀλλὰ περιέρχομαι πάντα τὸν κόσμον ἐπὶ ταῖς γυναιξί, καὶ ⌜στοχαζομένη τὴν ὥραν μαστεύω⌝ καὶ

MSS HLP = Recc. AB. c. XIII. (57) 14 Καὶ προσκυνήσας κύριον τὸν θεὸν τοῦ Ἰ(σρα)ὴλ ἐκελ. P | δαιμόνιον L 2 γύνη .. εἶδος ego: βοὺς μὲν τῷ εἴδει H, βοὺς με τὸ ἴδος L, πνεῦμα γυναικοειδὲς P | τὴν δὲ ... λυσίτριχος ego: τῆς δὲ μορφῆς καταπέμπουσαν ἅπαν τοῖς μέλεσιν λίαν τρίχων H, τὴν δεὺ μορφήν. καταπέμπουσαν ἅπ(αν) τοῖς μέλεσιν αὐτοῦ· λυσιν τριχῶν L, τὴν κορυφὴν κατέχουσα ἀπὸ παντὸς μέλους· καὶ τὰς λυσίτριχας P 3 § 2. εἶπον A: ἔφην P 4 αὐτήν P: αὐτὸν A | λέγε μοι σὺ P | εἶ LP: εἰσεὶ H | ἡ δὲ ... χρείαν P: — A | καὶ τίς σύ P^c ad marg. lat., in textu καὶ σὺ τίς εἶ prim. man. scri. subter σὺ τίς εἶ linea fracta ducta 5 καὶ ἔχεις A | μαθεῖν A: ἀκοῦσαι P | τὰ — L | πραγ. π. εἰσιν ὄντα L: πραγ. πεισηνόντα H, — P | * H f. 18^r | εἰ — L 6 μαθεῖν: + στήκω γὰρ δεδεμ(έν)η πρὸ προσώπου σου P | πορεύον L | * L f. 16^r 1 | ταμίοις σου L 7 σου — P | καὶ πάλιν H | καθεσθ. A: καθήσας P, ad marg. scr. σεις quod forte pro σας in καθήσας legendum est | ἐπὶ τ. θρον. A: πρὸ τοῦ βήματος P 8 καὶ ἐρώτησαί με ego: κ. ἐρώτησε ἡμῖν L, τότε ἐρωτήσεις με P, — H | τότε — P | μαθεῖς H: μαθεῖν L, μαθήση P | βασιλεὺς σολομῶν L | τὶ τίς H § 3. (58) 9 Σολομῶν: — L, + καθὼς συνέταξέ μοι, ἠνεσχόμην δὲ διὰ τὴν ἐνοῦσαν μοι σοφίαν, ἵνα δυνηθῶ ἀκοῦσαι τὰς πράξεις αὐτῆς, καὶ ἐλέγξαι αὐτάς, καὶ φανερῶσαι τοῖς ἀνθρώποις P | καθήσας LP | ἐπὶ ... εἶπον: ἔφησα πρὸς τὸν δαίμονα P 10 ἠρώτησα ego: ἐρώτησα L, ἐρωτίσαι H | αὐτὴν ego: αὐτὸν H, ἐγὼ L | λέγε μοι τίς H | σύ — P | ἡ δὲ ἔφη H (ὁ) L: καὶ εἶπεν P | Ὀβυζούθ: ἀβυζούθ L, ἡ βυζοῦθ καὶ ἰδιοὺθ H, ἐγὼ (* Mg 1336) λέγομαι παρὰ ἀνθρώποις ὀβιζοὺθ P, l. Ἀβυζοῦ? cf. Intro pp. 78 et 82 11 ἥτις ... καθεύδω ego; ἥτις ἐὰν ἐκτήσω καθεύδω H, καὶ τῆς ἐννυκτὶ οὐ καθ. L, ἥτις νυκτὸς οὐ καθ. P | περιερχόμενος H | τὸν — H 12 ἐπὶ HP: ἐν L | τ. τικτούσαις γυν. P | στοχαζ. ... μαστεύω ego: μαστίζομ(έν)η τὴν ὥραν μαστίζω H, στομαχιζόμην τὴν ὥραν· μαστίζω L, τὴν μὲν ὥραν στοχαζομένη σταματίζω (in marg. ἴσταμαι) P

πνίγω τὰ βρέφη, * καὶ καθ᾽ ἑκάστην νύκτα ἄπρακτος οὐκ ἐξέρχομαι. σὺ δὲ οὐ δύνασαί με διατάξαι. καὶ εἰς τὰ δυσηκῆ μέρη περιέρχομαι. 4. καὶ οὐκ ἔστι μου τὸ ἔργον εἰ μὴ βρέφων ἀναίρεσις καὶ ὀφθαλμῶν ἀδικία καὶ στομάτων καταδίκη καὶ φρενῶν ἀπώλεια
5 καὶ σωμάτων ἄλγησις.« 5. καὶ ταῦτα ἀκούσας ἐγὼ Σολομῶν ἐθαύμασα, καὶ τὸ εἶδος αὐτῆς οὐκ ἐθεώρουν ἀλλὰ σκότος τὸ σῶμα
* αὐτῆς ὑπῆρχε καὶ αἱ τρίχες αὐτῆς ἠγριωμέναι. 6. κἀγὼ δὲ Σολομῶν λέγω αὐτήν· »λέγε μοι, πονηρὸν πνεῦμα, ὑπὸ ποίου ἀγγέλου καταργεῖσαι.« ἡ δὲ εἶπέ μοι· »ὑπὸ τοῦ ἀγγέλου Ῥαφαήλ·
10 καὶ ὅτε γεννῶσιν αἱ γυναῖκες, γράψαι τὸ ὄνομά μου ἐν χαρτίῳ καὶ ἐγὼ φεύξομαι ἀπὸ τῶν ἐκεῖσε. 7. κἀγὼ ἀκούσας ταῦτα προσέταξε δεσμευθῆναι αὐτὴν ταῖς θριξὶ καὶ κρεμασθῆναι ἔμπροσθεν

MS P 1 pro πνίγω ... περιέρχομαι (l. 2) praebet haec: ἐὰν ἐπιτύχω ἔπνιξα. εἰ δὲ μή γε (* f. 12ʳ) ἀναχωρῶ εἰς ἕτερον τόπον· μίαν γὰρ νύκτα ἀποχωρῆσαι ἄπρακτος οὐ δύναμαι· πνεῦμα γὰρ χαλεπόν εἰμι, μυριώνυμον καὶ πολύμορφον, καὶ νῦν μὲν ὧδε, καὶ νῦν με εἶναι (l. νῦν ἐκεῖ με εἶναι) (νῦν ἐκεῖ [νεῦμα (sic) νῦν ἐκεῖ?] εἶναι FlMg, ponit πνεῦμα pro νεῦμα Mg)· καὶ εἰς τὰ δυτικὰ (δατικὰ Fl) μέρη περιέρχομαι. ἀλλ᾽ ὡς ἐστὶ νῦν περισφραγίσας με τῷ δακτυλιδίῳ τοῦ θεοῦ οὐκ ἐποίησας, οὐ παρέστηκά σοι ἐγὼ οὐδέν με διατάξαι δυνήσῃ
MSS HL = Rec. A. 1 ἐξερχόμενος H 2 με H: μὴ L | διατάξαι H: ὑποτάξαι L | δυσηκῆ ego: δισηκὰ H, δυσικὰ L, (westering Crtr, assignatas Mgtr)
MSS HLP = Recc. AB. 3 § 4. καὶ ... ἔργον A: οὐδέν μου γὰρ ἔστιν ἔργον P | ἀναίρεσις καὶ ὤτων κωφότης καὶ P | καὶ — H 4 ἀδικίας L | * H f. 18ᵛ | καταδίκη A: χαλινόδεσμα P 5 § 5. (59) καὶ — P 6 καὶ omisso, τὸ εἶδος cum ἐθαύμασα coniunxerunt LP | αὐτῆς H: αὐτοῦ LP | οὐκ A: — P | ἐθεωρ. ... ὑπῆρχε H (αὐτῆς: αὐτοῦ) L: ἐθεώρουν ἅπαν τὸ σῶμα αὐτῆς σκοτία· ἡ δὲ ὄψις αὐτῆς ὕλη λαμπρὰ διάχλωρος P 7 * L f. 16ʳ² | καὶ — P | ἠγριωμέναι: + ὡς δράκοντος, καὶ τὰ σύμπαντα μέλη αὐτῆς, ἀόρατα. Καὶ ἡ φωνὴ αὐτῆς κατάδηλος, ἤρχετο πρός με P | § 6. δὲ... αὐτήν A: κατασοφισάμενος εἶπον P 8 πν(εῦμ)α πον. P | ὑπὸ (bis) H: διὰ L, — P | ποίῳ ἀγγέλῳ P 9 καταργῇ συ P | ὁ δὲ L | εἶπέ μοι A: μοι ἔφη P
MS P = Rec. B. 9 pro ὑπὸ ... ἐκεῖσε praebet P haec: τῷ ἀγγέλῳ τοῦ θεοῦ τῷ καλουμένῳ ἀφαρώφ, ὃ ἑρμηνεύεται ῥαφαήλ, ὦ καὶ νῦν καταργοῦμαι εἰς τὸν ἀπάντα (ἁ super lineam adscr. Pᶜ, ἅπαντα Fl) χρόνον. οὗ τὸ ὄνομα ἐάν τις τῶν ἀν(θρώπ)ων ἐπίσταται καὶ ἐπὶ γεννώσῃ γυναικὶ γράψῃ, τότε οὐ δυνήσομαι εἰσελθεῖν· οὗ ὁ (super lin. adscr. Pᶜ) ψῆφος χμ
MSS HL = Rec. A. 10 ὅταν γεννήσῃ ἡ γυναῖκα L 11 ἀπό τ. ἐκ. — L
MSS HLP = Recc. AB. 11 § 7. κἀγὼ σολομῶν P, καὶ ἐγὼ A | ταῦτα καὶ δοξάσας τὸν κύριον P | προσετ. HP: ἐκέλευσα L 12 αὐτὴν ... κρεμασθ. — L | αὐτὴν ego: τούτοις H, αὐτῆς P | τὰς τρίχας P

τοῦ ναοῦ ἵνα πάντες οἱ διερχόμενοι υἱοὶ Ἰσραὴλ βλέποντες δοξάσουσι τὸν θεὸν τὸν δόντα μοι τὴν ἐξουσίαν ταύτην.* * *

XIV. Καὶ πάλιν ἐκέλευσα παρεῖναί μοι ἕτερον δαίμονα· καὶ ἦλθε πρός με τῷ εἴδει δράκων κυλινδούμενος, τὸ δὲ πρόσωπον ἔχων καὶ τοὺς πόδας ἀνθρώπου καὶ τὰ μέλη αὐτοῦ δράκοντος καὶ τὰ πτερὰ κατὰ νώτου. 2. καὶ ἰδὼν αὐτὸν ἔκθαμβος γενόμενος εἶπον αὐτῷ· »σὺ τίς εἶ καὶ πόθεν ἐλήλυθας;« καὶ εἶπέ μοι τὸ πνεῦμα· »τὸ μὲν πρῶτον παρέστηκά σοι, βασιλεῦ Σολομῶν, πνεῦμα θεοποιούμενον ἐν ἀνθρώποις, * νῦν δὲ κατηργημένον διὰ τῆς τοῦ θεοῦ δεδομένης σοι σφραγῖδος. 3. καὶ νῦν ἐγώ εἰμι ὁ λεγόμενος Πτεροδράκων, οὐ συγγινόμενος πολλαῖς γυναιξίν, ὀλίγαις δὲ καὶ εὐμόρφοις, αἵτινες ⌜τοῦ ξύλου⌝ τούτου τοῦ ἄστρου ὄνομα κατέχουσι. 4. καὶ ἀπέρχομαι πρὸς αὐτὰς ὡσεὶ πνεῦμα πτεροειδὲς συγγινόμενον διὰ γλουτῶν, καὶ ἡ μὲν βαστάζει ᾗ ἐφώρμησα καὶ τὸ γεννηθὲν ἐξ αὐτῆς Ἔρω⟨ς⟩ γίνεται· ὑπ' ἀνδρῶν δὲ μὴ δυνηθὲν βασταχθῆναι ἐψόφησεν ἄρα καὶ ἡ γυνὴ ἐκείνη. αὕτη

MSS HLP = Recc. AB. 1 τ. ναοῦ LP: μου καὶ τοῦ ναοῦ H, + τοῦ θεοῦ FP | οἱ ... Ἰσρ. ego: οἱ ἐρχόμενοι υἱοὶ Ἰ(σρα)ὴλ καὶ H, οἱ διερχόμενοι τῶν υἱῶν Ἰ(σρα)ὴλ L, οἱ (supra lin. adscr. P^c) υἱοὶ ἰσραὴλ διερχόμενοι καὶ P | ἐβλέποντες αὐτὴν καὶ L   2 δοξάσουσι ego: — H, δοξάζουσι LP | κύριον τ. θεὸν Ἰ(σρα)ὴλ P | ταύτην: + καὶ σοφίαν καὶ δύναμιν παρὰ θεοῦ (* f. 12^v) διὰ τῆς σφραγῖδος ταύτης P | ** H f. 19^r
C. XIV. (60) 3 δαιμόνιον L   4 πρός ... κυλινδ. H: πρ. με τὸ ἴδος ὡς ὑδράκοντος κυλινδ. L, πρὸ προσώπου δρακοντοειδὴς ἀνακυλινδ. P | καὶ τοὺς πόδας ἔχων P 5 κ. τ. μέλη αὐτ. H: τὸ δὲ ἕτερον σῶμα L, τὰ δὲ μέλη αὐτοῦ πάντα ἀπὸ τῶν ποδῶν P | δράκοντος HP: κοντὸς L   6 κατὰ νότον P, κατὰ νώτον H, ἐκ τὰ νότατον L | § 2. ἰδὸν vel ἰδοὺ P | αὐτὸν H (ex -ος corr.) P: τούτου L   7 καὶ εἶπον L | αὐτῷ H: αὐτὸν L, — P | σὺ — P | εἰ ὁ δαίμων· καὶ τίς λ(έ)γ(ει)· καὶ P | ἐλήλυθας εἰπέ μοι P | καὶ .. πνεῦμα H: κ. ἀποκριθεὶς τὸ πνεῦμα λέγει P, — L   8 τὸν μὲν H
θ πνεῦμά τε P | θεοποιημένον L | ἐν ἀνθρώποις δὲ νῦν καταργοῦμαι H
* L f. 16^v 1   10 τῆς ... σοι P: τῆς σῆς δεδομένης H, τοῦ θεοῦ δεδωμένου τοι L | σφραγῖδος καὶ σοφίας P | § 3. καὶ νῦν P: νῦν δὲ A | ἐγώ .....
δαιμόνιον (p. 48*, l. 5), i. e., XIV 3—XVI 1) om. mss. HL
MS P = Rec. B.   12 ξύλου certe falsum est: ξυλ. < (λ super υ posito) MS, ξύλι Fl errore, ξιφίον vel Σειρίου conj. Bn; stellae vel sideris nomen aut compendium falso enodavit scriptor; l. forte Τοξότου?   14 γλουτῶν Crtr nates): πλοῦτον P | βαστάζει ego: ἐβάσταζεν P | ᾗ Fl: ἦ P | ἐφώρμησα P   15 Ἔρως Fl: ἔρω punctis tribus incertum esse notatum P, ἤρως conj. Bn vix recte

μου ἡ πρᾶξίς ἐστιν. 5. θέσον οὖν μοι μόνον ἀρκεσθῆναι, τὰ δὲ λοιπὰ τῶν δαιμονίων ἐνοχλούμενα ὑπό σου καταρασσόμενα πᾶσαν μὲν ἀλήθειαν εἴπωσι· τὰ δὲ διὰ πυρὸς ποιήσουσιν ἀναλωθῆναι τὴν μέλλουσαν ὕλην τῶν ξύλων ὑπό σου συνάγεσθαι εἰς 5 οἰκοδομὴν ἐν τῷ ναῷ.« 6. καὶ ὡς ταῦτα ἐλάλησεν ὁ δαίμων, ἰδοὺ τὸ πνεῦμα ἀπὸ τοῦ στόματος αὐτοῦ ἐξελθὸν ἐνέπρησε τὸν δρυμῶνα τοῦ Λιβάνου καὶ ἐνεπύρισε πάντα τὰ ξύλα ἅπερ εἰς τὸν ναὸν τοῦ θεοῦ ἐθέμην. 7. καὶ εἶδον ἐγὼ Σρλομῶν ὃ πεποίηκε τὸ πνεῦμα καὶ ἐθαύμασα, καὶ δοξάσας τὸν θεὸν ἠρώτησα τὸν 10 δαίμονα τὸν δρακοντοειδῆ λέγων· »εἰπέ μοι ποίῳ ἀγγέλῳ καταργῇ σύ.« ὁ δέ μοι ἔφη· »τῷ μεγάλῳ ἀγγέλῳ τῷ ἐν τῷ δευτέρῳ οὐρανῷ καθεζομένῳ τῷ καλουμένῳ Ἑβραϊστὶ Βαζαζάθ.« 8. κἀγὼ Σολομῶν ἀκούσας ταῦτα καὶ ἐπικαλεσάμενος τὸν ἄγγελον αὐτοῦ κατέκρινα μάρμαρα πρίζειν εἰς οἰκοδομὴν τοῦ ναοῦ τοῦ θεοῦ.
15 XV. καὶ εὐλογήσας τὸν θεὸν ἐκέλευσα παρεῖναί μοι ἕτερον δαίμονα. * καὶ ἦλθε πρὸ προσώπου μου ἕτερον πνεῦμα ὡς γύνη μὲν τὸ εἶδος ἔχον, εἰς δὲ τοὺς ὤμους ἑτέρας δύο κεφαλὰς σὺν χερσίν. 2. καὶ ἠρώτησα αὐτήν· »λέγε μοι σὺ τίς εἶ.« ἔφη δέ μοι· »ἐγώ εἰμι Ἐνήψιγος, ἥτις καὶ μυριώνυμος καλοῦμαι.« 3. καὶ 20 εἶπον αὐτῇ· »ἐν ποίῳ ἀγγέλῳ καταργῇ σύ;« ἡ δέ μοι ἔφη· »τί ζητεῖς; τί χρήζεις; ἐγὼ μὲν μεταβάλλομαι ὡς θεὰ λεγομένη, καὶ μεταβάλλομαι πάλιν καὶ γίνομαι ἕτερον εἶδος ἔχουσα. 4. καὶ μὴ θελήσῃς κατὰ τοῦτο γνῶναι πάντα τὰ κατ' ἐμέ, ἀλλ' ἐπειδὴ πάρει μοι, εἰς τοῦτο ἄκουσον· ἐγὼ παρακαθέζομαι τῇ σελήνῃ 25 καὶ διὰ τοῦτο τρεῖς μορφὰς κατέχω. 5. ὅτε μὲν μαγευομένη ὑπὸ τῶν σοφῶν γίνομαι ὡς Κρόνος. ὅτε δὲ πάλιν περὶ τῶν καταγόντων με κατέρχομαι καὶ φαίνομαι ἄλλη μορφή· τὸ μὲν τοῦ στοιχείου μέτρον ἀήττητον καὶ ἀόριστον καὶ ἀκατάργητόν ἐστιν. ἐγὼ γοῦν εἰς τὰς τρεῖς μορφὰς μεταβαλλομένη κατέρχομαι καὶ 30 γίνομαι τοιαύτη ἥνπερ βλέπεις. 6. καταργοῦμαι δὲ ὑπὸ ἀγγέλου

MS P = Rec. B. 1 § 5. θέσον: θὲς Bn   2 καταρασσ.: καὶ ταρασσ. ἵνα Bn   4 μέλλουσαν corr. Bn: μέλουσαν P | σου ego: τοῦ P, τούτων conj. Bn   § 6. (62) 6 ἰδοὺ corr. Bn: ἴδον P | * Mg 1337 | ἐξελθὼν P 7 * f. 13ʳ
    MS P = Rec. B. c. XV. l. 16 * (64)   17 ἔχον ego: ἔχουσα P 18 § 2. ἐρώτησα P   § 3. 20 αὐτῇ: η incertum, αὐτῷ Fl   § 5. 28 ἀήττητον P: ἀνίττητον Fl errore

Ραθαναὴλ τοῦ καθεζομένου εἰς τρίτον οὐρανόν. διὰ τοῦτο οὖν σοι λέγω· οὐ δύναταί με χωρῆσαι ὁ ναὸς οὗτος.«

7. κἀγὼ οὖν Σολομῶν εὐξάμενος τῷ θεῷ μου καὶ ἐπικαλεσάμενος τὸν ἄγγελον ὃν εἶπέ μοι, Ραθαναήλ, ἐποίησα τὴν σφραγῖδα καὶ κατεσφράγισα αὐτὴν ἁλύσει τριττῇ, καὶ κάτω δεσμῶν τῆς ἁλύσεως ἐποίησα τὴν σφραγῖδα τοῦ θεοῦ. 8. καὶ προεφήτευσέ μοι τὸ πνεῦμα λέγον· »ταῦτα μὲν σύ, βασιλεῦ Σολομῶν, ποιεῖς ἡμῖν. μετὰ δὲ χρόνον τινὰ ῥαγήσεταί σοι ἡ βασιλεία σου, καὶ πάλιν ἐν καιρῷ διαρραγήσεται ὁ ναὸς οὗτος καὶ συνλευσθήσεται πᾶσα Ἱερουσαλὴμ ἀπὸ βασιλέως Περσῶν καὶ Μήδων καὶ Χαλδαίων· καὶ τὰ σκεύη τούτου τοῦ ναοῦ οὗ σὺ ποιεῖς δουλεύσουσι θεοῖς. 9. μεθ᾽ ὧν ἂν καὶ πάντα τὰ ἀγγεῖα ἐν οἷς ἡμᾶς κατακλείεις κλασθήσονται ὑπὸ χειρῶν ἀνθρώπων καὶ τότε ἡμεῖς ἐξελευσόμεθα ἐν πολλῇ δυνάμει ἔνθεν καὶ ἔνθεν καὶ εἰς τὸν κόσμον κατασπαρησόμεθα. 10. καὶ πλανήσομεν πᾶσαν τὴν οἰκουμένην μέχρι πολλοῦ καιροῦ ἕως τοῦ θεοῦ ὁ υἱὸς τανυσθῇ ἐπὶ ξύλου· καὶ οὐκέτι γὰρ γίνεται τοιοῦτος βασιλεὺς ὅμοιος αὐτῷ ὁ πάντας ἡμᾶς καταργῶν, οὗ ἡ μήτηρ ἀνδρὶ οὐ μιγήσεται. 11. καὶ τίς λάβῃ τοιαύτην ἐξουσίαν κατὰ πνευμάτων εἰ μὴ ἐκεῖνος; ὃν ὁ πρῶτος διάβολος πειρᾶσαι ζητήσει καὶ οὐκ ἰσχύσει πρὸς αὐτόν, οὗ ἡ ψῆφος τοῦ ὀνόματος χμδ, ὅ ἐστιν Ἐμμανουήλ. 12. διὰ τοῦτο, βασιλεῦ Σολομῶν, ὁ καιρός σου πονηρὸς καὶ τὰ ἔτη σου μικρὰ καὶ πονηρὰ καὶ τῷ δούλῳ σου δοθήσεται ἡ βασιλεία σου.«

13. Κἀγὼ Σολομῶν * ἀκούσας ταῦτα ἐδόξασα τὸν θεὸν καὶ θαυμάσας τῶν δαιμόνων τὰς ἀπολογίας ἕως τῶν ἀποβάσεων ἠπίστουν αὐτοῖς καὶ οὐκ ἐπίστευον τοῖς λεγομένοις ὑπ᾽ αὐτῶν. 14. ὅτε δὲ ἐγένοντο, τότε συνῆκα καὶ ἐν τῷ θανάτῳ μου ἔγραψα τὴν διαθήκην ταύτην πρὸς τοὺς υἱοὺς Ἰσραὴλ καὶ ἔδωκα αὐτοῖς ὥστε εἰδέναι τὰς δυνάμεις τῶν δαιμόνων καὶ τὰς μορφὰς αὐτῶν

MS P = Rec. B. 2 § 6. χωρῆσαι conj. Cr: χωρίσαι P 3 § 7. (65) 5 δεσμῶν ego: δεσμὸν P § 8. 9 συνλευσθ. ego: συνλευσθ. P, vox nibili cuius vis fortasse est 'congeries lapidum fiet', "shall be undone" = (συν)λυνθήσεται Cr, συνλουθήσεται (sic) Fl errore ˙ 13 § 9. κατακλείεις ego: κατακλύεις P 24 § 13. (66) * f. 14ʳ 27 § 14. * Mg 1340

C. XV 10. Apoc. XII 9 notat James
C. XV 11. Mt. IV 1—11; Lk. IV 1—13
C. XV 12. Gen. XVII 9 notat James

καὶ τὰ ὀνόματα αὐτῶν τῶν ἀγγέλων ἐν οἷς καταργοῦνται οἱ δαίμονες. 15. καὶ δοξάσας κύριον τὸν θεὸν Ἰσραὴλ ἐκέλευσα περιδεθῆναι τὸ πνεῦμα δεσμοῖς ἀλύτοις. XVI. Καὶ εὐλογήσας τὸν θεὸν ἐκέλευσα παρεῖναι ἕτερον πνεῦμα. καὶ ἦλθε πρὸ προσώπου μου ἕτερον δαιμόνιον * ἔχον τὴν μορφὴν ἔμπροσθεν ἵππου, ὄπισθεν δὲ ἰχθύος. καὶ λέγει μεγάλην τὴν φωνήν· »βασιλεῦ Σολομῶν, ἐγὼ θαλάσσιόν εἰμι πνεῦμα χαλεπόν. ἐγείρομαι οὖν καὶ ἔρχομαι ἐπὶ τοὺς πελάγους παρὰ * τῆς θαλάσσης καὶ ἐμποδίζω τοὺς ἐν αὐτῇ πλέοντας ἀνθρώπους. 2. διεγειρόμενος δὲ καὶ ἐμαυτὸν ὡς κῦμα καὶ μεταμορφούμενος ἐπεισέρχομαι τοῖς πλοίοις. καὶ αὕτη μου ἡ ἐργασία τοῦ ὑποδέχεσθαι τὰ χρήματα καὶ τοὺς ἀνθρώπους. ⌜λαμβάνω γὰρ καὶ διεγείρομαι καὶ διαρρίπτω τοὺς ἄνθρώπους ὑπὸ τῆς θαλάσσης, οὕτως εἰμὶ ἐπιθυμῶν σωμάτων, ἀλλ' ἐκρίπτω αὐτὰ ἔξω τῆς θαλάσσης ἕως τοῦ δεῦρο.⌝ 3. ἐπεὶ δὲ ὁ Βεελζεβοὺλ ὁ τῶν ἀερίων καὶ ἐπιγείων καὶ καταχθονίων πνευμάτων δεσπότης συμβουλεύει εἰς τὰς καθ' ἑνὸς ἑκάστου ἡμῶν πράξεις, διὰ τοῦτο κἀγὼ ἀνέβην ἐκ τῆς * θαλάσσης σκέψιν τινὰ λαβεῖν παρ' αὐτῷ.

MS P = Rec. B. **1** ante ἀγγέλων scriptum δαιμόν(ων) linea delevit prim. man.

C. XVI. (67) l. **5** * rursus inc. mss. HL

MSS HLP = Recc. AB. **6** μορφ. ἔχω H, μορφ. ἔχων L | ἔνπροστεν H | ὄπιστεν L | κ. λ. μεγάλη τὴν φωνὴν H, κ. λεγ(ει) μετὰ μεγάλης φωνῆς L, κ. φωνὴ ἦν αὐτῷ μεγάλη καὶ ἔλεγε πρός με P   **7** ἐγὼ πνεῦμα θαλάσσιον εἰμί P | θαλάσσιος L   **8** ἐγειρ. ... θαλάσσης: καὶ ἀποδέχομαι ἐν χρυσῷ καὶ ἀργύρῳ. ἐγὼ τοιοῦτον εἰμὶ πνεῦμα διεγυρόμενον καὶ ἐρχόμενον ἐπὶ τὰ ἁπλώματα τοῦ ὕδατος τῆς θαλ. P | οὖν H: δὲ L | ἐπὶ ... θαλάσσης H: διὰ τῆς θαλάσσης ἐπὶ τὰ πλεῖα (l. πλοῖα) L   **9** * H f. 19ᵛ | ἐν αὐτῇ πλ. HP: ἐν τῶ πλείω (l. πλοίῳ) L   **10** § 2. διεγειρ. ... μεταμορφ.: διεγύρω γὰρ ἐμαυτὸν εἰς κῦμα καὶ μεταμορφοῦμαι· ἐπιρίπτω καὶ P | διεγυρόμενοι L | καὶ — L | ἐμαυτὸν L: ἐμαυτοὺς H | ὡς κῦμα L: κεῖμαι H   **11** ἐπεισερχ. P: περιέρχομαι L | ὑπεισέρχομαι τοῖ πλείον H | μου ἐστὶν P   **12** τοῖς ἀν(θρώπ)οις L

MS P = Rec. B. **12** λαμβάνω ... δεῦρο (l. 15): — A

MSS HLP = Recc. AB. § 3. l. **15** ἐπεὶ ego: ἐπὶ Λ, ἐπειδὴ P | ὁ τῶν ... δεσπότης A: ἄρχων τῶν ἀερίων πνευμάτων κ. καταχθ. κ. ἐπιγ. δεσπόζει καὶ P   **17** ἐμβουλεύει L | εἰς τὰς P: τοῦ A | καθ' — P   **18** ἀνέβη LP: ἀναβαίνω H | ἐκ A: ἀπὸ P | * P f. 14ʳ | σκέψιν: σκῆψιν conj. Cr cum dubio | σκέψιν ... θαλάσσης (p. 49*, l. 2) P: om. per homoeoteleuton A

4. ἔχω δὲ καὶ ἑτέραν δόξαν καὶ πρᾶξιν· μεταμορφοῦμαι εἰς κύματα καὶ ἀνέρχομαι ἀπὸ τῆς θαλάσσης καὶ δεικνύω ἐμαυτὸν τοῖς ἀνθρώποις καὶ καλοῦσί με Κυνόπηγον ⌈ὅτι μεταμορφοῦμαι εἰς ἄνθρωπον· ἔστι μοι τὸ ὄνομα ἀληθές. ναυτίαν δὲ ἀποστέλλω τινὰ διὰ τῆς ἀνόδου μου εἰς τοὺς ἀνθρώπους. 5. ἦλθον οὖν εἰς τὴν συμβουλὴν τοῦ ἄρχοντος Βεελζεβοὺλ καὶ ἐδέσμευσέ με εἰς τὰς χεῖράς σου.⌉ νῦν δὲ παρέστηκά σοι καὶ διὰ τὸ μὴ ἔχειν ὕδωρ δύο ἢ τρεῖς ἡμέρας ἐκλείπει τὸ πνεῦμά μου τὸ λαλοῦν σοι.«* 6. κἀγὼ εἶπον αὐτῷ· »λέγε μοι ποίῳ ἀγγέλῳ καταργεῖσαι.« ὁ δέ λέγει· »διὰ τοῦ *Ἰαμέθ.« 7. κἀγὼ ἐκέλευσα αὐτὸν βληθῆναι εἰς φιάλην καὶ ὕδατος θαλάσσης δοχὰς δέκα περιχύνεσθαι καὶ περιέφραξα ἐπάνω μαρμάρῳ καὶ περιήπλωσα τῇ ἀσφάλτῳ καὶ πίσσῃ καὶ στυπείῳ τὸ στόμα τοῦ ἀγγείου καὶ σφραγίσας τῷ δακτυλιδίῳ ἐκέλευσα ἀποτεθῆναι εἰς τὸν ναὸν τοῦ θεοῦ.

XVII. Καὶ ἐκέλευσα παρεῖναί μοι ἕτερον πνεῦμα. * καὶ ἦλθε πνεῦμα ἀνθρώπου μορφὴν ἔχον σκοτεινὴν καὶ ὀφθαλμοὺς λάμ-

---

MSS HLP = Recc. AB. § 4. 1 κύματα conj. Cr: καύματα P 3 καὶ A ὡς οἱ ἐπίγειοι P | Κυνόπηγον H: κὖνόπιγω L, l. forte κυματόπηγον, κυνόπαστον P, l. κυνόσβατον, Κυνόσπαστον Cr cum Plin., HN XXIV 74

MS P = Rec. B. ll. 3—9 habet P textum peculiarem. ὅτι ... χεῖράς σου (l. 7) om. A 7—9 νῦν ... σοι: κἀγὼ παρέστιν ἐνώπιόν σου διὰ τῆς σφραγίδος ταύτης· καὶ σὺ νῦν βασανίζεις με, ἰδοὺ οὖν δύο· καὶ τριῶν ἡμερῶν ἐκλείπει τὸ πν(εῦμ)α τὸ λαλοῦν διὰ τὸ μὴ ἔχειν με ὕδωρ P
MSS HL = Rec. A. 4 δὲ: + παρέχω L 7 σοι H: σε L 8 ὅτι δύο τρεῖς ἡμέρας ponit post λαλοῦν σοι L 9 * L f. 16ᵛ 2

MSS HLP = Recc. AB. § 6. (69) 9 κἀγὼ .. αὐτ. HP: λέγω δὲ τοῦτον L | λέγε μοι — L | ἀγγέλων A | καταργῇ συ P 10 λέγει: ἔφη Pʳ | * H f. 20ʳ | Ἰαμέθ LP: ἰαβέθ H | § 7. κἀγὼ: + δοξάσας τὸν θεὸν P | κελεύσας H | αὐτ. βληθ. H: tr. L | αὐτὸν — P 11 εἰς φιαλ. βληθ. τὸ πνεῦμα P | φιάλην P: φυλακὴν A | περιχυν. A: ἀνὰ μετρητῶν β̄ P 12 ἐπάνω P: ἐπάνωθεν L, — H | μαρμάρῳ H; μαρμάρων LP | περιήπλωσα A: — P | τῇ ἀσφ. A: ἀσφάλτων P 13 πίσσῃ ego: πύσαν H, πίσα L, πίσσης P | κ. στυπείῳ ego: κ. στυπίων H, στιπίων L, — P | εἰς τὸ P | στόμα HP: σόμα L | ἀγγείου APCr: ἀγγέλου Fl errore | τὸ δακτυλίδιον H 14 ἐκέλ. ... θεοῦ — H | ἐν τῷ ναῷ L

C. XVII. 15 ἐκέλευσαν H | πνεῦμα HP: δαίμονα L | * (70) ἦλθε: + πρὸ προσώπου μου κατειδωλισμένον (καταλισμένον Mg, καταδουλισμένον Cr) ἕτερον P 16 ἔχον P: ἔχων L, ἔχουσαν H | σκοτεινὴν L: σκοτενὴν H, σκοτεινὸν P |. κ. ὀφθ. λαμπ. A: τοὺς ὀφθ. ἔχον λαμπ. καὶ ἐν τῇ χειρὶ φέρον σπάθην P

UNT. 9: McCown.

ποντας. καὶ ἐπηρώτησα αὐτὸν λέγων· »σὺ τίς εἶ;« ⸢ὁ δὲ ἔφη·
»ἐγώ εἰμι ὀχεικὸν πνεῦμα ἀνθρώπου γίγαντος ἐν σφαγῇ τετελευ-
τηκότος ἐν τῷ καιρῷ τῶν γιγάντων.¹« 2. καὶ εἶπον αὐτῷ·
»λέγε μοι τί διαπράττεις ἐπὶ τῆς γῆς καὶ ποῦ ἔχεις οἰκητήριον.«
5 ὁ δέ μοι ἔφη· »ἡ * κατοικία μου ἐν τόποις ἀβάτοις. ἡ ἐργασία
μου αὕτη· παρακαθέζομαι τοῖς τεθνεόσιν ἀνθρώποις ἐν τοῖς μνη-
μείοις καὶ ἐν ἀωρίᾳ παραμορφῶ * τοῖς τεθνεόσι καὶ εἰ λήψομαί**
τινα εὐθέως * ἀναιρῶ αὐτὸν τῷ ξίφει. 3. εἰ δὲ μὴ δυνηθῶ ἀναιρεῖν, ποιῶ αὐτὸν δαιμονίζεσθαι καὶ τὰς σάρκας αὐτοῦ κατατρώ-
10 γειν καὶ σιάλους ἐκ τῶν γενείων αὐτοῦ καταρρεῖν.« 4. ἔφην δὲ
αὐτῷ· »φοβήθητι τὸν θεὸν τοῦ οὐρανοῦ καὶ τῆς γῆς καὶ εἰπέ
μοι ποίῳ ἀγγέλῳ καταργεῖσαι.« ὁ δὲ ἔφη μοι· »ἐμὲ καταργεῖ ὁ
μέλλων κατελθεῖν σωτήρ, οὗ τὸ στοιχεῖον ἐν τῷ μετώπῳ, εἴ τις
γράψει, καταργεῖ με καὶ ἐπιτιμηθεὶς ἀποστρέψω ἀπ' αὐτοῦ τα-
15 χέως· τοῦτο δὲ τὸ σημεῖον σταυρός.« 5. ταῦτα δὲ ἀκούσας ἐγὼ
Σολομῶν κατέκλεισα τὸν δαίμονα ὥσπερ καὶ τἄλλα δαιμόνια.

MSS HLP = Recc. AB. 1 αὐτὸν A: αὐτὸ P | λέγων — P
MS P = Rec. B. 1—3 τὸ δὲ ... γιγάντων P, καὶ ὁ δαίμων ἔφη· τὸ ὄνομά
μου μαχθὸν L, — H | 1 ὁ δὲ cum rec. A infra: τὸ δὲ P   2 ὀχεικὸν ego,
i q., ὀχευτικὸν: ὀχικὸν P
MSS HLP = Recc. AB. 3 § 2. καὶ — P   4 καὶ — L   5 ὁ δέ μοι
H: ὁ δαίμων L, τὸ δὲ P | ἡ κατοικία ... ἐργασία: ἡ κακοία (l. κακία) H |
ἡ μὲν κατ. P | * P f. 15ʳ | τόποις ἀβάτοις L: τοῖς κατακάρποις τόποις P
| ἡ δὲ ἐργ. P   6 αὕτη HP: ἐτούτη εἶναι L, + ἐστὶν H | παρακαθίζω
ἐμαυτὸν P | τεθνεόσιν A: παρερχομένοις P   7 καὶ ἀλλ' ἐν H | παρα-
μορφῶ: + ἐμ H | * H f. 20ᵛ | τεθν. A: τελευτῶσι P | εἰ P: ἡ H, ὁ L
| ** L f. 17ʳ   8 εὐθέως post ξίφει ponit L | * Mg 1341 | ἀναιρῶ H:
ἀνερῶ P, ἀερῶ L | τῷ H: τὸ L, — P | § 3. μὴ L: μοι H, οὐ P | ἀναι-
ρεῖν A: ἀναιρῆσαι P   9 ποιῶ: ποιὸν L | αὐτοῦ: αὐτῶν L | κατατρώ-
γειν A: κατεσθίειν P   10 σιάλους ego: σὺ ἄλλοις H, σει ἄλλους L, τοὺς
σιέλους P | ἐκ A: ἀπὸ P | γενείων P: γονιῶν A | αὐτοῦ H: αὐτ(ῶν) L,
— P | καταρέειν H, καταρέων L | § 4. ἔφη A   11 αὐτῳ: + ὁ βασιλεὺς
σολομῶν φοβηθ. οὖν P | τοῦ ... τῆς HP: πν(εῦμ)α πονηρὸν L   12 ἀγγέ-
λων H | καταργῇ συ P | ὁ δὲ A: τὸ δ' P | μοι H: — LP | ὁ ἐμὲ H |
ἐμὲ καταργῇ με L   13 κατελθ. σωτ. A: σ(ωτ)ὴρ γενέσθαι ἄν(θρωπ)ος P |
καὶ εἴ A   14 γράψει: + αὐτῶ A, ἐπιγράψει P | καταργεῖ ... αὐτοῦ A:
ἡττήσει με καὶ φοβηθεὶς ἀποστραφήσομαι P   15 καὶ τοῦτο P | στ(αυ)-
ρ(ό)ς A: ἐὰν τις ἐπιγράφῃ φοβηθήσομαι P | § 5. ταῦτα δὲ A: καὶ τοῦτο P,
+ αὐτοῦ H   16 κατεκλ. A: καὶ δοξάσας κύριον τὸν θεὸν ἐπέκλεισα P |
τ. δαίμ. H. αὐτὸν L, τὸ δαιμόνιον P | τὰ ἄλλα L | δαιμόνια A: πν(εύμ)ατα P

XVIII, 1—4   τὰ λς´ στοιχεῖα   51*

XVIII. Καὶ ἐκέλευσα παρεῖναί μοι ἕτερον δαίμονα. καὶ ἦλθον πρός με τὰ τριάκοντα ἓξ στοιχεῖα, * αἱ κορυφαὶ αὐτῶν ὡς κύνες ἄμορφοι. ἐν αὐτοῖς δὲ ἦσαν ἀνθρωπόμορφα, ταυρόμορφα, θηριοπρόσωπα, δρακοντόμορφα, σφιγγοπρόσωπα, πτηνοπρόσωπα. 2, καὶ ταῦτα ἰδὼν ἐγὼ Σολομῶν ἐπηρώτησα αὐτὰ λέγων· »καὶ ὑμεῖς τίνες ἐστε;« αἱ δὲ ὁμοθυμαδὸν μιᾷ * φωνῇ εἶπον· »ἡμεῖς ἐσμεν τὰ τριάκοντα ἓξ στοιχεῖα, οἱ κοσμοκράτορες τοῦ σκότους τοῦ αἰῶνος τούτου. 3. ἀλλ᾽ οὐ δύνασαι ἡμᾶς, βασιλεῦ, ἀδικῆσαι οὐδὲ κατακλεῖσαι· ἀλλ᾽ ἐπειδὴ ἔδωκέ σοι ὁ θεὸς τὴν ἐξουσίαν ἐπὶ πάντων τῶν ἀερίων πνευμάτων καὶ ἐπιγείων καὶ καταχθονίων, ἰδοὺ παραστήκομεν ἔμπροσθέν σοι ὡς τὰ * λοιπὰ πνεύματα.«
4. Κἀγὼ δὲ Σολομῶν προσκαλεσάμενος τὸ ἓν πνεῦμα εἶπον

C. XVIII. MSS HLP = Recc. AB.   **1** (72) παρεῖναί μοι LP: — H | ἕτερον δαιμ. P: ἕτερα δαιμόνια L, πν(εύμ)ατα H | καὶ ἦλθον π. με: — L | ἦλθον P: ἤλθασιν H   **2** πρός με H: πρὸ προσώπου μοι P | τὰ λς στοιχ. H, τὰ λεγόμενα στοιχ. L, τριάκοντα ἓξ πν(εύμ)α P | * H f. 21ʳ | αἱ κορ. HP: καὶ ἡ κορυφῇ L | ὡς LP: ὡσεὶ H   **3** ἐν αὐτοῖς· ἦσαν δὲ H | ἦσαν καὶ L | ἀνώμορφα καὶ κατόμορφα· θηρ. δρακ. σφιγγωπ. πτερωτα· ἐν τὰ πρόσωπα H, ἀπὸ ἀνωμορφα· καὶ ταυρομ. καὶ θηρ. L, ἀνθρωπόμορφοι, ὀνοπρόσωποι, βοοοπρόσωποι, καὶ πτηνοπρόσωποι P   **5** § 2. καὶ ... Σολ. A: κἀγὼ σολομῶν ἀκούσας καὶ ἰδὼν αὐτὰ ἐθαύμασα καὶ P | αὐτὰ — H | καὶ — P   **6** αἱ HP: εἱ L | ὁμοθ. HP: ὁμοῦ L | μίαν φωνὴν L | * L f. 17ʳ² | εἶπαν μιὰ φωνή H   **7** ἐσμεν HP: ἐσταὶ L | τριακ. ἕξει δαιμόνια καὶ στοιχεῖα L | οἱ HP: — L | τὸ σκότος L   **8** τοῦ αἰῶνος A: — P   § 3. δυνήσῃ βασιλεῦ σολομῶν ἡμᾶς P | καὶ ἀδικεῖσαι L   **9** οὐδὲ κατακλ.: — L, + οὐδὲ κελεῦσαι ἡμῖν P | ἐπειδὴ LP: ἐπεὶ H | κύριος ὁ θεὸς P   **10** πάντων (+ ἡμῶν L) ... (καὶ — 1° — om. H) ... καταχθ. A: παντὸς πν(εύματο)ς ἀερίου τὲ καὶ ἐπιγείου καὶ καταχθονίου P   **11** ἰδοὺ A: διὰ τοῦτο καὶ ἡμεῖς P | παραστήκομεν H: παραστίκαμέν σοι L, παριστάμεθα P | ἔμπροσθέν H: pr. καὶ ἡμεῖς L, ἐνώπιον P | ὡς καὶ L | * P f. 15ᵛ   **12** πνεύματα: + ἀπὸ κριοῦ, καὶ ταύρου, διδύμου τὲ καὶ καρκίνου, λέοντος, καὶ παρθένου, ζυγοῦ τε καὶ σκΚορπίου (sic, κ = η?) τοξότου, αἰγωκέρωτος, ὑδροχόου, καὶ ἰχθύος P

MS P = Rec. B. § 4. ll. 13—p. 52*, 1 pro Κἀγὼ ... μοι praebet P haec: τότε ἐγὼ σολομὼν ἐπικαλεσάμενος τὸ ὄνομα κυρίου σαβαώθ, ἐπηρώτησα αὐτὰ καθ᾽ ἕνα ὁποῖος τρόπος αὐτῶν τυγχάνει, καὶ ἐκέλευσα αὐτοὺς ἕνα ἕκαστον εἰς τὸ μέσον ἐλθόντα εἰπεῖν τὴν ἑαυτοῦ πρᾶξιν. τότε προσελθὼν ὁ πρῶτος εἶπεν P

MSS HL = Rec. A. § 4. 1. 13 δὲ — L | τὸ — L

4**

αὐτῷ· »σὺ τίς εἶ;« ὁ δὲ ἔφη μοι »ἐγὼ δεκανὸς α΄ τοῦ ζῳδιακοῦ κύκλου, ὃς καλοῦμαι Ῥύαξ.⌉ 5. κεφαλὰς ἀνθρώπων ποιῶ ἀλγεῖν καὶ κροτάφους σαλεύω. ὡς μόνον ἀκούσω· »Μιχαήλ, ἔγκλεισον Ῥύαξ«, εὐθὺς ἀναχωρῶ.« 6. ὁ δεύτερος ἔφη· »ἐγὼ Βαρσαφαὴλ 5 καλοῦμαι. ἡμικράνους ποιῶ τοὺς ἀνθρώπους τοὺς ἐν τῇ ὥρᾳ μου κειμένους. ὡς δὲ ἀκούσω· »Γαβριήλ, ἔγκλεισον Βαρσαφαήλ«, εὐθὺς ἀναχωρῶ.«. 7. ὁ τρίτος ἔφη· »Ἀρτοσαὴλ καλοῦμαι. ὀφθαλμοὺς ἀδικῶ σφόδρα. ὡς δὲ ἀκούσω· »Οὐριήλ, ἔγκλεισον Ἀρτοσαήλ,« εὐθὺς ἀναχωρῶ.«
10   8. Ὁ τέταρτος ἔφη· »ἐγὼ καλοῦμαι * Ὀροπέλ. λαιμοὺς καὶ συνάγχας καὶ σηπεδόνας ἐπιπέμπω. ὡς δὲ ἀκούσω· »Ῥαφαήλ, ⌈ἔγκλεισον Ὀροπελ,«⌉ εὐθὺς ἀναχωρῶ.« 9. ὁ πέμπτος ἔφη· »ἐγὼ Καιρωξανονδάλον * καλοῦμαι. ἐμφράξεις ὠτίων ποιῶ. ἐὰν δὲ

MSS HL = Rec. A. § 4. 1 * H f. 21ᵛ | μοι — L

MS P = Rec. B. § 4. ll. 1—2 pro ἐγώ ... Ῥύαξ praebet P textum interpolatum hunc: ἐγώ εἰμι ὁ (πρῶτος) δεκανὸς τοῦ ζῳδιακοῦ κύκλου, ὃς καλοῦμαι κριός, καὶ μετ᾽ ἐμοῦ οἱ δύο οὗτοι. ἐπηρώτησα οὖν αὐτούς· τίνες καλεῖσθε; § 5. ὁ μὲν πρῶτος ἔφη· ἐγώ, κύριε, ῥύαξ καλοῦμαι
MS HL = Rec. A. § 4. ll. 1—2 ἐγώ ... Ῥύαξ dubitanter propono: ἐγὼ δεκαδᾶν (δεκάδων L) τοῦ ἐξοδίου (ἐξοδίῳν L) κυκλῶνος (κακόκλονος — κο supra lin. adscr. — H) καλοῦμαι καὶ κριὸς HL
MSS HLP = Recc. AB. § 5. 2 ποιεῖν H | ἀλγεῖν — A   3 καὶ — L | σαλεύειν H | μόνον: μὲν L | ἔγκλεισον ego: ἔκλυσον (forte recte, sed in ms. tribus punctis dubii indicandi notatum) P, ἔγγεισον H, ἔγγισον L   4 Ῥύαξ P: οὗ οὐρὸν H, οὐροὴλ L | § 6. (74) δεύτερος: numeros constanter per compendia scr. codd. omnes | ἔφη: λέγ < L | βαρσαβαὴλ L   5 ἡμίκρανος L, ἡ μικρανοες Mg | τοὺς ἀνθρ. A: ἀλγεῖν P   6 ὡς δὲ L: ἕως δὲ H, ἐὰν μόνον P | ἔγκλησον HP, ἔκλεισον (κ ex λ corr.) L   7 εὐθὺς semper scr. P, εὐθέως semper L, interdum εὐθὺς, interdum εὐθέως H | § 7. (75) καὶ ὁ L | Ἀρτοσαὴλ HL: ἀρωτοσαὴλ P   8 ὡς δὲ H: ὡς μόνον P, καὶ ἐὰν L | ἀκοίσαι P | οὐρονὲλ L | ἔγκλεισον P: ἔκκλεισον H, ἔκλεισον L | ἀρατοσαὴλ P, ἀρσαὴλ L
§ 8. sectionem 8 om. Fl cum nota hac: »Hic omisi quae v. in additam. sub signo *),« quae additamenta reperire non potui   10 ἔφη HP: εἶπεν L | * L f. 17ᵛ¹ | Ὀροπέλ P: ὀροπόλος L, ἀροπόλον H | λαιμοὺς ... ἐπιπέμπω P: λιμοὺς καὶ συμπεδώνας καὶ συν(εχὰς linea delet.) μπεδώνας καὶ συνοχὰς ἐμποιῶ H, λιτ(οὺς) καὶ σιπεδώνας κ. συνοχὰς ἐμπιῶ L   11 ὡς δὲ A: ἐὰν P   12 ἔγκλεισον Ὀρ. — A | § 9. (76) 13 καὶ ρωξανονδάλον H καιριξενονδάλων L, ἰουδὰλ P | " H f. 22ʳ | ἔμφραξιν P | ὠτίων HP: ὅτι L | ποιῶ H: ἐνμπιῶ L, καὶ σφήνωσιν ἀκοῶν ἐπιτελῶ P | δὲ — P

XVIII, 9—15   τὰ λς´ στοιχεῖα   53*

ἀκούσω· »Ούρουήλ, ⌈ἔγκλεισον Καιρωξανονδάλον,⌉ ευθύς * ἀναχωρῶ.« 10. ὁ ἕκτος ἔφη· »ἐγὼ Σφενδοναὴλ καλοῦμαι. παρυτίδας καὶ ὀπισθοτόνους ἐμποιῶ. ἐὰν ἀκούσω· »Σαβαήλ, ⌈ἔγκλεισον Σφενδοναήλ,⌉ εὐθὺς ἀναχωρῶ.« 11. ὁ ἕβδομος ἔφη· »ἐγὼ
5 Σφανδῶρ καλοῦμαι. ὤμων δύναμιν ἐλαττῶ καὶ χειρῶν νεῦρα παραλύω, καὶ μέλη κοπιάζω. ἐὰν ἀκούσω· »Ἀραήλ, ⌈ἔγκλεισον Σφανδῶρ,⌉ εὐθὺς ἀναχωρῶ.« 12. ὁ ὄγδοος ἔφη· »ἐγὼ Βελβὲλ καλοῦμαι. καρδίας ἀνθρώπων καὶ φρένας διαστρέψω .. ἐὰν ἀκούσω· »Καραήλ, ⌈ἔγκλεισον Βελβέλ,⌉ εὐθὺς ἀναχωρῶ.«
10 13. Ὁ ἔννατος ἔφη· »ἐγὼ Κουρταὴλ καλοῦμαι. στρόφους ἐγκάτων * ἐπιπέμπω. ἐὰν ἀκούσω· »Ἰαώθ, ⌈ἔγκλεισον Κουρταήλ,⌉ εὐθὺς ἀναχωρῶ.« 14. ὁ δέκατος ἔφη· »ἐγὼ Μεταθίαξ καλοῦμαι. νεφρῶν πόνους ποιῶ. ἐὰν ἀκούσω· * »Ἀδωναήλ, ⌈ἔγκλεισον Μεταθίαξ,⌉ εὐθὺς ἀναχωρῶ.« 15. ὁ ἑνδέκατος ἔφη· »ἐγὼ Κατα-
15 νικοταὴλ καλοῦμαι. μάχας καὶ αὐθαδείας κατ' οἴκους ἐπιπέμπω. ἐάν τις θέλει εἰρηνεύειν, γραψάτω εἰς ἑπτὰ φύλλα δάφνης τὰ

MSS HLP = Recc. AB. 1 ούριὴλ H | ἔγκλεισον Καιρ. ego: ἔγκλησον Ιουδὰλ P, — A | * P f. 16ʳ 2 § 10. Σφενδοναὴλ P: σφενδεναὴλ H, φεδοναὴλ L | παρυτιδ.: + ποιῶ· καὶ παρίσθμια P 3 ὀπιστοτόνους H, ὀπιστονότους L, ὀπισθότονα P | ἐμποιῶ A: — P | Σαβαὴλ (β ex λ corr.) P: Σαβραὴλ Mg errore, σαφαὴλ L, σφεβαὴλ H | ἐγκλ. Σφεν. — A 4 σφανδοναὴλ P | § 11. (78) ἔφη HP: εἶπεν L 5 Σφανδῶρ P: δορὸν H, φανδωρὸν L | ὤμων δυν. P: ἀν(θρώπ)ων (ἀνον H) δυνάμεις A | ἐλαττῶ P: ἐλαττόνω H, ἐλαττῶν L, + καὶ σαλεύω P, + ἐὰν ἀκούει L | καὶ — H | χειρῶν εὗρα H 6 παραλύω HP: παρχύω L, + καὶ ὀστᾶ παλαμῶν συντρίβω P | κ. μέλη κοπ. H: κ. μυελοὺς ἐμπιπύζω (ἐκπιπύζω Fl, l. ἐκπιπίλζω = ἐκπίνω) P, — L | ἐγκλ. Σφανδ. — A 7 § 12. (79) βοκβὲλ in βελβὲλ corr. L 8 διαστρέφω HP: ἀναστρέφω L 9 Καραὴλ A: ἀραὴλ P | ἐγκλ. Βελβ. — A
§ 13. (80) 10 ἔφη HP: εἶπεν L | Κουρταὴλ P: κουρταὴλ vel κοφταὴλ H, ἀκουρταραὴλ L 11 ἐγκάτων A: ἐν κοιλίᾳ P | * Mg 1344 | ἐπιπέμπω A: ἀποπέμπω, πόνους ἐπάγω P | ἐὰν ... ἀναχωρῶ — L | Ἰαώθ P: σαβαὼθ H | ἐγκλ. Κουρτ. — H 12 § 14. (81) ἔφη HP: εἶπεν L | Μεταθίαξ P: μεταθύαξ H, μετάθεαξ L 13 νεφρούς ποιῶ πονεῖν P | ἐὰν δὲ H | * H f. 22ᵛ | Ἀδωναήλ P: ἀδωναῖ H, ἀδωνὰν L | ἐγκλ. Μεταθ. — A 14 § 15. (82) ἔφη HP: εἶπεν L | Καταν. P: κανικοταὴλ L, νικοταὴλ H 15 αὐθαδείας A: ἀδικίας P | οἴκους: + ποιῶ καὶ σκληρίας P | * L f. 17ᵛ² 16 εἰρηνεύειν: εἰρηνεύει L, + εἰς τὸν οἶκον αὐτοῦ P | γραψάτω P: γράψαι H, ἃς γράφη L | εἰς ... με H: τὰ ἑπτὰ ὀνομ. τ. κατ. με εἰς ἐπ. φύλα δάννης ἐτοῦτα L, εἰς ἐπ. φύλλ < δάφνης τὸ ὄνομα τοῦ καταργοῦντος με ἀγγέλου, καὶ ταῦτα τὰ ὀνόματα P

ὀνόματα τὰ καταργοῦντά με· »ἄγγελε· ἐαέ· ἰεώ· σαβαώθ· ἐγκλείσατε Κατανικοταήλ,« καὶ πλύνας τὰ φύλλα τῆς δάφνης ῥανάτω τὸν οἶκον αὐτοῦ τῷ ὕδατι, καὶ εὐθὺς ἀναχωρῶ.« 16. ὁ δωδέκατος ἔφη· »ἐγὼ Σαφθοραὴλ καλοῦμαι. διχοστασίας ἐμβάλλω
5 τοῖς ἀνθρώποις καὶ εὐφραίνομαι αὐτοὺς σκανδαλίζων. ἐάν τις γράψει ταῦτα· * »ἰαέ· ἰεώ· υἱοὶ Σαβαώθ,« καὶ φορεῖ ἐν τῷ τραχήλῳ αὐτοῦ, εὐθὺς ἀναχωρῶ.«
17. Ὁ τρίτος καὶ δέκατος ἔφη· »ἐγὼ Φοβοθὴλ καλοῦμαι. νευρῶν χαλάσεις ποιῶ. ἐὰν ἀκούσω· »Ἀδωναΐ,« εὐθὺς ἀναχωρῶ.«
10 18. ὁ τέταρτος καὶ δέκατος ἔφη· »ἐγὼ Λερωήλ * καλοῦμαι. ψύχος καὶ ῥῖγος καὶ στομάχου πόνον ἐπάγω. ἐὰν ἀκούσω· »Ἰάζ, μὴ ἐμμείνῃς, ⌈μὴ θερμάνῃς, ὅτι καλλίον ἐστὶ Σολομῶν ἕνδεκα πατέρων,«⌉ εὐθὺς ἀναχωρῶ.« 19. ὁ πέμπτος καὶ δέκατος ἔφη· »ἐγὼ Σουβελτὶ καλοῦμαι. φρίκην καὶ νάρκην ἐπιπέμπω. ἐὰν μόνον

MSS HLP = Recc. AB. **1** ἄγγελε A: — P | ἐαέ H: ἰεαὲ L, ἰαὲ P | ἰεώ LP: ἰωεὼ H | σαβαώθ A: υἱοὶ σαβαώθ, διὰ τὸ ὄνομα τοῦ μεγάλου θεοῦ P | ἐγκλήσαται H, ἐγκλησάτω P, ἐγγίσατε L, + τῷ Fl errore **2** καὶ A: πλύνᾳ vel πλύνας P, πλύνων Fl | τ. φυλ. τ. δαφ. H: τὰς δάφας L, τὰ δαφόφυλλα P, τὰ δαφνόφυλλα Fl, + ἐπὶ τοῦ ὕδατος P | ῥεννάτω (sic) Fl errore **3** τὸν ... ὕδατι P: τοῦ οἴκου μετὰ τὸ ὕδωρ ἐκείνω L, τὸ ὕδωρ ἐπὶ τὸν οἶκον αὐτοῦ H, + ἀπὸ ἔσω ἕως ἔξω P | § 16. (83) **4** σαφαθωραὴλ P | ἐμβάλω P **5** εὐφρ. αὐτ. σκανδ. P: φρένας σκανδαλίζω (-ζων H) A **6** γράψει ταῦτα A: εἰς χάρτην ἐπιγράψῃ ταῦτα τὰ ὀνόματα τῶν (* f. 16ᵛ) ἀγγέλων P | ἰαέ· ἰεώ· (ἰαω· L) υἱοὶ Σαβ. A: ἰαεῶ· ἰειλῶ· (Ἰαελῶ Fl) ἰωελὲτ· σαβαώθ· ἰθοθ· βαὲ P, cf. supra § 15, l. 1, textum cod. ms. P | φορεῖ ... αὐτοῦ H: — L, πλίξας φορέσῃ τῷ τραχήλῳ, ἢ καὶ τὰς (scil. χάρτας?) πρὸς τὸ οὖς ἤθη (l. τιθῇ) P **7** ἀναχωρῶ: + καὶ τὴν μέθην λύω P

§ 17. (84) **8** Φοβοθὴλ A: βοθὴλ P **9** νευρ. χαλ. ego: νευρῶν κολάσσης H, νευρ. χαλάσας L, νευροχαλάσης P, νευροχρίλασεις (sic) Fl errore | ἐὰν ... Ἀδωναΐ H: ἐὰν ἀκ. ἀδ. δ. . L, ἐὰν ἐφαπτόμενος ἀκ. τοῦ μεγάλου ἀδοηὴλ τὸ ὄνομα ἔγκλησαν βοθοθὴλ P **10** § 18. (85) ἔφη P: εἶπε L, — H | ἐγὼ Λερωήλ ... ἀναχωρῶ (l. 13) et ἐγὼ Σουβελτι ... ἀναχωρῶ (l. 13—p. 55*, 1) tr. P | λερωὴλ L, ῥοκλὴδ P, Ῥοηλὴδ Fl | * H f. 23ʳ | ψύχος LP: ψυχρὸς H **11** κ. στ. πόνον P: κ. στόμαχον H, κ. στομαχὸν L | ἐπάγω A: ἐποιῶ P | ἐὰν A: ὡς μόνον P | Ἰάζ, μὴ ἐμμ. ego: ἰὰζ μὴ ἐμμενὴς H, ἰάζ μὴ ἐμμβείνης L, ἴαζ μὴ ἐμμείνης P **12** μὴ θερ. ὅτι κάλλιον ... ἐν δέκα πατ. P, — A **13** § 19. (86) ἔφοι ὁ ιε̄ H **14** Σουβελτὶ L: σουβελτὴ H, κουμελτὴλ P, Κουμεατὴλ Fl | φρικ. κ. ναρκ. ἐπιπ. P: — L, τὸν ⟨ν⟩οῦν καὶ σάρκας ἐμποιῶ H | ἐὰν A: ὡς P | μόνον — L

ἀκούσω· »Ῥιζωήλ, ἔγκλεισον Σουβελτί,¹ εὐθὺς ἀναχωρῶ.« 20. ὁ ἕκτος καὶ δέκατος ἔφη· »ἐγὼ Κατρὰξ καλοῦμαι. ἐπιφέρω τοῖς ἀνθρώποις πυρετοὺς ἀνιάτους. * ὁ θέλων ὑγιὴς γενέσθαι τριψάτω κολίανδρον καὶ ἐπιχριέτω τὰ χείλη λέγων· »ὁρκίζω σε κατὰ τοῦ Δάν, ἀναχώρησον ἀπὸ τοῦ πλάσματος τοῦ θεοῦ,« καὶ εὐθὺς ἀναχωρῶ.« 21. Ὁ ἕβδομος καὶ δέκατος ἔφη· »ἐγὼ Ἱεροπὰ καλοῦμαι. ἐπὶ τοῦ στομάχου τοῦ ἀνθρώπου καθέζομαι, καὶ ποιῶ ἀσπασμοὺς ἐν βαλανείῳ· καὶ ἐν ὁδῷ εὑρίσκω τὸν ἄνθρωπον καὶ πτωματίζω. ὃς δ᾿ ἂν εἴπῃ εἰς τὸν δεξιὸν ὠτίον τοῦ πάσχοντος ἐκ τρίτου· »ἰοῦδα ζιζαβοῦ.« ἰδέ, ποιεῖ με ἀναχωρεῖν.« 22. * Ὁ ὄγδοος καὶ δέκατος ἔφη· »ἐγὼ Μοδεβήλ καλοῦμαι. γυναῖκα ἀπὸ· ἀνδρὸς χω-

MSS HLP = Recc. AB. 1 Ῥιζωήλ H: ριζωὲλ L, ζωρωὴλ P | ἔγκλεισον Σουβ. ego cum dubio: — A, ἔγκλησον κουμενταὴλ P, de Κουμενταὴλ annotavit Fl: »diversa genera scripturae in una enuntiatione.« | ἀναχωρῶ ὅτι τὸν νοῦν καὶ σάρκας ἐμπιῶ L | § 20. (87) 2 ἐγὼ — H | Κατρὰξ H: ἰατρὰξ L, ἀτραξ P | ἐπιφέρω A: ἐγὼ καταστρέφω P | τοὺς ἀν(θρώπ)ους L 3 ἀνιατ.: + καὶ βλαβεροὺς P | * L f. 18ʳ¹ | ὁ ... γενέσθαι A: ἐὰν θέλῃς με ἐγκλῆσαι P | τριψ. κολ.: τρ. κολύατρον H, τρ. κολίαντρον L, κολ. κόψας P 4 καὶ — P | ἐπιχρ. τ. χειλ. L: ἐπίχριε τὰ χείλη αὐτοῦ H, ἐπίχριε τῶν χειλέ(ων) P | λέγων: + οὗτος H, + τὴν ἐπωδὴν ταύτην P | ὁρκίζω ... θεοῦ H (— ἀπὸ ... θεοῦ) L: τὸ πύρεθρον τὸ ἀπὸ ῥυπαρί(ας), ὁρκίζω σε κατὰ τοῦ θεοῦ τοῦ ὑψίστου τοῦ θρόνου, ἀναχώρει ἀπὸ ῥυπαρί(ας), καὶ ἀναχώρει ἀπὸ τοῦ πλάσματος τοῦ θεοῦ P 5 καὶ — H 6 ἀναχωρῶ : + ἀπὸ τὸ πλάσμα τ. θεοῦ L
§ 21. (88) 7 Ἱεροπὰ ego: ἱερωπὰ L, κεροπὰκ vel ἡεροπάη H, ἱεροπαὴλ P | ἐπὶ: pr. ἐὰν L 8 τοῦ — H | τ. ἀνθρ. A: τῶν ἀν(θρώπ)ων P | ποιῶ ἀσπασμοὺς H (i. q. σπασμοὺς, cf. Dieterich, Unters. p. 33, ἀσπασμένος): ποιώσας σπασμοὺς L, ποιῶ ἀσπαρμοὺς (sub ϱ lineam posuit man. prim.?) P | ἀσπ. ἐν βαλ. κ. ἐν ὁδῷ· scr. mss. omnes, sed ἐν ὁδῷ cum εὑρίσκω legendum est 9 εὑρίσκω H: εὕρω L, καὶ ὅπου δ᾿ ἂν εὑρεθῶ καὶ εὕρω P | τὸν — L | πτωματ. P: παραστοματίζω H, ἀποστοματίζω L 10 ὃς δ᾿ ἂν P: ὡς δ᾿ ἂν H, καὶ ἐὰν L | εἴπῃ H, εἴποι P, εἰπεῖ τις L | εἰς ... τρίτον L: εἰς ... ὠτίον (* f. 23ᵛ) τοῦ ἀν(θρώπ)ου ἐκ τρίτου H, τοῖς πάσχουσιν εἰς τὸν οὖς αὐτῶν, τὰ ὀνόματα ταῦτα ἐκ τρίτου εἰς τὸ δεξιὸν P 11 ἰοῦδα ... με ego: ἰούδαζιζαβοϊδέποι εἰ με H, ἰούδαζειζαβονιδέ· ποιοῦμαι L, ἰουδαριζὴ, ζαβουνὴ· δούνη P, Fl falso legit | ἀναχωρεῖν A: εὐθὺς ἀναχωρῶ P |
§ 22. (89) * P f. 17ʳ 12 ἔφη ὁ ἰῆ H | Μοδ. καλ. H: μοδιήλ καλ. L, καλ. βουλδουμὴχ P | γυναῖκα L: γυναῖκας HP | ἀνδρός P: ἄνδρα L, τοὺς ἑαυτῶν ἄνδρας H | χωρίζω P: χωρήζωμαι L, χορίζων H, + καὶ φθόνον ἐπιτελῶ P | γράψῃ P

ρίζω. ἐάν τις γράψει τῶν ὀκτὼ πατέρων τὰ ὀνόματα καὶ θήσει αὐτὰ ἐν προθύροις, εὐθὺς ἀναχωρῶ.« 23. ὁ ἔννατος καὶ δέκατος ἔφη· »ἐγὼ καλοῦμαι Μαρδέρω. ἐπιφέρω πυρετοὺς ἀνιάτους; καὶ ἐν οἴῳ δὲ οἴκῳ * γράψεις τὸ ὄνομά μου, εὐθὺς ἀναχωρῶ.« 24. ὁ εἰκο-
5 στὸς ἔφη· »ἐγὼ καλοῦμαι ʽΡὺξ Ναθώθω. εἰς γόνατα καθέζομαι τῶν ἀνθρώπων. ἐάν τις γράψει εἰς χάρτην· »Φνουνηβιήλ,« εὐθὺς ἀναχωρῶ.« 25. ὁ πρῶτος καὶ εἰκοστὸς ἔφη· „ἐγὼ ʽΡὺξ Ἀλὰθ καλοῦμαι. δύσπνοιαν τοῖς νηπίοις ἐμποιῶ. ἐάν τις γράψει· »ʽΡαριδέρις,« καὶ * βαστάζει, εὐθὺς ἀναχωρῶ.«
10 26. Ὁ δεύτερος καὶ εἰκοστὸς ἔφη· »ἐγὼ καλοῦμαι ʽΡὺξ Αὐδαμεώθ. καρδιόπονον ἐπιπέμπω. ἐάν τις γράψει· »ʽΡαιονώθ,« εὐθὺς ἀναχωρῶ.« 27. ὁ τρίτος καὶ εἰκοστὸς ἔφη· »ἐγὼ ʽΡὺξ Μαν-

MSS HLP = Recc. AB. 1 ὀκτὼ: ἢ vel fortasse ζ H, ἕξη L, σῶν P | ὀνόματα: + σολομῶν ἐν χάρτῃ P | θήσει LP: θέσει H   2 αὐτὰ — H | ἐν προθ. P: ἐμπροσθέραις H, ἐμπροσθύραις L, + τοῦ οἴκον αὐτοῦ P
MS P = Rec. B. pro εὐθὺς ἀναχωρῶ praebet textum hunc: ἐκεῖθεν ἀναχωρῶ. ἡ δὲ ἐπιγραφή ἐστιν αὕτη· κελεύει σοι ὁ θεὸς ἀβραὰμ, καὶ ὁ θ(εὸ)ς Ἰσαὰκ, καὶ ὁ θεὸς Ἰακώβ, ἀναχώρησον ἀπὸ τοῦ οἴκου τούτου μετ᾽ εἰρήνης, εὐθὺς ἀναχωρῶ
MSS HPL = Recc. AB. § 23. (90) 3 ἔφη ὁ ιθ H | Μαρδέρω ... μου (l. 4) et Ναθάθω ... Φνουνηβιήλ (ll. 5—6) tr. P | ἐγὼ καλοῦμαι Μαρδέρω P: ἐγὼ ῥὺξ καλοῦμαι μαδούωρ H, ἐγὼ μανδραβουροῦν καλοῦμαι δον L | ἐπιφ. πυρ. ἀνιατ. H: πυρ. ἀν. ἐπιφ. L, πυρετὸν ἐπιπέμπω ἀνίατον τοῖς ἀν(θρώπ)οις P | καὶ ... μου H: ἐνίῳ· οἴκῳ γράψει· τὸ ὄν. μου L, ἐάν τις (* Mg 1345) γράψῃ εἰς χάρτην βιβλίον· σφηνήρ, ῥαφαήλ, ἀναχώρημην (ἀναχώρημεν Fl), σύρον δούρον, καὶ τῷ τραχήλῳ περιάψῃ P   4 εὐθὺς P: εὐθέως L, — H | § 24. (91) 5 ἔφη — H | ἐγὼ ριξίνα θά· θω καλοῦμαι L | ʽΡὺξ Ναθώθω H: ναῶθ P | καὶ εἰς τὰ γόνατα P | τῶν ἀνθρ. P: τῶν ἀν(θρώπ)ω L, τοῦ ἀν(θρώπ)ου H   6 ἐπιγράψῃ P | εἰς χάρτην H: εἰς χαρτίον L, ἐν χάρτῃ P | Φνουνηβ. H: φνουνιφαήλ L, φνουνοβοηὸλ, ἔξελθε ναθάθ, καὶ τραχείλιν μὴ ἄψῃς P   7 § 25. (92) ἔφη ὁ κα H | ʽΡὺξ Ἀλὰθ ... βαστάζει (l. 9) et ʽΡὺξ Αὐδαμεώθ ... ῥαιονώθ (ll. 10—11) tr. H | ʽΡὺξ Ἀλὰθ ego: ῥηξ ὁ ἀλὰθ H, ρὶξ ὀλὰθ L, ἀλὰθ P   8 δύσπνοιαν P: δίσπνια H, δύσπνια L, pr. βῆχα καὶ P | νηπίοις L: παισὶν P, — H | γράψει ... βαστάζει (+ αὐτῷ) H: γραψ. καὶ βαστ.· ραριδερὶς L, ἐπιγράψῃ εἰς χάρτην· ῥορὴξ δίωξον σὺ ἀλὰθ, καὶ τῷ τραχήλῳ περιάψῃ P   9 * H f. 24ʳ
MSS HL = Rec. A. 10 § 26. ὁ δευτ. ... ἀναχωρῶ — P, errore Mg ὁ κβ´ pro ὁ κγ´ posito ὁ κγ´ (§ 27) omitteri videtur | sectiones 26 et 25 tr. H, cf. supra | ʽΡὺξ Αὐδαμ. H: ρὶξ αὐμαδεώθ (ante καλοῦμαι) L   11 καρδιοπ. ... ἀναχωρῶ H: ἐὰν τις γράψει ῥαιζώθ καλοῦμαι ἐὰν τῆς γράψει ραιζώθ καὶ βαστάζει ἀναχωρῶ ὅτι καρδιόπονος ἐπιμπέσει καὶ πέμπω L
MSS HLP = Recc. AB. § 27. (93) 12 ἔφη ὁ κγ H | ʽΡὺξ Μανθ.: ρὶξ μανθαδῶ L, ῥὺξ αὐθάδης H, νεφθαδᾶ P

θαδῶ καλοῦμαι. νεφροὺς ἀλγεῖν ποιῶ. ἐάν τις γράψει· »Ἰαώθ, Οὐριήλ,‹ εὐθὺς ἀναχωρῶ.« 28. ὁ τέταρτος καὶ εἰκοστὸς ἔφη· »ἐγὼ 'Ρὺξ Ἀκτονμὲ καλοῦμαι. πλευρὰς ἀλγεῖν ποιῶ. ἐάν τις γράψει ἐν ὕλῃ ἀπὸ πλοίου ἀστοχήσαντος· »ἀερίου Μαρμαραώθ,‹ εὐθὺς ἀναχωρῶ.« * 29. ** ὁ πέμπτος καὶ εἰκοστὸς ἔφη· »ἐγὼ 'Ρὺξ Ἀνατρὲθ καλοῦμαι. ζέσεις καὶ πυρώσεις εἰς σπλάγχνα ἀναστέλλω. ἐὰν ἀκούσω· »ἄφαρὰ ἀραρή,‹ εὐθὺς ἀναχωρῶ.« 30. ὁ ἕκτος καὶ εἰκοστὸς ἔφη· »ἐγὼ 'Ρὺξ ὁ Ἐναυθὰ καλοῦμαι. φρένας ἀποκλέπτω καὶ καρδίας ἀλλοιῶ. ἐάν τις γράψει· »Καλαζαήλ,‹ εὐθὺς ἀναχωρῶ.« 31. ὁ ἕβδομος καὶ εἰκοστὸς ἔφη· »ἐγὼ 'Ρὺξ Ἀξησβυθ καλοῦμαι. ὑπεκτικοὺς ποιῶ ἀνθρώπους καὶ αἱμορρόους. ἐάν τις ὁρκίσει με εἰς οἶνον * ἄκρατον καὶ δώσει τῷ πάσχοντι, εὐθὺς ἀναχωρῶ.« 32. Ὁ ὄγδοος καὶ εἰκοστὸς ἔφη· »ἐγὼ 'Ρὺξ Ἁπὰξ καλοῦμαι. ἀγρυπνίας ἐπιπέμπω. ἐάν τις γράψει »κόκ· φνηδισμός,‹ καὶ περιάψει τοῖς κροτάφοις, εὐθὺς ἀναχωρῶ.« 33. ὁ ἔννατος καὶ εἰκοστὸς ἔφη· »ἐγὼ 'Ρὺξ Ἀνοστὴρ καλοῦμαι. μητρομανίας ἐπιπέμπω καὶ πόνους ἐν τῇ κύστει ποιῶ. ἐάν τις εἰς ἔλαιον καθαρὸν τρεῖς

MSS HLP = Recc. AB. 1 ποιῶ: + καὶ στραγγισμοὺς οὔρων ἐπιτελῶ P | Ἰαώθ, Οὐριήλ H: ἰαώθ ὀριήλ L, εἰς λαμνὸν (in marg. dextr. πέταλ <) κασσιτήρινον, ἰαθώθ, οὐρουήλ, νεφθαδᾶ καὶ περιάψῃ τῷ ἰσχίῳ P 2 § 28. (94) ἔφη ὁ κδ H 3 ἐγώ — L | ῥὴξ ἀκτονμὲ H, ἐρίξ κτονμὲ L, ἄκτον μὲν P, + δίωξον transversa linea deletum P | πλευρὰς καὶ ψόας P | ἐμποιῶ H 4 γράψει: γλύψῃ P | ὕλῃ P: οἴλο H, ἡλίῳ L, + χαλκοῦ P | ἀπὸ .. εὐθύς — L | ἀπὸ πλ. ἀστοχ. P: ἀποπλού. ου ἀστολίσαντος H | ἀερίου Μαρμ. H: ἀρνίου μαρμαραώθ, σαβαώθ, ἄκτον μὲν δίωξον, καὶ περιάψῃ τῷ ἰσχίῳ P 5 * hic explicit in media col. cod. ms. L (f. 18ʳ²)
MSS HP = Recc. AB. § 29. (95) 5 ** P f. 17ᵛ 6 'Ρὺξ H: — P | ζέσεις κ. πυρέσεις H, καύσεις κ. πυρώσεις P | εἰς τὰ σπλ. ἀποστέλλω P 7 ἄραρα χάραρα P | § 30. (96) 8 'Ρὺξ ὁ Ἐν.: ἐνενούθ P 9 ἀλλοιῶ καὶ νοδὸν (l. νωδὸν) ποιῶ P | Καλαζαήλ H: ἀλλαζοωλ, δίωξον ἐνενούθ, καὶ περιάψῃ τὸν χάρτην P 10 § 31. (97) 'Ρὺξ Ἀξησβυθ H: φηθ P 11 αἱμοφόους H, αἱμορασίας (αἱμορραγίας) conj. Bn) ποιῶ P 12 τις γράψει ἢ H | * H f. 24ᵛ | οἶν. εὐώδη ἄκρατον P | δώσει H: κατὰ τοῦ ἐνδεκάτου ἐῶν (l. αἰῶνος Crtr) λέγων· ὁρκίζω σε κατὰ τοῦ ἐνδεκάτου ἐῶν παῦσαι ἀξιωφθιθ, καὶ δὸς ποιεῖν (l. πιεῖν Crtr) P
§ 32. (98) 14 'Ρὺξ Ἁπὰξ H: ἅρπαξ P 15 ἀγρυπνοπνίας P | γράψῃ P | κόκ ... περιάψῃ P, — H 16 § 33. (99) 17 'Ρὺξ — P | Ἀνοστὴρ P: ἀστὴρ H | ἐπιπέμπω: + ἐάν τις γράψῃ κόκ· φνηδισμός· καὶ περιάψῃ transversa linea deleta P 18 κύστει: κήτῃ H | εἰς: γράψει H

κόκκους δάφνης λεάνας ἐπαλείψει λέγων· »ὁρκίζω σε·κατὰ τοῦ
Μαρμαραώθ,« εὐθὺς ἀναχωρῶ.« 34. ὁ τριακοστὸς ἔφη· »ἐγὼ 'Ρὺξ
Φυσικορὲθ καλοῦμαι. μακρονοσίαν ποιῶ. ἐάν τις βαλεῖ ἅλας εἰς
ἔλαιον καὶ ἐπαλείψει τὸν ἀσθενὴν λέγων· »χερουβίμ, σεραφίμ,
5 βοηθεῖτε,« εὐθὺς ἀναχωρῶ.« 35. ὁ πρῶτος καὶ τριακοστὸς ἔφη·
»ἐγὼ 'Ρὺξ Ἀλευρὴθ καλοῦμαι. ὀστέα ἰχθύος καταπίνων, ἐάν τις
⟨τοῦ⟩ αὐτοῦ ἰχθύος ὀστέον ἐπιθήσει εἰς τὰ βύζια τοῦ πάσχοντος,
εὐθὺς * ἀναχωρῶ.« 36. ὁ δεύτερος καὶ τριακοστὸς ἔφη· »ἐγὼ
'Ρὺξ Ἰχθύον καλοῦμαι. νεῦρα παραλύω. * ἐὰν δὲ ἀκούσω· >Ἀδω-
10 ναΐ, μάλθη,< εὐθὺς ἀναχωρῶ.« 37. ὁ τρίτος καὶ τριακοστὸς ἔφη·
»ἐγὼ καὶ 'Ρὺξ Ἀχωνεώθ καλοῦμαι. ἐν τῷ φάρυγγι καὶ τοῖς
παρισθμίοις πόνον ποιῶ. ἐάν τις εἰς φύλλα κισσοῦ γράψει· »λει-
κουργός,« βοτρυδὸν ⌈ἀναχωρίς,⌉ εὐθὺς ἀναχωρῶ.«
38. Ὁ τέταρτος καὶ τριακοστὸς ἔφη· »ἐγὼ 'Ρὺξ Αὐτὼθ κα-
15 λοῦμαι. φθόνους φίλων καὶ μάχας ποιῶ. καταργεῖ με δὲ τὸ α´
καὶ β´ γραφόμενον.« 39. ὁ πέμπτος καὶ τριακοστὸς ἔφη· »ἐγὼ
καὶ 'Ρὺξ Φθηνεώθ καλοῦμαι. βασκαίνω πάντα ἄνθρωπον.
καταργεῖ με δὲ ὁ πολυπαθὴς ὀφθαλμὸς ἐγχαραττόμενος. 40. ὁ

MSS HP = Recc. AB. 1 λεώνας δάφνης H | σε·ἀνοστῆρ P 2 Μαρ-
μαραώθ H: μαρμαραῶ, παῦσον P | § 34. (100) 'Ρὺξ Φυσικ. ... βοήθειτε
(l. 5) et 'Ρὺξ Ἀλευρὴθ ... πάσχοντος (ll. 6—7) tr. P | 'Ρὺξ Φυσικ. H: ἡ
φησικιρὲθ P 3 βαλεῖ (βαλεῖν ms.) ... ἀσθενὴν H: εἰς ἔλαιον βαλὼν ἅλας
τριπτὸν ἐπαλείφη τὸν κάμνοντα P 4 σεραφὶμ· χερουβὶμ· βοηθήσατέ μοι P
5 § 35. (31) 6 ἐγὼ — H | 'Ρὺξ Ἀλ. H: ἀλλεβορὶθ P | sectiones 35 et
34 tr. P, v. supra | καταπίνων ego: καταπίνειν H 7 ὀστέα ... πάσχον-
τος: ἐάν τις νυκτοφαγήσῃ (sub v linea brevi ducta supra eandem η ponit ms.;
in marg. lat. ἰχθυο scr. man. prim.) ὀστέον καταπίῃ, καὶ ἄρας ὀστέον ἀπὸ
τοῦ ἰχθύος βήσσει P | βήζια H 8 * H f. 25ʳ | § 36. (102) 9 'Ρὺξ
— P | ἰχθύος H | παραλύω P: παλίω H, + καὶ συντρίβω P | * P f. 18ᵛ
| δὲ — P | Ἀδωναΐ, μάλθη H: ἀδοναὴθ βοήθει P 10 § 37. (103)
11 καὶ — P | 'Ρὺξ Ἀχων. H: ἀγχονίων P | ἐν ... ποιῶ: ἐν τοῖς σπαρ-
γάνοις καὶ ἐν τῷ φάρυγγι κεῖμαι P | φάραγγι H | παριθμίοις H 12 ἐὰν
... ἀναχωρίς H: καὶ ἐάν τις εἰς φύλλα συκῆς γράψῃ· λυκοῦργος, ἓν παρὰ ἓν
γράμμα (ἐνπαρὰ· ἐνγραμμὰ ms.), γράψῃ δὲ βοτρυδὸν (in marg. βο <)
13 ἀναχωρῶ: + λυκοῦργος ὑκοῦργος· κοῦργος· οὖργος· γὸς· ὃς P

§ 38. (104) 14 'Ρὺξ — P | Αὐτὼθ H: αὐτοθιθ P 15 φθον. ποιῶ
κ. μάχας P | καταρ. με: καταργοῦμαι H | δὲ ... γραφ. H: οὖν τὸ ἄλφα
καὶ τὸ ὠμέγα γραφόμενα P 16 § 39. (105) 17 κ. 'Ρὺξ Φθην.: φθηνοθ P
| παντὶ ἀν(θρώπ)ῳ P 18 κατ. με: καταργοῦμαι H | δὲ ... ὀφθαλ.: οὖν
ὀφθαλμὸς πολυπαθὴς P | ἐγχαραττόμενον H | § 40. (106)

ἕκτος καὶ τριακοστὸς ἔφη· »ἐγὼ καὶ ῾Ρὺξ Μιανὲθ καλοῦμαι. τῷ σώματι ἐπίφθονός εἰμι· οἴκους ἐρημῶ· σάρκας ἀφανίζω. ἐάν τις γράψει ἐν τοῖς προθύροις τοῦ οἴκου οὕτως· * »μέλπω ἀρδὰδ ἀναάθ,« φεύγω ἐγὼ τοῦ τόπου,« * 41. καὶ ταῦτα ἀκούσας ἐγὼ
5 Σολομῶν ἐδόξασα τὸν θεὸν τοῦ οὐρανοῦ καὶ τῆς γῆς καὶ ἐκέλευσα αὐτοὺς ὕδωρ φέρειν. 42. καὶ ηὐξάμην πρὸς τὸν θεὸν τοὺς τριάκοντα ἓξ δαίμονας τοὺς ἐμποδίζοντας τῇ ἀνθρωπότητι προσέρχεσθαι εἰς τὸν ναὸν τοῦ θεοῦ.

XIX. Καὶ ἤμην ἐγὼ Σολομῶν τιμώμενος ὑπὸ πάντων τῶν
10 ἀνθρώπων τῶν ὑποκάτω τοῦ οὐρανοῦ. καὶ ᾠκοδόμουν τὸν ναὸν τοῦ θεοῦ, καὶ ἡ βασιλεία μου ἦν εὐθύνουσα. 2. καὶ ἤρχοντο πάντες οἱ βασιλεῖς πρός με θεωρῆσαι τὸν ναὸν τοῦ θεοῦ ὃν ᾠκοδόμουν, καὶ χρυσίον καὶ ἀργύριον ἐκόμιζον πρός με, χαλκὸν

MSS HP = Recc. AB. 1 καὶ ῾Ρὺξ ego: χερὴξ H, — P | Μιανὲθ: βιανακὶθ P | τοῦ σώματος P 2 ἐπιφθ. P: ἐφθόμενον H | ἐρήμους H | ἀφανίζω: + καὶ ὅσα ἄλλα τοιαῦτα P 3 τοῖς — P | οὕτως: αὐτοῦ P | * H f. 25ᵛ | μηλτὼ· ἀρδοῦ· ἀναάθ P 4 ἐγὼ — P | * Mg 1348 | τόπου ἐκείνου P | § 41. (107) 5 κ. ἐκελ..: ἐκελ. δὲ P 6 φέρειν H: κομίζειν ἐν τῷ ναῷ τοῦ θεοῦ P

MS P = Rec. B pro § 42 textum interpolatum praebet hunc: § 42. καὶ ἔτι προσηυξάμην πρὸς κύριον τὸν θεὸν ὥστε τοὺς ἔξω δαίμονας καὶ ἐμποδίζοντας τὴν ἀνθρωπότητα συμποδίζεσθαι καὶ προσέρχεσθαι εἰς τὸν ναὸν τοῦ θεοῦ. § 43. ἐγὼ δὲ τοὺς μὲν τῶν δαιμόνων κατέκρινα ἐργάζεσθαι τὰ βαρέα ἔργα τῆς οἰκοδομῆς τοῦ ναοῦ τοῦ θεοῦ· τοὺς δὲ φρουραῖς (Fl, ex φρουροὺς corr. ms.) κατέκλεισα: § 44. ἑτέρους πυρομαχεῖν ἐκέλευσα χρυσίῳ καὶ ἀργυρίῳ καὶ μολύβδῳ καὶ φιάλῳ παρακαθέζεσθαι, καὶ τοῖς λοιποῖς δαίμοσι τρόπους ἡτοίμασθαι ἐφ' οἷς ὀφείλουσι κατακλεισθῆναι.

MS H = Rec. A in § 42 brevem textum praebet.

C. XIX. MS P = Rec. B pro c. XIX, ll. 9—p. 60*, 4, textum interpolatum praebet hunc: (108) Καὶ εἶχον πολλὴν ἡσυχίαν ἐγὼ σολομῶν (in marg. inf. add. βασιλεὺς ms.) ἐν πάσῃ (f. 18ᵛ) τῇ γῇ καὶ ἐν εἰρήνῃ διῆγον πολλῇ, τιμώμενος ὑπὸ πάντων ἀν(θρώπ)ων καὶ τῶν ὑπὸ τῶν οὐρανῶν, καὶ ᾠκοδόμουν τὸν ναὸν ὅλον κυρίου τοῦ θεοῦ, καὶ ἡ βασιλεία μου ἦν εὐθύνουσα καὶ ὁ στρατός μου ἦν μετ' ἐμοῦ, καὶ λοιπὸν ἀνεπαύσατο ἡ πόλις Ἱ(ερουσα)λὴμ χαίρουσα καὶ ἀγαλλιωμένη. § 2. καὶ ἅπαντες οἱ βασιλεῖς τῆς γῆς ἤρχοντο πρός με ἀπὸ τῶν περάτων τῆς γῆς θεωρῆσαι τὸν ναὸν ὃν ᾠκοδόμουν κ(υρί)ῳ τῷ θ(ε)ῷ, καὶ ἀκούσαντες τὴν σοφίαν τὴν δοθεῖσαν μοι προσεκύνουν μοι εἰς τὸν ναόν· χρυσίον καὶ ἀργύριον, καὶ λίθους τιμίους πολλοὺς διαφόρους, καὶ χαλκὸν καὶ σίδηρον, καὶ μόλιβδον, καὶ ξύλα κέδρινα, καὶ ξύλα ἄσηπτα προσέφερόν μοι εἰς τὴν κατασκευὴν τοῦ ναοῦ τοῦ θεοῦ.

MS H. § 1. l. 10 ἐκοδώμουν ms.

τε και σίδηρον και μόλυβδον και ξύλα προσέφερον εις την κατασκευήν του ναού. 3. εν οίς και ή Σάβα βασίλισσα Νότου γόης υπάρχουσα πολλή τη φρονήσει ήλθε και προσεκύνησεν ενώπιόν μου. XX. Και ιδού εις των τεχνιτών γηραιός έρριψεν αυτόν ενώπιόν μου λέγων· »βασιλεύ Σολομών υιός Δανείδ, ελέησόν με το γέρας.« και είπον αυτώ· »λέγε, γέρον, ο θέλεις.« 2. ο δε έφη· »δέομαί σου, βασιλεύ. υιόν έχω μονογενή, και ούτος καθ' εκάστην * ύβρεις επάγει μοι χαλεπάς, έτυπτέ μου γαρ το πρόσωπον και την κεφαλήν, ότι θάνατον πικρόν επαγγέλει μοι ποιήσαι. τούτου χάριν προσήλθον ίνα εκδικήσης μοι.« 3. εγώ δε ταύτα ακούσας εκέλευσα αγαγείν εμοί τον υιόν αυτού. τούτου δε ελθόντος είπον * αυτώ· »ούτως έχεις;« 4. ο δε έφη· »έως απονοίας εμπέπλησμαι, βασιλεύ, ώστε τον γεννήτορά μου παλάμη τινάξαι. ίλεώς μοι γενού, ώ βασιλεύ· αθέμιτον γαρ ακούσαι τοι-

---

MS P = Rec. B. § 3. εν οίς και βασίλισσα νότου γοής υπάρχουσα εν πολλή φρονήσει ήλθεν και προσεκύνησεν ενώπιόν μου επί την γην, και ακούσασα την σοφίαν μου εδόξασε τον θεόν του ί(σρα)ήλ· εν οίς και εδοκίμασε δοκιμασίαν τα της σοφίας μου πάντα, όσα εσοφισάμην αυτήν κατά την δοθείσαν μοι σοφίαν: και πάντες υιοί ί(σρα)ήλ εδόξασαν τον θεόν.

Parallela ad c. XX v. infra in ms. D c. IV.

C. XX. MSS HP = Recc. AB. (110) 5 ιδού εν ταίς ημέραις εκείναις P | γηραιός την ηλικίαν P   6 υιός Δ. — P | με: μου conj. James | το γερ.: ότι γηραιός υπάρχω P   7 κ. είπον αυτ. ego: κ. είπον αυτόν H, κελεύσας ούν αυτόν αναστήναι και φησίν P | λέγε: ειπέ P | § 2.   8 έχων H | ούτως P | καθ' εκ. (scil. ημέραν) — P   9 * P f. 19r | επαγάγη μου H | έτυπτε ego: έτυπον H, και τύψας P | μου ... προσωπ.: με κατά προσ. P   10 κεφαλήν μου διέτιλλεν P | ότι: και P | πικρόν: πονηρόν P | επαγγέλεται P | ποιήσαι — P   11 τούτον H | προσ. ... μοι: προεξίημοι (sic, προσίημαι? Fl; l. πρόσειμι) υμίν, εκδικήσόν με P | εκδικήσης conj. James: εκδικής εις H | § 3. (111) δε: + σολομών P   12 ακούσας κατενύγην αποβλέψας εις το εκείνου γήρας, και P | αγαγείν ego: αγγαγεν H, αχθήναι P | τούτου ... έχεις: του δε αχθέντος επερώτουν αυτόν ει ούτως έχει P   13 § 4. ο δε έφην H, ο δε νέος έφη P

MS P = Rec. B pro έως ... ταλαιπορίαν (ll. 13—p. 61*, 1) textum interpolatum praebet hunc: ούχ ούτως απονοία εγώ εμπεπλησμένος ώστε τον γεννήτορά μου π(ατέ)ρα παλάμη τύψαι. ίλεως γενού μοι βασιλεύς (ς finali transversa linea deleta). ου γ(αρ) αθέμιτα τοιαύτα τετόλμηκα ο ταλαίπορος εγώ MS H = Rec. A.   15 αθέμιτον ego: αθές μοι τον H αὐτὴν παραβολὴν καὶ ταλαιπορίαν.« 5. ἐγὼ οὖν Σολομῶν τοῦ νέου ἀκούσας παρεκάλουν τὸν πρεσβύτην εἰς ἔννοιαν ἐλθεῖν. ὁ δὲ οὐκ ἤθελεν ἀλλ' εἶπε· »θανατωσάτω αὐτόν. 6. Καὶ θεωρῶν τὸν δαίμονα Ὀρνίαν γελάσαντα ἐγὼ ἐθυμώθην λίαν ἐν τῷ γελάσαι αὐτὸν ἐνώπιόν μου, καὶ τοῦτον μεταστήσας ἐκέλευσα τὸν Ὀρνίαν ἐλθεῖν καὶ εἶπον αὐτῷ· »κατηραμένε, ἐμὲ προσεγέλασας;« 7. ὁ δὲ ἔφη· »δέομαί σου, βασιλεῦ· οὐ διὰ σὲ ἐγέλασα, ἀλλὰ διὰ τὸν δύστηνον γέροντα καὶ τὸν ἄθλιον νέον, * τὸν τούτου υἱόν· ὅτι μετὰ τρεῖς ἡμέρας τεθνήξεται, καὶ ἰδοὺ ὁ γέρων βούλεται αὐτὸν κακῶς ἀνελεῖν.« 8. καὶ ἐγὼ εἶπον· »ἢ ἀληθῶς * οὕτως ἔχει;« ὁ δαίμων εἶπε· »ναί, βασιλεῦ.« 9. καὶ ἐκέλευσα μεταστῆναι τὸν δαίμονα καὶ ἐλθεῖν τὸν γέροντα καὶ τὸν τούτου υἱόν, καὶ ἐκέλευσα αὐτοὺς εἰς φιλίαν γενέσθαι. 10. * καὶ εἶπον τῷ πρεσβύτῃ· »μεθ' ἡμέρας τρεῖς ἄγαγέ μοι τὸν υἱόν σου ὧδε.« οἱ δὲ προσκυνήσαντες ἀνεχώρησαν.

MSS HP = Recc. AB. 1 § 5. οὖν: δὲ P | τ. νέου ἀκ.: ταῦτ' ἀκ. παρὰ τ, νέου P   2 πρεσβύτερον P | ἔννοιαν HP: εὔνοιαν conj. James | ἐλθεῖν καὶ δέχεσθαι τοῦ υἱοῦ τὴν ἀπολογίαν P   3 ἀλλ'... αὐτ.: ἀλλὰ μᾶλλον θανατωθήτω P

MS P = Rec. B pro § 6 textum praebet hunc: ἐν δὲ τῷ μὴ πείθεσθαι τὸν πρεσβύτερον ἔμελλον τῷ νέῳ τιμωρίας ἀποφήνασθαι· καὶ θεωρήσας ὀρνίαν τὸν δαίμονα γελῶντα· ἐθυμώθην μεγάλως διὰ τὸ γελάσαι τὸν δαίμονα ἐνώπιόν μου· καὶ τούτους μεταστῆσαι ἐκέλευσα ὀρνίαν εἰς μέσον ἀχθῆναι τοῦ βήματος. τοῦ δὲ ἀχθέντος (Mg 1349) ἔφην αὐτῷ· ἐπικατάρατε, τί με προσχὼν ἐγέλασας;

MS H = Rec. A. § 6. 4 θεορῶ H | γελάσσαντα H   5 αὐτῷ ego: αὐτὸν H | κατηραμένε vel κατειρμένε ego: κατερειμένε H

MSS HP = Recc. AB. 6 § 7. δὲ: δαίμων P   8 τοῦτον τὸν δυστ. P   9 * H f. 27ʳ | τ. τουτ. υἱόν: υἱὸν αὐτῶν H | μετὰ... τεθν.: τρεῖς ἡμέρας καὶ ἐν ἀωρίᾳ τετελευτήσει ὁ υἱὸς αὐτοῦ P   10 κακῶς ἀναιρεῖν αὐτόν P

MS P = Rec. B in § 8 textum praebet hunc: (112) ἐγὼ δὲ σολομῶν ἀκούσας ταῦτα· ἔφην πρὸς δαιμόνιον· ἀληθῆ εἰσιν (* f. 19ᵛ) ἃ λέγεις; ὁ δὲ λέγει· ἀληθῆ ταῦτα, βασιλεῦ

MS H = Rec. A in § 8 textum breviorem praebet.

MSS HP = Recc. AB. 11 § 9. καὶ ἀκούσας ἐγὼ P   12 ἐλθεῖν πάλιν τὸν γηραιὸν μετὰ καὶ τοῦ υἱοῦ αὐτοῦ P   13 καὶ — P | εἰς φιλ. γεν.: φιλίᾳ τραπῆναι, καὶ τὰ εἰς τροφὴν αὐτοῖς παρασχόμενος P

MSS HPQ = Recc. AB. 14 * § 10. ⁓ post omissionem maximam hic rursus incipit ms. Q (cc. III—XX 9 omissis, v. supra p. 16*) | κ. εἶπον H: εἶπον οὖν B | ὧδε τ. υἱόν σου B, + καὶ διατάξω αὐτόν Q, + καὶ ἐπινοοῦμαι αὐτοῦ P   15 οἱ δὲ προσκυν. B: καὶ προσσεκύνησαν H

11. Καὶ ἐκέλευσα πάλιν ἀγαγεῖν τὸν Ὀρνίαν πρός με καὶ εἶπον αὐτῷ· »λέγε μοι πόθεν τοῦτο σὺ οἶδας ὅτι μετὰ τρεῖς ἡμέρας τεθνήξεται ὁ νέος.« 12. ὁ δὲ ἔφη· »ἡμεῖς οἱ δαίμονες ἀνερχόμεθα ἐπὶ τοῦ στερεώματος τοῦ οὐρανοῦ καὶ μέσον τῶν ἄστρων 5 ἱπτάμεθα καὶ ἀκούομεν τὰς ἀποφάσεις ** τὰς ἐξερχομένας ἀπὸ τοῦ θεοῦ ἐπὶ τὰς ψυχὰς τῶν ἀνθρώπων. 13. ⌜καὶ λοιπὸν ἐρχόμεθα καὶ εἴτε ἐν δυναστείᾳ, εἴτε ἐν πυρί, εἴτε ἐν ῥομφαίᾳ, εἴτε ἐν συμπτώματι μετασχηματιζόμενοι ἀναιροῦμεν.«⌝ 14. καὶ ἐπηρώτησα αὐτόν· »λέγε μοι οὖν πῶς ὑμεῖς δύνασθε εἰς τὸν οὐρα- 10 νὸν ἀναβαίνειν δαίμονες ὄντες.« 15. ὁ δὲ ἔφη μοι· »ὅσα ἐν οὐρανῷ ἐπιτελοῦντα, οὕτως καὶ ἐπὶ τῆς γῆς, αἱ γὰρ ἀρχαὶ καὶ ἐξουσίαι * καὶ δυνάμεις ἄνω ἵπτανται καὶ τῆς εἰσόδου τοῦ οὐρανοῦ ἀξιοῦνται. 16. ἡμεῖς δὲ οἱ δαίμονες ἀτονοῦμεν μὴ ἔχοντες

MSS HPQ = Recc. AB. (113) **1** Καὶ Q: — H, τούτων δὲ ἀπελθόντων P | ἐκελ. ... με H: πάλιν ἐκελ. ἐλθεῖν πρός με τὸν δαίμοναν Ὀρνίαν Q, ἐκελ. εἰς μέσον ἀχθῆναι τὸν ὀρνίαν P | εἶπον αὐτ. HP: λέγω πρὸς αὐτόν Q **2** τοῦτο ... νέος H: σὺ τὰ μέλλοντα γινώσκεις Q, σὺ ταῦτα οἶδας P **3** § 12. ἔφη H: εἶπεν P, λέγει μοι Q | ἀνερχόμενοι H **4** ἐπὶ τ. στερ. H: κατὰ τὸ στερέωμα B | ἀστέρων B **5** ἱπταμ. B: ἀπτώμεθα H | * H f. 27ᵛ | ** Q f. 12ᵛ | ἀπὸ τ. θ. H: παρὰ θεοῦ Q, — P, + πρὸς τοὺς ἀγγέλους Q

MS H = Rec. A pro § 13 textum praebet hunc: καὶ ἐρχόμεθα μετὰ δυναστείας· εἴτε ῥομφαία εἴτε ἐν πυρί· καὶ ἀνεροῦμεν αὐτοὺς μετασχημ.

MSS PQ = Rec. B. **6** § 13. ἐρχόμεθα εἰς τὴν γῆν Q | post ἀναιροῦμεν add. PQ glossam hanc: καὶ ἐάν τις ἀποθάνῃ ἐν ἀωρίᾳ ἢ βίᾳ τινί (καὶ ... τινί: καὶ ἐὰν μὴ ἐν ἀωρίᾳ τίς, ἢ βίᾳ τινὶ ἀποθ. P), μεταμορφούμεθα ἡμεῖς οἱ δαίμονες (+ εἰς τὸ ὄνομα τοῦ τεθνεότος, Q) ὥστε παραφαίνεσθαι (φαιν. P) τοῖς ἀνθρώποις καὶ σέβεσθαι ἡμᾶς (+ ἐπὶ τῆς — ex τοῖς corr. — ἀνθρωπίνης φύσεως P)

MSS HPQ = Recc. AB. **8** § 14. κ. ἐπ. αὐτόν H: (114) ἐγὼ δὲ (ἐγὼ γοῦν P) ταῦτα ἀκούσας ἐδόξασα κύριον τὸν θεὸν καὶ ἐπ. πάλιν τὸν δαίμονα B **9** οὖν et ὑμεῖς — B **10** ἀναβῆναι B | ὄντες: + καὶ μέσον τῶν ἀστέρων καὶ τῶν ἁγίων ἀγγέλων μιγῆναι B | § 15. μοι B

MSS PQ = Rec. B pro οὕτως ... ἀναπαύσεως (p. 63*, l. 1) praebent haec: οὕτως καὶ ἐπὶ τῆς γῆς (οἱ ἐπὶ γῆς Q) οἱ τύποι αὐτῶν· εἰσὶν γὰρ ἀρχαί, ἐξουσίαι, κοσμοκράτορες (* P f. 20ʳ). καὶ ἱπτάμεθα ἡμεῖς οἱ δαίμονες ἐν τῷ ἀέρι καὶ ἀκούομεν τῶν ἐπουρανίων τὰς φωνὰς καὶ (+ πάσας P) τὰς (+ ἐπουρανίας Q) δυνάμεις θεωροῦμεν (ἐπιθεωρ. P)· καὶ ὡς μὴ ἔχοντες βάσιν ἀναπαύσεως ἀτονοῦμεν

MS H = Rec. A. **12** ἵπτανται ego: ἥτταντε H **13** § 16. ἀτονοῦμεν (cf. Rec. B supra): αὐτὸν οὖν μὲν H, forte l. ἀκούομεν. μὴ δὲ ἔχοντες

§ 15. Eph. I 21; II 2

βάσιν ⌜ἀναβάσεως ἢ⌝ ἀναπαύσεως, καὶ ἐκπίπτομεν ὥσπερ φύλλα ἀπὸ τῶν δένδρων καὶ δοκοῦσιν οἱ θεωροῦντες ἄνθρωποι ὅτι ἀστέρες εἰσὶν οἱ πίπτοντες ἀπὸ τοῦ οὐρανοῦ. 17. οὐχ οὕτως ἐστί, * βασιλεῦ, ἀλλὰ πίπτομεν διὰ τὴν ἀσθένειαν ἡμῶν καὶ ἐν 5 τῷ μηδαμόθεν ἔχειν ἀντίληψιν καταπίπτομεν ὡς ἀστραπαὶ ἐπὶ τὴν γῆν, καὶ πόλεις καταφλέγομεν καὶ ἀγροὺς ἐμπυρίζομεν. οἱ δὲ ἀστέρες τοῦ οὐρανοῦ τεθεμελιωμένοι εἰσὶν ἐν τῷ στερεώματι.« 18. καὶ ταῦτα ἀκούσας ἐγὼ Σολομῶν ἐκέλευσα τὸν δαίμονα τηρεῖσθαι ἕως ἡμερῶν πέντε.
10 19. Μετὰ δὲ τὰς πέντε ἡμέρας μετακαλεσάμενος τὸν γέροντα οὐκ ἤθελεν ἐλθεῖν. εἶτα ἐλθών, εἶδα αὐτὸν τεθλιμμένον καὶ πενθοῦντα. 20. καὶ εἶπον αὐτῷ· »ποῦ ἐστιν ὁ υἱός σου, γέρον;« ὁ δὲ ἔφη· »ἄπαις ἐγενόμην, ὦ βασιλεῦ, καὶ ἀνέλπιστος τάφῳ υἱοῦ παραφυλάττω.« 21. ἐγὼ δὲ Σολομῶν ἀκούσας ταῦτα καὶ 15 γνοὺς ὅτι ἀληθῆ εἰσι τὰ παρὰ τοῦ δαίμονος * λαληθέντα μοι ἐδόξασα τὸν θεὸν τοῦ οὐρανοῦ καὶ τῆς γῆς. *

MSS HPQ = Recc. AB. 2 δοκοῦσιν ... πίπτοντες H. θεωροῦντες ἡμᾶς οἱ ἄνθρωποι δοκοῦσιν ὅτι (+ οἱ P) ἀστέρες πίπτουσιν B 3 § 17. οὐχ οὕτως ἐστί: οὐχ ὅτως ἔσται H, pr. ἀλλ' B 4 * H f. 28ʳ | ὦ βασ. P | ἀλλ' ἡμεῖς ἐσμέν. καὶ πίπτομεν ἐπὶ τὴν γῆν διὰ Q 5 μηδαμόθεν B: μὴ δυνάμεθα H | ἔχειν HPIs: ἔχημεν Q | ἀντιληψ.: ἀντιλέγειν Q | πίπτωμεν H | ἐπὶ τ. γῆν H: ἐν ἀωρίᾳ (πολλῇ ex πολλῆς corr. add. P) καὶ ἐξάπινα (αἰφνηδίως Q) B 7 δὲ HQ: γὰρ P | τοῦ οὐρανοῦ — B | τεθεμελ. HPIs: τε θέμελοι ὅμοιον P | στερεωμ. H: οὐρανῷ ὥσπερ ὁ ἥλιος καὶ ἡ σελήνη B 8 § 18. (115) τὸν ... πέντε: φρουρεῖσθαι τ. δαιμ. ἄχρι ἡμερῶν ε' B 9 ἡμέραις H
§ 19. 10 μετὰ δὲ ἡμ. ε̄' H | ἐπεκαλεσάμην Q | γέροντα H: γηραιὸν B, + ἔμπροσθέν μου Q, + ἤμελλον ἐρωτᾶν P 11 οὐκ ἤθελ. ... πενθ. H: ἐλθὼν δὲ ὁ γέρων πρός με κατὰ πένθος καὶ μελανῷ τῷ προσώπῳ P, καὶ ἐλθὼν πρός με ὁ ἄνθρωπος κατὰ πένθος καὶ μεμελα⟨σ⟩μένῳ τῷ προσώπῳ αὐτοῦ Q 12 § 20. καὶ — P | εἶπον P: εἶπα H, λέγω Q | αὐτῷ P: αὐτὸν H, πρὸς αὐτὸν Q, + εἰπὲ πρεσβύτα B | γέρον H: — B, + καί τί τό σχῆμα (+ τοῦτο P, + τοῦ προσώπου σου Q) B 13 ἔφη H: ἔφην Q, + ἰδού P, + ἰδού, κύριε, Q | ἄπαις: ἅπας H | ὦ βασ. — B | ἀνέλπιστα B 14 παραφυλ. ego]: παραφυλάττειν H, παρακαθέζομαι Q, παρακαθεζόμενος P, + ἤδη γὰρ ἡμέρας (ἡμέραι P) δύο νεκροῦ γεγονότος B | § 21. 15 ἀληθὲς H | εἰσι ... μοι: εἰσὶν ᾗ ἔφη μοι ὁ δαίμων Ὀρνίας, καὶ Q, μοι ἔφησεν ὁ δαίμων ὀρνί(ας) P | * H f. 28ᵛ 16 τοῦ ... γῆς: Ἰσραὴλ Q, τοῦ ἰ(σρα)ὴλ P | * Q f. 13ʳ

C. XX 17, 1 5 Lc. X 18 notat James.

XXI. Καὶ Σάβα ἡ βασίλισσα Νότου ἐθαύμασα καὶ εἶδε τὸν ναὸν ὃν ᾠκοδόμουν καὶ ἔδωκε μυρίους ** σίγλους χαλκοῦς. 2. καὶ εἰσῆλθεν εἰς τὸν ναὸν καὶ εἶδε τὸ θυσιαστήριον καὶ τὰ χερουβὶμ καὶ τὰ σεραφὶμ κατασκιάζοντα τὸ ἱλαστήριον καὶ τοὺς 5 διακοσίους λίθους τῶν λύχνων ἐξαστράπτοντας ἐκ διαφόρων χρωμάτων, λύχνοι καὶ σμαράγδων καὶ ὑακίνθου τῶν λίθων καὶ σαμφείρου. 3. καὶ εἶδε τὰ σκεύη τὰ ἀργυρᾶ καὶ χαλκᾶ καὶ χρυσᾶ καὶ τὰς βάσεις τῶν κιόνων ὑπὸ χαλκοῦ ἁλυσιδωτοῦ πεπλεγμένας. εἶδε καὶ τὴν θάλασσαν τὴν χαλκῆν ἔχουσαν ἐπισταθὸν καὶ τοὺς 10 τριάκοντα ἓξ ταύρους. 4. καὶ ἦσαν ἐν * τῷ ἱερῷ τοῦ θεοῦ ἐργαζόμενοι πάντες .... * μισθοῦ ταλάντου χρυσοῦ ἑνὸς χωρὶς τῶν δαιμόνων.

Parallela ad c. XXI v. infra ms. D c. V.
C. XXI. (116) MSS HPQ = Recc. AB. 1 Σάβα ... ἐθαυμ. καὶ Η: ἰδοῦσα ἡ βασ. νότου ταῦτα πάντα ἐθαυμ. δοξάζουσα τὸν θεὸν ἴ(σρα)ὴλ καὶ Ρ, — Q, supplevit ἡ βασ. Νότου Is | 2 ναὸν: + κυρίου Ρ, οἶκον κυρίου Q | ὃν ᾠκοδ. Η: οἰκοδομούμενον Β | * Mg 1352 | κ. ἔδωκε (δέδωκεν ms.) ... χαλκ. Η: κ. ἔδωκεν (** f. 20ᵛ) σίκλον χρυσίου καὶ ἀργυρίου μυριάδας ἑκατὸν, καὶ χαλκοῦ ἐκλεκτοῦ Ρ, ἐχαρίσατο ἐν τῷ ναῷ κυρίου χρυσίου καὶ ἀργυρίου καὶ χαλκοῦ ἐκλεκτοῦ λίτρας μυριάδας ῥ Q 3 § 2. εἶδε — Ρ | κ. τὰ χερ. ... ἱλαστ.: τοὺς ἀναφόρους τοὺς χαλκοὺς τοῦ θυσιαστηρίου Β 4 κατασκιάζοντα Η 5 διακοσίους Η: ἀναφόρους Q, — Ρ | λύγχνων Η 6 χρημάτων Q | λύχνοι ... σαμφείρου: καὶ λύχνη (λυχνίου Ρ) τοῦ (l. λυχνίτου) λίθου καὶ σμαράγδου καὶ ὑακίνθου καὶ σαμφύρου (σαπφείρου Ρ) Β 7 § 3. εἶδε — Q | τ. ἀργ. ... χρυσᾶ: τ. χρυσᾶ κ. (+ τὰ Q) ἀργυρᾶ κ. χαλκᾶ κ. ξύλινα κ. ἐκ δερμάτων ἁπλώματα ἠρυθροδανομένα (ἠρυθρηδανομένων Q) Β | καὶ (2°): pr. εἶδε Q, + ἴδε Ρ 8 κιόνων: + τοῦ ναοῦ κυρίου Β
MSS HQ = Recc. AB. 8—10 ὑπὸ ... θεοῦ — Ρ 8 ἁλυσιδωτοῦ: βαισιδώτου Q | πεπλεγμ.: πεπλημένας Η, πλοκῇ περιπεπλεγμένων Q 9 δὲ καὶ Q | ἔχουσαν ... ταύρους: ἔχουσα στάδιον κ. τ. λς̄ ταυρ. Η, ἣν ἐποίησα εἰς τὸ μῆκος ἔχουσα (ἔχουσα⟨ν⟩ Is) σταδίους καὶ ἐπὶ στάδιον καὶ τοὺς ῑς̄ ταύρους Q 10 § 4. ἦσαν ... ἑνὸς (l. 12): ἦσαν οἱ ἐργαζόμενοι εἰς τὸν ναὸν κυρίου (rursus ms. Ρ) οἱ πάντες χρυσίου ἑνὸς Q, οἱ παντ. χρ. ἑνὸς Ρ |
* Η f. 29ʳ 11 * textum depravatum enodari non potui: οἱ μελησιοι (apographum incertum) Η

MSS HPQ = Recc. AB. 12 δαιμόνων: + ὧν κατέκρινα ἐργάζεσθαι. καὶ ἦν εἰρήνη κύκλῳ τῆς βασιλείας μου (+ καὶ Ρ) ἐπὶ πάσης τῆς γῆς (πᾶσαν τὴν γῆν Q) Β

XXII. ᴦἈπέστειλε δὲ ἐπιστολὴν ὁ βασιλεὺς Ἀράβων Ἀδάρκης, ⟨λέγων οὕτως· »Βασιλεὺς Ἀράβων Ἀδάρκης⟩¹ βασιλεῖ Σολομῶντι χαίρειν. Ἰδοὺ ἠκούσαμεν τὴν δεδομένην σοι σοφίαν καὶ ὅτι ἄνθρωπος ὢν παρὰ κυρίου ἐδόθη σοι σύνεσις ἐπὶ πάν-
5 των τῶν πνευμάτων ἀερίων τε καὶ ἐπιγείων καὶ καταχθονίων. 2. πνεῦμα δέ ἐστιν ἐν τῇ Ἀραβίᾳ· ἐν γὰρ τῇ ἑωθινῇ ἔρχεται αὔρα ἀνέμου ἕως ὥραν τρίτην καὶ ἡ πνοὴ αὐτοῦ δεινὴ καὶ ἀποκτείνει ἀνθρώπους καὶ κτήνη καὶ * οὐ δύναται ζῆσαι πνοὴ οὐδεμία ἐναντίον τοῦ δαίμονος. 3. δέομαί σου οὖν, ἐπειδὴ ὡς
10 ἄνεμός ἐστι τὸ πνεῦμα, σόφισαί τι κατὰ τὴν δεδομένην σοι σοφίαν ὑπὸ κυρίου τοῦ θεοῦ σου καὶ καταξίωσον ἀποστεῖλαι δυνάμενον ἄνθρωπον συλλαβέσθαι αὐτό. 4. καὶ ἰδοὺ σοῦ * ἐσόμεθα, βασιλεῦ Σολομῶν, ἐγώ τε καὶ πᾶς ὁ λαός μου καὶ πᾶσα ἡ γῆ μου, καὶ εἰρηνεύσει πᾶσα Ἀραβία, ἐὰν τὴν ἐκδίκησιν ταύτην ποιή-

---

Parallela ad c. XXII v. infra in ms. D, c. VI 1—9
C. XXII. (117) MSS HPQ = Recc. AB. 1 Ἀπεστ.... Ἀδάρκης (l. 2) ego: ἀπέστειλεν δὲ βασιλεὺς αἰδάρκις περσῶν H, καὶ ἐγένετο ἐν τῷ εἶναι με ἐν τῇ βασιλείᾳ μου ἀπέστειλέ μοι ἐπιστολὴν ὁ βασ. ἀράβων ἀδάρης P, ἐν ταύταις δὲ ταῖς ἡμέραις ἀπέστειλέν με ἐπιστολὴν ὁ βασ. Ἀράβων Ἀδάρκης ὀνόματι Q, + ἡ δὲ γραφὴ τῆς ἐπιστολῆς ἔγραφεν οὕτως B   2 βασιλεῖ: βασιλεῦ H, + τῷ Q   3 χαιρ.: τὸ χέρειν H | τὴν... σοφίαν (+ παρὰ θεοῦ) H: καὶ ἀκουστὸν (ἀκουστὰ Q) γέγονεν εἰς (— εἰς Q) πάντα τὰ πέρατα τῆς γῆς τὴν (τῇ Q) ἐν σοὶ δεδομένην (-μένῃ Q) σοφίαν (σοφίᾳ Q) B   4 ὢν π. κυρ. H: ἐλεήμων παρὰ κυρίου (θεοῦ Q) εἰ σύ B | ἐδόθη σοι συν. H: καὶ συν. ἐδόθη σοι P, — Q | πνευματ.... καταχθ. B: ἀερίων κ. καταχθ. H   6 § 2. πνεῦμα ... Ἀραβ. H: ἐπειδὴ πν. πάρεστιν ἐν τῇ χώρᾳ τῆς Ἀραβίας τοιόνδε B | ἐν τῷ ἑωθινῷ B   7 τις αὔρα B | ὡρῶν τριῶν P (ḡ) Q | δεινὴ καὶ χαλεπὴ B | ἀποκτένει H   8 * P f. 21ʳ | οὐ δύν.... δαίμονος H: οὐ δυν. πνοὴ οὐδ. ζῆσαι ἐπὶ τῆς γῆς ἐναντίον τ. δαιμ. ἐκείνου P, οὐ δυνάμεθα οὐδεμία πνοῇ ζῶντες ἐπὶ τῆς γῆς ζῆσθαι ἀπὸ τὴν δύναμιν τοῦ πνεύματος ἐκείνου Q

MS H = Rec. A pro § 3 textum mutilatum praebet hunc: δέομαί σου οὖν φῆσασθαι ἐπ᾽ ἐμοὶ ποῖος ἄνεμος ἐστὶν τὸ πνεῦμα καὶ εἰπεῖν μοι
MSS PQ = Rec. B. 9 § 3. σου — P | οὖν — Q   10 σόφισαι Kurz: σόφισε PQIs | τι P: δὴ Q | σοι — Q   11 δυνάμενον P: δύναμιν καὶ Q   12 αὐτό Q: αὐτῷ P

MSS HPQ = Recc. AB. 12 § 4. σοῦ ego: ᾳν vel ου H, — B | * H f. 29ᵛ | ἐσώμεθα H, ἔσομαι B, pr. ἐγώ Q   13 πᾶς — P | πᾶσα ... μου H: ἡ γῆ μου ἅπασα (πᾶσα P) δοῦλοί (δούλη P) σου ἕως θανάτου B   14 ἐὰν δὲ H, ἐάνπερ P | ἐκδικ. H: δικαιοσύνην B
UNT. 9: McCown.

σεις ήμιν. 5. διὸ δεόμεθά σου, μὴ παραβλέψῃς τὴν ἱκεσίαν ἡμῶν, καὶ κύριος ἡμῶν γενοῦ ἀείδια πάντοτε. ⌜ἐρρῶσθαι τὸν ἐμὸν κύριον ἀεὶ διὰ παντός.«⌝

6. Ἐγὼ δὲ Σολομῶν ἀναγνοὺς τὴν ἐπιστολὴν ταύτην καὶ
5 πτύξας ἀπέδωκα τῷ δούλῳ μου εἰπὼν αὐτῷ· »μετὰ ἑπτὰ ἡμέρας ὑπομνήσεις μοι τὴν ἐπιστολὴν ταύτην.« 7. ⌜καὶ ἦν Ἱερουσαλὴμ ᾠκοδομωμένη καὶ ὁ ναὸς συνεπληροῦτο.⌝ καὶ ἦν λίθος ἀκρογωνιαῖος μέγας ὃν ἐβουλόμην θεῖναι εἰς κεφαλὴν γωνίας τῆς πληρώσεως τοῦ ναοῦ τοῦ θεοῦ. 8. καὶ πάντες οἱ τεχνῖται καὶ πάν-
10 τες οἱ δαίμονες οἱ συνυπουργοῦντες ἦλθον ἐπὶ τὸ αὐτὸ ἀγαγεῖν τὸν λίθον καὶ θεῖναι εἰς τὸ πτερύγιον * τοῦ ναοῦ καὶ οὐκ ἴσχυσαν σαλεῦσαι αὐτόν. * 9. μετὰ δὲ τὰς ἑπτὰ ἡμέρας μνησθεὶς ἐγὼ τῆς ἐπιστολῆς τοῦ βασιλέως Ἀράβων ἐκάλεσα τὸ παιδάριόν μου καὶ εἶπον αὐτῷ· »ἐπίσαξον τὴν κάμηλόν σου καὶ λάβε ἀσ-
15 κὸν καὶ τὴν σφραγῖδα ταύτην, 10. καὶ ἄπελθε εἰς Ἀραβίαν εἰς τὸν τόπον ἐν ᾧ τὸ πονηρὸν πνεῦμα πνέει, καὶ κρατήσας τὸν ἀσκὸν καὶ τὸ δακτυλίδιον ἔμπροσθεν * τοῦ στόματος τοῦ ἀσκοῦ.

MSS HPQ = Recc. AB. 1 § 5. διὸ — H | ἡμῶν: + καὶ μὴ ἐξουθενημένην τὴν σὴν ὑποτελεῖ καὶ ὑποτεταγμένην ἐπαρχίαν ἀποτελέσῃ P 2 καὶ ... πάντοτε H: ὅτι σου οἰκέται (ἱκέται P) ἐσμέν, ἐγὼ (+ τε P) καὶ ὁ λαός μου καὶ πᾶσα ἡ γῆ μου B | ἐρρῶσθαι ... παντός B: — H 3 ἀεὶ Q: — P § 6. (118) 4 ταύτην — P | κ. πτυξ. H: κ. ἀναπτυξ. P, — Q 5 ἀπέδωκα B: ἐπιδέδωκα H | δούλῳ H: λαῷ B | εἰπὼν αὐτῷ HP: εἰπόντες Q 6 ὑπομν. ... ταύτην H: ὑπομνήσεις (ὑπομνήσατέ Q) με περὶ τῆς ἐπιστολῆς ταύτης B | § 7. καὶ ἦν ... συνεπληρ. B: — H 7 οἰκοδομουμένη Q | ἀκρογων. κείμενος B 8 μέγας ἐκλεκτὸς P | ὃν H: ὅντινα B | εἰς τὴν κεφαλὴν τῆς γωνίας τῆς συμπληρώσεως B 9 τ. ναοῦ τ. θ.: αὐτοῦ P | § 8. 10 συνυπεργοῦντες Q | ἀγαγεῖν H: ὥστε ἀναγαγεῖν B 11 θεῖναι αὐτὸν B | εἰς H: ἐπὶ P, ὑπὸ Q | * H f. 30ʳ | ναοῦ: + τοῦ ἱεροῦ B 12 * P f. 21ᵛ | αὐτόν: + καὶ θεῖναι πρὸς τὴν γωνίαν τὴν θεματισμένην αὐτῷ P, + ἦν γὰρ ὁ λίθος ἐκεῖνος πάνυ μέγας καὶ χρήσιμος εἰς τὸ τεθῆναι ἐπὶ τῆς γωνίας (τὸ ... γων.: τὴν γωνίαν P) τοῦ ἱεροῦ B | § 9. (119) καὶ μετὰ τὰς B | ἐμνήσθην Q 13 ἐγὼ — B | τοῦ H: Ἀδάρκου Q, ἀδάρου P | ἐκάλεσα P: ἐπεκαλεσάμην Q, ἐκέλευσα H | τ. παιδ. H: τὸν παῖδα P, τὸν παιδί Q 14 τὴν H: τὸν B | λάβε: + μετά σου Q, σεαυτὸν P | λάβε δὲ καὶ B 15 φραγίδα P | § 10. εἰς τὴν Ἀρ. ἐπὶ τὸν B 16 πνέει B: πνῆ H | κρατήσας B: κατάργησον H 17 ἀσκὸν B: αἰκὸν H | καὶ τὸ ... ἀσκοῦ P: κ. τ. δακτ. θὲς ἐμπρ. τὸν ἐκὸν H, ἐπιτηδείως εἰς τὸ τόπον, ὅθεν ἐξέρχεται ἡ πνοὴ τοῦ δαίμονος, ὁμοίως δὲ τὸ δακτυλίδιον Q, + κατὰ τὴν πνοὴν τοῦ πνεύματος P | * Mg 1353

§ 7. Is XXVIII 16; I Pt. II 6

11. καὶ ἐν τῷ ἐμπνευσθῆναι τὸν ἀσκὸν εὑρήσεις ὅτι ὁ δαίμων ἐστὶν ὁ ἐκεῖσε ἐμπνέων. τότε σπουδαίως μετὰ βίας δῆσον τὸν ἀσκὸν καὶ σφραγίσας τὸ δακτυλίδιον ἐπίσαξον ἐπὶ τὴν κάμηλον καὶ κόμισον αὐτὸν ἐνθάδε, καὶ ἄπελθε ὑγιαίνων.« 12. Τότε ὁ παῖς κατὰ * τὰ ἐνταλθέντα ἐποίησε καὶ ἐπορεύθη εἰς Ἀραβίαν. καὶ οἱ ἄνθρωποι τοῦ τόπου ἐκείνου ἠπίστουν εἰ ἄρα δυνήσεται τὸ πονηρὸν πνεῦμα συλλαβέσθαι. 13. καὶ ὄρθρου * ἀναστὰς ὁ οἰκέτης ἔστη κατενώπιον τοῦ πνεύματος τῆς πνοῆς καὶ ἔθηκε τὸν ἀσκὸν ἐπὶ τὸ ἔδαφος, ἐπέθηκε δὲ καὶ τὸ δακτυλίδιον. * καὶ εἰσῆλθεν εἰς τὸν ἀσκὸν καὶ ἐπνευμάτωσεν αὐτόν. 14. ὁ δὲ παῖς σταθεὶς ἔσφιγξε τὸν ἀσκὸν ἐπὶ τῷ στόματι ἐν ὀνόματι κυρίου Σαβαὼθ καὶ ἔμεινεν ὁ δαίμων ἔσωθεν

MSS HPQ = Recc. AB. 1 § 11. ἐμπνευσθ. H: πνευματωθῆναι B | ἀσκὸν: αἶκὸν H | εὑρήσεις ego: εὑρέσεις H, τότε συνήσεις B 2 ὁ ἐκ. ἐμπν. — B | τότε σπουδ. H: κμὶ σπουδῇ B | μετὰ βίας — B | δῆσον τ. ἀσκ. (ἐκὸν) H: περιδήσας τὸ στόμα τοῦ ἀσκοῦ B 3 κ. σφραγ. τ. δακτ. H: κατασφράγισον αὐτὸν μετὰ τοῦ δακτυλιδίου καὶ P, σφράγισον αὐτὸν μὲ τὸ δακτ. καὶ Q | ἐπίσαξον αὐτὸν B | τὴν HP. τὸν B 4 κόμισον αὐτ. ἐνθ. H: κομ. μοι ἐνθ. P, ἐλθὲ πρὸς ἡμᾶς Q, + καὶ ἐὰν κατὰ τὴν ὁδὸν τάξει (τάξεται Q) σοι χρυσίον ἢ ἀργύριον (ἄργυρον Q, + ἢ θησαυροὺς P) ἵνα (ὅπως Q) ἀπολύσῃς αὐτόν, βλέπε μὴ πεισθῇς (+ καὶ ἀπολύσῃς αὐτόν Q). σύνταξον δὲ (ἀλλὰ σύνταξαι P, + αὐτοῦ Q) ἄνευ ὅρκου (+ ἀπολῦσαι P). καὶ ἐὰν ἀποδείξῃ (ὑποδείξῃ Q) σοι τόπους (τόπον ἔχοντα Q) χρυσίου ἢ (καὶ Q) ἀργυρίου, σημειωσάμενος τοὺς τόπους σφράγισαι τὴν σφραγίδα ταύτην (⟨σ⟩φράγισαι τὸν τόπον τοῦ χρήματος Q) καὶ ἄγαγέ μοι αὐτὸν (αὐτ. ἀγ. μοι ὦδε Q) B | καὶ H: ἤθη B
§ 12. (120) 5 κατὰ (* f. 30^v) τ. ἐνταλθ. H: τ. ἐντελόμενα Q, τὰ ἐντεταλμένα αὐτῷ P, + παρὰ τοῦ βασιλέως σολομῶν < H | ἐποίησε: + καὶ ἐπέσαξε τὴν (τὸν Q) κάμηλον καὶ ἔθηκε τὸν ἀσκὸν (+ ἐπὶ τὸν κάμηλον Q) B 6 εἰς τὴν Ἀρ. B 7 ἄρα ... συλλαβ. P: ἄρα τὸ πνεῦμα τὸ πονηρὸν δυνήσεται συλλαβ. Q, δυνατὸν ἄν(θρωπ)ον συλλαβ. H | § 13. κ. ὄρθρου ego: κ. ὀρθὸς H, ὄρθρου δὲ γενομένου B 8 * P f. 22^r | ὁ — H 9 ἐπέθηκε ... δακτ. H: καὶ τὸ δακτ. (* Q f. 14^r) ἐπὶ τὸ στόμα (τοῦ στόματος P) τοῦ ἀσκοῦ B 10 εἰσῆλθεν ... ἐπνευματ. αὐτ. ego: εἰσῆλθεν ... ἐμπνευσμάτισεν αὐτ. ἀπὸ τῆς πνοῆς τοῦ πονηροῦ πν(εύματο)ς H, ἐπνευματώθη ὁ ἀσκὸς Q, ἔπνευσεν ὁ δαίμων διὰ μέσον τοῦ δακτυλιδίου εἰς τὸ στόμα τοῦ ἀσκοῦ καὶ εἰσελθὼν ἐπνευμάτωσε τὸν ἀσκὸν P 11 § 14. παῖς HQ: ἄνθρωπος P | σταθεὶς H: ἐνσταθεὶς εὐθέως P, συντόμως Q | ἔσφιγξε (ἔσφηξε ms.) ... στόματι H: ἔσφιγξεν τῇ χειρὶ τὸ στόμα τοῦ ἀσκοῦ P, ἔδησεν τὸ στόμα τοῦ ἀσκοῦ Q 12 ἐν HP: ἐπὶ τῷ Q | κυρίου τοῦ θεοῦ P | ὁ δαιμ. ἐσωθ. H. ἔσω ὁ δαιμ. B

εἰς τὸν ἀσκόν. 15. ἔμεινε δὲ καὶ ὁ παῖς εἰς ἀπόδειξιν ἡμέρας τρεῖς, καὶ οὐκέτι ἔπνευσε τὸ πνεῦμα, καὶ ἐπέγνωσαν οἱ Ἄραβες ὅτι ἀσφαλῶς συνέκλεισε τὸ πνεῦμα. 16. τότε ἐπέσαξε τὸν ἀσκὸν εἰς τὴν κάμηλον. προσέπεμπον δὲ οἱ Ἄραβες τὸν παῖδα μετὰ 5 δώρων καὶ τιμῶν εὐφημοῦντες τὸν θεόν, ἔμειναν γὰρ ἐν εἰρήνῃ. εἰσήγαγε ⟨δὲ⟩ τὸ πνεῦμα ὁ παῖς καὶ ἔθηκεν αὐτὸ εἰς κεφαλὴν τοῦ ναοῦ.

17. Τῇ δὲ ἐπαύριον εἰσῆλθον ἐγὼ Σολομῶν εἰς τὸν ναόν· καὶ ἤμην ἐν λύπῃ περὶ τοῦ λίθου τοῦ ἀκρογωνιαίου. καὶ ἀναστὰς 10 ὁ ἀσκὸς καὶ περιπατήσας βήματα ἑπτὰ ἔστη ἐπὶ τὸ στόμα καὶ προσεκύνησέ μοι. 18 καὶ θαυμάσας ἐγὼ ὅτι μετὰ τοῦ ἀσκοῦ δυνάμεις ἔσχε καὶ περιεπάτησεν, ἐκέλευσα αὐτὸ ἀναστῆναι. καὶ ἀνέστη ὁ ἀσκὸς καὶ ἔστη ἐν τοῖς ποσὶν πεφυσιωμένος. 19. καὶ ἐπηρώτησα αὐτὸν λέγων· »σὺ τίς εἶ;« λέγει ἔσω τὸ πνεῦμα· *
15 »ἐγώ εἰμι δαίμων λεγόμενος Ἐφιππᾶς, ὁ ἐν τῇ Ἀραβίᾳ.«

MSS HPQ = Recc. AB. 1 ἐν τῷ ἀσκῷ Q | § 15. ἐμ. δὲ κ. H: καὶ μετὰ τοῦτο ἐμ. B | παῖς ἐν τῇ χώρᾳ ἐκείνῃ ἡμ. τρεῖς εἰς ἐπίδειξιν B 2 πνεῦμα: + πλέον τῇ πόλει ἐκείνῃ P, + πλεῖον ἐν τῇ χώρᾳ ἐκείνῃ Q | ἔγνωσαν πάντες οἱ B 3 § 16. (121) ἐπίσαξε B | ἀσκὸν: + ὁ παῖς B | τὴν HP: τὸν Q 4 προσεπ. δὲ H: καὶ προεπ. P, καὶ ἐξαπέστειλαν Q | τ. παιδ. οἱ Ἀρ. B | μετὰ... τιμῶν H: μετὰ τιμῆς πολλῆς καὶ δώρων πολυτίμων P, μ. τιμ. πολ. καὶ δῶρα πολλὰ ἐδωροφόρησαν τὸν παῖδα Q 5 εὐφ. τ. θ. H: εὐφημ. καὶ δοξάζοντες τὸν θεὸν Ἰσραὴλ P, ἐπαίνους καὶ δόξαν πεμψάμενοί μοι Q | ἔμειν. ... εἰρ. — B 6 εἰσηγ. ... παῖς H: ὁ δὲ παῖς εἰσηγ. τὸν ἀσκὸν B | αὐτὸ ego: αὐτῷ H, αὐτὸν Q, — P | κεφαλὴν H: τὸ μέσον B 8 § 17. εἰσῆλθον: ἐλθὼν B | ἐγὼ βασιλεὺς P | ναὸν τοῦ θεοῦ B 9 καὶ — B | λύπῃ πολλῇ B | καὶ ἐν τῷ εἰσέρχεσθαί μοι εἰς τὸν ναὸν (+ κυρίου Q) B 10 κ. περιπ. βημ. ἐπ. H: πεφυσημένος (— P) ἐπεριεπάτησεν ἐπ. βημ. B | ἔστη (ἔστι ms.) ... στόμα H: ἔπεσεν δὲ ἐπὶ στόμα P, καὶ ἐλθὼν ἔμπροσθέ μου ἔπεσεν ἔμπροσθέν μου κήπον (l. κύπτον Is) τὸ στόμα τοῦ ἀσκοῦ ἐπὶ τὴν γῆν Q 11 ἐπροσκύνησε Q | § 18. κ. θαυμ. ἐγὼ HP: ἐγὼ δὲ ταῦτα θεωρήσας ἐθαύμασα Q | ὅτι καὶ B | μετὰ τ. ἀσκοῦ H (— τοῦ) P: ἐν ἀσκῷ δεδεμένος ὁ δαίμων Q | δύναμιν B 12 ἔσχε ὁ δαίμων P | περιεπάτει B | ἐγὼ δὲ ἐκέλευσα Q | αὐτὸν B 13 κ. ἔστη — H | ἐν — P | πεφυσ. H: πεφυσυμένος P, πεφυσημένος Q | § 19. 14 σύ: pr. εἰπέ μοι B, — Q | λέγει ἔσω H: καὶ ἔφη ἔσωθεν B | * P f. 22ᵛ | ὁ δαίμων ὁ λεγόμενος B | ἐφιππὰς P, ἐφιππᾶς Q, ἔφιππας H, cf. supra VI 5, infra XXIV 1 | ὁ ὢν P, ὃ ἤμην Q

20. καὶ εἶπον αὐτῷ· »ποίῳ ἀγγέλῳ καταργεῖσαι;« ὁ δὲ λέγει· »τῷ διὰ παρθένου μέλλοντι γεννηθῆναι ἐπειδὴ αὐτὸν προσκυνοῦσι ἄγγελοι, καὶ ὑπὸ Ἰουδαίων μέλλοντι σταυρωθῆναι.«
XXIII. Ἐγὼ δὲ λέγω πρὸς αὐτόν· »τί μοι δύνασαι ποιῆσαι;« 5 ὁ δὲ ἔφη· »ἐγὼ δυνατός εἰμι ὄρη μεταστῆναι καὶ μεταφέρειν οἴκους καὶ βασιλεῖς καταβαλεῖν.« 2. καὶ εἶπον αὐτῷ· »εἰ δυνατὸς εἶ, ἔπαρον τὸν λίθον τοῦτον εἰς τὴν ἀρχὴν τῆς γωνίας τοῦ ναοῦ.« ὁ δὲ ἔφη. »οὐ μόνον τοῦτον τὸν λίθον ἐπαρῶ, βασιλεῦ, ἀλλὰ καὶ σὺν τῷ δαίμονι τῷ ἐν τῇ Ἐρυθρᾷ θαλάσσῃ τὸν ἐν τῇ 10 Ἐρυθρᾷ θαλάσσῃ κίονα τὸν ἀέριον, καὶ στήσεις αὐτὸν ὅπου θέλεις.« 3. καὶ ταῦτα εἰπὼν ὑπεισῆλθεν ὑποκάτω τοῦ λίθου καὶ ᾖρεν * αὐτὸν καὶ ἀνῆλθεν εἰς τὸν κλίμακα βαστάζων τὸν λίθων

MSS PQ = Rec. B pro § 20 praebent textum hunc: καὶ (ἐγὼ δὲ Q) εἶπον αὐτῷ· (+ τοῦτό σοι ἐστὶ τὸ ὄνομα; ὁ δὲ ἔφη· ναί· ὅπου γὰρ βούλομαι ἐφίπταμαι καὶ ἐμπυρίζω καὶ θανατῶ. καὶ εἶπον αὐτῷ· P) ποίῳ ἀγγέλῳ καταργεῖσαι (καταργῇ σὺ P); ὁ δὲ εἶπεν· ὁ μονάρχης θεὸς ὁ ἔχων ἐξουσίαν κατ' ἐμοῦ (+ καὶ ἀκούεσθαι P), ὁ διὰ παρθένου μέλλων γενᾶσθαι (ὁ καὶ μέλλων ἐκ παρθ. τίκτεσθαι Q) καὶ ὑπὸ Ἰουδαίων (+ μέλλει Q) σταυρωθῆναι ἐπὶ ξύλου, ὃν προσκυνοῦσι ἄγγελοι ἀρχάγγελοι, ἐκεῖνός με καταργεῖ καὶ ἀτονεῖ με ἐκ τῆς πολλῆς μου δυνάμεως (ἀτονεῖ μου τὴν πολλήν μου δύναμιν Q) τῆς δοθείσης μοι (μου Q) ὑπὸ τοῦ πατρός μου τοῦ διαβόλου.
MS H = Rec. A. 1 § 20. τοῦ δ. π. μέλλοντο < γενηθ. ms. 3 μελλ < ms.

Parallela ad c. XXIII v. infra in ms. D c. VI 10f.
C. XXIII. MSS HPQ = Recc. AB. 4 ἐγὼ ... αὐτὸν Q: ὁ δὲ λέγει αὐτῶν H, εἶπον δὲ αὐτῷ P | δύνασαί μοι Q | μοι — P 5 μεταστῆναι H: μεταφέρειν P, σαλεῦσαι Q | κ. μεταφ. ... καταβ. (καταβαλῶ ms.) H: οἰκίας βασιλέων καταβαλ. (καταλαβεῖν Q), δένδρα ἀπέταλα (ἀπέταλλα Q, -αλα Kurz) ξηραίνω (μαραίνω P) B 6 § 2. εἰ ... τοῦτον H: δύνασαι ἐπάραι τὸν λίθον τοῦτον καὶ θέσαι (ex θέσθαι corr. P) αὐτὸν B 7 γωνίας ταύτης τῆς οὔσης ἐν τῇ εὐπρεπείᾳ τ. ναοῦ B 8 οὐ μόνον HP: δύνομαι καὶ Q | τὸν λίθον — B | ἐπάραι B | βασιλεῦ, ἀλλὰ — Q 9 * Mg 1356 | σὺν ... θαλάσσῃ ego: σὺν τῷ δαίμονι τῷ ἐπὶ τῆς ἐρυθρᾶς θαλάσσης P, συντόμως ἕνα H, — Q | τὸν ἐν ... ἀέριον H: ἀναγάγω τὸν κίονα τὸν ἀερίστην P, τὸν κίονα τὸν ἐν βύθῳ τῆς θαλάσσης (f. 14ᵛ) τῆς Ἐρυθρᾶς θαλάσσης, ὅνπερ βαστάζει ἕτερος δαίμων φυλάττων αὐτὸ ἐκεῖ ἕως τὴν σήμερον Q 10 στήσεις ... θέλεις H: στήσω αὐτ. (αὐτ. θέσω Q) ὅπου βούλει (βούλῃ Q) ἐν Ἱερουσαλὴμ B 11 § 3. καὶ — B | ὑπεισῆλθεν ... λίθον H: ἠνάγκασα αὐτόν, καὶ ὡσεὶ ἐκφυσηθεὶς ὁ ἀσκὸς ἐγένετο καὶ ὑποδέδωκα τῷ λίθῳ καὶ διέζωσεν ἑαυτὸν P, ἐπέδειξα αὐτοῦ τὸν λίθον. ὁ δὲ ἀσκὸς ἐγένετο ὡσεὶ ἐκφυσηθεὶς καὶ διέζωσεν ἑαυτὸν Q 12 ᾖρεν αὐτ. H: ἐπῆρεν (+ τὸν λίθον Q, * P f. 23ʳ) ἐπάνω τοῦ ἀσκοῦ B | εἰς τ. κλιμ. H: ὁ ἀσκὸς τὰς κλίμακας P, ὁ ἀσκὸς τὰς σκάλας Q | * H f. 32ʳ

καὶ ἔθετο αὐτὸν εἰς τὴν ἄκραν τῆς εἰσόδου τοῦ ναοῦ. 4. ἐγὼ δὲ Σολομῶν ἐπαιρόμενος εἶπον· »ἀληθῶς νῦν ἐπληρώθη ἡ γραφὴ ἡ λέγουσα· ›λίθον ὃν ἀπεδοκίμασαν οἱ οἰκοδομοῦντες οὗτος ἐγενήθη μὲν εἰς κεφαλὴν γωνίας,‹ καὶ τὰ λοιπά.

5 XXIV. ⌈Καὶ πάλιν εἶπον αὐτῷ· »ἄπελθε, ἄγαγέ μοι ὃν εἶπας κίονα ἐν τῇ Ἐρυθρᾷ θαλάσσῃ. καὶ ἀπελθὼν ὁ Ἐφιππᾶς ἀνήγαγεν τὸν δαίμονα καὶ τὸν κίονα ἀμφότεροι βαστάζοντες ἀπὸ τῆς Ἀραβίας. 2. ἐγὼ δὲ κατασοφισάμενος⌉ ὅτι τὰ δύο πνεύματα ταῦτα ἐδύναντο πᾶσαν τὴν οἰκουμένην σαλεῦσαι ἐν μιᾷ
10 ῥοπῇ περιεσφράγισα ἔνθεν καὶ ἔνθεν τῷ δακτυλιδίῳ καὶ εἶπον· »φυλάττεσθε ἀκριβῶς.« * 3. καὶ ἔμειναν βαστάζοντες τὸν κίονα

MSS HPQ = Recc. AB. 1 ἔθετο HP: ἔθηκεν Q | τῆς ... ναοῦ Β: τοῦ ναοῦ τῆς ὁδοῦ Η | § 4. 2 ἐπαιρόμενος Η: ἰδὼν τὸν λίθον ἐπηρμένον καὶ τεθεμελιωμένον (+ ἐθαύμασα καὶ Q) B | νῦν ... λέγουσα Η (— νῦν) P: ἡ γραφὴ εἶπεν Q 3 ὃν ἀπεδοκ. B: ἀναπεδοκ. Η 4 μὲν — Β | καὶ τὰ λοιπά Η: ὅτι τοῦτο οὐκ ἔστιν ἐμὸν δοῦναι ἀλλὰ τοῦ θεοῦ τὸ κατισχύσαι τὸν δαίμονα ἐπάραι τὸν λίθον τηλικοῦτον καὶ ἀποθέσθαι αὐτὸν εἰς τόπον ὃν ἐβουλόμην P, ὅτι τοῦ θεοῦ τὸ θέλημά ἐστιν τῷ δώσαντι τὴν ἰσχὺν δαίμονος ⟨ἐ⟩πάραι λίθον τοσοῦτον μέγεθος καὶ ἀποτεθῆναι εἰς τὸν τόπον ὃν ἐβουλόμην Q
Parallela ad c. XXIV v. in ms. D c. VI 12—14
C. XXIV. MSS HPQ = Recc. AB. (124) textum eius capitis depravatum per conjecturam dubitanter emendavi 5 καὶ ... θαλάσσῃ Η: — Β 6–8 καὶ ... Ἀραβίας Q: καὶ ἀπῆλθεν καὶ ᾖρεν αὐτῶν. ἐγὼ δὲ εἶδον αὐτὸν ἄφνω ἐρχόμενον βαστάζοντα τὸν κίονα τὸν ἀέριον Η, + ὡς δὲ ἐθεασάμην τὸν κίοναν φέροντες εἰς ὕψος τοῦ ἀέρος βαστάζοντες πάντες οἱ θεωροῦντες τὰ θαῦμα ἐξεπλάγησαν Q (l. fortasse ὡς δὲ εἶδον αὐτὰ ἀμφότερα ἐρχόμενα βαστάζοντα τὸν κίονα τὸν ἀέριον cum κατεσοφισάμην, v. infra), καὶ ἤγαγεν Ἐφιππᾶς τὸν δαίμονα τὸν ἐν τῇ Ἐρυθρᾷ θαλάσσῃ μετὰ τοῦ κίονος, καὶ λαβόντες ἀμφότεροι τὸν κίονα ὑψώθησαν ἀπὸ τῆς γῆς P 8 § 2. ἐγὼ δὲ κατασ. Β: κατεσοφισάμην Η 9 ἐδύν. ... οἰκουμ. Η: ἠδύναντο τ. οἰκ. ὅλην (ὅλ. τ. οἰκ. Q) B, pr. μὴ Cr | σαλεῦσαι Β: σαλέαιι Η | μιᾷ ῥοπῇ Η: ῥυπῇ (l. ῥιπῇ Kurz) Q, στιγμῇ χρόνου P 10 καὶ περιεσφράγισα αὐτὸν Η | μετὰ τοῦ δακτυλιδίου Q 11 φυλαττ. ἀκριβ. Η: φυλάσσου ἀκριβ. P, πρὸς τοὺς δαίμονας· ἐπ' ὀνόματος κυρίου Ἰσραὴλ θεοῦ Σαβαὼθ στῆτε, δαίμονες. μετὰ τοῦ κιονίου εἰς τὸ ὕψος τοῦ ἀέρος ἐν τῷ τόπῳ τούτῳ, βαστάζοντες τὸν κίονα ἕως τῆς συντελείας τοῦ αἰῶνος Q | * H f. 32ᵛ | § 3. ἔμειναν: + τὰ πνεύματα Β, add. adhuc εἰς τὸν τόπον Q | βαστάζοντα P | τ. κίονα — P

§ 4. Ps. CXVIII 22; Mk. XII 10; Mt. XXI 42; Lk. XX 17; I Pt. II 6f. Mt. XX 23; Mk. X 40

εἰς τὸν ἀέρα μέχρι τῆς σήμερον ⌈εἰς ἀπόδειξιν τῆς δεδομένης μοι σοφίας. 4. καὶ ἦν κρεμάμενος ὁ κίων ὑπερμεγέθης διὰ τοῦ ἀέρος ὑπὸ τῶν πνευμάτων βασταζόμενος καὶ οὕτως κάτωθεν τὰ πνεύματα ἐφαίνοντο ὥσπερ ἀὴρ βαστάζοντα. 5. καὶ ἐν τῷ ἀτενίζειν ἡμᾶς ⟨ὑπόλοξος⟩ ἐγένετο ἡ βάσις τοῦ κίονος καὶ ἔστιν ἕως τῆς σήμερον.⌉ *

XXV. Καὶ ἐγὼ ἠρώτησα τὸν ἕτερον δαίμονα τὸν ἀνελθόντα ἐκ τῆς θαλάσσης μετὰ τοῦ κίονος· ⌈»σὺ τίς εἶ καὶ τί καλεῖσαι καὶ τί σου ἡ ἐργασία; ὅτι πολλὰ ἀκούω περὶ σου.« 2. ὁ δὲ δαίμων ἔφη· »ἐγώ, βασιλεῦ Σολομῶν, καλοῦμαι Ἀβεζεθιβοῦ· καί ποτε ἐκαθεζόμην ἐν πρώτῳ οὐρανῷ, οὗ τὸ ὄνομα Ἀμελούθ. 3. ἐγὼ οὖν εἰμι * πνεῦμα χαλεπὸν καὶ πτερωτὸν καὶ μονόπτερον, ἐπίβουλον πάσης πνοῆς ὑπὸ τῶν οὐρανῶν. ἐγὼ παρήμην ἡνίκα ὁ Μωϋσῆς εἰσήρχετο εἰς Φαραὼ βασιλέα Αἰγύπτου σκληρύνων αὐτοῦ τὴν καρδίαν. 4. ἐγώ εἰμι ὃν ἐπικαλοῦντο Ἰαννῆς καὶ Ἰαμβρῆς οἱ μαχόμενοι τῷ Μωϋσῇ ἐν Αἰγύπτῳ. ἐγώ εἰμι ὁ ἀντιπαλαίων τῷ Μωϋσῇ ἐν τοῖς τέρασι καὶ τοῖς σημείοις.«

MSS HPQ = Recc. AB. **1** εἰς τ. ἀέρα — B | μέχρι τ. (τὴν H) σημ. HP: ἕως καὶ τὴν σήμερον Q

MSS PQ = Rec. B. **1—6** εἰς ἀποδ. ... σήμερον magnem partem om. ms. H, v. infra ll. 4 f. **2** § 4, ὁ κίονας ἐν μεγέθει φρικτῷ εἰς τὸν ἀέρα Q **3** καὶ οὕτως ... βαστάζοντα om. Q per homoeoteleuton **4** § 5. καὶ ἐν .. κίονος (ὑπόλοξος ex P supplevi) H: κ. ἐν τ. ἀτεν. τις ὁ κίων ὑπόλοξος βαστάζόμενος ὑπὸ τῶν πνευμάτων P, φερόμενος ὡς ὑπὸ λοξήγον οὐχὶ ὀρθῶς Q **5** ἕως καὶ τὴν σήμερον Q **6** * P f. 23ᵛ

C. XXV. MSS HPQ = Recc. AB. (125) **7** ἠρώτησα H: Σολομῶν ἐπηρωτ. B | τὸν ἕτ. ... κίονος H: τὸ ἕτερον τὸ ἐν τῇ ἐν Ἀραβίᾳ τῆς Ἐρυθρᾶς θαλάσσης Q, τὸ πνεῦμα τὸ ἕτερον τὸ ἀνελθὸν μετὰ τοῦ κίονος ἀπὸ τοῦ βυθοῦ τῆς θαλάσσης τῆς ἐρυθρᾶς καὶ εἶπον αὐτῷ P

MSS PQ = Rec. B. §§ 1—5. ll. 8—p. 72*, **1** σὺ ... αὐτῷ — H | εἰ καὶ τί — Q **9** περί P: παρά Q | § 2. **10** Σολ. — Q | Ἀβεζεβιθοῦ Q | καί ποτε ἐκαθεζ. Q: ἀπόγονός εἰμι ἀρχαγγέλου, καθεζομένου μου P **11** ὄνομα: + τοῦ ἀγγέλου τοῦ καταργοῦντός με Q | Ἀβελούθ Q **12** § 3. οὖν — Q | χαλεπὸν (* f. 15ʳ) πνεῦμα Q -| καὶ (1°) — Q **13** ἐπιβουλ. ... οὐρανῶν P: πολλὰ κακὰ ἐνεργῶν Q | ἐγὼ παρ. ἡνίκα P: ὅθεν ἐγώ εἰμι, ὅταν Q **14** ὁ Μωϋσῆς Q: μωσῆς P | βασιλέως mss. **15** ἰανὶς καὶ ἰαμβρὶς P, Ἰανῆς κ. Ἰαμβρὶς Q | οἱ μαχόμενοι Q: οἱ καυχώμενοι P, οἰκουχώμενοι Fl **16** ἐν Αἰγ. ... Μωϋσῇ om. Q per homoeoteleuton **17** τέρασι καὶ Q: πέρασι P, τέρασι conj. Cr

5. εἶπον οὖν αὐτῷ⌐¹ »πῶς οὖν εὑρέθης ἐν τῇ Ἐρυθρᾷ θαλάσσῃ;« ὁ δὲ ἔφη· ⌐»ἐν τῇ ἐξόδου τῶν υἱῶν Ἰσραὴλ ἐγὼ ἐσκλήρυνα τὴν καρδίαν Φαραὼ καὶ ἀνεπτέρωσα αὐτοῦ τὴν καρδίαν καὶ τῶν θεραπόντων αὐτοῦ. 6. καὶ ἐποίησα αὐτοὺς ἵνα καταδιώξωσιν 5 ὀπίσω τῶν υἱῶν Ἰσραήλ, καὶ συνηκολούθησε Φαραὼ καὶ πάντες οἱ Αἰγύπτιοι. τότε ἐγὼ παρήμην ἐκεῖ καὶ συνηκολουθήσαμεν, καὶ ἀνήλθομεν ἅπαντες ἐν τῇ Ἐρυθρᾷ θαλάσσῃ. 7. καὶ ἐγένετο ἡνίκα διεπέρασαν οἱ υἱοὶ Ἰσραήλ,⌐¹ ἐπαναστραφὲν τὸ ὕδωρ ἐκάλυψε πᾶσαν τὴν παρεμβολὴν τῶν Αἰγυπτίων· τότε εὑρέθην ἐγὼ ἐκεῖ 10 καὶ συνεκαλύφθην ἐν τῷ ὕδατι ⌐καὶ ἔμεινα ἐν τῇ θαλάσσῃ τηρούμενος⌐¹ ὑποκάτω τοῦ κίονος ⌐μέχρι ἀνῆλθεν Ἐφιππᾶς.« * 8. κἀγὼ δὲ Σολομῶν ὥρκισα αὐτὸν βαστάζειν τὸν κίονα ἕως τῆς συντελείας. 9. καὶ σὺν θεῷ ἐκόσμησα τὸν ναὸν αὐτοῦ ἐν πάσῃ εὐπρεπείᾳ. καὶ ἤμην χαίρων καὶ δοξάζων αὐτόν.⌐¹

MSS PQ = Rec. B. 1 § 5. οὖν P: δὲ ἐγὼ Q   2 ἔφη P: λέγει μοι Q | ἐσκλήρουν Q   4 § 6. ἵνα καταδ. P: ὅπως καταδιώξουσιν Q   5 συνεκολούθησεν Q   6 ἐσυνηκολούθησάν με Q | § 7.   7 ἡνίκα P: ὅτε Q
MS H = Rec. A. §§ 5—7. pro ll. 1—2 πῶς ... ἔφη; praebet H haec: πῶς ἐν τῇ ἐριθρᾷ θαλάσσῃ οἰκῇς. ὁ δαίμων ἔφη   2—8 ἐν τῇ ... Ἰσραήλ — H

MSS HPQ = Recc.AB.   8 ἐπαναστραφὲν ... ἐκαλ. B: ὅταν ἐστράφη ὁ ὕδωρ καὶ ἐκάλειψεν H   9 πᾶσαν — H | Αἰγυπτ.: + καὶ πᾶσαν τὴν δύναμιν αὐτῶν B | τότε εὑρ. H: εὑρ. οὖν B   10 συνεκ. ἐν τ. ὑδ. H: ἐκάλυψέν με τὸ ὕδωρ B | κ. ἔμεινα ... τηρούμενος B: — H   11 κίονος τούτου B

MS H = Rec. A §§ 7—9, ll. 11—14 μέχρι ... αὐτόν: textum brevem praebet
MSS PQ = Rec. B eiusdem sectionis textum interpolatum praebent hunc: ὡς δὲ ἦλθεν Ἐφιππᾶς πεμφθεὶς παρὰ σοῦ ἐν ἀγγείῳ ἀσκοῦ (* P f. 24ʳ) ἐγκλεισθεὶς καὶ ἀνεβίβασέ με πρὸς σέ. § 8 (127) κἀγὼ (+ οὖν P) Σολομῶν ἀκούσας ταῦτα ἐδόξασα τὸν θεὸν καὶ ὥρκισα τοὺς δαίμονας ὥστε μὴ παρακοῦσαί μου ἀλλὰ μεῖναι βαστάζοντας (-τες Q) τὸν (τὴν P) κίονα. καὶ ὤμοσαν ἀμφότεροι λέγοντες· ζῇ κύριος ὁ θεός (+ σου P, + ὃς παρέδωκεν ἡμᾶς ὑποχειρίους σου Q), οὐ μὴ ἀποθώμεθα τὸν στῦλον τοῦτον ἕως τῆς συντελείας τοῦ αἰῶνος. ᾗ δ' ἂν * ἡμέρᾳ (ego: εἰ δ' ἂν ἡμέραν P, εἰς δ' ἂν ἡμέραν Q, εἰς δ' ἦν ἡμ. conj. Kurz, * Mg 1357) πέσῃ ὁ λίθος οὗτος, τότε ἔσται ἡ συντέλεια τοῦ αἰῶνος. § 9. (128) ἐγὼ δὲ (κἀγὼ P) Σολομῶν ἐδόξασα τὸν θεὸν καὶ (+ ἐδὸ linea deletum P) ἐκόσμησα τὸν ναὸν τοῦ κυρίου πάσῃ εὐπρεπείᾳ, καὶ ἤμην εὐπνυμῶν ἐν τῇ βασιλείᾳ μου καὶ εἰρήνη ἐν ταῖς ἡμέραις μου

XXVI. Ἔλαβον δὲ γυναῖκας ἀπὸ πάσης χώρας * καὶ βασιλείας, ὧν οὐκ ἦν ἀριθμός. καὶ ἐπορεύθην πρὸς τῶν Ἰεβουσαίων βασιλέα καὶ εἶδον γυναῖκα ἐν τῇ βασιλείᾳ αὐτῶν καὶ ἠγάπησα αὐτὴν σφόδρα, καὶ ἠθέλησα αὐτὴν μῖξαι σὺν ταῖς γυναιξί μου. 2 καὶ εἶπον πρὸς τοὺς ἱερεῖς αὐτῶν· »δότε μοι τὴν Σουμανίτην ταύτην, ὅτι ἠγάπησα αὐτὴν σφόδρα.« καὶ * εἶπον πρός με· »εἰ ἠγάπησας τὴν θυγατέρα ἡμῶν, προσκύνησον τοὺς θεοὺς ἡμῶν, τὸν μέγαν Ῥαφὰν καὶ Μολόχ, καὶ λάβε αὐτήν.« 3. ἐγὼ δὲ οὐκ ἠθέλησα προσκυνῆσαι, ἀλλ' εἶπον αὐτοῖς· »ἐγὼ οὐ προσκυνῶ θεῷ ἀλλοτρίῳ.« 4. αὐτοὶ δὲ παρεβιάσαντο τὴν παρθένον λέγοντες ὅτι· »ἐὰν γένηταί σοι εἰσελθεῖν εἰς τὴν βασιλείαν Σολομῶν⟨τος⟩, * εἰπὲ αὐτῷ· ›οὐ κοιμηθήσομαι μετά σου ἐὰν μὴ ὁμοιωθῇς τῷ λαῷ μου, καὶ λάβε ἀκρίδας πέντε καὶ σφάξαι

C. XXVI. MSS HPQ = Recc. AB. 1 Ἔλαβον δὲ H: καὶ ἔλαβ. P, ἐγὼ δὲ ἐλ. Q | γυναῖκας: + ἐμαυτοῦ P, + εἰς ἀνάπαυσίν μου Q | πάσας Q | * H f. 33ʳ | κ. βασιλείας — B   2 ὧν B: οὐ H | ἐπορεύθη H | τ. Ἰεβουσ. βασ. ego: τὸν ἰεβ. βασιλέων H, τοὺς Ἰεβουσαίους Q, τὸ ἰεβουσαῖον P 3 εἶδον HQ: ἰδὼν P | γυναῖκα ... αὐτῶν H: ἐκεῖ θυγατέρα ἀνθρώπου Ἰεβουσαίαν B | καὶ — P   4 σφόδρα: + ὡς πολλὰ ὡραίαν οὖσαν Q | ἠθέλησα ... μου H: ἠβουλόμην δέξεσθαι αὐτὴν μετὰ ταῖς γυναιξί μου εἰς γυναῖκα P, ἐζήτησα αὐτὴν ἵνα μου γυναῖκαν μετὰ τῶν ἑτέρων γυναικῶν Q § 2.   5 αὐτῶν: + κ. εἰπ. πρὸς τ. ἱερεῖς linea deleta P | μοι HQ: μου P | Σουμανίτην H: σονμανίτην P, παῖδα Q   6 ὅτι ... σφόδρα H: εἰς γυναῖκα (+ μου Q) B | * Q f. 15ᵛ | με: + οἱ (— Q) ἱερεῖς τοῦ Μολόχ B, add. etiam διότι εἴδωλα ἐσεβόντισαν Q | ἐὰν ἀγαπᾷς B   7 θυγατ. ἡμῶν H: παρθένον B, + εἴσελθε (+ δὲ Q) καὶ B   8 τὸν μέγαν: τῷ μεγάλῳ θεῷ P (+ ἡμῶν) Q | ῥαφὰμ H | Μολόχ: pr. τῶ καλουμένω θεῶ P | καὶ λάβε αὐτ. HQ: — P | § 3. δὲ: οὖν B, + τοῦτο H, + φοβηθεὶς τὴν δόξαν τοῦ θεοῦ (+ ἡμῶν Q) B   6 ἠθελ. HQ: ἠκολούθησα P | προσκυνῆσαι ... ἐγὼ P (καγὼ) Q: — H | οὐ: οὐδὲ H

MSS PQ = Rec. B in fine sectionis 3 (post ἀλλοτρίῳ) et pro sectionibus 4 et 5 praebent textum hunc: καὶ τίς δὲ (κ. τίς δὲ omisso spatioque puro relicto in marg. scr. τίς αὕτη P) ἡ (— Q) ὑπόθεσις ὅτι τοσοῦτον (τοῦτο Q) με ἀναγκάζετε ποιῆσαι; § 4. οἱ δὲ εἶπον· ἵνα ὁμοιωθῇς (ἵνα ὁμ. om. spatioque puro relicto ωθεὶς scr. P) τῶν πατέρων ἡμῶν. (129) ἐμοῦ δὲ πυθομένου ὅτι οὐδαμῶς (οὐδαμὴ Q) προσκυνήσω (προσθύσω Q) θεοῖς ἀλλοτρίοις, αὐτοὶ (καὶ P) παρήγγειλαν τὴν παρθένον τοῦ μὴ κοιμηθῆναί μοι, ἐὰν μὴ πεισθῶ θῦσαι τοῖς θεοῖς (+ αὐτῶν Q)

MS H = Rec. A. § 4. 12 αὐτῷ ego: αὐτῶν H | ad σφάξαι (l. 13) et ἔθυσα (ἔθησα ms.; p. 74*, 4) cf. Dial. Tim. et Aquil., p. 70, et mss. PQ infra; v. Intro p. 38.

αὐτὰς εἰς τὸ ὄνομα Ῥαφὰν καὶ Μολόχ.« 5. ἐγὼ δὲ διὰ τὸ ἀγαπᾶν με τὴν κόρην ὡς ὡραίαν οὖσαν πάνυ, καὶ ὡς ἀσύνετος ὤν, οὐδὲν ἐνόμισα τῶν ἀκρίδων τὸ αἷμα καὶ ἔλαβον αὐτὰς ὑπὸ τὰς χεῖράς μου καὶ ἔθυσα εἰς τὸ ὄνομα Ῥαφὰν καὶ Μολόχ τοῖς 5 εἰδώλοις, καὶ ἔλαβα τὴν παρθένον εἰς τὸν οἶκον τῆς βασιλείας μου.
 6. Καὶ ἀπήρθη τὸ πνεῦμα τοῦ θεοῦ ἀπ᾿ ἐμοῦ, καὶ ἀπ᾿ ἐκείνης τῆς ἡμέρας ἐγένετο ὡς λῆρος τὰ ῥήματά μου. καὶ ἠνάγκασέ με οἰκονομῆσαι ναοὺς τῶν εἰδώλων. 7. κἀγὼ οὖν ὁ δύστη-
10 νος ἐποίησα τὴν συμβουλὴν αὐτῆς καὶ τελείως ἀπέστη ἡ δόξα τοῦ θεοῦ ἀπ᾿ ἐμοῦ καὶ ἐσκοτίσθη τὸ πνεῦμά μου, καὶ ἐγενόμην γέλως τοῖς εἰδώλοις καὶ δαίμοσιν.
 8. Διὰ τοῦτο ἀπέγραψα ταύτην μου τὴν διαθήκην ἵνα οἱ

MSS PQ = Rec. B. § 5. κἀγὼ οὖν ὁ δόλιος (+ καὶ πανάθλιος Q) κινουμένου μου πικροῦ καὶ ἀσώτου βέλους τοῦ ἔρωτος τῆς κόρης, ἔδωκα ἐπίσχυσιν, καὶ (πικροῦ ... ἐπισχ. καὶ Q: ἔρως παρ᾿ αὐτῇ P) ἔφερέν μοι πέντε ἀκρίδας (P f. 24ᵛ) λέγων (+ μοι Q)· λάβε ταύτας τὰς ἀκρίδας καὶ σύντριψον αὐτὰς ἐπ᾿ ὀνόματος (·ατι Q) τοῦ θεοῦ Μολόχ (+ καὶ Ῥαφὰ Q), καὶ (+ νῦν P) κοιμηθήσομαι μετά σου. ὅπερ καὶ ἐτέλεσα (+ ἐγὼ τὴν ἀπώλειαν ταύτην Q).
MSS PQ = Rec. B pro § 6 textum praebent hunc: καὶ (+ ταῦτα ποιήσας ὁ ἄθλιος Q) εὐθὺς ἀπέστη (+ ἀπ᾿ ἐμοῦ Q) τὸ πνεῦμα (+ τὸ ἅγιον Q) τοῦ θεοῦ, (+ ἀπ᾿ ἐμοῦ P, + καὶ ἅπασα ἡ δόξα καὶ ἡ σοφία Q), καὶ ἐγενόμην ἀσθενὴς ὡσεὶ λῆρος τοῖς ῥήμασί μου (καὶ τὰ ῥήματά μου ὡς ἡ — ὡσεὶ Kurz — λῆρος Q)· ἐξ οὗ καὶ ἠναγκάσθην (·σθη P) παρ᾿ αὐτῆς (αὐτοῖς Q) κτίσαι ναὸν τῶν εἰδώλων τῇ Βαὰλ (Τηβὰλ Q) καὶ τῷ (— Q) Ῥαφὰ καὶ τῷ (τὸν) Μολὸχ καὶ τοῖς λοιποῖς εἰδώλοις (τῶν λοιπῶν εἰδώλων Q)
MS H = Rec. A. § 6. 7 ἀπήρθη ego: ἐπήρθη ms.

MS H = Rec. A pro sectione 7 textum, ut mihi videtur, interpolatum praebet nunc: ἐγὼ δὲ ὁ δύστινος ᾠκοδόμησα διὰ τὸ πάνη ἀγαπᾶν αὐτήν. καὶ διεράγη ἡ βασιλεία μου καὶ ὀλόλυξα μεγάλως, καὶ ἐσκορπίσθη τὸ πν(εῦμ)α καὶ ἐδόθη εἰς δουλείαν τὸν ὀβροὰμ (* f. 34ʳ) σκῆπτρα ί'· τὸ συνη (sic) κατὰ ⟨τὰ⟩ ῥηθέντα μοι ὑπὸ τῶν δαιμόνων, ὅτι ἔφησάν μοι· ὑπὸ τὰς χεῖρεις ἡμῶν μέλλεις τελευτῆσαι.«
MSS PQ = Rec. B a sectione 7 usque ad finem praebent breviorem et, ut mihi videtur, meliorem textum. § 7. 9 κἀγὼ οὖν P: ὅπερ ἐγὼ Q   10 ἐποίησα ... αὐτῆς P: κατηργασάμην ἅπαντα Q   11 ἀπ᾿ ἐμοῦ post ἀπέστη ponit Q | 12 καὶ παίγνιον τοῖς δαίμοσιν Q

MS H = Rec. A pro § 8 textum interpolatum praebet hunc: καὶ ἔγραψα τὴν διαθήκην μου ταύτην τοῖς ιουδαίοις καὶ κατέλιπον ταύτην αὐτοῖς εἰς μνημόσυνον πρὸς τελευτῆς μου. ἡ διαθήκη μου φυλαττέσθω παρ᾿ ὑμῶν (ἡμῶν ms.)
MSS PQ = Rec. B. § 8. 13 διὰ γὰρ Q

ἀκούοντες εὔχησθε καὶ προσέχητε τοῖς ἐσχάτοις καὶ μὴ τοῖς πρώτοις, ἵνα τελείως εὕρωσι χάριν εἰς τοὺς αἰῶνας· ἀμήν.

εἰς μυστήριον μέγαν κατὰ πνευμάτων ἀκαθάρτων ὥστε γνῶναι ὑμᾶς (ἡμῶν ms.) τῶν πονηρῶν δαιμόνων τὰς μηχανὰς καὶ τῶν ἁγίων (τὸν ἅγιον ms.) ἀγγέλων τὰς δυνάμεις· ὅτι ἐνισχύει μέγας κύριος σαβαὼθ ὁ θεὸς τοῦ ἰσραὴλ καὶ ὑπέταξεν ἐπ' ἐμοὶ πάντα τὰ δαιμόνια, ἐν ᾧ ἐδόθη μοι σφραγὶς διαθήκης αἰωνίου. ταῦτα οὖν ἔγραψον ἅπερ κατέλαβον μετὰ τῶν υἰῶν ἰσραὴλ ⌐πν(ευ-μάτ)ων τε πν(εῦμ)α τὸ ἀκαθάρτων (f. 34ᵛ) ὀνειδισμῶν προσφέρωσιν⌐ εἰς τὰ ἅγια τῶν ἁγίων. § 9. ἐγὼ οὖν σολομῶν υἱὸς δα(υεὶ)δ υἱοῦ ἰεσσαὶ ἔγραψα τὴν διαθήκην μου καὶ ἐσφράγισα αὐτὴν (αὐτῶν ms.) τῷ δακτυλιδίῳ τοῦ θεοῦ. καὶ ἀπέθανον ἐν τῇ βασιλείᾳ μου καὶ προσετέθην μετὰ τῶν π(ατέ)ρων μου ἐν εἰρήνῃ ἐν ἱ(ερουσα)λήμ. καὶ ἐπληρώθη ὁ ναὸς κυρίου τοῦ θεοῦ οὗ ὑπὸ θρόνου αὐτοῦ ποταμὸς (πυρὸς ex Dan. VII 10 suppl. James) ἕλκει· ᾧ παρειστήκεισαν μυριάδες ἀγγέλων καὶ χιλιάδες ἀρχαγγέλων καὶ χερουβὶμ ἐπικράζοντα σεραφὶμ κεκραγότα καὶ λέγοντα· ἅγιος, ἅγιος, ἅγιος κύριος σαβαὼθ καὶ εὐλογητὸς εἶ εἰς τοὺς αἰῶνας τῶν αἰώνων· ἀμήν.

§ 10. δόξα σοι, ὁ θεός μου, καὶ κ(ύριο)ς, δόξα σοι
σὺν τῇ ὑπ⟨ε⟩ρευκ⟨λεεῖ⟩(?) θ(εοτό)κῳ καὶ τῷ τιμίῳ
προδρόμῳ καὶ πάντας ἁγίους, δόξα σοι.

MSS PQ = Rec. B. 1 ἀκούοντες: λαχόντες P | εὔχησθε Q: εὔχεσθε P, + μοι ὅπερ ῥυσθῶ τοῦ σκότους καὶ τῆς κολάσεως τῆς πικρᾶς ὡς θεῷ παρήκοος (Kurz: παρήκωος ms.) Q | προσέχητε Q: προσέχετε P, + ὀφείλην τοῖς ἀνθρώποις Q | · καὶ μὴ P: τὰ μάλλον ἢ Q   2 τελείως — Q

Lectiones novas et emendationes ex ms. N (Sancti Saba) v. in App., infra p. 112ff.

ΔΙΑΘΗΚΗ ΣΟΛΟΜΩΝΤΟΣ

Recensio C

Prologus

1. Ἐγένετο μετὰ τὸ ἀποθανεῖν τὸν Δαυεὶδ τὸν βασιλέαν προσευξαμένου τοῦ υἱοῦ αὐτοῦ οἰκοδομεῖν τὴν Σιών, προσευχομένου δὲ αὐτοῦ ἦλθεν φωνὴ λέγουσα· »Σολομῶν υἱὸς Δαυείδ, κύριος ὁ θεὸς τῶν πατέρων σου αὐτὸς εἰσακούσας τῆς προσευχῆς σου δέδωκά σοι πᾶσαν τὴν ἰσχύν, καὶ ἰδοὺ ἔσῃ βλέπων πᾶσαν τὴν σοφίαν λελευκασμένην ὡς χιόναν ἐνώπιόν σου καὶ τῶν ὀφθαλμῶν σου.« 2. Ταῦτα ἀκούσας καὶ ὥσπερ ὑπό τινος αὐγῆς ἐλλαμφθεὶς καὶ ἐμπνευσθεὶς τὴν διάνοιαν ἦν παρακαλῶν καὶ δεόμενος τοῦ θεοῦ λέγων οὕτως· »θεὲ αἰώνιε«, ἔφη, »θεὲ ἀπερινόητε, ἄκτιστε καὶ ἀόρατε, ὁ πάντα κτίσας τῷ νεύματί σου μόνῳ, ἔπιδε τοῦ δούλου σου δέησιν καὶ διασάφησον τὴν τῶν χειρῶν σου ἐνέργειαν. 3. καὶ γὰρ ὅσα ἐποίησας σὺ ὁ θεός, πρὸς σύστασιν πάντων τῶν ἡμετέρων σωμάτων ἐποίησας καὶ ὠφέλειαν, τά τε καρποφόρα καὶ μὴ καρποφόρα δένδρα, θηρία τε καὶ πετεινά, καὶ αὐτὸν δὴ τὸν θεῖον ἀέραν ὃν πᾶσα φύσις ἐπιπνέει. 4. τὸ μέγιστόν σε τοίνυν δυσωπῶ ἵνα διανοιχθῶσί μου οἱ ὀφθαλμοὶ καὶ ὁρῶ τὴν ἀποκεκρυμμένην σοφίαν σου, ὅτι εὐλογητὸς εἶ εἰς τοὺς αἰῶνας· ἀμήν.« 5. ταῦτα τοίνυν εὐξαμένου φωνῆς

MSS VW. conspectum titulorum vide infra, p. 99*. **4** τὸν (1°): — V
6 αὐτοῦ: αὐτὸν V | φωνὴ: φο(νὴν) V **7** δ: — W | εἰσακούσει V
9 καὶ ἐν τοῖς ὀφθαλμοῖς σου W § 2. 1. **11** ἐλαμφῆς ἐπνευσθῆς (— καὶ) V
| παρακαλῶ V **12** οὕτως — V | ἀπεριν.: + θεὲ ἐών V **13** τὸν
εὔματι V **14** ἔπιδε: ἐπι ἐπι V § 3. 1. **16** ὑμετέρων V § 4. 1. **21** αἰῶνας τῶν αἰώνων W | § 5. τοίνυν: δεύτερον V

ἤκουσεν λεγούσης· »Σολομῶν, Σολομῶν, κύριος ὁ θεός σου ἐρεῖ· ἄρξαι κτίζειν μου οἶκον εἰς ὄνομα τῆς ἐπουρανίου μου Σιών.‹ καὶ ἤρξατο οἰκοδομεῖν τὴν Σιών.

8. Καὶ ταῦτα εἰπὼν ἔφη μετὰ κλανθμοῦ· * »δέομαί σου, βασιλεῦ Σολομῶν, ἵνα μή με κατακαύσῃς ὑπὸ τῆς σφραγῖδος, καὶ ὑπόσχομαί σοι ἐν ὅρκῳ ὅτι εἰς τὸ ὄνομα τοῦ Ὄντος προσφέρω ʼσοι πάντα τὰ δαιμόνια καὶ παραδώσω σοι ταῦτα ὑποχειρίους δι' ἑνὸς ἑκάστου σημείων καὶ τῶν δυνατῶν καὶ τῶν δυναμένων καὶ τῶν ἐξουσιαζόντων.« καὶ εἶπον ἐγὼ Σολομῶν· »εἰ τοῦτο ποιήσεις, ἔσῃ ἐλεύθερος.« 9. καὶ λέγει μοι· »λάμβανε ἐρίφους μελανοὺς ἀγεννήτους εἰς ἀριθμὸν ποσουμένων να', καὶ ἔνεγκέ μοι μάχαιραν καινὴν τρίκωλον μελανοκέρατον, καὶ ἐκδείραντες τὰς ἐρίφους.« 10. εἶτα προσέταξεν ἐναχθῆναι αἷμαν ἀνθρώπινον τοῦ δευθῆναι τὰ δέρματα καὶ ἔρραψεν αὐτὰ ἀνὰ δύο φύλλων καὶ ἔρρυψεν αὐτὰ ἐν τριωδίῳ, καὶ εὗρεν γεγραμμένον ἑνὸς ἑκάστου ὄνομα ἰδιοχείρως ἐν τοῖς δερματίοις καὶ τὸ ση-

MSS VW. 1 λεγούσης: + αὐτὸν W, + πρὸς αὐτὸν U
MSS UVW. πρὸς αὐτὸν· Σολομῶν... ἐρεῖ exscr. editores ex MS U cf. supra, Introd. p. 20f. | ἐρεῖ U: ἔρει V, ἐρεῖ W
MSS VW. Textus recensionis C cc. I—IX 7 cum recc. A et B supra pp. 5*—37* exhibitur. 4 § 8. κλαυμοῦ W | * V f. 439ᵛ 5 βασ. Σολ.: βασιλεύς V 7 παραδίδω V 8 ἑκάστου αὐτοῦ V | σημείων: + καὶ εἶπα ἐγὼ σολομῶν καὶ V | τ(ὸν) δυνατ(ὸν) καὶ τ(ὸν) δυνάμενον καὶ τ(ὸν) ἐξουσιάζοντα V 9 τοὺς ἐξουσιάζοντας W 10 ἔσῃ: ἔστο V
MSS TUVW. § 9. l. 10 καὶ λέγει μοι VW: Δαίμων σφραγισάμενος ὑπὸ Σαλυμῶνος τάδε εἶπε· δαιμονίων δυνάμεις καὶ ὀνόματα (ὀνομ. inter lineas sub δαιμ. δυναμ. scr.) hoc modo inc. fragmentum ms. U §§ 9—10. l. 10—14 καὶ ... δέρματα: ἔτερα πρᾶξις τῆς αὐτῆς. ὁμοίως παιδίον παρθένον καθαρὸν· κάθισον εἰς ἄμουλον (f. 39b²) καὶ ξύσον μετὰ ἐλαίου ἀπὸ τηγανίου κόλον εἰς τὴν παλάμην τοῦ παιδίου, καὶ λέγε ταῦτα τὰ ὀνόματα ἕως ἑπτὰ φορές· Ναχπιέλ· Ναχπιέλ· Χατμήν· Ἑρμήν· μελανοκέρατο τοῦ δευθῆναι τὰ δέρματα, καὶ μετὰ τοῦ δευθῆναι τὰ δέρματα λαβὼν ὁ βεελζεβοὺλ· τὰ $\overline{να}$ δέρματα hoc modo inc. sectio in Clavicula = ms. T § 9. l. 11 ἀγεννήτους: pr. καὶ + καὶ ἔλαβεν ἐκ πάντων τῶν θρεμμάτων αὐτοῦ V | ποσουμένων UW: ποσον V 12 τρίκωλον ego: τρῆκλον V, τρίκλον vel τρίηλον UW § 10. l. 14 δευθῆναι V | καὶ — TV | ἔρραψεν ... τριωδίῳ TV: ἐποίησα οὕτως καὶ ἔρρυψεν αὐτὰ ἐν τριωδίῳ ἀνὰ δύο φύλλων UW | ἔρραψεν ... ἔρρυψεν: ἔραψεν .. ἔρηψεν T, ἔρηψεν .. ἔρηψεν V, ἔρριψεν U, ἔρυψεν W 15 τριμδίῳ: l. fortasse τριόδῳ, pr. τῶ T | γεγραμμένα mss. 16 ἐν ... αὐτοῦ(3°) p. 78*, 1: — T | σημεῖον αὐτοῦ: σιμάδη του V

μεῖον αὐτοῦ καὶ τὴν ἐνέργειαν αὐτοῦ καὶ τὴν δεσποτείαν αὐτοῦ οὕτως·

X. Τζιανφιέλ· * δεσπόζει ρμ'· ἐνεργεῖ δὲ εἰς τὸ ἀναγγεῖλαι τὰ παρεληλυθότα καὶ τὰ ἐνεστῶτα καὶ τὰ μέλλοντα. 2. Φα-
5 ράν· * δεσπόζει ͵α· ἐνεργεῖ δὲ εἰς τὸ πληρεῖν πάντα τὰ θελήματα. δύναται καὶ πῦρ ἀναβιβάζειν εἰς τὸν ἀέρα καὶ ὕδωρ κατάγειν καὶ ἀστέρας ὑποδεικνύειν. 3. Μαχουμέτ· * δεσπόζει σ΄· ἐνεργεῖ εἰς τὸ γελᾶν ἀνθρώπους ἀλλήλων. ποιεῖ δὲ καὶ τετράποδα λαλεῖν ἀνθρωπίνως καὶ ἀναφαίνεσθαι τοὺς ἀνθρώπους
10 ἀκεφάλους. ποιεῖ δὲ τούτους * γυμνοὺς περιπατεῖν ἀλλὰ καὶ τὰ ἄλογα κτήνη βλέπειν ἀλλήλα ὡς θηρία ἄγρια. 4. Ναπούρ· * δεσπόζει ν΄· δύναται ἐν μιᾷ ὥρᾳ παρέχειν χρυσίον καὶ ἀργύριον ὅπερ διεπράξας πρὸς τῆς ἀπαντῆς σου τῆς ζωῆς καὶ τῆς γεννήσεως μέχρι τότε, ὁμοίως καὶ στολὰς μὴ ῥηγνυμένας. 5. Ῥοάπτ·
15 * δεσπόζει υ΄· ἐνεργεῖ δὲ εἰς τὸ γενέσθαι φρόνιμον καὶ νοῦν ἐμφύειν. 6. Παρέλ· * δεσπόζει κε΄· ἐνεργεῖ δὲ εἰς τὸ ἀνθῆσαι τὰ δένδρα παρὰ καιρόν, φῦναι δὲ καὶ βοτάνας εἰς ξηρὸν ξύλον.

MSS TUVW. 1 δεσπ. αὐτοῦ: ἀρχὴν του V   2 οὕτως UW: ταῦτα T, — V
C. X 1. l. 3 Τζιανφιέλ TV: Τζηαν. UW, pr. ā' T, pr. ὁ πρῶτος ἔχει ὄνομαν V. In hoc loco et in locis sequentibus asterisco denotatis mss. habent post nomen sive ante nomen signum (σημεῖον) daemonis; in hoc loco signum ante nomen ponunt UW; in marg. sin. apud nomina numeros ab α' ad ιϛ' scr. V, in textu ante nomina numeros ab initio ad finem scr. T | δεσπ.: + ἐνεργίαις T | ρμ': ρ' T | δὲ — V   4 § 2. A secundo ad extremum ante nomen scr. ὁ T | in locis XI (§§ 2, 3, 4, 5, 8, 11, 14, 17, 18, 29, 45) signum post δεσπόζει ponit T; in locis V (§§ 12, 38. 40, 42, 44) signum post numerum imperii (= δεσποτείας) ponit T   5 ͵α: η' U | πληρεῖν UW: πληρῇ V, πληροῦν T | πάντα — V   6 δύναται: pr. καὶ V | εἰς: + τω transversis lineis delet. U | ἀναβηβάζει V   7 κατάγει UVW | ὑποδεικνήει V § 3. l. 8 ἐνεργεῖ δὲ T | εἰς τὸ — T | ἀνθρώποις UVW | ἀλλήλων τοῖς ἀνθρώποις T | καὶ — T   9 ἀναφαιν. T: νὰ φαίνεσται V, φαίνεσθαι UW | τοὺς ἀνθρ. ἀκεφ. ego: οἱ ἀν(θρωπ)οι ἀκέφαλοι mss.   10 ᵏ L f. 40ʳ¹ | γυμνοὺς T: — UVW   11 τὰ ἀλ. κτήνη ego: τοῖς ἀλόγοις κτήνεσιν mss. | ἐβλέπει T | ἀλλήλα ego: ἀλλήλοις TUW, ἀλείης V | ὡς: ὁ V   § 4. l. 12 ἀργύριον καὶ χρυσίον T | ἄργυρ < U   13 τ. ἀπαντῆς U: τῆς ἀπαντῆ W, τὴν ἀπάντη V, τὴν T | τῆς ζωῆς καὶ — T   14 μέχρι τότε ὁμοίως V: — UW, ὁμοίως τότε μέχρι T | καὶ — T   § 5. l. 15 τινὰ ἀφρόνιμον T | φρένιμον V | κ. νοῦν ἐμφ. — T   16 ἐμφυῇ UVW | § 6. Παρελκοζίον (sine signo) κοζίου pro signo scr. T   17 δένδρι παρὰ καιρῷ V | φῦναι: φόνε T | δὲ — T

7. Ἀσμοδεῶ· δεσπόζει ξ'· δύναται ἐν τῷ θέρει παρέχειν χιόνας καὶ βρέχειν, ἀλλὰ καὶ κεράσια παρέχειν ἐν χειμῶνι. 8. Μπηλέτ· * δεσπόζει σ'· δύναται εἴ τι θέλει ποιῆσαι ἐν τῷ μέρει τῆς Παλαιστίνης. 9. Λασαράκ· * δεσπόζει τ'. δύναται ποιῆσαι πολέμους καὶ παρατάξεις καὶ νίκας καὶ ἀνδραγαθίας. 10. Ῥααμέτ· * δεσπόζει σ'· οὗτος προλέγει τὰ μέλλοντα καὶ πλουτοδοτεῖ. 11. Τζερεπόνες· * δεσπόζει ρν'· δύναται ποιῆσαι καὶ συντύχωσιν ἰστορίαι καὶ τὰ εἴδολα, ἀκούειν δὲ καὶ ὀρνέων * φωνάς. 12. Νταρωγάν· * δεσπόζει τ'· ἐνεργεῖ δὲ εἰς τὸ καθαριεῦσαι πᾶσαν ῥυπαρίαν καὶ τοὺς πτωχοὺς ὡς πλουσίους ποιῆσαι, καὶ εἰ ἔσται αὐτοῦ, βασιλεύει. 13. Πελών· * δεσπόζει α· ἐνεργεῖ δὲ εἰς τὸ παραδοῦναι κάστρα καὶ πόλεις καὶ χώρας. 14. Σουπιέλ· * δεσπόζει α· ἐνεργεῖ δὲ εἰς τὸ ποιῆσαι ἐπανάστησιν κατὰ τοῦ δεσπότου καὶ παραδοῦναι ἑτέρῳ τῷ ἄρχοντι εἰς τὸ ἄρχειν καὶ ἐλευθερῶσαι δεσμίους ἐν ταῖς φυλακαῖς ὁμοίως καὶ αἰχμαλότους. 15. Ὀριένς· * δεσπόζει φ' πνευμάτων τῶν ἀνατολικῶν· δύναται καὶ αὐτὸς ὁμοίως ὅσα δύνανται οἱ πάντες. 16. Ἀμεμῶν· * δεσπόζει μεσημβρινῶν πνευμάτων φ'· δύναται καὶ αὐτὸς ὁμοίως.

17. Ἐλτζήν· * δεσπόζει βορείων ** πνευμάτων φ'· δύναται καὶ αὐτὸς ὁμοίως. 18. Πανῶν· * δεσπόζει καὶ οὗτος τῶν πνευμάτων τῶν θαλασσίων χ'· ἐνεργεῖ δὲ καὶ αὐτὸς εἰς ἀνέμους

MSS TUVW. 1 § 7. ἀσμοδέος T, ἀσμοδεὼ U | ἐν τῷ ... δύναται (l. 3): — T | παρέχειν: κατεχ < V   2 βρέξει V | χειμωναν V
§ 8. 1. 4 Παλαιστίνης TU: παλεστ. V, παληστ. W   § 9 l. 5 ἀντραγαθίας V   6 § 10. Ῥααμέτ: ῥαεμέτ V, ραιμὲτ T, + καὶ αὐτὸς UW | οὗτος ... πλουτοδ.: δύναται τοῦ προλέγει⟨ν⟩ τὰ μελ. κ. πλουτοδοτεῖν T | πλουτωδωτή VW   7 § 11. τζερεπάωνες UW | καὶ: — W, l. fortasse ἵνα? 8 συντήχωσιν UW | συντειχόσην εστοριε V, συντυχοσιν ηδοριαι T | καὶ ἀκούην φωνὰς ὀρνέων πετεινῶν T | δὲ — V | * explicit fragmentum ms. U
MSS TVW. 9 § 12. ἰτάρογαν T | ἐνεργεῖ δὲ: δύναται T | καριεῦσαι πᾶσα T   § 13. l. 12 κάστρα ... χώρας: κάστοι κ. χώρας T   13 § 14. signum om. T ·| ‚α: μ' T | ἐπανάστασι V   14 τῷ ἀρχ. εἰς — T | 15 τὲς φυλακὲς W, τῆς φυλακῆς V   16 § 15. τῶν — V | ἀνατολικῶν τῶν πνευμάτων T   17 δύναται καὶ tr. V | δύνανται: δύνοντ(ο) T 18 § 16. ἀμαιμῶν V   20 § 17. ἐλτζεῖν V, ἐλτζὶν T | * V f. 440^r | βοριὴν V | ** W f. 269^v 21 ὁμοίως: οὕτως T   §§ 18—19. ll. 21—p. 80*, 1 καὶ οὕτως ... αὐτὸς — T   § 18. 1. 22 θαλασσίην V | καὶ — V

καὶ πλοῖα. 19. Βούλ· * δεσπόζει καὶ αὐτὸς πνευμάτων τῆς δύσεως φ'· δύναται καὶ αὐτὸς ὁμοίως. 20. Ἀμπατζούτ· δεσπόζει καὶ αὐτὸς ͵α· ἐνεργεῖ δὲ εἰς πᾶσαν τέχνην καὶ μάθησιν καὶ φρόνησιν καὶ γράμματα. 21. Ἀσταρώθ· * δεσπόζει ͵β· 5 ἐνεργεῖ δὲ εἰς τοὺς ἀπερχομένους καὶ ἐξερχομένους καὶ στήκοντας· ποιεῖ δὲ καὶ θησαυροὺς φανερωθῆναι. 22. Λουπήτ· * δεσπόζει ͵ε· ἐνεργεῖ δὲ εἰς τὸ ἀκούειν καὶ κράτειν καὶ πράττειν, κτίζειν καὶ χαλᾶν καὶ βλέπειν καὶ μεταφέρειν ἀπὸ τόπου εἰς τόπον. 23. Ἀπολήν· * δεσπόζει ͵ρ· ἐνεργεῖ δὲ εἰς τὸ πλουτῆσαι 10 καὶ παρέχειν χρυσίον καὶ ἄργυρον πολύν. 24. Ἀστερώθ· * δεσπόζει ͵α· ἐνεργεῖ δὲ εἰς βασιλείας καὶ πόλεις καὶ κάστρα καὶ πύργους καὶ κτίσματα. 25. Λάτζηφερ· * δεσπόζει ͵γ· ἐνεργεῖ εἰς πάντας τοὺς ἄρχοντας δηλαδὴ. καὶ εἰς τοὺς βασιλεῖς, καὶ δύναται καὶ ὅσα θέλει.. 26. Μαγώτ· * δεσπόζει καὶ αὐτὸς ͵δ· ἐνεργεῖ * 15 δὲ εἰς τὸ λέγειν καὶ ποιεῖν. 27. Καράπ· * δεσπόζει ͵ζ· ἐνεργεῖ δὲ εἰς πόλεις καὶ κάστρα καὶ οἴκους. 28. Οὔλεος· * δεσπόζει μιᾶς φυλῆς, ἤτοι ἅ. ποιεῖ δὲ μεγιστάνους καὶ στολὰς λαμπρὰς καὶ παίγνια καὶ παροφθαλμίας, καὶ ποιεῖ ὄνους τοὺς ἀνθρώπους καὶ ἄλλα ζῷα οἷα θέλεις. 29. Κρινέλ· * δεσπόζει ὄ· ἐνεργεῖ 20 δὲ εἰς τὸ ἀναιρεῖν ἄνδρας τε καὶ γυναῖκας, ποιεῖ δὲ μάχας καὶ ταραχὰς καὶ ὀχλήσεις. 30. Τουγέλ· * δεσπόζει ͵χ· ποιεῖ δὲ ἀγά-

MSS TVW. 1 § 19. πνευμάτων ... ὁμοίως: τῶν τ(ῆς) δύσεως πν(ευμάτ)ων δύναντ(αι) καὶ αὐτὸς ὅσα δύναντ(αι) οἱ πάντες T | καὶ pr. δὲ W | § 20. l. 3 δὲ — W | κ. μάθησιν — T 4 κ. γράμματα V: κ. πράγμα Τ, — W § 21. l. 5 δὲ καὶ αὐτὸς T | τοὺς — T | κ. ἐξερχομ. — T § 22. l. 7 ε' T | ἐνεργεῖν W | δὲ καὶ αὐτὸς T | τὸ: τοὺς T | καὶ (2°) — VW 8 κ. χαλᾶν ... βλέπειν — W | χαλᾶν ego: χαλνὰν T, χαλάτι V | μεταφέρει VW | τόπου: τόπον VW 9 § 23. Ἀπολήν V: ἀπόλην W, ἀπολιΐ T | ρ': φ' W 10 παρέχει TW | § 24. ἀστηρώθ W, ὁ ἕτερος ἀστηρώθ T | καὶ οὗτος δεσπόζει V 11 ἐνεργεῖ ... κάστρα: δύναται δὲ καὶ βασιλείαν πόλιν κάστρη T | κ. πύργους — W, πυργοὺς T 12 § 25. λατζιφέρ T | ͵γ· ἐνεργεῖ εἰς — T 13 δηλαδὴ: + δύνανται T | κ. δύνανται ... θέλει V: δύναται ὅσα θέλει T, — W 14 § 26. μαγότ W | καὶ αὐτὸς — T | ἐνεργεῖ: δύναται T | * T f. 40ᵛ² 15 λέγειν: + ἐνεργεῖν T § 27. l. 16 πόλιν κάστροι T | § 28. οὐλατὸς T 17 ἤτοι: ἤτι V, ἤτης T | α' T | ἐνεργεῖ δὲ ποιεῖν μεγιστάνους T 18 παροφθ. TW: παρεροα (α, ε, et o supra lin.) in fine lineae, ὀφθαλμίας in linea altera scr. V | ποιεῖ ego: ποιεῖν W, πιὴν V, ἢν T 19 ἀλία ζῷα οἱ καὶ θελ < V | θέλης T, θελ < W | § 29. σ' T | ἐνεργεῖν W 20 καὶ ποιεῖ δὲ T 21 κ. ὀχλησ. — T | § 30. τοῦγελ T | ἀγάπας καὶ φιλίας W

πας, πόλεις προς πόλεις και ανθρώπους μετά ανθρώπων και άνδρας μετά γυναικών. 31. Σεταριέλ· * δεσπόζει κ'· φανερεί θησαυρούς, ποιεί δε και τον χρώμενον αθεώρητον, παρά μηδενός θεωρούμενον. παρέχει δε και ταις γυναιξίν γνώμας χρηστάς. 32. Φακανέλ· * δεσπόζει ζ· ενεργεί δε εις πάντα τα θελήματα του βουλομένου. 33. Όέλ· * δεσπόζει γ· δύναται δε και αυτός όσα δύνανται οι πάντες αυτός μόνος. 34. Λένελ· * δεσπόζει λ'· ενεργεί δε εις το παρέχειν χρυσίον και αργύριον· και φέρει γυναίκας παρά μηδενός θεωρούμενος. 35. Σαρατιέλ· * δεσποζει ρ'· ενεργεί δε εις σεληνιαζομένους· δοκεί δε και την σελήνην καταβιβάζειν. 36. Μυρατζιέλ· * δεσπόζει β'· ενεργεί δε εις στρατείας και πολιορκίας και πόλεων αιχμαλωσίας. 37. Σανσωνιέλ· * δεσπόζει ςτ'· ενεργεί δε εις το ποιήσαι κλύδωνας μεγίστους και ανέμους σφοδρούς. 38. Ἀσιέλ· * δεσπόζει ι'· ενεργεί εις το φανερωθήναι τα κλεπτόμενα και τους κλέπτας και θησαυρούς τινας, επιγινωσκομένους μεν εις τόπον, μη γινωσκομένους δε εν ποίω μέρει κείνται του τόπου. 39. Καστιέλ· * δεσπόζει σ'· ενεργεί δε εις το υγιάναι πάσαν ασθένειαν. 40 Μεινγέτ· * δεσπόζει ξ'· δύνα-

---

MSS TVW. 1 πόλεις ego: πόλας V, πολλάς TW | πόλεις (2°) W: πόλας V, πόλιν T | άνθρωπον μετά ανθρώπου T 2 γυναικός (-κος bis, primum compendio, tum in linea altera scr.) T | 31. Σεταριέλ: σε in fine lineae, εταριέλ in linea altera scr. V | φανερεί... θεωρούμενον (l. 4): exscr. Gaulminius in notis ad Psellum, de oper. daem. (Migne, PG 122, col. 829, n. 25) φανερεί: εμφαίνει Gaulmin. 3 παρά: υπό Gaulmin. | ουδενός T 4 δε — T 5 § 32 και ενεργεί (εν. ex δύναμαι corr.) εις T § 33. l. 7 δύναται... μόνος: και οδάν (f. 41 r 1) ὁ δύναται οι πάντες αυτός μόνος ενεργεί, et ad marg. sup. in med. col. scr. λα' T | και δύναται αυτός δια δυν. ή δλη (l. οι όλοι) αυτός μόνος του V 7 § 34. Λένελ V: ὁ δελήνηλ T, νένελ W | λ' VW: σ' T 9 αργ. κ. χρυσ. T | κ. φόρει T: κ. φέρνει V, φέρει δε και W 10 μηδεν.: μιθεν < V § 35. l. 11 σεληνιαζ.: ελληνικά πάθη T 12 § 36. μιρατζηέλ W, μυρακιέλ T, + ὁ δαίμων και αυτός (ante signum) W | β'· β T | εις: ει V | στρατείας: αστραπάς T | και πόλεων: tr. W 13 § 37. σανσονιέλ T 14 ςτ': ς και τ' V | κλύδωνας: ς ex ν corr. W | μεγίστους T: μεγιστ < V, μεγάλους W 15 post σφοδρούς signum scr. V; post spatium purum parvulum relictum scr. * signum W; tum ενεργεί δε (— V) και αυτός ομοίως add. VW | § 38. ι' — T | και ενεργεί T 16 επιγιν.... μη — T 17 μεν: δε V | εν ... τόπου: εν ποίω τόπω κείνται W 18 κείται V | § 39. αστιέλ T | ενεργεί: οφελεί V 19 υγιένε V | § 40 μεινγέτ W, μηνγέτ V, μινγότ T

UNT. 9: McCown. 6*

ται ὄφεις καὶ δράκοντας ποιῆσαι. 41. Ἐνοδάς· * δεσπόζει ν'·
δύναται * εἰς τὸν ἀέραν πῦρ ἀνάγειν καὶ ἅρματα ἐμφανῶς κα-
τακαῦσαι. 42. Ἀτανιανούς· * δεσπόζει ͺα· δύναται δοῦναι πᾶσαν τέχνην καὶ γνῶσιν καὶ φρόνησιν τοῖς ἀνθρώποις.
5   43. Μυραγκούς· * δεσπόζει λ'· δύναται κρατεῖν τὸν ἥλιον
τοῦ μὴ φαίνεσθαι. 44. Ποτζέτιες· * δεσπόζει σ'· δύναται ποιῆσαι ἀνθρώπους καὶ ζῷα ἀνελθεῖν εἰς τὸν ἀέραν. 45. Ἄνετ·*
δεσπόζει ρ'· γνωρίζει δὲ ὅλας τὰς πέτρας καὶ τοὺς μαργάρους
ποιεῖ καὶ τὰ ἄλλα μέταλλα. 46. Παλτάφωτε· * δεσπόζει ι'·
10 ποιεῖ γνωρίζειν πάντα τὰ βότανα καὶ ποῦ ἕκαστον ἐνεργεῖ καί
ὠφελεῖ. 47. Σαπαρατζήλ· * δεσπόζει ν'· ποιεῖ γνωρίζειν τὰ
ὄρνεα πάντα καὶ ποῦ ἕκαστον ἐνεργεῖ. 48. Ταρσεύς· *δεσπόζει ξ'·
ποιεῖ δὲ γνωρίζειν τὰ δένδρα καὶ ποῦ ἕκαστον ἐνέργει. 49. Ναβέλ·
* δεσπόζει μ'· ποιεῖ δὲ γνωρίζει τὰ τετράποδα πάντα καὶ ποῦ
15 ἕκαστον ὠφελεῖ. 50. Σαταήλ· * δεσπόζει ε'· ἐνεργεῖ εἰς τοὺς
κροκοδείλους καὶ παρέχει * τούτους εἰς ὑποταγήν. 51. Ναπα-
λαικόν· * δεσπόζει ε'· δύναται ποιῆσαι τὴν ἡμέραν νύκταν καὶ
τὴν νύκταν ἡμέραν. 52. Μακατάκ· * δεσπόζει ε'· ἐνεργεῖ δὲ εἰς
τὸ πληθῦναι τὰ ποίμνια καὶ τοὺς ἵππους.
20   53. Ἐγὼ δὲ ἐν ἀποκρύφῳ θέμενος τόπῳ καταλιμπάνω τοῖς
τέκνοις μου ὅρκῳ παραδοὺς θεοῦ Σαβαὼθ ἁγίου ὀνόματος τοῦ

MSS TVW. 1 § 41. * L f. 41ʳ2   2 ἀέραν VW: ἄρα T | ἀνάγειν
VW: ἀναγαγῇ T   3 § 42. Ἀτανιανούς: ἀντιναός T, + καὶ αὐτὸς W
4 τέχνην: + δοῦναι T | τοὺς ἀνθρώπους T
  § 43. 1. 5 μιραγκούς W, μύρακος T | καὶ δύναται T   6 τοῦ Wv
— TV | § 44. ποτζέτιος T   7 ἀνελθεῖν T: — VW | ἀέρα T, ut semper·
§ 45. 1. 8 δύναται γνωρίζειν ὅλας T | πέτρας: + ποιεῖ T | τοὺς — W
9 ποιεῖ — T | § 46. παλταφάτε T | ι' T | * V f. 440ᵛ   10 γνορίζει V
| πάντα — T | ἐνεργεῖν T | ὠφελεῖ καὶ ἐνεργ. V | κ. ὠφελ. — T
11 § 47. σαρατήλ T | ποιεῖ ... πάντα: ἐνεργεῖ δὲ γνωρίζει πᾶν ὄρνεον T
| γνορείζει V   12 ὄρνεα super βότανα, quod linea expunxit, scr. pr. man.
W | πάντα — W | ἐνεργεῖ καὶ ὠφελεῖ W | § 48. ταρσές V, — T
13 ποιεῖν T | δὲ — W | γνωρίζει T, γνον < (l. γνῶναι) V, + πάντα T
| ἐνεργεῖ: ὀφειλ(εῖν) T | § 49. ναβάλ T   14 δὲ — W | ποιεῖ δὲ ... ὠφε-
λεῖ — T | γνωρίζει W, γνων < V   15 § 50. τασαήλ T | ͺε W | ἐνερ-
γεῖ δὲ T   16 παρέχειν T | * T f. 41ᵛ1 | § 51. ναμπαλαίκόν T   17 ͺε W
| ποιῆσαι κατὰ φαντασίαν T   18 § 52. μακκατάκ W, μαχατάκ V | ε' V:
ͺε W, — T   19 ἵππους: + καὶ ἔστην οὕτως, βασιλεῦ σολομῶν V, + τέλος T; explicit sectio haec Claviculae cod. T (cod. Harl. f. 41ᵛ1)

μηκέτι τινὶ μεταδοῦναι τοῦτο τὸ μέγα καὶ θεῖον μυστήριον, ἀλλ' ἐν ἀσφαλεῖ κατέχειν τόπῳ ὡς θησαυρὸν ἀδαπάνητον· ταῦτα * τοῖς πολλοῖς ἀθεώρητα καὶ ἀπόκρυφα διὰ τοὺς φρικτοὺς ἀπεχώρισα ὅρκους.

XI. Ἐρωτηθεὶς δὲ ὁ Βεελζεβοὺλ, ὃς Ἐντζιανφιὲλ καλεῖται παρ' ἐμοῦ, εἰ ἔστιν καὶ θήλεα δαιμόνια, τοῦ δὲ φήσαντος εἶναι, βουλόμην ἰδεῖν. 2. καὶ ἀπελθὼν ὁ τοιοῦτος ἤνεγκεν ἔμπροσθέν μου τὴν Ὀνοσκελοῦν καλουμένην μορφὴν ἔχουσαν περικαλλῆ καὶ σῶμα γυναικὸς εὐχρώτου, κτήμας δὲ ἡμιόνου. 3. ἐλθούσης δὲ αὐτῆς ἔφην αὐτὴν λέγων· »σὺ τίς εἶ;« ἡ δὲ ἔφη μοι· »ἐγώ Ὀνοσκελοῦ καλοῦμαι, πνεῦμα σεσωματοποιημένον. φωλεύω δὲ ἐπὶ τῆς γῆς· σπήλαιον οἰκῶ ἔνθα χρυσίον κεῖται. 4. ἔχω δὲ πολυποίκιλον τρόπον· ποτὲ μὲν ἀνθρώπους πνίγω ὡς δι' ἀγχόνης, ποτὲ δὲ ἀπὸ τῆς φύσεως ⌜ἐπιεγκόνων⌝ σκολιάζω αὐτούς. * 5. πλεῖστά μοι οἰκητήρια· πολλάκις δὲ καὶ συγγίνομαι τοῖς ἀνθρώποις ὡς γυναῖκάν με εἶναι, πρὸ δὲ τῶν ἄλλων τοὺς μελιχροὺς, οὗτοι γὰρ καὶ συναστροί μού εἰσιν· καὶ γὰρ τὸ ἄστρο μου οὗτοι λάθρα καὶ φανερῶς προσκυνοῦσιν.« 6. ἐπηρώτησα δὲ αὐτὴν ἐγὼ Σολομῶν· »πόθεν γεννᾶσαι;« ἡ δὲ ἔφη· »ἀπὸ φωνῆς βηρσαβεὲ ἱππικῆς χρηματικῆς.«

MSS VW. § 53. 2 ἀσφαλία mss. 3 * W f. 170ʳ | φρικτοὺς V: πολοὺς W C. XI. MSS T° (= T)VW. inc. narratio acephala de Onoskelou in cod. Harl. 5596 f. 7ʳ¹ (= T°, vel T). 5 ἐπηρώτησα δὲ ἐγὼ τὸν βεελζελοὺλ W | ὃς ... ἐμοῦ: ὁ καὶ τζιανφιὲλ Τ | ἐλτζιανφηὲλ V, ἐντζανφιὲλ W 6 εἰ — Τ | ἔστιν W: ἔστι T, εἰσι V | θήλεια W, θήλια V | τοῦ: τούτου Τ | δὲ: + μοι W | εἶναι T: ἔνι W, ἤναι φῆ V 7 § z. ὁ τοιοῦτος W: ὅτι οὗτος V, ὅτι οὗτος Τ | ἔμπροστέν μου W, ἔμπροστέ μου V, μοι (— ἔμπρ.) Τ 3 καλουμένη, ἔχουσα V | ἔχουσιν περικαλην W | περικαλὴ V, περιπερικαλὴ Τ 9 κνήμας: μνῆμος Τ | ἡμίονος Τ | § 3. δὲ — Τ 10 λέγων: λέγε μοι Τ | τίς εἶ σύ Τ | μοι — Τ | ὀνοσκελεὶς V 11 σεσωματωποιημένον W, σεσῶματοπηείμένω V, σεσωματωμένω Τ | φωλεύων W | δὲ — W 12 σπήλαιον οἰκῶ: ἐν σπηλαίω W § 4. 1. 13 ὡς δι' ἀγχ. — Τ 14 ἀπό: ὑπὸ Τ | ἐπιεγκόνων': ἐπιενγκόνων W, ἐπὶ εγκώνω V, ἐπὶ εγκόνων Τ; · ἐπιεγκονῶν, vel ἐπιεγχώνων (= ἐπί + ἐν + χώνω, pro χώννυμι)? | σχολιάζω W, σκωλιάζω V | * T f. 7ʳ² | § 5. πλεῖστα ἔσται μὴ οἰκ. V ιλ. μοι δὲ ἔσται οἰκ. V 16 με: μὲν Τ | πρὸ: πρὸς TW | τοὺς μελιχροὺς VW: τ. μελαχρόους Τ, 1. τοῖς μελιχροῖς 17 γὰρ (1°): + μου V | καὶ ιις om. Τ | τὸ γὰρ ἄστρο Τ | ἄστρον W | λαθ. προσκ. οὗτοι (— κ. φαν.) Τ 18 προσκ. λαθ. κ. ἐναργέως W | § 6. ἐρώτησα Τ 19 γενάσθαι W, γεναστ < V | ἔφη: εἶπεν T, + μὴ (1. μοι) V | βειρσαβεέ V, βηρφβεέ Τ, βηρσαβεὲλ N | ἱππ.: + καὶ Τ

7. Καὶ κατέκλεισα αὐτὴν ὑποκάτωθεν τεσσάρων λίθων μεγάλων. ἡ δὲ ἐβόησεν· »ἔξελέ με, ἔξελέ με, καὶ ἐνεγκῶ σοι τράπεζαν μετὰ φιάλου καὶ κύλικος, ἥντινα λαβὼν ἐπικρούσας μετὰ ἱμάσθλης πάντα προσφέρει σοι τὰ ὑποτεταγμένα βρωτὰ καὶ ποτά.« 8. καὶ κελεύσας ἀχθῆναι αὐτήν, ἤνεγκέ μοι τράπεζαν λιθίνην ἐκ λίθου ἰάσπιδος· μῆκος αὐτῆς ὡς πηχῶν τεσσάρων καὶ πλάτος πηχῶν τεσσάρων, ἔχουσα καὶ ἐν τοῖς κέρασιν μυρμηκολέοντας τέσσαρας λαλοῦντας ἀντ' ἐμοῦ ὅσα ἤθελον. 9. καὶ δὴ κελεύσας ὁμοῦ καὶ τὴν τράπεζαν ἐναχθῆναι ἐπεζήτουν καὶ τὴν * κύλικαν, μέντοι καὶ λίθον λυχνίτην κύλικος, καὶ περιέχον σχῆμα ἐπιδέδωκεν, καὶ ἡ μὲν τράπεζα ὅσα βρωτά, ἡ δὲ κύλιξ ὅσα ποτὰ παρεῖχεν ἐπιζητούμενα.

XII. Ἀνεζήτησα γὰρ ἐκ τῆς σφραγῖδος τὸ Παλτιὲλ Τζαμάλ, καὶ εὐθέως παραστὰς ἔφη μοι· »Σολομῶν, υἱὲ Δαυείδ, τί ἐκπειράζεις τοὺς δούλους σου καὶ τὰς δούλας σου; ἡμεῖς πάντες ἕως καιροῦ * σου καὶ δουλεύειν καὶ ὑπείκειν καθυποσχόμεθα καὶ τὰ ὀνόματα ἡμῶν ⌈ἔχειν⌉ ἐν ἀσφαλείᾳ ἐγράψαμεν καὶ τὰς δυνάμεις ἀνηγγείλαμεν ἀπάσας. 2. ὅντινα προστάσσεις, τὸ κελευόμενον ἐκπληρεῖν προθυμότατα. καὶ δεόμεθά σου ἵνα μὴ ἐάσῃς ἡμᾶς ἀπελθεῖν εἰς πέλαγος ἀχανές.«

3. Ἐγὼ δέ φησιν αὐτὸν εἰ ἔστιν ἀνάστασις τῶν τεθνεότων.

MSS TVW. 1 § 7. ὑποκάτω T   2 ἡ δὲ: καὶ W | ἐνεγκῶ T: ἐνορκομι (V, ἐν ὅρκῳ μοι W, 1. ἐνορκοῦμαι) δοῦναι VW   3 φιαλίον V | λαβὼν καὶ W   4 ἱμασθλῆς T, ἰσησμάλης W, ἠσασμάλης V | περιφέρει T   5 § 8. ἐκέλευσαν T | τράπεζα ληθήνη ἐκ ληθ < ἰασπίδος V   6 ἰάσπεως W | ὁ μίκος T | ὡς: + ἀπὸ V   7 καὶ (1°): — W | μυρμηγκολέοντας VW, μυρμυκωλευώντας T   8 ἀντ' ἐμοῦ: πάντας T | ἤθελα T   § 9. 1. 9 δὴ — T | ἐκέλευσα T | ὁμοῦ καὶ — T | ἐναχθῆναι μοι ὁμοῦ T | ἐπεζήτουν W: ἐπιζητῶν T, ἐπειζητὸν V   10 * T f. 7ᵛ¹ | μέντοι — T | λίθον λυχνήτην κοίλοικος W, λίθον ληχνείτι κύλεικος V, λίθον λιχνύτ(ων) κύλικες T | καὶ (2°) — T | περιέχοντα VW, ἐνπεριέχων T   11 ἐπιδέδοκεν W, ἐπιδώδεκα T | ὅσα: + περιεῖχεν T   12 ποτὰ — T | παρεῖχεν: περιεῖχεν T   C. XII. 1. 13 παλιτιὲλ T   14 εὐθέως — T | υἱὸς T   15 σου (1°) — T | ἡμεῖς: ἐμῆς V | πάντες: πάντοτε T   16 * V f. 441ʳ | σου — W | καὶ τὰ: πλὴν ἔπειτα V   17 ἡμῶν: εἰ μὴ V | ἔχειν T: ἔχων V, — W | ἀσφαλείᾳ: κεφαλῇ T | ἐγράψαμεν: ἐνγραφῆναι T   18 ἐναγκείλαμει TV | ἀπάσας ex ἀπάσης corr. V | § 2. ὅντινα ego: ὄντι W, ἥντηναν V εἴτινα T | προστάσσεις: + ἐκπληροῖ W   19 καὶ — T   20 ἀπελθεῖν — W   § 3. 1. 21 φησιν T: φήσας VW | τ. τεθνεότων: νεκρῶν T καὶ ἐφώνησεν φωνὴν μεγάλην λέγων· »ἔστιν, ἔστιν, μὰ τὸν ἰσχυρὸν θεὸν καὶ ζῶντα. καὶ ἡμεῖς γὰρ οἴησιν περιφερόμενοι ἐζοφώθημεν * φωτεινοὶ ὄντες τὸ πρότερον, καὶ ἔτι τῇ μετανοίᾳ οὐ προσεκλίναμεν. 4. λέγω δέ σοι ταῦτα, ὦ βασιλεῦ, θεὸς μόνος εἷς ἐστιν, ὃς τριὰ ὑμνολογεῖται παρὰ τῶν φωτεινῶν ἀγγέλων. αὐτὸς οὕτως σε ἡμᾶς παρέδωκεν, ἡμεῖς δὲ οἰκειοχείρως τὰ ὀνόματα ἡμῶν παρεδώκαμεν καὶ ἐπετάξαμεν καὶ ταῖς σφραγῖσιν ὁμοίως. 5. καὶ ὅστις, ὦ βασιλεῦ, γίνωσκε τ' ἀληθές, ἁγνίζει ἑαυτὸν ἡμέρας τρεῖς καὶ ἐπικαλεῖται τῇ ἁφῇ τῆς χειρὸς ἕναν ἡμῶν ὃν αἱρεῖται ἄρχοντα, ἐκπληροῖ τὸ κελευόμενον αὐτοῦ, καὶ ὥσπερ οἰκέτης τῷ ἰδίῳ δεσπότῃ πειθαρχεῖ, οὕτως ὁμοίως καὶ αὐτὸς τῷ κεκτημένῳ ἡμῶν τὰ ὀνόματα. 6. πρέπει οὖν ταῦτα ἐπιλέγειν τὰ ὀνόματα διὰ λίθου ἰάσπιδος ἐγγεγλυμμένης ζῳδίοις τοῖς δώδεκα· μέσον δὲ ὁ ὄφις καὶ λύρα, ἱστὸς καὶ ἄρκος, καὶ ὑπὲρ τὸν τύμπανον κυλικὴ φορὰ καὶ ἄνωθεν τούτου τὰ γράμματα ταῦτα· ZABARZHC, καὶ αὐτίκα ὑποτασσόμεθα τῷ κεκτημένῳ καὶ ἄκοντες.

XIII. Πλὴν, ὦ βασιλεῦ, καὶ τούτῳ προσεκτέον σοι· ἄνθρωποι

MSS TVW. 1 ἐφώνησεν: ἐβόησεν T | ἔστιν, ἔστιν ego: ἔστιν ἔστιν καὶ ἔστιν T, ἔστι ἔστη V, ἔστιν W 2 θεὸν — T | καὶ (2°) — T | οἴησιν ego: εἴησιν W, ᾕηση V, — T | περιφερόμενοι ego: προσφεράμενοι T, περιφερόμεθα VW 3 ἐζοφώθημεν ... πρότερον exscr. Gaulminius in notis ad Psellum, de oper. daem. (Migne, PG 122, 827, n. 19) | * L f. 7$^{v\,2}$ | ἔτι V: εἰς W, — T 4 οὐκ ἐκλίναμεν W § 4. l. 5 ὃς: ὡς T 6 αὐτὸς: οὗτος T | οὕτως: οὗτος TV | σε: l. σοι | παρέδωκεν: παραδωκὸς T | οἰκειοχ. ego: εἰκηοχύρος V, οἰχειόχειρος W, — T 7 παρεδώκαμεν: + ἰδιόχειρα T | ἐπεταξ. καὶ V: ἐγράψαμεν ὁμοίως καὶ T, — W 8 ὁμοίως: ἡμῶν T | post ἡμῶν punct. magn. argent. rubricumque ponit T, et posteaquam sequuntur quae verba infra ad l. 15 adducuntur §§ 5—6. ll. 8—16 καὶ ὅστις ... ταῦτα — T

MSS VW. § 5. l. 12 τῷ κέκτ. ego: τῶν κεκτημένων W, τὸν κεκτημένον V | § 6. πρέπει V: χρὴ W 13 ἐπιλέγι V | ἰασπίδος V, ἰάσπεως W | ἐνγκεγλυμμ(ένως) W 14 ἱστὸς W: εἰστὸς V, l. fortasse οἰστὸς | ὑπερι VW

MSS T. 16 ZABARZHC (rubric.) VW: ταῦτα δὲ ὀφίλην (l. ὀφείλει) βαστάζειν ἐπάνω σου, ἔστι γὰρ φύλαξ σου· ZABAPZHS T | explicit fragmentum MS T

MSS VW. 16 ὑποτασσόμ(ενα) W 17 ἀκῶντες W
C. XIII. l. 18 τοῦτο W | προσ. σοι. προσεκτέοσην V

πολλοὶ μέλλουσιν ζητεῖν τὸ τοιοῦτον μέγα μυστήριον ἵνα ὑποτασσώμεθα ὑπ' αὐτῶν, καὶ εἰ ἀκούσεις ἡμῶν ἐροῦμεν.« καὶ εἶπον· »λέγε, ἀποστάτα καὶ ἀπατεών.« 2. ὁ δὲ ἔφη· »σὺ καὶ τοῖς τέκνοις σου μόνοις ἐγκατάλειπε τὴν θησαυρὸν καὶ μὴ τοῖς
5 πᾶσῖν καὶ ἀφελεστέροις. ποίησον δὲ ἡμῖν σημεῖον ὅπως μετὰ τὸ ἀποθανεῖν σε Ἐζεκείᾳ τῷ βασιλεῖ ποιήσεις ἑτέραν διαθήκην τῷ κόσμῳ καὶ ἡ τοιαύτη ἔσται ἀποκεκρυμμένη καὶ μὴ φανερὰ τοῖς κοινοῖς καὶ ἀφελεστέροις, ἵνα μὴ ὁ θησαυρὸς ἐκλείπῃ τοῖς οἰκουμένοις. 3. οὐδεὶς γὰρ ἀπ' ἀρχῆς μέχρι τῆς σήμερον ἡμᾶς ἐδου-
10 λώσατο, καὶ μὴ παραχωρίσῃς ἡμᾶς θνητοῖς σώμασιν πειθαρχεῖν, 4. ὁ γὰρ Ἐζεκείας, ὦ βασιλεῦ, πολλὰ μὲν καὶ πατροπαράδοτα κατακαύσει καὶ ἄλλα πολλὰ μέν ἀφανίσει βιβλία, καὶ τὴν οἰκουμένην στηρίξει καὶ τὰ περιττὰ διακόψει.

5. Ἐγὼ δὲ Σολομῶν ἀκούσας εἶπον αὐτόν· »ἐξορκίζω σε εἰς
15 τὸν θρόνον τοῦ θεοῦ τὸ ἀσάλευτον καὶ εἰς τὸ ὄρνεον τὸ περιπετόμενον ἐπάνω τῆς κεφαλῆς αὐτοῦ ἵνα με εἴπῃς ἐν ποίῳ ἀγγέλῳ οἱ πάντες καταργεῖσθε.« 6. καὶ εἶπέν μοι· »βασιλεῦ Σολομῶν, ἡμεῖς πάντες ὑπὸ τοῦ θεοῦ δυνάμει καταργούμεθα καὶ ἐν τῷ ὀνόματι Ἀγλά, ἀλλ' ἐπειδὴ τῇ σφραγῖδι κατεδεσμεύσας ἡμᾶς
20 σὺ μόνος, ὑποτασσόμεθα μέχρι τινός. 7. ἐλεύσονται γὰρ ἡμέραι ἐν αἷς πολλὰ δεηθήσῃ, καὶ διὰ τοῦτο ἱκετεύομέν σοι ὅπως ἐν ταῖς ἐξῆς γενεαῖς ἕξομεν σημεῖον τῆς βασιλείας σου καὶ ὑποδείξομεν τοῦτο Ἐζεκείᾳ τῷ βασιλεῖ ὅπως δειχθῇ καὶ πλατυνθῇ εἰς τὴν οἰκουμένην ἣν δώσομεν αὐτῷ διαθήκην καινήν. 8. καὶ
25 ταύτην, ἐν ᾗ ἀληθινῶς τὰ ὀνόματα ἡμῶν ἐχαράξαμεν, κατακαύσει ἄνευ ἑνὸς μόνου ἥτις φυλαχθήσεται καὶ ἐν τῇ προσδοκου-

---

MSS VW. 1 μέλλωσιν W, μέλοσην V 2 ει — V | ἡμῶν ego: ὑμῶν VW | καὶ εἶπον W: ὁ δὲ ἔφη V 3 § 2. ὁ δὲ V: καὶ W 4 μόνοις V: — W 5 ἀφελεστέρης V, ἀσφελεσταίραις W 6 σε: ση V, σοι W | ἐζεκία τὸ βασιλεῖ VW | ποιήσῃ V | ἑτέρα διαθήκη V | τὸ κωσμ < V, — W 7 ἀποκεκρ. V: ἀποσφαλισμένη W 8 ἀσφαλεστέροις W 9 § 3. τη σημερον V, τὴν σημ. W 10 θνητοῖς ego: θικτοῖς W, θεικτεῖς V 11 § 4. μὲν W: δὲ V | πατροπαραδ. ego: παιδοπ(ατρό)ς W, πεδοπ(ατρό)ς V 12 ἄλλα W: ἄλον V

§ 5. l. 14 αὐτὸν VW: l. αὐτῷ 15 καί ... αὐτοῦ V: — W 16 με VW: l. μοι | ποίῳ ... πάντες W: πίω ἡ πάντες ἀγγέλων V § 6. l. 18 πάντες: pr. ἡ (l. οἱ) V 20 σὺ μόν(ος) VW: l. σοὶ μόνῳ cum ὑποτασσ.? § 7 l. 22 ἕξωμεν VW 23 πλατιθῇ V 24 αὐτὸ W, αὑτ < V

μένη τοῦ θεοῦ παρουσία πάλιν διαπλατυνθήσεται. 9. ἡ δὲ παρ' ἡμῶν δοθεῖσα τῷ Ἐζεκείᾳ ἐν ὅλῳ τῷ κόσμῳ παραδοθήσεται καὶ ὡς μέγα τι κειμήλιον παρὰ τοῖς σοφοῖς φυλαχθήσεται, ἥντινα ὡς παίγνιον καὶ ἀπάτην ἐκδώσομεν ἐν τῷ κόσμῳ. 10. Ταῦτα ἀκούσας ἐγὼ Σολομῶν ἐδεήθην τοῦ θεοῦ καὶ εἶπον· »θεὲ πατέρων, Ἀδωναΐ μέγας, ὁ τὴν σοφίαν τῷ δούλῳ σου χαρισάμενος, ἀποκάλυψόν μοι τί δεῖ ποιῆσαι.« 11. καὶ ἦλθεν φωνὴ λέγουσα· »Σολομῶν, Σολομῶν, ἔασον γραμμάτιον τῷ Ἐζεκείᾳ τῇ σφραγῖδι ταύτῃ ἐκσφραγισάμενος.« 12. καὶ καθίσας ἔγραψα· »τῷ Ἐζεκείᾳ τῷ μέλλοντι βασιλεῖ· Σολομῶν βασιλεύς, υἱὸς Δαυείδ, ἀπέστειλά σοι τάδε. λάβε ἐκ τοῦ Παλτιὲλ Τζαμὰλ διαθήκην ἣν δώσει σοι καὶ τῷ κόσμῳ παντὶ καταπλούτισον· τὴν δὲ ἐμὴν παραδοὺς πυρὶ πλὴν ἑνὸς ἥτις καὶ ἐν λαϊνέοις ἐντυπωθήσεται γράμμασιν ἕως ὁ μέγας καὶ ἰσχυρὸς θελήσαιεν.« 13. Ταῦτα γράψας παρέδωκα τῷ Τζαμὰλ, καὶ πάλιν ἠρώτησα αὐτὸν εἰ ἔστιν καλὸν τοῦ ὑγιαίνειν ὁλοσώματον καὶ ἀτραυμάτιστον ἐν τῷ κόσμῳ ἐᾶσαι πλοῦτον. καὶ εἶπέν μοι· »ἓν μόνον ἔασον δι' οἰκείας γραφῆς σου τῇ μέσῃ τῆς γῆς γράμμασιν ἀσημάντοις.« 14. καὶ δὴ καθίσας ἔγραψα χαλδαϊκοῖς γράμμασιν χερσὶν οἰκείαις τοῦ ὑγιαίνειν ὁλόσωμάτον καὶ ἀτραυμάτιστον (ἐᾶσαι) πλοῦτον, παραδοὺς μόνην τὴν Παλαιστίνην, ὡς, ὁπόταν φανήσεται, οὐ μόνον κεκτημένον ἀλλὰ καὶ ἅπαντα κόσμον ὀνήσῃ ὑγιαινὰ καὶ πλουτοποιὰ χαρίσματα παρέχῃ ἑκάστοτε, ἐπεὶ οὐρανόθεν ταῦτα κατέβησαν χερσὶν Ὑψίστου, μεγάλων κυδῶν κατέχουσι παλάμην, τοῦτο καὶ ἐπιδοῦσί μοι.

15. Ὧδε ἐγὼ Σολομῶν. εἰς δὲ τὸ ἑξῆς θεὸς ἰσχυρός, Ὕψιστος Σαβαώθ· ἀμήν.

MSS VW. § 8. 1. 1 διαπλατιδεί(σεται) V 4 ἥντινα ego: ἣν τινὲς VW
5 § 10. ἐδεήθη V 6 εἶπον W: ὕπαι (1. εἶπε) V § 12. 1. 11 παλτιὲ W,
πατιὲλ V 13 λαϊνέοις ego: λεανέες V, λεανὲς W 14 θελησῃ(εν) W,
θελεισίεν V
§ 13. 1. 16 τὸ εἰγΐενί V | ὁλὸ σῶματον V § 14. 1. 19 ἔγραψεν V
20 ὑγίην ὁλὸ σῶματον V | ἀτραμάτιστον πλούτων V 21 ἐᾶσαι addo |
* V f. 441ᵛ | μόνην τ. Παλ.: l. fortasse μόνῃ ἐν τῇ Παλαιστίνῃ? 22 ὀνήσῃ ego: ὃν εἰσι V, ὠνήσιν W 24 κυδῶν V: εἰδῶν W | κατέχουσι ego: κατέχουσα VW 25 τοῦτο ... μοι — W | ἐπιδοῦσι ego: ἐπιδούσαν V
§ 15. 1. 26 Ὧδε W: ὡς δὲ V | εἰς δὲ W: καὶ εἰς V

ΠΕΡΙ ΤΟΥ ΣΟΛΟΜΩΝΤΟΣ

1. Ὁ Σολομῶν υἱὸς Δαυεὶδ ἐγένετο ἐκ τῆς τοῦ Οὐρίου γυναικός· ἐγένετο δὲ οὕτως. ἐσκέψατο Δαυεὶδ ὁ βασιλεὺς τὴν τοῦ Οὐρίου γυναῖκα ἐν τῷ βαλανείῳ γυμνήν. καὶ ἐμβατεύσας ὁ Σατανᾶς εἰς τὴν καρδίαν αὐτοῦ ἔρωτα ἐπιθυμίας, ἐμοίχευσεν αὐτήν. 2. καὶ οὐ μόνον τὸ τῆς μοιχείας ἔργον εἰργάσατο, ἀλλὰ καὶ φονεῦσαι προήχθη τὸν Οὐρίαν τὸν ἄνδρα τῆς μοιχευθείσης ὁ ἀγαπητὸς τοῦ θεοῦ, ὁ μέγας προφήτης, ὁ ἐκλεκτὸς τοῦ θεοῦ, ὁ μέγιστος τοῖς πᾶσιν, ὁ τῆς ψαλμῳδίας καλλωπισμός, ὁ τῆς παλαιᾶς καὶ νέας διαθήκης σημειοφόρος, ὁ μεγαλώνυμος θεοπάτωρ. ἠπατήθη γὰρ παρὰ τοῦ Βελίαρ καὶ ἀρχεκάκου ἐχθροῦ· ἠπατήθη γὰρ ὡς ὁ πρωτόπλαστος ἐκεῖνος Ἀδάμ. 3. ἐφονεύθη δὲ Οὐρίας ἀποσταλεὶς παρὰ τοῦ Δαυεὶδ εἰς τὸν πόλεμον, καὶ ταχθεὶς βουλήσει αὐτοῦ καὶ θελήσει εἰς τὸ ἔμπροσθεν τοῦ πολέμου ὅπως καταληφθεὶς μόνος καὶ μὴ ἔχων τὸν βοηθοῦντα φονευθῇ. ὅπερ δὴ καὶ γέγονεν.

4. Πρὸ δὲ τοῦ ταῦτα γενέσθαι ἦλθεν ἄγγελος Κυρίου εἰς Νάθαν τὸν προφήτην λέγων αὐτῷ· »ἄπελθε εἰς τὸν Δαυεὶδ τὸν βασιλέα τὸν προφήτην καὶ δίδαξον αὐτὸν τοῦ μὴ ποιῆσαι * τὰ ἄθεσμα ἔργα τοῦ Σατανᾶ.« 5. ἐξελθὼν δὲ ὁ Νάθαν ἄπεισι πρὸς τὸν Δαυεὶδ καὶ ἐνεμποδίσθη παρὰ τοῦ Βελίαρ. εὗρε γὰρ ὁ διάβολος ἄνθρωπον ἐσφαγμένον γυμνὸν καὶ ἄρας αὐτὸν ἔθηκεν ἐν τῇ ὁδῷ τοῦ Νάθαν. 6. ἰδὼν δὲ τὸν νεκρὸν ἄνθρωπον ὁ Νάθαν ἐβουλήθη θάψαι αὐτόν· καὶ ἐν τῷ θάπτειν ἐπλήρωσεν ὁ Δαυεὶδ τὰ ἄθεσμα ἔργα τοῦ Σατανᾶ. καὶ ἐπιγνοὺς τοῦτο

MS D = codex 132 Monasterii Sancti Dionysii in Monte Atho (v. supra p. 7); incipit f. 367ʳ

10 ὁ μεγ. θεοπάτωρ, ὁ τῆς ... σημειοφόρος hoc ordine exscriptis, postea super ὁ μεγαλων. littera β, et super ὁ τῆς littera α scripta ordinem ut in textu indicavit scriptor 19 * f. 367ᵛ

Νάθαν ὁ προφήτης ἐθρήνει πικρῶς καὶ ἔλεγεν· »δι' ἐμὲ γέγονε τοῦτο τὸ ἁμάρτημα.« 7. καὶ πάλιν ἐλθὼν ὁ ἄγγελος πρὸς αὐτὸν ἔλεγε· »διὰ σοῦ γέγονε τὸ πτῶμα, διὰ σοῦ ἔσται καὶ ἡ διόρθωσις. ἄπελθε τοίνυν καὶ ἔλεγξον αὐτὸν τὴν ἀνομίαν.« καὶ λέγει Νάθαν πρὸς τὸν ἄγγελον· »πῶς ἐγὼ πένης ὢν ἐλέγξω βασιλέα;« 8. ὁ δὲ ἄγγελός φησι πρὸς αὐτόν· »ἐγὼ ἔσομαι μετὰ σοῦ· σὺ ἀνάγγειλον, ἐγὼ δὲ τὸν φόβον φέρω εἰς αὐτόν.« 9. καὶ ἀπελθὼν Νάθαν πρὸς τὸν Δαυεὶδ προσεκύνησεν αὐτῷ καὶ εἶπε· »δέσποτα βασιλεῦ, δίκην ἔχω μετά τινος, καὶ ἦλθον τοῦ εἰπεῖν πρὸς σὲ ταύτην.« ὁ δὲ βασιλεὺς πρὸς αὐτὸν λέγει· »τίς ἐστιν ἡ δίκη αὕτη;« 10. ὁ δὲ Νάθαν παραβολικῶς ἔλεγε· »δεσπότην ἔχω τὸν δεσπόζοντά με, καὶ κέκτηται ἀμνάδας ἑκατόν· καὶ εὐφραίνεται μετ' αὐτῶν. * ἐγὼ δὲ κέκτημαι ἀμνάδα μίαν. καὶ ἔλαβεν αὐτὴν ἀπ' ἐμοῦ ὁ τὰς ἑκατὸν ἔχων καὶ κατέφαγεν αὐτήν.« 11. τότε ἔγνω ὁ Δαυεὶδ τὸ σκευασθὲν αὐτῷ δρᾶμα καὶ ἀναστὰς ἐκ τῆς κλίνης αὐτοῦ στενάξας πικρῶς μετὰ δακρύων ἔλεγεν· »ἐγώ εἰμι ὁ ταῦτα διαπραξάμενος.« καὶ ἤρξατο κατανυκτικῶς λέγειν τὸν πεντηκοστὸν ψαλμόν, καὶ ὁ Νάθαν πρὸς αὐτόν. καὶ ἀφείλατο λοιπὸν κύριος ὁ θεὸς τὸ ἁμάρτημα.

12. Ἔτεκε Δαυεὶδ τὸν Σολομῶντα ἐκ τῆς τοῦ Οὐρίου. καὶ ἔλαβε τὴν βασιλείαν τοῦ πατρὸς αὐτοῦ Δαυεὶδ καὶ ἦν ἐληλακὼς εἰς ἄκρον σοφίας καὶ φρονήσεως· καὶ ἡ σειρὰ τῆς γενεαλογίας αὐτοῦ κατήντησε μέχρι καὶ τῆς θείας σαρκώσεως τοῦ κυρίου ἡμῶν Ἰησοῦ Χριστοῦ, ἐπεί ἐστι καὶ αὐτὸς ἐκ φυλῆς, μᾶλλον δὲ ἐξ ὀσφύος τοῦ θεοπάτορος Δαυεὶδ ἵνα καὶ ἡ προφητικὴ ῥῆσις πληρωθῇ ἡ λέγουσα· »οὐκ ἐκλείψει ἄρχων ἐξ Ἰούδα οὐδὲ ἡγούμενος ἐκ τῶν μηρῶν αὐτοῦ ἕως οὗ ἔλθῃ ᾧ ἀπόκειται.«

13. ἡ σοφία δὲ Σολομῶντος ὁμοία ἦν τῇ σοφίᾳ τοῦ πρώτου ἐκείνου ἀνθρώπου Ἀδάμ. ἐπαιδεύθη ταύτην τὴν σοφίαν τὴν μὲν παρὰ τοῦ θαυμασίου Σιράχ, τὴν δὲ παρὰ τῆς ἄνω προνοίας. τούτου δὲ τὴν σοφίαν ἐμφαίνων ὁ κύριος ἐν τοῖς εὐαγγελίοις ἔλεγεν, ὅτι »οὐδὲ σοφίαν * Σολομῶντος ὑψηλοτέραν οἶμαι τῶν ἄλλων,« ταύτην κρίνας ὥσπερ δῆτα καὶ ἦν.

---

4 αὐτὸν in αὐτῷ corr. prim. man. false § 10. l. 13 * f. 368ʳ
§ 12. l. 21 ἐληλακὸς ms. § 13. 31 σοφία ms. 32 * f. 368ᵛ

§ 12. ll. 26f. Gen. XLIX 10 — § 13. ll. 32f. Mt. XII 42; Lk. XI 31

II. Ταύτῃ τῇ σοφίᾳ θαρρήσας ὁ θαυμάσιος Σολομῶν ἐβουλήθη ἀνεγεῖραι οἶκον κυρίῳ τῷ θεῷ περικαλλῆ καὶ κρείττω πάντων τῶν ἀναθημάτων τῶν ἐπὶ τῆς γῆς. ἐγένετο δὲ καὶ ἀνηγείρετο ὁ οἶκος κυρίου τοῦ θεοῦ θελήσει καὶ σοφίᾳ καὶ δημιουργίᾳ θεοῦ διὰ τοῦ σοφοῦ Σολομῶντος καὶ τῆς τούτου προθυμίας. ἀνήγειρε τοίνυν μετὰ μεγάλης εὐπρεπείας τὸν τοιοῦτον ναὸν αὐτός τε καὶ οἱ παῖδες αὐτοῦ. 2. ἔσχε δὲ ἕνα ἀπὸ τῶν παίδων αὐτοῦ ποθεινότατον παρὰ πάντας, τὰ γὰρ σιτία καὶ τὰς τροφὰς καὶ τὰ ἱμάτια ἐπὶ τὸ διπλοῦν παρεῖχεν αὐτῷ. ἦν δὲ ὁ τοιοῦτος παῖς ἀηδὴς τῇ ὄψει καὶ τὸ πρόσωπον ἀκαλλώπιστος, καὶ ἐλυπεῖτο βλέπων αὐτὸν οὕτως ἔχοντα ὁ Σολομῶν. 3. ἐν μιᾷ δὲ τῶν ἡμερῶν φησι πρὸς αὐτόν· »πῶς οὕτως ἀηδὴς ἔχεις; τί σε τῶν παρόντων λυπεῖ; μὴ οὐ λαμβάνεις τὰ πάντα διπλᾶ παρ' ἐμοῦ;« 4. καὶ ὁ παῖς φησι πρὸς τὸν βασιλέα· »τὰ μὲν σιτία, δέσποτα βασιλεῦ, ἅπερ μοι παρέχεις πάντα καταναλίσκω. οὐκ εὐφραίνει δὲ ἀπὸ τούτων οὐδέν, καταλαμβάνει γὰρ ἐπ' ἐμὲ διὰ τῆς νυκτὸς δαιμόνιον πονηρὸν καὶ ἀκάθαρτον καὶ ὑποπιάζει καὶ ἐκθλίβει τὸ ἄκρον τοῦ δακτύλου μου. καὶ ἀπεργάζεται * τὴν ὄψιν μου τοιαύτην οἵαν ὁρᾷς ἀηδῆ καὶ σκυθρωπήν.«

5. Ἀκούσας δὲ τὸ ῥῆμα τοῦτο ὁ Σολομῶν ἐποίησεν ὑπὲρ τούτου ἔντευξιν καὶ παράκλησιν πρὸς κύριον τὸν θεόν. 6. καὶ ἀπεστάλη πρὸς αὐτὸν Μιχαὴλ ὁ ἀρχάγγελος μετὰ σφραγῖδος χαλκοῦ δακτυλίου, καὶ δέδωκε τὴν τοιαύτην σφραγῖδα πρὸς τὸν Σολομῶντα. 7. καί φησι· »ἐπίδος τῷ παιδὶ τὴν τοιαύτην σφραγῖδα καὶ κατεχέτω ταύτην ἐν τῇ κλίνῃ αὐτοῦ, καὶ ὁπόταν ἔλθῃ πρὸς αὐτὸν ὁ διάβολος, κρουσάτω τοῦτον μετὰ τῆς σφραγῖδος ἐπὶ τὸ στῆθος, καὶ δήσας ἀγαγέτω τοῦτον πρὸς σέ· μέλλεις γὰρ ὑποτάξαι πᾶν δαιμόνιον μετ' αὐτοῦ καὶ τῆς σφραγῖδος τοῦ θεοῦ, καὶ οἰκοδομῆσαι τὸν οἶκον τοῦ θεοῦ μετὰ τοῦ πλήθους τῶν δαιμόνων σὺν τοῖς ἀνθρώποις.« 8. λαβὼν δὲ ὁ Σολομῶν τὴν σφραγῖδα καὶ εὐχαριστήσας τῷ ἁγίῳ θεῷ, ἀπῆλθεν ἀπ' αὐτοῦ ὁ ἄγγελος. 9. καὶ προσκαλεσάμενος τὸν παῖδα δέδωκε τὴν σφραγῖδα, 10. ἀναγγείλας τὸ προσταχθὲν παρὰ τοῦ ἀγγέλου. 11. λαβὼν δὲ ὁ παῖς τὴν σφραγῖδα τοῦ θεοῦ, ἑσπέρας γενομένης ἀνε-

---

C. II. 1. 2 οἴκου ms. | κρείττονα Is 4 ἀνήγειρ. Kurz: ἀνεγ. ms. § 4. l. 18 * f. 369ʳ 19 σκυθρωπήν ms., σκηπτώπην Is κλίθη εἰς τὴν κοίτην αὐτοῦ, καὶ κατὰ τὸ εἰθισμένον παραγέγονε πρὸς αὐτὸν ὁ διάβολος. 12. καὶ ἀθρόον ὁ παῖς παίει τὸν ἐχθρὸν κατὰ τῆς καρδίας μετὰ τῆς τοῦ θεοῦ σφραγῖδος. * 13. ὁ δὲ σατανᾶς ἐλεεινῇ τῇ φωνῇ ἐβόησεν· »οἴμοι, οἴμοι, πῶς καταδουλοῦμαι βασιλεῖ Σολομῶντι;« καὶ δήσας τοῦτον εἰσήγαγε πρὸς τὸν βασιλέα Σολομῶντα. III. Καὶ θεασάμενος αὐτόν φησι· »εἰπὲ ἡμῖν, πονηρὸν πνεῦμα καὶ ἀκάθαρτον, τίς ἐστιν ἡ κλῆσίς σου καὶ τίς σου ἡ ἐργασία.« καὶ ὁ διάβολος ἔφη τῷ βασιλεῖ· »Ὀρνίας καλοῦμαι. ἡ δὲ ἐργασία μου εἰς πάντα ἐπιτήδεια.« 2. καὶ λέγει ὁ βασιλεύς· »τίς ὁ καταργῶν τὴν δύναμίν σου ἄγγελος;« καὶ ὁ διάβολος· »ὑπὸ τοῦ μεγάλου ἀρχαγγέλου Μιχαὴλ καταργοῦμαι αὐτός τε καὶ ἡ ἐμὴ δύναμις.« 3. καὶ ὁ βασιλεύς φησι· »δύνασαι ποιῆσαί τι εἰς τὸν ναὸν κυρίου καὶ εἰς τὴν οἰκοδομὴν αὐτοῦ χρησιμόν;« καὶ ὁ διάβολος· »δύναμαι μετὰ τῆς σφραγῖδος ταύτης ἐπισυνάξαι πᾶν δαιμόνιον ἔμπροσθέν σου καὶ ὑποτάξαι τῷ σῷ θελήματι καὶ οἰκοδομῆσαι, καὶ ἀνεγερεῖς μετὰ τῆς δουλείας καὶ ὑποταγῆς ἐκείνων τὸν ναὸν κυρίου παντοκράτορος.« 4. ταῦτα ἀκούσας ὁ Σολομῶν εὐχαρίστησε κυρίῳ τῷ θεῷ καὶ προέτρεψε τὸν Ὀρνίαν δαίμονα μετὰ τῆς σφραγῖδος καὶ τοῦ παιδίου ἀπελθεῖν καὶ ἐπισυνάξαι πᾶν δαιμόνιον. 5. καὶ ἀπῆλθον καὶ ἐπισυνήγαγον πάντα καὶ εἰσῆγον ταῦτα εἰς * τὸν βασιλέα Σολομῶντα. ἅμα δὲ τὸ πλησιάσαι ταῦτα εἰς τὸν βασιλέα προσεκύνουν αὐτῷ. 6. καὶ ἠρώτα ἓν ἕκαστον ὁ βασιλεὺς τῶν δαιμόνων τό τε ὄνομα καὶ τὴν ἐργασίαν καὶ ὑπὸ ποίου τῶν ἁγίων ἀγγέλων καταργεῖται. καὶ ὡμολόγουν τήν τε ἐργασίαν αὐτοῦ καὶ τὴν κλῆσιν καὶ τὸν καταργοῦντα ἄγγελον. 7. ἐπέτρεπε δὲ αὐτὰ ἐργάζεσθαι εἰς τὴν τοῦ ναοῦ οἰκοδομήν. καὶ ἐνήργει ἓν ἕκαστον τὴν δουλείαν εἰς ἣν δὴ καὶ ἐτάχθη παρὰ τοῦ σοφοῦ Σολομῶντος. 8. καὶ οὕτως ἦν ἰδεῖν θαῦμα ἐξαίσιον ἄνδρας μετὰ πλήθους δαιμόνων θελήσει κυρίου ἀνοικοδομοῦντας καὶ ἐκπληροῦντας τὸν ναὸν κυρίου εἰρηνικῶς μετὰ πάσης ἐπιμελείας τε καὶ σπουδῆς, μὴ τολμώντων τῶν

---

§ 12. l. 2 ἀθρόον ms.: ἀθρόων Is   3 * f. 369ᵛ
C. III 1. l. 10 ἐπιτήδεια Is: ἐπιτήδειος ms.   § 2. l. 12 ἡ — Is | ε in voce ἐμή primum omissum postea supra ἡ scr. ms.   13 § 3. δύνασε ms.
§ 5. l. 22 * f. 370ʳ   23 πλησιάσαι Is: πλησιᾶσαι ms., l. πλησιᾶσθαι?

δαιμόνων μηδὲ τὸ τυχὸν σκανδαλίσαι ἢ ἀδικῆσαι τοὺς ἀνθρώπους.

IV. Ἀπὸ δὲ τῶν ἀνδρῶν τῶν ἐχόντων ἀκριβῆ εἴδησιν εἰς τὴν τοῦ ναοῦ οἰκοδομὴν ἦλθεν εἷς εἰς φιλονεικίαν καὶ ἔριν μετὰ τοῦ υἱοῦ αὐτοῦ, καὶ ἐμάχοντο ἀλλήλοις θυμοῦ πνέοντες ἀλλήλους διασπαράξαι βουλόμενοι. 2. ὅλος δὲ τοῦ θυμοῦ ὁ πατὴρ γεγονὼς ἀπῆλθε πρὸς τὸν βασιλέα Σολομῶντα μετὰ δακρύων καὶ ὀδυρμῶν λέγων αὐτῷ· »δέσποτα βασιλεῦ· ἢ θανάτῳ τὸν ἐμὸν καταδίκασον * παῖδα ὡς ἐνυβρίσαντα παρανόμως εἰς ἐμὲ τὸν πατέρα, ἢ σαφῶς ἴσθι ὡς οὐδέποτε κινήσω τὴν χεῖρά μου εἰς τὴν τοῦ ναοῦ οἰκοδομήν.« 3. ἀκούων δὲ ταῦτα ὁ βασιλεὺς καὶ βουλευόμενος, ἦλθε καὶ ὁ υἱὸς ἐκείνου πρὸς τὸν βασιλέα ταὐτὰ ἐγκαλῶν. καὶ λέγων τῷ πατρί. 4. διαλογιζόμενος δὲ περὶ τούτου ὁ βασιλεὺς καὶ διαπορῶν τί ἄρα ἀποκρίνοιτο, στραφεὶς βλέπει τὸν Ὀρνίαν δαίμονα ἐργαζόμενον καὶ μειδιῶντα· καὶ λέγει πρὸς τοὺς κρινομένους· »ἀπόστητε μικρὸν ἀπ' ἐμοῦ.« 5. καὶ ἀποστάντων τὸν Ὀρνίαν μετακαλεῖται καί φησι πρὸς αὐτόν· »τί γελᾷς, ὦ Ὀρνία; τὴν βασιλείαν μου καταγελᾷς, ἢ τὴν κρίσιν μου, ἢ τὸν ναὸν κυρίου;« 6. καὶ ὁ Ὀρνίας πρὸς τὸν βασιλέα λέγει· »δέσποτα βασιλεῦ· σοφώτατε καὶ δικαιότατε Σολομῶν· οὔτε τὴν βασιλείαν σου κατεγέλασα, οὔτε τὴν κρίσιν σου, οὔτε τὸν ναὸν κυρίου, ἀλλὰ τούτους τοὺς ἀθλίους τοὺς κρινομένους, τὸν δύστηνον λέγω γέροντα καὶ τὸν τούτου υἱόν. οὐ μὴ γὰρ παρέλθωσι τρεῖς ἡμέραι καὶ τὸ τέλος διαδέξεται τὸν νέον.« 7. καὶ ὁ βασιλεὺς πρὸς τὸν Ὀρνίαν λέγει· »ἄπελθε καὶ ἐργάζου μετὰ σπουδῆς καὶ εἰρήνης καὶ ὑποταγῆς εἰς τὸν ναὸν κυρίου θεοῦ παντοκράτορος.« καὶ ἀπῆλθεν ἀπὸ τοῦ τόπου ἐκείνου ὁ Ὀρνίας καὶ * εἰργάζετο. 8. μετεκαλέσατο δὲ ὁ βασιλεὺς τοὺς δύο κρινομένους καί φησι πρὸς αὐτούς· »ἀπέλθατε καὶ ἐργάζεσθε τὸ ἔργον ὑμῶν ἄχρι πέντε ἡμέρας, καὶ μετὰ ταῦτα ποιήσομαι ἀπόφασιν καὶ τέλος τῆς κρίσεως ὑμῶν.« προσέταξε δὲ ὁ βασιλεὺς διορίσασθαι τὴν ἡμέραν καθ' ἣν ἔλεγε ταῦτα.

C. IV 1. l. 4 εἰς supplevi: τις conj. Is 6 § ϰ. ὅλος Is: ὅλως ms. 9 * f. 370ᵛ § 6. l. 22 δύστηνον: δύστυνον ms., δύστυχον Is errore 24 διαδέξεται conj. Is: διαδέξονται ms. § 7. l. 25 πρὸς supplevi 27 ᵏ f. 371ʳ

9. Παρελθουσῶν οὖν τῶν πέντε ἡμερῶν, ἦλθεν ὁ γέρων πρὸς τὸν βασιλέα κατηφὴς καὶ σπυθρωπὸς καὶ δάκρυα πρὸ τῶν ὀμμάτων ἀφεὶς φησι· »τέθνηκεν ὁ ἐμὸς υἱός, τέθνηκεν, καὶ οὐκ ἔτι ἴδῃς αὐτόν. ἐμὲ δὲ ἀπέλιπεν ἐν πένθει βαρυτάτῳ καὶ ὀδύνῃ καρδίας καὶ ἀφορήτῳ στεναγμῷ· οὐκ ἔτι γὰρ βλέψω αὐτόν· οὐκ ἔτι τὸ πρόσωπον ἐκείνου θεάσομαι. κατεκρύβη γὰρ ἐν τόπῳ ἀφεγγεῖ, ἐν τῇ σκοτεινῇ, ἐν τῇ ζοφερᾷ.« 10. ἐκπλαγεὶς οὖν ταῦτα ὁ βασιλεύς φησι· »ποίαν ἡμέραν τέθνηκεν;« καί φησι ὁ γέρων· »μετὰ τρίτην ἡμέραν ἀπέθανεν ἀφ᾽ ὅτου πρὸς τὸ σὸν κράτος ἤλθαμεν.« 11. καὶ λέγει ὁ βασιλεύς· »ἄπελθε ἐν εἰρήνῃ, ὁ γέρων, κύριος δὲ ὁ θεὸς ὁ πατὴρ τῆς παρακλήσεως καὶ παραμυθία τῶν θλιβομένων παρακαλέσαι σου τὴν καρδίαν εἰς τὸ μηκέτι λυπεῖσθαι. μνήσθητι γὰρ ὅτι ὁ σὸς υἱὸς ἄνθρωπος ἦν, πᾶς δὲ ἄνθρωπος θνητὸς ἦν. * μὴ τοίνυν λυποῦ, οὐ γὰρ ἀνύσεις οὐδὲν ὧν βούλεσαι.« ταῦτα ἀκούσας ὁ γέρων ἀπῆλθεν ἀναψυχθεὶς τὴν καρδίαν.

12. Καὶ μετακαλεσάμενος τὸν Ὀρνίαν φησίν· »εἰπὲ ἡμῖν πῶς ἐπιγινώσκεις τὸν θάνατον τοῦ ἀνθρώπου, πνεῦμα ἀκάθαρτον ὄν.« 13. Ὁ δὲ Ὀρνίας λέγει· »ἡμεῖς, δέσποτα, ἐκ τοῦ οὐρανοῦ ἐρρίφημεν κάτω, καὶ ἄγγελοι θεοῦ ὄντες καὶ φῶς περικείμενοι. νῦν δαίμονες καὶ ἀκάθαρτα πνεύματα καὶ σκότος, ὡς ὁρᾷς, ἐγενόμεθα, καὶ λειτουργοὶ θεοῦ τυγχάνοντες. νῦν σοῦ θεράποντες καὶ ὑπουργοί, θεοῦ κελεύοντος, γεγενήμεθα. 14. κάτω τοίνυν ἐξ οὐρανοῦ πεσόντες καὶ εἰς ᾅδην ῥιφέντες δεινῶς, πάλιν ἀνερχόμεθα εἰς τὸ κάτω τοῦ οὐρανοῦ πέταλον, καὶ τὰς τῶν ἀγγέλων ὁμιλίας ἀκούομεν, καὶ ἐξ αὐτῶν μανθάνομεν τὸν τοῦ ἀνθρώπου θάνατον πρὸ τεσσαράκοντα ἡμερῶν. 15. καὶ ἀκούσαντες τούτων ἐπιμελούμεθα καὶ ἀγωνιζόμεθα ἵνα τὸν τοῦ ἀνθρώπου θάνατον ἢ διὰ πυρὸς ἢ δι᾽ ὕδατος ἢ διὰ κρημνοῦ οἰκονομήσωμεν, ὅπως λάβωμέν τινα ἐξ αὐτοῦ μέριδα. 16. καὶ ἐν τῷ μὴ ἔχειν ἡμᾶς βάσιν ἀναπαύσεως ἐν τῷ πετάλῳ τοῦ οὐρανοῦ πίπτομεν ὥσπερ φύλλα ἀπὸ τῶν δένδρων, καὶ δοκοῦμεν τοῖς ἀνθρώποις ὡς

---

§ 9. l. 2 σκυθρωπὸς ms: σκυτρ. Is, corr. Kurz 4 ἔτι ms.: ἔστι Is, corr. Kurz | ἴδῃς conj. Is: ἴδοις ms. § 10. l. 9 ἀφ᾽ ὅτου Is: ἀφότου ms. § 11. l. 14 * f. 371ᵛ § 15. l. 28 τοῦ: supra lineam adscr. prim. man.

ἀστέρες χυνόμενοι, * ἵνα δοξαζώμεθα παρὰ τῶν ἀνθρώπων.«
17. καὶ ὁ βασιλεύς· »καὶ οἱ χυνόμενοι ἀστέρες, καὶ δοκοῦντες ἀστέρες, οὐκ εἰσιν ὄντες ἀστέρες;« καὶ ὁ Ὀρνίας· »οὐχί, βασιλεῦ· οἱ γὰρ τοῦ οὐρανοῦ ἀστέρες ἀθάνατοί εἰσι καὶ ἐστηριγμένοι καὶ
5 οὐ κινοῦνται.« 18. καὶ ἀκούσας ταῦτα ὁ βασιλεὺς ἀπέλυσε τὸν Ὀρνίαν εἰς ἔργον αὐτοῦ ἐργάζεσθαι.

V. Ὠικοδομεῖτο δὲ ὁ ναός· καὶ πάντες οἱ βασιλεῖς τῆς γῆς καὶ οἱ ἄρχοντες τῶν τιμίων καὶ βασίλισσα Νότου ἡ σοφὴ Σιβύλλα καὶ αὐτὴ ἦλθε θεάσασθαι τὸν ναὸν κυρίου, καὶ εἰσέφερε
10 καὶ αὐτὴ εἰς τὴν οἰκοδομὴν τοῦ ναοῦ ξύλα πολυτελῆ καὶ ἀξιόλογα.

VI. Ἀπέστειλε δὲ ὁ βασιλεὺς Ἀράβων ἐπιστολὴν πρὸς τὸν βασιλέα Σολομῶντα καὶ διελάμβανεν οὕτως· »βασιλεῦ Σολομῶν, χαίροις. γινωσκέτω ἡ βασιλεία σου ὅτι εἰς τὴν ἡμῶν χώραν
15 οἰκεῖ χαλεπὸν δαιμόνιον δυνατόν, καὶ κατὰ τρεῖς ἡμέρας ἀνεγείρει ἄνεμον ἰσχυρόν, καὶ ἐκριζοῖ οἰκίας καὶ δένδρα καὶ βουνοὺς καὶ ἀνθρώπους ἀπόλλυσι, ῥίπτων τούτους εἰς κρημνοὺς καὶ εἰς ὕδωρ καὶ εἰς πῦρ. 2. εἰ οὖν βούλει τὸ σὸν κράτος, ἀπόστειλον καὶ ἐξάλειψον καὶ ἐξολόθρευσον τοῦτον * ἀπὸ τῆς τοιαύτης χώρας.
20 εἰ οὖν τοῦτο ποιήσει ἡ βασιλεία σου, εἰσενέγκομεν εἰς τὴν τοῦ ναοῦ οἰκοδομὴν τάλαντα χρυσίου καὶ ἀργυρίου καὶ χαλκοῦ ἑκατὸν εἴκοσι πέντε.«

3. Ἀναγνοὺς οὖν τὴν ἐπιστολὴν ὁ βασιλεὺς ἐνετείλατο τῷ παιδαρίῳ τῷ ἔχοντι τὴν σφραγῖδα τάχιστα καταλαβεῖν πρὸς αὐ-
25 τόν· καὶ ἐλθόντος φησὶν ὅτι· »τάχιστα ἄπελθε εἰς τὸν τῶν Ἀράβων βασιλέα, καὶ λάβε μετά σου τὴν σφραγῖδα καὶ κάμηλον μίαν τὴν ταχίστην καὶ ἀσκὸν καινόν. 4. καὶ δειξάτω σοι τὸν τόπον ἔνθα πνεῖ τὸ πονηρὸν πνεῦμα· καὶ καταλαβὼν τὸν τόπον ἐκεῖνον ἐπίθες τὸν ἀσκὸν ἀνεῳγμένον ἔχοντα τὸ στόμα αὐτοῦ
30 πρὸς τῇ ὀπῇ τοῦ φωλεοῦ, καὶ παρατήρει τὴν ἡμέραν ἐν ᾗ ἐξέρχε-

---

§ 16. l. 1 * f. 374ʳ
C. V. l. 7 Ὠικοδομεῖτο ego: οἰκοδομήτο ms., -μεῖτο Is   8 σιβύλλα ms., (Σι-) Is, l. Σίβυλλα?
C. VI 1. l. 16 ἐκριζοῖ Is. ἐκριζεῖ ms.   18 § 2. βούλει: l. βούλεται?
19 * f. 374ᵛ   20 εἰσενέγκομεν Is: εἰσενέγκωμεν ms.   § 3. l. 26 ἀρράβων ms.   27 § 4. σοι ego: σε ms.   28 ἔχοντα ego: ἔχον ms.

ται τὸ πονηρὸν πνεῦμα. 5. καὶ ὅταν ἴδῃς τὸν ἀσκὸν πλησθέντα δίκην ἀνέμου, ἀσφάλισαι μετὰ τοῦ δακτυλίου τὸ στόμα αὐτοῦ τοῦ ἀσκοῦ, καὶ ἐπίθες αὐτὸν εἰς τὴν κάμηλον καὶ κατάλαβε ταχέως πρὸς ἡμᾶς.« 6. Καὶ ἀπῆλθε τὸ παιδάριον καὶ ἐποίησε πάντα κατὰ τὴν θέλησιν τοῦ βασιλέως Σολομῶντος. 7. ἐπαναστρέφοντος δὲ αὐτοῦ λέγει τὸ δαιμόνιον· »ἄνοιξόν μοι, ὦ παιδίον, καὶ ἐπιδείξω σοι τόπον ἐν ᾧ κέκρυπται πράσινος λίθος καὶ τὸ χρυσίον τὸ τίμιον.« τὸ δὲ παιδίον λέγει· »ἀπέλθωμεν πρῶτον πρὸς τὸν βασιλέα, καὶ μετὰ ταῦτα αὐτοῦ κελεύοντος ποιήσομεν.« 8. ὡς δὲ τὴν ὁδὸν ἤνυσαν καὶ τὸν τόπον κατέλαβον ἐν ᾧ ἦν, πεσὼν ἐκ τῆς καμήλου προσεκύνει ἄνω καὶ κάτω φερόμενος τὸν Σολομῶντα. 9. ὁ δὲ βασιλεύς φησι· »τίς εἶ καὶ τίς σου τὸ ὄνομα;« ὁ δέ φησι· »δαιμόνιόν εἰμι, Ἐφίππας καλούμενος.« 10. καὶ λέγει αὐτῷ· »δύνασαί ποιῆσαί μοί τι χρήσιμον;« καὶ ὁ Ἐφίππας· »δύναμαι ἆραι τὸν λίθον τὸν ἀκρογωνιαῖον ὃν ἀπεδοκίμασαν ἄνθρωποί τε καὶ δαίμονες καὶ θεῖναι τοῦτον εἰς κεφαλὴν γωνίας.« 11. καὶ ὁ βασιλεὺς προέτρεψε τὸν Ἐφίππαν ποιῆσαι ταῦτα. καὶ ἐποίησε τοῦτο ὁρώντων πάντων τοῦ τε βασιλέως καὶ τῶν περιεστηκότων ἀνδρῶν. 12. ἔκθαμβος δὲ γενόμενος ὁ βασιλεὺς ἤρετο τὸ Ἐφίππαν εἰ γινώσκοι καὶ ἕτερον πνεῦμα ὅμοιον αὐτῷ. καὶ λέγει ὁ Ἐφίππας· »ἔστι, βασιλεῦ, καὶ ἕτερον πνεῦμα * ἐν τῇ Ἐρυθρᾷ θαλάσσῃ καθήμενον καὶ ἔχον ἐν ἑαυτῷ τὸν πορφυροῦν κίονα.« 13. καὶ λέγει ὁ βασιλεύς· »ἄπελθε μετὰ τῆς σφραγῖδος καὶ ἄγαγέ μοι αὐτὸν ὧδε.« ἀπελθὼν δὲ ὁ Ἐφίππας μετὰ τῆς σφραγῖδος καὶ ἀνασπάσας αὐτὸν ἤγαγεν αὐτόν τε καὶ δαίμονας δύο βαστάζοντας τὸν κίονα καὶ φέροντας τοῦτον εἰς τὸν ἀέρα. 14. ἰδὼν δὲ ταῦτα ὁ βασιλεὺς καὶ ἔκθαμβος γενόμενος ἐκέλευσεν αὐτοῖς βαστάζειν τὸν κίονα καὶ κρέμασθαι εἰς τὸν ἀέρα μέχρι τῆς συντελείας τοῦ αἰῶνος καὶ μὴ ῥῖψαι τοῦτον ἐπὶ τῆς γῆς ποτε, μήπως λύμην τῷ τῶν ἀνθρώπων προξενήσωσι γένει.

---

§ 6. l. 6 * f. 373ʳ   § 7. l. 7 ἐπιδείξω Is: ἐπεδείξω ms.   § 8. l. 12 προσεκύνει ego: προσεκύνη ms., προσεκύνη σε Is   § 9. l. 14 Ἐφίππας Is: ἐφ' ἵππας ms.   § 11. l. 18 ποιῆσαι: ποιῆσαι Is   § 12. l. 21 γινώσκοι ego: γινώσκεις ms.   22 * f. 373ᵛ   23 ἔχων ms.

VII. Πάλιν οὖν ὁ βασιλεὺς πρὸς τὸν Ὀρνίαν λέγει· »ἔστι καὶ ἕτερον δαιμόνιον;« καὶ ὁ Ὀρνίας λέγει· »εἰσὶ μὲν πολλά, ὦ βασιλεῦ. ὑπάρχει δὲ ἀπὸ τούτων ἓν μεγίστην κεκτημένον τὴν δύναμιν.« 2. »ποῖον δὲ τοῦτο,« φησὶν ὁ βασιλεύς, »καὶ τίνα με-
5 γίστην ἔχει τὴν δύναμιν καὶ τί τούτῳ τὸ ὄνομα;« Ὁ Ὀρνίας λέγει· »Σαμαὴλ τὸ ὄνομα, ὦ βασιλεῦ, ἄρχων δὲ τοῦ τῶν δαιμόνων ὑπάρχει συστήματος· καὶ συμφέρον σοι ὑπάρχει, ὦ βασιλεῦ, τοῦ μὴ ἰδεῖν αὐτόν." 3. καὶ ὁ βασιλεύς· »μηδέν σοι * περὶ τοῦτο μελέτω, πονηρὸν καὶ ἀκάθαρτον πνεῦμα, ἀλλὰ λαβὼν
10 τὴν σφραγῖδα ἄγαγέ μοι αὐτὸν ὧδε κατὰ τάχος.« λαβὼν δὲ ὁ Ὀρνίας τὴν σφραγῖδα τοῦ θεοῦ ἀπῆλθε τὸ τοῦ βασιλέως πληρώσων θέλημα. 4. ὁ δὲ Σολομῶν ἐπὶ θρόνου καθήμενος ἦν τῷ τῆς βασιλείας κεκοσμημένος στέμματί τε καὶ διαδήματι καὶ τὸν Ὀρνίαν μετὰ τοῦ Σαμαὴλ ἐκδεχόμενος, σκῆπτρόν τε τὸ βασιλι-
15 κὸν ἀνὰ χεῖρα εἶχεν. 5. ἐλθόντων δὲ τοῦ τε Σαμαὴλ καὶ τοῦ Ὀρνία πρὸς τὸν βασιλέα, φησὶν ὁ βασιλεὺς πρὸς τὸν Σαμαήλ· »τίς εἶ, καὶ τί σου τὸ ὄνομα;« ὁ δέ φησι· »Σαμαὴλ κέκλημαι· ἄρχων δὲ τοῦ τῶν δαιμόνων ὑπάρχω συστήματος. 6. καὶ ὁ βασιλεύς· »δύνασαι ποιῆσαί μέ τι;« ὁ δέ φησι·« δύναμαι ἐμ-
20 φυσῆσαί σοι καὶ ἀπαγαγεῖν σε εἰς τὸ ἔσχατον τῆς γῆς.« καὶ ἅμα τῷ λόγῳ ἐνεφύσησεν αὐτὸν καὶ ἀπήγαγεν εἰς τὰ ἔσχατα τῆς γῆς.

VIII. Διεφημίζετο δὲ ἡ φήμη τοῦ βασιλέως εἰς πάντα τὰ πέρατα τῆς γῆς, καὶ προσκυνοῦντες ἦσαν αὐτῷ πάντες οἱ βασι-
25 λεῖς τῆς γῆς καὶ οἱ ἄρχοντες, καὶ χορηγοῦντες εἰς τὴν τοῦ ναοῦ οἰκοδομήν. 2. τῷ δὲ καιρῷ ἐκείνῳ * ἐρρητόρευσε τὸ ᾆσμα τῶν ᾀσμάτων. καὶ ἔλεγεν οὕτως· »ἐκτησάμην βασιλείαν· ἐκτησάμην ᾄδοντας καὶ ᾀδούσας.« καὶ καταλέξας τὰ πάντα τέλος ἐπάγει· »τὰ πάντα δὲ ματαιότης ματαιοτήτων· τὰ πάντα

---

§ 3. l. 8 * f. 372ʳ   § 6. l. 22 In hoc loco add. c. VIII 4 James forte c. VIII : post 2—7 ponendum
C. VIII. § 2. l. 26 ἐκείνῳ in marg. inf. scr. man. prim. | * f. 372ᵛ

§ 2. 27 cf. Ec. 2 : 7 ἐκτησάμην δούλους καὶ παιδίσκας, 2 : 8 ἐποίησά μοι ᾄδοντας καὶ ᾀδούσας   29 Ec. 1 : 2; 12 : 8f.

ματαιότης.« 3. ἔλεγε δὲ καὶ τοῦτο· »πάντων τῶν γραμμάτων ἄρχει τὸ χ̄. 4. εὐδοκίᾳ δὲ θεοῦ διεσώθη Σολομῶν εἰς τὰ αὐτοῦ βασίλεια. 5. καὶ ᾠκοδομεῖτο ὁ πάνσεπτος ναὸς τοῦ θεοῦ. ᾠκοδομεῖτο δὲ πάντα κατὰ μίμησιν τῆς ἀνατάξεως. 6. ὑπῆρχον τὰ χερουβὶμ καὶ τὰ σεραφὶμ καὶ τὰ ἐξαπτέρουγα· ὄπισθεν δὲ τοῦ θυσιαστηρίου τὰ πολυόμματα καὶ οἱ θρόνοι καὶ αἱ κυριότητες. 7. ἄρρητον δὲ τὸ κάλλος τοῦ τοιούτου ναοῦ καὶ ἀνερμήνευτον, καὶ τοιοῦτον οἷον οὔτε ἐγένετο οὔτε γενήσεται.

5. 11. 3—4 οἰκοδομεῖτο ms. (bis) § 7. 1. 7 κάλλος Is: κάλλους ms.

CONSPECTUS TITULORUM

Tituli Codicum Manu Scriptorum Recensionum A, B, et C
Titulus Codicum MSS PQ

Διαθήκη Σολομῶντος υἱοῦ Δαυείδ, ὃς ἐβασίλευσεν ἐν Ἱερου-
5 σαλὴμ καὶ ἐκράτησεν καὶ ὑπέταξεν πάντων ἀερίων, ἐπιγείων, καὶ
καταχθονίων πνευμάτων· δι᾽ ὧν καὶ πάντα τὰ ἔργα τοῦ ναοῦ τὰ
ὑπερβάλλοντα πεποίηκεν· καὶ τίνες αἱ ἐξουσίαι αὐτῶν κατὰ ἀνθρώπων, καὶ παρὰ ποίων ἀγγέλων οὗτοι οἱ δαίμονες καταργοῦνται. τοῦ σοφοῦ Σολομῶντος.

10   Titulus Codicis MS I

(Διαθήκη τ⟨οῦ⟩) Σολομῶντος υἱοῦ Δαυείδ, ὃς ἐβασίλευσεν ἐν
Ἱερουσαλήμ, καὶ περὶ τῶν δαιμόνων οὓς ἐκράτησε, καὶ τίνες εἰσὶν αἱ ἐξουσίαι δοθεῖσαι αὐτῷ ὑπὸ θεοῦ κατὰ τῶν δαιμόνων καὶ
παρὰ τίνων ἀγγέλων καταργοῦνται οἱ δαίμονες, καὶ τὰ ἔργα τοῦ
15 ναοῦ ἃ ὑπερβαλλόντως πεποίηκεν.

Titulus Codicis MS H

Διήγησις περὶ τῆς διαθήκης Σολομῶντος καὶ περὶ τῆς ἐλεύ-
σεως τῶν δαιμόνων καὶ περὶ τῆς τοῦ ναοῦ οἰκοδομῆς.

MSS PQ. Du C(angius in *Notae ad Zonorae Annalia*, p. 83), Fab(ricius, Cod. Pseudepigr. Vet. Test. I 1036 sq.)   4 Διαθήκη P: ἡ διήγησις Q | ὅς: ὡς Q   5—6 πάντων ... πνευμ. om. Q | ἐπιγείων om. DuC.   7 αἱ om. Q | ἀνθρ. pr. τῶν Q   8 οὗτοι PQ: εἶτοι DuC, αὐτοὶ conj. Fab | καταργοῦνται P: καταρχδῦνται DuC, καταργάζονται Q   9 τοῦ σ. Σολ. P: om. Q DuC Fab | Hic sequitur benedictio, cf. infra p. 99* l. 1 s.

MS I. 1. 11 Διαθήκη τοῦ: in marg. sup. negligenter exaratis litteris scr. man. alt. διαθήκη τ   14 οἱ: εἰ ms. | Sequitur benedictio

MS H. 1. 17 Sequitur benedictio, cf. infra

Tituli Codicum et Subscriptio   99*

Benedictio Codicum MSS HIPQ

Εὐλογητὸς εἶ, κύριε ὁ Θεός, ὁ δοὺς τῷ Σολομῶντι τὴν ἐξουσίαν ταύτην. σοὶ δόξα καὶ κράτος εἰς τοὺς αἰῶνας· ἀμήν.

Titulus Codicum MSS VW

Διαθήκη τοῦ σοφωτάτου Σολομῶντος μετὰ τῶν παραλλήλων αὐτῆς ὀνομάτων ἅτινα ὡς μυστήρια ὑπὸ τοῦ Ἐζεκίου μετὰ τὸ ἀποθανεῖν τὸν Δαυεὶδ τὸν βασιλέαν ἐφυλάχθησαν.

Subscriptio Codicis MS V

Τέλος τῆς διαθήκης τοῦ σοφωτάτου Σολομῶν²τος υἱοῦ Δαβίδ, ὅπερ ἐγράφη μετὰ τὸ ³ἀποθανεῖν Δα(βὶ)δ τὸν βασιλέαν ὃς ⁴ἐφυλάχθη ὑπὸ Ἐζεκίου τοῦ βασιλέως. ⁵ἐγράφη παρ' ἐμοῦ Ἰω(άννου) ἰατροῦ τοῦ αρο(?)· ἐν ἔτει ͵ϛЭμϑ´ ⁶(ἰνδικτιόνος) δ' ἐν μηνὶ Δεκε(μ)βρίῳ ιδ'. ⁷καὶ ὁ θεός ἐστι μεθ' ἡμῶν καὶ οὐδεὶς καθ' ἡμῶν.

MSS HIPQ. 1. 2 εἶ om. H | κύριε om. HQ | ὁ Θεός om. IQ | τ. ἔξουσ. ταυτ.: τοιαύτην ἐξουσίαν PQ   3 σοὶ ... ἀμήν PQ: om. I

MSS VW. 1. 5 παραλλ.: add. πνου̃ (l. πνευμάτων) V   6 ἅτινα ὡς W: εἷος (l. ἃ ὡς) V | μυστ.: add. ἐφυλάχθη V   7 ἀποθανὸν W | τὸν om. V `ἐφυλάχθησαν om. V | In πίνακι MS V scr. man. alt. titulum hunc: ἡ διαθήκη τοῦ σολομώντος περὶ τ(οὺς) δαίμονας πῶς ἐπίασ(εν) αὐτοὺς καὶ ἔκτισεν τὴν ἀγί(αν) σι(όν).

MS V. ll. 9—18 Numeri superiores ad lineas textus referunt. Τέλος ... αρο in notis Tironianis scriptum est   9 Δαβίδ: δαβηϑ ms.   10 ὅπερ l. ἥπερ | ὅς: l. ἥ   12 Δεκεμβ.: δεκενρίῳ ms.

SIGILLA ANULI SALOMONIS

PQ Ἡ δὲ γλυφὴ τῆς σφραγίδος τοῦ δακτυλιδίου τῆς πεμφθείσεις ἐστὶν πεντάλφα αὕτη.

L Ἡ δὲ σφραγὶς ταῦτα ἔλεγεν· ἰδοὺ αὕτη ἐστὶν ἡ σφραγίς·
5 x̄ ō θ̄ ρ̄ σ̄ β̄ ι ω̄ ν̄ x ā ω̄ ā ω̄ ε λ̄ ῑ γ ω̄ ι σ̄ ς γ ω̄ ᾱ ᾱ ε σ̄ ρ̄ οῡ ρ̄ ╪

HL Ἣν δὲ ἡ γλυφὶς αὐτοῦ* λέγων οὕτως· κ(ύρι)ε ὁ θεὸς ἡμῶν· λέων· λέων· σαβαώθ· βιωνίκ· ἀωᾶ· ἐλωί· αἰαῶ· αἰώ· ἰωασέ· σουγεωά· ἀιέ· ἀενίου· οὐ· οὐνίου· ἠρώ.

T Περὶ τοῦ δακτυλιδίου· Λαβὼν κηρὸν παρθένον, ποίησον
10 δακτυλίδιον ὥσπερ ὁρᾷς φορεῖν ἐν τῷ δεξιῷ σου δακτύλῳ τῆς χειρός σου. περιενδύσας αὐτῷ χαρτίον παρθένον ἐπίγραφε πᾶν μετὰ κονδυλίου τῆς τέχνης ταῦτα τὰ ιβ´ ὀνόματα· λέων· σαβαώθ· βιωνιά· ἐλωί· ἀωά· ἰαώ· ἰασού· σουιεωά· ἀενιού· οὐ· οὐνίου· ἰού· ἰρώ.

15 Vʳ. Τοῦ Σολομῶντος μεγάλου· λθλθῑ | μ̄ κ(ύρι)ε ὁ θ(εὸ)ς ἡμ|ῶν· λεων· σαβα|ωθ· αἰαῶ· βιονη|κα· ωαελοι· ιωα|σε· σουγεῶ· α|αιε· αε· νιουφυ|ουνη· ιαησ|ω.

MSS PQ = Rec. B. ll. 2–3. l. 3 in mss. pentalpha non est

MS L. ll. 4—5. l. 4 ταῦτα: αὐτὰ ms. | αὕτη ἐστὶν: οὕτη εἰσὶν ms.

MSS HI. ll. 6—8. l. 6 αὐτοῦ HIs: αὕτη I | * H f. 2ᵛ | λέγων: λέγοντος(?) Diels, l. fortasse λέγουσα 7 λέων: om. H, λέγων Is | post σαβαώθ scripta ἀωᾶ· ἐλωί· αἰαῶ· ἐλωί· transversis lineis delevit I | βιωνίκ H | ἀωᾶ I: ᾱ· ω̄· ά· H | αἰαῶ I: ἐαώ H, add. ἐλωί· I | αἰώ om. H 8 ἀῖὰ H, ἀγέ I | οὐ: om. I | οὐνίου: οὐρανίου Is | ἤρα H

MS T. ll. 9—14 vide Introductionem p. 19 s.   10 θρ(ας) ms. | χείρας ms.

MS Vʳ. ll. 15—17 vide Introductionem p. 24 s.

Sigilla Anuli Salomonis 101*

Rec. C. Ἦν δὲ ἡ ἐπιγραφὴ τῆς σφραγῖδος τοῦ δακτυλίου αὕτη· . . . . . * καὶ ἔδωκεν τῷ Σολομῶντι· αὗταί εἰσιν αἱ ἕνδεκα σφραγῖδαι ἃς ἔδωκεν ὁ ἄγγελος μετὰ τῶν δώδεκα λίθων· ἐξ ὧν ἡ μία σφραγῖδα ἔχει τῶν χαρισμάτων τὸ μέγεθος.

Sigilla Salomonis ex ms. L.

MSS VW. ll. 1—2 ⁷Ἦν . . . Σολομῶντι   2 αὕτη: ταύτης αὕτη ἡ σφρα-γ(ῖδα) τοῦ δακτυληδίου V | hic. sequuntur duodecim sigilla | * V f. 437ᵛ, W f. 267ᵛ | Σολομῶντι τὸν υἱὸν δᾱδ V
MSS VVᴮW. ll. 2—4 αὗται . . . μέγεθος   3 μετὰ . . . λίθων: τὸν σολομῶντα Vᴮ, add. τὸν τὰ προτία ἔχων τὸν ιβ' λιθ <. Μετὰ (δὲ) τὸ λα-β(εῖν) τ(ὴν) ᾱ σφραγῆδ(αν). ἐδόθισαν καὶ αὗται αἱ ἕνδεκα V | ἐξ ὧν VW: ἐξ οὗ Vᴮ   4 σφραγ. om. Vᴮ | τῶν . . μεγ.: τὸ χαρισμ < καὶ τὴν χάριδ < καὶ ιβ' λειθ < με (l. μετ') αὐτ(ῶν) Vᴮ

ΔΙΗΓΗΣΙΣ ΠΕΡΙ ΤΟΥ ΠΡΟΦΗΤΟΥ ΚΑΙ ΣΟΦΩΤΑΤΟΥ ΤΟΥ ΒΑΣΙΛΕΩΣ ΣΟΛΟΜΩΝΤΟΣ

I. *Διήγησις περὶ τοῦ σοφωτάτου βασιλέως Σολομῶντος πολὺ ὠφέλιμος, ὁποῦ ἦτον υἱὸς τοῦ προφήτου Δαυεὶδ τοῦ βασιλέως·* καὶ ἀκούσατε πῶς τὸν ἐγέννησεν τὸν Σολομῶν⟨τα⟩ ἀπὸ τοῦ Οὐρία τὴν γυναῖκα τὴν ὁποίαν τὴν εἶδεν ὁ προφήτης Δαυείδ. 2. ἀγναντεύοντες εἶδεν αὐτὴν ἀπὸ τὰ παραθύρια τοῦ παλατίου του καὶ τὴν ἠγάπησεν καὶ ἔστειλεν καὶ τὴν ἐπῆρεν καὶ ἔπεσεν μετ' αὐτῆς. καὶ ἐγγαστρώθη καὶ ἐγέννησεν αὐτὸν τὸν σοφώτατον Σολομῶν⟨τα⟩. 3. καὶ ὄχι μόνον πῶς ἔκαμεν τὴν μοιχείαν ἀλλὰ καὶ τὸν ταλαίπορον τὸν ἄνδρα της ἔστειλεν καὶ τὸν ἐφόνευσεν.

4. Καὶ ἰδὼν ὁ μεγαλοδύναμος θεὸς τὸ κακὸν ὁποῦ ἐποίησεν ὁ Δαυεὶδ καὶ θέλοντας νὰ τὸν γυρίσῃ εἰς ἐπιστρόφην καὶ εἰς μετάνοιαν ἵνα μὴν κολασθῇ αἰωνίως, ἔστειλεν τὸν ἀρχάγγελον αὐτοῦ Μιχαὴλ βαστῶντας εἰς τὰς χεῖρας αὐτοῦ ἕνα μαχαίρι δίστομον. 5. καὶ ἐπῆγεν εἰς τὸν προφήτην Νάθαν καὶ εἶπεν αὐτόν· »ὕπαγε ἔλεγχον τὸν προφήτην Δαυεὶδ τὸν βασιλέαν εἰς * τὴν μεγάλην ἁμαρτίαν ὁποῦ ἔκαμεν. καὶ ἐσὺ μὴν φοβᾶσαι τίποτες ὅτι ἐγὼ θέλω στέκεσθαι εἰς τοὺς νόμους ὀπίσω μὲ τοῦτο τὸ δίστομον σπαθὶ τὸ ξεγυμνωμένον. καὶ ἐσὺ Νάθαν θέλεις με βλέπειν καὶ ὁ Δαυεὶδ δὲν θέλει με βλέπειν οὐδὲ ποσῶς.

6. Καὶ οὕτως ἐγερθεὶς ὁ Νάθαν κατὰ τὸν λόγον τοῦ ἀρχαγγέλου καὶ ἐπῆγεν εἰς τὸν προφήτην Δαυεὶδ καὶ ἔλεγξεν αὐτὸν καὶ του ἔλεγεν παραβολικῶς· »βασιλέα καὶ προφήτη Δαυείδ, ἄνθρωπος εἶχεν ἐννενήκοντα ἐννέα προβατίνες. καὶ εἶχεν καὶ ἕνα δοῦλον, καὶ ὁ δοῦλός του ἐκεῖνος εἶχεν μόνον μίαν προβατίναν.

MS E = codex Monasterii Sancti Saba 290; inc. f. 177ᵛ. Ad. c. I cf. D
I 1—11. Tit.: add. λόγ⟨ος⟩ β   C. I § 1 l. 3 πολλὶ   18 ἔλεξον | * f. 178ᵛ
20 στέκεστε   24 ἔλεξον   25 βασιλέαν   26 ἐνέαν

καὶ ἐξήλευσέν τον καί του τὴν ἐπῆρεν καὶ εἰς τὸ τέλος ἔστειλεν καὶ τὸν ἐφόνευσεν καὶ ἐπῆρεν καὶ τὴν προβατίναν του. καὶ ὡς δικαιοκρίτης ὁποῦ εἶσαι, ἀποφάσισον τί μέλλει γενέσθαι ὁ ἄνθρωπος ἐκεῖνος;« 7. Καὶ ἀπεκρίθη ὁ προφήτης Δαυεὶδ καὶ εἶπεν ὅτι· »ἐκεῖνος ὁ ἄνθρωπος πρέπει νὰ σκάψουν ἕνα λάκκον καὶ τὸν ἐβάλουν μέσα ἕως τὴν μέσην καὶ νὰ τὸν ἐχώσουν μὲ τὸ χῶμα καὶ οὕτως νὰ τὸν λιθοβολήσουν«. 8. καὶ λέγει ὁ προφήτης Νάθαν· »ὦ βασιλεῦ, ἐσὺ εἶσαι ἐκεῖνος ὁποῦ ἔκαμες τὸν φόνον καὶ τὴν μοιχείαν«. 9. καὶ τότες ὁ Δαυεὶδ ὡσὰν ἄκουσεν, ἔτζι ἔμεινεν ὡσὰν νεκρὸς καὶ ἄλλαξεν ἡ ὄψις τοῦ προσώπου του. καὶ ἐγνώρισεν τὴν ἁμαρτίαν του ὁποῦ ἔκαμεν τὸ πῶς ἦτον μεγάλη. ὅμως * δὲν ὑπερηφανεύθηκεν ὡς βασιλέας ὁποῦ ἦτον ἵνα ὀργισθῇ κατὰ τοῦ προφήτου Νάθαν ὁποῦ τὸν ἔλεγξεν μεγάλως, ἀμμὴ παρευθὺς ἐσηκώθη ἀπὸ τὸν θρόνον του καὶ ἐπροσεκύνησεν τὸν προφήτην Νάθαν μετὰ δακρύων καὶ ἀναστεναγμῶν ἐξ ὅλης τῆς καρδίας καὶ εἶπεν· »ἀληθῶς ἐγὼ εἶμαι ὁποῦ ἥμαρτον ἐνώπιον τοῦ θεοῦ καὶ ἀνθρώπων«. 10. καὶ εὐθὺς ἔβγαλεν τὰ βασιλικὰ φορέματα ὁποῦ ἐβάσταζεν καὶ ἔβαλεν σάκκον τρίχινον καὶ εἰσέβη εἰς ἕνα λάκκον καὶ ἔλεγεν καὶ ἐθρήνει ὡς καθὼς ἔκαμεν τὴν ἀπόφασιν μὲ τὴν κρίσιν του καὶ ἐκεῖ ἥρμοσεν τὸ ψαλτήριον αὐτὸ ὁποῦ διαβάζομεν ἡμεῖς τὴν σήμερον ἡμέραν. καὶ μετ' ἐκείνην τὴν μετάνοιαν ἐσυγχώρεσέν τον ὁ θεὸς καὶ ἐκοιμήθη ἐν Κυρίῳ ἅγιος καὶ προφήτης καὶ βασιλέας.

II. Τὸ λοιπὸν ἂς ἔλθωμεν καὶ εἰς τὸν υἱόν του τὸν βασιλέαν Σολομῶντα ὁποῦ ἦτον μέγας καὶ σοφὸς καὶ ἦτον υἱὸς τοῦ προφήτου Δαυεὶδ καὶ ἐπαρέλαβεν τὸν θρόνον τοῦ πατρός του καὶ ἡ σοφία του ὑπὲρ πᾶσαν τὴν σοφίαν τοῦ κόσμου. καὶ ἐξήτησεν σοφίαν ἀπὸ τὸν θεὸν καὶ οὐχὶ πλοῦτον καὶ δόξαν καὶ τιμήν. ὅμως ὁ θεὸς ἔδωσέν του ὅλα τὰ καλά, τὴν σοφίαν, τὸν πλοῦτον καὶ τὴν δόξαν καὶ τὴν τιμήν. 2. καὶ ὅμως θαρρόντας εἰς τὴν σοφίαν τὴν πολλὴν ὁποῦ του ἔδωσεν ὁ θεὸς ἐβουλήθη νὰ κτίσῃ ἐκεῖνον τὸν ναὸν τοῦ θεοῦ ὁποῦ ἠθέλησεν νὰ τὸν ἀρχίσῃ ὁ πα-

---

9 § 9 l. ἔτσι   10 ἄλαξεν   11 * f. 178ᵛ   13 ἔλεξεν   14 ἀμὴ = εἰ μή   17 § 10. εὔγαλεν   19 ἐσέβη   21 ἐκύνον   22 τὸν: του
C. II. v. parallela in ms. D I 12—II   24 τοῦ υἱοῦ | τοῦ βασιλέως Σολομῶντος   30 § 2. θαρώντας   31 πολλὴν: τῆνλλυν scripto supra τὴν scr. no man. prim.

τέρας του ὁ Δαυείδ. καὶ ὁ Σολομῶν ἐβουλήθη νὰ τὸν ἀνακτίσῃ ἀπὸ θεμελίων ἐκλεκτὸν καὶ περίφημον ἵνα μὴ εὑρίσκεται κάτωθεν τοῦ οὐρανοῦ εἰς τὴν γῆν ἀπάνω ὡσὰν ἐκεῖνον τὸν ναόν. 3. ὅμως ἐσύναξεν τὴν κατασκευὴν ἅπασαν. λοιπὸν ἐσύναξεν τεχνίτας καὶ 5 μαϊστόρους ἐπιτηδείους τὸν ἀριθμὸν χιλιάδες τέσσαρις δίχως τῶν ἐργατῶν. καὶ ἄρχισαν νὰ κτίζουν τὸν ναὸν τοῦ θεοῦ εἰς ὄνομα τῆς ἁγίας Σιών.

3. Λοιπὸν ὁ βασιλεὺς Σολομῶν εἶχεν ἕνα παιδίον πολλὰ ὡραιότατον καὶ ποθεινότατον ἀπὸ ὅλα τὰ παιδία τοῦ παλατίου 10 του καὶ ἦτον σώφρον καὶ γνωστικὸν καὶ ἐπιτήδειον εἰς πᾶσα τέχνην, καὶ ἐχαίρετον ὁ βασιλεὺς βλέποντάς το καὶ τὸ ἔκαμεν ἐπίτροπον καὶ ἐπιτηρητὴν εἰς πᾶσαν του θέλησιν καὶ ἀγάπα το ὁ βασιλεὺς καὶ εἶχεν το ὡσὰν ἴδιον υἱόν. λοιπὸν τὸ ἔβαλεν ὁ βασιλεὺς τὸ παιδίον ἐκεῖνο ἀπάνω εἰς τοὺς μαϊστόρους ὁποῦ 15 ἐδούλευαν τὸν ναὸν τοῦ θεοῦ ἐπίτροπον καὶ ἐπιτηρητὴν καὶ ἑρμήνευεν τοὺς μαϊστόρους ὁποῦ ἐδούλευαν τὸν ναὸν τοῦ θεοῦ. καὶ ἔβλεπαν ὅλοι τὸ παιδίον καὶ αὐτὸς ὁ βασιλεὺς καὶ ἐθαύμαζαν εἰς τὴν γνῶσιν ὁποῦ εἶχεν. 4. ὅμως βλέποντας ὁ διάβολος ὁ ἐχθρὸς τῆς ἀληθείας δὲν ἠμπόριεν ὁ μιαρὸς νὰ βλέπῃ τὸ ἔργον 20 ὁποῦ ἐκαταπιάστηκεν ὁ βασιλεὺς Σολομῶν ὁποῦ οἰκοδόμα τὸν ναὸν τοῦ θεοῦ καὶ ἤθελεν νὰ κάμῃ καὶ τὸν βασιλέαν νὰ λυπηθῇ διὰ νὰ ἀμελήσῃ τὸ ἔργον τοῦ θεοῦ ἐκεῖνο διὰ νὰ μὴν φτειαστῇ τελείαν.

5. Ἀλλὰ θέλετε τὸ * ἀκούσῃ παρέμπροσθεν τί ἔπαθεν ὁ 25 μιαρὸς καὶ ἐγελάσθη καὶ ἐπιάσθη καὶ αἰσχύνθη. λοιπὸν εἰς ἐκεῖνες τὲς ἡμέρες ἄρχισεν ἐκεῖνο τὸ ὡραιότατον παιδίον καὶ ἔχανεν τὴν ὄψιν του καὶ τὸν νοῦν του καὶ ἔγινεν ὡσὰν ἐξεστηκόν. λοιπὸν ἤρχετον ἀοράτως ἀπὸ τὸν ἀέρα ἕνα πονηρὸν πνεῦμα καὶ ἀκάθαρτον δαιμόνιον καὶ ἐπείραζε τὸ παιδίον ὅποτε ἤθελεν 30 νὰ κοιμηθῇ εἰς τὴν κλίνην του καὶ τοῦ ἔδειχνεν ὁ μιαρὸς δαίμων λογιῶν φαντασίες. 6. καὶ βλέποντας ὁ βασιλεὺς τὸ παιδίον ἐκεῖνο ἐθαύμαζεν καὶ ἐλυπᾶτον πολὺ καὶ ἔδιδέν του ὁ βασιλεὺς διπλὸν τὸ φαγητὸν καὶ τὰ φορέματά του παρὰ τῶν ἄλλων παι-

---

1 * f. 179ʳ | νὰ ... θεμελίων per dittographiam bis scr. 5 τέσαρης
9 παιδίαν 12 πᾶσα του θέλημα corr. Pr. Bessarion 15 ἐδούλευεν
§ 4. l. 20 οἰκοδόμαν § 5. l. 24 * f. 179ᵛ 25 ἐπηάσθην | αἰσχύνθην
§ 6. l. 82 πολλὶ

δλων ὁποῦ εἶχεν εἰς τὸ παλάτιόν του ὅπως νὰ ἔλθῃ εἰς τὴν προτέραν του κατάστασιν καὶ εἰς τὴν τάξιν ὁποῦ εἶχεν, ἀλλὰ ἡ ὄψις τοῦ προσώπου του δὲν ἄλλαξεν ἀλλὰ μᾶλλον εἰς τὸ χειρότερον.

6. Καὶ μίαν τῶν ἡμερῶν ἐρώτησεν ὁ βασιλεὺς τὸ παιδίον καὶ ἔλεγεν του· »εἰπέ μου, τέκνον μου, διὰ τί εἶσαι κίτρινος καὶ σκυθρωπὸς εἰς τὴν ὄψιν καὶ ὁ νοῦς σου δὲν εἶναι μετὰ σοῦ μόνον εἶσαι παρηλλαγμένος«. 7. καὶ τὸ παιδίον δὲν ἤθελεν νὰ εἰπῇ τοῦ βασιλέως τί ἐπάθενε. καὶ βλέποντας τοῦτο ὁ βασιλεὺς πῶς δὲν τοῦ ἀπηλογᾶτον ἐθαύμαζε καὶ ἐλυπᾶτον πολὺ τὸ τί νὰ κάμῃ καὶ ἄρχισεν ὁ βασιλεὺς μετὰ ὀργῆς καὶ θυμοῦ καὶ ἔλεγεν πρὸς τὸ παιδίον »νὰ μοῦ εἰπῇς τὴν ἀλήθειαν ἀπὸ τί ἐκαταστάθεις ἔτζι εἰς τέτοιαν * θεωρίαν καὶ πῶς ἐβγῆκες ἔξαφνα ἀπὸ τὸν νοῦν σου, ἀμμὴ νὰ ἠξεύρῃς ὅτι πολλὰ βάσανα μέλλεις νὰ πάθῃς καὶ νὰ χάσῃς καὶ τὴν ζωήν σου. 8. ταῦτα ὡς ἤκουσεν τὸ παιδὶ ἐκεῖνο ἔλεγεν πρὸς τὸν βασιλέαν μετὰ δακρύων καὶ φόβου καὶ τρόμου· »αὐθέντη μου πολυχρονημένε, ἐμένα ὅλα τὰ καλά μου τὰ ἔχει ἡ βασιλεία σου δομένα καὶ τίποτες δέν μου λείπει. ἀπὸ τὰ καλὰ ὅλα αὐτὰ δὲν εὐφραίνεται ἡ καρδία μου, ἀλλὰ ἄκουσόν μου, αὐθέντη, νὰ σοῦ διηγηθῶ τί παθαίνω. ἐκεῖ ὁποῦ κοιμοῦμαι εἰς τὴν κλίνην μου ἔρχεται ἕνας ἄνθρωπος μαῦρος κατὰ πολλὰ ὡσὰν Ἀράπης καὶ μὲ πλακώνει εἰς τὴν καρδίαν καὶ πιάνει τὴν ἄκρην τοῦ δακτύλου μου τοῦ μικροῦ καὶ βυζάνει καὶ πίνει τὸ αἷμα μου καὶ πάλιν μοῦ φαίνεται τὴν ἡμέραν καὶ ἔρχεται ὡς ἄγγελος καὶ μοῦ λέγει ὅτι νὰ μὴν τὸ εἰπῶ τῆς βασιλείας σου αὐτὰ ὁποῦ παθαίνω καὶ ἐκεῖνος θέλει με ἐγλυτώσει ἀπὸ τὸν μαῦρον καὶ μοῦ εἶπεν ὅτι ἂν σοῦ τὸ εἰπῶ γλυτωμὸν δὲν ἔχω«.

9. Ταῦτα ἀκούσας ὁ βασιλεὺς ἐθαύμασεν καὶ εὐχαρίστησεν κύριον τὸν θεὸν καὶ ἐνόησεν ὁ βασιλεὺς ὅτι ἐκεῖνος ὁμοῦ ἐπείραζεν τὸ παιδίον μὲ τοιαύτες φαντασίες εἶναι πνεῦμα πονηρὸν καὶ ἀκάθαρτον δαιμόνιον. καὶ παρευθὺς ἔκαμεν ὁ βασιλεὺς δέησιν πρὸς τὸν θεὸν μετὰ δακρύων καὶ μετὰ συντετριμμένης καρδίας ἡμέραν καὶ νύκταν διὰ νὰ τοῦ ἀποκαλύψῃ ὁ θεὸς μὲ τί μόδον

---

§ 7. l. 8 ἤθελε   12 l. ἔτσι   13 * f. 180ʳ | εὐγῆκες | ἔξαφνα ego: ἔξα   14 ἀμὴ   § 8. l. 25 λέγει: λέη mss.   27 ὅτι ἂν ex ὁ ἂν   § 9. l. 32 καρδίαις

νὰ καταραθῇ τὸ δαιμόνιον ἐκεῖνο ὁποῦ ἐπείραξε τὸ παιδίον. 10. καὶ ἰδὼν ὁ θεὸς τὰ δάκρυα καὶ τοὺς κόπους του εἰσήκουσεν ὁ θεὸς τῆς δεήσεως Σολομῶν⟨τος⟩ καὶ παρευθὺς ἔστειλεν τὸν ἀρχάγγελον αὐτοῦ Μιχαὴλ μὲ μίαν βοῦλλαν ἤγουν σφραγῖδα καὶ τὴν ἔδωκεν τοῦ βασιλέως καὶ τοῦ εἶπεν ὅτι ἐκεῖνος ὁ Ἀράπης ἦτον πονηρὸν δαιμόνιον καὶ ἔρχεται ἀοράτως καὶ πειράζει τὸ παιδίον καὶ ὁ βασιλεὺς νὰ τὴν δώσῃ τοῦ παιδίου καὶ »ὅταν ὑπάγῃ πάλιν τὸ δαιμόνιον εἰς τὴν κλίνην νὰ τὸν πειράζῃ, νὰ τὸν κρούσῃ εἰς τὸ στῆθος μὲ τὴν σφραγῖδα τοῦ θεοῦ καὶ νὰ τὸν δέσῃ καὶ νὰ τὸν φέρῃ ἔμπροσθέν σου καὶ ἐσὺ Σολομῶν ἐξέταξον αὐτὸν ἵνα σου δείξῃ ὅλες του τὲς ἐπιβουλὲς καὶ ἐσὺ μετ' αὐτῆς τῆς σφραγῖδος θέλεις πατάξῃ πάντα διάβολον καὶ τὴν δύναμίν του καὶ νὰ τοὺς συνάξῃ ὅλους τοῦ ἀέρος καὶ τῆς γῆς καὶ τῆς θαλάσσης καὶ τῶν καταχθονίων καὶ νὰ οἰκοδομήσῃς τὸν ναὸν τοῦ θεοῦ μετ' αὐτῶν τῶν πονηρῶν δαιμόνων καὶ νὰ εἶνε ἐργάτες εἰς τοὺς τεχνίτας«. 11. καὶ ἐπῆρεν ὁ βασιλεὺς τὴν σφραγῖδα ἀπὸ τὸν ἀρχάγγελον Μιχαὴλ καὶ εὐχαρίστησεν τὸν θεὸν καὶ ἀπ' ἐκείνης τῆς σφραγῖδος ἐφτείασεν ὁ Σόλομῶν ἕνα δακτυλίδιον παρόμοιον ἀπὸ λίθου τιμῆς πολλῆς. καὶ ἔκραξεν τὸ παιδίον καὶ ἔδωκέν του τὴν βοῦλλαν τοῦ θεοῦ καὶ τοῦ εἶπεν ὡς καθὼς τοῦ ἐπαρήγγειλεν ὁ ἄγγελος.

12. Ἑσπέρας δὲ γενομένης ἔπεσεν τὸ παιδίον νὰ κοιμηθῇ εἰς τὴν κλίνην του· καὶ ἰδοῦ ἔφθασεν καὶ ὁ διάβολος κατὰ τὴν συνήθειαν ὁποῦ εἶχεν διὰ νὰ περικυκλώσῃ τὸ παιδίον. καὶ εἶχεν * τὴν ἔννοιαν κατὰ τὴν παραγγελίαν ὁποῦ τοῦ εἶπεν ὁ αὐθέντης του ὁ Σολομῶν καὶ ἐβούλλωσεν τὸν διάβολο⟨ν⟩ ἐπὶ τὸ στῆθος μὲ τὴν βούλλαν τοῦ θεοῦ. 13. ὁ δὲ σατανᾶς ἐβόησε φωνῇ μεγάλῃ καὶ εἶπεν· »οὐαί μοι τῷ ἀθλίῳ, πῶς ἐκαταδουλώθην καὶ ἔγινα ὑπόδουλος ὑπὸ τοῦ Σολομῶντος«. καὶ παρευθὺς ἐσηκώθη τὸ παιδίον ἀπὸ τὴν κλίνην του καὶ ἔδεσεν τὸν διάβολον καὶ τὸν ὑπῆγεν ἔμπροσθεν τοῦ βασιλέως.

III. Καὶ ὡς τὸν εἶδεν ὁ Σολομῶν ἐθαύμασεν καὶ εὐχαρίστησεν Κύριον τὸν θεόν, καὶ εἶπεν ὁ Σολομῶν πρὸς τὸ διάβολον· »εἰπέ

---

1 * f. 180ᵛ   § 10. l. 12 πάντα ex πᾶσα corr. Pr. Bessarion   13 δύναμιν ex δυν. corr. prim. man.   § 12. l. 23 εὔθασεν   25 * f. 181ʳ
C. III. cf. parallele in *Test. Sal.* II et ms. D. III   l. 32 εὐχαρίστησεν

μοι, πνεῦμα πονηρὸν καὶ ἀκάθαρτον, τί σοῦ ἐστιν ὄνομα καὶ τί⟨ς⟩ σου ἡ ἐργασία πρὶν μή σε τιμωρήσω εἰς τὸν τόπον τῆς γεέννης;« 2. καὶ ὁ δαίμων εἶπεν· »τὸ ὄνομά μου καλοῦμαι Ὀρνίας καὶ εἶμαι ὑπὸ ἀέρος τελώνιον καὶ ἡ ἐργασία μου εἶναι αὕτη· 5 σκανδαλίζω τοὺς ἀνθρώπους καὶ τὰς καρδίας των καὶ ἁμαρτάνουν καὶ λησμονοῦν τὸν ἐπουράνιον θεόν. καὶ πότε ὡσὰν γυναῖκα ἔμορφη φαντάζομαι εἰς τὸν ὕπνον τους καὶ ἁμαρτάνουν καὶ πότε ὡσὰν σκύλος γίνομαι καὶ πότε ὡσὰν γάϊδαρος καὶ πότε ὡσὰν ἀετὸς μετὰ πτέρα γίνομαι, καὶ πότε ὡσὰν λεοντάριν μὲ 10 ἄλλους δαίμονας γινόμεσθεν, καὶ πότε ἄλλων λογιῶν φαντασίες φανταζόμεσθεν εἰς τοὺς ἀνθρώπους. καὶ ὁπότε ἰδοῦμεν τὸν ἀρχάγγελον Μιχαὴλ καὶ τὸν Γαβριὴλ μᾶς ἐπιτιμοῦν μὲ τὴν δύναμιν τοῦ θεοῦ, καταργιζόμεσθεν«. 3. καὶ ταῦτα ἀκούσας ὁ βασιλεὺς Σολομῶν ἐδόξασε τὸν θεὸν καὶ * ἐπικαλέσθηκεν τοὺς 15 ἀρχαγγέλους τὸν Μιχαὴλ καὶ τὸν Γαβριήλ. καὶ εὐθὺς ἐφάνηκαν οἱ ἀρχάγγελοι ἀπὸ τὸν οὐρανὸν καὶ ἀλυσιδέσαντες τὸν Ὀρνίαν τὸν σατανᾶν μὲ τὸ τάγμα του ὅλον ὁρισάν τους οἱ ἀρχάγγελοι ὅτι νὰ ὑπάγουν ἀπὸ ἄκρον τῆς γῆς ἕως ἄκρον καὶ ἀπὸ θαλάσσης νὰ κουβαλήσουν μάρμαρα βαρύτατα. καὶ πάλιν ὡσὰν ἦλθαν 20 οἱ δαίμονες ἀπὸ ἐκείνην τὴν ὑπηρεσίαν τοὺς ἔβαλεν πάλιν ὁ βασιλεὺς καὶ ἔκοπταν μάρμαρα καὶ σίδερον διὰ τὴν οἰκοδομὴν τοῦ ναοῦ τοῦ θεοῦ.

IV. Καὶ πάλιν ὁ βασιλεὺς ἔκραξεν ἐκεῖνο τὸ ἐκλεκτὸν παιδίον καὶ εἶπεν του· »ἔπαρε, τέκνον, τὴν σφραγῖδα τοῦ θεοῦ καὶ 25 τὸν Ὀρνίαν τὸν σατανᾶν καὶ ὑπάγετε κατὰ τοὺς ἐρήμους τόπους καὶ ὅπου ἂν εὕρετε δαίμονας μὲ τὸ τάγμα του νὰ τοὺς βουλλώσετε ὅλους καὶ νὰ τοὺς φέρετε ἐδῶ εἰς ἡμᾶς«. 2. καὶ ἐπῆρεν τὸ παιδίον τὴν σφραγῖδα τοῦ θεοῦ καὶ τὸν Ὀρνίαν τὸν Σατανᾶν καὶ ὑπῆγεν κατὰ τοὺς ἐρήμους τόπους καὶ ἐκεῖ ηὗραν τὸν ἄρ-30 χοντα τῶν δαιμόνων τὸν Βεελζεβοὺλ καὶ λέγει ὁ Ὀρνίας ὁ σατανᾶς πρὸς τὸν Βεελζεβοὺλ τὸν ἄρχοντα τῶν δαιμόνων καὶ τοῦ λέγει· »καλεῖ σε ὁ βασιλεὺς Σολομῶν μὲ τὸν ὁρισμὸν τοῦ θεοῦ τοῦ σαβαώθ«. 3. καὶ λέγει ὁ Βεελζεβούλ· »καὶ ποῖος εἶναι αὐτὸς ὁ Σολομῶν ὁποῦ λέγεις;« καὶ τὸ παιδίον παρευθὺς ἔριξεν τὴν

---

2 ἐργασίαν   § 2. 1. 6 ἀλησμονοῦν   § 3. 1. 14 * f. 181ᵛ
C. IV. parallela l. c. in ms. D III. 1. 25. 29 τοὺς: τὰς

σφραγῖδα καὶ ἐκόλλησεν εἰς τὸν Βεελζεβούλ, καὶ εὐθὺς ἐσηκώθη μετὰ βίας μὲ ἕξι χιλιάδες δαιμόνια καὶ ἐπῆγαν ἔμπροσθεν τοῦ βασιλέως * Σολομῶν⟨τος⟩ καὶ τὸν ἐπροσκύνησαν ὅλοι οἱ δαίμονες καὶ ὁ βασιλεὺς εὐχαρίστησεν τὸν θεὸν τοῦ οὐρανοῦ καὶ τῆς γῆς ὁποῦ τὸν ἠξίωσεν τοιαύτης χάριτος καὶ τιμῆς καὶ τὸν ἐπροσκυνούσαν οἱ δαίμονες. 4. καὶ ἐπαράστησεν ὁ βασιλεὺς Σολομῶν τὸν Βεελζεβοὺλ τὸν σατανᾶν μὲ τὸ τάγμα τον ὅλον σιδεροδεμένους καὶ βουλλωμένους ὅλους μὲ τοῦ θεοῦ τὸ ὄνομα. εἶτα λέγει πρὸς τὸν Βεελζεβοὺλ τὸν πρῶτον διάβολον »τί σού ἐστι τὸ ὄνομα καὶ ἡ ἐργασία σου ἡ μιαρὰ ὁποῦ πράττεις;« 5. καὶ ὁ δαίμων εἶπεν· »ἐγὼ εἶμαι ὁποῦ ὀνομάζομαι Βεελζεβοὺλ καὶ εἶμαι ἄρχων ἕξι χιλιάδων δαιμόνων καὶ λέγομαι γαστὴρ θηλυμανίας, καὶ ἐγὼ ἤμουν ὁ πρῶτος ἄγγελος τοῦ οὐρανοῦ ὁ λεγόμενος Βεελζεβούλ. καὶ ἦτον μετ' ἐμοῦ καὶ ἄλλος πρῶτος σατανᾶς ὁ λεγόμενος Ἑωσφόρος, πλὴν ἐπετίμησέν τον ὁ θεὸς καὶ ἐκατακλείσθη ἐν ταρτάρῳ δεσμῷ. 6. καὶ ἐγὼ εἶμαι ὁποῦ κάμνω τοὺς δαίμονας καὶ εἶνε εἰς τὴν ἐξουσίαν μου. ἐγὼ εἶμαι ὁ ἄρχων τοῦ ἀέρος εἰς τὰ πονηρὰ καὶ ἀκάθαρτα πνεύματα. καὶ μετασχηματίζονται καὶ γίνονται ὡς ἄνθρωποι καὶ φαίνονται εἰς ὄνειρα καὶ εἰς φαντασίες κακὲς καὶ ἁμαρτάνουν. καὶ μικρὰ παιδία πνίγω σιμὰ εἰς τὲς μάνες των κοντά. 7. καὶ ὅποιος ἄνθρωπος κἂν ἄνδρας κἂν γυναῖκα καὶ εἶναι ἀπὸ ἐνεργείας ἐδικῆς μας καὶ νὰ καπνισθῇ μὲ χολὴν ὀψαρίου γλιανοῦ ὁποῦ εἶναι εἰς τὰ γλυκὰ τὰ νερὰ καὶ νὰ λέγῃ ἔτζι· »πρόφθασον Ῥαφαὴλ ὁ παρεστηκὼς ἐνώπιον τοῦ θεοῦ«, εὐθὺς ἀναιροῦμαι ἀπὸ ἐκεῖ. 8. ἐγὼ εἶμαι ὁποῦ ἀναγκάζω τοὺς βασιλεῖς καὶ πολεμοῦν ἕνας μὲ τὸν ἄλλον καὶ κάμνουν αἰχμαλωσίες πολλὲς κἄν τε εἰς θάλασσαν κἄν τε εἰς ξηρὰν γῆν. καὶ ποτὲ καλὸν τοῦ ἀνθρώπου δὲν θέλω«.

9. Καὶ ὁ βασιλεὺς Σολομῶν εἶπεν πρὸς αὐτούς· »ὑπὸ τίνος ἀγγέλου καταργεῖται ἡ δύναμίς σας«; καὶ εἶπεν ὁ Βεελζεβούλ· »ἀπὸ τοῦ παντοκράτορος θεοῦ κυρίου σαβαὼθ καταργεῖται ἡ δύναμίς μας καὶ ἀπὸ τοῦ ἀρχαγγέλου Ῥαφαήλ«. καὶ οἱ δαίμονες ἔτρεμαν μήπως καὶ ὁ βασιλεὺς τοὺς ἐπιτιμήσῃ καὶ τοὺς ὀργισθῇ

---

§ 3. l. 2 βίαν   3 * f. 182ʳ   § 4. l. 10 μιαρὰ ex μιχρὰ corr. man. alt.
§ 5. l. 12 ἄρχον ex ἄρσον corr. man. alt. | χιλιάδων ex χιάδων corr. man. alt.
§ 6. l. 20 παιδίαν   21 ἥτες μάναις τους   § 7. l. 24 * f. 182ᵛ

μὲ τοῦ θεοῦ τὸ ὄνομα. 10. εἶτα τοὺς ὥρισεν ὁ βασιλεὺς νὰ πριονίζουν μάρμαρα καὶ λίθους ὅλοι οἱ δαίμονες σιδεροδεμένοι. καὶ ὁ καθεὶς δαίμων ἐτάχθη νὰ δουλεύῃ εἰς τὸν ναὸν τοῦ θεοῦ ὅπου ἔκτιζεν ὁ Σολομῶν. 11. καὶ ἐκεῖ ὅπου ἐργάζουνταν οἱ δαίμονες πρᾶγμα ἦτον ἀνεκδιήγητον καὶ εἰς θαῦμα πολὺ τότες. ποῖος νὰ ἔβλεπεν καὶ νὰ μὴν ἐθαύμαζεν τοὺς ἀνθρώπους τοὺς τεχνίτας μὲ τόσον πλῆθος δαιμόνων νὰ ἐργάζουνται εἰς τὸν ναὸν τοῦ θεοῦ εἰρηνεμένα μετὰ πάσης ἐπιμελείας καὶ σπουδῆς. καὶ οὐδ' ὅλως ἐτολμοῦσαν οἱ δαίμονες νὰ πειράξουν ἵνα ἀδικήσουν κανέναν ἀπὸ τοὺς ἀνθρώπους. 12. καὶ τόσον τοὺς εἶχεν ὁ Σολομῶν ὅλους τοὺς δαίμονας βουλλωμένους μὲ τὴν σφραγῖδα ἐκείνην ὅπου τοῦ ἔστειλεν ὁ θεὸς μὲ τὸν ἀρχάγγελον αὐτοῦ Μιχαὴλ καὶ τόσον τοὺς ἐκατάστησεν ὅλους ὅτι ὡσὰν σκλάβους. ἔτζι ἔκοπταν μάρμαρα * καὶ λίθους καὶ ἀσβέστην, καὶ τὸ νερὸν τὸ ἐκουβαλοῦσαν μὲ κάδους βαρυτάτους. ὅλοι των ἁλυσοδεμένοι ἐδούλευαν τὸν ναὸν τοῦ θεοῦ.

V. Λοιπὸν ἐκεῖ εἰς τὸ κτίσιμον ὅπου ἔκτιζαν οἱ μαΐστόροι καὶ οἱ δαίμονες ἐργάζουνταν, ἕνας ἀπὸ τοὺς μαΐστόρους ἦλθεν εἰς φιλονεικίαν μὲ τὸν υἱὸν αὐτοῦ. ὁ δὲ πατέρας τοῦ παιδίου ἐπῆγεν εἰς τὸν βασιλέαν μετὰ πολλῶν δακρύων καὶ ἐγκάλεσεν τὸν υἱὸν αὐτοῦ τὸ πῶς τὸν ἀτίμησεν καὶ τὸν ὕβρισεν καὶ ἔλεγεν πρὸς τὸν Σολομῶν⟨τα⟩· »βασιλεῦ πολυχρονημένε, θανάτωσαι τὸν υἱόν μου ὅτι ἐμένα τὸν πατέρα του μὲ ἀσχήμισεν καὶ μὲ ὕβρισεν καὶ μὲ ἀτίμησεν. καὶ ἐὰν δὲν τὸν θανατώσῃς ἐγὼ πλέον δὲν βάνω τὸ χέριν μου νὰ δουλεύσω εἰς τὸν ναὸν τοῦ θεοῦ«. Καὶ ἰδοὺ μετὰ ὥραν ἱκανὴν ἐπῆγεν ὁ υἱὸς τοῦ μαΐστορος εἰς τὸν βασιλέαν Σολομῶν⟨τα⟩ καὶ ἐγκάλειε τὸν πατέρα του. 2. καὶ διαλογιζόμενος ὁ βασιλεὺς καὶ ἀπορῶντας τί ἀπόκρισιν νὰ δώσῃ καὶ τοὺς δύο νὰ τοὺς εἰρηνεύσῃ ἐστράφη εἰς τὸν ναὸν καὶ ἔβλεπεν καὶ εἶδεν τὸν Ὀρνίαν τὸν διάβολον καὶ δὲν ἐργάζατον νὰ δουλεύῃ ὡσὰν καὶ τοὺς ἄλλους δαίμονας, μόνον ἔστεκεν καὶ ἐγέλαν. καὶ λέγει ὁ βασιλεὺς πρὸς τοὺς δύο τὸν πατέρα καὶ τὸν

---

§ 10. l. 3 καθεεῖς   § 11. l.5 πολλύν   6 εὔλεπεν   § 12. l. 11 ἐκείνον   12 τοῦ: τους   13 ἐκατάσησεν   14 * f. 183ᵛ   15 κάδδους | των: τους

C V. Parallele in ms. D c. IV. l. 18 ἦλθαν   22 Βασιλεὺς   § 2. l. 29 τοὺς: τὸν | ἐστράφην

υἱὸν ὁποῦ ἐκρένουνταν· »ἀναχωρήσατε ὀλίγον ἀπ' ἐμοῦ«. καὶ οὕτως ἀνεχώρησαν καὶ οἱ δύο καὶ τότες ὁ βασιλεὺς ἔστειλεν ἐκεῖνο τὸ ἐκλεκτὸν παιδίον νὰ φέρῃ τὸν Ὀρνίαν τὸν σατανᾶν * μὲ τοὺς ἄλλους δαίμονας καὶ νὰ τοὺς φέρῃ ἔμπροσθέν του. καὶ ἐπῆγεν τὸ παιδίον καὶ τοὺς ἤφ⟨ερ⟩εν. 3. καὶ λέγει ὁ Σολομῶν πρὸς τὸν Ὀρνίαν· »ὦ πνεῦμα ἀκάθαρτον δαιμόνιον, διὰ τί γελᾷς τὴν βασιλείαν μου καὶ τὴν κρίσιν μου καὶ τὸν ναὸν τοῦ θεοῦ ὁποῦ οἰκοδομῶ«; 4. καὶ ὁ Ὀρνίας ὁ διάβολος ἔλεγεν πρὸς τὸν βασιλέαν· »οὐχί, δέσποτα βασιλεῦ, σοφώτατε καὶ δικαιότατε, οὔτε τὴν κρίσιν σου ἐγέλασα ποτέ μου, οὔτε τὴν βασιλείαν σου, οὔτε τὸν ναὸν τοῦ θεοῦ ὁποῦ οἰκοδομᾷς, ἀλλὰ αὐτουνοὺς τοὺς δύο ἀθλίους ὁποῦ ἦλθαν καὶ κρίνουνται εἰς τὴν βασιλείαν σου αὐτὸν τὸν γέροντα μὲ τὸν υἱόν του ὁποῦ μαλώνουν καὶ φιλονεικοῦν καὶ ὑβρίζουνται. ἀκόμη νὰ μὴν περάσουν τρεῖς ἡμέρες καὶ αὐτουνοῦ τοῦ γέροντος ὁ υἱὸς μέλλει νὰ ἀποθάνῃ«. 5. ταῦτα ἀκούσας ὁ βασιλεὺς παρὰ τοῦ Ὀρνίου τοῦ εἶπεν· »σύρε ἐργάζου εἰς τὸν ναὸν τοῦ θεοῦ μετὰ σπουδῆς καὶ εἰρήνης«. καὶ ἀπῆλθεν ὁ Ὀρνίας καὶ ἐργάζετον μετὰ φόβου καὶ τρόμου εἰς τὸν ναὸν τοῦ θεοῦ. καὶ πάλιν ὁ βασιλεὺς ἐκάλεσεν τοὺς δύο κρινομένους τὸν πατέρα καὶ τὸν υἱὸν ὁποῦ ἐφιλονεικοῦσαν καὶ ἐμάλωναν καὶ τοὺς ἔδωσεν διορίαν νὰ ἀναμείνουν ἡμέρας πέντε καὶ οὕτως νὰ κάμῃ τὴν κρίσιν τους. καὶ τοῦτο τὸ ἔκαμεν ὁ Σολομῶν διὰ τὸν λόγον ὁποῦ τοῦ εἶπεν ὁ Ὀρνίας ὅτι νὰ μὴν περάσουν τρεῖς ἡμέρες καὶ νὰ ἀποθάνῃ ὁ υἱὸς τοῦ γέροντος.

6. Καὶ ὡσὰν ἐπέρασαν αἱ πέντε ἡμέρες ἦλθεν ὁ πατὴρ τοῦ παιδίου ἐκείνου εἰς τὸν Σολομῶν⟨τα⟩ καὶ μετὰ δακρύων καὶ ὀδυρόμενος ἔλεγεν· »βασιλεῦ πολυχρονημένε, ἀπόθανεν ὁ υἱός μου καὶ πλέον δὲν θέλω ἰδεῖν αὐτόν«. λέγει του ὁ βασιλεύς· »καὶ πότε ἀπόθανεν ὁ υἱός σου, γέροντά μου«; λέγει του ὁ μαΐστορας· »ἀφότης ἐδικαστήκαμεν καὶ ἐμαλώσαμεν δὲν ἐπέρασαν τρεῖς ἡμέρες καὶ ἀπόθανεν«. λέγει τοῦ ὁ βασιλεύς· »ἄπελθε, γέροντά μου, εἰς τὸν καλὸν καὶ δόξαζε τὸν θεόν, καὶ ὁ κύριος νὰ σοῦ δώσῃ ὑπομονὴν εἰς τὴν θλῖψιν τῆς καρδίας σου«. καὶ ταῦτα παρη-

---

1 ἀπ' ἐμοῦ: ὁπονεμοῦ   3 * f. 183ᵛ   § 4. l. 12 ἀθλιγί | εἰς: ἡ
13 γέροντα: γέρων in τόων corr. man. alt. errore   § 5. l. 16 ἔργαζου
§ 6. l. 25 αἰ: ἡ   27 * f. 184ʳ

γορήσας τὸν γέροντα ἐκεῖνον, ἀπῆλθεν. 7. καὶ πάλιν ἔστειλεν ὁ βασιλεὺς τὸ παιδίον νὰ φέρῃ τὸν Ὀρνίαν τὸν δαίμονα. καὶ εὐθὺς τὸν ἤφερεν καὶ τὸν ἐπαράστησεν ἔμπροσθέν του. εἶτα λέγει ὁ Σολομῶν πρὸς ἐκεῖνον· »εἰπέ μοι, πνεῦμα πονηρὸν καὶ ἀκάθαρτον, πόθεν ἐγνωρίζεις τὸν θάνατον τοῦ ἀνθρώπου;« 8. καὶ ὁ διάβολος εἶπεν μετὰ φόβου καὶ τρόμου· »καὶ ἡμεῖς, δέσποτα βασιλεῦ, ἤμεσθεν πρῶτα ἄγγελοι καὶ ἀπὸ τὴν ὑπερηφάνειάν μας ὀργίστηκέν μας ὁ θεὸς ἀπὸ τοῦ οὐρανοῦ τὸν πρῶτον μας τὸν Ἑωσφόρον τὸν σατανᾶν καὶ ἐκεῖ ἔπεσεν κάτω εἰς τὴν ἄβυσσον. καὶ ὅταν ἐφώ(νη)σεν ὁ ἀρχάγγελος Μιχαὴλ καὶ εἶπεν το· »στῶμεν καλῶς«, καὶ καθὼς ὁ θεὸς ὅρισεν ἔτζι ἐσταθήκαμεν, καὶ ἡμεῖς ἤμεσθεν ἐναέρια τελώνια τῶν ψυχῶν, καὶ ἀπὸ φῶς θεοῦ ὁποῦ ἤμεσθεν καὶ ἄγγελοι ἐγίνημεν σκότος καὶ μαυρισμένοι ὡς καθὼς μᾶς ἐβλέπεις καὶ θεωρεῖς. 9. καὶ ἡμεῖς ἀνερχόμεθα εἰς τὸ κάτωθεν μέρος τοῦ οὐρανοῦ ὑμνοῦμεν καὶ δοξάζομεν τὸν θεὸν τὸ ἡμερόνυκτον, καὶ ἡμεῖς πετῶντας ἀκούομεν τῶν ἀγγέλων * τὲς ὁμιλίες καὶ τὰ γράμματα τοῦ καθενὸς ἀνθρώπου, καὶ μανθάνομεν τὸν θάνατον τοῦ ἀνθρώπου ἀπὸ σαράντα ἡμέρες καὶ πρωτύτερα, καὶ διὰ τοῦτο πάσχομεν καὶ ἡμεῖς νὰ τὸν κολάσωμεν καὶ νὰ πέσῃ εἰς κακὲς καὶ ἄτυχες πράξες ἕως ὁποῦ νὰ ἔλθῃ ἡ ζωὴ τοῦ ἀνθρώπου ἐκείνου εἰς ζημίαν θανάτου καὶ νὰ κολασθῇ νὰ τὸν κερδέσωμεν. 10. καὶ πετώμενοι τὸ κάτωθεν μέρος τοῦ οὐρανοῦ καὶ ὡς φύλλα ἀπὸ δένδρου ὁποῦ πέφτουν ὑπὸ ἀνέμου μεγάλου εἰς τὴν γῆν, οὕτῳ καὶ ἡμεῖς πέφτομεν ὑπὸ θεοῦ ῥοπῆς καὶ δὲν δυνάμεσθεν διὰ νὰ σταθοῦμεν. καὶ βλέποντάς μας οἱ ἄνθρωποι νομίζουν ὅτι εἶναι ἀστέρες τοῦ οὐρανοῦ χυνόμενοι καὶ μᾶς δοξάζουν οἱ ἄνθρωποι καὶ λέγουν ὅτι αἰχμάλοτος ἐλευθερώθη, καὶ ὁ θεὸς νὰ τὸν γλυτώσῃ«. 11. ὁ βασιλεὺς Σολομῶν ἔλεγεν πρὸς τὸν Ὀρνίαν· »αἱ γὰρ τοῦ οὐρανοῦ ἀστέρες χύνονται ποτὲ κάτω;« καὶ ὁ δαίμων ἔλεγεν· »οὐχί, δέσποτα, αἱ γὰρ ἀστέρες ἀνατέλουν καὶ βασιλεύουν καὶ περιπατοῦν μαζὶ μὲ τὸν οὐρανὸν καὶ εἶνε ἀσάλευτοι καὶ στερομένοι ὡσὰν τὸν ἥλιον καὶ τὴν σελήνην ἕως τὸν μέλλοντα αἰῶνα«.

---

§ 8. 1. 8 ὀργίθηκεν   14 εὐλέπεις   § 9. ἀνέρχομαι   16 * f. 184ᵛ
§ 10. 1. 23 ἀπὸ: ὑπὸ | πέφτουν: πέμπτουν   24 πέφτομεν: πέμπτομεν
26 χυνόμενοι: χιόμενοι   § 11. l. 29. 30 αἰ: ἡ, οἱ

12. Ταῦτα ἀκούσας ὁ βασιλεὺς Σολομῶν εὐχαρίστησεν τὸν θεὸν καὶ πάλιν ὅρισεν τὸν Ὀρνίαν νὰ δουλεύῃ εἰς τὸν ναὸν τοῦ θεοῦ μὲ τοὺς ἄλλους δαίμονας.

VI. Καὶ πάντες οἱ βασιλεῖς τῆς γῆς καὶ ἡ σοφὴ Σιβύλλα ἦλθαν καὶ αὐτὴ μετ᾽ αὐτοὺς νὰ ἰδοῦν τὸν ναὸν τοῦ θεοῦ καὶ ἐπήγασι καὶ κανίσκια μεγάλα τοῦ * βασιλέως Σολομῶν⟨τος⟩. καὶ ἤφεραν οἰκοδομὴν διὰ τὸν ναὸν τὴν ἁγίαν Σιών, καὶ πολυτελῆ καὶ ἀξιόλογον ὕλην καὶ σκεύη πολλὰ καὶ πολύτιμα καὶ τὰ ἀφιέρωσαν εἰς τὸν ναὸν τοῦ θεοῦ.

VII. Καὶ ὁ βασιλεὺς τῶν Ἀσσυρίων τῆς Ἀραβίας ἔστειλεν ἐπιστολὴν εἰς τὸν βασιλέαν Σολομῶν⟨τα⟩ καὶ ἔγραφεν οὕτως· »εἰς τὸν βασιλέαν τὸν Σολομῶν⟨τα⟩ τὸν σοφώτατον καὶ τιμιώτατον παρὰ ὅλους τοὺς βασιλεῖς τῆς γῆς χαίροις ἐν κυρίῳ τῷ θεῷ, ὑγίαινε κατὰ βασιλείαν Σόλυμα τῆς Ἰουδαίας καὶ Παλαιστίνης. νὰ τὸ ἐγνωρίζῃς καλὰ ἡ βασιλεία σου κατὰ Σόλυμα ὅτι ἐδῶ εἰς τὸν ἐδικόν μου τόπον καὶ τὴν χώραν κατοικεῖ ἕνα δαιμόνιον πονηρὸν καὶ δυνατὸν καὶ εἰς καθὲ τρεῖς ἡμέρας σηκώνει ἄνεμον δυνατὸν καὶ ῥίπτουνται σπίτια καὶ δένδρα καὶ βουνὰ καὶ τοὺς ἀνθρώπους τοὺς ῥίχνει εἰς τὸ πῦρ καὶ εἰς τὸ νερὸν τοὺς ἐγκρεμνίζει. καὶ ἤκουσα ὅτι μὲ τῆς σφραγίδος ὁποῦ σου ἔστειλεν ὁ θεὸς ἀπὸ τοῦ οὐρανοῦ μὲ τὸν ἀρχάγγελόν του καὶ ἐπάταξες πᾶσαν τὴν δύναμιν τῶν δαιμόνων. καὶ σὲ παρακαλῶ πολλὰ στεῖλε καὶ εἰς ἐμᾶς καὶ πέμψον νὰ τὸ ἐξολοθρεύσῃς τὸ πνεῦμα τὸ πονηρόν. καὶ ἐὰν τὸ κάμεις αὐτὸ ἡ βασιλεία σου, νὰ σοῦ στείλω ἔξοδον εἰς τὴν οἰκοδομὴν τοῦ ναοῦ τοῦ θεοῦ τάλαντα τριάντα χρυσίου καὶ ἀργυρίου· τὸ ἕνα τάλαντον κάμνει ἑκατὸν πενήντα λίτρες«.

2. Λαβὼν δὲ τὴν ἐπιστολὴν ὁ βασιλεὺς καὶ ἀναγνοὺς αὐτὴν εἶπεν τοῦ παιδίου νὰ πάρῃ * τὴν σφραγίδα τοῦ θεοῦ καὶ νὰ παγαίνῃ εἰς τὸν βασιλέαν τῆς Ἀραβίας τὸ γληγορότερον, καὶ ἔδωκέν του καὶ γραφὴν ὁποῦ τὸν ἐχαρέτα, καὶ εἶπεν τοῦ παιδίου ὅτι νὰ πάρῃ μαζί του καὶ ἕνα δερμάτι καινούριον καὶ ἕνα γοργοκάμηλον, καὶ ἔστειλεν τὸ παιδίον ὁ βασιλεὺς Σολομῶν μὲ

C. VI. l. 7 ~ f. 185ʳ
C. VII. l. 10 Ἀσσυρίων: ἀσαρίον ms., l. Ἀραβίων? 14 βασιλέαν σολομὲ 15 σολομε 16 δαιμόνον 23 νὰ τὸ: νὰ τον § 2. l. 29 * f. 185ᵛ

συνοδίαν ἀνθρώπων πολλῶν. καὶ ἐπαρήγγειλέν του· »κύτταξε, τέκνον μου, νὰ εὕρῃς τὸν τόπον ὁποῦ κατοικεῖ ὁ δαίμων καὶ ἰδὲς τὴν ὥραν καὶ τὴν ἡμέραν ὁποῦ μέλλει διὰ νὰ πνεύσῃ τὸν ἄνεμον. καὶ οὕτως ἔχε ἐσὺ τὸ δερμάτιον ἀνοικτὸν πρὸς τὴν πέτραν τῆς φωλεᾶς ὁποῦ κατοικεῖ ὁ δαίμων καὶ ὅταν ἰδῇς τὸν ἀσκὸν καὶ φουσκώσῃ ἄνεμον, ἐσὺ νὰ εἶσαι ἕτοιμος, ὀγλήγορα νὰ δέσῃς τὸ στόμα του τοῦ ἀσκοῦ καὶ νὰ τὸ βουλλώσῃς μὲ τὴν σφραγῖδα τοῦ θεοῦ καλούτσικα καὶ οὕτως βάλε τὸν ἀσκὸν ὁποῦ ἔχει τὸν δαίμονα ἀπάνω εἰς τὸν γοργοκάμηλον καὶ νὰ τὸν φέρῃς ἐδῶ εἰς ἡμᾶς«.

3. Καὶ ἀπῆλθεν τὸ παιδίον εἰς τὸν βασιλέαν τῆς Ἀραβίας καὶ ἔκαμεν ὡς καθὼς τοῦ ἐπαρήγγειλεν ὁ Σολομῶν. καὶ ἔτζι ἤφερεν τὸ παιδίον βουλλωμένον τὸν ἀσκὸν εἰς τὸν βασιλέαν. καὶ εἰς τὴν στράταν ὁποῦ ἤρχετον τὸ παιδίον μετὰ τοῦ δαίμονος ἔλεγεν ὁ δαίμων· »δέομαι, ὦ παιδίον, μήν με ὑπάγῃς εἰς τὸν βασιλέαν καὶ ἐγὼ νὰ σοῦ δείξω ποῦ εἶναι ὁ πράσινος ὁ λίθος καὶ τὸ χρυσίον τὸ τιμημένον καὶ κεκρυμμένον«. καὶ τὸ παιδίον ἔλεγεν πρὸς τὸν δαίμονα· »εἰς τὸν βασιλέαν τὸν Σολομῶν⟨τα⟩ καὶ εἴ τι ὁρίσῃ ἐκεῖνος, ἂς ποιήσῃ«. 4. καὶ ὡς * ἦλθαν ἔμπροσθεν εἰς τὸν βασιλέαν εὐθὺς ἔπεσεν ὁ ἀσκὸς κάτω ἀπὸ τὸ καμήλιον καὶ ἐκυλίετον ἄνω καὶ κάτω. καὶ πάντες ὅσοι ἦσαν ἐκεῖ ἐθαύμασαν. καὶ ἔλυσεν τὸ παιδίον τὸν ἀσκὸν καὶ εὐθὺς ἐβγῆκεν ὁ δαίμων ἔξω. 5. καὶ ἐβούλλωσεν αὐτὸν ὁ βασιλεὺς ἐπὶ τὸ στῆθος καὶ τὸν τράχηλον καὶ ἔδεσεν αὐτὸν καὶ ἔλεγεν ὁ βασιλεύς· »πῶς ὀνομάζεσαι;« καὶ ὁ δαίμων εἶπεν· »Ἐφίππας τὸ ὄνομά μου καλοῦμαι«. 6. λέγει ὁ βασιλεύς· »τί εἶναι ἡ ἐργασία σου ἡ μιαρά;« καὶ ὁ δαίμων εἶπεν· »ἡ ἐργασία μου εἶναι εἰς μύρια κακὰ ποιήματα. καὶ παρακαλῶ σε, ὦ βασιλεῦ, νὰ μήν με ἐπιτιμήσῃς μὲ τοῦ θεοῦ τὸ ὄνομα, καὶ ἐγὼ νὰ σοῦ φέρω τὸν λίθον τὸν ἀκρογωνιαῖον ὁποῦ φέγγει εἰς τὸ βάθος τῆς θαλάσσης ὑπὲρ τὸν ἥλιον τὸν ὁποῖον ἀπεδοκίμασαν οἱ ἄνθρωποι καὶ οἱ δαίμονες καὶ ἐγὼ νὰ σοῦ τὸν στήσω αὐτὸν εἰς τὴν πρώτην κεφαλαίαν τοῦ ναοῦ«.

---

3 l. διὰ νὰ πνεύσῃ Pr. Bessarion: διαναπεύσῃ   5 φωλεᾶς: φολεὰν
8 καλούτζικα   § 3. l. 14 ἤρχετον ex ἤχετον cor. prim. man.   17 τεμημένον   18 πρὸς bis scr.   § 4. l. 19 * f. 186ʳ   § 5. l. 23 στῆθι

7. Καὶ εὐθὺς ὅρισεν ὁ βασιλεὺς ἐκεῖνον τὸν Ἐφίππαν τὸν δαίμονα μὲ ἄλλους ἑτέρους δαίμονας. καὶ ὑπῆγεν καὶ ἤφεραν τὸν λίθον ἐκεῖνον τὸν ἀκρογωνιαῖον καὶ ἔστησάν τον εἰς τὴν μέσην τοῦ ναοῦ, καὶ οἱ πάντες ὅσοι ἦσαν ἐκεῖ ἐθαύμασαν ἰδόντες τὸ παράδοξον θαῦμα. 8. ἀλλὰ ἀφότης ἐκατέβη ὁ κύριος ἡμῶν Ἰησοῦς Χριστὸς ὁ υἱὸς καὶ λόγος τοῦ θεοῦ, τὸ φῶς τὸ ἀληθινὸν τὸ φῶς τῆς οἰκουμένης, ὁ ἥλιος ὁ ἀνέσπερος, ἐκεῖνος ὁ λίθος ἐσκοτίσθη ὁποῦ ἦτον ὑπὸ τοῦ βασιλέως Σολομῶν⟨τος⟩. καὶ ἀφότης ἔκτισεν ἐκεῖνον τὸν ναὸν τοῦ θεοῦ, ἤγουν τὴν ἁγίαν Σιών, ἕως ὁποῦ ἐγεννήθη ὁ κύριος ἡμῶν Ἰησοῦς Χριστός, ἐπέρασαν χρόνοι ψκζ, ἤγουν ἑπτακόσιοι εἴκοσι ἑπτά. ἀλλὰ ἃς ἐλθοῦμεν πάλιν ὅθεν ἀφήσαμεν τὸν λόγον μας.

VIII. Καὶ πάλιν εἶπεν ὁ βασιλεὺς τὸν Ἐφίππαν τὸν δαίμονα· »ὦ Ἐφίππα, ἠξεύρῃς καὶ ἕτερον δαιμόνιον ὡσὰν καὶ τοῦ λόγου σου«; καὶ ὁ δαίμων εἶπεν· »ἠξεύρω, ὦ δέσποτα, καὶ ἕτερον δαιμόνιον ἐν τῇ Ἐρυθρᾷ θαλάσσῃ καὶ καθοῦνται καὶ φυλάγουν τὸν στῦλον τὸν πορφυρόν«. 2. καὶ ὡσὰν ἤκουσεν ἔτζι ὁ βασιλεὺς εἶπεν τοῦ παιδίου· »τέκνον μου, ἔπαρε τὴν σφραγῖδα τοῦ θεοῦ καὶ τὸν Ἐφίππαν τὸν δαίμονα καὶ νὰ ὑπᾶτε εἰς τὴν Ἐρυθρὰν θάλασσαν, καὶ ὅσους δαίμονας καὶ ἂν εὕρῃς ἐκεῖ ὁποῦ φυλάγουν τὸν στῦλον τὸν πορφυρόν, σφράγισε τοὺς ὅλους ἀπάνω εἰς τὸ στῆθος καὶ ἃς πάρουν ἐκεῖνον τὸν κίονα τὸν πορφυρὸν ἀπάνω τους καὶ ἃς τὸν φέρουν ἐδῶ εἰς ἐμᾶς«. 3. καὶ οὕτως ὑπῆγεν ἐκεῖνο τὸ παιδίον μὲ τὸν Ἐφίππαν εἰς τὴν Ἐρυθρὰν θάλασσαν ναὶ ἐπλήρωσεν τοῦ βασιλέως τὸ θέλημα, καὶ ἐκεῖνο τὸ παιδίον ἐσφράγισεν ὅλους τοὺς δαίμονας μὲ τὴν σφραγῖδα τοῦ θεοῦ καὶ εἶπεν τους· »ἐπάρετε τὸν κίονα αὐτὸν καὶ ἐλᾶτε νὰ ὑπᾶμεν εἰς τὸν βασιλέαν τὸν Σολομῶν⟨τα⟩«. καὶ εὐθὺς οἱ δαίμονες ἐκεῖνοι ἐπῆραν τὸν κίονα τὸν πορφυρὸν ἀπάνω τους καὶ τὸν ἐβαστοῦσαν καὶ φέρνοντάς τον ἀπάνω εἰς τὸν ἀέρα. 4. καὶ ὁ βασιλεὺς ἰδὼν τοὺς δαίμονας τὸ πῶς φέρνουν ἐκεῖνον τὸν κίονα * ἐθαύμασεν καὶ ὅσοι ἦσαν ἐκεῖ ἔφριξαν ἰδόντες τὸ παράδοξαν τοῦ θαύματος. εἶτα ὥρισεν ὁ βασιλεὺς ἐκείνους τοὺς δαίμονας νὰ βαστοῦν ἐκεῖνον

§ 8. 1. 5 ἐκατεύη   7 τῆς: τὴς   9 * f. 186ᵛ
C. VIII. cf. parallela in Test. Sal. c. XXIV. § 2. l. 20 ἀνεεύρης ms., l. forte ἀνεύρεις   § 4. l. 31 * f. 187ʳ

τὸν κίονα ἀπάνω τους εἰς τὸν ἀέρα καὶ νὰ μὴν τὸν ἐρίξουν ποτὲ κάτω ἕως τὸν μέλλοντα αἰῶνα.

IX. Καὶ πάλιν ὥρισεν ὁ βασιλεὺς Σολομῶν, καὶ ἤφεραν τὸν Ὀρνίαν τὸν διάβολον ὁποῦ τὸν ἐπίασεν ἀπὸ τὴν ἀρχὴν ὁποῦ ἐδούλευεν καὶ ἐπαρέστησαν αὐτὸν ἔμπροσθεν τοῦ βασιλέως· καὶ λέγει τοῦ Ὀρνία· »εἶναι καὶ ἄλλα δαιμόνια καὶ πνεύματα πονηρὰ ὡσὰν καὶ αὐτά;« καὶ εἶπεν ὁ Ὀρνίας· »εἶνε, δέσποτα βασιλεῦ, πλὴν εἶναι ἕνα δαιμόνιον καὶ ἔχει δύναμιν περισσήν«. 2. καὶ ὁ βασιλεὺς εἶπεν· »καὶ ποῦ εἶναι αὐτὸ ὁποῦ κατοικεῖ;« καὶ ὁ Ὀρνίας εἶπεν· »εἶναι εἰς τοὺς τάφους τῶν ἀπεθαμμένων καὶ εἰς τόπους κρημνώδεις ἡ κατοικία, καὶ ἀφανίζει πολλοὺς τῶν ἀνθρώπων, καὶ ὀνομάζεται Σαμαήλ, καὶ εἶναι καὶ αὐτὸς ἄρχων εἰς ἕνα τάγμα τῶν δαιμόνων· καὶ δὲν εἶναι κανεὶς νὰ τοῦ ἀντισταθῇ ὅτε διασείει τὴν γῆν«. 3. καὶ ὁ βασιλεὺς λέγει πρὸ⟨ς⟩ τὸν Ὀρνίαν· »ἰδέν σε μέλει ἐσένα, πνεῦμα πονηρόν, διὰ τὴν δύναμιν ἐκείνου, μόνον σῦρε μὲ τὸ παιδίον καὶ μὲ τοῦ θεοῦ τὴν πρόσταξιν ὅπου καὶ ἂν εἶναι νὰ τὸν εὑρῆτε νὰ τὸν φέρετε ἐδῶ εἰς ἐμᾶς«. 4. εἶτα ἔκραξεν ὁ βασιλεὺς τὸ εὔμορφον παιδίον καὶ λέγει αὐτό· »ἔπαρε, τέκνον μου, τὴν σφραγῖδα τοῦ θεοῦ καὶ τὸν Ὀρνίαν καὶ σῦρτε νὰ εὑρῆτε τὸν σατανᾶν τὸν Σαμαὴλ * καὶ νὰ τὸν βουλλώσης καὶ νὰ τὸν δέσης καὶ νὰ τὸν φέρετε ἐδῶ«. 5. λαβών τε τὸ παιδίον τὴν σφραγῖδα τοῦ θεοῦ καὶ τὸν Ὀρνίαν καὶ ὑπῆγαν καὶ ηὗραν τὸν Σαμαὴλ τὸν δαίμονα μὲ τὸ τάγμα του. εἶτα εἶπεν τὸ παιδίον· »ἐν ὀνόματι κυρίου τοῦ θεοῦ τοῦ ὑψίστου νὰ σταθῆτε, ὅλα τὰ πονηρὰ καὶ ἀκάθαρ⟨τα⟩ πνεύματα, ⌈καὶ νὰ μὴν συσταθῆτε, ὅλα τὰ πονηρὰ καὶ ἀκάρθατα πνεύματα,⌉ καὶ νὰ μὴν συστῆτε ἀπὸ τὸν τόπον σας«, καὶ πλέον δὲν ἐσπάραξαν ἀπὸ τὸν τόπον τους. καὶ ὑπῆγεν τὸ παιδίον μὲ τὴν βούλλαν τοῦ θεοῦ καὶ τοὺς ἐβούλλωσεν ὅλους καὶ ἔδεσέν τους καὶ τοὺς ὑπῆγεν εἰς τὸν βασιλέαν.

6. Ὁ δὲ βασιλεὺς ἐκάθετον ἐπὶ θρόνου ὑψηλοῦ καὶ ἐνδυμένος μὲ βασιληκὸν στέμμα, καὶ εἶχεν εἰς τὸ χέριν του σκῆπτρον καὶ βίτζαν καὶ ἐβίγλιζαν εἰς τὸν ναὸν· τοῦ θεοῦ τὸ πῶς ἐδούλευαν οἱ μαΐστοροι καὶ οἱ δαίμονες ἐδούλευαν ὡσὰν ἐργάται καὶ ἐπριό-

---

C. IV. cf. parallele in ms. D VII   l. 5 ἐπαρέστησεν   § 2. l. 11 κατοικίαν   § 4. l. 20 * f. 187ᵛ   § 5. l. 25 ⌈ ⌉ certe dittogr.   29 ὑπῆγεν ex ὑπῆγαν cor. prim. man.

νιζαν λίθους καὶ μάμαρα. καὶ ἀπαντείχενεν ὁ βασιλεὺς τὸ παιδίον νὰ φέρῃ καὶ τοὺς δαίμονας. 7. καὶ ἰδοὺ μετὰ ὥραν ἱκανὴν ἔφθασεν καὶ τὸ παιδίον σύρνοντας καὶ τοὺς δαίμονας, καὶ τοὺς ἤφερεν ἔμπροσθεν τοῦ βασιλέως. καὶ ὁ βασιλεὺς ἰδὼν τοὺς δαίμονας ἐθαύμασεν καὶ εὐχαρί(στη)σεν τὸν θεὸν τοῦ οὐρανοῦ καὶ τῆς γῆς ὁποῦ τὸν ἠξίωσεν τοιαύτης χάριτος καὶ ἐκατίσχυνεν ὅλους τοὺς δαίμονας. καὶ ἦτον τὰ δαιμόνια ἐκεῖνα τὰ πρόσωπά τους μαῦρα. καὶ ἐρώτησεν τὸν * πρῶτον τους καὶ εἶπεν· »εἰπέ μοι, πνεῦμα πονηρὸν καὶ μιαρόν, τί τὸ σὸν ὄνομα καὶ τί εἶναι ἡ μιαρά σου ἐργασία;« 8. καὶ ὁ δαίμων εἶπεν· »τὸ ὄνομά μου λέγεται Χάθρου Σαμαήλ. ἥ τε ἐργασία μου εἶναι αὕτη· καθεζόμεσθεν εἰς τόπους τῶν διαβατῶν καὶ ⟨ἐ⟩γκρεμνίζομεν αὐτοὺς καὶ τοὺς πνίγομεν, καὶ ἔμπροσθεν εἰς τὰ κουφάρια τῶν ἀποθαμμένων καὶ εἰς τὰ μνήματα τῶν ἀποθαμμένων σεβαίνομεν καὶ σχηματιζόμεσθεν εἰς ἐκείνου τοῦ ἀνθρώπου τὴν μορφήν· καὶ κατατρόγομεν τὰς σάρκας τῶν ἀνθρώπων· ἕως ὁποῦ καὶ ἔρχωνται εἰς θάνατον. καὶ πάλιν ἐρχόμεσθεν ἐν τῷ ἀέρι καὶ κάμνομεν τοὺς ἀνθρώπους καὶ σεληνιάζουνται καὶ κατατρόγουν τὰς σάρκα(ς) των, καὶ ἀφρίζουν καὶ τρίζουν τοὺς ὀδόντας τους. καὶ ἄλλους πάλιν πνίγομεν εἰς γωνίες καὶ εἰς ⟨τὲς⟩ φάραγγες καὶ εἰς τοὺς ἐγκρεμνοὺς τοὺς ἐγκρεμνίζομεν καὶ θανατώνουνται αἰφνίδιον θάνατον καὶ κολάζομεν αὐτοὺς καὶ τοὺς κερδαίνομεν«. 9. καὶ εἶπεν ὁ βασιλεὺς πρὸς τὸν δαίμονα· »ἀμμὴ δὲν φοβᾶσαι τὸν θεὸν τοῦ οὐρανοῦ καὶ τῆς γῆς; ἀμμὴ ὑπὸ τίνος ἀγγέλου καταργεῖται ἡ δύναμίς σας;« καὶ εἶπον οἱ δαίμονες· »ὅποτε μέλλει νὰ ἔλθῃ ὁ σωτὴρ τοῦ κόσμου ὁ υἱὸς καὶ λόγος τοῦ θεοῦ ἐπὶ τῆς γῆς καὶ θέλει κάμνειν ἕνα στοιχεῖον εἰς ὅσους ἀνθρώπους θέλουν τὸν πιστεύσῃ εἰς ἐκεῖνόν τὸν βασιλέα⟨ν⟩ καὶ θέλουν ποιῇ οἱ ἄνθρωποι ἐκεῖνο τὸ στοιχεῖον εἰς * τὸ μέτωπον καὶ εἰς τὸ στῆθος μὲ τὴν δεξιάν τους τὴν χεῖρα«. τουτέστιν ἐπροέλεγεν ψξ χρόνους προτύτερα ἀπὸ τοῦ Χριστοῦ, τουτέστιν τὸν τίμιον σταυρόν. καὶ ἔλεγον οἱ δαίμονες· »τότε ἐμεῖς, δέσποτα, καταργεῖται ἡ δύναμίς μας, καὶ ἀναχωρίζομεν γοργὰ ἀπὸ τὸν ἄνθρωπον ἐκεῖνον«.

§ 7. l. 3 ἔφθασεν: εὔθασεν   8 * f. 188^r 10 ἐργασίαν   § 8. l. 20 φάραγγες   ἐγκρεμμοὺς ms., l. f. κρημνοὺς   § 9. l. 23 ἀμὴ (bis)   29 * f. 188^v

Cf. parallela ad §§ 8 f. in *Test*. c. XVII 2—4.

10. Καὶ ταῦτα ἀκούσας ὁ βασιλεὺς εὐχαρίστησεν τὸν κυρίον. εἶτα ἐπετίμησεν τὸν Σαμαὴλ καὶ τὸ τάγμα του ὅλον ὑπὸ κυρίου τοῦ θεοῦ καὶ ἐκατηργήθηκαν. καὶ ἐκατασιδέρωσεν τὸν Σαμαὴλ τὸν δαίμονα ἐπὶ τὸν τράχηλον καὶ ἐπριόνιζεν λίθους καὶ μάρ-
5 μαρα καὶ ἐκουβαλοῦσαν καὶ ἀσβέστην εἰς τὸν ναὸν τοῦ θεοῦ.

Χ. Καὶ εὐφημίσθη ὁ βασιλεὺς Σολομῶν καὶ πάντες οἱ βασιλεῖς καὶ οἱ ἄρχοντες καὶ οἱ μεγιστάνοι ὅλοι τους τὸν ἐπροσκυνοῦσαν ὡς βασιλέαν καὶ τιμημένον ἀπὸ ὅλους τοὺς βασιλεῖς τῆς γῆς καὶ τὸν εἶχαν εἰς μεγάλην φήμην εἰς ὅλον τὸν κόσμον καὶ
10 ἐθαύμαζαν ὅλοι τους καὶ εὐχαριστοῦσαν καὶ ἐδόξαζαν τὸν θεὸν τοῦ οὐρανοῦ καὶ τῆς γῆς ὁποῦ τὸν ἔδωσεν τοιαύτην ἐξουσίαν καὶ ὥρισεν ὅλους τοὺς δαίμονας τῆς γῆς καὶ τοῦ ἀέρος καὶ τῆς θαλάσσης καὶ τῶν καταχθονίων. 2. καὶ μετὰ τὴν συμπλήρωσιν τοῦ ναοῦ τοῦ θεοῦ ἐμάζωξεν ὁ βασιλεὺς Σολομῶν ὅλα τὰ δαιμόνια
15 καὶ ἀκάρθατα πνεύματα καὶ ἐπαράστησεν ἔμπροσθέν του ἀμέτρητον πλῆθος δαιμόνων καὶ ὥρισεν νὰ ἔλθουν ἄνθρωποι τεχνίτες καὶ καλοὶ ὁποῦ ἐδούλευαν τὰ * χαλκώματα καὶ ὥρισεν ὁ βασιλεὺς νὰ φτειάσουν ἀγγεῖα χαλκωματένια. καὶ τότες ἐπίασεν καὶ τὰ ἔκαμεν παρόμοια ὡσὰν πιθάρια κάδους τρανοὺς καὶ μὲ τοῦ θεοῦ
20 τὸ ὄνομα ὥρισεν ὁ βασιλεὺς ὅλους τοὺς δαίμονας καὶ ἐσέβησαν μέσα εἰς ἐκεῖνα τὰ ἀγγεῖα τὰ χαλκωματένια. καὶ τότες ἐπίασεν ὁ βασιλεὺς ἀτός του καὶ τοὺς ἐσφάλισεν καὶ ἐβούλλωσεν τὰ ἀγγεῖα μὲ τὴν βούλλαν τοῦ θεοῦ. καὶ ἦταν αἱ βούλλες ἀργυρὲς καὶ ἦταν οἱ δαίμονες μέσα. καὶ πλέον δὲν ἐτολμοῦσαν διὰ νὰ ἔβ-
25 γουν ἔξω.

3. Καὶ ἐχαίρετον ὁ βασιλεὺς Σολομῶν εἰς τὴν πλήρωσιν τῆς οἰκοδομῆς τῆς ἁγίας Σιών, καὶ τὸν καιρὸν ἐκεῖνον ἐρητόρευσε τὸ ᾆσμα τῶν ᾀσμάτων. καὶ ἐκατοίκησεν ἡ χάρις τοῦ ἁγίου πνεύματος εἰς τὸν ναὸν ἐκεῖνον τὸν ἱερόν. καὶ ἦτον τὸ μῆκος του
30 πῆχες οβ καὶ τὸ πλάτος κδ, καὶ ὁ πῆχυς ἐκεῖνος θέλουν νὰ εἰποῦν το πῶς ἦτον δέκα ἑπτὰ ποδάρια. καὶ ἀπὸ τοῦ γύρου τοῦ ναοῦ ἔκαμεν πολλὰ κελλιὰ διὰ νὰ κατοικοῦν οἱ ἱερεῖς καὶ διὰ νὰ βάνουν καὶ τὰ ἱερὰ σκεύη ὁποῦ τὰ εἶχαν οἱ προπάτορες ἀρχιερεῖς

C. X. cf. parallele in *Test. Sal.* XVIII 42—44 (ms. P) —XIX. l. 6 εὐφημίσθην   8 τιμημένοι   § 2. l. 17 τὰ bis scr. | * f. 189ʳ   18 ἀγγείαν
19 κάδδους   24 ἦταν: ταν bis scr. et postea primum eras.   § 3. l. 30 πῆχας
32 κελλιᾶν (sic)

ὁπού ἐλειτουργοῦσαν ἐκεῖ εἰς τὰ ἅγια τῶν ἁγίων. 4. καὶ ἐκεῖ εἰς τὸ βῆμα τοῦ ναοῦ ἦταν ἡ πλάκες ὁπού εἶχαν τὸν θεόγραφον νόμον ὁπού ἔδωκεν ὁ θεὸς τοῦ προφήτου Μωυσέως. ἦτον ἡ στάμνος ὁπού εἶχεν τὸ μάννα μέσα. ἦτον καὶ ἡ κιβοτός, ἦτον
5 καὶ ἡ ῥάβδος τοῦ Ἀαρών, τὸ χρυσοῦν * θυμιατήριον, ἡ λυχνία, ἡ ἁγία τράπεζος, καὶ ἄλλα πολλὰ ἦσαν ἀφιερωμένα τῷ θεῷ τῷ ὑψίστῳ. καὶ ἐκεῖ εἰς τὸ ἅγιον βῆμα δὲν ἐσέβαινεν κανεὶς μόνον ὁ ἀρχιερεὺς καὶ ἐκεῖνος μίαν φορὰν τὸν χρόνον μὲ τοὺς ἱερεῖς του ὡς καθὼς τὸ εἶχαν συνήθειαν. 5. τὸν καιρὸν ἐκεῖνον καὶ
10 ἦτον ὁ ναὸς ἐκεῖνος ὑψηλὸς ἕως ρκδ πῆχες καὶ τὸν ἐσκέπασεν ὁ βασιλεὺς τὸν ναὸν ἀπὸ πάνω ὅλον μὲ χρυσάφι καθαρὸν καὶ ἁγνὸν μάλαγμα. καὶ ἦτον κτισμένος μὲ δέκα λογιῶν μάμαρα πελεκητά. καὶ ἔφεγγεν ὁ ναὸς ἐκεῖνος ὡσὰν τὸν οὐρανὸν ὡς καθὼς φαίνεται εἰς τὴν ἐξαστερίαν μὲ τὸν ἥλιον καὶ μὲ τὴν
15 σελήνην.

6. Καὶ ὁ Σολομῶν ὡσὰν ἐτελείωσεν τὸν ναὸν ἐκεῖνον τὴν ὀνομαζομένην ἁγίαν Σιὼν ἐστάθη καὶ ἔκαμεν προσευχὴν εἰς τὸν θεὸν μὲ ὕμνους καὶ δοξολογίας καὶ νηστεύων καὶ ἀγρυπνιζόμενος καὶ παρακαλῶν διὰ τὰ ἁγιάσῃ τὸν ναὸν ὁπού ἔκτισεν. καὶ ἤκου-
20 σεν ὁ θεὸς τὴν δέησιν τοῦ Σολομῶν⟨τος⟩ καὶ ἐφάνη ὁ θεὸς καὶ εἶπεν του ὅτι· »ἤκουσα τῆς φωνῆς τῆς δεήσεάς σου καὶ ἡγίασα τὸν ναὸν ἐτοῦτον καὶ ὑπάρχοντα χερουβὶμ καὶ τὰ σεραφὶμ καὶ τὰ ἐξαπτέρυγα καὶ οἱ θρόνοι καὶ αἱ κυριότητες ὄπισθεν τοῦ θυσιαστηρίου τοῦ ναοῦ ἔσωθεν καὶ ἔξωθεν«. τό τε κάλλος τοῦ
25 ναοῦ ἐκείνου οὔτε ἔγινεν εἰς τὴν γῆν οὔτε θέλει γένῃ εἰς τὸν αἰῶνα.

XI. Καὶ ἐπέρασαν ἀπὸ τὸν καιρὸν τοῦ Σολομῶν⟨τος⟩ τοῦ * υἱοῦ Δαυεὶδ ἕως τοῦ Σεδεκίου τοῦ βασιλέως τῆς Ἱερουσαλὴμ χρόνοι 425. καὶ εἰς ἐκεῖνον τὸν καιρὸν ἦτον καὶ ὁ προφήτης Ἱερε-
30 μίας ἱερεὺς τοῦ θεοῦ τοῦ ὑψίστου μὲ τὸν Βαροὺχ καὶ τὸν Ἀβιμέλεχ, καὶ ἦσαν εἰς τὸν ναὸν τοῦ θεοῦ ἐκεῖνον ὁπού ἔκαμεν ὁ βασιλεὺς Σολομῶν καὶ ἔκαμναν προσευχὲς καὶ δεήσεις πρὸς τὸν θεὸν καὶ ὑμνοῦσαν καὶ ἐδοξολογοῦσαν τὸν θεὸν νύκταν καὶ ἡμέ-

---

5 * f. 189ᵛ | λυχνίαν   8 τῶν χρόνων   § 6. l. 17 προσευχήθη
23 οἱ: αἱ
C. XI. l. 27 * f. 190ʳ

ραν. 2. ὅμως βλέποντας ὁ θεὸς τὴν ὑπερηφάνειαν καὶ τὴν σκληροκαρδίαν τοῦ Σεδεκίου τοῦ βασιλέως εἶπεν τὸν Ἰερεμίαν τὸν προφήτην ὅτι νὰ ὑπάγῃ εἰς τὸν ναὸν καὶ πάρῃ τὰ ἅγια σκεύη τοῦ ναοῦ καὶ νὰ παραδώσῃ τὴν γῆν. καὶ τότες ὁ προφήτης Ἰερεμίας ἐπῆγεν εἰς τὸν ναὸν τοῦ θεοῦ καὶ ἐπῆρεν τὰ ἅγια σκεύη τῆς ἁγίας Σιὼν καὶ ἐπαρέδωκεν αὐτὰ τὴν γῆν καθὼς τὸν ἐπαρήγγειλεν ὁ θεὸς καὶ ἐπῆρεν καὶ τὰ κλειδία ἀπὸ τὸ ἅγιον θυσιαστήριον τοῦ ναοῦ καὶ τὰ ἔριψεν κάτω εἰς τὴν γῆν ἔμπροσθεν τοῦ ἡλίου καὶ εἶπεν ὁ προφήτης· »ἔπαρε αὐτὰ καὶ φύλαξέ τα ἕως ὁποῦ νὰ ἐξετάσῃ κύριος ὁ θεὸς δι' αὐτά, ὅτι ἡμεῖς δὲν εὑρεθήκαμεν ἄξιοι διὰ νὰ τὰ φυλάξωμεν«.

3. Καὶ τότες ἦλθεν καὶ ὁ βασιλεὺς ὁ Ναβουχοδονόσωρ ἀπὸ τὴν Βαβυλῶνα καὶ ἐπαρέλαβε τὴν Ἰερουσαλὴμ καὶ ἐκούρσευσεν αὐτὴν καὶ τότες ἐκάει τὸ σκέπασμα τοῦ ναοῦ ὁποῦ ἔκτισεν ὁ βασιλεὺς Σολομῶν ὁποῦ τὸν εἶχεν σκεπασμένον τὸν ναὸν ὅλον μὲ ἁγνὸν μάλαμα, καὶ καίοντας ἔτρεχεν * τὸ μάλαμα ὡσὰν ποτάμι μεγάλον. καὶ τὸν Σεδεκίαν τὸν βασιλέαν τῆς Ἰερουσαλὴμ ἔκοψεν τὴν γυναῖκα του καὶ τὰ παιδία του ἔμπροσθεν εἰς τ' ἀμμάτιά του καὶ αὐτὸν τὸν ἐτύφλωσεν καὶ τὸν ἐπῆρεν αἰχμάλωτον μὲ τὸν λαὸν ὅλον τῆς Ἰερουσαλὴμ εἰς τὴν Βαβυλῶνα. 4. οἱ δὲ Χαλδαῖοι ὁποῦ ἐκούρσευσαν τὴν Ἰερουσαλὴμ καὶ κουρσεύοντας ηὗραν ἐκεῖνα τὰ ἀγγεῖα τὰ χαλκωματένια ὁποῦ εἶχεν ὁ βασιλεὺς Σολομῶν τοὺς δαίμονας σφαλισμένους καὶ βουλλωμένους μὲ τὴν σφραγίδα ὁποῦ τοῦ ἔστειλεν ὁ θεὸς ἀπὸ τοὺς οὐρανοὺς μετὰ τοῦ ἀρχαγγέλου Μιχαήλ. καὶ βλέποντας οἱ Χαλδαῖοι τὲς βοῦλλες τὲς χρυσὲς καὶ τὰ ἀγγεῖα ἐκεῖνα τὰ χαλκωματένια ὁποῦ ἦτον εἰς τὴν γῆν χωσμένα, καὶ ἐφαίνουνταν ὡσὰν πηγάδια βουλλωμένα ἐθάρρεψαν οἱ Χαλδαῖοι ὅτι εἶναι θησαυρὸς κεκρυμμένος ⟨καὶ⟩ ἐπῆγαν καὶ ἐξεβούλλωσαν ἀπὸ ἐκεῖνα τὲς βοῦλλες τὲς χρυσὲς καὶ τὲς ἐξεβούλλωσαν καὶ ἔφυγον οἱ δαίμονες ἀπὸ ἐκεῖ πάλιν καὶ ἐπῆγαν πάλιν εἰς τὲς πρῶτες ὀργισμένες κατοικίες καὶ πάλιν πειράζουν τοὺς ἀνθρώπους.

XII. Λοιπὸν αὐτὰ τὰ κατορθώματα ὁποῦ ἔκαμεν ὁ βασιλεὺς Σολομῶν δὲν ἦτον ἀπὸ ἐδικήν του δύναμιν οὐδὲ ἀπὸ τὴν σοφίαν

§ 2. l. 7 κλυδίαν § 3. l. 16 ποταμὴν § 4. l. 21 ε pro κουρσεύοντας scr. postea eras. 22. 26 ἀγγίαν

του την πολλήν ἀλλὰ ἡ δύναμις ἦτον τοῦ μεγάλου θεοῦ τοῦ ὑψίστου τοῦ μονογενοῦς υἱοῦ τοῦ θεοῦ ὅπου ἔμελλεν ἀπὸ τοῦ Σολομῶντος τοῦ βασιλέως τὴν φυλὴν νὰ σαρκωθῇ καὶ ἕως τὸν καιρὸν ὅπου ἦλθεν καὶ ἐσαρκώθη ὁ κύριος ἡμῶν Ἰησοῦς Χριστὸς
5 χρόνοι 726 καὶ ἔκαμεν εἰς τὴν γῆν σωματικῶς χρόνους λγ, καὶ ἐσταυρώθη καὶ ἐτάφη καὶ ἀνέστη ἐκ τῶν νεκρῶν. καὶ ἡμᾶς ἐχάρισεν ζωὴν τὴν αἰώνιον καὶ μὲ τὴν ἐνέργειαν τοῦ τιμίου καὶ ζωοποιοῦ σταυροῦ ἐκατίσχυνεν τὸν μέγαν διάβολον τὸν ἐχθρὸν τῆς ψυχῆς μας. 2. λοιπὸν καὶ ἐκείνη ἡ σφραγίδα εἶχεν τὸν τύ-
10 πον τοῦ τιμίου καὶ ζωοποιοῦ σταυροῦ καὶ ἐπάταξεν ὅλους τοὺς δαίμονας καὶ ὄχι μόνον τοὺς ἔδεσεν ἀλλὰ καὶ ἐπάταξέν τους καὶ τὸ ἐν ὑστέροις πάλιν ὡσὰν ἐτελείωσεν τὸν ναὸν τοῦ θεοῦ πάλιν τοὺς ἐσφάλισεν καὶ τοὺς ἐφυλάκωσεν ὅλους εἰς ἐκεῖνα τ⟨α⟩ ἀγγεῖα τὰ χαλκοματένια. 3. λοιπὸν εἰς ἐτοῦτον τὸν καιρὸν ὅσοι
15 πιστεύουν τὸν κύριον ἡμῶν Ἰησοῦν Χριστὸν τὸν δι' ἡμᾶς σταυρωθέντα καταδεξάμενον μὲ καλὴν πίστιν καὶ μὲ καλὰ ἔργα μὲ τὸ σημεῖον τοῦ τιμίου καὶ ζωοποιοῦ σταυροῦ τοὺς δένει καὶ τοὺς καταργεῖ διότι μεγάλη ἁλυσίδα εἶναι ὁ τίμιος καὶ ζωοποιὸς σταυρὸς ὅπου μᾶς ἀφῆκεν νὰ κάμνομεν νὰ τὸν ὑμνοῦμεν καὶ νὰ τὸ
20 δοξάζομεν διὰ νὰ μᾶς γλυτώνῃ ἀπὸ ἐχθροὺς ψυχικοὺς καὶ σωματικοὺς καὶ νὰ μᾶς ἀξιώσῃ ἐν τῇ βασιλείᾳ τῶν οὐρανῶν ἧς γένοιτο πάντας ἡμᾶς ἐν Χριστῷ τῷ θεῷ, ᾧ ἡ δόξα καὶ κράτος τοῦ πατρὸς καὶ τοῦ υἱοῦ καὶ τοῦ ἁγίου πνεύματος νῦν καὶ ἀεὶ καὶ εἰς τοὺς αἰῶνας τῶν αἰώνων. ἀμήν.

C. XII. 1. 8 * f. 191ʳ   § 2. l. 13 ἀγγεῖαν   § 3. l. 21 βασιλείαν

Emendationes in Textum.

P. L.
11* 7 διαλογισάμενος ἃ μέλλει σοι φράσαι cum I et N.
12* 1 φλέγον cum HIN.
14* 6 ἐμφαίνω: add. ὑπὸ πάντων τῶν δαιμόνων κελευόμενος cum N.
16* 1 om. καὶ ἔρριψεν ... μοῖραν cum A et N.
    2 κἀκείνῃ οὗτος cum N.
25* 5 Pro λευκοῦ l. λύων cum NP.
26* 7 ὃν εἶπας γένος τὸ ἐν τῇ Ἐρυθρᾷ θαλάσσῃ τρεφόμενον cum LN.
    8 ἐγὼ αὐτὸν οὐκ ἀνενέγκω πρός σε cum LN.
27* 6 τὸν Ἐλωί, τὸ μέγα; cf. N.
29* 2 ἡ αὔρα ἐκείνη cum LN et C.
32* 4 θεαὶ cum N, cf. P.
    6 αὐτὰς cum NP.
    7 ἀπὸ τῆς πρώτης cum HN.
    9 ἡ δευτέρα, 33*, 1 ἡ τρίτη. etc.
34* 3 δὲ καὶ cum NP, ἡ ἕκτη cum HNP.
    8 ἐμοὶ δὲ κατέναντι ἐπιθυμίαν τῆς σοφίας N.
37* 10 κατασχών cum HN.
38* 14 ἄγαγέ μοι ὧδε τὸν δαίμονα N.
39* 5 ὡσεὶ κερασίου (vel κερατίου) τὸ εἶδος ὁμοῖος cum A et N.
40* 4 Pro γάρ l. δέ cum N.
    5 Pro ὄνομα l. ἅμα, pro ὃν λεγεῶνες l. λεγεῶσι.
    6 Λεοντόφρων cum HLN.
41* 5 Λεοντόφρονα cum HLN.
    11 Pro παιδία l. νήπια cum HN.
51* 6 οἱ δὲ cum LN.
56* 3 καλοῦμαι Ῥὺξ Μαρδέρω, cf. N et H.
57* 4 Pro ὕλῃ l. ἥλῳ cum HN.
71* 10 Ἀβεζεβιθοῦ cum NQ.
74* 9 Pro secc. 7 et 8 lege cum HN: 7. ἐγὼ δὲ ὁ δύστηνος ᾠκοδόμησα διὰ τὸ πάνυ ἀγαπᾶν αὐτήν, καὶ διεράγη ἡ βασιλεία μου καὶ ὠλόλυξα μεγάλως, καὶ ἐσκορπίσθη τὸ πνεῦμά μου καὶ ἐδόθη εἰς δουλείαν τῷ Ἱεροβοὰμ σκῆπτρα δέκα. τότε συνῆκα τὰ ῥηθέντα μοι ὑπὸ τῶν δαιμόνων ὅτι ἔφησάν μοι· »ὑπὸ τὰς χεῖρας ἡμῶν μέλλεις τελευτῆσαι«.

Emendationes in Textum

8. Καὶ ἔγραψα τὴν διαθήκην μου ταύτην ⌜τοῖς Ἰουδαίοις⌝ καὶ κατέλιπον ταύτην αὐτοῖς εἰς μνημόσυνον πρὸ τελευτῆς μου. ἡ διαθήκη μου φυλαττέσθω παρ᾽ ὑμῶν εἰς μυστήριον μέγα κατὰ πνευμάτων ἀκαθάρτων ὥστε γνῶναι ὑμᾶς τῶν πονηρῶν δαιμόνων τὰς μηχανὰς καὶ τῶν ἁγίων ἀγγέλων τὰς δυνάμεις· ὅτι ἐνισχύει μέγας κύριος Σαβαὼθ ὁ θεὸς Ἰσραὴλ καὶ ὑπέταξεν ἐπ᾽ ἐμοὶ πάντα τὰ δαιμόνια, ἐν ᾧ ἐδόθη μοι σφραγὶς διαθήκης αἰωνίου. 9. καὶ ἀπέθανον ἐν τῇ βασιλείᾳ μου καὶ προσετέθην μετὰ τῶν πατέρων μου ἐν εἰρήνῃ, καὶ ἐπληρώθη ὁ ναὸς κυρίου τοῦ θεοῦ, ᾧ πρέπει τιμὴ καὶ προσκύνησις εἰς τοὺς αἰῶνας τῶν αἰώνων· ἀμήν.

Corrigenda.

P. L.
48   5 *L.* a nail *pro* wood
7*   5 ἐπεδίδοντο, *app.* ἐπεδίδον τὸ
9*   2 *App.* ὁ δυνόμενος *in* ὀδυνώμενος *cor.* Windisch
9*   7 *App.* φόβου
22* 6 πρόσκαιρός
26*   *App.* § 4, *l.* 4 ἀπόλωνται
27*   *App.* § 7, *l.* 4 Ῥωμαίων
28* 11 *App.* εἴγειρεν H. *L.* 13 *App.* εἶπεν P
32* 7 *App.* ἐγὼ W
36* 6 τότε
39* 3 *App.* § 9, *l.* 2 ἀναφέρουσιν
40* 3 ἑτέραν
44* Head Ὀβυζούθ
46* 2 *App.* καταταρασσ.
64* 11 *L. fortasse* ὡς μέλισσαι
67* 2 *App.* καὶ *pro* κμὶ
85* 14 *Ante* ὑπερι *pr.* 15
86* 15 δρᾶμα (MS δράμα)
92* 1 ἢ
96* 27 ᾆσμα τῶν ᾀσμάτων
100* 6 *Pro* HL *l.* HI
103* Head Σολομῶντος
118* 1 *Post* αὐτὸς *add.* ἀναγογεῖν

INDEXES

References in Indexes I to IV are to chapter and section of text, in Indexes V and VI to pages of Introduction. * Hapax legomena; † conjecturally restored; (?) Probable copyist's errors.

I. Index of Grammar and Syntax

A complete exhibit is not attempted

Adverbs and conjunctions
Ἀλλά I 2 C, V 3 PC, VIII 5, 6, 8, IX 7, XI 5, XIII 2, 3, 5, XV 4 P, XVI 2 P, XVIII 3 (*bis*), XX 5, 7, 17, XXV 8 B, XXVI 3; C V 3, XIII 6; D VII 3; cf. οὐ μόνον
ἄν *c. ind.* X 6; *c. subj.* I 9, XVIII 21, XXV 8 P
ἄρα I 2 L, XIV 4, XXII 12 B; D IV 4

Γάρ IV 7, VIII 12 (*bis*), IX 2, X 2, 3†, XII 3, XVI 2 P, XX 2 H, C IV 6, V 3 (PC), VIII 12, XI 5, D I 2 (*bis*), 5, II 1, *et pas.*; cf. καὶ γάρ
γέ XIII 3 P
γοῦν IX 5 V, XV 5

Δέ I 1 L, C, 2 AL, C (*bis*), 3, 4, 11, 12, II 4, 5, 6, C X 1, 2, 3, D I 1, 3, 4, 5, 6, 8, 9, 10, *et pas.*
δὲ καί II 3, IV 6, V 9, XIV 3, C I 3, 4, 11, IV 5, VII 2, VIII 5, X 3, 6, 11, 21, D II 1, VIII 3, *et pas.*; cf. ὁ δέ under Article, and μέν ... δέ
δή I 3 C. 4 Q; C Pro 3, XI 9, XIII 14; D I 3, III 7

δηλαδή C X 25
δῆτα D I 13
διό I 1 L, XXII 5 P; διότι IV 9, V 10 P, 12, VII 6, XXVI 2 Q

Ἐάν *ι. ind.* VIII 11, XVIII 15 (?), 35;
c. subj. I 12 W, 13, VI 8, 10 (*bis*), VII 5, XI 5, XVII 4 P, XXVI 4 (*bis*); *ι. ind. vel subj.* XVIII 9, 10, 11, 12 *et pas.*
εἰ = *whether* IV 1, XXII 12; C XI 1; XII 3, XIII 13; D VI 12; = *if, c. ind. praes.* VI 10, XIII 2, XXIII 2; C X 8; *ι. ind. aor.* XXVI 2; *ι. ind. fut.* XVII 2, 4; C IX 8, X 12, XIII 1; D VI 2; *ι. subj.* XVII 3
εἰ μή XIII 3 P, 4, XV 11 P
εἶτα XVIII 15 P, XX 19 H; L I : (*bis*), II 1, 5, III 4, IV 1, 12, V 12 (*pas.*), VII 8 (*bis*); C IX 10
εἴτε XX 13 (*pas.*)
ἔνθα IV 4 PCC°; C XI 3; D VI 4
ἐπεί XVI 3 A, XVIII 3 H; C XIII 14; D I 12
ἐπειδή XV 4 P, XVI 3 P, XVIII 3 LP, XXII 3 B, 20; C XIII 6

I. Index of Grammar and Syntax

ἔπειτα V 8, XII 6 L
ἔτι C XII 3; D IV 9
ἕως c. *ind. fut.* II 5 L; c. *subj.* XV 10 P; D I 12; c. *opt.* C XIII 12

Ἤ XI 5, XIII 2 P, XVI 5 P, XVIII 16 P, XX 8 H, 16 H, XXII 11 B; D III 8, IV 2, 5, 15
ἤγουν I 2 W
ἤδη I 9 L: VII 5, XX 20 B
ἡνίκα XXV 3 P, 7 P
ἤτοι C X 28

Ἵνα c. *subj.* V 13 L, VI 4 P, XIII 7 (*ind. fut., mss.*), XX 2 H. XXV 6 P, XXVI 4 B, 8 B; C Pro 4, IX 8, XII 2, XIII 1, 2, 5; D I 12, IV 15, 16

Καθώς I 14, VI 11, XII 5
καί I 1, 2, 3, *et pas.*; = *etiam* I 1 L, IV 9, V 12, VII 7, VIII 7, 8, 11, *et pas.*, C IV 6, X 2, 4, 14, *et pas.*; D I 3, 7, 12 (*tris*), *et pas.*; = ἵνα C X 11; καὶ γάρ IV 6, V 4, 5, 10, VI 2, 6, XV 10 P; C Pro 3, XI 5, XII 3

Μέν VIII 12, XV 3, 5, XXIII 4 H; μὲν ... δέ IV 4 HI, 5 HIP, V 3 PC, IX 1 A, XIII 1, 3 P, XIV 2, XV (P) 1, 5, 8, XVIII 43 P; C V 3, X 38, XI 4, 9; D I 13, II 4, VII 1; μὲν ... καὶ V 3; μέν ... μέν C XIII 4
μέντοι C XI 9
μέχρι c. *ind.* IX 8 A, XXV 7; c. *subj.* IX 8 P
μή c. *subj.* I 12, 13, V 10, 11, VI 6, XV 4 P, XVII 3, XVIII 18 (*bis*), 24 P, XXII 5, 11 B, XXVI 4, 8 P; C IX 8, XII 2, XIII 2 (*bis*), 3; c. *gen. abs.* II 7, V 5; c. *inf.* I 14, VIII 7, 8, X 2, XVI 5, XX 6 P; C X 43; D I 4; IV 16, VI 14, VII 2; c. *part.* I 9 I, XIV 4, XX 16; C X 38, D I 3, III 8; c. *adj.* C Pro 3; μὴ οὐ D II 3
μηδέ D III 8
μήπως D VI 14

Νῦν VI 3, XI 6, XII 3, XIII 3 P (*bis*), 6 P, XIV 2, 3, XVI 5, XXIII 4; C V 4; D IV 13 (*bis*)

Ὅθεν XXV 3 Q
ὁπόταν c. *ind. fut.* C XIII 14; c. *subj.* II 3 B; D II 7
ὅπου XXII 20 P, XXIII 2
ὅπως c. *ind. fut.* C XIII 2, 7; L I 5; c. *subj.* I 5, XXII 11 Q, XXV 6 Q; C XIII 7; D I 3; IV 15; c. *inf.* I 9 L
ὅταν II 5 I, VII 7 CL, XIII 6 L, XXV 3 Q, 7 H; c. *subj.* C VII 7; D VI 4
ὅτε II 5 H, VII 7 HP, VIII 11, IX 5, XIII 6, XV 5 (*bis*) P, 14 P, XXV 7 Q
ὅτι = *because* IV 6, V 11, 12 L, XX 11, 16, 21, XXII 1, 11, 15, 18, XXIII 2, XXVI 3 H; C IX 8; D IV 11, VI 1; = *that* II 1 L, IV 6, V 5 P, 10 (*bis*), XVI 4 P, XVIII 18 P, 19 L, XX 2 H (?), 7, 11 H, XXIII 4 B, XXIV 2, XXV 1 B, XXVI 2 H, 7 H, 8 H; C Pro 4; in direct address XXVI 4; D I 13, VI 3
οὐ, οὐκ, οὐχ I 2 C, 4 L, VI 5, XX 17, *et pas.* οὐ μή c. *ind. fut.* I 13; c. *subj.* XXV 8 B; D IV 6; οὐ μόνον ... ἀλλὰ καί I 2 W, XI 5, XXIII 2; C XIII 14; D I 2
οὖν II 5 L, VII 7, IX 7 P (*bis*), X 3, XII 6, XIV 5, XV 6 P, 7 P, XVI 1 H, 5 P, XVIII 4 P, XX 5 H, 14 H, XXII 3, XXV 3 P, 5 B (*bis*); C II 3, XII 6; D IV 9, 10, VI 2 (*bis*), 3, VII 1
οὔτε ... οὔτε D IV 6, VIII 7

Πλήν C XIII 1, 12
πόθεν II 1 L, IV 8, IX 4, 5, XIV 2, XX 11; C XI 6
πότε II 5 L
ποτέ XXV 3; D VI 14; ποτὲ μὲν ..., ποτὲ δέ II 3, IV 5, VIII 4; C XI 4
ποῦ II 1 L, IX 3, XVII 2, XX 20; C X 46, 47, 48, 49
πού I 4
πῶς I 3, V 3, VI 6, 10, IX 2, XI 5, XII 6, XX 14, XXV 5; D I 7, II 3, 13, IV 12

I. Index of Grammar and Syntax 125*

τέ D VII 4; τὲ ... καί I 3 P, 7 A, XIX
2 H, XXII 1 B, 4; C Pro 3 (bis), X 29;
D II 1, III 2, 6 (bis), 8, VI 10, 11, 13,
VII 4, 5
τοίνυν C Pro 4, 5; D I 7, II 1, IV 11, 14

ὡς = like, as I 10, II 3, III 4, V 5,
VI 11 P, VII 1 LC, VIII 4, IX 2 A, 6,
X 1, 8 LP, XI 1 H, XV (P) 1, 3, 5,
XVI 2, XVIII 1, 3, 18 P, 19 P, XX 17 H,
XXII 3 B, XXVI 1, 5 (bis); Tit C; D
I 2, IV 2, 16; c. inf. C XI 5; = about
C XI 8; = when III 5, XIV 6, XXIV
1 Q, XXV 7 B; D IV 13, VI 8; c. subj.
vel ind. fut. XVIII 5, 6, 7, 8; = ἵνα
c. subj. XIII 14; = ὅτι D IV 2
ὡσεί c. gen. VII 1 HP, X 9; c. nom. XIV 4,
XVIII 1 H, XXIII 3 P, XXVI 6 B
ὥσπερ V 12, X 8 H, XX 16, 17 B; C Pro
2; D IV 16; c. ind. C XII 5; D I 13;
Sig T
ὥστε c. inf. I 1 H, 2 C (τοσοῦτον), I 10,
IV 12, V 5, 8 P, XV 14, XVIII 8 H

Anacoluthia H II 4, 7, V 9, VII 3, VIII
7, et pas.; I II 4, 7, V 9; L I 1, 2, 3,
4, 5, 6, 9, 10, V 9, VII 7, VIII 1—3,
et pas.; P I 4, II 3, 4, 6, IV 8, V 13,
VI 2, 8, 10, VII 2, 3, 6, VIII 11, XI
5, 6, XIII 3, et pas.; Q II 9; C Pro 1,
I 4, II 7, IV 1, 7, IX 9, XI 1, 5, 6,
XII 6, XIII 8, 12; see Cases-solecism

Article
Demonstrative — ὁ δέ, ἡ δέ, etc. IV 4,
8, 9, 10, 11, V 2, 3, 8, 10, etc., VIII 2,
XIV 5, XVIII 2, XX 10, et pas.; ὁ μέν,
ἡ μέν, VIII 12, XIV 4, XVIII 5 P
With infinitive, see Verbs — inf.
Omitted In prepositional phrases I 2, 3 C,
4, II 5, 6, 7, III 4, IV 9, et pas.; with
infinitive XI 6; with θεός C XII 4;
cf. IX 8 (φίλος)

Asyndeta I 4, 12, II 1 AQ, III 6, IV 5,
V 4 A, VIII 6, IX 2 C, A, 3, 6; C X 3,

7, 8, 9, 10, et pas., XI 7, 8, XII 1, 2,
4, XIII 10, 13; D I 2, 7, 8, 12, 13,
IV 9, VII 2, VIII 2, 6

Attic forms διαπράττω, εἰλέω, ἐλαττῶ,
ἡττάω, κρείττω, περιττός, τριττός,
ὑποτάττω, φρίττω, φυλάττω (XXIV
2 H, XXVI 8 H); see Index III

Cases
Nom. pendens I 1 L, 2 L, 3 W, 4 B, XII 4,
XVIII 1, XX 19 H; C XI 1; D IV 3
Gen. absolute I 1, 2 A, 4, II 3, 4 L, 6, 7,
IV 1, 3, V 5, VI 3, VIII 8, IX 5, XX 3,
XXII 13 B; C Pro 1 (bis), XI 1, 3; D
II 11, III 8, IV 9, 13, VI 7 (bis), 11,
VII 5; noun om. C Pro 5, II 7; D IV 5,
VI 3
Gen. of time, age, etc. I 5 B, VI 5 (er-
rore), IX 3, 5, XVI 5 P (errore), XXII
13 H; C VII 5, XI 8
Gen. with adj. III 5, V 13; D IV 2;
with comparative XVIII 18 P; D I 13,
II 1; see preps. παρά, ὑπέρ
Gen., possessive, in predicate VI 8,
XXII 4, XXIII 4 H†; C X 12
Gen. with verbs I 2 L, 4, 9 C, II 6, IV 1,
V 10, VI 2, 8, VII 6, XVIII 40, XX
2, 5, 7, 15, XXII 3, 5, 9, (cf. acc.
XXII 6); C Pro 1, 2, 5, IX 8, X 15
—19, 38, XII 2, 5, XIII 10; D IV 1

Dative, indirect object I 1, 3, 3 C, 5—10,
12—14, II 1, 2, 6, 9, III 1, 2, 5, 6, 7,
IV 2, 3, V 3, et pas.; C Pro 1, IX 8,
9, X 42, 53, XII 1, 5, XIII 2, 3, 8—13;
D I 4, II 7, 8, III 1, 4, IV 16, VI 3,
4, 7, VII 3
Dat. of advantage and disadvantage
I 9 (?), II 7, VIII 4, IX 2, XV 8, XVIII
44 P; C X 53; D I 11, II 1
Dat., possessive in predicate I 1, IV 5,
XI 3, XVI 4 P, XXVI 4; C XI 5; D
VII 2
Dat., associative III 4, VIII 8, XXV 4,
XXVI 4; D IV 1; c. adj. VIII 8, XV
10; D I 13, IV 3, VI 12

I. Index of Grammar and Syntax

Dat. of cause, specification, manner, means I 2V, 3L, 4C, 14, III 4P, V 3, 11, VI 3, VII 3, 7, VIII 2CP, 11, IX 6, X 6, 7, XI 1, 4P, 7, XIII 1H, 7, XIV 1, XVI 6, 7, XVII 2, 4, XVIII 2, 15, 43 P, 44 P, XIX 3, XX 4, XXII 20, XXIV 2; C Pro 2, XIII 6, 11, 13, 14; D I 3, II 1, 2, 10, III 8, VII 4
Dat. of time I 8, XXII 17; D VIII 2
Dat. with compound verbs I 3C, 4CL, 9, II 6, 7, III 7, IV 6, V 4 VI 11, VII 1, VIII 8, IX 1 PC, 6, X 1, 3, 8, XI 2, 3, XIII 1, XIV 1, 2, 3, XV 1, 4, 8, XVI 2, 5, 6, 7, XVII 2, 4, XVIII 15, 42, XX 4, XXII 20, XXIV 2; C Pro 2, X 31, 53, XI 5 (cf. acc. infra), 7, XIII 6, 11, 13, 14; D II 4, 10, III 3
Dat. for prepositional phrase I 14, II 6, 9, IV 9 PC, XX 3, 10, XXIV 1; C IX 8, 9, XI 7, 8; D VI 13, VII 3
Dat., see below under Acc.

Accusative of extent of time or space I 5, IV 12, VII 5, X 18, XVI 5, XXII 15, 17; C XII 3, 5
Acc. for time when D IV 10
Acc. of specification, manner, etc. I 3C, 11H, III 4L, VI 9P, VIII 1 PL, IX 1, X 1, 9, XI 4 H, XIII 1, XIV 1 L, XVI 1, XX 1; C Pro 2, VII 5, XII 3, 4; D IV 10, 11
Acc. subj. of infinitive I 1C, 4, 6, 7 (?), IV 6, V 13, VI 2, 6, 9, X 2, XX 6, XXII 5B, 11, XXIV 5, XXVI 5H; C Pro 1, XI 5, XIII 2; D I 4, IV 16
Acc. double with ὁρκίζω XI 6
Acc. or Dat. with προσκυνέω XXII 17, XXVI 3; D I 8, III 5, VIII 1 (Dat.); XXII 20, XXVI 2; C XI 5; D VI 8 (Acc.); σφραγίζω VII 3, VIII 12, X 6, 7, XVI 7, XXVI 9 (Dat.); XII 5, XXII 11 H, B (Acc.)
Vocative I 3C, 4, 7C, 14, II 6, III 5, V 9, VI 10, VII 3, IX 2, X 1, 2 (bis), XI 1, XII 4 (bis), XIII 2, XV 12, XVI 1, XVIII 3, 5, XX 1 (bis), 2, 4 (bis), pas.,

XXII 4, XXIII 2, XXV 2; C Pro 1, 2 (pas.), IX 8, XII 1, 4, 5, XIII 1 (bis), 4, 6, 10; D I 9, II 4, III 1, IV 2, 5, 6, 13, 17, VI 1, 7, 12, VII 1, 2, 3
Solecisms
Nom. for Dat. I 4 L, VI 1
Nom. for Acc. I 1 L
Dat. for Gen. C I 5, II 6, XIII 7 (σοι)
Dat. for Acc. XXVI 5 H†, C I 5, III 3 W, 4, VII 6, XIII 2; D I 7
Acc. for Gen. I 5 L, IV 6 H, X 6 L (μετὰ τούτους), XXII 2 Q
Acc. for Dat. IV 6 A, VI 11 H, XX 20 H; C I 1, 3V, 8W, II 1, III 7, V 3, X 42, XI 3, XII 3, 4, XIII 5, 14; D VII 6 (bis)

Comparison of adjective sand adverbs
Comparative I 1 A, 3 L, 4 L, 6 L, V 4, 6, VI 1 P, IX 6, XVIII 18 P; C XIII 2; D I 13, II 1
Superlative I 1, 7, II 5 L, VIII 11, XI 6, XVIII 20 P; D II 2

Compound words
ἀνακαλύπτω VI 3 P
ἀνακυλινδέω XIV 1 P
ἀναπτύσσω XXII 6 P
ἀπαραλάκτως I 3 C
ἀπερινόητος C Pro 2
ἀρρενοβατία VI 4 P
βοοπρόσωπος XVIII 1 P
γυναικοειδής XIII 1 P
δαφνόφυλλον† XVIII 15 P
ἐξαποστέλλω XXII 16 Q
ἐπεξουσιάζω I 5 L
ἐπικαπνίζω V 9 P
ἐρυθροδανόω XXI 3 B
ἡμιπρόσωπον VII 1 C
καθυπόσχομαι C XII 1
κατακληρονομέω IX 5 P
κατανύσσομαι XX 3 P
καταπεριπολεύω V 10 P
κρημνοβατέω XI 6 P
λυχναψία IX 7 P
μαρμαροκοπεῖν (?) X 10 P

I. Index of Grammar and Syntax

μελανοκέρατος IX 9 C
γευροχάλασις XVIII 17 P
νυκτοφαγήση (?) XVIII 35 P
ξυλοφορέω XI 7 P
ὀνοπρόσωπος XVIII 1 P
πλινθουργέω XII 6 P
πορφυροδανόμενος XII 4 P
προεπιστρέφω V 2 L
πρωτομαίστωρ I 2 B
πτηνοπρόσωπος XVIII 1 P
στραγγισμός XVIII 27 P
ὑπογινώσκω V 13 L
ὑποπροτάσσω X 6 L
φοβερόχροος XII 1
χαλινόδεσμα XIII 4 P

Crasis κἀγώ pas., κἀκεῖ VIII 5 P; κἀκεῖνος IX 7 P, -ως II 8; τἄλλα XVII 5; τἀληθές C XII 5; ταὐτά D IV 3

Elision, cf. ἀλλά, ἀντί, ἀπό, ἐπί, κατά, μετά, παρά; not observed VI 11 (ταῦτα ἀκούσας); IX 7 P (ἐπὶ αὐτό)

Gender—solecisms I 1 HI, 14 CQ, II 2; C IX 8, XII 2

Hebraisms ἐγένετο, καὶ ἐγένετο, etc.
I 6, XXII 1 P, XXV 7 B; C Pro 1; D II 1; εἰς χεῖρας I 5; ζῇ κύριος ὁ θεός I 13, V 12, XXV 8 B; πρὸ προσώπου cf. πρό under Prepositions

Hiatus P VI 11, IX 7; C XIII 10, 12

Indirect Discourse—Questions IV 1, XXII 12; cf. Inf. with subj. Acc.

Latinisms κάστρον C X 13, 24, 27; Λεγεών XI 3, 5, 6, 7; λίτρα XXI 1 Q; ὅ ἐστιν P XI 6, XV 11; πρὸ τεσσ. ἡμερῶν D IV 14

Nouns — case endings
ἄνδρες = Acc. I 1 L
ν in Acc. Third Declension ι 5 HL,

X 8 L; C I 3, 4, 6, 8, 9, 11, 14, II 9, IX 8, 10, X 51, XII 5
σφραγίδα, -δαι Sig C
φάραγγει C III 5

Prepositions
Ἅμα c. dat. X 6, XIII 1; D VII 6; c. acc. D III 5, VII 4
ἀνά ι. gen. C IX 10; c. acc. D VII 4
ἄνευ XXII 11 B; C XIII 8
ἀντί C XI 8
ἄνωθεν C XII 6
ἀπό c. gen. I 1 L, (= ὑπό), C, 2 P, 4, 4 B, II 1, III 4, IV 8 et pas.; = contrary to IV 5; C XI 5; c. dat. II 5 L; c. acc. XVIII 20 L, XXII 2 Q
ἄχρι ι. gen. XX 18 B; c. acc. D IV 8
Διά c. gen. agent, means, etc., I 6, 7, IV 7, V 3, 8, 11, VI 4; et pas.; C IV 5, IX 8, XI 4, XIII 13; D I 7, II 1, IV 15; place, I 5, IX 6, X 3, XIV 4, XXIV 4; C XII 6; time, D II 4; c. acc. cause, II 2, V 4, 13, VI 1, 2, 6, 9, VII 6, et pas.; C I 1, 3, XIII 2; D I 6, means C X 53; δ. παντός XXII 5 B
δίκην D VI 5
Ἔγγιστα C, ἔγγιστεν P, ἐγγύθεν A III 7
εἰς I 1, 3 C, 4, 9, II 3, 5, 7, 8, 9, III 3, 5, et pas.; C Pro 4, IX 9, X 2, 6, 18, 20, 21, 24, 25, et pas.; D I 1, 3, 4, B, 12, II 11, et pas.; ἐνεργεῖν εἰς C X 1, 2, 3, 5, 6, 12, 13, 14 (bis), 22, 23, 26, 29, 34, 35, 36, 37, 38, 39, 52; εἰς τὸ ὄνομα XXVI 4, 5; C IX 8; εἰς ὄνομα C Pro 5; εἰς = ἐν XV 6, XXII 14; XXIV 3 (?); D VI 1
ἐκ I 2 L, 4, 4 L, 5, 6 L, II 8, VI 5, X 9, XIV 2, XVI 3, XXVI 3, XXI 2, XXV 1 H; C IV 11, XI 8, XII 1, XIII 12; D I 1, 11, 12 (5), IV 13, 14 (bis), 15, VI 8; ἐκ τρίτου I 2 L, XVIII 21
ἔμπροσθεν ι. gen. IV 2 C, VI 1, XIII 7, XX 19 Q, XXII 10; D III 3; C IV 2, XI 2
ἐν I 1, 3 (tris), II 1 (bis), IV 4, 5, 8, 9 (tris), 10, et pas.; C IX 10, X 8, 14,

38, 53 (*bis*), *et pas.*; D I 1, 13, II 7,
et pas.; means, manner, V 9, VII 6,
7 (*bis*), X 5, XI 6 (*tris*), XII 2, 3, XV
3, 14, XX 13 (4); C XIII 5, 6, 12;
XV 9, XXV 9; C IX 10, XII 1; D
IV 11; *c. infin.* = *while, since*, I 4, 6,
7, VI 9, XX 6, 17, XXII 11, XXIV 5;
D IV 16; ἐν = εἰς I 5 C, X 5, XIII
2, 6, XVIII 28 (cf. 24, 27), 40; C I 5,
XIII 9; D I 5

ἐναντίον XXII 2 HP

ἐνώπιον V 9, IX 7, XIX 3, XX 1, 6;
C Pro 1

ἔξω XVI 2 P

ἐπάνω I 2 L, 9 L, II 5 L, XXIII 3 B;
C XII 6 T, XIII 5

ἐπί *c. gen.* I 2 AB, 3 P, 4 I, 10 L, II 8,
III 1 P, IV 4, 5 CC°, V 9, *et pas.*; C II 1,
VIII 9, XI 3; *c. dat.* I 1, II 6 L, III 3 W,
XIII 3, 6 P, XVIII 44 P, XXII 14, XXVI
5 B, 8 H; D VI 14, VII 4; *c. acc.* I 1 L,
C, 2 A, 10 L, 11, 14 L, II 2, 3, III 3 V,
V 5, *et pas.*; D II 2, 4, 7; ἐπὶ πολύ
VII 2; ἐπὶ πλεῖστον VII 5; ἐπὶ τὸ
διπλάσιον I 1 C, (διπλοῦν) D II 2;
ἐφ' ἑκάστης ἡμέρας I 2 Q, 3 B, ἐφ'
ἑκάστην ἡμέραν I 2 H, 3 A

ἕως *c. gen.* V 8, VI 11 P, XV 13 P, XVI
2 P, XX 4 H, 18 B, XXII 2 B, 4 B, XXIV
2 Q, 5, XXV 8; C XII 1; *c. dat.* XX
18 H; *c. acc.* XXII 2 H, XXIII 2 Q,
XXIV 5 Q; ἕως ἔξω XVIII 15 P; ἕως
ἐπὶ πολύ VII 2; ἕως ἑπτὰ φορές
C IX 9 T; ἕως οὗ D I 12

Καθώς I 10 L

κατά *c. gen.* I 1, 2, 4, III 7, V 5, IX 3
XI 6, XIII 2, XV 11, XVIII 20, XXII
20 B, XXVI 8 H; C X 14; D II 10;
Tit BI, Sub V; *c. acc.* I 1, 2, 10, VII 3,
VIII 11, X 2, XV 3, XVIII 21, XIX
3 P, XX 2 P, 12 B, 19 B, XXII 3 B, 12,
XXVI 7 H; C X 51 T; D II 9, VI 6,
VIII 5; καθ' ἕνα XVIII 4 P; καθ'
ἑνὸς ἑκάστου XVI 3 A; καθ' ὑπεροχήν, ὑπερβολήν X 2, P; κατὰ B, περὶ
C, I 2

κατενώπιον XXII 13

κάτω *c. gen.* D IV 14; *c. acc.*(?) XV 7

Μά C XII 3

μέσον I 1 L, XX 12, 14 B

μετά *c. gen.* I 6 L, II 5 L, III 4, V 2 P,
3 P, 9, 13, VI 3, IX 8, X 6 (*bis*), XI
5, 6, XV 9, XVI 1 L, XVIII 4, 22 P,
XIX 1 P, XX 9 P, XXII 11, 16, 18,
XXIV 1 P, 2 Q (*bis*); XXV 1, XXVI 8 H,
9 H; C IX 8, 9 T, X 30 (*bis*), XI 7 (*bis*);
D I 8, 9, 10, II 1, 6, 7 (*tris*), 12,
III 3 (*bis*), 4, 8 (*bis*), IV 1, 2, 7, VI 3,
5, 13, VII 4; Tit C, Sub V, Sig T,
C; *c. dat.* I 4 H, XXVI 1 B; *c. acc.*
I 2 L, 4, 4 L, XI 6, XV 8, XX 7, 10,
11, 19, XXII 6, 9; C Pro 1, XIII 2;
D IV 8, 10, VI 7; Tit C, Sub V

μέχρι V 4, XV 10 P, XXIV 3; C X 4,
XIII 3, 6; D I 12, VI 14

Ὄπισθεν D VIII 6

ὀπίσω XXV 6 B

Παρά *c. gen.* I 1 I, 2 C, P, 6, 9 IC, Q, 11,
V 11, VI 6, XVI 1, XX 12 Q, 21, XXII
1, XXV 7 B, XXVI 6 P, 8 H; C I 14,
X 31, 34, XI 1, XII 4, XIII 9; Sub V;
D I 2, 3, 5, 13 (*bis*), II 3, 10, III 7,
IV 16; *c. dat.* V 7 P, VI 4, 6, 8, P;
C XIII 9; *c. acc.* I 1 A, 3 B, 11 H, II 5,
XVIII 37 P; C X 6; D II 2

περί *c. gen.* I 4 H, VI 10, XV 5 P, XXII
17, XXV 1 P; D IV 4; Tit H, I, Sig T;
c. acc. I 2 C; D VII 3

πλήν C XIII 12

πρό I 14, IV 6; X 2; C XI 5; D I 4,
IV 9; πρὸ προσώπου VII 1, X 1, XII
1, XIII 1, XV 1, XVI 1; πρὸ τεσσ.
ἡμερῶν D IV 14

πρός *c. gen.* I 14 H, XXVI 8 H; C X 4;
c. dat. D VI 4; *c. acc.* I 1 A, 4 H, 6,
8, 9, 11, 12 (*bis*), 13, 14, II 7, *et pas.*;
C II 3, V 5, Pro 3, X 30; D I 5, 8,
II 5, 6, *et pas.*; for indirect obj. I 4 B,
13 BW, VI 6 P, XII 6 L, XIII 2, 3 P,
XV 14 P, XVI 1 P, XXIII 1 Q, XXVI
2 (*bis*); C I 9, 13; D I 7 (*bis*), 8, 9 (*bis*),
11, II 3, 4, 6, IV 4—8, VII 1, 5

I. Index of Grammar and Syntax

Σύν V 4P, XV 1P, XXIII 2, XXV 9H; D II 7
Ὑπέρ *c. gen.* D II 5; *c. acc.* I 1L, 3A; C XII 6
ὑπό *c. gen.* I 1 H, 2, 6L, 9P, II 4, IV 11, VI 8 (*bis*), IX 6, 7P, XI 6, XII 3, XIII 6 (*bis*), XIV 4, 5 (*bis*), XV 5, 6, 9, 13, XIX 1, XXI 3, XXII 3B, 20, XXIV 4, XXV 3, XXVI 7H, 9H; C Pro 2, IX 8; D III 2, 6; *c. dat.* C XIII 6; *c. acc.* XI 3, 5, XXII 8 Q, XXVI 5 H, 7 H
ὑποκάτω XI 7, XIX 1, XXIII 3 H, XXV 7
ὑποκάτωθεν C XI 7
Χάριν XX 2
χωρίς XXI 4
Ὡς VII 1 C
ὡσεί VII 1

Pronouns

αὐτός Third Person, *passim*; = *idem* V 3; XVIII 35 H, XXII 8; C IX 9 T; D IV 3; = *ipse* VII 6, IX 7P; C Pro 1, 3, X 15—20, XII 5; D I 12, II 1, III 2, V 1 (*bis*)
ἐγώ *passim*
εἷς as indef. pron. I 1 A, 3, XX 1; C XII 5
ἐμαυτοῦ, ἑαυτοῦ IV 6, VI 3P, IX 2, 3P, 6, 7P, XI 5, XVI 2, 4, XVIII 4P; C XII 5; D VI 12, cf. VI 3
ἐμός V 4, VI 4P, IX 5, X 3, XXIII 4P; C XIII 12; D III 2, IV 2, 9
ἡμέτερος C Pro 3
σύς I 4Q, III 5, X 5; D IV 10, 11, VI 2
σύ *passim*
τις, τίς *passim*

Verbs — Inflexion

Augment ἠνεσχόμην XIII 3 P; προεφήτευσε XV 8

Future from Subjunctive (Aor.) ἀγαγῶ II 6, VI 5, X 5
εἴπωσι XIV 5P
ἐνέγκω VI 5H; C XI 7Y; D VI 2
εὕρωμεν V 5 C
ἔχωμεν V 5 A
ἴδῃς D IV 9
μαθεῖς XIII 2 H
παρέλθωσι D IV 6
Periphrastic tenses I 1, 2, XVI 2P, XX 17, XXI 4, XXII 7B, XXV 9H, XXIV 4B, C Pro 1, 2; D I 12, VII 4, VIII 1
Reduplication σεσωματοπεποιημένον IV 4P

Verbs — Syntax

Infinitive with Art. in oblique cases
Gen. I 14, II 5, 7C, 8, V 6L, VII 4; C IX 10, X 43, 53, XIII 13, 14; D I 4 (*bis*), 9; = Nom. XVI 2; D VII 2
Dat. I 4, 7, VI 9, XX 17, XXII 1P, 11, 17B, XXIV 5; D I 6, IV 16
Acc. I 1, 2L, 4, V 13, VI 2, VII 2, XVI 5, XX 6P, XXVI 5, 7H; C Pro 1, X 1, 2, 3, *et pas.*, XIII 2; D III 5(?), IV 11
As noun without Art. XI 6
Optative C XIII 12 θελήσαιεν; D IV 4 ἀποκρίνοιτο, VI 1 χαίροις, 12 γινώσκοι
Participle
Unnecessary XI 3 ὄν, XIII 2 ὄντα
Future of purpose D VII 3
Perfect for Aorist II 9 CL; D I 3, II 6, 8, 9, 11
Subjunctive
With ἄν, ἐάν, εἰ, ἕως, ἵνα, ὅπως, ὡς cf. *supra* Adverbs
Hortatory D VI 7
In oath P XXV 8
Prohibitions I 12, 13, V 10, 11, VI 6, XV 4P, XVIII 18 (*bis*), XXII 5; C XIII 3

II. Index of Angelology, Astrology, Demonology, Magic

ἃ καὶ β' XVIII 38
Ἀβεζεθιβοῦ XXV 2 HP, -εβιθον Q
Ἀβελούθ XXV 2 Q, cf. Ἀμελούθ
Ἀβραάμ XVIII 22 P
Ἀβυζού(θ) XIII 2 L
ἄγγελος v. XVIII 15 and Index III
Ἄγλα C XIII 6
Ἀγχονίων XVIII 37 P, cf. Ἀχωνεώθ
Ἀδωναήλ P XVIII 14, 17, cf. Ἀδωναΐ
Ἀδωναΐ XVIII 14 H, ἀδωνάν L, XVIII 17 A, Ἀδωναήλ P, XVIII 36 H, ἀδοναήθ P
ἀενιον Sig A, T, V^r
ἀερίου XVIII 28 H, ἀρνίου P
Ἀζαήλ VII 7
αἰαώ Sig A, T (ἰαώ), V^r
Αἰγώκερας XVIII 3 P
ἀιέ Sig A, V^r
ἀιώ Sig A
Ἀκέφαλος δαίμων IX 1, X 8
Ἀκουρταραήλ XVIII 13 L
Ἀκτονμέ XVIII 28 H, κτονμέ L, ἄκτον μέν P
Ἀλάθ XVIII 25 HP, ὀλάθ L
ἀλακαρταναν I 9 C
Ἀλενρήθ XVIII 35 H, ἀλλεβορίθ P
Ἀλλαζοώλ XVIII 30 P, cf. Καλαζαήλ
Ἀλλεβορίθ XVIII 35 P, cf. Ἀλενρήθ
ἄμαξα V 4
Ἀμελούθ XXV 2, cf. Ἀβελούθ
Ἀμεμῶν C X 16, ἀμαιμῶν V
Ἀμπατζούτ C X 20
ἀναάθ XVIII 40
Ἀνατρέθ XVIII 29
Ἄνετ C X 45
Ἀνοστήρ XVIII 33 P, ἀστήρ H
Ἀντιναός C X 42 T, cf. Ἀτανιανούς
Ἀξησβύθ XVIII 31 H, φηθ, ἀξιωφθιθ P
Ἁπάξ XVIII 32 H, ἅρπαξ P
Ἀπάτη VIII 3, 5
Ἀπολήν C X 23
Ἀραήλ XVIII 11
ἀραρά ἀραρή XVIII 29 H, ἄραρα χάραρα P

Ἀραψ XI 4, ῥάθ P
ἀρδάδ XVIII 40 H, ἀρδοῦ P
ἀρνίον XVIII 28 P, cf. ἀερίου
Ἅρπαξ XVIII 32 P, cf. Ἀπάξ
Ἀρτοσαήλ XVIII 7 A (bis), L, ἀρωτοσαήλ, ἀρατοσαήλ P, ἀρσαήλ L
Ἀσιέλ C X 38
Ἀσμοδαῖος V 1, 7, 9, 11, 12, 13, Ἀσμοδεῶ C X 7 UVW, ἀσμοδέος T
Ἀσταρώθ C X 21, 24 T, cf. Ἀστερώθ
Ἀστεραώθ VIII 10 PW, ἀστεραέθ V, cf. περαωθ
Ἀστερώθ C X 24 V, ὁ ἕτερος Ἀσταρώθ T, ἀστηρώθ W
Ἀτανιανούς C X 42 VW, cf. Ἀντιναός
Ἄτραξ XVIII 20 P, cf. Κατράξ
Αὐδαμεώθ XVIII 26 H, αὐμαδεώθ L
Αὐθάδης XVIII 27 H, cf. Μανθαδώ
Αὐτοθίθ P, αὐτώθ H, XVIII 38
Ἀφαρώφ XIII 6 P
Ἀχωνεώθ XVIII 37 H, ἀγχονίων P
ἀωᾶ Sig A, L (αωαω), T

βαέ XVIII 16 P
Βαζαζάθ XIV 7
Βαλθιούλ VIII 9 P
Βαρουχιήλ VIII 6 C, -χιαήλ H, -χιαχήλ P
Βαρσαφαήλ XVIII 6 (bis), -σαβαήλ L
Βεελζεβούλ III 1, 3, 4, 5 C, 6, IV 2, VII 1, 2, 4 P, 9, 10, IX 8, XVI 3 A, 5 P; C IX 9 T, X 1; βελζεβουήλ H III 1, etc., V III 3; βεελζεβονέλ L saepe, βελζεβούλ W III 3
βειρσαβεέ IV 8 V°, C XI 6, cf. βηρσαβεέ, -βεέλ
Βελβέλ XVIII 12
βηροσαβεέ C XI 6, -βεέλ IV 8 W°, C XI 6 W, βειρσαβεέ V, βηρφβεέ T
βιανακίθ XVIII 40 P, cf. Μιανέθ
βιωνίx Sig L(?), A (βιωνιά), V^r (βιονηκα)
Βοθήλ, Βοθοθήλ XVIII 17 P, cf. Φοβοθήλ

II. Index of Angelology, Astrology, Demonology, Magic 131*

βολβοί θαλάσσης VI 10
βούλ C X 19, VII 6 VW
Βουλδουμήχ XVIII 22P, cf. Μοδεβήλ
βουλταλά VII 6
Βριαθός X 11 H, βριαθαονήλ L, βριεώ P, Βριάριος Bn
Βυζοῦθ. ἡ XIII 3 H, cf. Ὀβυζούθ,. Ἀβυζούθ

Γαβριήλ XVIII 6
Γλαμεχιήλ VIII 5 H, cf. Δαμεχιήλ, Χλαμεήλ
γλάνος V 9

Δάν XVIII 20 A
δάφνη XVIII 15
δαφνῶν I 3 W, cf. διαφ.
δεκανός XVIII 4
δεσπόζω XVI 3 P; C X 1, 2, etc.; D I 10
δεσποτεία C IX 10
διάβολος III 5 PC, XV 11, XXII 20 B; D I 5, II 7, 9, III 1, 2, 3
διαφνών I 3 V, cf. δαφν.
Δίδυμος XVIII 3 P
Δορόν XVIII 11 H, cf. Σφανδῶρ
δούνη XVIII 21 P
δοῦρον XVIII 23
δρακοντόπαις V 4 LP
δρακοντόπους V 4 HIC
δράκων VI 10, XII 1, 6, XIII 5 P, XIV 1; C X 40
Δύναμις VIII 3, 10; C IX 9 U
δύναμις cf. Index III

ἐαέ XVIII 15 H, ἱεαέ L, ἰαέ P
Ἐλβουρίων IX 7 P
ἐλεήθ VI 8 P, cf. Ἐλωΐ
Ἐλτζήν C X 17
Ἐλτζιανφηέλ C XI 1 V, cf. Ἐντζ.
Ἐλωΐ VI 8 L, ἐλωιθ H, ἐλεήθ P; Sig L(?), A, T, Vʳ
Ἐμμανουήλ VI 8, XI 6, XV 11
Ἐνανθά XVIII 30 H, ἐνενούθ P
Ἐνήψιγος XV 2 P
Ἐνοδάς C X 41

Ἐντζιανφιέλ C XI 1, ἐλτζιανφηέλ V, ἐντζανφιέλ W, τζιανφιέλ T
Ἔρις VIII 3, 6, 8
ἔριφος C IX 9
Ἑρμήν C IX 9 T
Ἔρως? XIV 4
Ἑσπερία VI 7 A
Ἐφιππᾶς VI 5, XII 4, XXII 18, XXIV 1, XXV 7; Ἐφίππας D VI 9, 10, 11, 12, 13

Ζαβαρζης C XII 6
ζαβουνή XVIII 21 P
Ζάλη VIII 3, 8, 11 C
ζιζαβοῦ XVIII 21 A
Ζυγός XVIII 3 P
ζωδιακός XVIII 4 P
ζῴδιον II 2; C XII 6
Ζωρωήλ XVIII 19 P, cf. Ῥιζωήλ

ἡμιτριταῖος VIII 6, 7
ἠρώ Sig A, cf. ἰρώ

θαλλάλ VII 6

ἰαέ XVIII 16 A, cf. ἐαέ
ἰαεῶ XVIII 16 P
Ἰάζ XVIII 18
ιαησω Sig Vʳ
Ἰαθώθ XVIII 27 P, cf. Ἰαώθ
Ἰακώβ XVIII 22 P
Ἰαμέθ XVI 6 LP, ἰαβέ H
Ἴαξ IX 8 P
Ἰατράξ XVIII 20 L, cf. Κατράξ
ἰαώ XVIII 16 L, Sig T
Ἰαώθ XVIII 13 P, σαβαώθ H, XVIII 25 A, ἰαθώθ P
Ἰδιούθ XIII 3 H, cf. Ἀβυζοῦθ
ἰεαέ XVIII 15 L, ἰαέ P, cf. ἐαέ
ἰειλῷ XVIII 16 P
Ἱεροπά XVIII 21 L, ἱεροπάκ H, ἱεροπαήλ P
ἰεώ XVIII 15 LP, ἰωεώ H, 16 H
ἰθόθ XVIII 16 P
ἰού Sig T
ἰοῦδα XVIII 21 A, ἰουδαρίζη P

9**

132*   II. Index of Angelology, Astrology, Demonology, Magic

Ἰουδάλ XVIII 9 P, cf. Καιρωξανονδάλον
ἱρώ Sig T, cf. ἠρώ
Ἰσαάκ XVIII 22 P
Ἰτάρογαν C X 12 T, cf. N ταρωγάν
Ἰχθύον XVIII 36 P, ἰχθύος H
Ἰχθύς XVIII 3 P
ἰωασέ Sig A, Vʳ
ἰωελέτ XVIII 16 P
ἰωεώ XVIII 15 H, cf. ἰεώ

Καιρωξανονδάλον XVIII 9 H, καιριξενονδάλων L, ἰουδάλ P
Κακίστη VIII 3, 11
Καλαζαήλ XVIII 30 H, ἀλλαζοώλ P
Κανωνήλ VIII 11 V, κανγρυήλ W
Καραήλ XVIII 12
Καράπ C X 27
Κάρκινος XVIII 3 P
Καστιέλ C X 39
Κατανικοταήλ XVIII 15 HLP, also κανικοταήλ L, νικοταήλ H
Κατράξ XVIII 20 H, ἰατράξ L, ἀτραξ P
Κλωθώ VIII 3, 7
κόκ XVIII 32
Κορυφὴ δρακόντων XII 6
Κουμελτήλ Κουμεντάήλ XVIII 19 P, cf. Σουβελτί
Κουρταήλ XVIII 13 HP, κοφταήλ? H, ἀκουρταραήλ L
Κρινέλ C X 29
Κριός XVIII 3 P, 4
κρόκος VI 10
Κρόνος XV 5
Κτονμέ, cf. Ἀκτονμέ
Κυνόπηγος XVI 4 (-ον) H, κυνόπιγω L, κυνόπαστον P, Κυνόσπαστον Cr, l. κυνόσβατον?
Κύων X 1, 2, 8

Δαμεχιήλ VIII 5 C, λαμεχαλαλ P, cf. Γλαμεχιήλ
Δασαράκ C X 9
λεγεῶν XI 3 (bis), 5 (bis), 6, 7
Δεικουργός XVIII 37 H, λυκοῦργος P

Δένελ C X 34 V, νένελ W, δελήνήλ T
Δεοντοφόρον XI 4 P, λεοντόφρον A XI 4, 7, λεοντόμορφος P
Δερωήλ XVIII 18, ῥοκλήδ P
Δέων XVIII 3 P, Sig A, T, Vʳ
λίβανος VI 10
Δὶξ Τέτραξ VII 4
Δουπήτ C X 22
Δυκοῦργος XVIII 37 P, cf. Δεικ.
λύχνος VI 10

μαγατά I 3 C
Μαγώτ C X 26 TV, μαγότ W
Μακατάκ C X 52 T, μακκατάκ W, μαχατάκ V
μάλθη XVIII 36 H
Μανθαδῶ XVIII 27 L, αὐθάδης H, νεφθαδᾶ P
Μαρδέρω XVIII 23 P, μαδούωρ H, μανδραβουροῦν L
Μαρμαραώ(θ) XVIII 28, 33
Μαρμαρώθ VIII 7 V, μαρμαροώθ W, μαρτυρώθ H, μετύρον L, μαρμαράθ P
Μαχατάκ cf. Μακατάκ
Μαχθόν XVII 1 L
Μαχιθιούμ VIII 8 C
Μαχουμέτ C X 3
Μεινγέτ C X 40 W, μηνγέτ V, μινγότ T
μέλπω XVIII 40 H, μηλτῶ P
μελχάλ VII 6, μελχάγ W, μελχαγί V
Μελχοῦ VIII 8 H, μελχουήλ L
Μεταθίαξ XVIII 14
μηλτῶ cf. μέλπω
Μιανέθ XVIII 40 H, βιαναχίθ P
Μινγότ cf. μεινγέτ
Μιραγκούς C X 43 W, cf. Μυραγκούς
Μιρατζηέλ C X 36 W, cf. Μυρατζιέλ
Μιχαήλ I 6, II 4 A, 5 I, XVIII 5; D II 6 III 2
Μοδεβήλ XVIII 22 H, μοδιήλ L, βουλδουμήχ P
Μπηλέτ C X 8
Μυραγκούς C X 43 V, μυρακός T, μιρ. W
Μυρατζιέλ C X 36 V, μυράκιελ T, μιρατζηέλ W

II. Index of Angelology, Astrology, Demonology, Magic 133*

Ναβέλ C X 49 VW, ναβάλ T
Ναθώθω XVIII 24 H, ναθαθώ(?) L, ναώθ, ναθάθ P
Ναπαλαικόν C X 51 VW, ναμπαλαικόν T
Ναπούρ C X 4
νάρδος VI 10
Ναχπιέλ C IX 9 T
Ναχτιέλ C IX 9 T
Νένελ cf. Δένελ
Νεφθαδᾶ cf. Μανθαδῶ
Νικοταήλ XVIII 15 H, cf. Κατανικ.
Νταρωγάν C X 12, ἰτάρογαν T

Ὀβυζούθ XIII 3 P, cf. Ἀβυζούθ, Βυζοῦθ
Ὀέλ C X 33
Ὀελήνήλ cf. Δένελ
Ὀλάθ cf. Ἀλάθ
Ὀνοσκελίς IV 2, 4, Ὀνοσκελοῦ IV 2 WC°, 4 WT°W°
Ὀριένς C X 15
Ὀρνίας I 2, 4 H, 10, 14 H, II 1, 9, III 1, 3, 4 PC, IX 3, XX 6, 11; D III 1, 4, IV 4, 5, 6, 7, 12, 13, 18, VII 1, 2, 3, 4, 5
Ὀροπέλ XVIII 8 P, ὀροπόλος L, ἀροπόλον H
οὐ Sig A, T, V^r (φυ)
Οὔλεος C X 28
οὐνίου Sig A, T, V^r (ουνη)
Οὐριήλ II 4 Q, 8, VIII 9 P, XVIII 7, 9 H, XVIII 27 H (ὀριήλ) L; οὐρουήλ II 4 C, VIII 9 A, XVIII 9, XVIII 27 P; οὐρονέλ II 7 L, XVIII 7 L; οὐρικά VIII 9 C
Οὐροήλ XVIII 5 L, ου ουρον H, cf. Ῥύαξ
ὀφθαλμός, ὁ πολυπαθής XVIII 39

παλιπούλ I 3 C
Παλιτιέλ C XII 1 T, cf. Παλτιέλ
Παλτάφωτε C X 46 VW, παλταφάτε T
Παλτιὲλ Τζαμάλ C XII 1 VW, Παλιτιὲλ Τζ. T, XIII 12 πατιέλ V, παλτιέ W
παντοκράτωρ θεός VI 8
Πανῶν C X 18

Παρέλ C X 6, παρελκοζίον T
Παρθένος II 2, XVIII 3 P
Πατικῇ VI 8 H, πατικεῖ L, cf. πευστικῶ
Πελών C X 13
πεντάλφα Sig B
Περαώθ VIII 10 H, περεώθ L, cf. Ἀστεραώθ
πευστικῶ VI 8 P, cf. Πατική
Πιστηφούμ I 9 W, πιστιρούμ V
Πλάνη VIII 3, 9
Ποτζέτιες C X 44 VW, ποτζέτιος T
Πτεροδράκων XIV 3

Ῥααμετ C X 10 UW, ῥαεμέτ V, ῥαιμέτ T
Ῥάβδος X 4
Ῥάθ XI 4 P
Ῥαθαναήλ XV 6, 7
Ῥαιονώθ XVIII 26 H, ῥαιζώθ L
Ῥαριδέρις XVIII 25 A, ῥορήξ P
Ῥαφαήλ V 9, XIII 6, XVIII 8, 23 P
Ῥιζωήλ XVIII 19 H, (-ωέλ) L, ζωρωήλ P
Ῥοάπτ C X 5
Ῥοκλήθ XVIII 18 P, cf. Δερωήλ
Ῥύαξ XVIII 5 P (bis), cf. Οὐροήλ
ῥύξ XVIII 24—40, sometimes ῥίξι or ῥήξ

Σαβαήλ XVIII 10 P, σαφαήλ L, σφεβαήλ H
Σαβαώθ XVIII 13, cf. Ἰαώθ, XVIII 15, 16, 28 P, Sig A, T, V^r
Σαμαήλ D VII 2, 4, 5
Σανσωνιέλ C X 37
Σαπαρατζήλ C X 47 VW, σαρατήλ T
Σαρατιέλ C X 35
Σαταήλ C X 50 VW, τασαήλ T
Σαφαήλ cf. Σαβαήλ
Σαφθοραήλ XVIII 16 A, θαφαθοραήλ P
σεραφίμ XVIII 34
Σεταριέλ C X 31
Σκορπίος XVIII 3 P
Σουβελτί XVIII 19 A, κουμελτήλ P
σουγεωά Sig A, σουιεωά T, σουγεω V^r
Σουπιέλ C X 14
στακτή VI 10

σύρòν XVIII 23 P
Σφανδῶρ XVIII 11 P, δορόν H, φανδωρόν L
Σφεβαήλ cf. Σαβαήλ
Σφενδοναήλ XVIII 10 P, σφενδεναήλ H; φενδοναήλ L
σφήνηρ XVIII 23 P
σφραγίζω cf. Index III

ταγιθαμάν VII 6 VW
τάλ VII 6 H
Ταρσεύς C X 48 W, ταρσές V
Τασαήλ C X 50 T; cf. Σαταήλ
Ταῦρος XVIII 3 P
Τέτραξ cf. Αἴξ
Τζαμάλ C XII 1, XIII 12, 13, cf. Παλτιέλ
Τζερεπόνες C X 11, -ώνες UW
Τζιανφιέλ C X 1 TV, ζηαν. UW, XI 1 T, cf. Ἐλτζιανφιέλ
Τοξότης XVIII 3 P
Τουγέλ C X 30

Ὑδροχόος II 2 (bis), XVIII 3 P
υἱοί Σαβαώθ XVIII 15 P, 16 A

φαθαλά I 9 C
Φακανέλ C X 32
Φανδωρόν XVIII 11 L, cf. Σφανδῶρ
Φαράν C X 2
Φενδεναήλ XVIII 10 L, cf. Σφενδ.
Φήθ XVIII 31 P, cf. Ἀξησβύθ
Φησικιρέθ XVIII 34 P, cf. Φυσικορέθ
Φθηνεώθ XVIII 39 H, φθηνοθ P
φνηδισμός XVIII 32
Φνουνηβιήλ XVIII 24 H, φνουνιφαήλ L, φνουνοβοηόλ P
Φοβοθήλ XVIII 17 A, βοθήλ P
Φόνος IX 2
Φυσικορέθ XVIII 34 H, cf. Φησικιρέθ

χαλκός XVIII 28
Χατμήν C IX 9 T
χερουβίμ XVIII 34
Χλαμεήλ VIII 5 L, cf. Γλαμεχήλ
χμ' XIII 6 P
χμδ' VI 8 P, XI 6 P, XV 11 P

ὠμέγα XVIII 38 P, cf. α'

III. Index of Greek words

Ἄβατες XVII 2
ἄβυσσος II 8 BC
ἀγαθός — κρείττων D II 1
ἀγαλλιάω XIX 1 P
ἄγαν I 1 I
ἀγαπάω I 1, 2, 3, 3 L, XXVI 1, 2, 5 H, 7 H
ἀγάπη C X 36
ἀγαπητός D I 2
ἀγγεῖον XV 9 P, XVI 7, XXV 7 B
ἄγγελος IV 10, V 3, 5, 9, VI 2, 8; C XII 4, XIII 5; D I 4, 7, 8, II 8; Tit B, I, Sig C, et pas.
ἀγέννητος I 3 C; C IX 9
ἅγιος IV 12, V 9 L, VI 4, 8, XX 14 B, XXVI 8 H, 9 H, 10 H; C X 53; D II 8, III 6

ἀγκών IV 5 P
ἁγνίζω C XII 5
ἄγριος C X 3
ἀγριόω XIII 5
ἀγρός VII 5, XX 17
ἀγρυπνία XVIII 32
ἀγχόνη IV 5 PCC°; C XI 4
ἄγω I 12 BC, 13 C, II 5 B, 9, III 7; C XI 8; D II 7, et pas.
ἀγωνίζομαι II 1 L; D IV 15
Ἀδάμ D II 2, 13
ἀδαπάνητος C X 53
Ἀδάρκης XXII 1 HQ, -ρης P
ἀδελφή VIII 8 C
ἀδελφός VIII 8, 9
ᾅδης D IV 14

III. Index of Greek words

ἀδιαλείπτως III 7
ἀδικέω XVIII 3, 7; D III 8
ἀδικία XIII 4, XVIII 15 P
ᾄδω D VIII 2
Ἀδωναΐ C XIII 10, cf. Index II
ἀεί XXII 5 Q
ἀείδιος XXII 5 H
ἀέριος XVI 3, XVIII 3, XXII 1, XXIII 2, XXIV 1 H; Tit B
ἀέριστος* XXIII 2 P
ἀηδής D II 2, 4
ἀηδῶς D II 3
ἀήρ VII 1, XX 15 B, XXIV 1 Q, 2 Q, 3, 4; C Pro 3, X 2, 41, 44; D VI 13, 14
ἀήττητος XV 5
ἀθάνατος D VI 17
ἀθέμιτος X.2 P, XX 4
ἄθεος VI 3
ἀθεράπευτος IX 7
ἄθεσμος X 2; D I 4, 6
ἀθεώρητος C X 31, 53
ἄθλιος XX 7, XXVI 6 Q; D IV 6
ἀθρόος D II 10
ἀθυμία I 3 L
αἰγιαλός II 5
Αἰγύπτιος XXV 6, 7
Αἴγυπτος XXV 3, 4
αἷμα XXVI 5; C IX 10
αἱμορασία (?) XVIII 31 P
αἱμόρροος XVIII 31 H
αἰνέω XII 5
αἵρεσις VI 4 P, VIII 5
αἱρέω C XII 5
αἴρω II 5, X 9, XII 4, XXIII 3; D I 5, VI 10
αἰτέω IX 1
αἰτία XI 2
αἰφνιδίως XX 18 Q
αἰχμαλωσία C X 36
αἰχμάλωτος C X 14
αἰών I 1, XVIII 2, 31 P (?), XXIV 2 Q, XXV 8 B, XXVI 8 B, 9 H; C Pro 4; D VI 14
αἰώνιος XXVI 8 H; C Pro 1
ἀκάθαρτος II 5 L, III 7, XXVI 8 H; D II 4, III 1, IV 12, 13

ἄκαιρος IV 8
ἀκαλλώπιστος D II 2
ἀκατάργητος XV 5
ἀκέφαλος IX 1; C X 3
ἀκολουθέω III 4
ἀκόλουθος I 14 L
ἀκοντίζω VII 8
ἀκουστός XXII 1 B
ἀκούω I 2, 3 C, 4, 5, 9, 12, II 5, VI 10, IX 5, XV 4, XVIII 5, XXII 1, XXV 1, XXVI 6 Q; C X 11, 22, XIII 1; D IV 14, et pas.
ἄκρα XXIII 3
ἄκρατος XVIII 31
ἀκριβής D IV 1, -ῶς X 6, XXIV 2
ἀκρίς XXVI 4, 5 H, VIII 11 P
ἀκροατής (?) IV 8 H
ἀκρογωνιαῖος XXII 7, 17; D VI 10
ἄκρον VII 6; D I 12, II 4
ἄκτιστος C Pro 2
ἄκωλος† XII 2 P
ἄκων C XII 6
ἀλαλάζω I 2 L, VI 9
ἀλγέω II 3, XVIII 5 P, 27, 28
ἄλγησις XIII 4
ἀλήθεια XIV 5
ἀληθής V 11, XVI 4 P, XX 8 P, 21; C XII 5
ἀληθινῶς C XIII 8
ἀληθῶς XX 8 H, XXIII 4
ἀλίσκομαι VIII 7 H.
ἄλκιμος I 1 A
ἀλλά cf. Index I, Adverbs and Conjunctions
ἀλλάσσω VIII 4
ἀλλήλων C X 3: D IV 1
ἀλλοιόω V 7, XVIII 30
ἄλλος VIII 1, 8, XV 5, XVIII 40; C X 28, 45, XI 5, XIII 4; D I 13
ἀλλότριος XXVI 3
ἀλλόφυλος VI 4 P
ἄλογος C X 8
ἅλς XVIII 34
ἀλυσιδωτός XXI 3
ἄλυσις XV 7
ἄλυσσος (?) II 6 L

ἄλυτος V 11, XV 15
ἅμα I 11 L; cf. Index I, Prepositions
ἁμάρτημα D I 6, 11
ἁμαρτία V 8, VI 4 P
ἀμελέω I 9 H
ἀμήν I 1, XXVI 9 H; C Pro 4
ἀμνάς D I 10
ἄμορφος XVIII 1
ἀμφότερος XXIV 1, XXV 8 B
ἄν cf. Index I
ἀνά cf. Index I
ἀναβαίνω XVI 3, XX 14
ἀνάβασις XX 16 H
ἀναβιβάζω XXV 7; C X 2
ἀναγγέλλω C X 1, XII 1, D I 8, II 8
ἀναγινώσκω
 ὁ ἀναγινώσκων L I 2, II 5, 6, V 9, 12, VI 10
 ἀναγνούς XXII 6; D VI 3
ἀναγκάζω VII 8, XXIII 3 P, XXVI 3 B, XXVI 6
ἀνάγω II 6, 9 I, XXII 8 B, XXIII 2 P, XXIV 1; C X 41
ἀναζητέω C XII 1
ἀνάθημα D II 1
ἀναίρεσις XIII 4
ἀναιρέω X 3, XVII 2, 3, XX 7, 13; C X 29
ἀνακαλύπτω VI 3 P
ἀνακλίνω D II 9
ἀνακράζω I 12 C, III 4, IV 11
ἀνακραυγάζω VI 9 P
ἀνακρίνω I 3 A
ἀνακτίζω I 1 L
ἀνακυλινδέω* XIV 1 P
ἀναλίσκω XIV 5
ἀνάπαυσις XX 16, XXVI 1 Q; D IV 16
ἀναπαύω I 4, XIX 1 P
ἀναπηδάω IX 3
ἀναπτερόω XXV 5
ἀναπτύσσω XXII 6 P
ἀνάπτω VI 10 L
ἀνασπάω D VI 13
ἀνάστασις C XII 3
ἀναστέλλω XVIII 29 H
ἀναστρέφω XVIII 12 L
ἀνατολή IX 7 P

ἀνατολικός C X 15
ἀνατρίβω V 12
ἀναφαίνω C X 3
ἀναφέρω(?) ἀναφέρεσιν X 9 L
ἀναφορεύς X 9 P
ἀνάφορον XXI 2 B
ἀναχωρέω XIII 3 P, XVIII 5 ff. (pas.), XX 10
ἀναχωρίς(?) XVIII 37 H
ἀναψύχω D IV 11
ἀνδραγαθία C X 9
ἀνεγείρω D II 1, III 3, VI 1
ἀνέλπιστος XX 20
ἄνεμος XXII 2, 3; C X 18, 37; D VI 1
ἀνένδοτος XI 2
ἀνερμήνευτος D VIII 7
ἀνέρχομαι XI 1 L, XVI 4, XX 11, XXIII 3, XXV 1, 6, 7; C X 44; D IV 14, VI 7
ἄνεσις VI 10 P
ἄνετος II 6
ἄνευ cf. Index I
ἀνέχω XIII 3 P
ἄνηβος II 3 C
ἀνήρ V 4 L, XIV 4, XV 10, XVIII 22; C X 29, 30; D I 2, III 8, IV 1, VI 11
ἀνθέω C X 6
ἄνθραξ V 9
ἀνθρώπινος XX 13 P; C IX 10
ἀνθρωπίνως C X 3
ἀνθρωπόμορφος XVIII 1
ἄνθρωπος II 3, IV 5, 6; C X 3, 30; D I 5, 6 et pas.
ἀνθρωπότης V 5, XVIII 42
ἀνίατος XVIII 20, 23
ἀνιμάω VII 6
ἀνιστάω VIII 10
ἀνίστημι II 1, III 4, VII 3, XX 1 P, XXII 13, 17, 18; D I 11
ἄνοδος IX 5 P, XVI 4 P
ἀνοίγνυμι D VI 4, 7
ἀνοικοδομέω I 1, D III 8
ἀνομία D I 7
ἀντί C XI 8
ἀντίληψις XX 17
ἀντιπαλαίω XXV 4
ἀντίχειρ I 2, 4
ἀντίχειρον I 2 W, 4 C

III. Index of Greek words 137*

ἀντίχειρος I 2, 4
ἀνύω D IV 11, VI 8
ἄνω V 12 L, VII 1, 2, XX 15; D I 13, VI 8, VIII 5
ἄνωθεν cf. Index I
ἀνωφερής, ἀνωφέρεσιν? X 9 H
ἀξιόλογος D V 1
ἄξιος I 1
ἀξιόω V 11, XX 15
ἀξίωμα V 4
ἀόρατος I 2 L, XIII 5 P; C Pro 2
ἀόριστος XV 5
ἀπάγω I 12 A, 13, X 5, D VII 6
ἀπαίρω XXVI 6
ἄπαις XX 20
ἀπαιτέω III 7
ἀπαντή C X 4
ἀπαραλλάκτως I 3 C
ἅπας I 3 C, XIII 6 P, XIX 2 P, XXV 6, XXVI 6 Q; C XII 1, XIII 14
ἀπατάω IV 6 C, D I 2
ἀπατεών C XIII 1
ἀπάτη VIII 5; C XIII 9
ἀπειλητικός V 2
ἄπειμι D I 5
ἀπεργάζομαι D II 4
ἀπερινόητος C Pro 2
ἀπέρχομαι pas.
ἀπέταλος XXIII 1 B
ἀπιστέω XV 13, XXII 12
ἅπλωμα XVI 1 P, XXI 3 B
ἀπό cf. Index I
ἀπόβασις XV 13
ἀπόγονος II 4, XXV 2 P
ἀπογράφω XXVI 8 B
ἀποδείκνυμι XXII 11 P
ἀπόδειξις XXII 15 H, XXIV 3
ἀποδέχομαι XVI 1 P
ἀποδίδωμι I 1 C, 2 L, 12 P, XXII 6
ἀποδοκιμάζω XXIII 4; D VI 10
ἀποθνήσκω XX 13 B, XXVI 9 H; C Pro 1, C XIII 2; D IV 10, Tit C, V
ἀποκαλύπτω I 3 C; C XIII 10
ἀπόκειμαι XII 4; D I 12
ἀποκλέπτω XVIII 30
ἀποκρίνω II 2, V 3, VII 3, 4, XI 1, XIV 2 P; D IV 4

ἀπόκρισις I 4 H
ἀποκρύπτω C Pro 4, XIII 2 V
ἀπόκρυφος C X 53
ἀποκτείνω VIII 9, XXII 2
ἀπολείπω D IV 9
ἀπόλλυμι VI 4 P; D VI 1
ἀπολογέομαι V 6
ἀπολογία XV 13, XX 5 P
ἀπόλυσις I 4 A
ἀπολύω I 4, XXII 11; D IV 18
ἀπομερίζω VIII 8 P
ἀπόνοια XX 4
ἀποπέμπω IX 7 P
ἀποπλανάω VIII 9
ἀποπνίγω II 2
ἀποστάτης C XIII 1
ἀποστέλλω I 7, XII 5, XVI 4 P, XVIII 29 P, XXII 1, 3; C XIII 12; D I 3, II 6, VI 1, 2
ἀποστοματίζω XVIII 21 L
ἀποστρέφω XVII 4
ἀποσφαλίζω C XIII 2 W
ἀποσχίζω VIII 8 PC
ἀποτελέω VI 4, XXII 5 P
ἀποτέμνω IX 6
ἀποτίθημι XVI 7, XXIII 4 B, XXV 8 B
ἀποφαίνω XX 6 P
ἀπόφασις II 6 L, XX 12; D IV 8
ἀποχωρέω XIII 3 P
ἀποχωρίζω V 5 C, 7 P, 8, VIII 8 LP^c; C X 53
ἄπρακτος XIII 3
ἅπτω II 3, VI 10, VII 5, XVIII 24 P
ἀπώλεια VI 4 P, XIII 4, XXVI 5 Q
ἄρα I 2 L, XIV 4, XXII 12 B; D IV 4
Ἀραβία II 5, XII 4, XXII 2, 4, 12, 19, XXIV 1, XXV 1 Q
Ἄραψ XXII 1, 9, 15, 16; D VI 1, 3
ἀργύριον I 12, 14, XVIII 44, XIX 2, XXI 1 B, XXII 11 B; C X 4, 34; D VI 2
ἄργυρος XVI 1 P; C X 23
ἀργυροῦς XXI 3
ἀριθμός XXVI 1; C IX 9
ἀρκέω XIV 5
ἄρκος C XII 6
ἅρμα VI 10; C X 41
Ἄρο Sub V

III. Index of Greek words

ἁρπάζω VII 7
ἀρρενοβατία VI 4 P
ἄρρητος D VIII 7
ἀρσενικός I 7
ἄρσην I 7 B
Ἄρτεμις VIII 11
ἀρχάγγελος I 6, II 4, 5, 7, V 9 P, VII 7, XXII 20 B, XXV 2 P, XXVI 9 H; D II 5, III 2
ἀρχέκακος D I 2
ἀρχή III 6 W, XII 4, XX 15, XXIII 2; C XIII 3
ἀρχιτεχνίτης* I 1 C
ἄρχω V 9 L, VI 9, VIII 5, XII 4; C Pro 5, C X 14; D I 11, VIII 3
ἄρχων II 9, III 5, 6 V, XVI 3 P, 5 P; C X 14, 25, XII 5; D I 12, V 1, VII 2, 5, 8
ἀσάλευτος C XIII 5
ἄσβεστος XI 7
ἀσήμαντος C XIII 13
ἀσήπτος XIX 2 P
ἀσθένεια XX 17; C X 39
ἀσθενέω I 2 C
ἀσθενής XVIII 34 H, XXVI 6 B
ἀσκός XXII 9, 10, 11, 13, 14, 16, 17, 18 XXIII 3 B, XXV 7 B; D VI 3, 4, 5
Ἆσμα τῶν ᾀσμάτων D VIII 2
ἀσπαρμός(?) XVIII 21 P
ἀσπασμός(?) XVIII 21 H
Ἀσσυρία V 10 P
Ἀσσύριοι V 10
ἀστήρ XX 12 B, 14 B, 16, 17; C X 2; D IV 16, 17
ἀστοχέω XVIII 28
ἀστραπή IX 7, XX 17
ἄστρον IV 6, 9, V 4, VI 7, VII 6, VIII 4, X 2, 3, XIV 3, XX 12 H; C XI 5
ἀσύνετος XXVI 5
ἀσφάλεια C XII 1
ἀσφαλής C X 53, XIII 2 W (ἀσφελέστερος)
ἀσφαλίζω D VI 5
ἄσφαλτος XVI 7
ἀσφαλῶς IV 12 L, XXII 15
ἀσώματος II 5 L
ἄσωτος XXVI 5 B

ἀτενίζω XXIV 5
ἀτονέω XX 16, XXII 20 B (= ἀτονόω)
ἀτραυμάτιστος C XIII 13, 14
αὐγή C Pro 2
αὐθάδεια XVIII 14 A
αὐλή I 14 B, II 1 P
αὔρα VII 3, XXII 2
αὐτίκα C XII 6
αὐτός cf. Index I Pronouns
ἀφαιρέω I 4; D I 11
ἀφανής VI 8
ἀφανίζω V 7, XVIII 40; C XIII 4
ἀφελής C XIII 2
ἄφεσις VI 10 A
ἀφεγγής D IV 9
ἀφή C XII 5
ἀφίημι I 2 L, IV 8; D IV 9
ἀφίστημι XXVI 7 B; D IV 4, 5
ἄφνω XXIV 1 H
ἀφόρητος V 13 P ᵍ; D IV 9
ἀφορμάω(?) XI 2 L
ἀφρίζω XII 2
ἀφρόνιμος* C X 5 T
ἀχανής C XII 2
ἀωρία IX 6, XVII 2, XX 7 P, 13 B, 17 B

Βαάλ XXVI 6 B
βαλανεῖον XVIII 21; D I 1
βάλλω V 12 L, XVI 7, XVIII 34
βαρύς II 5 L, XVIII 43 P; D IV 9
βασανίζω V 5, XI 6, XVI 5 P
βάσανος I 3
βασίδωτος* XXI 3 Q
βασιλεία I 14 BC, XV 8, 12, XIX 1, XXI 4 B, XXV 9 B(?), XXVI 1, 4 H, 5, 7 H, 9 H; C X 24, XIII 7; D I 12, IV 5, 6, VI 1, 2, VII 4, VIII 2
βασίλεια, τὰ II 1 P; D VIII 4
βασίλειον, τὸ V 5
βασιλεύς saepe
βασιλεύω C X 12; Tit AB, I
βασιλικός I 14 L, II 1 C, XIII 2; D VII 4
βασίλισσα XIX 3, XXI 1; D V 1
βάσις XX 16, XXI 3, XXIV 5; D IV 16
βασκαίνω XVIII 39
βαστάζω I 14, W, XIV 4, XVIII 26 L,

III. Index of Greek words

XXIII 2Q, 3, XXIV 1, 2Q, 3, 4, XXV
 8; D VI 13, 14
βαστάω* I 14V
Βελίαρ D I 2, 5
βέλος XXVI 5
βῆμα VI 1P, XIII 2P, XX 6P, XXII 17
βήξ XVIII 25P
βήσσω XVIII 35P
βία III 4, XX 13B, XXII 11
βιβλίον XVIII 23P; C XIII 4
βλαβερός IX 6, XVIII 20P
βλάπτω IV 6, X 3
βλέμμα V 2, 3
βλέπω V 2I, IX 3, 4, XIII 7; C Pro 1
 C X 3, 22; D II 2, IV 4, 9
βλοσυρός V 2I
βοάω II 5L, 6L; C XI 7; D II 10
βοήθεια II 7
βοηθέω XVIII 34, 36P; D I 3
βόλβιτον† IV 8
βολβός VI 10P
βόλος VI 10A
βοοπρόσωπος* XVIII 1P
βόρειος C X 17
βοτάνη I 3C; C X 6
βότανον C X 46
βοτρυδόν XVIII 37
βουλεύω D IV 3
βουλή VII 4, XII 3
βούλησις D I 3
βούλομαι I 1L, IV 1, XX 7, XXII 7,
 20P, XXIII 2B, 4B; C X 32, XI 1;
 D I 6, II 1, IV 1, 11
βούνευρον V 7
βουνός D VI 1
βοῦς XIII 1A
βρέφος XIII 3, 4
βρέχω C X 7
βροτός V 7P
βρυχάομαι XI 1
βρυχίζομαι* (= βρυχάομαι) I 12L
βρῶμα I 1C
βρωτόν C XI 7, 9
βυζάνω I 2L
βύζιον* XVIII 35, cf. Index IV, βυζί
βυθός VI 5, 6, XXIII 2Q, XXV 1P
βωβός IX 5, XII 2P

Γάρ cf. Index I
γέ cf. ibid.
γελάω XX 6P, 7; C X 3; D IV 5
γέλως XXVI 7B
γεμάω* V 12L
γενεά C XIII 7
γενεαλογία D I 12
γένειον XVII 3
γεννάω IV 8, V 3, 10, IX 5P, XIII 6,
 XIV 4, XXII 20; C XI 6
γέννησις C X 4
γεννήτωρ XX 4
γένος V 3, VI 3, XI 4; D VI 14
γέρων XX 1, 7, 9H, 19, 20; D IV 6;
 10f.
γῆ I 6, 8, 12, 14, II 1, 5, 8, 9, et pas.
γηγενής V 3
γηραιός XX 1, 9P, 19B
γῆρας XX 3P
γίγας XVII 1P
γίνομαι I 5, 8, 14L, II 3, et pas.
γινώσκω V 5, XV 4, XX 11Q, 21, XXVI
 8H; C XII 5; D I 11, VI 1, 12
γλουτός† XIV 4
γλυφή I 6, Sig B
γλυφίς Sig A
γλύφω XVIII 28P
γνώμη C X 31
γνωρίζω C X 45, 46, 47, 48, 49
γνῶσις C X 42
γογγύζω VIII 12P, IX 3
γόης XIX 3
γονεύς II 2
γόνος VI 3P, VII 5PC
γόνυ XVIII 24
γοῦν cf. Index I
γράμμα XVIII 37 P; C X 20, XII 6,
 XIII 12, 13, 14; D VIII 3
γραμμάτιον C XIII 11
γραφή XXII 1B, XXIII 4; C XIII 13
γράφω XIII 6, XV 14, XVII 4, XVIII
 saepe, XXVI 8H; C IX 10, XII 1, XIII
 12, 13, 14
γυμνός C X 3; D I 1, 5
γυναικοειδής XIII 1P
γυνή IV 6, V 7P, 8P, XII 2, XIII 1, 3

140* III. Index of Greek words

6, XIV 3, 4, XV 1, XVIII 22, XXVI 1;
C X 29, 30, 31, 34, XI 2, 5; D I 1
γυπότερος? (= ὑπόπτερος) II 3 C
γωνία V 12 L, VII 5, XXII 7, 8 B, XXIII
2, 4; D VI 10

Δαβίδ, cf. Δανείδ, Sub V
δαιμονίζομαι XVII 3
δαιμονικός 1 2
δαιμόνιον saepe
δαίμων saepe
δάκρυ D I 11, IV 2, 9
δακτυλίδιον I 6, 8 B, 9, 9 B, 10 L, 11, 12,
  12 W, II 5 L, III 1, 4, VII 3, VIII 12,
  X 6, XIII 3 P, XVI 7, XXII 10, 11, 13,
  XXIV 2, XXVI 9 H; Sig BT
δακτύλιος I 6 C, 8 C, 12 W, III 1 C, 3 C,
  X 6 P; D II 6, VI 5; Sig C
δάκτυλος I 2 C; D II 4; Sig T
Δανείδ I 1, 7, V 10, XX 1, XXVI 9 H;
  C Pro 1, C XII 1, XIII 12; D I 1, 3,
  4, 5, 6, 9, 11, 12; Tit BIC; cf. Δαβίδ
δάφνη XVIII 15, 33
δαφνόφυλλον† XVIII 15 P
δέ cf. Index I
δέησις C Pro 2
δεῖ I 7 P; C XIII 10
δείδω VI 8
δείκνυμι IV 2, X 7; C XIII 7; D VI 4
δεικνύω XVI 3
δειλιάω I 9 P (δειλιάζω?) Q
δεινός XXII 2
δεινῶς V 12; D IV 14
δεῖπνον I 1 C
δέκα V 12, IX 5, XVI 7, XXVI 7 H
δεκανός XVIII 4
δέκατος XVIII 14
Δεκέμβριος Sub V
δεκτικός XI 3 P
δέμας† IV 2
δένδρον XX 16, XXIII 1 B; C Pro 3, C
  X 6, 48; D IV 16, VI 1
δεξιός I 2, 3, 4, XVIII 21, Sig T
δέομαι I 4, 5, 14 BC, II 7, V 11 P, XX
  2, 7, XXII 3; C Pro 2, IX 8, XII 2,
  XIII 7, 10

δέρμα IV 2 W, XXI 2 B; C IX 9
δερμάτιον C IX 10
δεσμεύω V 6, 11, VI 5, XI 5, 6, XIII 7,
  XVI 5 P
δέσμιος III 7; C X 14
δεσμός IV 2 P, V 11, VI 3, VIII 11, XV
  7, 15
δεσμόω Fleck (errore) V 6, 11; cf. δεσμεύω
δεσπόζω cf. Index II
δεσποτεία cf. Index II
δεσπότης I 4 L, 14 BC, XVI 3 A; C X 14,
  XII 5; D I 9, 10, II 4, IV 2, 6, 13
δεσποτικός V 12 L
δεῦρο I 9, 11, 13 B, III 1, 3 HI, XVI 2 P
δεύτερος VI 3, VIII 3, XIV 8, XVIII 6
δεύω C IX 10
δέχομαι XX 5 P, XXVI 1 P
δέω I 14, II 6 L, III 7 I, IV 12 L, 12, V 1,
  X 8, XI 1, XIII 2 P, XXII 11, 14 Q;
  D II 7
δή cf. Index I
δηλαδή cf. Index I
δημιουργία D II 1
δῆτα cf. Index I
διά cf. Index I
διάβολος cf. Index II
διάγω I 1 H, XIX 1 P
διαδέχομαι D IV 6
διάδημα D VII 4
διαζώννυμι XXIII 3 B
διαθήκη V 9 L, 12 L, XV 14, XXVI 8,
  9 H; C XIII 2, 9, 12; D I 2; Tit B, I(?),
  H, C, Sub V
δίαιτα XI 2 P
διαπονέω IX 6 P
διάκονος VI 10 L
διακόπτω C XIII 4
διακόσιοι VIII 12, X 9, XXI 2 H
διαλαμβάνω D VI 1
διαλογίζομαι I 9 I; D IV 4
διάνοια C Pro 2
διανοίγω C Pro 4
διαπεράω XXV 7
διαπλατύνω C XIII 8
διαπορέω D IV 4

III. Index of Greek words

ʽιαπράσσω VIII 11, XVII 2; C X 4;
  D I 11
διάπυρος X 8P
διαρρήγνυμι V 5, XV 8, XXVI 7H
διαρρίπτω XVI 2P
διασαφέω C Pro 2
διασπαράσσω D IV 1
διαστρέφω XVIII 12HP
διασώζω D VIII 4
διατάσσω XIII 3
διατίλλω XX 2P
διαφαιρέω I 4V
διαφημίζω D VIII 1
διάφορος XIX 2P, XXI 2
διάχλωρος XIII 5P
διδάσκω VIII 9; D I 4
διδράσκω I 4L
Δίδυμος cf. Index II
δίδωμι I 1, 3IP, V 12P, VIII 1, et pas.
διεγείρω VI 4P, XVI 2, 2P
διέρχομαι IV 9, XIII 7
διηγέομαι VI 10
διήγησις Tit H
δίκαιος D IV 6
δικαιοσύνη XXII 4B
δίκη D I 9
δίκην cf. Index I
διό cf. Index I
διόρθωσις D I 7
διορίζω D IV 8
διορυκτής VIII 9
διότι IV 9, V 10P, 12
διπλάσιος I 1 C, 3B
διπλός I 11; D II 3
διπλοῦς I 1, 3; D II 2
διχοστασία XVIII 16
διώκω V 9, XVIII 25 P
δοκέω VI 1, X 2, 5, XX 16; C X 35;
  D IV 16, 17
δοκιμάζω XIX 3P
δοκιμασία XIX 3P
δόλιος XXVI 5B
δόξα V 5, XI 3P, XVI 4, XXII 16Q,
  XXVI 6Q, 7B, 10H
δοξάζω I 8, II 5, 9, et pas.
δουλεία XXVI 7; D III 3, 7
δουλεύω XV 8; C XII 1

δούλη C XII 1
δοῦλος V 13P, VI 4P, XV 12P, XXII
  4B, 6H; C XII 1, XIII 10
δουλόω C XIII 3
δοχή XVI 7
δρακοντοειδής XIV 1P, 7
δρακοντόμορφος XVIII 1
δρακοντόπαις cf. Index II
δρακοντόπους cf. Index II
δράκων VI 10, XII 1, 6, XIII 5P, XIV 1;
  C X 40
δρᾶμα D I 11
δρομαίως I 9, 11, 14B
δρυμός XI 7
δρυμών XIV 6
δύναμαι II 1 L, VI 6, et pas.
δύναμις II 4, III 5, V 11, VI 8P, VIII
  10, IX 6, XI 6P, XV 9, 14, XVIII 11,
  XXII 18, 20B, XXV 7B, XXVI 8H;
  C XII 1, XIII 6; D III 2, VII 1, 2; cf.
  also Index II
δυναστεία XX 13
δυνατός V 13, XXIII 1, 2; C IX 8; D VI 1
δυσηχής XIII 3A
δύσις C X 19
δυσμή I 2, 4
δύσπνοια XVIII 25
δύστηνος XX 7, XXVI 7; D IV 6
δυσωπέω C Pro 4
δυτικός XI 3A, XIII 3P(?)
δῶρον I 7, XXII 16
δωροφορέω XXII 16Q

Ἐάν cf. Index I
ἑαυτοῦ cf. Index I
ἐάω II 6; C XII 2, XIII 11, 13, 14
Ἑβραῖος VI 8
Ἑβραϊστί XIV 7
ἐγγίζω XVI 5 A, 15 L
ἔγγιος(?) IV 11
ἔγγιστα, -στεν cf. Index I
ἐγγλύφω C XII 6
ἔγγραφος I 3 C
ἐγγύθεν cf. Index I
ἐγείρω VI 4, VII 2, XVI 1
ἐγκαλέω D IV 3

ἔγκατα XVIII 13 A
ἐγκαταλείπω C XIII 2
ἐγκέφαλος XII 3
ἐγκλείω XVIII 5—15, XXV 7 B
ἐγκώνων(?) IV 5 CC°
ἐγχαράττω XVIII 39
ἐγχοανῆς(?) IV 8 C
ἐγώ cf. Index I
ἔδαφος XXII 13
ἐδωδή(?) IX 5 C
Ἐζεκίας C XIII 2, 4, 7, 9, 11, 12; Tit C, V
ἐθίζω I 10; D II 9
εἰ cf. Index I
εἶαρ† X 9
εἴθησις D IV 1
εἶδον I 13 L, II 1, III 5, et pas.; cf. Index I; v. ὁράω
εἶδος II 3, VIII 1, X 9, XIII 1, 5, XV 1, 3
εἴδωλον XXVI 5 H, 6, 7 B; C X 11
εἰκῶδες(?) XII 2 P
εἰλέω VI 10, VII 1
εἰμί pas.
εἶπον pas.
εἰρηνεύω VIII 7, XVIII 15, XXII 4
εἰρήνη XVIII 22 P, XXI 4 B, XXII 16, XXV 9 B, XXVI 9 H; D IV 11
εἰρηνικῶς D III 8, IV 6
εἰς cf. Index I
εἷς cf. Index I
εἰσάγω XXII 16; D III 5
εἰσακούω C Pro 1
εἰσέρχομαι I 5, 10 C, VIII 1 C, XIII 6 P, XXI 2, XXII 13, 17, XXV 3, XXVI 4
εἴσοδος XX 15, XXIII 3
εἰσφέρω D V 1, VI 2
εἶτα cf. Index I
εἴτι(?) I 2 L
ἐκ cf. Index I
ἕκαστος I 1 C, 2 A, 2, 3, III 7 PC, V 12 L, VIII 5 P, XIII 3, XVI 3, XVIII 4 P; C IX 8, X 46, 47, 48, 49
ἑκάστοτε C XIII 14
ἐκδέρω C IX 9
ἐκδέχομαι D VII 4
ἐκδίδωμι C XIII 9

ἐκδικέω XX 2
ἐκδίκησις XXII 4 H
ἐκεῖ V 10, VII 6, XII 3, XIII 3 P, XXIII 2 Q, XXV 6, 7, XXVI 1
ἐκείνῃ IV 8 C
ἐκεῖνος IV 4 L, V 10, VI 5, 6, VII 3, et pas.
ἐκείνως II 8 HIP
ἐκεῖσε I 1, XIII 6 A, XXII 11
ἔκθαμβος XIV 2; D VI 12, 13
ἐκθηλάζω I 2 C
ἐκθλίβω D II 4
ἐκλείπω XVI 5; C XIII 2; D I 12
ἐκλεκτός VI 4, XXI 1 B, XXII 7 P; D I 2
ἐκλύω XVIII 5 P
ἐκπειράζω C XII 1
ἐκπετάννυμι II 1 L
ἐκπιπίζω XVIII 11 P
ἐκπίπτω XX 16
ἐκπληκτικός X 2
ἐκπληρέω C XII 2
ἐκπληρόω C XII 5; D III 8
ἐκπλήσσω VI 9 P; D IV 10
ἐκριζόω D VI 1
ἐκρίπτω XVI 2 P
ἐκσφραγίζω C XIII 11
ἐκτείνω IX 3
ἐκφυσάω XXIII 3 B
ἔλαιον XVIII 33, 34
ἐλαττόω XVIII 11 PL, ἐλαττόνω(?) H
ἐλαύνω D I 12
ἐλέγχω XIII 3 P, D I 7
ἐλεεινός D II 10
ἐλεέω XX 1
ἐλεήμων XXII 1 B
ἐλεύθερος C IX 8
ἐλευθερόω C X 14
ἔλευσις I 14 H, III 4 H, V 1 H; Tit H
ἕλκος IX 6
ἕλκω XXVI 9 H
ἐλλάμπω G Pro 2
Ἕλλην VI 8 P
Ἑλληνιστής VI 8 A
ἐμβάλλω XI 3, XVIII 16
ἐμβατεύω D I 1
ἐμβλέπω V 2 P
ἐμβουλεύω*(?) XVI 3 L

III. Index of Greek words 143*

ἐμμένω XVIII 18
ἐμός cf. Index I
ἐμπαίζω II 3B
ἐμπεριέχω C XI 9T
ἐμπίπλημι XX 3
ἐμπίπρημι XIV 6
ἐμπλέκω V 8P
ἐμπνέω XXII 11; C Pro 2
ἐμποδίζω XVI 1, XVIII 42
ἐμποιέω IX 6, XVIII 8A, 9L, 10A, 19A, 25
ἔμπροσθεν XVI 1; D I 3; cf. also Index I
ἐμπυρίζω VII 5, XIV 6, XX 17, XXII 20P
ἔμπυρος IX 7
ἐμφαίνω II 3, D I 13
ἐμφανίζω III 7
ἐμφανῶς C X 41
ἔμφραξις XVIII 9
ἐμφυσάω D VII 6
ἐμφύω C X 5
ἐν cf. Index I
ἐνάγω C IX 10, XI 9
ἐναλλαγή VIII 2L
ἐναντίον cf. Index I
ἐναργέως IV 6WW°; C XI 5W
ἔνδοξος VI 1P
ἔνειμι XIII 3P
ἐνεμποδίζω(?) D I 5
ἐνέργεια VIII 11W; C Pro 2, IX 10
ἐνεργέω VI 4P; C X saepe; D III 7
ἔνθα IV 4PCC°: C XI 3; D VI 4
ἐνθάδε X 6P, XXII 11
ἔνθεν καὶ ἔνθεν XV 9, XXIV 2
ἐνθυμίζω VIII 5
ἐνίστημι XXII 14P; C X 1
ἐνισχύω XXVI 8H
ἔννοια XX 5
ἐνοχλέω XIV 5
ἐνταῦθα V 1C
ἐντέλλω I 14, XXII 12; D VI 3
ἔντευξις D II 5
ἐντυγχάνω IX 3H
ἐντυπόω C XIII 12
ἐνυβρίζω D IV 2
ἐνώπιον cf. Index I
ἐξαιρέω C XI 7

ἐξαίσιος D III 8
ἐξαλείω D VI 2
ἐξάπινα XX 17P
ἐξαποστέλλω XXII 16Q
ἐξαπτέρουγον D VIII 6
ἔξαρχος III 6
ἐξαστράπτω XXI 2
ἐξέρχομαι II 1 BC, 5L, V 6L, XIII 3, XIV 6, XV 9, XVIII 24P, XX 12; C X 21; D I 5, VI 4
ἑξῆς C XIII 7
ἐξηχεία* (ἐξηχέω) X 3
ἔξοδος XXV 5
ἐξολοθρεύω D VI 2
ἐξομολογέομαι I 5
ἐξορκίζω V 6L; C XIII 5
ἐξουθενέω XXII 5P
ἐξουσία I 1, V 13, VIII 1, XIII 7, XV 11 XVIII 3, XXII 15, 20B; Tit BI
ἐξουσιάζω I 5; C IV 8
ἔξω I 14, XVIII 15P, 42, P; cf. also Index I
ἐπαγγέλλω III 7, XX 2
ἐπάγω VI 4, XVIII 18A, XX 2; D VIII 2
ἔπαινος XXII 16Q
ἐπαίρω XXIII 2. 3B, 4
ἐπαλείφω XVIII 33, 34
ἐπαναπαύω VII 7P
ἐπανάστασις C X 14
ἐπαναστρέφω XXV 7B; D VI 6
ἐπανέρχομαι VI 3P
ἐπάνω XVI 7; cf. also Index I
ἐπαρχία XXII 5P
ἐπαύριον I 8, XXII 17
ἐπαφίημι IX 7P
ἐπεί cf. Index I
ἐπειδή cf. Index I
ἐπεῖδον C Pro 2
ἐπεῖπον I 9C, 11C
ἐπεισέρχομαι II 3L, IX 5, XVI 2
ἔπειτα cf. Index I
ἐπεξουσιάζω I 5L
ἐπερωτάω III 6, IV 8, et pas.
ἐπεύχω* IX 7P
ἐπί cf. Index I
ἐπιβάλλω VI 4P
ἐπιβουλεύω IX 7P

III. Index of Greek words

ἐπίβουλος V 7, XXV 3
ἐπίγειος XVI 3, XVIII 3, XXII 1; Tit B
ἐπιγίνομαι IX 8 L
ἐπιγινώσκω XXII 15; C X 38; D I 6, IV 12
ἐπιγραφή XVIII 22P; Sig C
ἐπιγράφω XVIII 25P; Sig T
ἐπιδείκνυμι X 5, XXIII 3Q; D VI 7
ἐπίδειξις XXII 15
ἐπιδίδωμι I 2 L, 3; C XI 9; D II 7
ἐπιδινέω XII 2
ἐπιεγκόνων(?) C XI 4
ἐπιεγχώνω† C XI 4
ἐπιεικής I 1C
ἐπιζητέω C XI 9
ἐπιθεωρέω XX 15P
ἐπιθυμέω IX 2, XVI 2P
ἐπιθυμία II 2, 3, VI 3, VIII 11, D I 1
ἐπικαθίζω VI 1P
ἐπικαλέω IX 7P, XIV 8, XV 7, XVIII 4P, XX 19Q, XXV 4; C XII 5
ἐπικαπνίζω* V 9P
ἐπικατάρατος XX 6P
ἐπίκειμαι V 12 L
ἐπικράζω XXVI 9 H
ἐπικλείω XVII 5P
ἐπικρούω C XI 7
ἐπιλέγω C XII 6
ἐπιμέλεια D III 8
ἐπιμελέομαι D IV 15
ἐπιμελής V 6
ἐπιμένω I 1H
ἐπινοέω XX 10P
ἐπιπέμπω IX 6, XVIII 8P, 13A, 15, 19P, 23P, 32, 33
ἐπιπνέω C Pro 3
ἐπισάττω XXII 9, 11, 16
ἐπισταδόν XXI 3
ἐπίσταμαι V 11, XIII 6P
ἐπιστολή XXII 1, 6, D VI 1, 3
ἐπιστρέφω VIII 11
ἐπισυνάγω III 3, 4
ἐπισφραγίζω VII 8
ἐπίσχυσις XXVI 5B
ἐπιτάσσω X 6; C XII 4
ἐπιτελέω V 8P, IX 7P, XVIII 9P, XX 15
ἐπιτέμνω VI 3

ἐπιτήδειος D III 1
ἐπιτίθημι II 6L, VII 8L, XVIII 35, XXII 13; D VI 4, 5
ἐπιτιμάω VI 11, XVII 4
ἐπιτρέπω D III 7
ἐπιτυγχάνω IX 3, XIII 3P
ἐπιφαίνω II 3L
ἐπιφέρω II 3C, VII 1, XVIII 20, 23
ἐπίφθονος XVIII 46
ἐπιχρίω XVIII 20
ἐπουράνιος II 3L, 5L, VI 10, XX 15; C Pro 5
ἐργάζομαι I 1, 3, X 8, XVIII 43P, XXI 4; D I 2, III 7, IV 4, 7, 8, 18
ἐργασία I 1, 44, II 5, V 6, 7P, VIII 5, X 5, XVI 2, XVII 2, XXV 1; D III 1, 6
ἔργον I 2 L, 4, 9 L, 10 L, IV 12, VI 3P, 4P, X 2, XII 2, XIII 4, XVIII 43P; D I 2, 4, 6, IV 8, 18, Tit B I
ἐρεθίζω IV 6, VIII 5 PC
ἐρείδω VI 10P
ἐρευνάω VIII 9
ἐρημόω XVIII 40
ἐρίζω VIII 6
ἔρις D IV 1, cf. also Index II
ἔριφος cf. Index II
ἑρμηνεύω XIII 6P
ἔρομαι D VI 12
ἐρυθροδανόω XXI 3B
Ἐρυθρός VI 3, 5, 6, XII 4, XXIII 2, XXIV 1, 1P, XXV 1B, 5, 6; D VI 12
ἔρχομαι I 2, 4, 9 L, II 7, et pas.
ἔρως XXVI 5B; D I 1, cf. also Index II
ἐρωτάω I 3C, IV 11, V 5PC, VI 6, VII 2, 3, 4, XIII 2, XIV 7, XV 2, XXV 1; C XI 1, XIII 13; D III 6
ἑσπέρα I 2 L, 9 L; D II 11
ἔσχατος XXVI 8B; D VII 6
ἔσω XII 4, XVIII 15P, XXII 14B, 18H
ἔσωθεν XXII 14H, 18B
ἑταῖρος† V 11Bn
ἕτερος V 1, 8P, 11, et pas.
ἑτοιμάζω XVIII 44P
ἔτος XV 12; Sub V
ἔτυμος† V 11Bn
Εὐαγγέλιον D I 13
εὐαγγέλλω* II 6Q

III. Index of Greek words

εὐδηλότερον IX 5 P
εὐδοκία D VIII 4
εὐθέως II 7, V 1 P, XVII 2, XXII 14 P; C XII 1, cf. εὐθύς
εὐθυμέω XXV 9 B
εὐθύνω XIX 1
εὐθύς VIII 11 C
εὐθύς or εὐθέως XVIII 5—37
εὔκοσμος II 3 AB
εὐλογέω I 1 A, VII 1, XI 1 P, XV 1 P, XVI 1 P
εὐλογητός I 1 AP, III 5, XXVI 9 H; C Pro 4
εὔμορφος VIII 1, XIV 3
εὐπρέπεια XXIII 2 B, XXV 9, D II 1
εὑρίσκω V 5 C, 10, VII 5, 6, IX 7 P, XII 5, XVIII 21, XXII 11, XXV 5, 7, XXVI 8 B; C IX 10; D I 5
εὐσέβεια VIII 9
εὐσχημόνως VIII 7
εὐσχημος VIII 1
εὔτονος VIII 12 P
εὐφημέω XXII 16
εὐφραίνω I 1 A, XVIII 16; D I 10, II 4
εὐχαριστέω II 1, III 6, VII 4; D II 8, III 4
εὔχομαι II 5, 7, VII 7, X 11 P, XV 7, XVIII 42, XXVI 8 B; C Pro 5
εὔχρωτος* IV 2; C XI 2
εὐώδης XVIII 31 P
ἐφάπτω XVIII 17 P
ἐφίπταμαι XXII 20 P
ἐφίστημι I 9
ἐφοράω XI 2 P
ἐφορμάω XIV 4
ἐχθρός D I 2, II 10
ἔχω I 1, 3 C, 4, 4 P ͨ, 6, II 3, et pas.
ἑωθινός XXII 2
ἕως V 8, VI 11, VII 2, XV 10, XVIII 15 P; C XIII 12, cf. also Index I

Ζάω XXII 2, XXV 8 B; C XII 3
ζέσις XVIII 29 H
ζητέω XV 3, 11, XXVI 1; C XIII 1
ζοθερός D IV 9
ζοφόω C XII 3

ζωδιακός XVIII 4 P
ζῴδιον II 2; C XII 6
ζωή C X 4
ζῷον C X 28, 44

Ἡγέομαι D I 12
ἡδέως IX 2 PC
ἡδονή IX 5 A
ἡλικία XX 1 P
ἥλιος I 2, 4, VI 10, 10 HP; C X 43
ἧλος XVIII 28
ἡμέρα I 2, 2 A, 3, 5. et pas.
ἡμίκρανος* XVIII 6 (= ἡμικρανικός)
ἡμίονος IV 2; C XI 2
ἡμιπρόσωπον* VII 1 C
ἥμισυς I 2, 4
ἡμιτριταῖος VII 6
ἧπαρ V 9, 13
ἥσυχος I 4
ἡττάω XVII 4 P
ἦχος IV 8

Θάλασσα II 5, 8, VI 3, 5, 6, 10, XII 4, XVI 1, 2, 3, 4, 7, XXI 3, XXIII 2, XXIV 1, 1 P, XXV 1, 5, 6, 7; D VI 12
θαλάσσιος XVI 1; C X 18
θαμβέω VII 2
θάνατος XV 14, XX 2, 4; D IV 2, 12, 14, 15
θανατόω XX 5, XXII 20 P
θάπτω D I 6
θαρρέῳ D II 1
θαῦμα D III 8
θαυμάζω VIII 2, XIII 5, XIV 7, XVIII 2 P, XXI 1, 18
θαυμάσιος D I 13
θεά VIII 4 P, XV 3
θεάομαι XXIV 1 Q; D III 1, IV 9, V 1
θεῖος I 1, 4 C, 10 L, C Pro 3; C X 53; D I 12
θέλημα C X 2, 32; D III 3, VII 3
θέλησις D I 3, II 1, III 8, VI 6
θέλω II 6, IV 7, VII 3, 4, 7, et pas.
θεματίζω XXII 8 P
θεμέλιος VIII 12

θεμελιόω XX 17, XXIII 4B
θεοπάτωρ D I 2, 12
θεοποιέω XIV 2
θεός I 4, 5, 6, 7, 8 et saepe
θεοτόκος XXVI 10H
θεραπεύω IX 7P
θεράπων XXV 5, D IV 13
θερμαίνω XVIII 18P
θέρος VII 5; C X 7
θεωρέω II 1P, XIII 5, XIX 2, XX 6, 15, 16, XXIV 1Q; C X 31, 34
Θηβαῖος VI 9
θηλάζω I 2, 4
θηλυκός I 7, II 3, VIII 1P
θηλυμανία V 8
θῆλυς IV 1; C XI 1
θηρίον C Pro 3; C X 3
θηριοπρόσωπος XVIII 1
θησαυρός I 14V, X 10, XXII 11P; C X 21, 31, 38, 53, XIII 2
θικτός(?) C XIII 3; cf. θνητός
θλίβω I 4, XX 19H; D IV 11
θνήσκω XVII 2, XX 7H, 11, 13Q; C XII 3; D IV 9, 10
θνητός C XIII 3† (MSS θικτός); D IV 11
θρασύς II 8B
θρέμμα C IX 9V
θρηνέω D I 6
θρίαμβος(?) VI 3
θρίξ XIII 1, 5, 7
θρόνος II 1, III 5, V 4, 9P, XIII 2, 3, XVIII 20, XXVI 9H; C XIII 5; D VII 4, VIII 6
θυγάτηρ V 3, XXVI 1B, XXVI 2
θυμιάω VI 10
θυμός V 2P; D IV 1, 2
θυμόω XX 6
θύρα I 14BC
θυσιαστήριον X 9, XXI 2; D VIII 6
θύω XXVI 4B, 5H

Ἰαμβρῆς XXV 4
Ἰαννῆς XXV 4
ἰάομαι VII 6, XI 2
ἰασαφήτην*(?) I 3C
ἴασπις† I 3C; C XI 8, XII 6

ἰατρός Sub V
ἴδιος VI 3; C XII 5
ἰδιοχείρως C IX 10
ἰδοῦ I 1I
ἰδού I 1, 4, 10, 14, XIV 6, XVIII 3, XX 1, 7, XXII 1, 4; C Pro 1, Sig L
Ἰεβουσαῖοι XXVI 1
ἱερεύς VI 4
ἱερόν XXI 4, XXII 8B
Ἱεροσόλυμα I 1P
Ἱερουσαλημ (fere compendio scr. sic, ἰλημ I 1, 7, XV 8, XIX 1P, XXII 7, XXIII 2B, XXVI 9H; Tit B I
Ἰεσσαί XXVI 9H
Ἰησοῦς Χριστός D I 12
ἱκεσία XXII 5
ἱκετεύω C XIII 7
ἱλαστήριον XXI 2H
ἵλεως XX 4
ἱμάσθλη C XI 7
ἱμάτιον D II 2
ἰνδικτιών Sub V
Ἰουδαῖος XXII 20, XXVI 8H
Ἰούδα D I 12
ἱππικῆς? IV 8C°; C XI 6
ἵππος XVI 1; C X 52
ἵπταμαι XX 12, 15
Ἰσραήλ IV 12A, XII 1, XIII 1P, XIX 3P XX 21B, XXII 16P, XXIV 2Q, XXVI 8H
ἵστημι VII 3, XII 4, XXII 13, 17, et pas.
ἱστορία C X 11
ἱστός C XII 6
ἰσχίον XVIII 27P, 28P
ἰσχυρός C XII 3, XIII 12; D VI 1
ἰσχύς C Pro 1
ἰσχύω X 2, XV 11, XXII 8
ἰχθύς V 9, 10, 13, XVI 1, XVIII 35
ἴχνος VIII 11
Ἰωάννης Sub V

Καθαιρέω VI 4, VIII 10
καθαριεύω C X 12
καθαρός VI 10, XVIII 33; C IX 9T
καθέζομαι XII 4P, XIII 2, XIV 7, XV 6, XVIII 21, 24, XXV 2
καθεύδω XIII 3

κάθημαι XIII 2P, 3LP; D VI 12, VII 4
καθίζω XIII 3H; C IX 9T XIII 12, 14
καθυπόσχομαι*(?) C XII 1
καινός C IX 9, XIII 7; D VI 3
καιρός V 5, VI 3, VII 5, XV 8, 10, 12, XVII 1; C XII 1; D VIII 2
καίω III 4
κακός I 4, VI 4P, VIII 5, X 2
κακουργέω VII 7
κακουργία V 7, VIII 11C
κακοῦργος IV 6
κακόω VIII 11
κακῶς XX 7
καλάμιον V 13P
κάλαμος V 6
καλέω I 3LP, 8BL, 9, 11, et pas.
κάλλος V 7; D VIII 7
καλλωπισμός D I 2
καλός XVIII 18P; C XIII 13
καλύπτω XXV 7
καλῶς IV 7
κάμηλος XXII 9, 11, 16; D VI 3, 5, 8
κάμινος XI 7
κάμνω XVIII 34P
κάνναβις IV 12
καπνίζω V 9
καρδία V 7, XVIII 12, 30, XXV 3, 5; D I 1, II 10, IV 9, 11
καρδιόπονος XVIII 26
καρποφόρος C Pro 3
κασσιτήρινος(?) XVIII 27P
κάστρον C X 13, 24, 27
καταβάλλω XXIII 1
καταβιβάζω C X 35
καταγελάω D IV 5, 6
κατάγω XI 6, XV 5; C X 2
καταδαπανάω IX 6
καταδεσμεύω C XIII 6
κατάδηλος XIII 5P
καταδικάζω D IV 2
καταδίκη XIII 4
καταδιώκω XXV 6
καταδουλίζω† XVII 1 Cr
καταδουλόω D II 10
κατάκαρπος XVII 2P
κατακαίω C IX 8, X 41, XIII 4, 8
κατάκειμαι XI 2

κατακλείω VI 3, IX 5, XV 9, XVIII 3, 43P, 44P; C XI 7
κατακληρονομέω IX 5P
κατακρίνω V 11, XI 7, XIV 8, XVIII 43, XXI 4B
κατακρύπτω D IV 9
καταλαμβάνω XXIII 2Q, XXVI 8H; D II 4, VI 3, 4, 5, 8
καταλέγω D VIII 2
καταλείπω XXVI 8H; D I 3
καταλιμπάνω C X 53
καταναλίσκω D II 4
καταντάω D I 12
καταννυκτικῶς D I 11
κατανύσσομαι XX 3P
καταξιόω XXII 3
καταπέμπω XIII 1H
καταπεριπολεύω* V 10P
καταπίνω XVIII 35
καταπίπτω XII 2, XX 17
καταπλουτίζω C XIII 12
καταπρίζω XI 7
καταράομαι XX 6
καταράσσω XIV 5
καταργέω II 4, IV 10, 12, V 9, 13, VI 8, VII 5, 7, VIII 5, 6, 7, 8, 9, 10, IX 7, X 11, XI 5, 6, XII 3, XIII 6P, XIV 2, XV 3, 6, 10, 14, XVI 6, XVII 4, XVIII 15, 38, 39, XXII 20, XXV 2Q; C XIII 5, 6; D III 2, 6, Tit B I
καταρρέω XVII 3
καταρτίζω V 12H
κατασκευάζω X 2
κατασκευή V 12P, XIX 2P
κατασκιάζω XXI 2
κατασκοπεύω X 6
κατασοφίζομαι XIII 6P, XXIV 2
κατασπείρω XV 9
καταστρέφω XVIII 20P
κατασφραγίζω XV 7, XXII 11B
καταταράσσω† XIV 5
κατατρώγω XVII 3A
καταφάγω D I 10
καταφλέγω XX 17
καταχθόνιος XVI 3, XVIII 3, XXII 1; Tit B
κατειδωλίζω* XVII 1 P

κατεργάζομαι V 12, VIII 12, IX 2, XII 2, XXVI 7 Q
κατέρχομαι II 7, VI 2 P, 8, XV 5, XVII 4
κατεσθίω IX 2, XVII 3 P
κατέχω X 2, XIII 1, XIV 3, XV 4; C X 53; D II 7
κατηφής D IV 9
κατισχύω XXIII 4 P
κατισχύω XXIII 4 P
κατοίκησις IV 4
κατοικία I 10 L, XVII 2
κατορθόω X 5
κάτω D IV 13, 14, VI 8
κάτωθεν XXIV 4
καῦμα(?) XVI 4 P
καῦσις XVIII 29 P
κέδρινος XIX 2
κεῖμαι II 2, 5, IV 4 PCC°, VII 6, XVIII 6; C X 38, XI 3
κειμήλιον C XIII 9
κέλευσμα VI 6 P
κελεύω I 1, 8, 14 B, et pas.
κέρας VII 6; C XI 8
κεράσιον X 9; C X 7
κερατίζω IV 2 P
κεφάλαιον XII 3 P
κεφαλή IV 2, V 6 L, IX 2, 5, 6, XV 1, XVIII 5, XX 2, XXII 7, 16, XXIII 4; C XIII 5; D VI 10
κηρός Sig T
κῆτος II 8
κικλήσκω† VIII 7
κινέω XXVI 5 B; D IV 2, 17
κιόνιον XXIV 2 Q
κισσός I 3 C†, XVIII 37
κίων XII 4, XXI 3, XXIII 2, XXIV 1, 2 Q, 3, 4, 5, XXV 1, 7, 8; D VI 12, 13, 14
κλάζω XV 9
κλαίω IX 5
κλάσμα V 13
κλαυθμός C IX 8
κλέπτης C X 38
κλέπτω C X 38
κληρονομέω IX 5
κλῆσις II 1; D III 1, 6
κλῖμαξ XXIII 3 HP

κλίνη D I 11, II 7
κλίνω C XII 4 W
κλύδων C X 36
κνήμη IV 2; C XI 2
κοιλία XII 2, XVIII 13 P
κοιμάω XXVI 4
κοινός C XIII 2
κοίτη D II 9
κόκκος XVIII 33
κοκκύζω IX 3 C
κολαπτός I 61
κολίανδρον XVIII 20
κόλον C IX 9 T
κόλπος II 3 W
κόμη? V 12
κομίζω XVIII 41 P, XIX 2 H, XXII 11
κονιορτός VII 2, 3
κοπιάζω XVIII 11 H
κόπτω II 5 Q, 8, X 10
κόρη XXVI 5
κορυφή XII 6, XIII 1 P, XVIII 1
κοσμέω X 5, XXV 9; D VII 4
κοσμοκράτωρ VIII 2, XVIII 2, XX 14 B
κόσμος V 7, VI 4 P, X 2, XIII 3, XV 9; C XIII 2, 12, 13, 14
κοχλίας VII 1
κόχλος VII 1 H
κράζω I 14, III 4 L, XXVI 9 H
κρατέω X 3, 8 L, XXII 10; C X 21, 43; Tit B I
κράτος I 1 AB, D IV 10, VI 2
κραυγάζω I 12, 14 QC
κρείττων D II 1
κρεμάννυμι XIII 7, XXIV 4; D VI 14
κρημνοβατέω XI 6 P
κρημνός IV 5, XI 6; D IV 15, VI 1
κρίνω X 8; D I 13, IV 4, 6, 8
κρίσις D IV 5, 6, 8
κρόκινος V 9
κροκόδειλος C X 50
κρόκος VI 10
κρόταφος XVIII 5, 32
κρούω IV 11; D II 7
κρύπτω V 10; D VI 7
κτάομαι C XII 5, 6, XIII 14; D I 10, VII 1, VIII 2
κτῆμα II 1 L

III. Index of Greek words   149*

κτῆνος XXII 2; C X 3
κτίζω ΙΙ 1 L, XII 4, XXVI 6B; C Pro 2, 5, X 22
κτίσμα IV 12; C X 24
κυκλικός C XII 6
κυκλίσκομαι(?) VIII 7
κύκλος XVIII 4P, XXI 4B
κυλινδέω XIV 1A
κύλιξ C XI 7, 9
κῦμα XVI 2, 4
κύριος I 6, 7, 8L, 9I, et pas.
κυριότης D VIII 6
κύσα(?) I 3C
κύστις XVIII 33
κύων X 1, 2, 11, XVIII 1
κώμη V 12H
κωφός IX 5P, XII 2
κωφότης XIII 4P

Λάβρος VII 2
λαγχάνω XXVI 8P
λάθρα IV 6; C XI 5
λαιμός X 8P, XVIII 8P
λαΐνεος C XIII 12
λαλέω IX 3, 5, X 1, XIV 6, XVI 5, XX 21; C X 3, XI 8
λαμβάνω I 2, 4, 9IC, 10L, et pas.
λαμνός* XVIII 27P
λαμπάς X 8
λαμπρός XIII 5P; C X 28
λάμπω X 8, XVII 1
λαός XXII 4, 6B, XXVI 4H
λάρυγξ X 3
λαύρα VII 3HC
λεαίνω XVIII 33
λέγω I 2, 2L, 3C, IV 11, et pas.
λειτουργέω XII 6H
λειτουργός D IV 13
λεοντόμορφος XI 7P
λεπτός XI 7
λεπτουργέω XII 6L
λεπτύνω I 2, 3, 4
λευκαίνω C Pro 1
λευκός† V 13
λέων II 3 XI 1
λῆρος XXVI 6

λίαν I 1H, XIII 1H, XX 6H
λίβανος VI 10
λίθινος C XI 8
λίθος I 3C, II 5, VII 8, VIII 6, X 5, 7, 8, 9, 10, XIX 2P, XXI 2, XXII 7, 8, 17, XXIII 2, 3, 4, XXV 8; C XI 7, 8, 9, XII 6; D VI 7, 10; Sig C
λιθοτομία II 5
λιθοτόμος II 5C
λιμός XVIII 8H
λιτός(?) XVIII 8L
λίτρα XXI 1Q
λογίζομαι I 9, IV 11
λόγος XI 1
λοιπόν XIX 1P, XX 12B; D I 11
λοιπός XIV 5, XVIII 3, 44P, XXVI 6B
Λυδία VIII 4
λύμη D VI 14
λυπέω D II 2, 3, IV 11
λύπη I 5L, XXII 17
λύρα C XII 6
λυσίθριξ XIII 1
λύσσα V 8P
λυχναψία IX 7P
λυχνεῖον XXI 2P
λυχνίτης C XI 9
λύχνος VI 10, XXI 2
λύω XVIII 16P
λωβός† XII 2Fü

Μαγεύω XV 5
μάθησις C X 20
μακρονόσια XVIII 34
μᾶλλον D I 12
μανθάνω VI 6, IX 5, XIII 2; D IV 14
μανιάκης V 12L
μαραίνω XXIII 2P
μάργαρος C X 45
μαρμαροκοπεῖν(?) X 10P
μάρμαρον VI 9, 11, X 10, XIV 8, XVI 7
μασθός IX 4H
μαστεύω† XIII 3
μαστίζω V 6P, XIII 3HL
μαστός IX 4LC
ματαιότης D VIII 2
μάχαιρα· C IX 9

III. Index of Greek words

μάχη VIII 3PH, 7P, XVIII 15, 38; C X 29
μάχομαι VIII 7, XXV 4; D IV 1
μεγαλόφωνος I 2L
μεγαλώνυμος D I z
μεγάλως XX 6P. XXVI 7H
μέγας I 1, 14, II 8, III 4, et pas.
μέγεθος XXIII 4Q; Sig C
μεγιστᾶνος C X 28
μεθέτεροι II 5L
μέθη XVIII 16P
μεθίστημι XX 6, 9, XXIII 1
μειδιάω V 12; D IV 4
μελαίνω XX 19Q
μελανοκέρατος* C IX 9
μελανός XX 19P; C IX 9
μελονόχροος IV 6L
μελήσιοι(?) XXI 4H
μελίχροος. -χρους IV 6
μελιχρός IV 6C; C XI 5
μέλλω I 9, V 13P, XIV 5, XVII 4, XX 6P, 11Q, XXII 20, XXVI 7H; C X 1, 10, XIII 1, 12; D II 7
μέλος IX 1, 6, XIII 1, 5P, XIV 1, XVIII 11H
μέλω D VII 3
μένω XXII 14, 15, 16, XXIV 3, XXV 7B
μερίζω VIII 8
μερίς II 8A; D IV 15
μέρος I 2C, V 10, VII 8L, XIII 3P; C X 8, 38
μεσημβρινός C X 16
μέσον C XII 6
μέσος XVIII 4P, XX 6P, 11P, XXII 13P, 16B; C XIII 13
μεταβάλλω II 3, 5L, XV 3, 5
μεταδίδωμι C X 53
μετακαλέω XX 19; D IV 5, 8
μεταλαμβάνω II 2C
μέταλλον C X 45
μεταμορφόω II 3B, XVI 2, 4, 4P, XX 13B
μετάνοια C XII 3
μετασαλεύω X 5
μετασχηματίζω XX 13
μεταφέρω XXIII 1; C X 22
μετοικισμός X 9

μετρητής XVI 7P
μέτρον XV 5
μέτωπον V 12L, XVII 4
μηδαμόθεν XX 17
μηδείς I 9; C X 31, 34; D VII 3
Μῆδοι XV 8
μηδόλως XI 1
μηκέτι C X 53; D IV 11
μῆκος VIII 12, XXI 3Q; C XI 8
μήν Sub V
μηρός D I 12
μήτηρ XV 10
μητρομανία XVIII 33
μηχανή XXVI 8H
μίγνυμι XV 10, XX 14B, XXVI 1H
μικρός V 4, VIII 4, XV 12; D IV 4
μικροφανής VIII 4PC
μίμησις D VIII 5
μιμνήσκω XXII 9; D IV 11
μισθίον I 2L, 3L
μισθός I 1A, 2, 3, 4, 10, XXI 4H
μνημεῖον XVII 2
μνήμη(?) IV 7
μνημόσυνον XXVI 8H
μοῖρα II 8BC, 9
μοιχεία D I 2
μοιχεύω D I 1, 2
Μολόχ XXVI 2, 4, 5
μόλυβδος IV 8, XVIII 44P, XIX 2
μονάρχης XXII 20B
μονογενής XX 2
μόνον I 2C, 12, XI 5, XIV 5, XVIII 5, 18P, 19HP, XXIII 2; C XIII 14
μονόπτερος XXV 3
μόνος V 8, 10, VI 1, 2; C Pro 2, X 33, XIII 2, 6, 8, 13, 14; D I 3
μορφή II 3, IV 2, XIII 1, XV 4, 5, 14, XVI 1, XVII 1; C XI 2
μυελός XVIII 11P
μυριάς XXI 2B, XXVI 9H
μυρίκινος V 9P
μύριος XXI 1
μυριώνυμος XIII 3P, XV 2P
μυρμηκολέων C XI 8
μυστήριον XXVI 8H; C X 53, XIII 1; Tit C
Μωϋσῆς XXV 3, 4

III. Index of Greek words

Νάθαν D I 4, 5, 6, 7, 9, 10, 11
ναί XX 8H, XXII 20P
ναός I 1, 3, 4, 5, 8, II 5, IV 12, *et pas.*
νάρδος VI 10H, νάρδιν L, νάρσιν P
νάρκη XVIII 19
ναυτία XVI 4P
νεανίας I 10L, 13L
νεκρός XX 20B; D I 6
νεόνυμφος V 7
νεός I 1, 10L, XX 5, 6, 7, 11; D I 2
νεώτερος I 2L, 3L, 4L
νεῦμα C Pro 2
νευρά XVIII 17A
νεῦρον XVIII 11, 36
νευροχάλασις * XVIII 17P
νεφρός XVIII 14, 27
νήθω IV 12
νήπιος XVIII 25L
νίκη C X 9
νίπτω XIII 2
νοέω XI 1P
νομή V 5
νομίζω IV 6, XXVI 5H
νόσημα XI 2
νότος VII 6, XIX 3, XXI 1; D V 1
νοῦς XVIII 19A; C X 5
νυκτοφαγήσῃ * XVIII 35P
νύξ I 3, C, 5, IV 12, V 8, VII 5, IX 5, *et pas.*
νωδός XVIII 30P
νῶτον XIV 1

Ξηραίνω II 8, XXIII 1Q
ξηρός C X 6
ξίφος VIII 6, XVII 2
ξύλινος XXI 3B
ξύλον VIII 6, IX 6, XI 7, XII 3, XIV 3, 6, XV 10, XIX 2; C X 6; D V 1
ξυλοφορέω XI 7P
ξύω C IX 9T

Ὅδε I 3C; C IX 9U
ὁδεύω IV 9
ὁδοδή(?) XII 2A
ὁδός VIII 11C, XVIII 21, XXII 11B; D I 5, VI 8
ὁδούς V 13†, XI 7 P, XII 2

ὀδύνη D IV 9
ὀδυρμός D IV 2
οἶδα IV 1AP, 6, V 13, XX 11; D IV 2
οἰδαίνω V 7
οἴησις† C XII 3
οἰκεῖος C XIII 13, 14
οἰκειοχείρως C XII 4
οἰκέτης X 6, XXII 13; C XII 5
οἰκέω IV 4CC°, VIII 4, XII 3; C XI 3; XIII 2; D VI 1
οἰκητήριον IV 5, XVII 2; C XI 5
οἰκία I 14L, VI 10; D VI 1
οἰκοδομέω I 1, 7, XIX 1, 2, XXI 1, XXII 6, XXIII 4, XXVI 7H; C Pro 1, 5; D II 7, III 3, V 1, VIII 5
οἰκοδομή I 1, 1A, II 8, X 10, XIV 5, 8 XVIII 43P; D III 3, 7, IV 1, 2, V 1, VI 2, VIII 1; Tit H
οἰκονομέω I 1P, XXVI 6; D IV 15
οἶκος I 5L, VII 5, XVIII 15, *et pas.*
οἰκουμένη XV 10, XXIV 2; C XIII 4, 7
οἶμαι D I 13
οἴμοι IX 3; D II 10
οἶνος XVIII 31
οἷος IX 2HP, XVIII 23; C X 23; D II 4 VIII 7
οἰστός† C XII 6
ὀλίγος IV 7, V 5, VII 2, VIII 11C, XIV 3
ὀλολύζω XXVI 7H
ὅλος I 5, V 7, 12, VI 9, XIII 5P, XIX 1P; C X 45, XIII 9; D IV 2
ὁλοσώματος C XIII 13, 14
Ὄλυμπος VIII 4
ὅλως IX 5P
ὁμιλία D IV 14
ὄμμα V 2C; D IV 9
ὄμνυμι XXV 8B
ὁμοθυμαδόν VIII 2PC, XVIII 2
ὅμοιος VIII 8, X 9, XV 10; D I 13, VI 12
ὁμοιόω XXVI 4
ὁμοίως VIII 7, 10, 11, X 8P; C IX 9, X 4, 14—19, XII 4, 5
ὁμολογέω D III 6
ὁμόνοια VIII 4P
ὁμοῦ VIII 4, 11C; C XI 9

ὀνειδισμός XXVI 8 H
ὀνίνημι+ C XIII 14
ὄνομα I 2 V, 3, 11 C, II 5, IV 12, V 5,
   6 L, 9, 10, VI 5, 6, 8, VII 6, 7, IX 7 P,
   X 4, XI 3, 4, 5, 6, XIII 6, XIV 3,
   XV 11, 14, XVI 4 P, XVIII 4 P, 15,
   XXII 14, XXIV 2 Q, XXV z, XXVI
   4 H, 5; C Pro 5, IX 8, 10, X 53, XII
   1, 4, 5, 6, XIII 6, 8; D III 6, VI 9,
   VII 2, 5; Tit C, Sig T
ὀνοπρόσωπος XVIII 1 P
ὄνος C X 28
ὄνυξ XI 7 H
ὀπή D VI 4
ὄπισθεν XVI 1
ὀπισθότονος XVIII 10
ὅπλον VIII 6
ὁποῖος XVIII 4 P
ὁράω I 3 L, 4 L, VI 10; C Pro 4; D II
   4, IV 13, VI 11; Sig T
ὄργανον VIII 2 C
ὀργή V 2 P, 3 P
ὀργίζω V 6 L
ὄρεξις V 8 P
ὀρθός XI 1 H
ὄρθρος VI 10, XXII 13
ὀρθῶς XXIV 5 Q
ὁρίζω I 10 A, VI 10 H, 11
ὁρκίζω V 9, VI 8, XI 6, XVIII 20, 31,
   33, XXV 8
ὅρκος C IX 8, X 53
ὄρνεον C X 47, XIII 5
ὄρνις C X 11
ὄρος VIII 4, X 3, XXIII 1
ὁρόω VI 10 L
ὀρύσσω VIII 12, XII 4
ὅς I 1, 2 C, 3 L, 7, 9, et pas.
ὅσος I 4 Pᵠ, IX 5, XVIII 40 P, XX 15;
   C Pro 3, C X 15, 25, 33, XI 8, 9
ὅσπερ I 2, 7 C, V 11, VII 1 C, IX 2 C,
   XII 4, XIV 6, XV 5, XVIII 2 Q, XXVI
   5 B, 8 H; C X 4; D I 3, II 4; Sub V
ὀστέον XVIII 35
ὅστις IX 8 P, XIII 3, XIV 3, XV 2; C
   XI 7, XII 2, 5, XIII 8, 9, 12; D IV 10;
   Tit C
στοῦν XVIII 11 P

ὀσφύς D I 12
οὐ, οὐκ, οὐχ I 2 C, 4 L, VI 5, 6, et pas.
οὐδαμῶς XXVI 4 B
οὐδέ XVIII 3; D I 12, 13
οὐδείς V 3, 11, VI 5, XIII 3 P, 4 P, XXII
   2; C XIII 3; D II 4, IV 11
οὐδέποτε D IV 2
οὐκέτι XV 10, XXII 15
οὔπω IX 7 P
οὐράνιος II 3, V 3, VI 2, 10 P
οὐρανός I 3, 6, 8, II 1 L, 5, et pas.
Οὐρίας D I 1, 2, 3, 12
οὖρον XVIII 27 P
οὖς I 3 C, XII 2, XIII 4 P, XVIII 16 P
οὗτος I 2 C, 7, 9, 12, II 1, et pas.
οὕτως I 4, 6 L, II 8 A, IV 12, et pas.
οὐχί I 3; D IV 17
ὀφείλω XVIII 44 P
ὀφθαλμός XIII 4, XVII 1, XVIII 7, 39;
   C Pro 1, 4
ὄφις C X 40, XII 6
ὀχεικός* XVII 1; l. ὀχευτικός(?)
ὄχλησις C X 29
ὀχλούμενος L: I 2, II 5, IV 12, V 6, 9,
   12, VII 8
ὀψία I 4 L
ὄψις I 3 L, II 3, XIII 5 P; D II 2, 4

Πάθος IX 4 P
παίγνιον XXVI 7 Q; C X 28, XIII 9
παιδάριον I 2 B, C, 3, 4 B, 9 B, et pas.
παιδεύω D I 13
παιδίον I 1, 1 HI, z, 4 A, 8, II 3, et pas.
παιδοπάτηρ(?) C XIII 4
παῖς I 1, 2, 2 A, 3 W, 4 H, III 5, 6 L,
   et pas.
παίω D II 10
παλαιός D I 2
Παλαιστίνη C X 8, XIII 14
παλάμη XVIII 11 P, XX 4; C IX 9 T,
   XIII 14
πάλιν II 9, III 7, V 5, 6 L, 8, et pas.
πανάγιος I 3 C
πανάθλιος XXVI 5 Q
πανσέληνος IV 9
πάνσεπτος D VIII 5

III. Index of Greek words 153*

παντελώς V 7 P
παντοκράτωρ III 5, 7 L, VI 8; D III 3
IV 7
πάντοτε III 7, XXII 5 H
πάνυ I 1, 2P, 3, XXVI 5 H, 7
παραβιάζομαι XXVI 4
παραβλέπω XXII 5
παραβολή XX 4
παραβολικώς D I 10
παραγγέλλω XXVI 4 B
παραγίνομαι IX 8; D II 9
παραδίδωμι XVI 5 P, XXV 8 B; C IX 8, X 13, 14, 53, XII 4, XIII 9, 12, 13, 14
παρακαθέζομαι XV 4, XVII 2, XVIII 44P, XX 20B
παρακαθίζω XVII 2P
παρακαλέω XX 5; C Pro 2; D IV 11
παράκλησις D II 5, IV 11
παρακολουθέω VIII 8, X 3
παρακούω XXV 8B
παραλλάσσω I 3 L
παράλληλος Tit C
παραλύω XVIII 11, 36
παραμορφόω XVII 2
παραμυθία D IV 11
παράνομος VI 4P
παρανόμως D IV 2
παραπίπτω X 8P
παραστήκω XVIII 3 HL
παραστοματίζω* XVIII 21 H
παράταξις C X 9
παρατηρέω D VI 4
παραφαίνω XX 13 Q
παραφυλάττω XX 20H
παραχωρέω C XIII 3
πάρεδρος III 5
πάρειμι VII 1, VIII 1, IX 1P, 3, X 1,
XIII 1, XIV 1, XV 1, XVI 1, XVII 1,
XVIII, 1, XXII 2B, XXV 3, 6; D II 3
παρεισέρχομαι XI 2P
παρεμβολή XXV 7
παρέρχομαι XI 1, XVII 2; C X 1; D IV 6, 9
παρέχω IV 7, VIII 10, XX 9P; C X 4, 7, 23, 31, 34, 50, XI 9, XIII 14; D II 2, 4

παρθένος (noun) V 7, XXVI 4, 5; (adj.)
C IX 9T; Sig T
παρίσθμιον XVIII 10P, 37H
παρίστημι V 4C, 9, VI 1, IX 1C, XIII 3P, XIV 2, XVI 5, XVIII 3, XXVI 9H; C XII 1
παρουσία C XIII 8
παροφθαλμία* C X 28
παρωτίς XVIII 10
πᾶς I 1, 3, 4, 7, 12, 14, II 6, et pas.
πάσχω I 4 L, XI 6, XII 3, XVIII 21, 31, 35
πατήρ V 4, 12, XVIII 18P, 22, XXVI 4, 9H; C Pro 1, XIII 10; D I 12, IV 2, 3, 11
πατροπαράδοτος† C XIII 4
παύω VII 7, XVIII 31P
πειθαρχέω C XII 5, XIII 3
πείθω XX 6P, XXII 11B, XXVI 4B
πειράζω XV 11
πέλαγος XVI 1; C XII 2
πέμπω I 1C, XXII 16Q; Sig B
πένης D I 7
πενθέω XX 19H
πένθος D II 7, IV 9
πεντάλφα Sig B
πέρας XIX 2P, XXII 1B; D VIII 1
περιαπλόω XVI 7
περιάπτω P: XVIII 25, 27, 28, 32(?P)
περιδέω XV 15
περίειμι II 9
περιεισέρχομαι XI 2 L
περιενδύω Sig T
περιέρχομαι IX 1 H, XI 2 H, XIII 3, XVI 2 H
περιέχω VIII 7; C XI 9 VW
περιηχέω XI 6
περιίστημι D VI 11
περικαλλής IV 2; C XI 2; D II 1
περίκειμαι D IV 13
περικλείω X 10
περικλυτός† V 7
περικριτός† V 7
περιπατέω XXII 17, 18; C X 3
περιπέτομαι C XIII 5
περιπλέκω XXI 3Q
περιποιέω IX 2PC

περιπολεύω VI 3 P
περισφίγγω V 6 L
περισφραγίζω X 8, XIII 3P, XXIV 2
περιττός C XIII 4
περιφέρω V 8P, X 8H; C XII 3
περιφράσσω XVI 7
περιχαρής I 8
περιχύνω XVI 7
περιχώννυμι V 12
Πέρσαι XV 8
πέταλον D IV 14, 16
πετεινός C· Pro 3
πέτρα C X 45
πηλός V 12
πῆχυς VIII 12; C XI 18
πιέζω I 2 C
πικρία V 13
πικρός XX 2H, XXVI 5B
πικρῶς V 12H; D I 6, 11
πίμπλημι D VI 5
πίνω XVIII 31 P
πίπτω XX 16, 17, XXV 8B; D IV 14, 16, VI 8
πίσσα XVI 7
πιστεύω VI 4P, XV 13
πιστός VI 4P
πλανάω VIII· 9, XV 10
πλάσμα XVIII 20
πλάτος C XI 8
πλατύνω C XIII 7
πλέκω VIII 5, XXI 3
πλευρά XVIII 28
πλέω XVI 1
πλῆθος D III 8; πληθύς VII 5 L
πληθύνω C X 52
πλημμελῶς IV 6 C
πλήν C XIII 1, 12
πληρέω* C X 2 UW
πλήρης V 13
πληρόω XXIII 4, XXVI 9 H; D I 6, 12, VII 3
πλήρωσις XXII 7
πλησιάζω V 4P, D III 5
πλίκω†* (plico) XVIII 16P
πλινθουργέω XII 6 P
πλοῖον XVI 2, XVIII 28; C X 18
πλοκή XXI 3 Q

πλοκολογέω* VIII 5 C
πλούσιος C X 12
πλουτέω C X 23
πλουτοδοτέω C X 10
πλουτοποιός C XIII 14
πλοῦτος XIV 4P?; C XIII 13, 14
πλύνω XVIII 15
πνεῦμα I 2 L, II 5 L, IV 4, VII 1PC, 4C, VIII 1, IX 5, 7P, XI 1, XII 2, XIII 3P, XIV 2, 4, 6, 7, XV 1, 11, 15, XVI 1, 5, XVII 1, 4L, 5P, XVIII 3, 4, XXII 1, 2, 3, 10, 12, 13, 15, 16, XXVI 6, 7; C X 15, 16, 17, 18, XI 3; D III 1, IV 12, 13, VI 4, 12, VII 3; Tit B
πνευματόω XXII 11, 13
πνέω XXII 10, 15; D IV 1, VI 4
πνίγω IV 5, XIII 3; C XI 4
πνοή XXII 2, 13, XXV 3
ποθεινότατος D II 2
ποθέω I 3 L
ποιέω I 1, 2 C, 3 C, 9 L, 12, IV 4 VW, et pas.
ποίημα II 1 L
ποιητής II 1 L, 9 B, III 5 P
ποίμνιον C X 52
ποῖος II 2, IV 9, 10, V 9, VI 7, 8, et pas.
πόλεμος VI 4; C X 9; D I 3
πολιορκία C X 36
πόλις I 1, XIX 1P, XX 17; C X 13, 24, 27, 30, 36
πολλάκις IV 6; C XI 5
πολύμορφος XIII 3
πολυόμματος D VIII 6
πολυπαθής XVIII 39
πολυποίκιλος IV 4; C XI 4
πολύς I 1, 2 L, 5 L, IV 5, V 5, 7 P, et pas.
πολλά I 1, IV 6, 9, IX 6, X 2
πολυτελής D V 1
πολύτιμος XXII 16P
πονέω XVIII 14P, D VI 11
πονηρός I 2 L, 4, 4 L, 9 L, 10 L, V 1, 6 L, VI 4P, XV 12, XX 2P, XXII 10, 12, XXVI 8H; D II 4, III 1, VI 4, VII 3
πόνος XVIII 14A, 18P, 33, 37 H
πορεύω I 9 L, 10 L, X 6P, XIII 2, et pas.
πορίζω IV 7
πορφύριος XII 4 H

III. Index of Greek words 155*

πορφυροδανόμενος* XII 4P
πορφυροῦς XII 4L; D VI 12
ποσόω C IX 9
ποταμός V 10, XXVI 9H
ποτόν C XI 7, 9
πούς V 11P, IX 6, XIV 1
πρᾶγμα XIII 2
πρᾶξις VI 3, VII 5, XI 3, XIV 4, XVI 3, 4, XVIII 4; C IX 9T
πρᾶος I 4C
πράσινος X 5, 7; D VI 7
πράσον X 9
πράττω C X 22
πρέπω X 3H; C XII 6
πρεσβύτερος XX 5P, 6P
πρεσβύτης XX 5H, 10, 20B
πρίζω VI 9, 11, XIV 8
προάγω D I 2
προγινώσκω V 13L
προγνωστικός V 12
προδότης IX 3
πρόδρομος XXVI 10H
προεδρεύω III 7AP
προεπιστρέφω* V 2L
προέρχομαι V 1P, XII 1
προέχω V 3
προθυμία I 1, 2, 2A; D II 1
πρόθυμος I 1; C XII 2
προθύμως I 1
πρόθυρον II 1BC, XVIII 22, 40
προλέγω C X 10
πρόνοια D I 13
προξενέω D VI 14
προορίζω XII 3
προπέμπω XXII 16P
προσαγορεύω VI 2
προσάγω VI 5P
προσγελάω XX 6H
προσδέω X 8P
προσδοκέω C XIII 8
προσεδρεύω III 7C
πρόσειμι XX 2P (εἶμι)
προσεῖπον I 3C
προσεκτέον C XIII 1
προσέρχομαι XVIII 4P, 42, XX 2
προσευχή C Pro 1
προσεύχομαι I 5L, 6, XVIII 42P; CPro 1

προσέχω XXVI 8B
προσθύω XXVI 4Q
προσκαθίζω VI 1
πρόσκαιρος V 5
προσκαλέω XVIII 4; D II 8
προσκλίνω C XII 3
προσκυνέω IV 6, 7, XII 1, XIII 1P, et pas.
προσοικέω VI 7L
προσπέμπω XXII 16
προστάσσω I 11P, VI 11P, VII 8, XIII 7; C IX 10, XII 2; D II 8, IV 8
προστίθημι IX 6, XXVI 9H
προσφέρω VI 5, IX 1, XIX 2, XXVI 8H; C IX 8, XI 7
προσψαύω II 6
πρόσωπον VII 1, X 1, XI 1P, et pas.
προτάσσω VI 11L
πρότερος I 9L; C XII 3
προτρέπω D III 4, VI 11
προφητεύω XV 8
προφήτης D I 2, 4, 6
προφητικός D I 12
πρωτομαΐστωρ I 2 (-ορος P, -ορον Q)
πρωτόπλαστος D I 2
πτεροειδής XIV 4
πτερόν XIV 1
πτερύγιον XXII 8
πτέρωτος XVIII 1H, XXV 3
πτηνοπρόσωπος XVIII 1P
πτύσσω XXII 6
πτύω VII 3
πτῶμα D I 13
πτωματίζω XVIII 21P
πτωχός C X 12
πύλη I 14
πυνθάνομαι IV 1, XXVI 4B
πῦρ I 3C, 10, III 4, VII 5, IX 6, 7P, XIV 5, XX 13; C X 2, 41, XIII 12; D VI 1
πύργος C X 24
πύρεθρον XVIII 20P
πυρετός XVIII 20, 23
πυρομαχέω XVIII 44P
πυρόω IX 6
πύρωσις XVIII 29P, πύρεσις H
πώγων V 12L

III. Index of Greek words

ῥαβδίζω V 6
ῥαίνω XVIII 15
ῥάπτω C IX 10
Ῥαφάν XXVI 2, 4, 5
ῥήγνυμι VII 1, IX 3, XV 8; C X 4
ῥῆμα V 3, 10, XXVI 6; D II 4
ῥῆσις D I 12
ῥητορεύω D VIII 2
ῥῖγος XVIII 18
ῥιπή XXIV 2
ῥίπτω I 9, 11, II 8, III 3, 4 P, et pas.
Ῥοβοάμ XXVI 7 H
ῥομφαία XX 13
ῥοπή XXIV 2 H
ῥυπαρία XVIII 20P; C X 12
ῥύπτω C IX 10
Ῥωμαῖος VI 8 P
ῥώννυμι XXII 5 B

Σάβα XIX 3, XXI 1
Σαβαώθ I 6, 7, III 7 L, V 9, XI 6 P, XXIV 2 Q; C X 53
σαλεύω XVIII 5, 11 P, XXII 8, XXIII 1 Q, XXIV 2
Σαλυμών C IX 9 U, cf. Σολομῶν
σάμφειρος XXI 2
σάρκωσις D I 12
σάρξ XVII 3, XVIII 19 A, 40
Σατανᾶς D I 1, 4, 6, II 10
σαφῶς D IV 2
σέβομαι V 5, 10, VI 4. XX 13 B
σειρά D I 12
σεισμός VI 10
σελήνη IV 9, VII 6, XV 4; C X 35
σεληνιάζομαι C X 35
σεραφίμ XXI 2 H, XXVI 9 H; D VIII 6
σημεῖον XXV 4; C IX 8, 10, XIII 2, 7
σημειοφόρος D I 2
σημειόω XII 3, XXII 11 B
σήμερον V 4, XXIII 2 Q, XXIV 3, 5; C XIII 3
σηπεδών XVIII 8
σίαλος XVII 3 (σίελος P)
Σιβύλλα D V 1
σίγλος, σίκλος X 9 P, XXI 1 B H
σίδηρος II 6, V 12, XIX 2

Σιράχ D I 13
σιτίδια, τὰ*† I 1 (A), 3 H
σιτίον I 1, 3, 4; D II 2, 4
Σιών I 1 L; C Pro 1, 5.
σιωπάω VI 11
σκάλα XXIII 3 Q
σκανδαλίζω XVIII 16; D III 8
σκελιάζω* IV 5 HI
σκέπτομαι D I 1
σκευάζω D I 11
σκευή V 8
σκεῦος XV 8, XXI 3
σκέψις XVI 3
σκῆπτρον XXVI 7 H; D VII 4
σκῆψις† XVI 3 Cr
σκληρία XVIII 15 P
σκληρύνω XXV 3, 5
σκολιάζω IV 5; C XI 4
σκορπίζω VII 5 C, XXVI 7 H
σκοτεινός XVII 1; D IV 9
σκοτία XIII 5 P
σκοτίζω VII 5 AP, VIII 11 C, XXVI 7 B
σκότος VIII 2, XIII 5. XVIII 2; D IV 13
σκυθρωπάζων I 3 L
σκυθρωπός D II 4, IV 9
σμάραγδος XXI 2
Σολομῶν I 1, 3, 4, 5, 7, 9, 11, et saepe
Σουμανίτης XXVI 2 H (σουμανίτης P)
σοφία III 5, IV 11, V 13P, et pas.
σοφίζω VII 4, XIX 3P, XXII 3
σοφός III 5 P, VIII 11, XV 5, et pas.
σπάθη XVII 1 P
σπάργανον XVIII 37 P
σπασμός† XVIII 21
σπήλαιον IV 4, 5; C XI 3
σπλάγχνον XVIII 29
σπορά V 3 P
σπουδαίως XXII 11
σπουδή D III 8, IV 7
στάδιον XXI 3 HQ
στακτή VI 10
σταλάσσω V 12 L
σταυρόω XXII 20
στέμμα D VII 4
στεναγμός D IV 9
στενάζω V 12; D I 11
στερέωμα XX 12, 17

III. Index of Greek words

στῆθος I 9, 11, III 3, IX 3; D II 7
στήκω I 14, XIII 2P; C X 21
στηρίζω VI 3P; C XIII 4; D LV 17
στιγμή XXIV 2P
στοιχεῖον VIII 2, XV 5, XVII 4, XVIII 1, 2
στολή C X 4, 28
στόμα XIII 4, XIV 6, XVI 7, XXII 10, 13B, 14, 17; D VI 4, 5
στομαχήζω(?) XIII 3L
στόμαχος XVIII 18, 21
στοχάζομαι XIII 3P
στραγγισμός* XVIII 27P
στρατεία C X 36
στρατιώτης IV 11, VII 1
στρατός XIX 1P
στρέφω XXV 7H; D IV 4
στρόφος VII 5, XVIII 13
στυγνάζω I 4L
στῦλος XXV 8B
στυππεῖον XVI 7
στύραξ V 13
συγγενής VII 5A, VIII 8W
συγγίνομαι IV 6, XIV 3, 4; C XI 5
συγκαλύπτω XXV 7
συγκλείω I 7, XXII 15
σύγκοιτος VIII 8C
συκῆ XVIII 37P
συλλαμβάνω XXII 3, 12
συλλεύω†* XV 8
συμβάντα, τά I 4
συμβασιλεύω(?) XVI 3P
συμβουλεύω XVI 3
συμβουλή XVI 5, XXVI 7B
συμμαχέω VI 4P
συμμίγνυμι V 7P
συμπάρειμι (εἰμί) II 9W, V 4
σύμπας XIII 5P
συμπλέκω VIII 1
συμπληρόω XXII 7
συμπλήρωσις XXII 7B
συμποδίζω XVIII 42P
σύμπτωμα XX 13B
συμφέρον D VII 2
συμφορά V 7P
συνάγχη XVIII 8P
συνάγω I 1, II 5C, XIV 5
συνακολουθέω XXV 6

συνάντημα IX 6
συναστρός* IV 6; C XI 5
συνδέω VIII 1
συνέρχομαι II 7B
σύνεσις XXII 1
συνήθης I 10
συνίημι XV 14, XXII 11B
συνοχή XVIII 8A
συντάσσω XXII 11B
συντέλεια XXIV 2Q, XXV 8; D VI 14
συντελέω II 8
σύντομος VIII 12P
συντόμως XXII 14Q, XXIII 2H
συντρίβω XVIII 11P, 36P, XXVI 5B
συντυγχάνω C X 11
συνυπουργέω XXII 8
σύρω VI 10
σύστασις C Pro 3
σύστημα D VII 2, 5
σφαγή XVII 1
σφάζω XXVI 4H; D I 5
σφάλμα VII 6
σφήνωσις XVIII 9P
σφιγγοπρόσωπος XVIII 1·
σφίγγω XXII 14
σφόδρα I 1, 2, 3L, II 6L, XVIII 7 XXVI 1, 2H
σφοδρός C X 37
σφραγίδιον II 9B
σφραγίζω II 5, IV 12, VII 3, 8LC, VIII 12, IX 3, X 6, 7, XII 5, XVI 7, XXII 11, 11B, XXVI 9H; C IX 9U
σφραγίς I 6, 7, 8, II 5L, 9, V 11, X 6, XIV 2, XV 7, XXII 9, 11B, XXVI 8H; C IX 8, XII 1, 4, XIII 6, 11; D II 6, 7, 8, 9, 10, III 3, 4, VI 3, 13, VII 3; Sig B, L; plural σφραγίδαι Sig C
σχῆμα II 5, X 1, XI 1, 1LP
σχοινίον IV 12
σχοῖνος, ἡ IV 12P
σχολάζω I 10L
σχολιάζω(?) IV 5WW°
σῶμα I 4, IV 2C, V 12L, VII 1H, et pas.
σωματοποιέω IV 4V°W°P; C XI 3VW
σωματόω II 5L, IV 4AT°; C XI 3T
σωτήρ XVII 4
σωφρονέω VIII 8

Ταλαίπωρος XX 4
τάλαντον XXI 4 H; D VI 2
ταμεῖον XIII 2
τανύω XV 10
τάξις D VIII 5
ταραχή C X 29
Τάρταρος VI 3
τάσσω II 5, V 5, VIII 12, XXII 11; D I 3, III 7
ταυρόμορφος XVIII 1
ταῦρος XXI 3
τάφος VIII 9, XX 20
ταχέως D VI 5, τάχιστα D VI 3, τάχυ IV 2
τάχιστος D VI 3
τάχος D VII 3
τεῖχος V 12 L, VII 8 L
τέκνον C X 53, XIII 2
τελείως XXVI 7 B, 8 B
τελευτάω XVII 1, 2 P, XX 7, XXVI 7
τελέω XXVI 5 B
τέλος D IV 6, 8, VIII 2; Sub V
τέμνω I 2 C, II 5
τέρας XXV 4
τετράπους C X 3, 49
τέφρα VI 5 P
τέχνη C X 20, 42; Sig T
τεχνίτης I 1, 3, VII 8, X 8, XX 1, XXII 8
τηγάνιον C IX 9 T
τηλικοῦτος XXIII 4 P
τηρέω X 8 P, XX 18 H, XXV 7
τίθημι XIV 5, 6, XVIII 22, et pas.
τίκτω XIII 3 P, XXII 20; D I 12
τιμάω XIX 1
τιμή XXII 16, I 6 C (?)
τίμιος I 6, VI 8, XIX 2 P, XXVI 10 H; D V 1, VI 7
τιμωρέω V 3
τιμωρία XX 6 P
τινάσσω VII 3, XX 4
τοιόσδε XXII 2 B
τοιοῦτος I 2 C, II 1 L, IV 2 C, XV 5, 10, 11, XVI 1 P, XVIII 40, XX 4; C XI 2, XIII 1; D II 1, 2, 4, 6, 7, VI 2, VIII 7
τοιούτως I 4 L
τοῖχος VII 5
τολμάω XX 4 P; D III 8

τόπος I 1, II 3, VII 3, VIII 6, et pas.
τοσοῦτος XXIII 4 Q, XXVI 3 P, adv. I 2 C
τότε VII 1 L, 3, IX 5, XIII 2, 6 P, et pas.
τράπεζα I 1 C; C XI 7, 8, 9
τράχηλος II 6 L, V 12, IX 6, XVIII 16, 23 P, 24 P, 25 P
τρέμω II 1, VI 8
τρέπω X 3 LP, XX 9 P
τρέφω VI 3, 5
τρέχω I 9 C, X 9 H (?)
τρίβολος XII 2 A, τριβόλαιος P
τρίβω V 12 L, XVIII 20
τρίζω XII 2
τρικέφαλος XII 1 P
τρίκλος (?) C IX 9
τρικυμία V 8
τρίχωλος † C IX 9
τριπτός XVIII 34 P
τριττός XV 7
τριφδίον (?) C IX 10
τρόπαιον IV 4 C
τρόπος IV 4, XVII 3, XVIII 4 P, 44 P; C XI 4
τροφή XX 9 P; D II 3
τυγχάνω IX 6, XVIII 4 P; D III 8, IV 13
τύμπανον C XII 6
τύπος XX 15 B
τύπτω V 6 L, XII 2, XX 2
τυραννέω V 5 P
τύραννος VI 4, VIII 10
τυφλόω XII 2 P

Ὑάκινθος XXI 2
ὕβρις XX 2
ὑγιαίνω XXII 11; C X 39, XIII 13, 14
ὑγιής XVIII 20 A
ὑδρία V 12
ὕδωρ V 10 L, 11, XI 6, XVI 1 P, et pas.
υἱός I 1, 7, V 3, 10, XIII 7, et pas.
ὕλη IV 8, V 12 L, VI 10, XIV 5, XVIII 28
ὑμνέω I 8, XII 6 L
ὑμνολογέω C XII 4
ὑπακούω VI 4 P
ὑπακτικός XVIII 31
ὑπάρχω XIII 5, XIX 3, XX 1 P, et pas.
ὑπείκω C XII 1
ὑπεισέρχομαι IX 5 C, XVI 2 H, XXIII 3

III. Index of Greek words

ὑπεναντίος VIII 10
ὑπερβάλλω Tit B, ὑπερβαλλόντως Tit I
ὑπερβολή X 2P
ὑπερευκλεής†* XXVI 10H
ὑπερήφανος V 3
ὑπερί C XII 6
ὑπερισχύω X 2P
ὑπερμεγέθης XXIV 4
ὑπεροχή X 2
ὕπνος II 3B
ὑπνωτικός II 3
ὑπογινώσκω* V 13L
ὑποδείκνυμι XXII 11Q; C XIII 7
ὑποδεικνύω C X 2
ὑποδέχομαι XVI 2
ὑποδέω XXIII 3P
ὑπόδυνα(?) XII 2P
ὑποδύνω VII 5
ὑπόθεσις XXVI 3B
ὑποκαίω V 13
ὑποκαπνίζω I 3C
ὑποκάτωθεν C XI 7
ὑπόκαυσις XI 7P
ὑπολαμβάνω I 4L
ὑπολείπω VI 2, VII 1
ὑπόλοιπος VII 1P
ὑπόλοξος XXIV 5
ὑπομένω XI 6
ὑπομιμνήσκω XXII 6
ὑποπιάζω D II 4
ὑποπροτάσσω* X 6L
ὑπόπτερος II 3
ὑπόσχομαι C IX 8
ὑποταγή C X 50; D III 3, IV 6
ὑποτάσσω II 5L, 7, 8, III 5, et pas.
ὑποτελέω XXII 5P
ὑποτελής XXIII 5P
ὑπουργός D IV 13
ὑποχείριος XXV 8B; C IX 8
ὑψηλός VII 1, 8; comp. D I 13
ὕψιστος I 7, XI 6, XVIII 20P
ὕψος VI 8, XXIV 1Q
ὑψόω XXIV 1P

Φαίνω II 3B, VIII 4, XV 5, et pas.
φανερέω.* C X 31

φανερός C XIII 2
φανερόω XIII 3P; C X 21, 38
φανερῶς IV 6, VI 6P, XII 3; C XI 5
φαντασία III 7; C X 51T
φάντασμα VIII 9C
φάραγξ IV 5
Φαραώ XXV 3, 5, 6
φάρυγξ XVIII 37
φαῦλος VIII 9
φέρω I 7, VI 4P, VIII 6, XI 7, et pas.
φεύγω XIII 6A, XVIII 40
φήμη D VIII 1
φημί passim
φθάνω IX 5P
φθονέω I 2A
φθόνος VI 4, XVIII 38
φιάλη XVI 7P
φίαλος* XVIII 44P; C XI 7
φιλία XX 9
φιλολογέω X 2P
φιλονεικία D IV 1
φίλος VIII 11, IX 8, XVIII 38
φλέγω I 10
φλόξ III 4
φοβερός I 3C
φοβερόχροος* XII 1
φοβέω II 6, V 9, VI 10L, XVII 4
φόβος I 4L; D I 8
φονεύω V 8; D I 2, 3
φόνος V 8P, VI 4
φορά C IX 9T, XII 6
φορέω V 12, XVIII 16; Sig T
φράζω VI 8L
φρένιμος (cf. φρόνιμος)* I 1C; C X 5 V
φρενιτιάω X 3P
φρήν X 3, XIII 4, XVIII 12, 30
φρίκη XVIII 19P
φρικτός XXIV 4Q; C X 53
φρίσσω II 1
φρόνησις XIX 3; C X 20, 41; D I 12
φρόνιμος (cf. φρένιμος) C X 5UW
φρουρά XVIII 43P
φρουρέω XX 18B
φυλακή XVI 7A; C X 14
φυλάσσω XXIII 2Q, XXIV 2HP, XXVI 8H; C XIII 8, 9; Tit C, Sub V
φυλή C X 28; D I 12

φύλλον XVIII 15, 37, XX 16; C IX 10; D IV 16
φυσάω XXII 17Q, 18 Q
φυσιόω XXII 18
φύσις IV 5, XX 13P; C Pro 3, XI 4
φύω C X 6
φωλεός D VI 4
φωλεύω IV 4, V 4; C XI 3
φωνέω C XII 3
φωνή I 3C, 4, IV 8, V 13, VIII 2PC; et pas.
φῶς D IV 13
φωτεινός C XII 3, 4

X, τὸ D VIII 3
χαίρω I 2, 14BC, X 1, XIX 1, XXII 1, XXV 9; D VI 1
χάλαξις XVIII 17
χαλάω C X 22
Χαλδαῖοι XV 8, χαλδαϊκός C XIII 14
χαλεπός I 2C, 10, 14H, V 13P, XIII 3P, XVI 1, XX 2, XXII 2B, XXV 3; D VI 1
χαλινόδεσμα* XIII 4 P
χαλκός XIX 2, XXI 1B; D II 6, VI 2
χαλκοῦς XVIII 28P, XXIV, 2B, 3
χαμαί VII 3
χαρακτήρ XI 6
χαράσσω C XIII 8
χαρίζομαι XXI 1Q; C XIII 10
χάρις II 5, XX 2, XXVI 8B
χάρισμα C XIII 14; Sig C
χαροποιέω C X 12T
χάρτης I 3C, XVIII 16P, 23P, 24, 25 P
χαρτίον XIII 6A, XVIII 24L; Sig T
χεῖλος XVIII 20
χειμών C X 7
χείρ I 2, 3C, 4, 5, II 1L, V 6L, et pas.
χερουβίμ XXI 2H, XXVI 9 H; D VIII 6
χιλιάς XXVI 9 H
χιών C Pro 1; C X 7
χλεύη IV 11
χολή V 9, 13
χορηγέω D VIII 1
χορηγία V 12

χορτάζω IX 2
χράομαι C X 31
χρεία XIII 2
χρῄζω XV 3
χρῆμα XVI 2, XXII 11Q
χρηματικῆς(?) IV 8 C°; C XI 6
χρήσιμος D III 3, VI 10
χρηστός C X 31
Χριστός D I 12
χρίω V 12 L
χρόνος V 5, XIII 6P, XV 8, XXIV 2P
χρυσίον I 12, 14, IV 4PCC°, 6, XII 4, XVIII 44P, XIX 2, XXI 1B, 4B, XXII 11; C X 4, 23, 34, XI 3; D VI 2, 7
χρύσιος IV 4P
χρυσός XVI 1 P
χρυσοῦς XXI 3H, 4 H
χρῶμα XXI 2
χύνω VIII 7 (χέω?) P; D IV 16, 17
χώρα I 1, XXVI 1; C X 13; D VI 1, 2
χωρέω XV 6
χωρίζω VIII 8, XVIII 22

Ψαλμῳδία D I 2
ψαλμός D I 11
ψῆφος VI 8P, XI 6P, XIII 6P, XV 11P
ψιλός† V 12 L
ψόα XVIII 28P
ψοφέω XIV 4
ψυχή I 4, 5, VIII 9, XX 12
ψῦχος XVIII 18LP
ψυχρῶς XVIII 18 H

Ὦ I 4C; C XII 4, 6, XIII 1, 4; D IV 5, VII 2
ὧδε II 9, VI 3, IX 7 P, XIII 3P, XX 10; D VI 13, VII 3
ὦμος VII 8 L, XV 1, XVIII 11
ὥρα I 3BC, 4C, 9, 10, XIII 3, XVIII 6, XXII 2; C X 4
ὡραῖος XXVI 1Q, 5 H
ὠτίον XVIII 21
ὠφέλεια C Pro 3
ὠφελέω C X 46, 49

IV. Index of Modern Greek
(Not including MS E´)

Ἀμουλα C IX 9 T
ἀρτίκου(?) V 6 L
ἅς VII 4 L XVIII 15 L
ἄστρο C XI 5 TV

Εἰμί: ἤμουν I 1 I(?), ἤτον I 1 L
ἕνας I 1 L
ἔρχομαι: ἤρχετον I 2 L
ἐτούτη XVII 2 L, ἐτοῦτα XVIII 15 L

Ζαλίζω VIII 11 C

Καθεμίαν I 2 C
καθρέπτης Intro. p. 19
κονδύλιον Sig T
κράτος D IV 10, VI 2

μέ = μετά XXII 11 Q
Σταματίζω XIII 3 P
στρώνω† V 8
Τρεκλός† C IX 9
τυφλόνω XII 2 A

V. Index of Subjects and Persons

Aaron, a magician 102
Abezethibu (or, -bithu) 44, 82
Abraxas 70
Aēšma daēva 55
Agla 84
ἀκέφαλος δαίμων 67
Amulets 18, 21, 23, 24f., 47, 72, 75, 77 and n. 5, 103; *see also* Pentacles
Anastasius Sinaites 96, 98, 99
Angelology 4, 46; Arabian 79; Christian 4, 70; Jewish 59, 61
Angels, fallen 43, 79; names 47, 75; *see also* Gabriel, Michael, Raphael, Uriel, and Index II, of Magic and Demonology
Apharoph 42, 82
Apocalypse of Noah 60
Apocalypticism 49 f.
Apotropaic materials 48
Arabian Nights 1, 79, 84, 86
Aro, or Aron, *see* John of
Ašakku marsu 53 f.
Asia, province of 109 f.
Asmodaeus 55, 61 f., 71, 81, 86
Assyria 52
Astrology 46, 91; Egyptian 57
Athos, Mount 10, 13
Azhi Dahāka 56

Babylonia 52 f.
Bath qol 43

Beelzebul 44 f., 50, 68, 83
Bengali magic 52
Bibliothèque Nationale 12, 15, 25; *see also* Manuscripts I, P, W
Bilkis 4
Bologna University Library 21
Book of the Dead 56 f.
Bornemann, Friedrich August 28, 105; *see also* Bibliographies II and III
British Musem 13, 18
Burkitt, F. Crawford 75

Cabalism 82 f.
Carmina 90
Cedrenus, Georgius 95, 96, 99
"Chaldeans" 2
Christianity 2 f., 50 f., 83; early Church 70—75; mediaeval 75—78
Clavicula Salomonis, *see* Solomon, apocryphal books
Colbert, Jean Baptiste 15, 16, 17
Collectio Herovalliana 103
Conybeare, F. C. 27, 29, 51, 68 f., 105 f., 108
Conclusions 43, 87 f., 104, 106 ff., 109
Cross in magic 51
Cryptography 18, 22, 23
Cup, magic 84

Date, *see* Manuscripts, Testament
Dead, Book of, *see* Book of Dead
Dead, burial of 85

UNT. 9: McCown.

V. Index of Subjects and Persons

Decani 34, 42, 45, 46, 47, 57 f., 71, 101
Decretum Gelasianum 103
Deissmann, Adolf VIII, 11 n. 3
Demoniac, Gadarene 50 f.
Demonology 82; of Apocrypha and Pseudepigrapha 59 f.; Arabian 78 f., 80; Babylonian 52 f., Byzantine 77 f.; Christian 2 f., 70—75; Galilean 65; Hellenistic 66 f.; Jewish 59 ff., pre-Talmudic 3, 65, Talmudic 62 f.; Mazdian 54 ff.; New Testament 68 f.; Palestinian 3, 65; of Testament 43 ff.
Demons 4, 44, 45; appearance 80, build Temple 3, 49, 80; hierarchy 44, 84; list of fifty-one 20, 84, 101, 102, see also Decani; names of 44, 45, see also Abezebithu, ἀκέφαλος δαίμων, ašakku marsu, Asmodaeus, Azhi Dakāka, Beelzebul, Eltzianphiel, Empusa, Enepsigos, Ephippas, Hekate, Iblis, Kunopegos, Lix Tetrax, Lucifer, Mastema, Obyzuth, Onoskelis (-lu), Ornias, Paltiel Tzamal, Saḫr, and Index II, of Magic and Demonology; nature 43 f., see also Demonology; origin 43, 83; prophecy of 5, 44, 62; punishment 80; works 45
Dialogue of Timothy and Aquila 38, 76, 106
Dream books 22, 26
Du Cange 17

Editions, etc., of Testament 28—30
Egypt 56 ff., 109 f.
Elements, 68; see also Decani, κοσμοκράτορες, Seven spirits
Eleven, mystical number 82
Eltzianphiel 83
Empusa 45
Enepsigos 67, 82
England, manuscripts used in, see British Museum, Holkham Hall, and Manuscripts H and L (T)
I Enoch 59 ff.
Ephesia grammata 47, 67
Ephippas 44, 53
Eros 48

Ethiopia 71 ff.
Eusebius, "Archaeological History"(?) 98, 99
Fabricius 17 n. 1, 28, Bibliography III 1
Faust literature 1
Faustina 2
Fleck, F. F. 15, 17, 28, 105, Bibliography I 1
Folklore 1; Arabian 78 ff.; Christian 71 ff.; motifs: aerial column 73; burial of dead 85; immovable cornerstone 69, 73; demons used in building 4, 49, 80; falling stars 79 f.; father and son, quarrel of 32, 73; future, knowledge of 5, 44, 62; magic ring, see Solomon, ring of; seduction to idol worship by beautiful woman 71 f.; Solomon as builder, fall of, glory and wealth, power ower animals, visit of Queen of Sheba, wisdom, see Solomon; Testament 4, 32; see also Locusts, sacrifice of
France, manuscripts, see Bibliothèque Nationale
Fürst, J. 15, 28, Bibliography II 2

Gahriel 42, 81
Galilee 109
Gaster, M. 42, 108, 109
Gaulmin, Gilbert 17 and n. 6, 27
Gelasius, decree of 103
Georgios Monachos 95, 96, 98 f.
Georgian legend 73
Ginzberg, Louis 30 and Bibliography II 5
Glycas, Michael 95, 96, 99
Gnosticism 70 f., 82, 84 f., 110
Greek, modern 19

Haggadah 1
Harnack, Adolf 29, 105, 108
Healing, magical 101
Heidelberg, University Library 13 n. 1
Hekate 67, 82 n. 4
Hellenism 66 ff.
Hermaneia, see Solomon, apocryphal books
Hermetic writings 26
Herovalliana, Collectio, see Collectio

V. Index of Subjects and Persons

Hezekiah 36, 92, 96 ff., 99, 102
Hippolytus 96 f.
Holkham Hall, Library 11
Hygromanteia, *see* Solomon, apocryphal books

Iblis 81
Incantations 90
Inventiones Nominum 73
Iranian influences 54 ff.
Isidor (pseudo-), de muneris 103
Isis 4
Istrin, V. M. 10, 12, 17, 18, 29, 105
Italy, Greek manuscripts 14 n. 1, 15 n. 1, 19, 20, 25, 26 f.; *see also* Bologna, University Library; Milan, Ambrosian Library; and Manuscripts U, V, and W

James, Montague Rhodes 11 n. 3, 29, 49, 60, 91
Jantsch, Heinrich 10 n. 1, 20 n. 3
Jerusalem, manuscripts, *see* Appendix, manuscripts E and N pp. 112—115
Jesus Christ 2, 50 f., 74, 83
Jeu, First Book of 85, Second Book of 70
Jewish elements in Testament 59—66
Jinn 78 ff., *see also* Solomon, jinn of
Johannes Canabutzes 12
John of Aron (Aro?) 23
Judaism 59—66

Key of Solomon, *see* Solomon, apocryphal books, Clavicula
Kohler, Kaufman 3 n. 1, 30, 65, 106, 108
κοσμοκράτορες 45, 60, *see also* Elements
Kurz, E. 29
Kynopeges 44, 45

Language of Testament 38—43
Legend, *see* Folklore, Solomon
Leicester, Earl of 11
Letter formulae 40 ff.
Lix Tetrax 67
Locusts as sacrifice 49, 64, 72, 81
Lucifer 45

Magianism 54 f., 85
Magic 47 f.; Arabian 78 f.; Christian 2 f., 74; Egyptian 56 f; Ethiopian 72; Hellenistic 67 f.; Jewish-Aramaic 65 f.; materials used 48; mediaeval 84 f.; medicine and magic 4, 13, 32, 47 f., 90; *see also* Cup, Demonology, Incantations, Table
Maimonides 93
Manuscripts consulted; Austrian, *see* Vienna; English, *see* England; French, *see* France; German, *see* Munich; Italian, *see* Italy; Russia, *see* Moscow; *see also* Jerusalem, Mount Athos; relationships 5—9, 30—33; manuscript D 10 f., 29, 31, 32 f., 38 f., 85 f., 111; E, *see* Appendix; H 11 f., 31, 37; I 12 f., 29, 31, 37; L 13 ff., 31, 86; N, *see* Appendix; P 15 ff., 28, 31, 37, 50; Q 18 ff., 29, 31; S 15, 18, 31 f.; T 18 f., 23, 31 f.; U 20 f., 23; V 14 ns. 2, 3, 15, 18, 20, 21—25, 26, 31 f.; W 14 and n. 1, 18, 20, 25—27, 31 f.
Marcus Aurelius 1 f.
Mastema 61
Mazdaism, *see* Magianism
Mediates, George 25, 27
Mesmes, de, Henri and Jean Jacques, 16, 17 and n. 5
Michael 46, 49, 54, 72
Middle Ages, science 22, 26
Migne, Abbé 15, 29
Milan, Ambrosian Library 20
Minas, Minoides 12 f.
Montgomery, James A. 65
Moscow 27, 58
Moses as magican 93
Mount Athos 14 n. 1, 27
Munich 14 n. 1, 20
Mysticism, cosmic 71
Myths, motifs, *see* Folklore

Name, power of 4, 47, 74
Names, magic, *see* Angels, Demons, Re
Nathan 85
New Testament 68 f.
Nino, *see* St. Nino
Notaricon 82, 84

Obsequies of the Virgin (Syriac) 73
Obyzuth 78, 82

V. Index of Subjects and Persons

Omont, H. 13 n. 1, 16 n. 5. 17 and ns. 1, 5, 26
Onoskelis (-lu) 15, 19, 67, 83
Ornias 44, 73, 78
Origen 99

Palestine 109f,
Paltiel Tzamal 19, 36, 102
Pamphilus 92.
Papyri, magic 84, 85
Parousia 34
Pentacles 100, see also Amulets
Pistis Sophia 70f., 85
Pleiades 70
Poseidon 67
Procopius of Gaza 95, 96
Psellus. Michael 27, 78, 97
Psychology; popular 1 f.
Pythagorean writings (so-called) 14f., 20, 22, 26

Queen of Sheba, see Sheba
Quran 85 and n. 9

Raphael 42, 82
Rashi 93
Re 4
Recensions of Testament 35f.; Rec. A 31, 32f., 37f.; 40, 82, 86, 108, 111; Rec. B 31, 32f., 37, 40, 77, 82f., 86, 107, 108, 111; Rec. C 32, 33f., 39f., 83f., 87, 99f., 100f., 102, 108, 111; Rec. C, Prologue 32, 83f.
Remedies, magical, see Magic and medicine
Ring of Solomon, see Solomon
Rufinus 73

Sahr 80, 81
St. Augustine 1
St. Nino 73
Salzberger, Georg 30, 80, 106
Schürer, Emil 29, 105, 109
Seals of demons 84, see also Solomon, Seal of
Seal of Solomon, see Solomon

Semiphoras, see Solomon, apocryphal books
Sepher Raziel, see Solomon, apocryphal works
Seven demons 82
Sheba, queen of 4, 48, 75
Sheintob ben Isaac 93
Shem-ha-meforash 42
Shunamite 3, 49, 64f.
Signs, magic 86, see also Amulets
Solomon 48f.; apocryphal books and writings 90—103; Clavicula Salomonis 1, 9 n. 6, 14 and n. 1, 15, 19f., 26, 77, 83, 85, 86f., 100, 101, 102, 103; Ἑρμανεία 14 n. 1; Interdictio (or Contradictio) 103; τὸ κληδὴν τῆς ὑγρομαντείας 14 n. 1, see also Clavicula; Phylacteria 103; πράξεις Σολομῶντος 24f.; Semiphoras 100, Sepher Raziel 100; τέχνη τοῦ Σολομῶντος 22; Ὑγρομαντεία 14, 20, 100; Christ and 76ff.; demons and 48, 49, 85 n. 1, 91; exorcisms ascribed to 91ff., 94; fall of 3, 5, 48f., 62ff., 71f., 81; favorite slave 3; flying through air 85 f.; jinn of 65, see also demons and; legend of 49, 55f., 63, 79, Arabic 94, Christian 94—104, Jewish 90—94; as magician 48, 68, 77f., 90ff.; medicine, founded by 95, writings on 101f.; ring 3, 4, 18, 26, 49, 64, 81, inscription on 82, see also seal; seal 13f., 18, 23, 65, 86f., see also ring; Temple building 3, 4, 56, 59; wisdom and glory 4, 90ff,, 95f.; medical wisdom 92f.
Sorcery 2
South, queen of, see Sheba
Style of Testament 3, 38—43
Subscription of MS V 23
Suidas 98
Summaries, see Conclusions
Superstitions, wandering of 85
Syncretism 51f, 66

Table, magic 84
Takhma Urupa 56

Talmud 56, 62
Tartarus 44, 46
Testament, author 43, 47, 88f; date 2, 105ff., 108; manuscripts, see Manuscripts; original 33, 35, 38, 40, 87, 105; recensions, see Recensions; sources analyzed 87—90; style, see Style; subjekt matter 48—90; textual principles of edition 36ff.; translation, question of 42f.
Thou, de, Jaques August 17 and n. 5
Thraētaona 56
Thundering Legion 2
Timothy and Aquila, see Dialogue of

Timothy and Aquila
Tobit, Book of 55
Toy, C. H. 105, 109

Uriel 42

Vienna, manuscripts 18, 23, 24 n. 2, 58
Virgin birth 83
Virgin, Obsequies of 73
Vivonne, Duchesse de 16, 17.

Yima 55f.

Zahravi 93
Zonaras 95

VI. Index of Quotations from Ancient Authors

1. The Bible and Apocrypha.

Gen VI 1—4   59
I Kgs III   90
I Kgs IV 26—29   96
I Kgs IV 33   63
I Kgs V 9—14   90
Ps CXVIII 22   61, 69
Is XXVIII 16   69

Tob I 19; II 3ff.   85 n. 6
Sap VII 1   61
Sap VII 16—21   96
Sap VII 17—22   91
Sap IX 4   61

I Enoch VIf.   59
I Enoch XVf.   59
I Enoch XXXVII—LXXI   60
I Enoch LXXIX 1—12   60
Jub VII 21ff.   59
Jub X 5   59
Jub X 7—9   60
Test Reub III 3—6   60

Mt XXI 42   61
I Pt II 6f.   61, 69

2. Rabbinical writings.

Aboth di R. Nathan 37 3   62f.
Mishna
  Berakoth 10a   92f.
  Pesachim 56a   92f.
  Hagiga 16a   62f.
Targum Sheni Esther 63

3. Greek, Roman etc.

Anastasius Sinaites
  Quaest XII   98
  Quaest XLI   96f.
Citharismus regis Dauid   60, 91
Clemens Alex , Theodoti exc.   71, 72   74
De magis, incantoribus, et divinis (Syriac)   75
Dialogue of Timothy and Aquila   103f.
Pseudo-Epiphanius, Vitae prophetarum   85 n. 6
Glycas, Michael, Ann.   97, 99, 102
Pseudo-Gregentius, Disputatio   77
Hippolytus, Refutatio IIf.   2 n. 3
Jerome, In Eccl. XII 13f.   97
Josephus Christianus
  Hypomnesticon LXXIV   98, 101
  Hypomnesticon CXX   97

Josephus, Flavius, Ant VIII 25   91 f.
Kebra Nagast LXIV   72
Leontius, In med. Pentecostem   76
Marcus Aurelius I 6   2 n. 1
Nicetas Acominatus, History P 95   101 f.
Origen, In Mt com. 110   94
Ps.-Philo, de antiquitatibus biblicis   91
Syncellus, Georgius, Chron. B 776 f.   97f.
Theodoret, Quaest. X et XVIII in III Reg.   95 f.

4. Manuscripts.

Bologna University Library, No. 3632   14 ns. 2, 3, 20, 21—25, 87
British Museum, Harleian, No. 5596   13 ff., 18, 20, 86; Harleian 6483   85 n. 1
Cambridge, Trinity College, No. 1404 (French)   85 n. 1
Holkham Hall, No. 99   11 f.
Milan, Ambrosian, No. 1030   15 n. 1, 20
Mount Athos
  Andreas Monastery, No. 73   18
  Dionysius Monastery, No. 132   10 f.
  Dionysius Monastery, No. 282   14 n. 1
  Koutloumousios Monastery, No. 3221 27
Munich Greek, No. 70   14 n. 1, 20 n. 1
Paris, Bibliothèque Nationale
  Anc. fonds grecs No. 38   15 ff.
  Anc. fonds grecs No. 2419   14 n. 1, 25 ff., 58
  Supplément grec No. 500   12 ff.
  Supplément grec No. 574 (great magic papyrus) ll. 850, 853, 3040 64 n. 2, 68
Vaticanus graecus, No. 1809   25
Vienna
  Philos.-graec. No. 108   18, 58
  Medic. No. 23 (ol. 50)   58

www.ingramcontent.com/pod-product-compliance
Lightning Source LLC
Chambersburg PA
CBHW020324170426
43200CB00006B/267